C. Nelson

D1482941

BAHÁ'U'LLÁH
THE KING OF GLORY

By the same author

Bahá'u'lláh
A brief life, followed by an essay entitled
THE WORD MADE FLESH

The Báb
The Herald of the Day of Days

'Abdu'l-Bahá
The Centre of the Covenant of Bahá'u'lláh

Edward Granville Browne and the Bahá'í Faith

Muḥammad and the Course of Islám

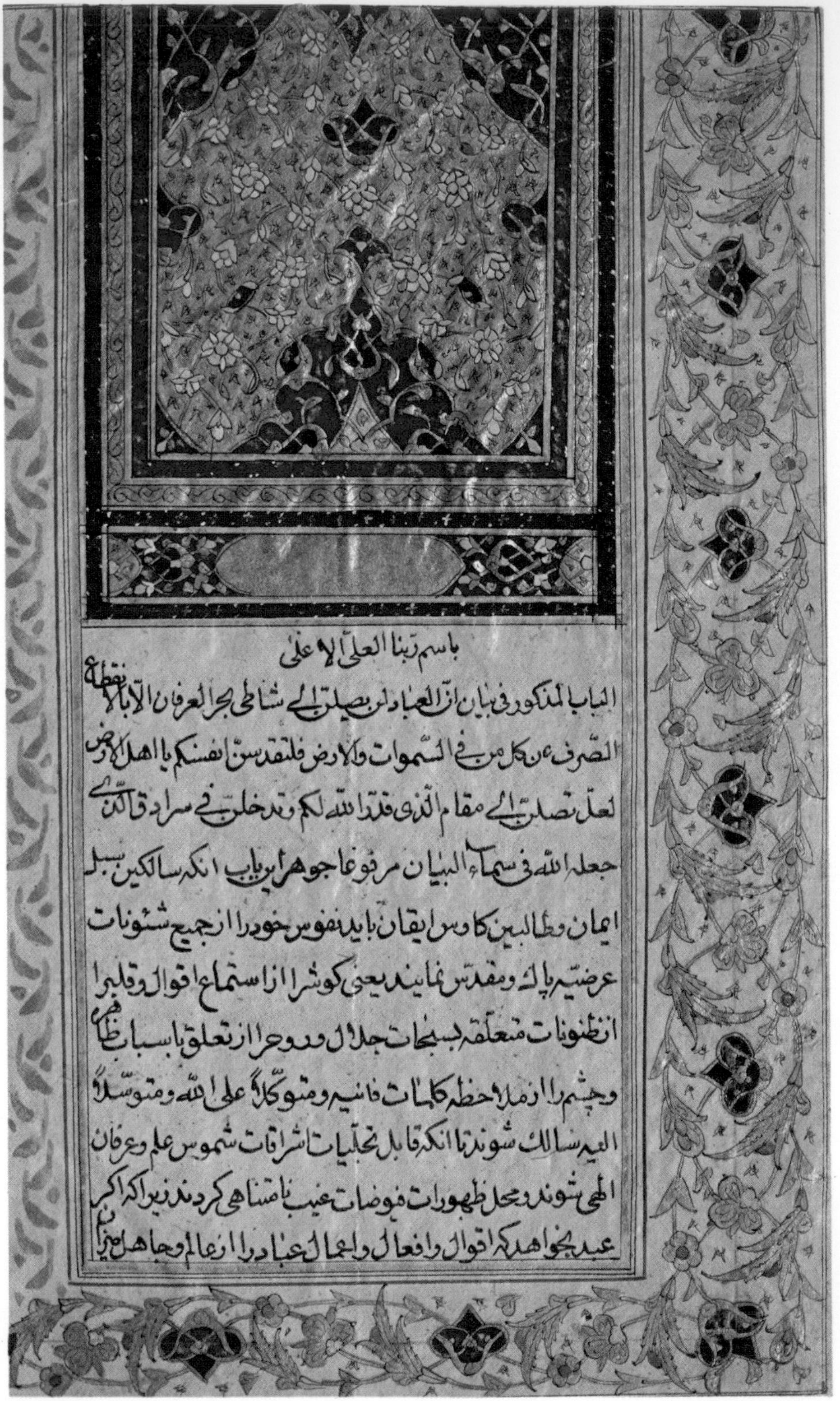
باسم ربنا العلی الاعلی

الباب المذکور فی بیان ان العباد لن یصلن الی شاطئ بحر العرفان الا بالانقطاع
الصرف عن کل من فی السموات والارض فلتقدسن انفسکم یا اهل الارض
لعل تصلن الی مقام الذی قدر الله لکم و تدخلن فی سرادق الذی
جعله الله فی سماء البیان مرفوعا جوهر این باب آنکه سالکین سبل
ایمان و طالبین کاوس ایقان باید نفوس خود را از جمیع شئونات
عرضیه پاک و مقدس نمایند یعنی گوش را از استماع اقوال و قلب را
از ظنونات متعلقه بسبحات جلال و روح را از تعلق باسباب ظاهره
و چشم را از ملاحظه کلمات فانیه و متوکلا علی الله و متوسلا
الیه سالک شوند تا آنکه قابل تجلیات اشراقات شموس علم و عرفان
الهی شوند و محل ظهورات فیوضات غیب نامتناهی گردند زیرا اگر
عبد بخواهد که اقوال و افعال و اعمال عباد را از عالم و جاهل میزان

Opening page of the Kitáb-i-Íqán *of Bahá'u'lláh from a copy dated 1871 in the handwriting of Áqá Mírzá Áqáy-i-Rikáb-Sáz, the first Bahá'í martyr of Shíráz*

BAHÁ'U'LLÁH

The King of Glory

by

H. M. BALYUZI

GEORGE RONALD
OXFORD

GEORGE RONALD, Publisher
46 High Street, Kidlington, Oxford, OX5 2DN

©H. M. BALYUZI 1980
All Rights Reserved

Third Printing 1980

Extracts from the following works reprinted by permission:
By Bahá'u'lláh: *Epistle to the Son of the Wolf*, Copyright 1941, 1953, © 1969 by National Spiritual Assembly of the Bahá'ís of the United States; *Gleanings from the Writings of Bahá'u'lláh*, Copyright 1952, © 1976 by National Spiritual Assembly of the Bahá'ís of the United States; *The Hidden Words*, published by National Spiritual Assembly of the Bahá'ís of the United States; The *Kitáb-i-Íqán: The Book of Certitude*, Copyright 1931, 1950 by National Spiritual Assembly of the Bahá'ís of the United States. By 'Abdu'l-Bahá: *Memorials of the Faithful*, Copyright © 1971 by National Spiritual Assembly of the Bahá'ís of the United States; *Some Answered Questions*, Copyright 1930, 1954, © 1964 by National Spiritual Assembly of the Bahá'ís of the United States. By Shoghi Effendi: *God Passes By*, Copyright 1944, © 1972, 1975 by National Spiritual Assembly of the Bahá'ís of the United States. By Nabíl-i-A'ẓam: *The Dawn-Breakers*, published by National Spiritual Assembly of the Bahá'ís of the United States. By Esslemont: *Bahá'u'lláh and the New Era*, Copyright 1950, © 1970, 1976, 1978 by National Spiritual Assembly of the Bahá'ís of the United States. By Lady Blomfield: *The Chosen Highway*, published by National Spiritual Assembly of the Bahá'ís of the United States

ISBN 0 85398 090 X

Printed in the United States of America

The humanitarian and spiritual principles enunciated decades ago in the darkest East by Bahá'u'lláh and moulded by Him into a coherent scheme are one after the other being taken by a world unconscious of their source as the marks of progressive civilization. And the sense that mankind has broken with the past and that the old guidance will not carry it through the emergencies of the present has filled with uncertainty and dismay all thoughtful men save those who have learned to find in the story of Bahá'u'lláh the meaning of all the prodigies and portents of our time. *Shoghi Effendi*

This is the story of Bahá'u'lláh, dedicated to the unfading glory of His great-grandson, the writer of the above lines, the Guardian of the Bahá'í Faith.

Preface

PRIOR to anything else in this preface, I must express my deepest and ever-abiding gratitude to the Universal House of Justice, the Supreme Body of the Bahá'í World Community, for their gracious encouragement at every stage, without which this book could never have been written. I am also most grateful for the approval accorded to my translations from Scriptures.

Next, I wish to offer my sincere and grateful thanks to the Hands of the Cause resident in the Holy Land, for devoting much of their time to read and review for publication this book, which is the first of four volumes on the life and times of Bahá'u'lláh. This volume presents a complete biography.

Apart from a variety of documents and sundry accounts, my chief sources have been: the unpublished part of the immortal chronicle by Mullá Muḥammad-i-Zarandí, Nabíl-i-A'ẓam; the reminiscences of Áqá Ḥusayn-i-Á<u>sh</u><u>ch</u>í; and the narrative of Áqá Muḥammad-Riḍáy-i-Qannád-i-<u>Sh</u>írází.

Áqá Ḥusayn was the son of Áqá Muḥammad-Javád-i-Ká<u>sh</u>ání, a Bábí of early days. Orphaned, when a young boy, he was taken to Ba<u>gh</u>dád, where he grew up in the household of Bahá'u'lláh, eventually becoming His cook. For that reason he came to be known as Á<u>sh</u><u>ch</u>í (Broth-maker).

When, in December 1924, Áqá Ḥusayn-i-Á<u>sh</u><u>ch</u>í was at an advanced age and on his death-bed, Shoghi Effendi, the Guardian of the Bahá'í Faith, instructed Áqá 'Abdu'r-Rasúl-i-Manṣúr-i-Ká<u>sh</u>ání to sit by his bedside and take down all that the dying man could remember of the events of seven decades. It is a fascinating story that Á<u>sh</u><u>ch</u>í had to tell; and what is particularly striking is the amazing rapport between the reminiscences of an elderly man, very soon to die, and the narrative of Áqá Riḍáy-i-Qannád.

Áqá Riḍá, a native of <u>Sh</u>íráz and a confectioner (Qannád) by trade, was a devout follower of Bahá'u'lláh, and was closely beside Him from Ba<u>gh</u>dád days until His ascension. He later served 'Abdu'l-Bahá with equal zeal and devotion, until his death in 1912, while 'Abdu'l-Bahá was in America.

Áqá Riḍáy-i-Qannád-i-Shírází

Áqá Ḥusayn-i-Áshchí of Káshán

Áqá Riḍá states that he wrote his narrative at the request of Nabíl-i-A'ẓam, and he put his pen to paper some time in the early eighties of the last century. The exact date is unknown because, unfortunately, in the copy made available to me, the final pages of his all-absorbing narrative are missing. It is to be hoped that somewhere a complete copy exists and will come to light, although it is possible that Áqá Riḍá may not have finished his invaluable account.

The great value of both Áqá Riḍá's narrative and Áqá Ḥusayn's reminiscences lies in the fact that they are eye-witness accounts, and not recollections and anecdotes told them by someone else. Both men were personally involved in and with the events they describe.

The narrative of Nabíl-i-A'ẓam hardly needs any introduction. That superb volume, *The Dawn-Breakers*, has already made it known. In that part of his chronicle which is unpublished, Nabíl, like Áqá Riḍá and Áqá Ḥusayn, relates mostly the events and incidents in which he himself was involved, which he saw with his own eyes.

The autobiography of Ḥájí Mírzá Ḥabíbu'lláh Afnán, dealing as it does with months lived in close proximity to the residences of Bahá'u'lláh, has a unique importance. I am most grateful to my cousin, Abu'l-Qásim Afnán, for lending me this invaluable document from the pen of his father, and for providing me with other material of great historical interest.

It should be stressed that the spoken words of Bahá'u'lláh, quoted in these pages, cannot be equated with His Writings. No one could have been taking notes at the time, although it cannot be ruled out that some may be the very words spoken. The reporting of Nabíl, however, is in a different category, because he usually read to Bahá'u'lláh what he had heard Him say. Nevertheless, none of these reported words of Bahá'u'lláh has scriptural value.

Quotations are reproduced in their original form, even though differing from the spelling and transliteration of Persian words adopted in this book. Translations from Arabic and Persian are my own, unless otherwise attributed. For Constantinople, Adrianople, and Smyrna, I have used at times their Turkish names: Istanbul, Edirne (Adirnih), Izmír, which are common usage today for referring to those cities.

That the many Persian names in the book may present difficulties to the Western reader is clear, but the innumerable persons, who, in one way or another, had some connexion with Bahá'u'lláh, cannot be omitted from His biography. They can be identified only by the names they used, however difficult. For a guide to the construction of Persian

Nabíl-i-A'ẓam, Mullá Muḥammad-i-Zarandí

names, the reader may wish to refer to my earlier book, *The Báb*, where a preliminary note deals with this subject.

Immense indeed, as in the past, is my indebtedness to Marion Hofman. Without her prodigious editorial work, the contents of this book would have remained loosely-jointed and diffused.

I am profoundly grateful to Moojan Momen, whose help and assistance to me have been of inestimable value. Throughout this book and its addenda, there are biographical notes, historical accounts of cities and localities in which Bahá'u'lláh dwelt, as well as other material written by him, based on his assiduous and able research.

I am very thankful to Mr Horst Kolo for his excellent production of the frontispiece and a number of other photographs. The contribution of the Audio-Visual Department of the Bahá'í World Centre, Haifa, Israel, in providing the major number of illustrations, is deeply appreciated, and I also acknowledge gratefully certain photographs from the National Spiritual Assembly of the Bahá'ís of Írán, as well as from several others to whom due attribution is given. Some old engravings and photographs from books are reproduced and acknowledged (see bibliography for details).

For permission to quote from published works, I am much indebted to the Universal House of Justice, Bahá'í World Centre, Haifa; to the Bahá'í Publishing Trusts of the United States and the United Kingdom; and to Dorothy Anderson, Hutchinson & Co., Jonathan Cape Ltd, Macmillan (London and Basingstoke), and Oxford University Press. The extracts from the Public Record Office files are used with the permission of the Controller of Her Majesty's Stationery Office. The text of the Authorized Version of the Bible is Crown copyright and the extracts used herein are reproduced by permisson. A number of works now out of copyright have also been quoted. Full acknowledgement of all sources is given in the bibliography and notes.

I also wish to thank, in addition to those mentioned above, Mr Stratford Caldecott for his meticulous copy editing, and Mr Rustom Sabit for his additional careful proof reading.

And, finally, I wish to pay my tribute to my wife's share in the writing and the shaping of this book. Her support constantly eased my path.

H. M. BALYUZI

London
June 1979

CONTENTS

ADDENDA

Illustrations and maps are indexed under the relevant headings.

Introduction

THE ancient land of Írán, from which the voice of Zoroaster was heard some three thousand years ago, calling men to right thought, right speech, right deed, is the cradle of the Bábí-Bahá'í Faith. It is a vast land, 628,000 square miles, where towns and cities are situated 5,000 feet above sea-level. On the Íránian plateau there are high peaks reaching up to 18,934 feet, which is the height of Mt Damávand in the north. Its snow-clad top is visible from the capital, Ṭihrán. Beyond the Alburz range, of which Mt Damávand forms a part, lie the Caspian provinces of Gílán and Mázindarán, covered with lush vegetation and thick forests. The Zagros range in the west descends to the flat plain of 'Iráq – the historic land of two rivers, the Tigris and the Euphrates. There was a time when 'Iráq was part of the Íránian Empire, whose rulers had a winter capital on the bank of the Tigris: the renowned city of Ctesiphon, where the world-famed Arch of Chosroes still stands. In the centre and to the east of the Íránian plateau, there are extensive tracts of desert – Dasht-i-Kavír and Dasht-i-Lúṭ – and there are numbers of oasis cities on the fringes of these inhospitable deserts, cities such as Yazd and Kirmán that have stood up bravely, in the course of centuries, to the ravages of man and nature. In the north-east, near the frontier with the Soviet Union, lies the holy city of Mashhad, which harbours the mausoleum of the eighth Imám, 'Alí Ibn Músá, ar-Riḍá. The Mosque of Gawhar-Shád, of which the Shrine of Imám Riḍá is an integral part, is a gem of architecture and design, one of the most beautiful structures of the world. It was thus beheld and described by an Englishman, who, dressed as a Persian, dared to enter its holy precincts:

> I hastened down the dark bazaar, found the dome where I turned to the left, and was greeted, on coming out into the court, by such a fanfare of colour and light that I stopped a moment, half blinded. It was as if someone had switched on another sun.

The whole quadrangle was a garden of turquoise, pink, dark red, and dark blue, with touches of purple, green, and yellow, planted among paths of plain buff brick. Huge white arabesques whirled above the ivan* arches. The ivans themselves hid other gardens, shadier, fritillary-coloured. The great minarets beside the sanctuary, rising from bases encircled with Kufic the size of a boy, were bedizened with a network of jewelled lozenges. The swollen sea-green dome adorned with yellow tendrils appeared between them. At the opposite end glinted the top of a gold minaret. But in all this variety, the principle of union, the life-spark of the whole blazing apparition, was kindled by two great texts: the one, a frieze of white *suls*† writing powdered over a field of gentian blue along the skyline of the entire quadrangle; the other, a border of the same alphabet in daisy white and yellow on a sapphire field, interlaced with turquoise Kufic along its inner edge, and enclosing, in the form of a three-sided oblong, the arch of the main ivan between the minarets. The latter was actually designed, it says, by 'Baisanghor, son of Shah Rukh, son of Timur Gurkani (Tamerlane), with hope in God, in the year 821 (AD 1418).' Baisanghor [Báysunqur] was a famous calligrapher; and being the son of Gohar Shad also, he celebrated his mother's munificence with an inscription whose glory explains for ever the joy felt by Islam in writing on the face of architecture.[1]

Írán's second holy city is Qum, directly south of the capital, where we come upon another famed mausoleum, that of Ma'ṣúmih, a sister of the eighth Imám. Here in Qum, around the shrine of Ma'ṣúmih, some of the Ṣafaví and the Qájár monarchs are buried. Still further to the south, two of Írán's most celebrated cities are situated: Iṣfahán, the beloved city of 'Abbás the Great – of which it has been said: 'Iṣfahán, Niṣf-i-Jahán: Iṣfahán, half the world' – right in the heart of Írán, at a distance of 414 kilometres from Ṭihrán; and more to the south, at a distance of 895 kilometres from the capital, the city of S͟híráz, where the Dawn broke in the year 1844, the city of Sa'dí and Ḥáfiẓ, beloved and enriched by that exemplary and benevolent ruler, Karím K͟hán-i-Zand – in praise of which Sa'dí wrote and sang:[2]

O, blessed and blissful is that dawn,
When myself, once again, I shall find atop
the Alláh-u-Akbar Pass of S͟híráz-town.

O, to see once again that Paradise on Earth,
Where security dwells, not oppression of want and dearth.

* *Ayván*: portico, open gallery. (HMB)
† *T͟hult͟h*: a style of calligraphy. (HMB)

Under the Qájárs, in the course of the nineteenth century, these two cities of high renown suffered both neglect and desecration. Ághá Muḥammad Khán, the founder of the dynasty, laid hands on structures majestically reared by Karím Khán in Shíráz. And in Iṣfahán, Sulṭán-Mas'úd Mírzá, the Ẓillu's-Sulṭán, the eldest son of Náṣiri'd-Dín Sháh, began defacing the beauties lavished on his city by 'Abbás the Great. In close vicinity to Shíráz stand the monumental ruins of Persepolis: the magnificent palace of Apádáná, raised by Darius and Xerxes, and set on fire by Alexander, the Macedonian; also Naqsh-i-Rustam, where the Achaemenian kings were entombed.

Between Shíráz and the Persian Gulf littoral, there are ranges of high peaks and difficult passes, before the plateau descends to sea-level. And in the south-west lie both oil wells and the remains of the ancient city of Susa (Shúsh), which knew the presence of great kings and of Daniel, the Prophet of the Israelites. Over Khúzistán, the province of oil wells, are the provinces of Luristán and Kurdistán, haunts of the Lurs and the Kurds, heirs of great traditions and of stalwart warriors. The Zagros range, with the very high peak of Alvand, cuts through the territories of the Lurs and the Kurds, embraces rocks on which mighty kings of old (such as Darius the Achaemenian) had their stories inscribed, and holds in its fold two other renowned cities: Kirmánsháh and Hamadán. Close to Hamadán is the site of the Median city of Ecbatana. And in the north west, close to both the Turkish and the Soviet frontiers, is the city of Tabríz, illustrious in the past – the capital of Sháh Ismá'íl, the founder of the Ṣafavid dynasty – and in the mid-nineteenth century its earth sanctified by the sacred blood shed upon it. Here the Báb was executed in 1850.

Once territories north of the river Aras formed part of the Íránian Empire, until they were wrenched away from Írán in the reign of Fatḥ-'Alí Sháh. Not far from the river Aras (Araxes of the Greeks) the Báb spent many months in captivity. And it was Ḥáfiẓ of Shíráz, the city where the glorious Báb first saw the light of day, who wrote:[3]

> Over the banks of Aras shouldst thou, O Zephyr, pass,
> Kiss the earth of that vale and refreshen thy breath thereby.

This is Írán of the present day, which the followers of Bahá'u'lláh, wherever they be, know as 'the sacred Land of Írán', the cradle of their Faith. Of its future, 'Abdu'l-Bahá, the Son of Bahá'u'lláh and the

Centre of His Covenant, has written: 'The government of the native land of the Blessed Perfection will become the most respected government of this world . . . and Írán will become the most prosperous of all lands.'[4]

But, when the nineteenth century opened, Írán was fast becoming the darkest of all lands. The monstrous yoke of the Qájárs had just come to rest on the neck of a nation stunned by blow after blow. Ruled by ignorant and avaricious kings, and lorded over by venal officials and rapacious landlords taking their example from their brutish sovereigns, Persians sank into a stupor; the worst of human nature and the most loathsome of human characteristics took the upper hand; ferocity and greed and cruelty abounded; Írán became intellectually starved and morally corrupt. Self-willed and self-seeking clerics veered a credulous people one way and the other with their insensate rivalries, their false judications, their contradictory pronouncements; and Írán became spiritually moribund. Some seven decades ago, in a sea-town of Írán where many foreign nationals resided and traded, the Governor, sensing the great need for a civil court, instituted such a court and put at its head a learned man, turbaned and well-versed in Islamic jurisprudence. Immediately the cry went up from the clerics of the town, denouncing the civil court as *Ṭághút*, an idol of pre-Islamic Arabia. Thereupon, the Governor told them that should they choose one among themselves to be the judge and the adjudicator, with the rest promising to obey and enforce his verdicts, he, the Governor, would at once dissolve the civil court. But they would not and could not take the step which would concede supremacy to one amongst themselves. And the civil court remained and prospered to the discomfiture of the clerics. Of course there were outstanding exceptions to these degradations, but those exceptions only tended to prove the rule.

The Manifestation of God has always appeared amongst the most depraved, the most demoralized people of His age, in the most benighted, downtrodden land. Moses came to a people who had become enslaved, had lost their self-respect and fallen a prey to their idle fancies. He challenged both the might of the tyrant and the waywardness of His own people, and both did He vanquish. Jesus stepped out of the lowest ranks of the same people, the children of Israel, who had once again forfeited their birthright, fallen into serfdom, and forgotten the warnings and counsels of their Prophets. He suffered grievously both at their hands and at the hands of their brutal oppressors. But triumph was His in the final count. Muḥammad, the Arabian Prophet, rose up amongst idolaters, uncouth and unbridled, who buried their daughters alive, who were lawless and predatory. He made of a people, disparate and forlorn, a single and single-minded nation, gave it law, vision and understanding, and taught it to worship the One True God. And in the nineteenth century, in the ancient land of Írán, amongst a people wallowing in the depths of ignominy, there arose two Manifestations of God: One of pure lineage, a descendant of the Arabian Prophet, the Other a scion of the royal house of Írán that ruled the Empire before the advent of Islám. They had the power to recreate lives, to confer on men the gift of second birth. In the almost impenetrable gloom, the darkness of fanaticism, ignorance and rapacity that had enshrouded the people of Írán, the star of Their Faith shone as brightly as a million suns, illuminating the paths of countless men and women to heroic action. Their call was directed not only to the inhabitants of Írán, but to the entire concourse of mankind. They too suffered grievously, as had Jesus of Nazareth and Muḥammad of Mecca. But Their persecutors paid the penalty in the end a hundredfold, as had the persecutors of Jesus and Muḥammad. History does not show a single instance of anyone who dared to raise his hands to harm and injure the Báb, Bahá'u'lláh or Their followers, who escaped the consequences of his actions.

These pages will relate the story of Bahá'u'lláh, as well as the story of the retrogression of a nation under the yoke of the Qájárs.

Prologue

THE towering grandeur, the compelling majesty, and the tender beauty of the life of a Manifestation of God cannot be comprehended by events usually associated with a saintly life. The immensity of such a life presents itself in that mysterious influence which it exerts over countless lives – an influence which does not function through social status and prestige, wealth, secular power or worldly dominion, indeed not even through the medium of superior knowledge and the force of intellectual achievement.

The Manifestation of God is the Archetype, and His life is the supreme pattern. His vision, not arrested by time and space, encompasses the future as well as the past. He is the only and the necessary link between one cycle of social evolution and another. Without Him history is meaningless and co-ordination is impossible. Furthermore, the Manifestation of God releases deep reservoirs of spiritual power and quickens the forces latent in Man. By Him, and by Him alone, can Man attain 'second birth'. Through Him, and Him alone, can Man know God.

Mírzá Ḥusayn 'Alí Núrí, Whom history knows as Bahá'u'lláh – the Glory of God – was born at dawn on 2 Muḥarram AH 1233, 12 November 1817, in Ṭihrán, the capital of Persia.

I

The Ancestry of Bahá'u'lláh

BAHÁ'U'LLÁH was descended from the pre-Islamic monarchs of Írán. He came from a region of the country, bordering on the Caspian Sea and well protected by the high peaks of the Alburz range, whose dwellers, for scores of years after the victory of Arab arms, continued to defy the invader, refusing to accept the new ordering and new Faith. And when they finally bowed to the inevitable, they submitted not to the system accepted by the generality of Muslims and represented by the Caliphate in Baghdád, but to the Shí'ism of the Zaydí variety. In the succeeding centuries there were a number of dynasties and petty kingdoms which held sway and guarded their autonomy in the fastnesses of mountains and in the depths of thick forests by the Caspian Sea. And strangely enough, when Sháh Ismá'íl united all of Írán in allegiance to the apostolic Imáms of the House of the Prophet, Áqá Rustam-i-Rúzafzún, the last of these proud potentates, refused to recognize his authority, and chose to put his trust in Muḥammad Khán-i-Shaybání (also known as Shaybak Khán), the Sunní Uzbak ruler of Transoxania, to overthrow the Ṣafavid upstart. But fate decreed otherwise, and it was Shaybak Khán who met defeat and lost his life. Áqá Rustam, it is said, died of fright when a devotee of Sháh Ismá'íl threw the severed hand of the Uzbak ruler onto his lap.

It is to Yazdigird III, the last Sásánian monarch to occupy the throne of Írán, that the genealogy of Bahá'u'lláh can be traced. Ustád Javánmard, the principal of the Zoroastrian school of Yazd, presented seven queries to Bahá'u'lláh, the seventh of which concerned His ancestry. The Tablet known as *Shír-Mard* (Lion of a Man) – thus called because the recipient was so addressed by Bahá'u'lláh – was sent to him in reply. (This Tablet is also known as *Lawḥ-i-Haft-Pursish*.) Answering his questions one by one, to the seventh query Bahá'u'lláh responded by referring him to the genealogy which Mírzá Abu'l-Faḍl-i-Gulpáygání had gathered and compiled. Many years later, in the

Mírzá 'Abbás, known as Mírzá Buzurg, Vazír-i-Núrí, father of Bahá'u'lláh

year AH 1320 (10 April 1902–30 March 1903), Áqá K͟husraw Bimán, who was also of Zoroastrian origin, was visiting the Holy Land. He asked resident Bahá'ís* for information regarding the ancestry of Bahá'u'lláh. They presented his request to 'Abdu'l-Bahá, who also referred them to Mírzá Abu'l-Faḍl-i-Gulpáygání, then visiting the United States. Mírzá Abu'l-Faḍl's answer to Áqá K͟husraw Bimán's letter was published in Bombay, at a later date, as a pamphlet.

Mírzá Abu'l-Faḍl, designated by the Guardian of the Bahá'í Faith as one of the nineteen 'Apostles of Bahá'u'lláh', was a man of rare erudition and a degree of scholarship so far unequalled amongst the followers of Bahá'u'lláh, whether in the East or in the West. In his reply to Áqá K͟husraw Bimán, he describes how his interest was aroused in the genealogy of Bahá'u'lláh, and how his researches led him to Yazdigird III, the last of the Sásánian monarchs of Írán. He goes on to state, however, that his work, which Bahá'u'lláh had mentioned in the Tablet addressed to the schoolmaster of Yazd, was lost when he and a number of other Bahá'ís were arrested in Ṭihrán in the early months of 1883 by the order of Kámrán Mírzá, the Náyibu's-Salṭanih, son of Náṣiri'd-Dín S͟háh.

Mírzá Abu'l-Faḍl writes that he was, in the course of his investigation, particularly impressed by the fact that so severe and unsympathetic a critic of the Bahá'í Faith (and so hostile a commentator) as Riḍá-Qulí K͟hán-i-Hidáyat,† entitled the Amíru's͟h-S͟hu'ara' (The Emir of Poets), had admitted in the Niz͟hád-Námih (The Book of Ancestry), that the Núrís of Mázindarán are descended from Chosroes I, the renowned Sásánian monarch known as 'Ádil (The Just). And final confirmation came from Ḥájí Mírzá Riḍá-Qulí, a half-brother of Bahá'u'lláh, who told Mírzá Abu'l-Faḍl categorically, in answer to his query, that the Núrís possessed a genealogical table tracing their line back to Yazdigird the Sásánian.

The father of Bahá'u'lláh was Mírzá 'Abbás-i-Núrí, the son of Mírzá Riḍá-Qulí Big,‡ of the village of Tákur, in the district of Núr, of the province of Mázindarán. Mírzá 'Abbás came to be known as

---

* He names them, in a pamphlet published in Bombay, as Zaynu'l-Muqarrabín, Áqá Muḥammad-Riḍáy-i-Qannád and Mírzá Maḥmúd-i-Kás͟hání.
† Poet and historian of the nineteenth century, author of the supplement to the Rawḍatu's̱-Ṣafá of Mírk͟hund. See E. G. Browne. A Literary History of Persia, vol. IV; also H. M. Balyuzi, The Báb, pp. 141, 142.
‡ Mírzá Riḍá-Qulí Big's father was also named Mírzá 'Abbás, son of Ḥájí Muḥammad-Riḍá Big, son of Áqá Muḥammad-'Alí, son of Áqá Fak͟hr, son of S͟háhríyár-Ḥasan.

Mírzá Buzurg-i-Vazír (Mírzá Buzurg, the Vizier). And this is how it happened. One day Fatḥ-'Alí Sháh (reigned 1797–1834) was shown a masterpiece of calligraphy by Mír 'Imád, the celebrated calligrapher. Marvellous was the beauty of that piece of handwriting, and Fatḥ-'Alí Sháh wondered if anyone living could match its excellence. Ḥasan-'Alí Mírzá, the Shujá'u's-Salṭanih, the sixth son of the Sháh, mentioned the name of Mírzá 'Abbás-i-Núrí. He was sent for, shown the work of Mír 'Imád, and challenged to produce its like. Thereupon Mírzá 'Abbás took Mír 'Imád's masterpiece, copied it, and after that exercise wrote his own lines, had them suitably illuminated and presented them to Fatḥ-'Alí Sháh. The Sháh's admiration was boundless. A royal decree bestowed upon Mírzá 'Abbás the name Mírzá Buzurg, and invested him with a robe of honour – a garment which the monarch himself had worn. At the same time the Sháh exempted the people of the village of Tákur from the payment of taxes. A few years later, Mírzá Buzurg was appointed vizier to Imám-Virdí Mírzá, the twelfth son of Fatḥ-'Alí Sháh, who was the *Ílkhání* (chief of the clans) of the Qájár tribe (to which the royal family itself belonged).

Mírzá Buzurg prospered in the service of the State, until the days of Muḥammad Sháh (reigned 1834–48), when he encountered the ill will of that monarch's notorious grand vizier, Ḥájí Mírzá Áqásí, and lost his position and much of his considerable wealth.

2

The Family of Bahá'u'lláh

MÍRZÁ Buzurg, Vazír-i-Núrí, the father of Bahá'u'lláh, had seven wives, three of whom were concubines. It was his father, Riḍá-Qulí Big, who arranged his first marriage to a relative of the family, named Khán-Nanih, before Mírzá Buzurg left the district of Núr in Mázindarán to make his fortune in Ṭihrán. Two sons, Mírzá Áqá, the elder, and Mírzá Muḥammad-Ḥasan, were born of this union. Bahá'u'lláh mentions an occasion in His childhood, in the Persian *Lawḥ-i-Ra'ís* – a Tablet addressed to 'Álí Páshá, the Ottoman grand vizier – when, during the nuptial fête of His brother, Mírzá Áqá, who did not have long to live, His attention was drawn to a puppet show. Afterwards, Mírzá Buzurg gave the widow in marriage to his second son, Mírzá Muḥammad-Ḥasan. This lady was a cousin of Mírzá Áqá Khán-i-Núrí, the second grand vizier of Náṣiri'd-Dín Sháh.

Mírzá Buzurg's second wife was Khadíjih Khánum, who had been married once before and was widowed. She had one son and two daughters by her first marriage, namely, Mírzá Muḥammad-'Alí, Sakínih Khánum and Ṣughrá Khánum. Mírzá Buzurg took Khadíjih Khánum as his wife and wedded her daughter, Sakínih Khánum, to his younger brother, Mírzá Muḥammad. Khadíjih Khánum was the mother of Bahá'u'lláh (Mírzá Ḥusayn-'Alí). The first-born of that marriage was a daughter, Sárih Khánum; she is generally known as 'Ukht', Arabic for sister, because Bahá'u'lláh has thus referred to her. The next was a son, Mírzá Mihdí, who died in his father's lifetime; and Mírzá Ḥusayn-'Alí (Bahá'u'lláh) was the third-born. The fourth was another son, Mírzá Músá, entitled Áqáy-i-Kalím in later years, and the fifth was another daughter, Nisá' Khánum, who was married eventually to Mírzá Majíd-i-Áhí, a secretary of the Russian Legation.

The third wife of Mírzá Buzurg was Kulthúm Khánum-i-Núrí, by whom he had five children. The first was a daughter, Sháh-Sulṭán Khánum (also called 'Izzíyih Khánum), who became a firm supporter

Two of the sons of Mírzá Buzurg-i-Núrí: on the left is Mírzá Músá, Áqáy-i-Kalím, full brother of Bahá'u'lláh. On the right is Mírzá Riḍá-Qulí.

of Mírzá Yaḥyá (Ṣubḥ-i-Azal). Next came three sons: Mírzá Taqí, a poet with the sobriquet Paríshán, who became a Shaykhí much opposed to Bahá'u'lláh; Mírzá Riḍá-Qulí, who earned the designation 'Ḥájí' by his pilgrimage to Mecca, and who kept apart from Bahá'u'lláh, even trying to conceal the fact of their relationship (see p.443), although his wife, Maryam, was greatly devoted to Him; and the third son, Mírzá Ibráhím, who also died in his father's lifetime. The fifth child of that marriage of Mírzá Buzurg was another daughter, Fáṭimih-Sulṭán Khánum, who also chose to follow Mírzá Yaḥyá into the wilderness.

The next three wives of Mírzá Buzurg were concubines. The first was Kúchik Khánum of Kirmánsháh, the mother of Mírzá Yaḥyá. The second was a Georgian lady, Nabát Khánum, and by her Mírzá Buzurg had another daughter, Ḥusníyyih Khánum, of whom not much is known. The last concubine, Turkamáníyyih, was the mother of Mírzá Muḥammad-Qulí who was greatly devoted to Bahá'u'lláh.

And then came Mírzá Buzurg's marriage to a daughter of Fatḥ-'Alí Sháh. This lady, who was entitled Ḍíyá'u's-Salṭanih* – like her husband, a noted calligraphist – was overbearing, haughty and grasping. Their marriage was to bring the Vazír-i-Núrí nothing but misfortune and, in the end, to prove his undoing.

* According to I'timádu's-Salṭanih's *Muntaẓim-i-Náṣirí* (Ṭihrán 1300, p. 161), her name was Sháh Bigum.

Two of the sons of Mírzá Buzurg-i-Núrí: on the left is Mírzá Muḥammad-Qulí, half-brother of Bahá'u'lláh who shared His exile. On the right is Mírzá Yaḥyá, Ṣubḥ-i-Azal.

Ḥájí Mírzá Áqásí, the Prime Minister, was both vain and vengeful, and, as mentioned in the preceding chapter, he was antagonistic to Mírzá Buzurg. One reason which prompted his enmity was Mírzá Buzurg's particular friendship with the celebrated Qá'im-Maqám, Mírzá Abu'l-Qásim of Faráhán. These two thought very highly of each other, as evidenced by letters contained in the Compendium of Letters by the great Minister.* In June 1835 the Qá'im-Maqám was treacherously put to death by Muḥammad Sháh. The very manner of his fall from power and his execution, which was followed by the rise to high office of Ḥájí Mírzá Áqásí, left no doubt in the mind of Mírzá Buzurg that the sad fate of his dear friend was to be attributed to the low cunning of the monster who was now in the saddle, and he could not hide his feelings of horror and disgust. One of his letters condemnatory of Ḥájí Mírzá Áqásí fell into the hands of the Grand Vizier, who, before long, retaliated with force. As soon as he conveniently could, he struck at Mírzá Buzurg. First, he had Mírzá Buzurg dismissed from the governorship of Burújird and Luristán. This post, which included control over a sizeable part of the Bakhtíyárí territory – a very disturbed and rebellious region – had been entrusted to Mírzá Buzurg by his great friend, Mírzá Abu'l-Qásim, the Qá'im-Maqám, soon after

* This Compendium was compiled and edited, in later years, at the instance of Ḥájí Farhád Mírzá, the Mu'tamidu'd-Dawlih, a brother of Muḥammad Sháh. It has been printed several times, under the title *Munshí'át-i-Qá'im-Maqám*, to provide a guide to and an example of excellence of style and diction.

the accession of Muḥammad S͟háh to the throne. A document exists in the handwriting of Muḥammad S͟háh himself, commending and praising the services rendered by Mírzá Buzurg in this capacity.* Next, Ḥájí Mírzá Áqásí stopped Mírzá Buzurg's annual allowance. Then, he did all in his power to disturb the relationship between Mírzá Buzurg and his last wife, Ḍíyá'u's-Salṭanih, the daughter of Fatḥ-'Alí S͟háh. Through her nephew, Firaydún Mírzá, the Farmán-Farmá – who had been his favourite for the governorship of the province of Fárs – he induced Ḍíyá'u's-Salṭanih to seek and obtain divorce from her husband. Mírzá Buzurg was already in dire financial straits, for he had a very large family, and the yearly allowance, which was rightly his, was no longer available because of the malice of Ḥájí Mírzá Áqásí. He had had to sell a part of his properties and mortgage others, including the complex of houses in Ṭihrán in which he and his family resided. For a while, these houses had passed out of his possession, until he had bought them back through his son, Mírzá Ḥusayn-'Alí (Bahá'u'lláh). Mírzá Buzurg had the added misfortune of losing the better part of the palatial mansion which he had built and richly furnished in Tákur, by the descent of floods upon the town.

Ḍíyá'u's-Salṭanih, with the backing of the Grand Vizier and her powerful nephew, Firaydún Mírzá, forced through her divorce. But the marriage settlement was of such proportions that the Vazír-i-Núrí, enmeshed as he was in financial difficulties, could not pay it immediately. Ḍíyá'u's-Salṭanih then had Mírzá Buzurg imprisoned in his own house, and set men to beat him daily and torture him so as to extort the

* It appears that for a time Mírzá Buzurg was also vazír of this province – the official responsible for the collection of taxes. Mírzá Buzurg seems to have been particularly successful in organizing and levying taxes among the unruly and remote Lurí tribesmen – a feat that eluded most of his predecessors and successors in this post. In his 'Notes on a March from Zohab to Khuzistan', Sir Henry Rawlinson remarks: 'The valuation of kátir [the unit of taxation, usually about 100 *túmáns*] varies . . . according to the state of the province; but under the late Wazír, Mírzá Buzurg, who administered the revenues with eminent success for about ten years, it was raised to the rate of 200 old tómáns, or 333⅓ of the present currency; the 120 kátirs [being the assessment of the tribes of Pís͟h-Kúh] were, therefore, equivalent to 40,000 tómáns, and the amount annually realized from Písh-Kúh alone rather exceeded than fell short of this sum. [Rawlinson then sets out the classification of the tribes and the revenue system as observed by Mírzá Buzurg] . . . The system of revenue of Písh-Kúh is very simple; when the 120 kátirs have been duly distributed among the tribes . . . each subdivision determines the amount of share to be paid by the different camps of which it is composed . . . But in a wild country like this, where many of the tribes live in a state of open rebellion . . . the governor would certainly fail in his contract to the crown, unless he had indirect means of raising an extraordinary revenue to make up for many defalcations. Mírzá Buzurg, therefore, introduced an extensive system of fees and fines; and, where robberies and murder were of almost daily occurrence, he did not want opportunities of exaction; indeed he is said to have realized about 20,000 tómáns annually in this manner, and that, too, without cruelty or injustice.'[1]

money from him. At last, Mírzá Buzurg was obliged to sell, once again, his complex of houses in Ṭihrán, and part with the valuable carpets and other furnishings which they contained. In the *Epistle to the Son of the Wolf*, Bahá'u'lláh refers to the sale of these houses:

> In the early days we all lived in one house, which later on was sold at auction, for a negligible sum, and the two brothers, Farmán-Farmá [Firaydún Mírzá] and Ḥisámu's-Salṭanih [Sulṭán-Murád Mírzá], purchased it and divided it between themselves. After this occurred, We separated from Our brother.* He established his residence close to the entrance of Masjid-i-Sháh [the Mosque of the Sháh], whilst We lived near the Gate of Shimírán [Shimrán].[2]

Kulthúm Khánum, the third wife of Mírzá Buzurg and mother of Ḥájí Mírzá Riḍá-Qulí, had inherited the house 'close to the entrance of Masjid-i-Sháh' from her father. Mírzá Buzurg moved to that house. Mírzá Ḥusayn-'Alí (Bahá'u'lláh) rented the house 'near the Gate' of Shimrán, and took His mother, His wife, His other step-mothers and the rest of His brothers and sisters to live with Him. This rented house remained His residence for the remaining years He spent in Írán. It was near the Madrisiy-i-Mírzá Ṣáliḥ, the theological college where Mullá Ḥusayn-i-Bushrú'í would stay when bearing the message of the Báb to Ṭihrán. The children of Bahá'u'lláh – 'Abdu'l-Bahá (the Most Great Branch), Bahá'íyyih Khánum (the Greatest Holy Leaf) and Mírzá Mihdí (the Purest Branch) – were all born in this rented house; their mother was his first wife, Ásíyih Khánum.

After the storms subsided, Mírzá Buzurg made an effort to regain the houses which he had had to sell under duress 'for a negligible sum'. A document exists in the handwriting of Bahá'u'lláh, drawn up for the purpose of eliciting from those in the know their testimony to the fact that the sale of the houses had taken place under unlawful pressure. But it did not produce the desired effect and no restitution was made.†

Mírzá Buzurg then decided to retire to 'Iráq, but death supervened. He passed away in 1839, and his body was taken to 'Iráq and buried at Najaf, where the tomb of 'Alí – the cousin of the Prophet Muḥammad, the first apostolic Imám and the fourth caliph – is situated. He was survived by seven sons and five daughters. Apart from the Central

* This brother mentioned by Bahá'u'lláh was Mírzá Riḍá-Qulí. (HMB)

† Two other documents are also extant, issued by two of the noted divines of the capital, one the brother of the Imám-Jum'ih, pronouncing the illegality of the sale by auction of the houses of Mírzá Buzurg-i-Núrí.

Figure of this history, we shall, time and again, meet in its course other sons of this remarkable and highly-respected Núrí minister. Manuscripts exist in his superb and much-admired handwriting, in various collections both in and outside of Írán. There is one such scroll in the International Archives of the Bahá'í Faith on Mount Carmel.

Ḍíyá'u's-Salṭanih, after obtaining her divorce and receiving her marriage settlement, married Ḥájí Mas'úd-i-Garmrúdí, who held the post of Foreign Minister of Írán for a considerable time. They had a daughter, named Sháhansháh Bigum, who embraced the Faith of Bahá'u'lláh; always she deplored what her mother had done to Mírzá Buzurg. Of the two daughters of Sháhansháh Bigum herself, one was married to Ibn-i-Aṣdaq, one of the four Hands of the Cause of God appointed by Bahá'u'lláh, and the other to Intiẓámu's-Salṭanih, who was greatly devoted to 'Abdu'l-Bahá, and whose sons rose high in the service of the State.

3

Childhood and Early Life

BAHÁ'U'LLÁH was born and brought up in Ṭihrán, in a house in the district known as Darvázih Shimrán (Shimrán Gate). In those days this district was on the edge of the city, close to the moat which was filled in during the reign of Náṣiri'd-Dín Sháh. Another moat was dug much further away: that too has now disappeared. But the house of Mírzá Buzurg and its adjuncts still stand today.

The infancy of Bahá'u'lláh was a cause of astonishment to His mother, as 'Abdu'l-Bahá recalled one day. He never cried, never showed restlessness. Mírzá Buzurg had come to realize that amongst all his sons and daughters, this son, Mírzá Ḥusayn-'Alí, was one apart. It will be remembered that Tákur, in the district of Núr, was the home of Mírzá Buzurg and his ancestors. There he had built a palatial house, and Bahá'u'lláh always spent part of the year in Tákur, usually in the summer months. Mírzá Buzurg, in his own masterly calligraphic hand, had written the following lines in a prominent place in that mansion:

> When thou reachest the threshold of the Beloved say 'Aye',
> For there neither 'salám' nor ''alayk' can find a way.*
> This is the vale of Love, hold thy steps;
> This is holy ground, shed thy foot-gear.†

To this day, those lines written by Mírzá Buzurg have endured.

When Bahá'u'lláh was a child of five or six years, He dreamt that He was in a garden where huge birds were flying overhead and attacking Him, but they could not harm Him; then he went to bathe in the sea, and there he was attacked by fishes, but they too could cause Him no injury. Bahá'u'lláh related this strange dream to His father, and Mírzá Buzurg sent for a man who claimed to interpret dreams. After making his calculations, he told Mírzá Buzurg that the expanse of the sea was

* *Salám* means 'Peace'; *'alayk* means 'upon thee'.
† That is what Moses heard on Mount Sinai, as He approached the Burning Bush.

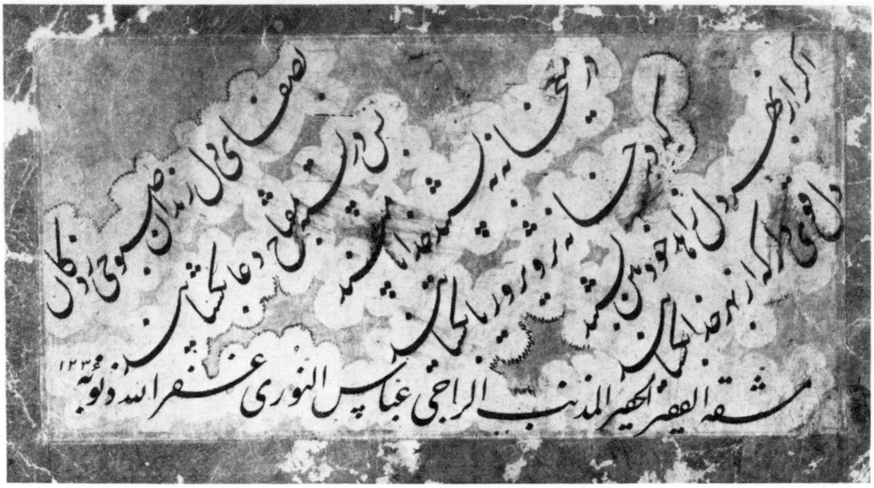

Specimen of the calligraphy of Mírzá Buzurg-i-Núrí

this world in its entirety, and the birds and fishes were the peoples of the world assailing his Son, because He would promulgate something of vital importance related to the minds of men. But they would be powerless to harm Him, for He would triumph over them all to achieve a momentous matter.

It is related that one day, when Mírzá Ḥusayn-'Alí was seven years old, as He was walking His parents were watching Him, and His mother remarked that He was a little short in stature. His father replied: 'That matters not. Do you not know how intelligent He is and what a wonderful mind He has!'.

The education and instruction which Mírzá Ḥusayn-'Alí received was limited both in nature and extent, as He Himself states in the Tablet addressed to Náṣiri'd-Dín Sháh: 'The learning current amongst men I studied not; their schools I entered not. Ask of the city wherein I dwelt, that thou mayest be well assured that I am not of them who speak falsely.'

In those days, the scions of noble houses were taught such matters as befitted their station in life, such as riding, handling a gun, wielding a sword, calligraphy, acquaintance with the works of the great classical poets of the land, a good reading knowledge of the Holy Book, the Qur'án, and hardly ever anything more. They were given such instruction by tutors, specially engaged by the parents, who were also required to teach them good manners.

But as Mírzá Ḥusayn-'Alí, the son of the Vazír-i-Núrí, grew up, the fame of His keen intelligence, His alert mind, His upright character, His benign, compassionate, benevolent nature, spread.

By the time Mírzá Ḥusayn-'Alí was fourteen, His rare understanding, His complete mastery of argument, and His unparalleled powers of exposition were remarked in all circles. Yet He was never assertive nor argumentative; rather, always courteous and patient. Only one thing aroused His ire, and that was any disrespectful reference to the Messengers of God and His Chosen Ones. Even then He would admonish the offender with kindliness and calm.

In a Tablet addressed to a Bahá'í of Shíráz, Bahá'u'lláh Himself tells of an incident in His childhood, when two hugely-turbaned divines were expounding theological questions to ladies in purdah. One such was whether the angel Gabriel had a higher station than Qanbar, the slave of 'Alí (the first Imám), who was greatly devoted to his master. Another concerned the station of 'Abbás, the brother of Ḥusayn (the third Imám), who suffered a martyr's death with the Imám in Karbilá; had he a rank higher than Salmán the Persian (Salmán-i-Fársí), who was one of the companions of the Prophet Muḥammad? Bahá'u'lláh recalls in that Tablet that He was astonished by this line and tone of argument, for if Gabriel, as stated in the holy Book, was the One by Whom the Holy Spirit descended upon the heart of the Apostle of God, then even the master of Qanbar could have no entry to that sphere.

In Yálrúd there lived a mujtahid, Shaykh Muḥammad-Taqí (see Addendum V), well-famed throughout the land. He had a thousand scholars of divinity around him, whom he taught and, from time to time, presented with a complex question to resolve. Whenever He returned to His home in Tákur, Bahá'u'lláh would usually stop for a while in Yálrúd, and here He would visit the mujtahid, who was distantly related to His family.* 'Abdu'l-Bahá has described how His own grandmother, who lived in Yálrúd, went one day at dawn to the house of the mujtahid to pray. After the morning prayer, Shaykh Muḥammad-Taqí told her that he had some excellent news for her. He had had a dream in which he had found himself outside a house which no one was allowed to enter, because, said the door-keeper, within it the Qá'im of the House of Muḥammad was closeted with Mírzá

* Yálrúd was the home of Ásíyih Khánum, the future wife of Bahá'u'lláh.

Ḥusayn-'Alí of Núr. At first the mujtahid had expressed his surprise that the son of a vizier should be so privileged; but on remembering their distant kinship, he had ascribed the privilege to this fact.

During a visit to Yálrúd, when Mírzá Ḥusayn-'Alí was sitting in the company of Shaykh Muḥammad-Taqí and other scholars and divines, He was asked to resolve a question they had been unable to answer to the mujtahid's satisfaction. The problem was this: an Islamic tradition states that 'Fáṭimih is the best of the women of this world, but for the one born of Mary'. But since Mary had no daughter, what did this conundrum mean? Bahá'u'lláh replied that the initial statement emphasized the impossibility of its alternative, since there could be no other woman comparable to Fáṭimih. It was like saying that a certain monarch is the greatest of the kings of this world, except for the one who comes down from Heaven; since no king has or will come down from Heaven, the uniqueness of that one monarch is stressed. Bahá'u'lláh's explanation left the great mujtahid silent, but next day he upbraided his disciples for having let him down badly. 'I have taught and trained you for years on end,' he complained, 'but when the need arises, I find you wanting in understanding, whereas an unturbaned youth has brilliantly explained the problem I had presented to you.'

At another time, Shaykh Muḥammad-Taqí had a dream of coming upon a room filled with trunks, which, he was told, belonged to Bahá'u'lláh. On opening one of them, he found it packed with books, and all the lines of those books studded with gems, the brilliance of which awakened him, he said.

Mírzá Abu'l-Faḍl-i-Gulpáygání relates in one of his works what he himself heard from a divine. In a gathering where Bahá'u'lláh was present, Mírzá Naẓar-'Alí of Qazvín (see Addendum V), the celebrated Ṣúfí *murshid* who was highly esteemed by Muḥammad Sháh, was holding forth on the station that a human being can attain. Referring to himself, he said, 'Should my servant come to me and say that Jesus the Christ was at the door, asking for me, my detachment is such that I would express no wish to see Him.' Some of those present kept silent, while others out of flattery murmured assent. Only Mírzá Ḥusayn-'Alí spoke up. He turned to the Qazvíní braggart, who had expressed such disrespect for a Manifestation of God, and said:* 'You are very close to the person of the sovereign and he is very devoted to

* The words spoken by Bahá'u'lláh in this anecdote are not an exact quotation.

you, but if the chief executioner with ten of his men were to come to this door and tell you that the monarch wanted to see you, would you take it calmly or would you be perturbed?' Mírzá Naẓar-'Alí paused for a while before replying, 'In truth, I would feel anxious.' 'In that case,' said Bahá'u'lláh, 'you should not make such an assertion.' Bahá'u'lláh's authoritative statement, according to Mírzá Abu'l-Faḍl, left them all speechless.

When Bahá'u'lláh was nearly fifteen years old, His elder sister Sárih Khánum and Mírzá Maḥmúd, the son of Mírzá Ismá'íl-i-Vazír of Yálrúd, were married. This Mírzá Maḥmúd, who never espoused the new Faith, had a younger sister, Ásíyih Khánum: winsome, vivacious and exceedingly beautiful. As soon as she came of age, and Bahá'u'lláh was nearly eighteen, Sárih Khánum requested her father, Mírzá Buzurg, to ask the hand of this sister-in-law for her Brother, Mírzá Ḥusayn-'Alí. Their marriage took place in Jamádíyu'l-Ukhrá (Jamádíyu'th-Thání) AH 1251 (about October 1835). Ásíyih Khánum was the mother of 'Abdu'l-Bahá.

Even those who were inimical towards His father, held Bahá'u'lláh in high esteem. One such was the Grand Vizier, Ḥájí Mírzá Áqásí. Rightly, Mírzá Buzurg had suspected that Ḥájí Mírzá Áqásí was largely responsible for the dismissal and the murder of that great man, his very good friend, Mírzá Abu'l-Qásim, the Qá'im-Maqám. At one time it was rumoured that Muḥammad Sháh had replaced the Ḥájí

Mírzá Abu'l-Qásim-i-Faráhání,
Qá'im-Maqám

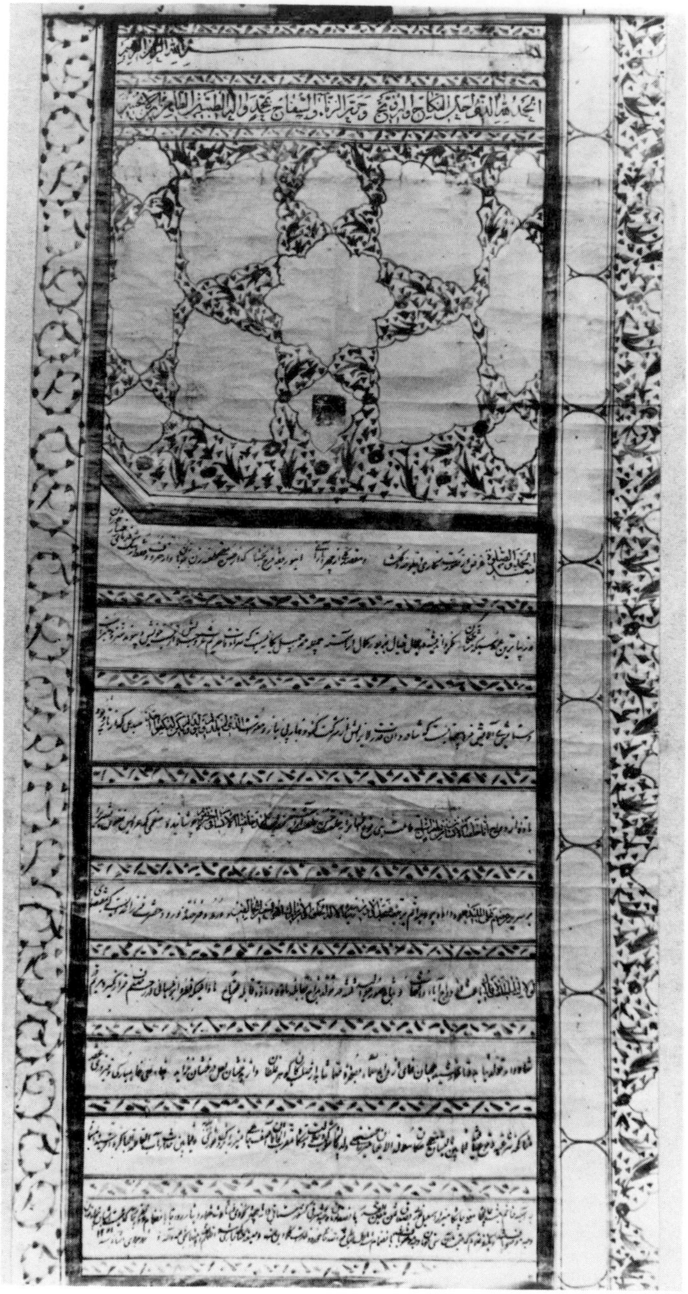

Marriage certificate of Bahá'u'lláh

with another grand vizier, namely Amír-Niẓám of Kirmánsháh. Mírzá Buzurg, who was then the Governor of Burújird and Luristán, expressed his delight in a letter to Prince Bahman Mírzá – a stormy petrel of Persian politics who eventually fled to Russia – and included this line:

'May this satyr be kept away from the Sháh.'

Bahman Mírzá, who was not at all friendly towards Mírzá Buzurg, showed this letter to Ḥájí Mírzá Áqásí. Infuriated, the latter sent for Mírzá Ḥusayn-'Alí and gave Him the letter His father had written to Bahman Mírzá, saying, 'See this; I do not know what I have done to your father to deserve this.' Mírzá Ḥusayn-'Alí kept silent. Then Mírzá Shafí' Khán, the Ṣáḥib-Díván, who was present, took the letter, had a good look at it and, in order to smooth matters, said, 'This is not written by Mírzá Buzurg. Someone has imitated him', whereat Ḥájí Mírzá Áqásí exclaimed, 'Impossible! There is no one who can produce such a beautiful specimen of calligraphy and such a wonderful piece of writing, such prose!' Still Mírzá Husayn-'Alí kept silent. Once again the Ḥájí turned to Him: 'What shall I, what can I do? He is your father. For your sake I will try to forget this and let bygones be bygones; but write to your father and advise him not to do it again.'

4

The Dawn

It was during the reign of Muḥammad S͟háh, in the year 1844, that the dawn of the long-awaited Day of God, foretold by all the Scriptures of mankind, appeared resplendent in the famed and delectable city of S͟híráz – the home and the resting-place of two of the greatest figures in the literary history of Írán, Sa'dí and Ḥáfiẓ, both of whom, in their own ways, prophetically foresaw the coming glory of their city and the rise of that wondrous Orb, the Sun of Truth, in the person of the Báb.

Ḥáfiẓ wrote:[1]

> S͟híráz shall tumultuous be, and One sweet-lipped
> there shall be,
> The wonders of whose lips shall set Bag͟hdád
> a-trembling.

And Sa'dí:[2]

> By God! This realm merits not darkness and gloom,
> This throne-seat of Solomon and of the Mystery of God.

In the centennial year of that effulgent dawn, the Guardian of the Bahá'í Faith wrote:

'May 23, 1844, signalizes the commencement of the most turbulent period of the Heroic Age of the Bahá'í Era, an age which marks the opening of the most glorious epoch in the greatest cycle which the spiritual history of mankind has yet witnessed. No more than a span of nine short years marks the duration of this most spectacular, this most tragic, this most eventful period of the first Bahá'í century. It was ushered in by the birth of a Revelation whose Bearer posterity will acclaim as the '*Point round Whom the realities of the Prophets and Messengers revolve*,' and terminated with the first stirrings of a still more potent Revelation, '*whose day*', Bahá'u'lláh Himself affirms, '*every Prophet hath announced*,' for which '*the soul of every Divine*

Messenger hath thirsted,' and through which '*God hath proved the hearts of the entire company of His Messengers and Prophets.*' . . . In sheer dramatic power, in the rapidity with which events of momentous importance succeeded each other, in the holocaust which baptized its birth, in the miraculous circumstances attending the martyrdom of the One Who had ushered it in, in the potentialities with which it had been from the outset so thoroughly impregnated, in the forces to which it eventually gave birth, this nine-year period may well rank as unique in the whole range of man's religious experience. We behold, as we survey the episodes of this first act of a sublime drama, the figure of its Master Hero, the Báb, arise meteor-like above the horizon of Shíráz, traverse the sombre sky of Persia from south to north, decline with tragic swiftness, and perish in a blaze of glory. We see His satellites, a galaxy of God-intoxicated heroes, mount above that same horizon, irradiate that same incandescent light, burn themselves out with that self-same swiftness, and impart in their turn an added impetus to the steadily gathering momentum of God's nascent Faith. . . .

'The opening scene of the initial act of this great drama was laid in the upper chamber of the modest residence of the son of a mercer of Shíráz, in an obscure corner of that city. The time was the hour before sunset, on the 22nd day of May, 1844. The participants were the Báb, a twenty-five year old siyyid, of pure and holy lineage, and the young Mullá Ḥusayn, the first to believe in Him. Their meeting immediately before that interview seemed to be purely fortuitous. The interview itself was protracted till the hour of dawn. The Host remained closeted alone with His guest, nor was the sleeping city remotely aware of the import of the conversation they held with each other. No record has passed to posterity of that unique night save the fragmentary but highly illuminating account that fell from the lips of Mullá Ḥusayn.

'"I sat spellbound by His utterance, oblivious of time and of those who awaited me,"* he himself has testified, after describing the nature of the questions he had put to his Host and the conclusive replies he had received from Him, replies which had established beyond the shadow of a doubt the validity of His claim to be the promised Qá'im. "Suddenly the call of the Mu'adhdhin [muezzin], summoning the

* They were his brother, nephew and other companions, who had come together from Karbilá to Shíráz, as if drawn by a magnet, in their quest. Their teacher and mentor, Siyyid Káẓim-i-Rashtí (who had died some months before) had told them to keep watch, because the advent of the Ṣáḥibu'z-Zamán (the Lord of the Age), the Qá'im of the House of Muḥammad, was close at hand. (HMB)

faithful to their morning prayer, awakened me from the state of ecstasy into which I seemed to have fallen. All the delights, all the ineffable glories, which the Almighty has recounted in His Book [the Qur'án] as the priceless possessions of the people of Paradise – these I seemed to be experiencing that night. Methinks I was in a place of which it could be truly said: '*Therein no toil shall reach us, and therein no weariness shall touch us;*' '*no vain discourse shall they hear therein, nor any falsehood, but only the cry, "Peace! Peace!"*'; '*their cry therein shall be, "Glory be to Thee, O God!" and their salutation therein, "Peace!", and the close of their cry, "Praise be to God, Lord of all creatures!"*' Sleep had departed from me that night. I was enthralled by the music of that voice which rose and fell as He chanted; now swelling forth as He revealed verses of the Qayyúmu'l-Asmá', again acquiring ethereal, subtle harmonies as He uttered the prayers He was revealing. At the end of each invocation, He would repeat this verse: '*Far from the glory of thy Lord, the All-Glorious, be that which His creatures affirm of Him! And peace be upon His Messengers! And praise be to God, the Lord of all beings!*'" . . .

'A more significant light, however, is shed on this episode, marking the Declaration of the Mission of the Báb, by the perusal of that "*first, greatest and mightiest*" of all books in the Bábí Dispensation, the celebrated commentary on the Súrih of Joseph, the first chapter of which, we are assured, proceeded in its entirety, in the course of that night of nights from the pen of its divine Revealer. The description of this episode by Mullá Ḥusayn, as well as the opening pages of that Book attest the magnitude and force of that weighty Declaration. A claim to be no less than the mouthpiece of God Himself, promised by the Prophets of bygone ages; the assertion that He was, at the same time, the Herald of One immeasurably greater than Himself; the summons which He trumpeted forth to the kings and princes of the earth; the dire warnings directed to the Chief Magistrate of the realm, Muḥammad Sháh; the counsel imparted to Ḥájí Mírzá Áqásí to fear God, and the peremptory command to abdicate his authority as grand vizir of the Sháh and submit to the One Who is the "*Inheritor of the earth and all that is therein*"; the challenge issued to the rulers of the world proclaiming the self-sufficiency of His Cause, denouncing the vanity of their ephemeral power, and calling upon them to "*lay aside, one and all, their dominion,*" and deliver His Message to "*lands in both the East and the West*" – these constitute the dominant features of that initial contact that marked the birth, and fixed the date, of the inception of the most glorious era in the spiritual life of mankind.'[3]

The Báb (the Gate) laid the injunction on Mullá Ḥusayn-i-Bushrú'í – who was soon to be known as Bábu'l-Báb (the Gate of the Gate) – not to divulge His name (Siyyid 'Alí-Muḥammad) to anyone. Nor should he show any sign that he had reached the end of his quest, had been led to the Qá'im of the House of Muḥammad, the Ṣáḥibu'z-Zamán, had recognized Him, believed in Him and given Him wholehearted allegiance. The secret of that most auspicious night was, for the time being, to remain a secret. Seventeen others, the Báb said, must seek Him, find Him and recognize Him, entirely by themselves.

The Guardian of the Bahá'í Faith continues: 'Not until forty days had elapsed, however, did the enrollment of the seventeen remaining Letters of the Living commence. Gradually, spontaneously, some in sleep, others while awake, some through fasting and prayer, others through dreams and visions, they discovered the Object of their quest, and were enlisted under the banner of the new-born Faith.'[4]

The last thus to enlist, who was destined to rank above them all, was a 22-year-old youth, Mullá Muḥammad-'Alí of Bárfurúsh (today named Bábul) in the province of Mázindarán. On the very hour of his arrival in Shíráz, he came face to face with the Báb in a thoroughfare, and without any questioning immediately recognized Him by His bearing and His gait as the Qá'im of the House of Muḥammad. On him the Báb conferred the title of Quddús, which means 'most holy and pure'.

The circle of the Ḥurúf-i-Ḥayy* – the eighteen Letters of the Living – was now complete. They were all in Shíráz, all but one. That solitary figure was a woman, some thirty years of age, learned, eloquent, a composer of noble verse, the daughter, niece and wife of famed and influential clerics of Qazvín. So assured and certain was she that the Lord of the Age had indeed come, and that whoever laid claim to that exalted station must be believed, that when Mírzá Muḥammad-'Alíy-i-Qazvíní, the husband of her younger sister and a stalwart disciple of Siyyid Káẓim-i-Rashtí, was setting out from Karbilá on his quest to find and offer his allegiance to the Qá'im, she gave him a

* *Ḥurúf* is the plural of *Ḥarf*: a letter of the alphabet. *Ḥayy*, which means Living, is numerically equal to eighteen.

sealed letter to present to that Lord of the Age, and these words to say to Him:[5]

> The effulgence of Thy face flashed forth, and the rays
> of Thy visage arose on high;
> Then speak the word, 'Am I not your Lord?' and 'Thou art,
> Thou art!' we will all reply.

Her name was Umm-Salamih. Siyyid Káẓim had called her Qurratu'l-'Ayn – the Solace of the Eyes. Bahá'í history knows her best as Ṭáhirih – the Pure – a designation bestowed on her by Bahá'u'lláh. Although she never attained the presence of the Báb, yet she arose with burning zeal, all ardour and steadfastness and with unsurpassed determination, to declare and promote His Faith, giving up kith and kin and finally life itself in His path.

Now, the Báb summoned His Letters of the Living to His presence and addressed them:

'O My beloved friends! You are the bearers of the name of God in this Day. You have been chosen as the repositories of His mystery. It behoves each one of you to manifest the attributes of God, and to exemplify by your deeds and words the signs of His righteousness, His power and glory. The very members of your body must bear witness to the loftiness of your purpose, the integrity of your life, the reality of your faith and the exalted character of your devotion. . . . Ponder the words of Jesus addressed to His disciples, as He sent them forth to propagate the Cause of God. In words such as these, He bade them arise and fulfil their mission: "Ye are even as the fire which in the darkness of the night has been kindled upon the mountain-top. Let your light shine before the eyes of men. Such must be the purity of your character and the degree of your renunciation, that the people of the earth may through you recognize and be drawn closer to the heavenly Father who is the Source of purity and grace. . . . You are the salt of the earth, but if the salt have lost its savour, wherewith shall it be salted? . . ." O My Letters! Verily I say, immensely exalted is this Day above the days of the Apostles of old. Nay, immeasurable is the difference! You are the witnesses of the Dawn of the promised Day of God. . . . You are the first Letters that have been generated from the Primal Point [the Báb] . . . I am preparing you for the advent of a mighty Day. . . . The secret of the Day that is to come is now concealed. It can neither be divulged nor estimated. The newly born babe of that Day excels the wisest and most venerable men of this time . . . Scatter throughout the length and breadth of this land, and, with steadfast feet and sanctified hearts prepare the way for His coming. Heed not your weaknesses and frailty; fix your gaze upon the invincible power of the Lord, your God, the Almighty. Has he not, in past days, caused Abraham, in spite of His seeming helplessness, to triumph over the forces of Nimrod? Has He not enabled Moses, whose staff was His only companion, to vanquish Pharaoh and his hosts? Has He not established the ascendancy of Jesus, poor and lowly as He was in the eyes of men, over the combined forces of the Jewish people? Has He not subjected the barbarous and militant tribes of Arabia to the holy and transforming discipline of Muḥammad, His Prophet? Arise in His name, put your trust wholly in Him, and be assured of ultimate victory.'[6]

The Báb specifically directed Mullá 'Alíy-i-Basṭámí to 'Iráq – the stronghold of the Shí'ih clerics.* He chose Quddús to accompany Him on pilgrimage to Mecca and Medina, and He gave the Bábu'l-Báb a mission, holy and exalted and of immeasurable significance, to accomplish in the capital city of Írán.

* Mullá 'Alí was before long caught up in a furore of agitation and oppression, was apprehended, put on trial and condemned to death. It has always been assumed that he was put to death somwhere in 'Iráq (either in Mosul or beyond), while being taken to Istanbul, because nothing more was ever heard of him after he reached Mosul. But recent research in official archives has established the fact that he arrived in the Ottoman capital, was once again put on trial and was condemned to hard labour in the dockyards. Then all trace of him is again lost. (For this information the author is much indebted to Mr Sami Doktoroglu.)

5

To the Capital City of Írán

> To Sheba I send thee, O Zephyr, Lapwing of the Morn;
> Behold well, whence thou goest and whither I send thee.
> – Ḥáfiẓ

THE glorious mission entrusted to Mullá Ḥusayn was truly enviable. Its nature was intimated to him by the Báb in assuring words: 'In this pilgrimage upon which We are soon to embark, We have chosen Quddús as Our companion. We have left you behind to face the onslaught of a fierce and relentless enemy. Rest assured, however, that a bounty unspeakably glorious shall be conferred upon you. Follow the course of your journey towards the north, and visit on your way Iṣfahán, Ká<u>sh</u>án, Qum, and Ṭihrán. Beseech almighty Providence that He may graciously enable you to attain, in that capital, the seat of true sovereignty, and to enter the mansion of the Beloved. A secret lies hidden in that city. When made manifest, it shall turn the earth into paradise. My hope is that you may partake of its grace and recognize its splendour. From Ṭihrán proceed to <u>Kh</u>urásán,* and there proclaim anew the Call. From thence return to Najaf and Karbilá, and there await the summons of your Lord. Be assured that the high mission for which you have been created will, in its entirety, be accomplished by you. . . .'[1]

And when the hour came for Mullá Ḥusayn to depart, the Báb strengthened him with words of utmost encouragement: 'Grieve not that you have not been chosen to accompany Me on My pilgrimage to Ḥijáz. I shall, instead, direct your steps to that city which enshrines a Mystery of such transcendent holiness as neither Ḥijáz nor <u>Sh</u>íráz can hope to rival. My hope is that you may, by the aid of God, be enabled to remove the veils from the eyes of the wayward and to cleanse the

* Bu<u>sh</u>rúyih, the home town of Mullá Ḥusayn, is situated in that province. (HMB)

minds of the malevolent. . . . The hosts of the invisible Kingdom, be assured, will sustain and reinforce your efforts. The essence of power is now dwelling in you, and the company of His chosen angels revolves around you. His almighty arms will surround you, and His unfailing Spirit will ever continue to guide your steps. He that loves you, loves God; and whoever opposes you, has opposed God. Whoso befriends you, him will God befriend; and whoso rejects you, him will God reject.'[2]

Mullá Ḥusayn was well known in Iṣfahán. He had visited that renowned city in the lifetime of Siyyid Káẓim-i-Ras͟htí on his behalf, to gain the approval of the celebrated mujtahid, Ḥájí Siyyid Muḥammad-Báqir-i-S͟haftí, who had since died. Now his son, Ḥájí Siyyid Asadu'-lláh, proved friendly, as his father before, and so did Ḥájí Muḥammad-Ibráhím-i-Kalbásí, another leading and remarkable divine of Iṣfahán. Even more crucial was the attitude of no less a person than Manúchihr K͟hán, the Mu'tamidu'd-Dawlih, the Georgian Governor of Iṣfahán, who refused to pay any heed to those who were already opposing Mullá Ḥusayn. With circumspection, because he was not yet allowed to mention the Báb by name, Mullá Ḥusayn led a number of people to recognize and give their allegiance to the newly-born Faith. The first convert, whom the Báb has immortalized in His Book, the *Bayán*, was a simple, ardent youth named Mullá Ja'far, known usually by his occupation: Gandum-Pák-Kun, the Sifter of Wheat, who fell at S͟hayk͟h Ṭabarsí. And the most outstanding of these new converts was Mullá Ṣádiq-i-Muqaddas-i-K͟hurásání, a notable disciple of Siyyid Káẓim, who in later years was one of the few to come safely through the holocaust at Ṭabarsí. He attained the presence of Bahá'u'lláh within the city-walls of 'Akká, became as stalwart a Bahá'í as he had been a Bábí, was honoured by Bahá'u'lláh with the designation Ismu'-lláhu'l-Aṣdaq (the Name of God, the Most Truthful), and remained true and loyal to the end of his life.* His son, Ibn-i-Aṣdaq, was one of the four Hands of the Cause of God appointed by Bahá'u'lláh, while Mullá Ṣádiq himself was named posthumously a Hand of the Cause by 'Abdu'l-Bahá in *Memorials of the Faithful* (p. 5).

* Some of those designated Ismu'lláh later broke the Covenant of Bahá'u'lláh – men such as Siyyid Mihdíy-i-Dahijí (Ismu'lláhu'l-Mihdí), Áqá Muḥammad-Javád-i-Qazvíní (Ismu'lláhu'l-Javád), and Áqá Jamál-i-Burújirdí (Ismu'lláhu'l-Jamál). Others remained true: Mullá Ṣádiq (Ismu'lláhu'l-Aṣdaq), Zaynu'l-Muqarrabín (Ismu'lláhu'l-Zayn), Siyyid 'Abdu'r-Raḥím-i-Iṣfahání (Ismu'lláhi'r-Raḥím), and Jináb-i-Munír (Ismu'lláhu'l-Muníb), who died in Smyrna in 1868. There were still others, not all of whom have as yet been identified.

Some of the personalities of the court of Muḥammad Sh͟áh: The young boy in the centre of the picture is Náṣiri'd-Dín, the Crown Prince, later to become Náṣiri'd-Dín Sh͟áh. Behind him on his right is Mírzá Abu'l-Qásim, Qá'im-Maqám, while to his left is Ḥájí Mírzá Áqásí. At the extreme left of the picture is Manúc͟hihr K͟hán, Mu'tamidu'd-Dawlih, the Governor of Iṣfahán. Between the latter and Qá'im-Maqám is Mírzá Abu'l-Ḥasan K͟hán-i-Ílchí, Persian envoy to Britain and the original for the character 'Mirza Firouz' in Morier's Hajji Baba of Ispahan. *(Another version of this same picture names the central figure as 'Abbás Mírzá, Násiri'd-Dín's half-brother.)*

In Kás͟hán, Mullá Ḥusayn tarried only a short while, but delivered the tidings of the dawn of the Day of God to Ḥájí Mírzá Jání, a prominent merchant of that town. Proceeding next to Qum, he found no one ready to hear him and so made his way to Ṭihrán, the capital city. Here dwelt the 'Mystery' spoken of by the Báb, He Whom the Báb's message and petition had to reach. Mullá Ḥusayn did not know in which direction or in which way he should seek that Mystery. But God had led him to the Qá'im, and he felt assured that, once again, he would be guided to the goal of his quest. He went to lodge in a theological college called the Madrisih (School) of Mírzá Ṣáliḥ, alternatively the Madrisih of Páminár (Páy-i-Minár), which was that district of Ṭihrán in which the college was situated. Ḥájí Mírzá Muḥammad-i-K͟hurásání, who stood at the head of the S͟hayk͟hís of the capital, was also the head of the Madrisiy-i-Mírzá Ṣáliḥ. In vain did Mullá Ḥusayn try to wake him to the truth of the dawning Day of God. Instead, Ḥájí Mírzá Muḥammad reprimanded Mullá Ḥusayn for deviating from the path of Siyyid Káẓim. Even more, he regarded Mullá Ḥusayn's sojourn in Ṭihrán as most undesirable, a menace to the safety and the integrity of the Shaykhí community. Mullá Ḥusayn assured him that he would not stay long in Ṭihrán and, in any case, he did not consider that he had said or done anything to denigrate the station and the position of Shaykh Aḥmad-i-Aḥsá'í or Siyyid Káẓim-i-Rashtí.

Not to antagonize Ḥájí Mírzá Muḥammad-i-Khurásání any more, Mullá Ḥusayn stayed away as much as he could from the Madrisih of Mírzá Ṣáliḥ. After all, it was an infinitely higher purpose than entanglement with this Shaykhí divine, that had brought him to Ṭihrán. He would leave the college early in the morning, and come back to his room after sunset. Mullá Muḥammad-i-Mu'allim (teacher or tutor), a native of the district of Núr in the province of Mázindarán, has given this account of how Mullá Ḥusayn reached the end of his quest and fulfilled the high mission entrusted to him by the Báb:

> ... I was in those days recognized as one of the favoured disciples of Ḥájí Mírzá Muḥammad, and lived in the same school in which he taught. My room adjoined his room, and we were closely associated together. On the day that he was engaged in discussion with Mullá Ḥusayn, I overheard their conversation from beginning to end, and was deeply affected by the ardour, the fluency, and learning of that youthful stranger. I was surprised at the evasive answers, the arrogance, and contemptuous behaviour of Ḥájí Mírzá Muḥammad. That day I felt strongly attracted by the charm of that youth, and deeply resented the unseemly conduct of my teacher towards him. I concealed my feelings, however, and pretended to ignore his discussions with Mullá Ḥusayn. I was seized with a passionate desire to meet the latter, and ventured, at the hour of midnight, to visit him. He did not expect me, but I knocked at his door, and found him awake seated beside his lamp. He received me affectionately, and spoke to me with extreme courtesy and tenderness. I unburdened my heart to him, and as I was addressing him, tears, which I could not repress, flowed from my eyes. 'I can now see,' he said, 'the reason why I have chosen to dwell in this place. Your teacher has contemptuously rejected this Message and despised its Author. My hope is that his pupil may, unlike his master, recognize its truth. What is your name, and which city is your home?' 'My name,' I replied, 'is Mullá Muḥammad, and my surname Mu'allim. My home is Núr, in the province of Mázindarán.' 'Tell me,' further inquired Mullá Ḥusayn, 'is there today among the family of the late Mírzá Buzurg-i-Núrí, who was so renowned for his character, his charm, and artistic and intellectual attainments, anyone who has proved himself capable of maintaining the high traditions of that illustrious house?' 'Yes,' I replied, 'among

his sons now living, one has distinguished Himself by the very traits which characterized His father. By His virtuous life, His high attainments, His loving-kindness and liberality, He has proved Himself a noble descendant of a noble father.' 'What is His occupation?' he asked me. 'He cheers the disconsolate and feeds the hungry,' I replied. 'What of His rank and position?' 'He has none,' I said, 'apart from befriending the poor and the stranger.' 'What is His name?' 'Ḥusayn-'Alí.' 'In which of the scripts of His father does He excel?' 'His favourite script is shikastih-nasta'líq.' 'How does He spend His time?' 'He roams the woods and delights in the beauties of the countryside.' 'What is His age?' 'Eight and twenty.' The eagerness with which Mullá Ḥusayn questioned me, and the sense of delight with which he welcomed every particular I gave him, greatly surprised me. Turning to me, with his face beaming with satisfaction and joy, he once more inquired: 'I presume you often meet Him?' 'I frequently visit His home,' I replied. 'Will you,' he said, 'deliver into His hands a trust from me?' 'Most assuredly,' was my reply. He then gave me a scroll wrapped in a piece of cloth, and requested me to hand it to Him the next day at the hour of dawn. 'Should He deign to answer me,' he added, 'will you be kind enough to acquaint me with His reply?' I received the scroll from him and, at break of day, arose to carry out his desire.

As I approached the house of Bahá'u'lláh, I recognized His brother Mírzá Músá, who was standing at the gate, and to whom I communicated the object of my visit. He went into the house and soon reappeared bearing a message of welcome. I was ushered into His presence and presented the scroll to Mírzá Músá, who laid it before Bahá'u'lláh. He bade us both be seated. Unfolding the scroll, He glanced at its contents and began to read aloud to us certain of its passages. I sat enraptured as I listened to the sound of His voice and the sweetness of its melody. He had read a page of the scroll when, turning to His brother, He said: 'Músá, what have you to say? Verily I say, whoso believes in the Qur'án and recognizes its Divine origin, and yet hesitates, though it be for a moment, to admit that these soul-stirring words are endowed with the same regenerating power, has most assuredly erred in his judgment and has strayed far from the path of justice.' He spoke no more. Dismissing me from His presence, He charged me to take Mullá Ḥusayn, as a gift from Him, a loaf of Russian sugar and a package of tea, and to convey to him the expression of His appreciation and love.

I arose and, filled with joy, hastened back to Mullá Ḥusayn and delivered to him the gift and message of Bahá'u'lláh. With what joy and exultation he received them from me! Words fail me to describe the intensity of his emotion. He started to his feet, received with bowed head the gift from my hand, and fervently kissed it. He then took me in his arms, kissed my eyes, and said: 'My dearly beloved friend! I pray that even as you have rejoiced my heart, God may grant you eternal felicity and fill your heart with imperishable gladness.' I was amazed at the behaviour of Mullá Ḥusayn. What could be, I thought to myself, the nature of the bond that unites these two souls? What could have kindled so fervid a fellowship in their hearts? Why should Mullá Ḥusayn, in whose sight the pomp and circumstance of royalty were the merest trifle, have evinced such gladness at the sight of so inconsiderable a gift from the hands of Bahá'u'lláh? I was puzzled by this thought and could not unravel its mystery.

A few days later, Mullá Ḥusayn left for Khurásán. As he bade me farewell, he said: 'Breathe not to anyone what you have heard and witnessed. Let this be a secret hidden within your heart. Divulge not His name, for they who envy His position will arise to harm Him. In your moments of meditation, pray that the Almighty may protect Him, that, through Him, He may exalt the downtrodden, enrich the poor, and redeem the fallen. The secret of things is concealed from our eyes. Ours is the duty to raise the call of the New Day, and to proclaim this Divine Message unto all people. Many a soul will, in this city, shed his blood in this path. That blood will water the Tree of God, will cause it to flourish, and to overshadow all mankind.'[3]

Once again Divine Providence had led Mullá Ḥusayn-i-Bushrú'í to the end of his quest – the most momentous in the history of mankind.

As for the obscure Shaykhí student of theology, Mullá Muḥammad-i-Mu'allim-i Núrí – whom that same Providence had guided to seek the company of Mullá Ḥusayn and consort with him, that he might point the way to the goal and perform a service unmatched, holy and supremely meritorious – he would shed his blood on the same battlefield as Mullá Ḥusayn. There an implacable enemy would tear his frail body into shreds.

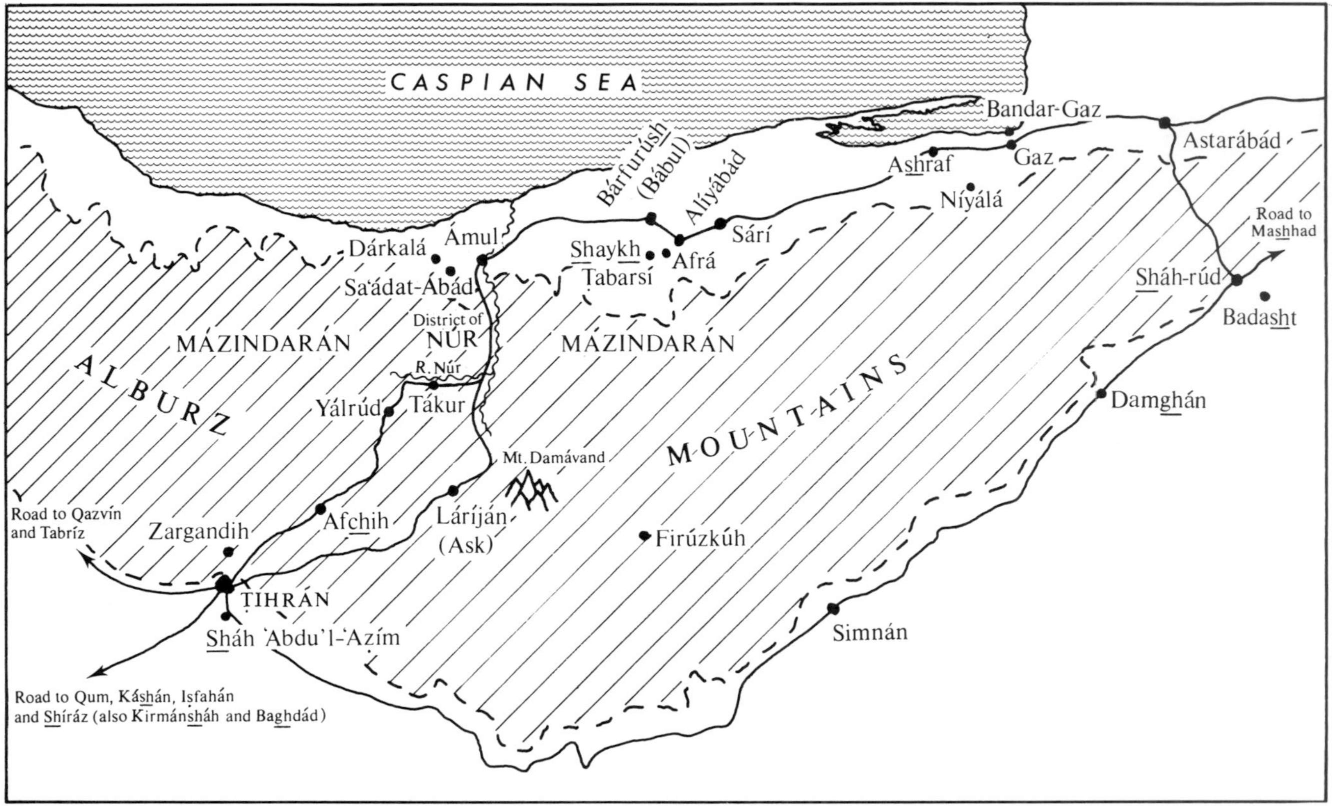

Map of northern Írán, showing Mázindarán, Ṭihrán, and some of the places associated with the early years of Bahá'u'lláh's life

6

In the Home of His Ancestors

FROM the day Mírzá Ḥusayn-'Alí, the Son of the Vazír-i-Núrí, gave His allegiance to the Cause of the Báb, He arose with all His vigour to promote that Cause. It was a fact well known that He had never attended a theological college, nor ever sat at the feet of a famed theologian, teacher, philosopher or guide. It was also well known that He was a master of argument, a fount of knowledge, a model of eloquence. Now, as an Exponent of the Faith of the Báb, these high qualities which He had evinced became more keen, more acute and more penetrating.

His first journey to propagate the Cause of the Báb was to Mázindarán, to the home of His ancestors. Shaykh Muḥammad-Taqí, the influential divine of Núr, whom we have met before in these pages, was now dead, and his seat of authority was occupied by his son, Shaykh Muḥammad. The latter knew that he could never surpass, nor even match, Bahá'u'lláh's powers of expression and exposition, and that, in truth, he was certain to fall far short. So when Bahá'u'lláh's ceaseless exertions to spread, throughout the district of Núr, the knowledge of the advent of the Báb, had brought a large number of its prominent citizens, including Mírzá Muḥammad-Ḥasan, His brother, and the heroic Muḥammad-Taqí Khán, one of His close relatives, under the banner of the new Faith, provoking at the same time intense opposition and hostility among a number of others – the chief of whom was Mírzá 'Azízu'lláh, an uncle of Bahá'u'lláh – Shaykh Muḥammad remained silent and held his peace. His students, however, would not leave him alone, and insisted that he should make an effort to counter Bahá'u'lláh's activities. They pressed him so hard that he finally gave way, appointing two of the most learned and accomplished of his pupils – his brothers-in-law Mullá 'Abbás and Mullá Abu'l-Qásim – to go to meet Bahá'u'lláh and challenge Him. Just then Bahá'u'lláh was at Dárkalá. Arriving there, the two went straight to an assemblage where a large number had congregated to listen to Bahá'u'lláh. He was expounding for them the inner essence of the very first súrih of the Qur'án. The two emissaries sat down, listened with rapt attention, and found themselves totally captivated. Mullá 'Abbás was first to get to his feet, and trembling, with tears streaming down his cheeks, he told his compatriots, 'You do as you wish, but as for me, I am struck dumb; no memory and no speech is left to me; go and tell Mullá Muḥammad that henceforth my duty is service at the threshold of Mírzá Ḥusayn-'Alí.' Mullá Abu'l-Qásim too had been overwhelmed; he told Mullá 'Abbás, 'Like you, I shall never abandon Him to serve anyone else. My place too is at His door.'

Then Bahá'u'lláh Himself went to the village of Sa'ádat-Ábád to visit Mullá Muḥammad. The latter, aware of his own inability, would not enter into a discussion with Him and found all manner of pretext to evade the issue. Finally, he decided to consult the Qur'án. He took up the holy Book, opened it at random, but soon shut it, saying lamely that the verses on that page did not omen well.

Travelling throughout the homeland of His ancestors, Bahá'u'lláh one day encountered a young dervish sitting by a brook, busy with his cooking. When Bahá'u'lláh asked what he was doing, the young man replied, 'Oh, I am cooking God to eat Him.' Bahá'u'lláh was highly amused by the simplicity of this response and showed great kindness to him.

That dervish, whose name was Muṣṭafá Big, was a native of Sanandij in Kurdistán, a poet using the sobriquet of Majzúb (the Attracted). He became so attracted and attached to Bahá'u'lláh that he followed Him, singing His praises and calling out to Bahá'u'lláh to 'tear asunder the veils, . . . tear asunder the veils.' Many who witnessed his behaviour were in their turn attracted, and devoted themselves to Bahá'u'lláh.

7

The First Imprisonment

BAHÁ'U'LLÁH'S first imprisonment was in connection with the murder of Ḥájí Mullá Taqíy-i-Baraghání, the uncle and father-in-law of Qurratu'l-'Ayn. Ḥájí Mullá Taqí (who has come to be known as Shahíd-i-Thálith – the Third Martyr) was an obscurantist divine, extremely narrow-minded and extremely hostile towards the persons and teachings of Shaykh Aḥmad-i-Aḥsá'í and Siyyid Káẓim-i-Rashtí. From his pulpit he would thunder against them in abusive language. And this was why he was murdered in his mosque, in the dim light of dawn. He who committed the murder was a fervent admirer of Shaykhí tenets, and publicly confessed that he had stabbed Ḥájí Mullá Taqí in the mouth, because of that divine's intemperate language. He was a native of Shíráz, variously named as Mírzá Ṣáliḥ, Mullá 'Abdu'lláh and Mírzá Ṭáhir, the Baker, who, by his own testimony at his trial in Ṭihrán, had never been a convinced Bábí, but was on his way to Máh-Kú to visit the Báb and investigate His Cause. But Mullá Muḥammad, the husband of Qurratu'l-'Ayn, was a man as fanatical and vindictive as his father, and he cast his net widely to secure the arrest of a number of innocent Bábís, who were transported to Ṭihrán.

One day in August 1919, 'Abdu'l-Bahá, speaking to a number of Bahá'ís gathered in the drawing-room of His Haifa residence, related the story of that first imprisonment of Bahá'u'lláh. He said that four men, one of whom was the actual assassin, were taken to Ṭihrán and detained in the house of Khusraw Khán. Bahá'u'lláh requested Mírzá Shafí' Khán, the Ṣáḥib-Díván, to tell Ḥájí Mírzá Áqásí what the true situation was. Ṣáḥib-Díván, a man free from prejudice, had great influence over the Grand Vizier; he gave him Bahá'u'lláh's message, which seemed to please him. Then, Bahá'u'lláh went with His retinue to visit the detainees, and gave them whatever money they required. Soon all of Ṭihrán came to hear of it.

The man who had murdered the mujtahid of Qazvín, and was

openly confessing it, finding that his confession had been useless, decided to escape. One night, when it was snowing, he broke gaol (with his fetters) and made his way to the house of Riḍá Khán, the Turkoman, an officer in the service of Muḥammad Sháh. Cunningly, instead of running to the gate of the house, he sent his walking-stick flying at it. The gate was opened, and a plank was put on the snow, over which the escapee walked into the house. When a search was instituted in the morning, they found no trace of the footsteps of the escapee. Because Bahá'u'lláh had been to see the detainees and had given them money, the relatives of the murdered mujtahid came from Qazvín to accuse Bahá'u'lláh of having helped the self-confessed assassin to escape. Bahá'u'lláh, undaunted, rode over, accompanied by *farráshes* and horsemen, to the place of the detention of the prisoners. He was put under arrest and also imprisoned. However, it was soon proved that the accusations were baseless, and Bahá'u'lláh was freed after a short spell in prison. But what these relatives of Ḥájí Mullá Taqíy-i-Baraghání did not know was that it was Bahá'u'lláh Who had ordered and arranged the rescue of Qurratu'l-'Ayn from their clutches.[1]

As for the murderer of the mujtahid, Riḍá Khán took him out of Ṭihrán. 'Abdu'l-Bahá said that when it was discovered what had happened, a thousand horsemen were sent in pursuit of Riḍá Khán, but he was never caught. Eventually both of them reached the fortress of Shaykh Ṭabarsí, and met there the death of martyrs.

8

The Conference of Badasht

THE Conference of Badasht was unique and unparalleled in the religious annals of mankind. Never before, in the lifetime of a Manifestation of God, had His followers gathered to take counsel together, as one body, regarding the nature of their Faith and their future course of action. The moving Genius and the Convener of that unprecedented conference was no less a person than Mírzá Ḥusayn-'Alíy-i-Núrí, Who subsequently became known in the Bábí community as Jináb-i-Bahá.* As the Guardian of the Bahá'í Faith has particularly remarked: 'The primary purpose of that gathering was to implement the revelation of the Bayán by a sudden, a complete and dramatic break with the past – with its order, its ecclesiasticism, its traditions, and ceremonials. The subsidiary purpose of the conference was to consider the means of emancipating the Báb from His cruel confinement in Chihríq. The first was eminently successful; the second was destined from the outset to fail.'[1]

Badasht was a hamlet, situated on the borders of Mázindarán. When Bahá'u'lláh reached this hamlet, He rented three gardens: one He assigned to Quddús, Ḥájí Mullá Muḥammad-'Alíy-i-Bárfurúshí, the eighteenth and the last of the Báb's Letters of the Living, and the first of them in rank. A second garden was specified as the residence of Qurratu'l-'Ayn, whom Bahá'u'lláh had rescued from the perils surrounding her in Qazvín, her native town. Bahá'u'lláh, Himself, stayed in the third garden. Nabíl-i-A'ẓam writes:

> . . . Those who had gathered in Badasht were eighty-one in number, all of whom, from the time of their arrival to the day of their dispersion, were the guests of Bahá'u'lláh. Every day, He revealed a Tablet which Mírzá Sulaymán-i-Núrí chanted in the presence of the assembled believers. Upon

* It ought to be noted that the name 'Bahá'u'lláh' was first mentioned by the Báb in His Book, the Persian *Bayán*; and that it was as 'Jináb-i-Bahá' that Mírzá Ḥusayn-'Alíy-i-Núrí became known in the Bábí community, after the Conference of Badasht.

each He bestowed a new name. He Himself was henceforth designated by the name of Bahá; upon the Last Letter of the Living was conferred the appellation of Quddús, and to Qurratu'l-'Ayn was given the title of Ṭáhirih [the Pure]. To each of those who had convened at Badasht a special Tablet was subsequently revealed by the Báb, each of whom He addressed by the name recently conferred upon him. When, at a later time, a number of the more rigid and conservative among her fellow-disciples chose to accuse Ṭáhirih of indiscreetly rejecting the time-honoured traditions of the past, the Báb, to whom these complaints had been addressed, replied in the following terms: 'What am I to say regarding her whom the Tongue of Power and Glory has named Ṭáhirih . . .?'[2]

It was indeed Qurratu'l-'Ayn, the Pure, who, on that never-to-be-forgotten day, in the beginning of summer 1848, first raised the resonant clarion call to emancipation from the man-made fetters of the past, to the horror and consternation of a large number of her fellow-believers. She appeared before them, with her veil discarded, her face adorned and uncovered for all to see. To many of them it seemed as if the Day of Resurrection had overtaken them – as, in truth, it had. One of them, 'Abdu'l-Kháliq-i-Iṣfahání, cut his own throat – so horrified and scandalized he felt – and, screaming, with blood pouring out, rushed from the assemblage of his co-religionists. A number of others followed him, walked out and away from the Faith of the Báb. Quddús was furious; he had his bare sword in his hand, and it looked as if, at any moment, he would use it on Ṭáhirih. Nabíl writes, quoting Shaykh Abú-Turáb:

> His threatening attitude failed, however, to move her. Her countenance displayed that same dignity and confidence which she had evinced at the first moment of her appearance before the assembled believers. A feeling of joy and triumph had now illumined her face. She rose from her seat and, undeterred by the tumult that she had raised in the hearts of her companions, began to address the remnant of that assembly. Without the least premeditation, and in language which bore a striking resemblance to that of the Qur'án, she delivered her appeal with matchless eloquence and profound fervour. She concluded her address with this verse of the Qur'án: 'Verily, amid gardens and rivers shall the pious dwell in the seat of truth, in the presence of the potent King.' As she uttered these words, she cast a furtive glance towards both Bahá'u'lláh and Quddús in such a manner that those who were watching her were unable to tell to which of the two she was alluding.[3]

Qurratu'l-'Ayn's bold bid for emancipation happened on a day when Bahá'u'lláh was indisposed. Quddús had gone to visit Him in

His garden, and other companions had also gathered there around Him. Then Ṭáhirih came in, and her entry, as we have seen, was exactly like a thunderbolt. 'I am the Word', she declared, 'which the Qá'im is to utter, the Word which shall put to flight the chiefs and nobles of the earth!' And, at the very end, she said: 'This day is the day of festivity and universal rejoicing, the day on which the fetters of the past are burst asunder. Let those who have shared in this great achievement arise and embrace each other.'[4]

After the pandemonium had subsided, Bahá'u'lláh quietly took command. Nabíl-i-A'ẓam writes:

> That memorable day and those which immediately followed it witnessed the most revolutionary changes in the life and habits of the assembled followers of the Báb. Their manner of worship underwent a sudden and fundamental transformation. The prayers and ceremonials by which those devout worshippers had been disciplined were irrevocably discarded. A great confusion, however, prevailed among those who had so zealously arisen to advocate these reforms. A few condemned so radical a change as being the essence of heresy, and refused to annul what they regarded as the inviolable precepts of Islám. Some regarded Ṭáhirih as the sole judge in such matters and the only person qualified to claim implicit obedience from the faithful. Others who denounced her behaviour held to Quddús, whom they regarded as the sole representative of the Báb, the only one who had the right to pronounce upon such weighty matters. Still others who recognized the authority of both Ṭáhirih and Quddús viewed the whole episode as a God-sent test designed to separate the true from the false and distinguish the faithful from the disloyal.
>
> . . . This state of tension persisted for a few days until Bahá'u'lláh intervened and, in His masterly manner, effected a complete reconciliation between them. He healed the wounds which that sharp controversy had caused, and directed the efforts of both along the path of constructive service.[5]

Bahá'u'lláh had the fifty-sixth súrih of the Qur'án, 'al-Wáqi'ah' ('The Event', or 'The Terror' in the translation of A. J. Arberry), read to that assemblage, and when their minds comprehended the meaning and the allusions and the purport of those verses of the Qur'án, they understood that indeed the Day of Resurrection had overtaken them:

> * When the Terror descends
> (and none denies its descending)
> abasing, exalting,
> when the earth shall be rocked

and the mountains crumbled
and become a dust scattered,
and you shall be three bands –

Companions of the Right (O Companions of the Right!)
Companions of the Left (O Companions of the Left!)
and the Outstrippers: the Outstrippers
those are they brought nigh the Throne,
in the Gardens of Delight
(a throng of the ancients
and how few of the later folk)
upon close-wrought couches
reclining upon them, set face to face,
immortal youths going round about them
with goblets, and ewers, and a cup from a spring
(no brows throbbing, no intoxication)
and such fruits as they shall choose,
and such flesh of fowl as they desire,
and wide-eyed houris
as the likeness of hidden pearls,
a recompense for that they laboured.
Therein they shall hear no idle talk, no cause of sin,
only the saying 'Peace, Peace!'[6]

Bahá'u'lláh stayed in Badasht for twenty-two days. Then, the Bábís – those who had remained constant and steadfast – with their faith fortified, set out from the environs of that epoch-making conference; but at the village of Níyálá they were attacked on all sides. Bahá'u'lláh, Himself, related to Nabíl:

'We were all gathered in the village of Níyálá and were resting at the foot of a mountain, when, at the hour of dawn, we were suddenly awakened by the stones which the people of the neighbourhood were hurling upon us from the top of the mountain. The fierceness of their attack induced our companions to flee in terror and consternation. I clothed Quddús in my own garments and despatched him to a place of safety, where I intended to join him. When I arrived, I found that he had gone. None of our companions had remained in Níyálá except Ṭáhirih and a young man from Shíráz, Mírzá 'Abdu'lláh. The violence with which we were assailed had brought desolation into our camp. I found no one into whose custody I could deliver Ṭáhirih except that young man, who displayed on that occasion a courage and determination that were truly surprising. Sword in hand, undaunted by the savage assault of the inhabitants of the village, who had rushed to plunder our property, he sprang forward to stay the hand of the assailants. Though himself wounded in several parts of his body, he risked his life to protect our property. I bade him desist from his act. When the tumult had subsided, I approached a number of the inhabitants of the village and was able to convince them of the cruelty and shamefulness of their behaviour. I subsequently succeeded in restoring a part of our plundered property.'[7]

9

From Bada<u>sh</u>t to <u>Shaykh</u> Ṭabarsí

FROM Bada<u>sh</u>t Bahá'u'lláh went to His native district of Núr. He placed Ṭáhirih in the charge of <u>Shaykh</u> Abú-Turáb-i-I<u>sh</u>tahárdí, to be taken to a place of safety. Meanwhile, adversaries in the capital (no doubt one of them being Ḥájí Mírzá Áqásí, the Antichrist of the Bábí Revelation) were poisoning the mind of Muḥammad <u>Sh</u>áh against Bahá'u'lláh, making it appear that He had incited rebellion. Then a day came, according to Nabíl, that Muḥammad <u>Sh</u>áh declared: 'I have hitherto refused to countenance whatever has been said against him. My indulgence has been actuated by my recognition of the services rendered to my country by his father. This time, however, I am determined to put him to death.'[1] Ḥájí Mírzá Áqásí, accordingly, obtained an edict from Muḥammad <u>Sh</u>áh and instructed one of the notables of Mázindarán to put Bahá'u'lláh under arrest.

Bahá'u'lláh states in one of His Tablets that after leaving Bada<u>sh</u>t, He travelled to Núr by easy stages. He visited <u>Sh</u>áh-rúd, the district of Hizárjaríb, Jaz (Gaz) – to the south of Bandar-Jaz (Bandar-Gaz) on the Caspian Sea – and A<u>sh</u>raf – 'village by village, town by town' – until He arrived at Núr. It was probably while Bahá'u'lláh was at Bandar-Jaz during the course of this journey that the following incident occurred. 'Abdu'l-Bahá has related that when Bahá'u'lláh arrived at Bandar-Jaz, He was taken ill. In this sea-town lived a Bábí, named Mírzá Masíḥ, a man of superior qualities. 'Abdu'l-Bahá describes him as 'spirit personified', one who, 'having read just one verse from the pen of the Primal Point, observed: "Just let this Báb be mine; you may have everyone else"'. At this very time, while Bahá'u'lláh was at Bandar-Jaz, Mírzá Masíḥ passed away. Bahá'u'lláh held a memorial meeting for him, and also wrote a prayer of visitation for this wonderful man.

It was while Bahá'u'lláh was at Bandar-Jaz that the edict came from Muḥammad <u>Sh</u>áh ordering His arrest. Bahá'u'lláh was at this time the

Muḥammad Sháh

guest of some of the notables of the town, and these, together with the Russian agent at Bandar-Jaz, who was a Persian, came to Bahá'u'lláh offering Him a passage in a Russian ship which was at anchor there. But Bahá'u'lláh did not accept it and did not run away. Next day, Bahá'u'lláh was the guest of a notable of that area. The Russian agent had also been invited to that banquet. Many of the prominent men of that district of Mázindarán were there to meet Bahá'u'lláh. Then a courier arrived, bringing news of Muḥammad Sháh's demise. The edict of Muḥammad Sháh for Bahá'u'lláh's arrest had lost its authority.

Amidst these happenings, Quddús had been arrested and imprisoned in the town of Sárí, in the house of Mírzá Muḥammad-Taqí, one of the prominent divines of the province of Mázindarán. Ṭáhirih had also been detained. She was taken to Ṭihrán where she was held under house arrest in the residence of Maḥmúd Khán, the kalántar (mayor) of the capital. There she remained until her martyrdom in the blood-bath of August 1852.

At Badasht, Mullá Ḥusayn, the Bábu'l-Báb, had been a notable absentee. He was a guest, at the time, of Ḥamzih Mírzá, the Ḥishmatu'd-Dawlih – a brother of Muḥammad Sháh (see Addendum V), and the Governor-General of Khurásán – where he was treated with courtesy and consideration. After leaving the camp of the Governor-General, he intended to go to Karbilá, but now a Tablet reached him from the Báb which totally changed his plans. In it the Báb had conferred on him a new name, Siyyid 'Alí, had sent him a green turban of His own to wear, and had directed him to go to Mázindarán to aid and support Quddús, with a black standard unfurled and carried before him. This black standard would be that of which the Prophet Muḥammad had given tidings: 'Should your eyes behold the Black Standards proceeding from Khurásán, hasten ye towards them, even though ye should have to crawl over the snow, inasmuch as they proclaim the advent of the promised Mihdí, the Vicegerent of God.'[2] In the course of his long march from Khurásán to Mázindarán, the Bábu'l-Báb was joined by Bábís who had been at Badasht. And as they went on, more and more came to enlist under the Black Standard. Thus the number of the companions reached 300 and beyond. At Bárfurúsh (Bábul) – the home of Quddús, who was still a captive in Sárí – because of the intense hostility of Sa'ídu'l-'Ulamá, the vindictive leading divine of that district, the Bábís had to use arms to defend themselves, and then because of treachery and broken pledges, they had, hurriedly, to throw up a wall and build a fortress around the mausoleum of <u>Shaykh</u> Ṭabarsí, in the heart of the forests of Mázindarán, and stay beleaguered within it.

Hearing of these events, while at Núr, Bahá'u'lláh decided to visit <u>Shaykh</u> Ṭabarsí. With His preparations completed, He moved to the village of Afrá, which belonged to a certain Naẓar-'Alí <u>Kh</u>án. There He stopped to order a sumptuous dinner for the inmates of the fortress and sent <u>Shaykh</u> Abú-Turáb-i-I<u>sh</u>tahárdí to inform them of His impending arrival. Then, accompanied by Naẓar-'Alí <u>Kh</u>án, He went to the fortress, to be received very warmly by the Bábu'l-Báb. It ought to be recalled that it had been Mullá Ḥusayn, the Bábu'l-Báb, who had conveyed, some four years before, the message of the Báb to Bahá'u'lláh, and thus he knew how exalted was the station of Mírzá Ḥusayn-'Alíy-i-Núrí, now known as Jináb-i-Bahá. Mullá Ḥusayn was lost in wonderment as he gazed at Bahá'u'lláh and heard Him for the first time. All his attention was riveted on Him. Bahá'u'lláh approved of all the arrangements made at <u>Shaykh</u> Ṭabarsí, but what was much missing there, He observed, was the person of Quddús. It ought to be emphasized that the Bábís had not gathered at the mausoleum of <u>Shaykh</u> Ṭabarsí in order to stage a rebellion against the government of their country, but rather to seek safety.

Bahá'u'lláh instructed Mullá Mihdíy-i-<u>Kh</u>u'í to take six men with him to Sárí and demand the release of Quddús. This was done, and Mírzá Muḥammad-Taqí, the leading mujtahid of that town, feared not to comply. In this manner, Quddús was released after ninety-five days of detention, and joined the companions at <u>Shaykh</u> Ṭabarsí. Bahá'u'lláh Himself left the fortress, together with Naẓar-'Alí <u>Kh</u>án and <u>Shaykh</u> Abú-Turáb, and by way of Núr went to the capital city of Írán, intending to return at a later date to the fortress, to bring provisions and other necessities for the companions. This was the promise that He made to the Bábu'l-Báb.

10

The Downfall of Ḥájí Mírzá Áqásí

THE wily Ḥájí Mírzá Áqásí, the Antichrist of the Bábí Revelation, well knew that with the death of Muḥammad Sháh in September 1848, his hold on power would become tenuous and the reins of affairs would slip from his incompetent hands. And so, as soon as it became evident that the Sháh was dangerously ill, the Grand Vizier kept away from the royal residence. And when Muḥammad Sháh breathed his last, the Grand Vizier was nowhere to be seen. He had made many enemies, and to whom could he turn in his hour of need?

As was usual after the demise of a monarch, the whole country, or most of it, was plunged into a state of unease or restiveness. In Shíráz, for example, Ḥusayn Khán – the Ájúdán-Báshí (honoured with the titles Niẓámu'd-Dawlih and Ṣáḥib-Ikhtíyár), who had governed with a fist of iron, bringing Shíráz and indeed the whole province of Fárs to respect order – was now facing a combination of two of the most powerful and influential grandees of the province, who were determined to oust him: the chieftain of the Qashqá'í tribe, and the ever-diplomatic and cautious Ḥájí Mírzá 'Alí-Akbar, the Qavámu'l-Mulk. And the common people had fallen in line with them. It was this Ḥusayn Khán who had subjected the Báb to indignities and inflicted punishments on His followers and the members of His family. Now even he, who had succeeded in subduing an unruly people, who had driven out two governors in the past – one of whom, Firaydún Mírzá, was a brother of Muḥammad Sháh – could not on this occasion force his will on an alliance of the mob and the grandees, and had to quit. He was not heard of again after this débâcle, and his stormy career came to an abrupt end.

As to the circumstances of the downfall of the Prime Minister himself, let Jahángír Mírzá, a brother of Muḥammad Sháh and author of *Táríkh-i-Naw* (New History), who was an eyewitness, describe what happened to Ḥájí Mírzá Áqásí. Already the Epistle of the Báb, addressed to him, had been delivered to this Antichrist of His Faith by Mullá Muḥammad 'Alíy-i-Zanjání (Ḥujjat), and it must have struck terror into his craven heart.

The following is the gist of what Jahángír Mírzá writes, although not an exact translation:

After the passing of the late sovereign, Ḥájí Mírzá Áqásí called in the Russian and British ministers, and together they wrote a letter which conveyed the news to the heir apparent in Tabríz. Ḥájí Mírzá Áqásí was then overcome by fear, and for reasons of his own [whatever they were] wanted to take 'Abbás Mírzá, a younger son of the late sovereign, to 'Abbásábád (the Ḥájí's own property), and he sent Maḥmúd Páshá y-i-Mákú'í to bring 'Abbás Mírzá from Tajrísh – the summer resort in the district of Shimrán, where the late sovereign had passed away – but it could not be done. Then Ḥájí Mírzá Áqásí

Ḥájí Mírzá Áqásí, grand vizier to Muḥammad Sháh and Antichrist of the Bábí Revelation

remained the night in 'Abbásábád, collected about fifteen hundred Mákú'ís and Íravánís round himself and set out for the royal citadel in the capital, which he took into his own possession, and sat there waiting. In Tajrísh, Mírzá Naṣru'lláh, the Ṣadru'l-Mamálik, gathered together the kháns and the courtiers who were there, and they decided to summon all the grandees and princes then in the capital, have the 'ulamá and the mujtahids wash and shroud the body of the late sovereign, after which they would all proceed to Ṭihrán to place the body in the garden of Lálihzár, and thence to the royal citadel. But after preparing the body for interment, for fear of some untoward event in the royal citadel which was occupied by Ḥájí Mírzá Áqásí, they delayed its removal, and the grandees and princes returned to the capital. At this point, the mother of the heir apparent, Mahd-i-'Ulyá, took affairs into her own hands and informed the foreign envoys that the presence of Ḥájí Mírzá Áqásí in the royal citadel, with all his following, was most undesirable. And Prince Bahrám Mírzá [the Mu'izzu'd-Dawlih, brother of Muḥammad Sháh] went to the citadel and counselled the Ḥájí to leave. The artillery officer in charge of the guards at the citadel was also advised by the mother of the heir apparent to force the Ḥájí to leave, and he trained his cannon on the house of Ḥájí Mírzá Áqásí, which was in the neighbourhood. Ḥájí Mírzá Áqásí had also heard of the forgathering of all the princes and grandees in Tajrísh, and that added to his alarm and distress.

At last, after a stay of twenty-four hours in the citadel, the Ḥájí rode out, together with his Mákú'ís and Íravánís, most of whom left him to go to the garden of Khán-Bábá Khán-i-Sardár. The Grand Vizier was now almost alone, and to whatever village he went, the people there would not let him enter. So, helplessly, with only fifty or sixty horsemen, he took the road to Karaj. By the river, Núru'lláh Khán-i-Sháhsavan, who had set out in his pursuit, reached him. The Ḥájí had fully armed himself with rifles and pistols (some carried on his own person and some tied to the saddle) and also with daggers, a mace and a sword. He fired at Núru'lláh Khán and set his horse galloping towards the Shrine of Sháh 'Abdu'l-'Aẓím. Núru'lláh Khán pursued him to the very precincts of the shrine, but the Ḥájí fled into its enclave. Núru'lláh Khán then possessed himself of the Ḥájí's horse and belongings and what appertained to the Ḥájí's men, leaving them almost naked.

As soon as Mírzá Naṣru'lláh, the Ṣadru'l-Mamálik, heard how the Ḥájí had fared, he intervened once again, informed the mother of the heir apparent of these events, and then in the company of all the princes, the courtiers, the grandees, and the foreign envoys, brought the body of the late sovereign to the capital with full military honours, and placed it in safe keeping in the garden of Lálihzár. He then wrote to Tabríz to inform the new sovereign of all that had occurred.

With Ḥájí Mírzá Áqásí out of the way, deserted, discredited, and a *bastí* [one who takes refuge in a *bast*, or sanctuary] in the Shrine of Sh̲áh 'Abdu'l-'Aẓím, what happened next, according to Jahángír Mírzá, was something unheard of, for certain persons gathered round Mírzá Naṣru'lláh, who apparently had ambitions of his own, to speak of something amounting to a republic or, at least, constitutional government. The new Sh̲áh had not yet arrived from Tabríz, but, as Jahángír Mírzá puts it, his determined, energetic mother was equal to the occasion and would have none of that nonsense. She took immediate steps to safeguard the royal treasures, and then by quiet diplomacy won over most of those who had congregated around Ṣadru'l-Mamálik. She also made handsome presents of money to a number of divines, such as Áqá Muḥammad-Ṣáliḥ of Kirmánsh̲áh (who was then sent to his home town to ensure the loyalty of its people), and Mírzá 'Askarí, the Imám-Jum'ih of Mas̲h̲had, who was directed to that holy city for the same purpose. Nevertheless, disturbances of diverse sorts were rife, some of which were nipped in the bud – such as the activities of Muḥib-'Alí K̲h̲án, the Governor of Kirmánsh̲áh, and of Sayfu'l-Mulúk Mírzá, a son of Fatḥ-'Alí Sh̲áh; and also the moves of Alláhyár K̲h̲án, the Áṣafu'd-Dawlih, and of 'Alí-Sh̲áh, the Ẓillu's-Sulṭán, in 'Iráq (stopped in time by the British representative in Bag̲h̲dád and the Ottoman válí there).

At last, Náṣiri'd-Dín and his Minister, Mírzá Taqí K̲h̲án, the Vazír-Niẓám – who, *en route*, had been elevated to the rank of Amír-Niẓám and was soon to be further honoured by the title Amír Kabír – reached the capital. By a royal rescript the new Grand Vizier occupied the houses of the *bastí* Antichrist, and Ḥájí Mírzá Áqásí himself, who had aged considerably during those weeks, was shorn of his wealth and given a safe conduct to 'Iráq, where, nine months later, he died in the holy city of Karbilá.

II

The Second Imprisonment

IN December 1848, to fulfil His promise to visit Shaykh Ṭabarsí for a second time, Bahá'u'lláh set out with a number of the Bábís intending to visit the besieged fortress. Those who went with Him included Ḥájí Mírzá Jáníy-i-Káshání,* Mullá Báqir-i-Tabrízí (one of the Báb's Letters of the Living), Shaykh Abú-Turáb-i-Ishtahárdí, Áqá Siyyid Ḥasan-i-Khu'í, Áqá Siyyid Ḥusayn-i-Turshízí (one of the Seven Martyrs of Ṭihrán), 'Abdu'l-Vahháb Big, Muḥammad-Taqí Khán-i-Núrí and Mírzá Yaḥyá, Ṣubḥ-i-Azal.

But Bahá'u'lláh did not succeed in fulfilling His intention, for He and His companions were arrested and detained when they reached a village some nine miles from Shaykh Ṭabarsí. People of that village had abandoned it and night had fallen when Bahá'u'lláh and His entourage arrived there. They put the arms which they had with them in one room, away from any fire, and settled down for the night. The next day they were to make their way into the fortress. But in the course of the night, informed by guards and spies from the royal army stationed around Shaykh Ṭabarsí, an officer surrounded the abandoned village with a considerable number of riflemen, and apprehended Bahá'u'lláh, taking Him with His companions to the town of Ámul. Because 'Abbás-Qulí Khán, the general who was also Governor of Ámul, had gone to the camp of Prince Mihdí-Qulí Mírzá, the Deputy-Governor, Muḥammad-Taqí Khán-i-Láríjání, recognizing Bahá'u'lláh, lodged Him and His companions in his own house. But Ámul was soon in turmoil, on hearing of the detention of a number of Bábís whom the Deputy-Governor had respectfully taken to his own house, instead of putting them in fetters and chains. And, as usual, the clergy, always on the alert to make mischief, were agitating. The divines of Ámul were particularly marked for their rapacity

* The merchant who had acted as host to the Báb in Káshán, and the first chronicler of His Faith, who was martyred in August 1852.

Mosque at Ámul, where Bahá'u'lláh was interrogated and bastinadoed

(as 'Abdu'l-Bahá has described them). They demanded from Muḥammad-Taqí Khán that Bahá'u'lláh be taken to the mosque. So strident was their clamour that the Deputy-Governor, although reluctant and apprehensive, had no alternative but to comply. Then the divines declared that the people ought to come to the mosque, fully armed. Next day they all arrived: the butcher with his axe, the carpenter with his hatchet. It was their intention to make a rush at Bahá'u'lláh and murder Him. Surrounded by the crowd, Bahá'u'lláh was led to the mosque, where He sat under one of the arches. Two merchants from Shíráz, guests of the Governor, also came in and took their seats. The divines were there, of course, in full force.

This is how 'Abdu'l-Bahá related the story of that day and that event, one evening in August 1919, in the drawing-room of His house in Haifa. One of the Shírází merchants mentioned a dream he had had the previous night, and wished it to be interpreted for him. When invited by Bahá'u'lláh to say what his dream was, the merchant replied: 'I dreamt that the Qá'im of the House of Muḥammad was in this mosque, holding a finger between his teeth.' 'But that is blasphemy', shouted one of the divines. Bahá'u'lláh asked the impetuous priest to desist, because it was nothing of the kind: holding a finger between one's teeth was a sign of astonishment. The two merchants were much attracted to Bahá'u'lláh. In the pocket of Ḥájí Mírzá Jání when he was searched, a letter had been found in the handwriting of Siyyid Ḥusayn-i-Kátib, written with great speed, which they could not read. Someone suggested that only Mullá 'Alí-Ján could read that type of hand-writing. So he, who in the past had been generously treated by Bahá'u'lláh, was sent for. Now he chose to forget Bahá'u'lláh's kindness, took up the letter, but, finding that he could not read it, his eyes caught a word which he considered to have been wrongly spelt. He exclaimed that this was a composition of the Báb, indicative of His ignorance and illiteracy. By quoting an incident in the life of Muḥammad, and the Prophet's saying, Bahá'u'lláh proved to Mullá 'Alí-Ján that this particular word was not at all what he thought it should be – that it was the right word and correctly spelt. Mullá 'Alí-Ján was abashed.

By now the divines were downcast but would not give up. They insisted that Bahá'u'lláh should be bastinadoed. Muḥammad-Taqí Khán was alarmed and told them that he could not carry out their verdict without permission from the Sardár. He would write to him about the matter, but it would take a horseman about four hours to reach Shaykh Ṭabarsí and deliver his letter; meanwhile, they ought to wait. His pleading had no effect on the divines, who clamoured that their verdict should be carried out there and then. However, Muḥammad-Taqí Khán found a way to thwart them. As mentioned, Bahá'u'lláh was sitting in the mosque, under an arch next to the clay wall. He set his men to take away the clay bricks from outside, one by one, until they reached the last thickness. Then suddenly they brought down the wall and, through the passage made, Bahá'u'lláh was led to a place of safety. When armed men surrounded the house of Muḥammad-Taqí Khán, he went to the roof to tell them that Mírzá Ḥusayn-'Alí was in his custody, nor would he deliver Him to them until he had heard from the Sardár. His own men, fully armed, took up defensive positions with their rifles trained on the excited mob, who were egged on by the divines. Finding how matters stood the mob dispersed.

The next day Muḥammad-Taqí Khán received a letter from 'Abbás-Qulí Khán, the Governor, reprimanding him for having arrested Bahá'u'lláh in the first instance. Should any harm come to Mírzá

Ḥusayn-'Alí, he declared, he would burn down the city of Ámul. He did not want a blood-feud to be perpetuated between his family and the family of Mírzá Buzurg-i-Núrí. Muḥammad-Taqí K͟hán took this letter to the divines, but they refused to be placated, claiming that matters of faith concerned them and were no concern of the K͟hán. Muḥammad-Taqí K͟hán had a brother named Mírzá Ḥasan, described by 'Abdu'l-Bahá as 'a man of ferocious character'. He arrived the next midnight and made straight for his brother's house. As soon as he set foot in it, he enquired where Bahá'u'lláh was, and whether 'Abbás-Quli K͟hán's letter had reached them. When informed that Bahá'u'lláh was within, and that the Sardár's letter had indeed arrived, he calmed down. In turn, he was asked why he had come away from the royal camp. The answer was simple: he had fled. So had Prince Mihdí-Qulí Mírzá and 'Abbás-Qulí K͟hán, and nobody knew where they were. The Bábís, he said, had made a sortie, broken through all the fortifications, set the whole army to flight and burned down the house (made of logs) in which the princes were lodged. Then Mírzá Ḥasan began a verbal attack on the divines, which he continued on the morrow, when they came to get a definite reply from Muḥammad-Taqí K͟hán. He used such choice epithets as '*pidar-súk͟htih*' (burnt father) which caught them thoroughly by surprise. 'If you are men of your word,' he told them, 'and want a *jihád*, why do you not come out to S͟hayk͟h Ṭabarsí?' But they were poltroons, and thus challenged they gave up and went away.

Now, both Muḥammad-Taqí K͟hán and Mírzá Ḥasan were full of apologies and wished to make restitution for all the stolen property, but Bahá'u'lláh would have none of it. 'It was all given in the path of God', He said.

Nabíl-i-A'ẓam has also given an account of this episode which conforms in general to the paragraphs above, as based on the talk by 'Abdu'l-Bahá. The significant addition is that the Deputy-Governor, much embarrassed by the insistence of the divines, who were interrogating Bahá'u'lláh in the mosque, that He and His companions be put to death as Bábís, attempted 'to hold in check the passions which had been aroused', by ordering 'his attendants to prepare the rods and promptly inflict a befitting punishment upon the captives', and promising to hold them in prison until the Governor's return. At this point, Bahá'u'lláh intervened to prevent His companions receiving the bastinado, and requested that the punishment be inflicted upon Him in their stead. The Deputy-Governor 'was reluctantly compelled to give orders that Bahá'u'lláh alone be chosen to suffer the indignity which he had intended originally for His companions.'[2] The Guardian of the Bahá'í Faith has stated, in a letter to the believers in the East, dated January 1929, that Bahá'u'lláh suffered the bastinado in Mázindarán.

Nabíl also gives Bahá'u'lláh's own description of this episode, in which he reports Him as saying:

> Mírzá Taqí succeeded, in spite of the tumult Our arrival had raised, and in the face of the opposition of the 'ulamás, in releasing Us from their grasp and in conducting Us to his house. He extended Us the warmest hospitality. Occasionally he yielded to the pressure which the 'ulamás were continuously bringing to bear upon him, and felt himself powerless to defeat their attempts to harm Us. We were still in his house when the Sardár, who had joined the army in Mázindarán, returned to Ámul. No sooner was he informed of the indignities We had suffered than he rebuked Mírzá Taqí for the weakness he had shown in protecting Us from Our enemies. . . . 'You should have been satisfied with preventing the party from reaching their destination and, instead of detaining them in this house, you should have arranged for their safe and immediate return to Ṭihrán.'[3]

In the *Epistle to the Son of the Wolf*, Bahá'u'lláh refers to His imprisonment in these words: 'While confined in the prison of the Land of Mím (Mázindarán) We were one day delivered into the hands of the divines. Thou canst well imagine what befell Us.'[4]

The peril being averted, Bahá'u'lláh returned to Núr, and from Núr proceeded to Ṭihrán.

12

A Momentous Year

THE ensuing year, from the summer of 1849 to the summer of 1850, witnessed a number of signal events in the ministry of the Báb. May 1849 had marked the termination of the eleven-month-long Mázindarán upheaval at Shaykh Ṭabarsí and the martyrdom of Quddús, the last Letter of the Living and the foremost disciple of the Báb. Persecution of the Bábís erupted with unprecedented ferocity in the opening months of 1850. In Ṭihrán occurred the episode of the Seven Martyrs; in Yazd, Siyyid Yaḥyáy-i-Dárábí (Vaḥíd) became embroiled in agitation against the Faith of the Báb and had to leave, but in Nayríz (in the province of Fárs in the south of Persia), he and his companions were surrounded, and fell eventually to treachery on the part of his opponents; at Zanján, in the north, the Shí'ih 'ulamá incited the people against the redoubtable Mullá Muḥammad-'Alí (Ḥujjat), a conflict that was to continue to the end of the year, with an outcome equally tragic. Finally, the Báb, Himself, was martyred in July 1850 in Tabríz. In the words of Nabíl-i-A'ẓam:

> That year, rendered memorable by the magnificent heroism which those staunch supporters of His Faith displayed, not to speak of the marvellous circumstances that attended His own martyrdom, must ever remain as one of the most glorious chapters ever recorded in that Faith's bloodstained history. The entire face of the land was blackened by the atrocities in which a cruel and rapacious enemy freely and persistently indulged. From Khurásán, on the western confines of Persia, as far west as Tabríz, the scene of the Báb's martyrdom, and from the northern cities of Zanján and Ṭihrán, stretching south as far as Nayríz, in the province of Fárs, the whole country was enveloped in darkness, a darkness that heralded the dawning light of the Revelation which the expected Ḥusayn was soon to manifest, a Revelation mightier and more glorious than that which the Báb Himself had proclaimed.[1]

Bahá'u'lláh, too, played a major role in these events. His house in Ṭihrán became a focal point for the Bábís of the capital city, and those

Bábís who were passing through Ṭihrán also received His hospitality. Among the Bábís who at this time frequented the house of Bahá'u'lláh was Vaḥíd, who was to go from there to earn eternal fame and glorious martyrdom at Nayríz. Another visitor was Mírzá 'Alíy-i-Sayyáḥ (Mullá Ádí Guzal of Marág͟hih), who was acting as courier for the Báb and was commissioned by Him to perform a pilgrimage to S͟hayk͟h Ṭabarsí and pray at the graves of those distinguished martyrs (see Addendum V for a note on his life). Yet another who called on Bahá'u'lláh was Mullá 'Abdu'l-Karím-i-Qazvíní (Mírzá Aḥmad), bringing with him the pen-case, seals and rings of the Báb. A frequent caller of those days was Mullá Muḥammad-i-Zarandí (Nabíl-i-A'ẓam), who has recorded some of the incidents connected with Bahá'u'lláh in that memorable year, one of these being the arrival and reception of Sayyáḥ:

> I have heard Áqáy-i-Kalím, who received Sayyáḥ at the entrance of Bahá'u'lláh's home in Ṭihrán, relate the following: 'It was the depth of winter when Sayyáḥ, returning from his pilgrimage, came to visit Bahá'u'lláh. Despite the cold and snow of a rigorous winter, he appeared attired in the garb of a dervish, poorly clad, barefooted, and dishevelled. His heart was set afire with the flame that pilgrimage had kindled. No sooner had Siyyid Yaḥyáy-i-Dárábí, surnamed Vaḥíd, who was then a guest in the home of Bahá'u'lláh, been informed of the return of Sayyáḥ from the fort of Ṭabarsí, than he, oblivious of the pomp and circumstance to which a man of his position had been accustomed, rushed forward and flung himself at the feet of the pilgrim. Holding his legs, which had been covered with mud to the knees, in his arms, he kissed them devoutly. I was amazed that day at the many evidences of loving solicitude which Bahá'u'lláh evinced towards Vaḥíd. He showed him such favours as I had never seen Him extend to anyone. The manner of His conversation left no doubt in me that this same Vaḥíd would ere long distinguish himself by deeds no less remarkable than those which had immortalized the defenders of the fort of Ṭabarsí.'
>
> Sayyáḥ tarried a few days in that home. He was, however, unable to perceive, as did Vaḥíd, the nature of that power which lay latent in his Host. Though himself the recipient of the utmost favour from Bahá'u'lláh, he failed to apprehend the significance of the blessings that were being showered upon him. I have heard him recount his experiences, during his sojourn in Famagusta: 'Bahá'u'lláh overwhelmed me with His kindness. As to Vaḥíd, notwithstanding the eminence of his position, he invariably gave me preference over himself whenever in the presence of his Host. On the day of my arrival from Mázindarán, he went so far as to kiss my feet. I was amazed at the reception accorded me in that home. Though immersed in an ocean of bounty, I failed in those days, to appreciate

the position then occupied by Bahá'u'lláh, nor was I able to suspect, however dimly, the nature of the Mission He was destined to perform.'[2]

'Abdu'l-Bahá has also recounted this episode, in a somewhat different form. One day when travelling by train from Salt Lake City to San Francisco, during the course of His historic journey in the United States and Canada in the evening of His Life, He recalled a day more than six decades before when, as a small child in Ṭihrán, he had been seated next to Vaḥíd in His Father's house. Of a sudden an unkempt dervish, wild in appearance, came into the room, his feet covered with mud. He was Mírzá 'Alíy-i-Sayyáḥ. Hearing that he had just returned from Máh-Kú where the Báb was imprisoned, Vaḥíd knelt to kiss his mud-stained feet, for those feet had trod the earth where the Báb had stood.

Sayyáḥ was also the bearer of a message from Bahá'u'lláh to the Báb, which was dictated to Mírzá Yaḥyá (Ṣubḥ-i-Azal) and sent in his name. Nabíl describes the significant reply:

> Shortly after, a reply, penned in the Báb's own handwriting, in which He commits Mírzá Yaḥyá to the care of Bahá'u'lláh and urges that attention be paid to his education and training, was received. That communication the people of the Bayán have misconstrued as an evidence of the exaggerated claims which they have advanced in favour of their leader. Although the text of that reply is absolutely devoid of such pretensions, and does not, beyond the praise it bestows upon Bahá'u'lláh and the request it makes for the upbringing of Mírzá Yaḥyá, contain any reference to his alleged position, yet his followers have idly imagined that the letter constitutes an assertion of the authority with which they have invested him.[3]

It is probable that the following episode related by 'Abdu'l-Bahá years later, when staying as a guest in Lady Blomfield's house in London, also occurred during the course of this year when Qurratu'l-'Ayn (Ṭáhirih) was being held a prisoner at the house of Maḥmúd Khán-i-Kalántar. (The fact that she was to be found visiting Bahá'u'lláh's house is not particularly surprising, since someone of Bahá'u'lláh's eminence could without difficulty arrange to act as guarantor for her temporary release from confinement.) Lady Blomfield writes:

> He, being a little boy, was sitting on the knee of Qurratu'l-'Ayn, who was in the private parlour of His mother, Ásíyih Khánum; the door of this room being open, they could hear, from behind the curtain, the voice of Siyyid Yaḥyáy-i-Dárábí, who was talking and 'arguing with my Father'.

Qurratu'l-'Ayn, that beautiful, fearless poetess, addressing the Siyyid with her musical, yet penetrating voice, said: 'O Siyyid this is not the time for arguments, for discussions, for idle repetitions of prophecies or traditions! It is the time for deeds! The day for words has passed!

'If you have courage, now is the appointed hour for manifesting it; if you are a man of deeds, show a proof of your manhood by proclaiming day and night:

"The Promised Herald has come!

"He has come, the Qá'im, the Imám, the Awaited One has come! He has come!"'

'Abbás Effendi told us that He remembered this episode very distinctly; the expression of enthusiasm on her lovely, radiant face as she spoke those inspiriting words from behind the curtain, which hung before the door, was wonderfully impressive.

'Abbás Effendi added:

'She used often, during her short visit, to take me on to her knee, caress me, and talk to me. I admired her most deeply.'[4]

The significant delivery to Bahá'u'lláh of the seals and other personal effects of the Báb has also been described by Nabíl:

Forty days before the arrival of that officer at Chihríq,* the Báb collected all the documents and Tablets in His possession and, placing them, with His pen-case, His seals, and agate rings, in a coffer, entrusted them to the care of Mullá Báqir, one of the Letters of the Living. To him He also delivered a letter addressed to Mírzá Aḥmad, His amanuensis, in which He enclosed the key to that coffer. He urged him to take the utmost care of that trust, emphasized the sacredness of its character, and bade him conceal its contents from anyone except Mírzá Aḥmad.

Mullá Báqir departed forthwith for Qazvín. Within eighteen days he reached that town and was informed that Mírzá Aḥmad had departed for Qum. He left immediately for that destination and arrived towards the middle of the month of Shá'bán (12 June–11 July AD 1850). I was then in Qum, together with a certain Ṣádiq-i-Tabrízí, whom Mírzá Aḥmad had sent to fetch me from Zarand. I was living in the same house with Mírzá Aḥmad, a house which he had hired in the Bágh-Panbih quarter. In those days Shaykh 'Aẓím, Siyyid Ismá'íl, and a number of other companions likewise were dwelling with us. Mullá Báqir delivered the trust into the hands of Mírzá Aḥmad, who, at the insistence of Shaykh 'Aẓím, opened it before us. We marvelled when we beheld, among the things which that coffer contained, a scroll of blue paper, of the most delicate texture, on which the Báb, in His own exquisite handwriting, which was a fine Shikastih script, had penned, in the form of a pentacle, what numbered

* This was the officer sent to bring the Báb from the fortress of Chihríq where he was imprisoned, to Tabríz, following the orders of the Amír-Niẓám. (HMB)

> about five hundred verses, all consisting of derivatives from the word 'Bahá'. That scroll was in a state of perfect preservation, was spotlessly clean, and gave the impression, at first sight, of being a printed rather than a written page. So fine and intricate was the penmanship that, viewed at a distance, the writing appeared as a single wash of ink on the paper. We were overcome with admiration as we gazed upon a masterpiece which no calligraphist, we believed, could rival. That scroll was replaced in the coffer and handed back to Mírzá Aḥmad, who, on the very day he received it, proceeded to Ṭihrán. Ere he departed, he informed us that all he could divulge of that letter was the injunction that the trust was to be delivered into the hands of Jináb-i-Bahá [Bahá'u'lláh] in Ṭihrán.[5]

Within that same month of Sha'bán, on 9 July 1850, occurred the martyrdom of the Báb. Ḥájí Sulaymán Khán had left Ṭihrán for Tabríz as soon as he heard of the danger which threatened the Báb. Although he arrived too late to effect the Báb's deliverance, he succeeded in rescuing His remains and those of His companion. Under Bahá'u'lláh's direction they were brought to Ṭihrán and there concealed.

13

One Year at Karbilá

SOON after the martyrdom of the Báb, Mírzá Taqí Khán, the Ṣadr-i-A'ẓam (Grand Vizier), who was responsible for and had ordered the death of the Báb, sought a meeting with Bahá'u'lláh. At this meeting he stated courteously but in no uncertain terms that had it not been for Bahá'u'lláh's support and guidance, the Bábís would not have lasted for such a considerable period of time, resisting well-tried, well-equipped government forces at Shaykh Ṭabarsí and elsewhere; yet he had never discovered proof which would establish, beyond any measure of doubt, Bahá'u'lláh's involvement and complicity. Mírzá Taqí Khán then expressed his regret that such superb abilities, which Bahá'u'lláh unquestionably possessed, had never been put to the service of the State. Nevertheless, he intended to recommend that the Sháh appoint Him to the post of Amír-i-Díván (Head of the Court). At the moment, however, the Sháh was about to leave for Iṣfahán, and during his absence it would be advisable for Bahá'u'lláh also to go away temporarily from the capital. Although couched politely, this was tantamount to an order by the Ṣadr-i-A'ẓam. Bahá'u'lláh, as courteously, refused the offer of employment by the Government, and informed Mírzá Taqí Khán of His wish to go on pilgrimage to the holy cities of 'Iráq. Mírzá Taqí Khán was delighted and relieved. Accordingly Bahá'u'lláh left for Karbilá, a few days after that meeting with the Grand Vizier. Bahá'u'lláh Himself told Nabíl-i-A'ẓam: 'Had the Amír-Niẓám been aware of My true position, he would certainly have laid hold on Me. He exerted the utmost effort to discover the real situation, but was unsuccessful. God wished him to be ignorant of it.'[1]

At the very time when Bahá'u'lláh was on the point of leaving Ṭihrán, the casket containing the remains of the Báb and His faithful disciple reached the capital. Acting on the instructions of Bahá'u'lláh, His brother Mírzá Músá (Áqáy-i-Kalím) and Mírzá Aḥmad-i-Kátib

(Mullá 'Abdu'l-Karím-i-Qazvíní) hid the casket in a safe place, within the precincts of the Shrine of Imám-Zádih Ḥasan.

Attending Bahá'u'lláh on His journey to 'Iráq were Áqá Shukru'-lláh-i-Núrí and Mírzá Muḥammad-i-Mázindaráni, the latter one of the survivors of Shaykh Ṭabarsí. Bahá'u'lláh spent most of August 1851, the month of Ramaḍán (the Muslim month of fasting), in Kirmánsháh. There, both Nabíl-i-A'ẓam and Mullá 'Abdu'l-Karím-i-Qazvíní attained His presence. He directed Mullá 'Abdu'l-Karím to go to Ṭihrán, and Nabíl to take Mírzá Yaḥyá with him and stay in the vicinity of Sháh-rúd.

Bahá'u'lláh stopped in Baghdád for a few days, and reached Karbilá on 28 August 1851. Ḥájí Siyyid Javád-i-Karbilá'í and Shaykh Sulṭán, an Arab Bábí converted to the Faith of the Báb by Ṭáhirih, were both residents of Karbilá, and both had been beguiled by a certain Siyyid-i-'Uluvv, who claimed to be a personification of the Holy Ghost. Bahá'u'lláh dealt with this Siyyid kindly but firmly, and persuaded him to renounce any such fantastic claim and promise never to indulge in it again. Shaykh Sulṭán and Ḥájí Siyyid Javád-i Karbilá'í realized how mistaken they had been, and reverted to their true allegiance, which they held firmly to the hour of death.

Shaykh Ḥasan-i-Zunúzí, who had served the Báb during His captivity in Ádharbáyján, was now living in Karbilá, having been directed by the Báb Himself to go to that holy city and make it his home. Shaykh Ḥasan had been a disciple of Siyyid Káẓim-i-Rashtí, and had first attained the presence of the Báb during the Báb's pilgrimage to the holy cities of 'Iráq, in the lifetime of Siyyid Káẓim. Later, Shaykh Ḥasan served Him as amanuensis, at Máh-Kú and then at Chihríq. When the Báb came to know that both Quddús and the Bábu'l-Báb were besieged in Mázindarán, He urged the Bábís to go to their aid, and He said to Shaykh Ḥasan: 'Had it not been for My incarceration in this mountain fastness, I would have felt it My bounden duty to go in person to help My beloved Quddús. But such is not the case with you. I want you to go to Karbilá, and await the day when with your own eyes you can behold the Beauty of the Promised Ḥusayn. On that day remember Me, and offer Him My love and submission. I am giving you a very important commission. Beware lest your heart shall falter and forget the glory given unto you.'[2]

Shaykh Ḥasan did as he was bidden, and was now in Karbilá, until one day in October 1851 he came face to face with Bahá'u'lláh for the first time, inside the Shrine of Imám Ḥusayn, and in Bahá'u'lláh he recognized that Ḥusayn of Whom the Báb had spoken. He would have shouted it from roof-tops, but Bahá'u'lláh restrained him.

Many others, during those months of Bahá'u'lláh's sojourn in the holy cities of 'Iráq, attained His presence and became devoted to Him. Among them were Mírzá 'Abdu'l-Vahháb, that glorious youth of Shíráz (see Chapter 18); Shaykh-'Alí Mírzá, also of Shíráz and the nephew of Shaykh Abú-Turáb, the imám-jum'ih of that city who had stood up to protect the Báb; and Mírzá Muḥammad-'Alí, a well-known physician of Zanján, who, many years later, met a martyr's death.

During this period of Bahá'u'lláh's absence from Írán, dramatic changes had taken place. Surprisingly, owing to jealousy and fear, Náṣiri'd-Dín Sháh had dismissed Amír Kabír and ordered him to Káshán, commissioning Ḥájí 'Alí Khán, the Ḥájibu'd-Dawlih – who would, before long, persecute the followers of the Báb with callous butchery – to proceed to that town and have the fallen Minister put to death. Mírzá Naṣru'lláh-i-Núrí, known as Mírzá Áqá Khán, had been appointed Grand Vizier, and he wrote and asked Bahá'u'lláh to return to Írán.

14

The Fall of Amír Kabír

NÁṢIRI'D-DÍN SHÁH, the fourth king of the Qájárs, the obscurantist monarch who richly deserves the epithet 'Tyrant of Írán', had begun his five-decade-long, disastrous reign in September 1848. (See Addendum I.) It was the adroit skill and the iron will of Mírzá Taqí Khán-i-Faráhání, the Amír-Niẓám – soon to be given the title Amír Kabír, the Great Emir, by which he is generally known – that had secured the throne firmly for the eighteen-year-old Náṣiri'd-Dín. Yet within three years of his accession, Náṣiri'd-Dín Sháh had this Grand Vizier put to death.

Mírzá Taqí Khán, whose father had been a cook in the service of the great Mírzá Abu'l-Qásim-i-Qá'im-Maqám, was undoubtedly a very capable man, well devoted to the service of his country. But he was also rash, merciless and self-willed. In recent times, as a modern Persian writer has put it, he has been almost deified in Írán. His virtues were abundant and abundantly clear, but so were his deficiencies and shortcomings. He it was who had used all his considerable power to crush and eradicate the Faith of the Báb and wipe out its followers. He it was who took upon himself to ordain the execution of the Báb. He it was who almost destroyed 'Abbás Mírzá, the Náyibu's-Salṭanih (later entitled Mulk-Ará), the half-brother of Náṣiri'd-Dín Sháh, of whom the sovereign's mother was inordinately jealous; had it not been for the intervention of Colonel Farrant, the British chargé d'affaires, 'Abbás Mírzá would certainly have lost his life through her machinations. Mírzá Taqí Khán was imperious and unbending, but even he could not deter that uneasy, incompetent poltroon, Áṣafu'd-Dawlih, and his highly ambitious, daring, reckless and charming son, Ḥasan Khán (known as Sálár), from rebelling in Khurásán for the second time. Sulṭán-Murád Mírzá, the Ḥisámu's-Salṭanih, uncle of the young Náṣiri'd-Dín, was given the task of bringing the Sálár to his knees and pacifying the whole of the province of Khurásán, which he did with

Mírzá Taqí Khán-i-Faráhání, Amír Kabír, grand vizier to Náṣiri'd-Dín Sháh

alacrity and ruthlessness – a characteristic of all the Qájár princes of the first rank. He laid siege to Mashhad, and Sálár and his unfortunate father were overthrown.

But now it was not in Khurásán that heroic efforts were to be looked for – Khurásán which had witnessed, shortly before, the historic and crucial Conference of Badasht, and the exodus of the fearless Bábu'l-Báb. Now great and tragic events were moving to a climax in the forests of Mázindarán, in the town of Nayríz (in the province of Fárs), and in the city of Zanján. Here, in all three, a few hundred Bábís, persecuted, hounded and beleaguered, were forced to take up arms and fight, putting armies to flight, and in the end being overcome only by treachery and false promises. The indomitable Mullá Ḥusayn, the stout-hearted Quddús and seven others of the Báb's Letters of the

Living fell at Shaykh Ṭabarsí in Mázindarán, together with scores of other heroic men; the undaunted Ḥujjat (the outspoken cleric, Mullá Muḥammad-'Alí of Zanján) and his stalwart supporters – amongst whom was Zaynab, a young girl dressed as a youth, who took the masculine name of Rustam-'Alí and kept watch over the ramparts – fought every inch of the ground before falling with unparalleled bravery; at Nayríz the erudite Siyyid Yaḥyáy-i-Dárábí, surnamed Vaḥíd, whom Muḥammad Sháh himself had commissioned to go to Shíráz and investigate the claim and the Cause of the Báb – and who had given Him his total allegiance – met a martyr's death in circumstances reminiscent of the martyrdom of the third Imám, the Prince of the Martyrs, while with him also fell many an intrepid soul, equally dedicated and unflinching in devotion to the Lord of the Age, the Qá'im of the House of Muḥammad.

In the capital city of Írán, seven men – one of whom was the venerable Ḥájí Mírzá Siyyid 'Alí, the maternal uncle of the Báb who reared Him when He was orphaned – were beheaded in public; and as these Seven Martyrs of Ṭihrán walked resolutely and with firm steps to present their heads to the executioner, they were vilified, loaded with imprecations and mocked by a barbarous mob, who afterwards heaped insults on their corpses and set them on fire.

Then, one day in midsummer 1850, in a square of the city of Tabríz, the glorious Báb, Himself, together with a disciple whom no earthly attachment, not even the sight of his infant child, could induce to deviate from the path of His Lord and renounce his faith, were riddled with bullets.

The heroism of these 'God-intoxicated' souls was truly unmatched.

But now it was the turn of Mírzá Taqí Khán, in whose time as Grand Vizier the Báb and His followers had so greatly suffered, to be sent the same way as his predecessor, the ignorant, scheming Antichrist of the Bábí Dispensation. He was summarily dismissed from office by his whimsical, ungrateful monarch, whose own sister, 'Izzatu'd-Dawlih, he had married. The fallen Minister was ordered to go to Káshán. It is claimed that the intervention of the Russian Minister on his behalf angered the young and unstable Náṣiri'd-Dín, who commissioned one of his courtiers, Ḥájibu'd-Dawlih, to travel covertly to Káshán and murder Mírzá Taqí Khán. Ḥájibu'd-Dawlih bided his time until one day, when the fallen Grand Vizier was in his bath, he crept into the bath-house and told him of his commission. Mírzá Taqí Khán faced death bravely. He chose to have his veins opened, and to die as his life-blood slowly oozed away. When 'Izzatu'd-Dawlih learned what had befallen her husband, it was too late to save him. Soon after his murder, Náṣiri'd-Dín Sháh forced his widowed sister to marry Niẓámu'l-Mulk, a son of his new Grand Vizier: Mírzá Áqá Khán-i-Núrí. But as soon as Mírzá Áqá Khán was also dismissed (though not put to death), 'Izzatu'd-Dawlih obtained a divorce from him.

Mírzá Taqí Khán left two daughters who, decades later, were married to two sons of Náṣiri'd-Dín Sháh: Táju'l-Mulúk (later entitled Ummu'l-Khaqán – 'the Mother of the Sovereign') to Muẓaffari'd-Dín Mírzá, who eventually came to the throne; and Hamdamu'l-Mulúk (later entitled Hamdamu's-Salṭanih) to Sulṭán-Mas'úd Mírzá, the Ẓillu's-Sulṭán.

Of the ministry, dismissal and murder of Mírzá Taqí Khán, Sir Percy Sykes writes:

> It is said that people have the rulers they deserve and, if so, Persia is to be sincerely pitied; for she is ruled, as Europe was in mediaeval times, by officials whose main desire is to amass wealth *per fas aut nefas*. However this may be, the regrets which the traveller feels when visiting the charming gardens and pavilions of Fin [Fín, in the environs of Káshán, where Mírzá Taqí Khán was murdered] are rendered more poignant when he reflects that, had this Minister governed for twenty years, he might have trained up some honest, capable men to succeed him. The execution of Amir-i-Nizam was, indeed, a calamity for Persia; for it arrested the progress which had been so painfully achieved and, as the near future was to prove, it had an equally disastrous effect on her external relations.[1]

It must be admitted, in fairness, that despite all the appalling injuries that Mírzá Taqí Khán inflicted on the newly-born Faith, right in its cradle, he was a zealous, upright reformer, honest and hard-working. The imprint of his many good deeds remained to remind his nation, many decades later, of the benefits gained by the short and eventful vizierate of this enigmatic man. He it was who laid the foundations of modern education in Írán, by instituting a college called 'Dáru'l-Funún' (The Abode of Arts and Sciences), and employing European instructors, Austrian and French, to teach in that college. He it was who took the first steps to introduce journalism on Western lines into

Írán, with its concomitant, a properly-run printing-press. But all his reforms and innovations, which included much else, do not equate him with being an advocate of democracy and democratic, constitutional government, which his over-zealous admirers have been attributing to him, in recent years. Both by temperament and by practice, he was a despot of the same mould as his whimsical royal master.

15

The Mad Attempt to Assassinate Náṣiri'd-Dín Sháh

BAHÁ'U'LLÁH had hardly returned from His pilgrimage to the holy cities of 'Iráq, and while he was still an honoured guest of the Grand Vizier, a storm of titanic force and dimension broke over the heads of the Bábís of Ṭihrán. It decimated their ranks, shook their diminishing community to its foundations and almost wiped it out of existence. The Bábís had no one to blame for their dire misfortune but the rashness and hot-headedness of some of their members. Bahá'u'lláh had already counselled them to walk in the ways of wisdom and moderation. But they had chosen to disregard His warnings.

Mullá Shaykh-'Alí, entitled 'Aẓím (Great) of Turshíz (now Káshmar) in Khurásán, a veteran of the Faith, was living in Ṭihrán and had a cluster of the Bábís round him. They met in various homes, including that of Ḥájí Sulaymán Khán, another veteran of the Faith, the same brave and devoted man who had, at the behest of Bahá'u'lláh, gone to Tabríz to recover the remains of the martyred Báb and bring them to Ṭihrán. Amongst those Bábís attached to Mullá Shaykh-'Alí were three young men, Ṣádiq of Tabríz, a confectioner, Fatḥu'lláh, an engraver of Qum, and Ḥájí Qásim of Nayríz. It so happened that Ḥájí Qásim had suffered much at the hands of the adversaries of his Faith. In the eyes of these youths, the young Sháh was the source of all the calamities that had befallen them, and so they plotted to assassinate him. It is not known how many were involved in this criminal folly, but Mullá Shaykh-'Alí certainly was. By the testimony of Bahá'u'lláh, as reported by Nabíl-i-A'ẓam, Mullá Shaykh-'Alí made a full confession, and his frank and unhedged admissions convinced the authorities that Bahá'u'lláh had never been privy to such an evil design.

Ṣádiq, Fatḥu'lláh, and Ḥájí Qásim waylaid Náṣiri'd-Dín Sháh on Sunday, 15 August 1852, in one of the summer resorts of the district of

Náṣiri'd-Dín Sh̲áh

Sh̲imrán. Today the summer resorts of Sh̲imrán adjoin and have become part of the capital city, but in those days appreciable distances separated them from Ṭihrán. The Sh̲áh and his retinue had just left his summer palace at Níyávarán on a hunting expedition, when the three young men approached him as petitioners seeking redress and justice. They were far from being professional assassins, and attempted their dastardly deed in a clumsy way. Their weapons were inadequate: short daggers and pistols that fired pellets. They tried to drag the Sh̲áh from his horse, and inflicted pellet wounds on him which were not serious. By this time the members of the Sháh's retinue had reached him to protect him, and beat off the assailants. Ṣádiq was killed on the spot. His body was cut in two, and each half was hoisted and left dangling over one of the several gates of the capital – Darvázih Shimrán, the gate on the road to the summer resorts, and Darváziy-i-Sháh 'Abdu'l-'Aẓím,* the gate on the road south to the tomb of the saint of that name. Fatḥu'lláh, who would not say a word under torture, was taken to be deaf and dumb. Molten lead was poured down his throat. Ḥájí Qásim too was soon dispatched.

* The tomb of Sháh 'Abdu'l-'Aẓím or Ḥaḍrat-i-'Abdu'l-'Aẓím, a descendant of the Prophet, was in those days several miles distant from Ṭihrán. But today the village that bore the name of the saint has been renamed Shahr-i-Ray and adjoins the capital.

Mírzá Áqá Khán-i-Núrí, I'timádu'd-Dawlih, second grand vizier of Náṣiri'd-Dín Sháh and distant relative of Bahá'u'lláh

Now Ṭihrán fell into turmoil. There was a full hue and cry seeking the Bábís. The mother of the young Sh̲áh was particularly vociferous in demanding vengeance. Ḥájí 'Alí K̲h̲án, Ḥájibu'd-Dawlih (see Addendum V) of Marág̲h̲ih, the farrás̲h̲-bás̲h̲í of the royal court, set about frenziedly seeking, finding and arresting as many of the Bábís as he could. At this juncture 'Abbás, the man-servant of Ḥájí Sulaymán K̲h̲án, who had accepted the Faith of the Báb, turned coat and betrayed his master and his fellow believers. He had come to know personally many of the leading Bábís of Ṭihrán, and informed Ḥájibu'd-Dawlih of the meeting of his co-religionists in the house of his master. Therewith Ḥájí Sulaymán K̲h̲án's house was surrounded and entered, and all the Bábís found there were arrested. All told, eighty-one Bábís were apprehended, of whom thirty-eight were leading members of the community. They were thrown into the Síyáh-C̲h̲ál – the Dark Pit.

Bahá'u'lláh was, at this moment, staying in a summer residence at Afjih (Afc̲h̲ih), in the vicinity of Ṭihrán. Ja'far-Qulí K̲h̲án, the brother of Mírzá Áqá K̲h̲án, the Ṣadr-i-A'ẓam (Grand Vizier), was still His host. The Grand Vizier himself sent word to inform Bahá'u'lláh of the engulfing tide, and particularly pointed out the venom of the anger and hatred of the mother of the Sh̲áh directed against His person. His friends offered to hide Him from the wrath of His ill-wishers until the danger had passed. But Bahá'u'lláh remained calm and composed. He had nothing to fear, and the next day He rode towards the royal quarters. On the way He alighted at the home of Mírzá Majíd K̲h̲án-i-Áhí, in the village of Zargandih. Mírzá Majíd K̲h̲án, secretary to the Russian envoy, was the husband of His sister, Nisá' K̲h̲ánum. The news of His approach reached Ḥájibu'd-Dawlih, who promptly informed the Sh̲áh. And the sovereign immediately ordered His arrest. But His enemies were confounded, for while they were looking for Him to arrest Him, He was coming to them, of His own accord. But when had Bahá'u'lláh ever shown fear or panic?

They laid their rough hands upon His Person. On the road to the dungeon in Ṭihrán, a big crowd gathered to jeer at Him and to heap insults upon Him. He Who had been their friend and defender, their shield and support in need, was now the victim of their blazing hatred.

People did the same to Jesus. On Palm Sunday they went out to greet Him. They gave Him a royal welcome. And Jerusalem echoed with 'Hosanna to the Son of David'. 'Blessed is He', they cried, 'that cometh in the Name of the Lord; Hosanna in the Highest.' A few days later, in the courtyard of Pontius Pilate, they were given a choice. Which should die? Barrabas, the proved and convicted criminal, or Jesus, the Light of the World? They asked for the death of Jesus. They rejected the Christ. 'Crucify Him', they cried.

Thus has the world ever treated its true friend.

Among the crowd, which hurled abuse at Bahá'u'lláh and pelted Him with stones, was an old woman. She stepped forward with a stone in her hand to strike at Him. Although frenzied with rage, her steps were too weak for the pace of the procession. 'Give me a chance to fling my stone in His face', she pleaded with the guard. Bahá'u'lláh turned to them and said, 'Suffer not this woman to be disappointed. Deny her not what she regards as a meritorious act in the sight of God.' Such was the measure of His compassion.

About the attempt on the life of the Sháh, Bahá'u'lláh writes in His *Epistle to the Son of the Wolf:*

> By the righteousness of God! We were in no wise connected with that evil deed, and Our innocence was indisputably established by the tribunals. Nevertheless, they apprehended Us, and from Níyávarán, which was then the residence of His Majesty, conducted Us, on foot and in chains, with bared head and bare feet, to the dungeon of Ṭihrán. A brutal man, accompanying Us on horseback, snatched off Our hat, whilst We were being hurried along by a troop of executioners and officials. We were consigned for four months to a place foul beyond comparison. As to the dungeon in which this Wronged One and others similarly wronged were confined, a dark and narrow pit were preferable. Upon Our arrival We were first conducted along a pitch-black corridor, from whence We descended three steep flights of stairs to the place of confinement assigned to Us. The dungeon was wrapped in thick darkness, and Our fellow-prisoners numbered nearly a hundred and fifty souls: thieves, assassins and highwaymen. Though crowded, it had no other outlet than the passage by which We entered. No pen can depict that place, nor any tongue describe its loathsome smell. Most of these men had neither clothes nor bedding to lie on. God alone knoweth what befell Us in that most foul-smelling and gloomy place![1]

16

The Birth of the Bahá'í Revelation

Síyáh-Chál – the Black Pit – was a subterranean dungeon in the capital of Írán, dim, damp and dismal, never knowing the rays of the sun. At one time it had been the water reservoir of a public bath. Few people survived who were kept there for long. Now, in the summer of 1852, they herded together all the Bábís on whom they could lay their hands in Ṭihrán, cast them into this dungeon and chained and fettered them. Amongst them were men from all walks of life: from distinguished courtiers to humble artisans, from well-to-do merchants to learned students of theology.

Bahá'u'lláh, Himself, was one of their number. Around His neck they placed one or other of the two most dreaded chains in the whole land. Under its ponderous weight His whole frame was bent. In the *Epistle to the Son of the Wolf*, Bahá'u'lláh speaks of those awesome chains:

> Shouldst thou at some time happen to visit the dungeon of His Majesty the Sháh, ask the director and chief jailer to show thee those two chains, one of which is known as Qará-Guhar, and the other as Salásil. I swear by the Day-Star of Justice that for four months this Wronged One was tormented and chained by one or the other of them. 'My grief exceedeth all the woes to which Jacob gave vent, and all the afflictions of Job are but a part of My sorrows!'[1]

Bahá'u'lláh and a glorious Shírází youth, 'Abdu'l-Vahháb (see Chapter 18), were chained together. Though outwardly degraded in the eyes of men, and fettered as a dangerous criminal, Bahá'u'lláh had visitors in Síyáh-Chál of such eminence as Dúst-'Alí Khán, the Mu'ayyiru'l-Mamálik* and Niẓámu'd-Dawlih, and Ḥájí Mírzá

* Some sixty years later, the third Mu'ayyiru'l-Mamálik, Dúst-Muḥammad Khán – the son of Dúst-'Alí Khán and a son-in-law of Náṣiri'd-Dín Sháh – met 'Abdu'l-Bahá in London and became so devoted to Him that he sought His presence almost every day, and accompanied Him wherever He went. One day, Mírzá Maḥmúd-i-Zarqání, 'Abdu'l-Bahá's secretary and the chronicler of His journeys, came upon Dúst-Muḥammad Khán, gazing on 'Abdu'l-Bahá with tears running down his cheeks.

Maḥmúd, the Niẓámu'l-'Ulamá, who had been the tutor of Náṣiri'd-Dín Sháh in his youth and had assisted at the trial of the Báb in Tabríz. They went into His presence in that verminous dungeon, sat down courteously beside Him and spoke to Him with great respect.

Nabíl, the immortal historian of the Bahá'í Faith, recounts in his work the words which he himself heard from Bahá'u'lláh, describing the torments of those days:

> We were all huddled together in one cell, our feet in stocks, and around our necks fastened the most galling of chains. The air we breathed was laden with the foulest impurities, while the floor on which we sat was covered with filth and infested with vermin. No ray of light was allowed to penetrate that pestilential dungeon or to warm its icy coldness. We were placed in two rows, each facing the other. We had taught them to repeat certain verses which, every night, they chanted with extreme fervour. 'God is sufficient unto me; He verily is the All-Sufficing!' one row would intone, while the other would reply: 'In Him let the trusting trust.' The chorus of these gladsome voices would continue to peal out until the early hours of the morning. Their reverberation would fill the dungeon, and, piercing its massive walls, would reach the ears of Náṣiri'd-Dín Sháh, whose palace was not far distant from the place where we were imprisoned. 'What means this sound?' he was reported to have exclaimed. 'It is the anthem the Bábís are intoning in their prison,' they replied. The Sháh made no further remarks, nor did he attempt to restrain the enthusiasm his prisoners, despite the horrors of their confinement, continued to display.
>
> One day, there was brought to Our prison a tray of roasted meat which they informed Us the Sháh had ordered to be distributed among the prisoners. 'The Sháh,' We were told, 'faithful to a vow he made, has chosen this day to offer to you all this lamb in fulfilment of his pledge.' A deep silence fell upon Our companions, who expected Us to make answer on their behalf. 'We return this gift to you,' We replied, 'we can well dispense with this offer.' The answer We made would have greatly irritated the guards had they not been eager to devour the food We had refused to touch. Despite the hunger with which Our companions were afflicted, only one among them, a certain Mírzá Ḥusayn-i-Mutivallíy-i-Qumí, showed any desire to eat of the food the sovereign had spread before us. With a fortitude that was truly heroic, Our fellow-prisoners submitted, without a murmur, to endure the piteous plight to which they were reduced. Praise of God, instead of complaint of the treatment meted out to them by the Sháh, fell unceasingly from their lips – praise with which they sought to beguile the hardship of a cruel captivity.
>
> Every day Our gaolers, entering Our cell, would call the name of one of Our companions, bidding him arise and follow them to the foot of the gallows. With what eagerness would the owner of that name respond to

that solemn call! Relieved of his chains, he would spring to his feet and, in a state of uncontrollable delight, would approach and embrace Us. We would seek to comfort him with the assurance of an everlasting life in the world beyond, and, filling his heart with hope and joy, would send him forth to win the crown of glory. He would embrace, in turn, the rest of his fellow-prisoners, and then proceed to die as dauntlessly as he had lived. Soon after the martyrdom of each of these companions, We would be informed by the executioner, who had grown to be friendly with Us, of the circumstances of the death of his victim, and of the joy with which he had endured his sufferings to the very end.[2]

It was in the murk, the gloom, the twilit world of the Síyáh-Chál that the Bahá'í Revelation was born – in Ṭihrán, the same city where the Bearer of that Revelation Himself first saw the light of day. This dismal prison, where dangerous criminals were thrown, had been chosen to lodge the broken and shattered remnants of a once proud and flourishing community. All around Bahá'u'lláh, chained and fettered, lay the Bábís, once carrying their heads high, but now bearing the stigma and the dishonour of would-be regicides. The enemy, fully aroused, knew no mercy and showed them none. They were doomed men, and they suffered horrible tortures before their lives were stifled.

The community of the Báb, become a shepherdless, aimless flock, courted disaster. Was it for this futility, this dubious, unedifying end, this seeming disgrace, one might well have asked, that the glorious Báb had gladly given His life, that the brave, the indomitable Bábu'l-Báb, the gentle, unwavering Quddús, the fearless, courageous Ḥujjat, the erudite, steadfast Vaḥíd and hundreds of other heroic souls, had fallen on the battlefield?

The answer would have been an emphatic, a thousandfold 'No', because the Bábís, no matter how demoralized, how subject to influences alien to the truth of their Faith, or far strayed from the righteous purposes of the Báb, had kept aglow in their hearts the hope born of the promise of the near advent of 'Him Whom God shall make manifest'.

It was in the path of that Supreme Manifestation of the Godhead that the Báb had shed His blood. It was to pave the way for His coming that martyrs had fallen at Shaykh Ṭabarsí, at Zanján, at Nayríz. Indeed the whole *raison d'être* of the Bábís was to know and acknowledge 'Him Whom God shall make manifest'. 'I am preparing you for the advent of a mighty day' – these had been the words of the glorious Báb addressed to the Letters of the Living, His first disciples, when He laid upon them the mandate to go out, 'scatter throughout the length and breadth' of the land and with 'steadfast feet and sanctified hearts, prepare the way for His coming'. The Báb had assured His people of 'ultimate victory', but that 'ultimate victory' had surprisingly and cruelly eluded them. It must, therefore, of a certainty, be theirs under the standard of that Supreme Manifestation of the Godhead, Whose advent had also been promised to them, and Whom they eagerly awaited.

Bahá'u'lláh, Himself, has given us a vivid and overpowering account of those hours when He became conscious of His Divine Mission:

'During the days I lay in the prison of Ṭihrán, though the galling weight of the chains and the stench-filled air allowed Me but little sleep, still in those infrequent moments of slumber I felt as if something flowed from the crown of My head over My breast, even as a mighty torrent that precipitateth itself upon the earth from the summit of a lofty mountain. Every limb of My body would, as a result, be set afire. At such moments My tongue recited what no man could bear to hear.'

'One night, in a dream, these exalted words were heard on every side: "Verily, We shall render Thee victorious by Thyself and by Thy pen. Grieve Thou not for that which hath befallen Thee, neither be Thou afraid, for Thou art in safety. Ere long will God raise up the treasures of the earth – men who will aid Thee through Thyself and through Thy Name, wherewith God hath revived the hearts of such as have recognized Him." '

'While engulfed in tribulations I heard a most wondrous, a most sweet voice, calling above My head. Turning My face, I beheld a Maiden – the embodiment of the remembrance of the name of My Lord – suspended in the air before Me. So rejoiced was she in her very soul that her countenance shone with the ornament of the good-pleasure of God, and her cheeks glowed with the brightness of the All-Merciful. Betwixt earth and heaven she was raising a call which captivated the hearts and minds of men. She was imparting to both My inward and outer being tidings which rejoiced My soul, and the souls of God's honored servants. Pointing with her finger unto My head, she addressed all who are in heaven and all who are on earth, saying: "By

God! This is the Best-Beloved of the worlds, and yet ye comprehend not. This is the Beauty of God amongst you, and the power of His sovereignty within you, could ye but understand. This is the Mystery of God and His Treasure, the Cause of God and His glory unto all who are in the kingdoms of Revelation and of creation, if ye be of them that perceive.'"[3]

These words are unique in the Scriptures of mankind.

17

Bábí Martyrs of 1852

THE savageries perpetrated, and cruelties inflicted, on the Bábí martyrs in the summer of 1852 were truly revolting, so revolting that an Austrian officer, Captain von Goumoens, in the employment of Náṣiri'd-Dín Sháh, sent in his resignation and wrote this bitter letter to a friend; it is dated 29 August 1852:

'Dear Friend, My last letter of the 20th inst. mentioned the attempt on the King. I will now communicate to you the result of the interrogation to which the two criminals were subjected. In spite of the terrible tortures inflicted, the examination extorted no comprehensive confession; the lips of the fanatics remained closed, even when by means of red-hot pincers and limb-rending screws they sought to discover the chief conspirator. All that transpired was that they belonged to the Bábí sect. These Bábís are heretics . . . This sect was founded . . . by a certain *Báb*, who was shot by the King's command. The most faithful of his adherents fled to Zanján, where, two years ago, they were reduced by the Royal Troops, and, as was generally believed, were exterminated without regard for age or sex. Like all religious intolerance, this unmeasured persecution produced exactly the opposite of the effects intended. The Báb's teaching gained more and more ground, and is at the present moment diffused through the whole country. Since the government obstinately clung to the system of persecution, the schismatics found occasion to steel their resolution, and to develop qualities which, contrasted with the effeminate luxury of the State Religion, compelled respect. Very skilfully had the Prophet [*i.e.* the Báb] pointed out to the disciples of his teaching that the way to Paradise lay through the torture-chamber. If he spoke truly, then the present Sháh has deserved great merit, for he strenuously endeavours to people all the realms of the Saints with Bábís! His last edict still further enjoins on the Royal servants the annihilation of the sect. If these simply followed the Royal command and rendered harmless such of the fanatics as are arrested by inflicting on them a swift and lawful death, one must needs, from the Oriental standpoint, approve of this; but the manner of inflicting the sentence, the circumstances which precede the end, the agonies which consume the bodies of the victims until their life is extinguished in the last convulsion are so horrible that the blood curdles in my veins if I now endeavour to depict the scene for you, even in outline. Innumerable blows with sticks which fall heavily on the back and soles of the feet, brandings of different parts of the body with red-hot irons, are such usual inflictions that the victim who undergoes only such caresses is to be accounted fortunate. But follow me my friend, you who lay claim to a heart and European ethics, follow me to the unhappy ones who, with gouged-out eyes, must eat, on the scene of the deed, without any sauce, their own amputated ears; or whose teeth are torn out with inhuman violence by the hand of the executioner; or whose bare skulls are simply crushed by blows from a hammer; or where the *bázár* is illuminated with unhappy victims, because on right and left the people dig deep holes in their breasts and shoulders and insert burning wicks in the wounds. I saw some dragged in chains through the *bázár*, preceded by a military band, in whom these wicks had burned so deep that now the fat flickered convulsively in the wound like a newly-extinguished lamp.

'Not seldom it happens that the unwearying ingenuity of the Orientals leads to fresh tortures. They will skin the soles of the Bábís' feet, soak the wounds in boiling oil, shoe the foot like the foot of a horse, and compel the victim to run. No cry escaped from the victim's breast; the torment is endured in dark silence by the numbed sensation of the fanatic; now he must run; the body cannot endure what the soul has endured; he falls. Give him the *coup de grâce*! Put him out of his pain! No! The executioner swings the whip, and – I myself have had to witness it – the unhappy victim of hundred-fold tortures runs! This is the beginning of the end. As for the end itself, they hang the scorched and perforated bodies by their hands and feet to a tree head-downwards, and now every Persian may try his marksmanship to his heart's content from a fixed but not too proximate distance on the noble quarry placed at his disposal. I saw corpses torn by nearly 150 bullets. The more fortunate suffered strangulation, stoning or suffocation: they were bound before the muzzle of a mortar, cut down with swords, or killed with dagger thrusts, or blows from hammers and sticks. Not only the executioner and the common people took part in the massacre: sometimes Justice would present some of the unhappy Bábís to various dignitaries and the Persian [recipient] would be well content, deeming it an honour to imbrue his own hands in the blood of the pinioned and defenceless victim. Infantry, cavalry, artillery, the *ghuláms* or guards of the King, and the guilds of butchers, bakers, etc., all took their fair share in these bloody deeds. One Bábí was presented to the crack officers-corps of the garrison; the general in command dealt the first blow, and afterwards each one as his rank determined. The Persian troops are butchers, not soldiers. . . . Would to God that I had not lived to see it! But by the duties of my profession I was unhappily often, only too often, a witness of these abominations.'[1]

Such was the measure of the disgust and revulsion of an upright and civilized Austrian officer. But those who ordered, sanctioned, and committed such savageries, not only committed them but pleasurably gloried in their abominable deeds, as the reportage in the pages of the official gazette of the time, *Rúznámiy-i-Vaqáyi'-i-Ittifáqíyyih*, amply testifies.

One of that band of brave and unflinching souls, who died in the holocaust of 1852, was Sulaymán Khán, the same fearless spirit who, at the bidding of Bahá'u'lláh, had rescued the mangled, inseparable remains of the glorious Báb and His faithful disciple. They bored nine holes in his body (even assisted by himself) and placed nine lighted candles in them. Thus they paraded him in the streets and bazars, with a howling, yelling, crazed mob jeering at his heels. Sulaymán Khán was a young courtier, in the full vigour of his manhood, accustomed to power and display. On this day of his martyrdom he stopped in the midst of his tortures and exclaimed: 'What greater pomp and pageantry than those which this day accompany my progress to win the crown of glory! Glorified be the Báb, who can kindle such devotion in the breasts of His lovers, and can endow them with a power greater than the might of kings!' As the candles flickered in his wounds, he said, 'You have long lost your sting, O flames, and have been robbed of your power to pain me. Make haste, for from your very tongues of fire I can hear the voice that calls me to my Beloved!'[2] And when one of his brutal tormentors reviled him, he answered with these lines:

> Clasping in one hand the wine-cup, in one hand
> the Loved One's hair,
> Thus my doom would I envisage dancing through
> the market-square.[3]

Thus died Sulaymán Khán.

Another distinguished victim in this tornado was Ṭáhirih, the beautiful, talented poetess of Qazvín – the same heroic soul who, at the Conference of Badasht, raised the call of the emancipation of her downtrodden sex. Now, in the dead of night, they strangled her and cast her body into a pit of which no trace was left. But the memory of her supreme constancy, courage and devotion will for ever endure. No matter how maligned and denigrated she may be (or may have been) by those blinded to truth, because of their jealousy and fanaticism, the bright star of the silver-tongued poetess of Qazvín will dazzlingly shine to the end of time. Ṭáhirih knew of her approaching death and was ready for it. To her hostess, the wife of the magistrate in whose custody she was placed, Ṭáhirih said on the day preceding the night of her martyrdom: 'I am preparing to meet my Beloved, and wish to free you from the cares and anxieties of my imprisonment.'[4] She was in bridal array.

Such was the fortitude of the Bábís and such was the magnitude of their sacrifice.

Siyyid Ḥusayn-i-Kátib of Yazd, surnamed 'Azíz, one of the Báb's Letters of the Living, His amanuensis and companion in the mountain-prisons of Ádharbáyján, was another prominent Bábí who quaffed the cup of martyrdom in that summer of 1852. He was handed over to the Ájúdán-Báshí and officers of the highest rank in the army, who hacked him with their swords.

Mullá 'Abdu'l-Karím-i-Qazvíní (known as Mírzá Aḥmad-i-Kátib) was torn apart by artillery men with their daggers. His brother, Áqá 'Abdu'l-Ḥamíd, also met a martyr's death.

The martyr mentioned by Captain von Goumoens to have been shod like a horse and made to run was, according to the official gazette, Áqá Muḥammad-Taqí, a native of Shíráz. The perpetrators of that barbarous deed were Asadu'lláh Khán, Náṣiri'd-Dín Sháh's Master of the Horse, and his crew in the royal stables.

Even the young students of the Dáru'l-Funún – the college recently instituted by Amír Kabír – were made to take part in those savageries. Their victim was Mírzá Nabí of Damávand, a learned man, resident in Ṭihrán. They cut him down with swords and spears.

Ḥájí Mírzá Jání, the faithful merchant of Káshán, who had acted as host to the Báb in that city, and was the first chronicler of His Faith,* became the victim of Áqá Mihdí, the Maliku't-Tujjár (the King of the Merchants), and the leading traders of the capital, who set upon him with a variety of weapons.

Another figure of note who met a martyr's death was Luṭf-'Alí Mírzá of Shíráz, a survivor of the holocaust of Shaykh Ṭabarsí. Luṭf-'Alí Mírzá was a scion of the Afshárid kings. He wrote a historical account of the episode of Shaykh Ṭabarsí in Mázindarán, which remained unfinished. The Sháṭir-Báshí (the chief runner or courier) and the *sháṭirs* (couriers) serving under him, put Luṭf-'Alí Mírzá to death by making him the target of stones, knives, daggers and sticks.

All these barbarities are reported in the official gazette with relish and pride. Sháṭir-Báshí had rendered signal services to the Sháh, that very day when the attempt was made on his life, and therefore Náṣiri'd-Dín Sháh wished to spare Mírzá Sulaymán-Qulí, known as Kháṭibu'r-Raḥmán (the Orator of the Merciful), who was the brother of Sháṭir-Báshí. But the latter, himself, brought about Mírzá Sulaymán-Qulí's death, saying that he did not wish to have a brother who was a Bábí.

Ḥusayn-i-Mílání, known as Ḥusayn-Ján (Beloved Ḥusayn), who had put forward a claim and had acquired a following, was another martyr in that August, that month of horrors. Soldiers of various regiments killed him with their spears, in their own fiendish way.

According to Nabíl-i-A'ẓam, thirty-eight Bábís met a martyr's death, in the fashions described, at the hands of various groupings of people. Enough has been said to show the barbarities committed by a vengeful enemy. Now, we shall only record the names of the other martyrs, as reported in the offical gazette. No grave, no tombstone is there in the capital city of Írán, to remind one of their supreme sacrifice. But the pages of history will enshrine their glories and bear witness, throughout centuries unborn, to the heroism which they displayed, and to the infamy and eternal shame of their persecutors.

* His short chronicle has been tampered with, beyond all recognition, and made the repository of hallucinations under the title *Nuqṭatu'l-Káf*. See Balyuzi, *Edward Granville Browne and the Bahá'í Faith*. It is said that Mírzá Áqá Khán, the Grand Vizier, wished to save Ḥájí Mírzá Jání.

The rest of the martyrs are named as: Siyyid Ḥasan-i-Khurásání (Ḥájí Mírzá Ḥasan-i-Raḍaví, one of the survivors of Shaykh Ṭabarsí), Mullá Ḥusayn-i-Khurásání, Mullá Zaynu'l-'Ábidín-i-Yazdí, Mullá Fatḥu'lláh-i-Qumí (one of the assailants of the Sháh, according to the official gazette), Shaykh 'Abbás-i-Ṭihrání, Áqá Muḥammad-Báqir-i-Najafábádí, Mullá Mírzá Muḥammad-i-Nayrízí (according to the official gazette, he had fought at Mázindarán, Zanján and Nayríz, his body bearing many scars of wounds received in those campaigns), Áqá Muḥammad-'Alíy-i-Najafábádí, Áqá Mihdíy-i-Káshání, Ṣádiq-i-Zanjání (said to have been a native of Tabríz, he was one of those who attempted the life of Náṣiri'd-Dín Sháh, and died the same day at the hands of the Sháh's entourage), Ḥájí Qásim-i-Nayrízí (he met his death with Sulaymán Khán, and in the same manner, their bodies being cut into halves, each half to swing on a city-gate), Mírzá Rafí'-i-Núrí, Mírzá Maḥmúd-i-Qazvíní, Najaf-i-Khamsi'í, Ḥasan-i-Khamsi'í, and Muḥammad-Báqir-i-Quhpáy'í.

The same official gazette reports that Náṣiri'd-Dín Sháh sentenced the following to life imprisonment, because their guilt had not been proved: Mírzá Ḥusayn-'Alíy-i-Núrí (Bahá'u'lláh), Mírzá Sulaymán-Qulí (whose own brother, as we have seen, encompassed his death), Mírzá Maḥmúd, Áqá 'Abdu'lláh (son of Áqá Muḥammad-Ja'far), Mírzá Javád-i-Khurásání, and Mírzá Ḥusayn-i-Qumí, of whom the official gazette adds: 'Though not quite guiltless, was kept for questionings' – most probably to make him incriminate 'Abbás Mírzá, the half-brother of Náṣiri'd-Dín Sháh, whose tutor Mírzá Ḥusayn had been at Qum. Eventually, both he and 'Abbás Mírzá were banished to 'Iráq.

Apart from those whose names were given in the official gazette, the following are also known to have been martyred in that summer of 1852: Ḥájí Muḥammad-Riḍáy-i-Iṣfahání, Ibráhím Big-i-Khurásání, Mírzá 'Alí-Muḥammad-i-Núrí (a cousin of Bahá'u'lláh, son of a paternal aunt), Mullá 'Abdu'l-Faṭṭáḥ (an old man, eighty years old, who was brought from Tákur, and died as soon as he was cast into the Síyáh-Chál), Mullá 'Alí Bábá and Áqá Muḥammad-Taqí (both natives of Tákur and brought from there to Ṭihrán, where both died within the prison-walls).

And it is certain that there were other martyrs in Ṭihrán whose names have not been recorded by friend or foe.

In Tákur, in the district of Núr, the native town of the father of Bahá'u'lláh, occurred an incident for which responsibility can be laid at the door of Mírzá Yaḥyá. Prior to the attempt on the life of Náṣiri'd-Dín Sháh, Mírzá Yaḥyá, who knew of the plans concocted by 'Aẓím and Ḥusayn-Ján-i-Mílání and others, left the capital for Tákur. So certain was he of the success which would attend the plans of his misguided fellow believers in Ṭihrán that he took covert steps to consolidate his own position in Tákur, and indeed in the whole district of Núr. Mullá 'Alí Bábá was a divine of advanced years in Tákur. Mírzá Yaḥyá persuaded him to lay aside his garb of a divine, a man of learning, to put on the garments of a fighting man, bedecked with weapons, and to wear on his head a hunting-cap. Muḥammad-Taqí Khán, who was young and impressionable, followed suit, with a few others, and thus rumours spread that the Bábís were planning an uprising. Soon, news came that an attempt had been made to assassinate the Sháh and had signally failed. Mírzá Yaḥyá was extremely frightened, gave out that he was leaving for Ṭihrán, and rode out of Tákur in haste, only to return the same night and go into hiding. When he emerged from his hiding-place it was as a dervish, and in that disguise, together with his uncle, Mírzá (or Mullá) Zaynu'l-'Ábidín, and another man named Mullá Ramaḍán, they went roaming in the forests of Mázindarán, until they reached the sea-town of Mashhad-Sar (now Bábulsar). There, Mírzá Yaḥyá and his uncle took a boat to Anzalí, in the Caspian province of Gílán. From Anzalí, they made their way to Baghdád. The people of Tákur had, however, been thoroughly alarmed and, led by Shaykh 'Azízu'lláh (that uncle of Bahá'lláh who was hostile), kept sending exaggerated reports to Ṭihrán which greatly angered Náṣiri'd-Dín Sháh. He ordered Mírzá Áqá Khán, the Ṣadr-i-A'ẓam, to give a salutary lesson to the Bábís of Tákur. Mírzá Áqá Khán was a Núrí himself and knew how distorted the news of Tákur was, but he had to do something to satisfy the Sháh. So he chose a regiment of cavalrymen, gave command to Ḥasan-'Alí Khán-i-Qájár, and made his own nephew, Mírzá Abú-Ṭálib Khán, the adviser of Ḥasan-'Alí Khán. Mírzá Abú-Ṭálib Khán's sister was the wife of Áqa Muḥammad-Ḥasan, a brother of Bahá'u'lláh. Despite this relationship and despite the Grand Vizier's warnings and injunctions, and Ḥasan-'Alí Khán's protestations, Mírzá Abú-Ṭálib Khán took high-handed action. He refused to meet his own brother-in-law, terrorized the countryside, and let his soldiers loose upon the people of Tákur, many of whom fled to the hilltops and mountain peaks. Bábá Khán, Muḥammad-Taqí Khán and ʻAbdu'l-Vahháb Big were three of the leading Bábís who took to the hills. Bábá Khán managed to get away. Muḥammad-Taqí Khán, beholding from his vantage point the riotous, unbridled behaviour of the soldiers and the sorry plight of his fellow believers, told his companion that he would go back to give whatever aid he could to the suffering inhabitants of Tákur. ʻAbdu'l-Vahháb Big tried to stop him, seeing how hopeless the situation was. But Muḥammad-Taqí Khán was adamant and ʻAbdu'l-Vahháb Big, together with his servant, accompanied him. On their descent into Tákur they were fired on. ʻAbdu'l-Vahháb Big and Muḥammad-Taqí Khán both fell, while the servant threw himself into the river and was carried away by its current.

ʻAbdu'l-Bahá spoke, one evening in August 1919, in the drawing-room of His house at Haifa, of Muḥammad-Taqí Khán of Tákur, his high qualities and his bravery. Muḥammad-Taqí Khán, He said, had been brought up in the lap of luxury, and was survived by an old mother, eighty years of age, who was constancy personified. All that had been left to her was a wrecked house, the contents of which had been pillaged. Throughout the night, ʻAbdu'l-Bahá related, she praised God and rendered thanks to Him: 'My Lord! I had but one son, and him I gave in Thy path. All praise be unto Thee!'

A month later, ʻAbdu'l-Bahá added, a certain Ḥájí Ḥasan-i-Kujúrí came to Muḥammad-Taqí Khán's mother, to pay back, being a very honest man, something which he said he had owed to her martyred son. But the old lady, although in great need, refused to accept it, no matter how Ḥájí Ḥasan pleaded to be allowed to make the repayment. She said, 'My son's wife and children are in Ṭihrán; take it to them.'

Mírzá Abú-Ṭálib Khán arrested about twenty of the leading Bábís, amongst whom were the aged Mullá ʻAbdu'l-Faṭṭáḥ, Mullá ʻAlí Bábáy-i-Buzurg (the Elder) and Mullá ʻAlí Bábáy-i-Kúchik (the Younger), and herded with a number of women, they were sent to Ṭihrán. The men were taken to the Síyáh-Chál. The above-mentioned three with three others, one of whom was named Muḥammad-Taqí Big, died in that dungeon, in the presence of Bahá'u'lláh. He closed the eyelids of Mullá ʻAlí Bábáy-i-Buzurg, as death overtook him. ʻAbdu'l-Bahá has related that when a man was ordered by Mírzá Abú-

Áqá Muḥammad-Ḥasan, elder half-brother of Bahá'u'lláh

Ṭálib Khán to cut off the beard of Mullá 'Abdu'l-Faṭṭáḥ, he cruelly cut off also part of his chin. That aged Bábí was more dead than alive, and expired on arrival at the Síyáh-Chál. The presumptuous, wayward Mírzá Abú-Ṭálib Khán even forced his own brother-in-law to abandon Tákur. Áqá Muḥammad-Ḥasan, who had charge of the properties of the family there, left his son, Mírzá Ghulám-'Alí, in his own stead and proceeded to Ṭihrán. When Mírzá Abú-Ṭálib Khán was received by Náṣiri'd-Dín Sháh, he boasted of all that he had achieved; but the Sháh, turning to Ḥasan-'Alí Khán, enquired in Turkish what actually had occurred. The Qájár chieftain was quite truthful and told Náṣiri'd-Dín Sháh that he had found no sign of rebellion in

Tákur, and taking troops there had only resulted in the death of a number of innocent men, the devastation of a large area of the country-side, the destruction of the house of Mírzá Buzurg, and the pillage of all the valuable contents of that house. Náṣiri'd-Dín Sháh, it is said, felt ashamed and abashed. Mírzá Áqá Khán reprimanded his nephew, although that young upstart received a commission in the army and was given a regiment to command.

But history records that this is what happened to those guilty of transgressions at Tákur. Mírzá Abú-Ṭálib Khán went down with cholera within a month. At the hour of his death, his head was resting on the knees of Áqá Muḥammad-Ḥasan, the brother-in-law whom he had slighted and scorned. Now that husband of his sister showed him all kindliness and compassion, to the astonishment of Mírzá Áqá Khán. Mírzá Khalíl-i-Yálrúdí, who had committed atrocities in the course of the same year, fell off a bridge with his horse and was fatally wounded. Ṭahmásb-Qulí Khán-i-Kujúrí, also guilty of atrocities, was torn to pieces by his own entourage. Nabí, the man who by his own confession had shot Muḥammad-Taqí Khán, during the army's march back from Tákur, fell from his steed and was killed.

18

The Story of a Shírází Youth

THIS is the story of a Shírází youth – a glorious youth who immolated himself, because his pure heart brimmed with love for Bahá'u'lláh. His story goes back to the opening months of the new Dispensation. It has been told by Bahá'u'lláh; it has been told by 'Abdu'l-Bahá; and Nabíl has recorded it.

When Mullá 'Alíy-i-Basṭámí – one of the Báb's Letters of the Living instructed by Him to go to 'Iráq – left for his destination, he had gone only a short distance from Shíráz before he was overtaken by a youth. His name, the young man said, was 'Abdu'l-Vahháb. His purpose was very simple: to be with Mullá 'Alí wherever he was going. And he had a strange tale to tell. Let Nabíl-i-A'ẓam take up the story:

> 'I beseech you,' he tearfully entreated Mullá 'Alí, 'to allow me to accompany you on your journey. Perplexities oppress my heart; I pray you to guide my steps in the way of Truth. Last night in my dream, I heard the crier announce in the market-street of Shíráz the appearance of the Imám 'Alí, the Commander of the Faithful. He called to the multitude: "Arise and seek him. Behold, he plucks out of the burning fire charters of liberty and is distributing them to the people. Hasten to him, for whoever receives them from his hands will be secure from penal suffering, and whoever fails to obtain them from him, will be bereft of the blessings of Paradise." Immediately I heard the voice of the crier, I arose and, abandoning my shop, ran across the market-street of Vakíl to a place where my eyes beheld you standing and distributing those same charters to the people. To everyone who approached to receive them from your hands, you would whisper in his ear a few words which instantly caused him to flee in consternation and exclaim: "Woe betide me, for I am deprived of the blessings of 'Alí and his kindred! Ah, miserable me, that I am accounted among the outcast and fallen!" I awoke from my dream and, immersed in an ocean of thought, regained my shop. Suddenly I saw you pass, accompanied by a man who wore a turban, and who was conversing with you. I sprang from my seat and, impelled by a power which I could not repress, ran to overtake you. To my utter amazement, I found you standing upon the very site which I had witnessed in my dream, engaged in the

recital of traditions and verses. Standing aside, at a distance, I kept watching you, wholly unobserved by you and your friend. I heard the man whom you were addressing, impetuously protest: "Easier is it for me to be devoured by the flames of hell than to acknowledge the truth of your words, the weight of which mountains are unable to sustain!" To his contemptuous rejection you returned this answer: "Were all the universe to repudiate His truth, it could never tarnish the unsullied purity of His robe and grandeur." Departing from him, you directed your steps towards the gate of Kázirán [Kázirún]. I continued to follow you until I reached this place.'

Mullá 'Alí tried to appease his troubled heart and to persuade him to return to his shop and resume his daily work. 'Your association with me,' he urged, 'would involve me in difficulties. Return to Shíráz and rest assured, for you are accounted of the people of salvation. Far be it from the justice of God to withhold from so ardent and devoted a seeker the cup of His grace, or to deprive a soul so athirst from the billowing ocean of His Revelation.' The words of Mullá 'Alí proved of no avail. The more he insisted upon the return of 'Abdu'l-Vahháb, the louder grew his lamentation and weeping. Mullá 'Alí finally felt compelled to comply with his wish, resigning himself to the will of God.

Ḥájí 'Abdu'l-Majíd, the father of 'Abdu'l-Vahháb, has often been heard to recount, with eyes filled with tears, this story: 'How deeply,' he said, 'I regret the deed I committed. Pray that God may grant me the remission of my sin. I was one among the favoured in the court of the sons of the Farmán-Farmá,* the governor of the province of Fárs. Such was my position that none dared to oppose or harm me. No one questioned my authority or ventured to interfere with my freedom. Immediately I heard that my son 'Abdu'l-Vahháb had forsaken his shop and left the city, I ran out in the direction of the Kázirán gate to overtake him. Armed with a club with which I intended to beat him, I inquired as to the road he had taken. I was told that a man wearing a turban had just crossed the street and that my son was seen following him. They seemed to have agreed to leave the city together. This excited my anger and indignation. How could I tolerate, I thought to myself, such unseemly behaviour on the part of my son, I, who already hold so privileged a position in the court of the sons of the Farmán-Farmá? Nothing but the severest chastisement, I felt, could wipe away the effect of my son's disgraceful conduct.

'I continued my search until I reached them. Seized with a savage fury, I inflicted upon Mullá 'Alí unspeakable injuries. To the strokes that fell heavily upon him, he, with extraordinary serenity, returned this answer: "Stay your hand, O 'Abdu'l-Majíd, for the eye of God is observing you. I take Him as my witness, that I am in no wise responsible for the conduct of your son. I mind not the tortures you inflict upon me, for I

* Most probably Ḥusayn-'Alí Mírzá, son of Fatḥ-'Alí Sháh. The next Farmán-Farmá, also for a short while the Governor of Fárs, was Firaydún Mírzá, brother of Muḥammad Sháh. (HMB)

stand prepared for the most grievous afflictions in the path I have chosen to follow. Your injuries, compared to what is destined to befall me in future, are as a drop compared to the ocean. Verily, I say, you shall survive me, and will come to recognize my innocence. Great will then be your remorse, and deep your sorrow." Scorning his remarks, and heedless of his appeal, I continued to beat him until I was exhausted. Silently and heroically he endured this most undeserved chastisement at my hands. Finally, I ordered my son to follow me, and left Mullá 'Alí to himself.

'On our way back to Shíráz, my son related to me the dream he had dreamt. A feeling of profound regret gradually seized me. The blamelessness of Mullá 'Alí was vindicated in my eyes, and the memory of my cruelty to him continued long to oppress my soul. Its bitterness lingered in my heart until the time when I felt obliged to transfer my residence from Shíráz to Baghdád.'[1]

Next, we meet this God-intoxicated youth in Káẓimayn,* the holy city adjacent to Baghdád, where he had set himself up in a shop. The year is 1851. Bahá'u'lláh is temporarily in 'Iráq, having gone there on the advice of Mírzá Taqí Khán, the Amír Kabír.

Káẓimayn with its two sacred shrines was frequently visited by Bahá'u'lláh. It was inevitable that the Shírází youth should encounter Bahá'u'lláh and, having encountered Him, become fervently attached to Him. Now he knew no peace save in the presence of Bahá'u'lláh, Who was still known only as Jináb-i-Bahá by the Bábís, and as Mírzá Ḥusayn-'Alíy-i-Núrí by the world at large. Mírzá 'Abdu'l-Vahháb's dearest wish was to travel back to Írán in the company of Bahá'u'lláh. But Bahá'u'lláh persuaded him to remain where he was, with his father, and gave him a sum of money to enlarge and extend his trade.

> Whither can a lover go but to the land of his beloved? And what seeker findeth rest away from his heart's desire? To the true lover reunion is life, and separation is death. His breast is void of patience and his heart hath no peace. A myriad lives he would forsake to hasten to the abode of his beloved.[2]

Thus did the Most Sublime Pen inscribe, years later in Baghdád.

'Abdu'l-Vahháb could not but follow Bahá'u'lláh to Ṭihrán. He reached the capital at the time when the misguided attempt had been made on the life of the Sháh and Ṭihrán was in turmoil. 'Abdu'l-Bahá,

* It is also stated that it was in Karbilá that this young man had his shop, and it was there that he met Bahá'u'lláh.

relating in a Tablet the story of that glorious youth, speaks of the officials searching everywhere for the Bábís, and 'Abdu'l-Vahháb, undaunted, giving praise to his Lord in the market-place. He was seized and thrown into the Síyáh-Chál. Mírzá 'Abdu'l-Vahháb-i-Shírází had, at long last, found that repose, that peace of heart and mind which his whole being craved, for he was continuously in the presence of his Lord. He was chained with Bahá'u'lláh.

And Bahá'u'lláh, one day, told Nabíl:

'We were awakened one night, ere break of day, by Mírzá 'Abdu'l-Vahháb-i-Shírází, who was bound with Us to the same chains. He had left Káẓimayn and followed Us to Ṭihrán, where he was arrested and thrown into prison. He asked Us whether We were awake, and proceeded to relate to Us his dream. "I have this night," he said, "been soaring into a space of infinite vastness and beauty. I seemed to be uplifted on wings that carried me wherever I desired to go. A feeling of rapturous delight filled my soul. I flew in the midst of that immensity with a swiftness and ease that I cannot describe." "Today," We replied, "it will be your turn to sacrifice yourself for this Cause. May you remain firm and steadfast to the end. You will then find yourself soaring in that same limitless space of which you dreamed, traversing with the same ease and swiftness the realm of immortal sovereignty, and gazing with that same rapture upon the Infinite Horizon."

'That morning saw the gaoler again enter Our cell and call out the name of 'Abdu'l-Vahháb. Throwing off his chains, he sprang to his feet, embraced each of his fellow-prisoners, and, taking Us into his arms, pressed Us lovingly to his heart. That moment We discovered that he had no shoes to wear. We gave him Our own, and, speaking a last word of encouragement and cheer, sent him forth to the scene of his martyrdom. Later on, his executioner came to Us, praising in glowing language the spirit which that youth had shown. How thankful We were to God for this testimony which the executioner himself had given!'[3]

'Abdu'l-Vahháb kissed the knees of Bahá'u'lláh; then he sang and danced all the way into the embrace of death. All the fiendish cruelties, all the unspeakable tortures, which, at the hour of death, the rapacious enemy inflicted upon that glorious youth of Shíráz, never made a dent in his constancy, because his blessed eyes were gazing 'upon the infinite Horizon'. His pure heart brimmed with love and joy.

Thus died 'Abdu'l-Vahháb, a simple youth from Shíráz.

And now we move with the years: sixty years after the martyrdom of 'Abdu'l-Vahháb. 'Abdu'l-Bahá, the Centre of the Covenant of

Bahá'u'lláh, is in the United States of America, travelling from the shores of the Atlantic to the shores of the Pacific. One day, He relates the story of that Shírází youth to a number of American Bahá'ís. Lua Getsinger (whom the Guardian of the Bahá'í Faith has honoured with the designation of the 'mother teacher of the West') is amongst those privileged to hear 'Abdu'l-Bahá tell that stirring story. Reaching the crucial moment when 'Abdu'l-Vahháb took leave of Bahá'u'lláh to go to his martyrdom – but let Juliet Thompson complete the picture:

> Suddenly Abdul Baha's whole aspect changed. It was as though the spirit of the martyr had entered into Him . . . With His head thrillingly erect, snapping His fingers high in the air, beating on the porch with His foot till we could scarcely endure the vibrations set up – such electric power radiated from Him – He sang the martyr's song, ecstatic and tragic beyond anything I had ever heard. This was what the Cause meant then! This was what it meant to live near Him! Another realm opened to me – the realm of Divine Tragedy.
>
> 'And thus,' ended Abdul Baha, 'singing and dancing he went to his death – and a hundred executioners fell on him! And later his old parents came to Baha'o'llah, praising God that their son had given his life in the Path of God!'
>
> He sank back in His chair. Tears swelled in my eyes, blurring everything. When they cleared I saw a yet stranger look on His face. His eyes were unmistakably fixed on the invisible. They were as brilliant as jewels and so filled with delight that they almost made His vision real to us. A smile of exultation played on His lips. Very low, so that it sounded like an echo, he hummed the martyr's song. 'See!' He exclaimed, 'the effect that the death of a martyr has in the world. It has changed my condition.' There was a moment of silence; then He said: 'What is it, Juliet, that you are pondering so deeply?' 'I was thinking of the look on your face when you said that your condition was changed. I was thinking I had seen a flash of the joy of God over those who die happily for humanity.'[4]

Ḥájí 'Abdu'l-Majíd, the father of 'Abdu'l-Vahháb – who inflicted such hard punishment on Mullá 'Alíy-i-Basṭámí – and his wife, took unhesitatingly the same path as their glorious son, as soon as they came face to face with Bahá'u'lláh.

19

Release and Exile

THE mother of Náṣiri'd-Dín Sháh was vociferous in demanding the blood of Bahá'u'lláh, and Ḥájibu'd-Dawlih would, no doubt, have had Him executed, if he could have found a way to do it; but every time they took 'Abbás, the page-boy who had been in the employment of the martyred Ḥájí Sulaymán Khán, to Síyáh-Chál to identify Bahá'u'lláh, he stoutly maintained that he had never seen Him in the company of the Bábís, in the house of his master. In the meantime, Bahá'u'lláh's brothers and sisters were making every effort to bring about His release, but Náṣiri'd-Dín Sháh was adamant. He had decided that Bahá'u'lláh should be kept in prison to the end of His days.

Mírzá Áqá Khán-i-Núrí, the Ṣadr-i-A'ẓam who had replaced Mírzá Taqí Khán, owed much to Bahá'u'lláh. At a time when he had fallen into disgrace during the premiership of Ḥájí Mírzá Áqásí, and was bastinadoed and fined, Bahá'u'lláh paid a good deal of the fine for him. And later, when Mírzá Áqá Khán found himself in dire financial straits during his exile in Káshán, Bahá'u'lláh again came to his rescue, and through Mírzá Shafí', the Ṣáḥib-Díván, got him an annuity of nineteen hundred *túmáns*. Still later, Bahá'u'lláh helped Káẓim Khán and his wife – he was the son of Mírzá Áqá Khán – to join his father in Káshán. Now, in 1852, the relatives of Bahá'u'lláh sent handsome and valuable presents and even a large sum of money to Mírzá Áqá Khán.

Urged by Mírzá Majíd-i-Áhí, the secretary of the Russian Legation – as previously noted, he was married to a sister of Bahá'u'lláh – Prince Dolgorouki, the Russian Minister, also pressed the Government to come soon to a decision and release Bahá'u'lláh. On the other hand, enemies were doing their utmost to bring about His death, particularly those who desired to obtain the patronage of the vengeful mother of Náṣiri'd-Dín Sháh. Having failed in their attempt to gain an admission from the page-boy of Ḥájí Sulaymán Khán, they tried to poison Bahá'u'lláh. Some noxious substance was introduced into the food

Mírzá Majíd-i-Áhí, secretary to the Russian Legation and brother-in-law of Bahá'u'lláh

brought from His home, but the effect of that poison became so noticeable that Bahá'u'lláh ceased to partake of that food.

Mullá Shaykh-'Alíy-i-Turshízí, surnamed 'Aẓím, was also still languishing in the Síyáh-Chál. Prince Dolgorouki insisted that his representative, together with Ḥájibu'd-Dawlih and a representative of the Ṣadr-i-A'ẓam, should visit the Síyáh-Chál and interrogate Mullá Shaykh-'Alí. 'Aẓím completely exonerated Bahá'u'lláh; he told them that Bahá'u'lláh was never involved in any plot directed against the Sháh, and he took upon himself all responsibility for the attempt on the Sháh's life. Bahá'u'lláh has lauded the courage and truthfulness of Mullá Shaykh-'Alí of Turshíz, and has said that he was truly 'Aẓím – Great. However, Mírzá Ḥusayn-i-Mutavallí, in order to curry favour, tried to inculpate Bahá'u'lláh. This effrontery was too much even for Ḥájibu'd-Dawlih, who gave Mírzá Ḥusayn a hard slap in the face.

This fickle man, from the time of his defection at Shaykh Ṭabarsí, when he dared to spit on the face of Quddús, had always betrayed the Faith which he had once so warmly espoused. Now, having been in Qum a tutor to 'Abbás Mírzá, the ill-starred half-brother of Náṣiri'd-Dín Sháh, he was under grave suspicion; to show that he was guiltless, he took up a penknife and cut off an ear of Mullá Shaykh-'Alí. But this despicable deed did not save him from torture; he was branded and his screams rang throughout the dungeon.

Despite the fact that Mullá Shaykh-'Alí had clearly confessed to his own crucial part in the attempt to assassinate the Sháh, Mírzá Abu'l-Qásim, the Imám-Jum'ih of Ṭihrán, would not consent to his execution. The rapacious Ḥájibu'd-Dawlih tricked the Imám-Jum'ih, got a verdict from him by false pretences, and had Mullá Shaykh-'Alí immediately put to death, an infamous action which greatly angered the Imám-Jum'ih. 'Aẓím was the last martyr of the holocaust of summer 1852.

At last, Náṣiri'd-Dín Sháh agreed to let Bahá'u'lláh go, and decreed that He should be banished from Írán. Bahá'u'lláh had lingered in chains for four agony-laden months. Mírzá Áqá Khán sent a confidant named Ḥájí 'Alí to bring Him out of the Síyáh-Chál. The sight of the appalling condition of the dungeon and the enfeebled condition of Bahá'u'lláh deeply shocked Ḥájí 'Alí, who assured Bahá'u'lláh that they had had no idea of the terrible circumstances He had endured all those months. Ḥájí 'Alí then offered his own cloak to Bahá'u'lláh, which He refused, preferring to appear before Mírzá Áqá Khán and the others of the Government in the rags He was wearing.

The Guardian of the Bahá'í Faith writes:

> No sooner had He presented Himself before them than the Grand Vizir addressed Him saying: 'Had you chosen to take my advice, and had you dissociated yourself from the Faith of the Siyyid-i-Báb, you would never have suffered the pains and indignities that have been heaped upon you.' '*Had you, in your turn,*' Bahá'u'lláh retorted, '*followed My counsels, the affairs of the government would not have reached so critical a stage.*' Mírzá Áqá Khán was thereupon reminded of the conversation he had had with Him on the occasion of the Báb's martyrdom, when he had been warned that '*the flame that has been kindled will blaze forth more fiercely than ever.*' 'What is it that you advise me now to do?' he inquired from Bahá'u'lláh. '*Command the governors of the realm,*' was the instant reply, '*to cease shedding the blood of the innocent, to cease plundering their property, to cease dishonoring their women, and injuring their children.*' That

same day the Grand Vizir acted on the advice thus given him; but any effect it had, as the course of subsequent events amply demonstrated, proved to be momentary and negligible.[1]

Bahá'u'lláh was given one month to leave the country. At the time of His release from the Síyáh-Chál, He was too ill to set out on a long journey. He had no home of His own now. His house had been wrecked and pillaged, and His two wives and children had found temporary accommodation in an obscure quarter of the capital. He went to live in the house of His brother, Mírzá Riḍá-Qulí, whose wife Maryam, the sister of Bahá'u'lláh's second wife and devoted to Him, made adequate arrangements for Him to rest and recuperate.

The Guardian of the Bahá'í Faith writes:

> This enforced and hurried departure of Bahá'u'lláh from His native land, accompanied by some of His relatives, recalls in some of its aspects, the precipitate flight of the Holy Family into Egypt; the sudden migration of Muḥammad . . . from Mecca to Medina; the exodus of Moses, His brother and His followers from the land of their birth, in response to the Divine summons, and above all the banishment of Abraham from Ur of the Chaldees to the Promised Land – a banishment which, in the multitudinous benefits it conferred upon so many divers peoples, faiths and nations, constitutes the nearest historical approach to the incalculable blessings destined to be vouchsafed, in this day, and in future ages, to the whole human race, in direct consequence of the exile suffered by Him Whose Cause is the flower and fruit of all previous Revelations.[2]

On the twelfth day of January 1853, Bahá'u'lláh and His family left Ṭihrán, together with two of His brothers – Mírzá Músá, known in later years as Áqáy-i-Kalím, and Mírzá Muḥammad-Qulí – and accompanied by a representative of the Imperial Government of Írán, and an official of the Russian Legation. Bahá'u'lláh's youngest son, Mírzá Mihdí, the Purest Branch, then a young child, had to be left behind with relatives, and it was some years before he could be reunited with his parents. The Russian Government had offered Bahá'u'lláh a refuge in its own territories, but He chose to go to 'Iráq. The time allowed Him to prepare had been too short, and particularly so since He needed a long period of rest before embarking on this journey in the heart of winter, over the high peaks and mountain passes of western Írán. He, His family and His brothers had not been able to provide themselves with all that was required for adequate protection against the intense cold of those heights.

Mírzá Riḍá-Qulí, half-brother of Bahá'u'lláh and husband of Maryam

The Guardian of the Bahá'í Faith has further written:

> In a prayer revealed by Him at that time, Bahá'u'lláh, expatiating upon the woes and trials He had endured in the Síyáh-Chál, thus bears witness to the hardships undergone in the course of that '*terrible journey*': '*My God, My Master, My Desire! . . . Thou hast created this atom of dust through the consummate power of Thy might, and nurtured Him with Thine hands which none can chain up. . . . Thou hast destined for Him trials and tribulations which no tongue can describe, nor any of Thy Tablets adequately recount. The throat Thou didst accustom to the touch of silk Thou hast, in the end, clasped with strong chains, and the body Thou didst ease with brocades and velvets Thou hast at last subjected to the abasement of a dungeon. Thy decree hath shackled Me with unnumbered fetters, and cast about My neck chains that none can sunder. A number of years have passed during which afflictions have, like showers of mercy, rained upon Me. . . . How many the nights during which the weight of chains and fetters allowed Me no rest, and how numerous the days during which peace and tranquillity were denied Me, by reason of that wherewith the hands and tongues of men have afflicted Me! Both bread and water which Thou hast, through Thine all-embracing mercy, allowed unto the beasts of the field, they have, for a time, forbidden unto this servant, and the things they refused to inflict upon such as have seceded from Thy Cause, the same have they suffered to be inflicted upon Me, until, finally, Thy decree was irrevocably fixed, and Thy behest summoned this servant to depart out of Persia, accompanied by a number of frail-bodied men and children of tender age, at this time when the cold is so intense that one cannot even speak, and ice and snow so abundant that it is impossible to move.*'[3]

As Bahá'u'lláh neared the frontier, a period drew to its close. Were the people of Írán aware of the loss they sustained? Steeped in ignorance, sunk in bigotry, blinded by prejudice, led by self-seeking men, beguiled by falsehoods, theirs was not to see and know. And thus the Redeemer of the world passed out of their midst. He Who once was loved and respected by rich and poor, high and low, prince and peasant alike, was now deserted by the same people on whom He had lavished mercy, love, justice and charity at all times. Írán lost the presence of Bahá'u'lláh, but could His spirit ever be absent from that or any other land?

Despite the hardships of that long journey, all along the road Bahá'u'lláh received every consideration. He stopped any forcible levy on the peasantry for provisions, and He refused offers of presents made by landlords and owners of villages. In Kirmánsháh, he stayed for a few days. A number of the Bábís who lived in that city attained

His presence. Among them were Mírzá 'Abdu'lláh, a dealer in shoes, whose native town was Qazvín, and Áqá Ghulám-Ḥusayn, a merchant of Shúshtar. Nabíl relates that later he found this merchant firmly devoted to Bahá'u'lláh. Pilgrims on their way to the holy cities of 'Iráq gathered in Kirmánsháh, joining the entourage of Bahá'u'lláh to ease and expedite their departure.

At Karand, which has been a centre of 'Alíyu'lláhís,* the Governor, Hayát-Qulí Khán, who belonged to that sect, greeted Bahá'u'lláh with marked reverence. 'He was shown, in return,' the Guardian of the Bahá'í Faith writes, 'such kindness by Bahá'u'lláh that the people of the entire village were affected, and continued, long after, to extend such hospitality to His followers on their way to Baghdád that they gained the reputation of being known as Bábís.'[4]

As the frontier was reached, on Bahá'u'lláh's instructions Mírzá Músá went ahead to Khániqayn and rented an orchard, redolent with flowers, as it was springtime and the days of Naw-Rúz. Water ran through its brooks and the birds were singing. On one side there was an orangery and on the other palm trees. Bahá'u'lláh stopped there and rested. He told His entourage that all that His enemies had devised had come to nought.

* Those who equate the Imám 'Alí with God. They are known for their tolerance, charity and compassion.

20

Baghdád – the First Year

Bahá'u'lláh reached Baghdád on 8 April 1853.* He had been travelling for three months, in the heart of winter, over the bleak, snow-bound heights of the western Íránian plateau. After the rigours He had suffered in the dungeon of Ṭihrán, a journey of that length, over such ground and in such a climatic condition, would have taxed any physical frame beyond endurance. But He had come through His ordeal strong and unswerving.

After a few days in Baghdád, He moved to the township of Káẓimayn, three miles away, which harbours the shrines of the seventh and the ninth Imáms. Mírzá Ibráhím Khán of Tabríz, – the Consul-General of Persia from 1846 until his death in December 1858 – calling to pay his respects, suggested that because of the fanaticism of the populace and the pilgrims it might be more convenient for Bahá'u'lláh to return to Baghdád and live in the old quarter, which was close to Káẓimayn. Bahá'u'lláh agreed and a search was made for a suitable house. About a month later, He and His family came back to Baghdád and settled in the house of Ḥájí 'Alí Madad, which had been rented for Him.

At this time, Baghdád was a provincial centre of the Ottoman Empire, with a population of about 60,000. Little there was to bespeak its renowned history as the city built, between AD 762 and 766, by the 'Abbásid Caliph al-Manṣúr, and called by him Madínatu's-Salám – the City of Peace. Al-Manṣúr had made his city the capital of a vast empire stretching from Egypt to the confines of China. Subsequent caliphs enlarged and beautified it, until by the tenth century it was some 8½ kilometres in length and 7¼ kilometres in width, filled with the finest palaces, most magnificent mosques, and most extensive bazars of that age. Its population at that time is estimated to have been some 1½ million. From this time on there was a general decline in

* 28 Jamádíyu'th-Thání AH 1269

View of Baghdád and the Tigris River

Baghdád's fortunes, until two successive sackings by the Mongols in 1258 and 1401 put a complete end to its former glory. In 1534, the Ottoman Sulṭán, Sulaymán the Magnificent, took Baghdád and, in the next century, it was ruled alternately by Ottomans and Ṣafavids, until in 1638 it settled into its role as an Ottoman provincial centre until the First World War.

When Bahá'u'lláh took up residence in Baghdád, where He would live for the next ten years, what had remained of the disconsolate, bewildered and decimated community of the Báb learned to turn to Him for advice, for guidance, for protection, because Mírzá Yaḥyá, who was known as the 'nominee' of the Báb, was nowhere to be seen. Having managed, as we have seen, to escape from Tákur in the company of his uncle, Mírzá Zaynu'l-'Ábidín, he was now living in Baghdád under the assumed name of Ḥájí 'Alíy-i-Lás Furúsh, in the street of the charcoal-vendors (Dhughál-Furúshán). It was Bahá'u'lláh's wish that he should return to Persia, there to serve the Faith of the Báb, as His own words make clear:

> . . . About two months after Our arrival in 'Iráq, following the command of His Majesty the Sháh of Persia – may God assist him – Mírzá Yaḥyá joined Us. We said unto him: 'In accordance with the Royal command We have been sent unto this place. It is advisable for thee to remain in Persia. We will send Our brother, Mírzá Músá, to some other place. As your names have not been mentioned in the Royal decree, you can arise and render some service.' Subsequently, this Wronged One departed from Baghdád, and for two years withdrew from the world. Upon Our return, We found

that he had not left, and had postponed his departure. This Wronged One was greatly saddened.[1]

One of the very first to recognize in Bahá'u'lláh that true mentor, counsellor and guide which the community of the Báb sorely needed, was Ḥájí Há<u>sh</u>im-i-'Aṭṭár, a wealthy Persian merchant who lived in new Bag<u>h</u>dád. Having once attained the presence of Bahá'u'lláh, he became devoted to Him, and in the end gave Him his allegiance. We shall meet him in these pages in future years. Áqá Muḥammad-Ḥasan, a merchant of Iṣfahán; Siyyid Muḥammad-Riḍá and Siyyid Muḥammad-Taqí, two brothers, sons of Siyyid-i-Buká'; Ḥájí 'Abdu'l-Majíd-i-<u>Sh</u>írází – the father of that glorious martyr, Mírzá 'Abdu'l-Vahháb – and his brother, Mírzá Ḥasan, who was known as 'Gul-i-Guláb' (Red Rose, literally, 'the flower of the rose-water') – all Persians who lived in Káẓimayn – rallied round Him. And so did the Arab Bábís of Bag<u>h</u>dád, notably <u>Sh</u>ay<u>kh</u> Sulṭán and Áqá Muḥammad-Muṣṭafá. Another veteran of the Faith of the Báb, who very soon came to see that the hopes of the Bábís must be centred in the person of Bahá'u'lláh, was Ḥájí Siyyid Javád-i-Karbilá'í.

<u>Sh</u>ay<u>kh</u>-'Alí Mírzá of <u>Sh</u>íráz, a distinguished figure related to the imám-jum'ih* of that city, as well as Siyyid 'Abdu'r-Raḥím of Iṣfahán (honoured in later years with the designation of Ismu'lláhi'r-Raḥím – the Name of God, the Merciful), and Mírzá Muḥammad-'Alí, the physician of Zanján, who was to meet a martyr's death, were the most notable of the Bábís in Írán who, from that early time, became convinced that only by turning to Jináb-i-Bahá could they find that sure anchor which could and would steady the storm-tossed ship of their Faith.

But winds of dissension were already blowing, and rifts were making their mark. Whilst bound in chains in the Síyáh-<u>Ch</u>ál of Ṭihrán, at a time when Mírzá Yaḥyá was constantly running for shelter, Bahá'u'lláh had vowed to arise and regenerate the shattered community of the Báb. Now, from the obscurity he had chosen, Mírzá Yaḥyá was secretly engaged in engineering opposition to Bahá'u'lláh, in company with Siyyid Muḥammad-i-Iṣfahání, who had established himself in Karbilá.

* Two imám-jum'ihs of <u>Sh</u>íráz, <u>Sh</u>ay<u>kh</u> Abú-Turáb and his son, Ḥájí <u>Sh</u>ay<u>kh</u> Yaḥyá, who lived to be over ninety years of age, from the days of the Báb onwards always strove to give aid and afford protection to the followers of the Bábí-Bahá'í Faith. And they succeeded well beyond all expectation.

The Guardian of the Bahá'í Faith writes:

> Little wonder that from the pen of Bahá'u'lláh, Who was as yet unable to divulge the Secret that stirred within His bosom, these words of warning, of counsel and of assurance should, at a time when the shadows were beginning to deepen around Him, have proceeded: '*The days of tests are now come. Oceans of dissension and tribulation are surging, and the Banners of Doubt are, in every nook and corner, occupied in stirring up mischief and in leading men to perdition. . . . Suffer not the voice of some of the soldiers of negation to cast doubt into your midst, neither allow yourselves to become heedless of Him Who is the Truth, inasmuch as in every Dispensation such contentions have been raised. God, however, will establish His Faith, and manifest His light albeit the stirrers of sedition abhor it. . . . Watch ye every day for the Cause of God. . . . All are held captive in His grasp. No place is there for any one to flee to. Think not the Cause of God to be a thing lightly taken, in which any one can gratify his whims. In various quarters a number of souls have, at the present time, advanced this same claim. The time is approaching when . . . every one of them will have perished and been lost, nay will have come to naught and become a thing unremembered, even as the dust itself.*'[2]

There was one person, however, to whom Bahá'u'lláh vouchsafed a view of that 'Secret that stirred within His bosom'. He was a Bábí youth of Káshán named Mírzá Áqá Ján. This youth had a dream, in which the Báb appeared, and then he came upon some of the writings of Bahá'u'lláh. Ascertaining that Jináb-i-Bahá was in Baghdád, he made his way to 'Iráq, and in Karbilá attained His presence. No matter how grievous Mírzá Áqá Ján's waywardness would become – for eventually he chose to break the Covenant of Bahá'u'lláh and stray into the wilderness – this distinction remains his, that he was the first to recognize in the person of Bahá'u'lláh the Promised One of the Bayán – the Promise of All Ages. In later years, Bahá'u'lláh honoured him with the title of Khádimu'lláh – Servant of God.

The Guardian of the Bahá'í Faith writes:

> This same Mírzá Áqá Ján, recounting to Nabíl his experiences, on that first and never to be forgotten night spent in Karbilá, in the presence of his newly-found Beloved, Who was then a guest of Ḥájí Mírzá Ḥasan-i-Ḥakím-Báshí, had given the following testimony: 'As it was summer-time Bahá'u'lláh was in the habit of passing His evenings and of sleeping on the roof of the House. [Áqá Mírzá Muḥammad-Qulí and I sprinkled water on the roof, swept and carpeted it, until He came. He talked to us, had His dinner and retired to rest.] That night, when He had gone to sleep, I,

Mírzá Áqá Ján of Ká<u>sh</u>án, <u>Kh</u>ádimu'lláh

according to His directions, lay down for a brief rest, at a distance of a few feet from Him. No sooner had I risen, and . . . started to offer my prayers, in a corner of the roof which adjoined a wall, than I beheld His blessed Person rise and walk towards me. When He reached me He said: '*You, too, are awake.*' Whereupon He began to chant and pace back and forth. How shall I ever describe that voice and the verses it intoned, and His gait, as He strode before me! Methinks, with every step He took and every word He uttered thousands of oceans of light surged before my face, and thousands of worlds of incomparable splendor were unveiled to my eyes, and thousands of suns blazed their light upon me! In the moonlight that streamed upon Him, He thus continued to walk and to chant. Every time He approached me He would pause, and, in a tone so wondrous that no tongue can describe it, would say: '*Hear Me, My son. By God, the True*

One! This Cause will assuredly be made manifest. Heed thou not the idle talk of the people of the Bayán, who pervert the meaning of every word.' In this manner He continued to walk and chant, and to address me these words until the first streaks of dawn appeared. . . . Afterwards I removed His bedding to His room, and, having prepared His tea for Him, was dismissed from His presence.[3]

Nabíl writes that Mírzá Áqá Ján further related to him that the Abhá Beauty (Bahá'u'lláh) said to him: '"If you see Me in the market-place, do not show any sign of recognition, unless I call you Myself." That day, when I went out to the bazar, I encountered His Blessed Person. He called out loudly for me and I ran into His presence. For a while, an hour or more, He spoke to me there in the market-place. Afterwards, He went to Najaf. He instructed me: "Stay in Karbilá. When I return [from Najaf], should I pass this way, I shall take you with Myself to Baghdád, and, should I go [to Baghdád] by way of Ḥillih, I shall send for you." I stayed in Karbilá for three months. I used to gather thorn, and sell it to the bath-keepers. One day, Shaykh Abú-Turáb [-i-Ishtahárdí] told me, "If I could get hold of a copy of the Persian *Bayán*, I would read something out of it to you." I said: "It can be found." "Where?" enquired Shaykh Abú-Turáb. I replied that Ḥájí 'Abdu'l-Majíd-i-Shírází in Káẓimayn had a copy, and I left that very hour for Káẓimayn to obtain it. When I neared Baghdád I ran into Abu'l-Qásim-i-Káshání and enquired about Ḥaji 'Abdu'l-Majíd. At first, he thought that I intended to meet Azal, but when he realized that my heart had been captivated by someone else, he asked me for a reason, and, when I mentioned the gait and the speech of the Abhá Beauty, he gave me a luminous Tablet revealed for me, in which the People of Bahá and the qualities of the Abhá Beauty had been mentioned. When the news of my coming was given to His Blessed Person, He summoned Me and said that He had intended to send for me.'[4]

Thus began Mírzá Áqá Ján's forty-year-long service to Bahá'u'lláh as attendant, amanuensis and companion.

The Guardian of the Bahá'í Faith writes:

The confidence instilled in Mírzá Áqá Ján by this unexpected and sudden contact with the spirit and directing genius of a new-born Revelation stirred his soul to its depths – a soul already afire with a consuming love born of his recognition of the ascendancy which his newly-found Master had already achieved over His fellow-disciples in both 'Iráq and Persia. This intense adoration that informed his whole being, and which could neither be suppressed nor concealed, was instantly detected by both Mírzá Yaḥyá and his fellow-conspirator Siyyid Muḥammad.[5]

It was at this time that Ḥájí Mírzá Kamálu'd-Dín-i-Naráqí came to Baghdád. He was a grandson of Ḥájí Mullá Aḥmad-i-Naráqí, a distinguished divine of past times, and was himself a man of learning. Through Áqáy-i-Kalím, he asked Mírzá Yaḥyá to write for him a commentary on the Qur'ánic verse: 'All food was allowed to the children of Israel'. Of course as soon as Mírzá Yaḥyá became aware of the fact that the Bábís of Naráq had learned of his whereabouts, fear overcame him. Nevertheless, he wrote a commentary, but it was an affront to the intellect of such a man as Ḥájí Mírzá Kamálu'd-Dín, who saw clearly Mírzá Yaḥyá's incompetence. Instead he looked to Bahá'u'lláh for guidance and enlightenment, and in response to his request Bahá'u'lláh revealed a Tablet which is known as the *Tablet of Kullu'ṭ-Ṭa'ám* (All Food). In this Tablet, as the Guardian of the Bahá'í Faith writes,

> . . . Israel and his children were identified with the Báb and His followers respectively – a Tablet which by reason of the allusions it contained, the beauty of its language and the cogency of its argument, so enraptured the soul of its recipient that he would have, but for the restraining hand of Bahá'u'lláh, proclaimed forthwith his discovery of God's hidden Secret in the person of the One Who had revealed it.[6]

The fame of the *Tablet of Kullu'ṭ-Ṭa'ám* aroused fresh jealousy in the heart of Mírzá Yaḥyá, who could not realize his own inability. Siyyid Muḥammad-i-Iṣfahání, the Antichrist of the Bahá'í Revelation, was pushing Mírzá Yaḥyá more and more to oppose and thwart Bahá'u'lláh. Friends were gathering around Bahá'u'lláh from every side, not only from the ranks of the Bábís, who were just beginning to hold their heads high once again, but from circles well beyond. The Válí of Baghdád had come to see that this Exile, recently arrived from Írán, was of a different category from the many Persian princes and princelings banished to 'Iráq or who had fled there. Bahá'u'lláh was well in the public eye. It was He Who had suffered months of inhuman incarceration in the dungeon of Ṭihrán, whereas Mírzá Yaḥyá's cowardice had condemned him to feel always insecure, to be always on the run and, not daring to use his own name, to pursue an obscure existence in a dilapidated corner of Baghdád.

Mírzá Zaynu'l-'Ábidín, the uncle with whom Mírzá Yaḥyá had fled from Tákur, whom Bahá'u'lláh had just named Aḥmad and the Bábís called Jináb-i-Bábá,* was, about this time, Bahá'u'lláh's guest in Baghdád. Mírzá Áqá Ján described to Nabíl the sequel to the revealing of the *Tablet of Kullu'ṭ-Ṭa'ám*, who recorded it thus: 'Jináb-i-Bábá came along and told me that He [Bahá'u'lláh] had gone to Káẓimayn. Without thinking I hurried there, and not knowing where to go, I was standing on a corner. Then I saw a siyyid coming towards me. He asked me: "Are you the Káshání youth?" and then added: "Come with me; He [Bahá'u'lláh] has asked for you." Afterwards, I found out that this siyyid was Siyyid Muḥammad-Taqí, the son of Siyyid-i-Buká', who lived in Káẓimayn. That day, when I attained His Blessed Presence, He was saying to Áqá Muḥammad-Ḥasan, the Iṣfahání merchant: "Prior to your coming, Ḥájí Mírzá Kamálu'd-Dín-i-Naráqí was here. He had asked a question regarding the verse, Kullu'ṭ-Ṭa'ám, from there [meaning Azal], but not having understood anything from his answer, he asked Me the same. I wrote an answer for him, read it to him, but did not give it to him. I want to read it to you now." He began to chant and read. How can I describe what hearing every word, uttered in that blessed tone, did to one? In between, He read a number of verses in the same tone He had used that first night in Karbilá, on the roof of the Dáru'sh-shafá [the House of Treatment]. When He reached the end, He said: "What do you say?" I offered the comment: "If there be fairness, all of the learned men ['ulamá] should bow their heads." His Blessed Person replied: "As thou sayest, if there be fairness."'[7]

That uncle of Bahá'u'lláh, Jináb-i-Bábá, according to Mírzá Áqá Ján, many a time swore that had he not attained the presence of his Nephew, he would have lost his faith completely.

Mírzá Áqá Ján further related to Nabíl that, one day in Káẓimayn, when both he and Áqá Muḥammad-Ḥasan-i-Iṣfahání were in the presence of Bahá'u'lláh, in the house of Ḥájí 'Abdu'l-Majíd-i-Shírází, He asked the host whether he wished to hear the Badí' (Unique) language, which, He said, was the language used by the denizens of one of the worlds of God. He then proceeded to chant in that language. Mírzá Áqá Ján said that hearing this language had a wonderful effect on the listener. One day, Mírzá Áqá Ján related, Bahá'u'lláh said to Ḥájí 'Abdu'l-Majíd: 'Ḥájí, you have heard the Badí' language,

* Bábá means father.

and witnessed God's supremacy over His worlds. Render thanks for this bounty and appreciate its worth.'

Mírzá Yaḥyá had never lifted a finger to protect the Faith of which he was supposed to be the nominal head. Now, incited and aided by Siyyid Muḥammad and a few, very few, others of the same nature, Mírzá Yaḥyá began a secret campaign to discredit Bahá'u'lláh. He circulated wild rumours, ascribed to Bahá'u'lláh actions, opinions, views and intentions totally at variance with truth. These undercurrents and innuendoes became so perilous for the integrity of the Faith of the Báb, threatening it with bitter controversies and even fatal divisions, that Bahá'u'lláh reached the decision to take Himself away from Baghdád and from the society of men whom He knew and who knew Him. Such seclusion from the gatherings of men has always occurred in the lives of the Manifestations of God. Moses went out to the desert of Sinai. Buddha sought the wilds of India. Christ walked the wilderness of Judaea, Muḥammad paced the sun-baked hillocks of Arabia.

> Mírzá Áqá Ján himself has testified: 'That Blessed Beauty evinced such sadness that the limbs of my body trembled.' He has, likewise, related, as reported by Nabíl in his narrative, that, shortly before Bahá'u'lláh's retirement, he had on one occasion seen Him, between dawn and sunrise, suddenly come out from His house, His night-cap still on His head, showing such signs of perturbation that he was powerless to gaze into His face, and while walking, angrily remark: '*These creatures are the same creatures who for three thousand years have worshipped idols, and bowed down before the Golden Calf. Now, too, they are fit for nothing better. What relation can there be between this people and Him Who is the Countenance of Glory? What ties can bind them to the One Who is the supreme embodiment of all that is lovable?*' 'I stood,' declared Mírzá Áqá Ján, 'rooted to the spot, lifeless, dried up as a dead tree, ready to fall under the impact of the stunning power of His words. Finally, He said: "*Bid them recite: 'Is there any Remover of difficulties save God? Say: Praised be God! He is God! All are His servants, and all abide by His bidding!' Tell them to repeat it five hundred times, nay, a thousand times, by day and by night, sleeping and waking, that haply the Countenance of Glory may be unveiled to their eyes, and tiers of light descend upon them.*" He Himself, I was subsequently informed, recited this same verse, His face betraying the utmost sadness. . . . Several times during those days, He was heard to remark: "*We have, for a while, tarried amongst this people, and failed to discern the slightest response on their part.*" Oftentimes He alluded to His disappearance from our midst, yet none of us understood His meaning.'[8]

21

Sulaymáníyyih

ONE morning, the household of Bahá'u'lláh awoke to find Him gone. And no one knew where to seek Him. That day was 10 April 1854.

It was to Sulaymáníyyih, in the heart and uplands of Kurdish 'Iráq, that Bahá'u'lláh had turned for seclusion. Some eight years later He described that episode in the *Kitáb-i-Íqán – The Book of Certitude* – which He revealed for Ḥájí Mírzá Siyyid Muḥammad, a maternal uncle of the Báb:

> We fain would hope that the people of the Bayán will be enlightened, will soar in the realm of the spirit and abide therein, will discern the Truth, and recognize with the eye of insight dissembling falsehood. In these days, however, such odours of jealousy are diffused, that – I swear by the Educator of all beings, visible and invisible – from the beginning of the foundation of the world – though it hath no beginning – until the present day, such malice, envy, and hate have in no wise appeared, nor will they ever be witnessed in the future. For a number of people who have never inhaled the fragrance of justice, have raised the standard of sedition, and have leagued themselves against Us. On every side We witness the menace of their spears, and in all directions We recognize the shafts of their arrows. This, although We have never gloried in any thing, nor did We seek preference over any soul. To everyone We have been a most kindly companion, a most forbearing and affectionate friend. In the company of the poor We have sought their fellowship, and amidst the exalted and learned We have been submissive and resigned. I swear by God, the one true God! grievous as have been the woes and sufferings which the hand of the enemy and the people of the Book inflicted upon Us, yet all these fade into utter nothingness when compared with that which hath befallen Us at the hand of those who profess to be Our friends.
>
> What more shall We say? The universe, were it to gaze with the eye of justice, would be incapable of bearing the weight of this utterance! In the early days of Our arrival in this land, when We discerned the signs of impending events, We decided, ere they happened, to retire. We betook Ourselves to the wilderness, and there, separated and alone, led for two years a life of complete solitude. From Our eyes there rained tears of anguish, and in Our bleeding heart there surged an ocean of agonizing

> pain. Many a night We had no food for sustenance, and many a day Our body found no rest. By Him Who hath My being between His hands! notwithstanding these showers of afflictions and unceasing calamities, Our soul was wrapt in blissful joy, and Our whole being evinced an ineffable gladness. For in Our solitude We were unaware of the harm or benefit, the health or ailment, of any soul. Alone, We communed with Our spirit, oblivious of the world and all that is therein. We knew not, however, that the mesh of divine destiny exceedeth the vastest of mortal conceptions, and the dart of His decree transcendeth the boldest of human designs. None can escape the snares He setteth, and no soul can find release except through submission to His will. By the righteousness of God! Our withdrawal contemplated no return, and Our separation hoped for no reunion. The one object of Our retirement was to avoid becoming a subject of discord among the faithful, a source of disturbance unto Our companions, the means of injury to any soul, or the cause of sorrow to any heart. Beyond these, We cherished no other intention, and apart from them, We had no end in view. And yet, each person schemed after his own desire, and pursued his own idle fancy, until the hour when, from the Mystic Source, there came the summons bidding Us return whence We came. Surrendering Our will to His, We submitted to His injunction.[1]

Bahá'u'lláh had taken only one companion with Him, Áqá Abu'l-Qásim-i-Hamadání. Eventually, as we shall see, it was because of a mishap that led to Áqá Abu'l-Qásim's death, in the western regions of Írán, that the Family of Bahá'u'lláh learned where to seek Him. But in Sulaymáníyyih, Bahá'u'lláh had totally concealed His identity. Dressed in the garb of a dervish (*darvísh*), He had assumed the name of Darvísh Muḥammad-i-Írání, and lived the life of a hermit in the caves above Sulaymáníyyih. (The *kashkúl* which He had with Him in the mountains of Kurdistán is preserved today in the International Bahá'í Archives on Mount Carmel.) Many years later, Bahá'u'lláh described His situation: 'We sought shelter upon the summit of a remote mountain which lay at some three days' distance from the nearest human habitation. The comforts of life were completely lacking. We remained entirely isolated from Our fellow men . . .'[2]

From time to time, Bahá'u'lláh came into Sulaymáníyyih from the caves in search of the necessities of life. Áqá Abu'l-Qásim also visited Him and carried provisions to Him. Then a time came when Áqá Abu'l-Qásim had to leave Bahá'u'lláh and go to Írán to obtain money and certain goods. At the frontier, on his return, he was set upon either by highwaymen or frontier patrols and was mortally wounded. When he was found he was near to death, but was able to say that his name was Abu'l-Qásim, that he was a native of Hamadán, and that whatever he carried of money and goods belonged to Darvísh Muḥammad-i-Írání, whose haunts were the uplands of Kurdish 'Iráq.

In a Tablet addressed to Maryam (Mary), the wife of His brother, Ḥájí Mírzá Riḍá-Qulí, soon after His return from Sulaymáníyyih, Bahá'u'lláh wrote:

> The wrongs which I suffer have blotted out the wrongs suffered by My First Name [the Báb] from the Tablet of creation. . . . After countless afflictions, We reached 'Iráq at the bidding of the Tyrant of Persia, where, after the fetters of Our foes, We were afflicted with the perfidy of Our friends. God knoweth what befell Me thereafter! At length I gave up My home and all therein, and renounced life and all that appertaineth unto it, and alone and friendless, chose to go into retirement. I roamed the wilderness of resignation, travelling in such wise that in My exile every eye wept sore over Me, and all created things shed tears of blood because of My anguish. The birds of the air were My companions and the beasts of the field My associates. . . . By the righteousness of God! I have borne what neither the oceans, nor the waves, nor the fruits, nor any created thing, whether of the past or of the future, hath borne or will be capable of bearing.[3]

Today Sulaymáníyyih is a very pleasant small town, at a distance of about 200 miles from Baghdád, built amidst three hills and surrounded by trees and verdure. But it must have been otherwise in Bahá'u'lláh's time, for Commander James F. Jones of the Indian Navy, who accompanied Sir Henry Rawlinson on a tour of Kurdistán in 1844, writes thus of Sulaymáníyyih as he found it:

> Sulimaniyeh, the capital of the Pachalic, is a collection of small and ruinous houses, bearing a more mean appearance than, I believe, the most wretched hamlet in England. This is, however, not attributable to the poverty of the Kurds alone, but to the nomade habits of its occupants, who, in the spring, summer, and autumn, abandon the town, and spread themselves over the country . . . After its second foundation by Ibrahim Pacha [sixty-two years previously], it gradually improved, and in Rich's time boasted of about a thousand houses. I believe, at the present time, it scarcely contains half that number of tenable dwellings, and is, moreover, considered unhealthily situated when compared with the more salubrious and less confined region of the adjoining plain. Built on the skirt of a low and barren range, which rises up immediately behind it, it is either entirely shut out from the cooler breezes that sweep the plain, or is visited by constant hot winds which blow from the E. and NE. over the heated ridge during the summer months.[4]

There are many of its prominent citizens who treasure tenderly the memory of Bahá'u'lláh's sojourn amongst their forefathers. At first, the people, although much impressed by Him, took Him only to be as He presented Himself, an itinerant dervish from Írán, until a fragment of His writing came into the hands of a disciple of Shaykh Ismá'íl, a Ṣúfí *murshid* of that region. This man took it to his mentor, who found it irresistible. Shaykh Ismá'íl and some of his disciples then hurried into the presence of Bahá'u'lláh and learned much from Him. One day, they asked Him to explain to them the intricacies of the book, *al-Futúḥát al-Makkíyyah*, by the great Andalusian mystic, Shaykh Muḥyí'd-Dín Ibnu'l-'Arabí. Bahá'u'lláh replied that He had never read it and did not know its contents, but would grant them their wish. So, every day, a page would be read in His presence and He would expound and explain the views of that celebrated mystic seer. Then they begged Him to compose an ode in the style of the famous *Tá'íyyih* ode of another celebrated mystic, the Egyptian Ibnu'l-Fáriḍ. And He agreed to grant them that request as well. The result was a poem of utmost eloquence which gained widespread fame and acceptance as the *Qaṣídiy-i-'Izz-i-Varqá'íyyih*. It originally consisted of 2,000 couplets, but Bahá'u'lláh chose 127 of them, which He allowed to be copied and preserved. No one previously had dared to compose such an ode in such a style as that of Ibnu'l-Fáriḍ.

Thus, the fame of Darvísh Muḥammad-i-Írání began to reach areas beyond the confines of the small Kurdish town.

Whenever Bahá'u'lláh came into Sulaymáníyyih, to make use of the public bath or to make any purchases, He would stay in the *Takyih*, the theological seminary of Mawláná Khálid. The original mosque of which Mawláná Khálid had been the custodian was destroyed in later times, but had been rebuilt to the same proportions. Mawláná Khálid was, at the time of Bahá'u'lláh's sojourn, an old man highly revered amongst the Kurds. He requested Darvísh Muḥammad to draw up a document which would perpetuate the custodianship of his institution for his descendants. That and other works from Bahá'u'lláh's pen are now owned by families in Sulaymáníyyih, who refuse to part with them at any price. Some three decades ago, a possessor of such a highly-valued relic stated that even should he be offered a million *dínárs* (a million pounds) he would still refuse to let that priceless document go, because he was certain all bounties would be cut off

Takyih *of Mawláná Khálid in Sulaymáníyyih, where Bahá'u'lláh stayed*

from him and his family, should it leave their possession. A figure highly revered by the Kurds in Sulaymáníyyih is Káká Aḥmad, a saint of past ages. But as compared with Íshán,* the designation given out of veneration to Darvísh Muḥammad-i-Íránî, they had no doubt that the latter ranked higher. Even the particular mountain, called Sar-Galú, which Bahá'u'lláh had especially made His home, is held to be a place holy and sacred.†

In those years of Bahá'u'lláh's absence from Baghdád, the fortunes of the Bábís had touched their nadir. Mírzá Yaḥyá, incompetent, terror-stricken, helpless, could and would do nothing to halt the ebb, the impending disaster of total, irreparable disintegration. Earnest, dedicated souls in Írán, finding life impossible – not only because of the tyrannies of the times and the venom injected into society by selfish divines, but also because of the lawlessness which still held the terribly reduced community of the Báb in its grip – would, with very great

* Íshán means 'they', and Bahá'u'lláh was known by this designation even before going to Sulaymáníyyih.

† The author is indebted to Mr Mas'ud Berdjis for details of Sulaymáníyyih and its inhabitants during recent years.

Sar-Galú, where the caves in which Bahá'u'lláh lived are situated

effort, make their way to Baghdád, only to be told that Mírzá Yaḥyá, the nominee of the Báb, could not be reached. He had forbidden even the mention of the name of the street in which he lived. One such distinguished proponent of the Faith, who had travelled to Baghdád both to escape the increasing hostility of the people and to seek solace in consorting with Mírzá Yaḥyá, was Mullá Zaynu'l-'Ábidín of Najaf-Ábád (in the environs of Iṣfahán), who was destined to shine brilliantly in future years in the galaxy of the apostles of Bahá'u'lláh, honoured by the designation Jináb-i-Zaynu'l-Muqarrabín conferred upon him by the Most Sublime Pen. Unable to meet Mírzá Yaḥyá, in despair he retraced his steps to his homeland, but hearing at the frontier of fresh outbursts of fanatical assaults, took the weary road once again to Baghdád. He was well rewarded because, soon after, Bahá'u'lláh came back from Sulaymáníyyih and Mullá Zaynu'l-'Ábidín found all that his soul craved.

The Guardian of the Bahá'í Faith has described those days and the shameful deeds perpetrated by Mírzá Yaḥyá and his henchmen:

> While the foundations of Bahá'u'lláh's future greatness were being laid in a strange land and amidst a strange people, the situation of the Bábí

> community was rapidly going from bad to worse. . . . Mírzá Yaḥyá, closeted most of the time in his house, was secretly directing, through his correspondence with those Bábís whom he completely trusted, a campaign designed to utterly discredit Bahá'u'lláh. In his fear of any potential adversary he had dispatched Mírzá Muḥammad-i-Mázindarání, one of his supporters, to Ádhirbáyján for the express purpose of murdering Dayyán [Mírzá Asadu'lláh of Khuy], the 'repository of the knowledge of God' [so designated by the Báb], whom he surnamed 'Father of Iniquities' [Abu'sh-Shurúr] and stigmatized as 'Ṭághút' [an idol of Pre-Islamic Arabia], and whom the Báb had extolled as the '*Third Letter to believe in Him Whom God shall make manifest*'. In his folly he had, furthermore, induced Mírzá Áqá Ján to proceed to Núr, and there await a propitious moment when he could make a successful attempt on the life of the sovereign. . . . He even, as a further evidence of the enormity of his crimes, ordered that the cousin of the Báb, Mírzá 'Alí-Akbar,* a fervent admirer of Dayyán, be secretly put to death – a command which was carried out in all its iniquity. As to Siyyid Muḥammad, now given free rein by his master, Mírzá Yaḥyá, he had surrounded himself, as Nabíl who was at that time with him in Karbilá categorically asserts, with a band of ruffians, whom he allowed, and even encouraged, to snatch at night the turbans from the heads of wealthy pilgrims who had congregated in Karbilá, to steal their shoes, to rob the shrine of the Imám Ḥusayn of its divans and candles, and seize the drinking cups from the public fountains . . .[5]

The Bábís, if they were to escape total annihilation, desperately needed a guiding hand, but it could not be the trembling, ineffectual hand of Mírzá Yaḥyá. Twenty-five men, as 'Abdu'l-Bahá has stated, had presumed to claim the station of the Promised One of the Bayán. Some of them were men of deep guile and duplicity, some simple, misguided souls, and some saw themselves as standing head and shoulders above Mírzá Yaḥyá. Some were irretrievably lost, but others came to do penance at the door of Bahá'u'lláh.

When the news reached Baghdád of the death of Áqá Abu'l-Qásim-i-Hamadání, who had been missed at the same time that Bahá'u'lláh had disappeared from His home, it became evident that Darvísh Muḥammad-i-Írání, who dwelt in the mountains of the Kurdish north, and whose fame had also reached Baghdád, could be no other than the person of Bahá'u'lláh. At the instance of the Most Great Branch, who was no more than twelve years old, and of Áqáy-i-Kalím, the faithful brother of Bahá'u'lláh, Shaykh Sulṭán – the father-in-law of Áqáy-i-Kalím and a Bábí of Arab origin converted by the efforts of

* See genealogy, p. 404.

Ṭáhirih – left Baghdád accompanied by Javád the Ḥaṭṭáb (wood-cutter), who was also of Arab origin, to seek Bahá'u'lláh in Sulaymáníyyih and implore Him to return. Mírzá Yaḥyá, now in dire straits, renounced and rejected by such remaining stalwarts of the Faith of the Báb as Mírzá Asadu'lláh-i-Dayyán and Ḥájí Mírzá Músáy-i-Qumí, also wrote to beg Him to come back.

To Shaykh Sulṭán Bahá'u'lláh said: '*But for My recognition of the fact that the blessed Cause of the Primal Point was on the verge of being completely obliterated, and all the sacred blood poured out in the path of God would have been shed in vain, I would in no wise have consented to return to the people of the Bayán, and would have abandoned them to the worship of the idols their imaginations had fashioned.*'[6]

And as they neared Baghdád, on '*the banks of the River of Tribulations*',* He told Shaykh Sulṭán that the few days still left were the last days for Him of peace and tranquillity on this earth – '*days*' which He said '*will never again fall to My lot*'.[6]

They reached Baghdád on 19 March 1856.† Exactly two lunar years had passed since Bahá'u'lláh's departure, and He Himself has described the situation which then confronted Him: '*We found no more than a handful of souls, faint and dispirited, nay utterly lost and dead. The Cause of God had ceased to be on any one's lips, nor was any heart receptive to its message.*'[7]

* Such is the way Bahá'u'lláh referred to the city of the 'Abbásids and its stream: the Tigris.

† 12 Rajab AH 1272. Shaykh Sulṭán has written a book, describing his quest, his journey and his return in the company of Bahá'u'lláh.

22

Baghdád – Friend and Foe

On His return to Baghdád, Bahá'u'lláh found the Bábís demoralized and degraded. The effect of this situation upon Him has been described by the Guardian of the Bahá'í Faith: 'Such was the sadness that overwhelmed Him on His arrival that He refused for some time to leave His house, except for His visits to Káẓimayn and for His occasional meetings with a few of His friends who resided in that town and in Baghdád.'[1]

Bahá'u'lláh's own words, in the *Kitáb-i-Íqán*, are a sufficient testimony to the condition of the Bábí community in those days, and to the spirit in which He arose to revive the Cause of the Báb:

> What pen can recount the things We beheld upon Our return! Two years have elapsed during which Our enemies have ceaselessly and assiduously contrived to exterminate Us, whereunto all witness. Nevertheless, none amongst the faithful hath risen to render Us any assistance, nor did any one feel inclined to help in Our deliverance. Nay, instead of assisting Us, what showers of continuous sorrows, their words and deeds have caused to rain upon Our soul! Amidst them all, We stand, life in hand, wholly resigned to His will; that perchance, through God's loving kindness and His grace, this revealed and manifest Letter may lay down His life as a sacrifice in the path of the Primal Point, the most exalted Word. By Him at Whose bidding the Spirit hath spoken, but for this yearning of Our soul, We would not, for one moment, have tarried any longer in this city. 'Sufficient Witness is God unto Us.' We conclude Our argument with the words: 'There is no power nor strength but in God alone.' 'We are God's, and to Him shall we return.'[2]

Shortly after Bahá'u'lláh's return from Sulaymáníyyih, there occurred an event which caused Him great sorrow. We have already seen that Mírzá Yaḥyá had (in his book *Mustayqiẓ)* openly reviled Mírzá Asadu'lláh-i-Dayyán for having advanced a claim, and during Bahá'u'lláh's absence had despatched Mírzá Muḥammad-i-Mázindarání to Ádharbáyján for the express purpose of murdering that distinguished believer. As it happened, Dayyán had simultaneously set out from

Á<u>dh</u>arbáyján for Ba<u>gh</u>dád, and so Mírzá Muḥammad failed to find him. It was at this time that Bahá'u'lláh returned from Sulaymáníyyih and Dayyán attained His presence and renounced all claims he had made for himself. Mírzá Yaḥyá, however, was not to be turned aside from his purpose. One day Mírzá Muḥammad tricked Dayyán into accompanying him from Káẓimayn to Ba<u>gh</u>dád and there fell upon him and encompassed his death.

Gradually, Bahá'u'lláh began to rebuild the Bábí community and restore its self-respect, integrity and prestige, until He had extricated the Bábís (those few who were left) from the depths of ignominy to which they had sunk, during His absence in the mountains of Kurdistán. They could now hold their heads high, and were no longer the butt of every sort of foul abuse.

On one occasion some retainers of 'Alí-<u>Sh</u>áh, the Ẓillu's-Sulṭán (see Addendum V), cursed a Bábí who was passing the door of that exiled prince's residence. Bahá'u'lláh sent a message to Ẓillu's-Sulṭán to ask his men to hold their tongues. The Prince obeyed. Before long his sons, <u>Sh</u>ujá'u'd-Dawlih and Sayfu'd-Dawlih, were *habitués* of the *bírúní* of the house of Bahá'u'lláh. Zaynu'l-'Ábidín <u>Kh</u>án, the Fa<u>kh</u>ru'd-Dawlih, another nobleman from Írán, was often heard to say: 'I cannot explain it, I do not know how it is, but whenever I feel gloomy and depressed, I have only to go to the house of Bahá'u'lláh to have my spirits uplifted.'

As for the notables of the city, whoever met Bahá'u'lláh and came into His presence became attracted and devoted to Him. <u>Sh</u>ay<u>kh</u> 'Abdu'l-Qádir (possibly al-Gílání, an 'ulamá famous for his calligraphy, who died in 1897), 'Abdu's-Salám Effendi (who is mentioned by Bahá'u'lláh in the *Kitáb-i-Badí'*), Ibn-Álúsí, and Siyyid Dawúdí, all men of learning; 'Abdu'lláh Pá<u>sh</u>á of Sulaymáníyyih and his vizier, Maḥmúd Áqá, and Mullá 'Alí-Mardán (the controller of customs), men of public affairs, were equally devoted to Him.* There

*'Abdu's-Salám Effendi – probably <u>Sh</u>ay<u>kh</u> 'Abdu's-Salám a<u>sh</u>-Shawwáf – was born about 1819 and attended the classes of <u>Sh</u>ay<u>kh</u> Maḥmúd al-Álúsí. He then became one of the teachers at the al-Qádiriya theological college. He died in 1900.

Ibn-Álúsí – one of the five sons of the famous <u>Sh</u>ay<u>kh</u> Maḥmúd al-Álúsí, who died in 1854. It is not clear which son is referred to here, but he is probably one of the three eldest: 'Abdu'lláh, Bahá'u'd-Dín; 'Abdu'l-Baqí; and Siyyid Na'mán, <u>Kh</u>ayru'd-Dín.

Siyyid Dawúdí is probably Siyyid Dawúdí an-Naq<u>sh</u>bandí al-<u>Kh</u>álidí, who was one of the 'ulamá and a <u>sh</u>ay<u>kh</u> of the <u>Kh</u>álidíya section of the Ṣúfí Naq<u>sh</u>bandí order. He died in 1882.

'Abdu'lláh Pá<u>sh</u>á was one of the Bábán family, hereditary pá<u>sh</u>ás of Sulaymáníyyih.

were numbers of Persian princes living in exile in Baghdád, some of whom we have already noted, and to name one more: Riḍá-Qulí Mírzá, the Náyibu'l-Íyálih (the eldest son of the pretender, Ḥusayn-'Alí Mírzá, the Farmán-Farmá) – all were to be seen reverentially attending Bahá'u'lláh in the *bírúní* of His residence.

So many were the devotees of Bahá'u'lláh, among all classes of the population and particularly the ruling class, that anyone who dared to say a word derogatory to Him would be silenced in no time.

Áqá Muḥammad, a Kurd from Írán, had come to Baghdád and opened a shop to sell *kabáb* (kebab). Towards the Bábís he was not at all well disposed. Under his influence people in the bazar, particularly the Persians, had waxed bold in abusing the Bábís. One day a confectioner named Ḥasan used a foul epithet in reference to some of the Bábís who accompanied Bahá'u'lláh as He passed by. One of them went back and gave Ḥasan a sound beating. Next day, Áqá Muḥammad took that Bábí to task, telling him: 'You should not have punished Ḥasan yourself, but should have come to me, the leader of this bazar, with your complaint.' Knowing full well that Áqá Muḥammad was the source of all the mischief in the bazar, this Bábí told him so to his face and gave him a beating as well. The Kurd, enraged, stood up on a platform in his shop to shout that the vile Bábís had now become so aggressive as to beat him. 'I will go', he threatened, 'to their leader and demand justice. Should he not heed me, I know what to do; I will take the matter into my own hands.' The next day he stopped Bahá'u'lláh while He was on His way to a coffee-house, and complained bitterly of the behaviour of the Bábí youth. Bahá'u'lláh assured him that He would summon all those who had seen the incident and question them. Whoever had misbehaved would be punished. Áqá Muḥammad went back to his shop, greatly surprised that Bahá'u'lláh had said He would punish the guilty person, rather than putting the case to the Consul. The Persian consul at this time was Mírzá Ibráhím Khán, who was away in Karbilá. When Áqá Muḥammad ran to the Consulate with his complaint, the Vice-Consul sent an agent to Bahá'u'lláh's house to find out what had happened. He was informed in no uncertain terms that should the shopkeepers in the bazar not cease their foul language, they would all receive their due. The agent said no more, nor did he approach the person of Bahá'u'lláh, but the Vice-Consul took steps to put an end to this misbehaviour. He also had both Áqá Muḥammad and Ḥasan brought in, berated them and kept them in custody. After a few days, when their families came crying to Bahá'u'lláh's door that they had no one to look after them, Bahá'u'lláh sent word to the Vice-Consul and both were released. When the Consul returned from Karbilá, and heard what had happened in his absence, he was angered by the insulting behaviour of the shopkeepers and ordered the re-arrest of the two ringleaders. As the river was in flood with no bridge crossing, they were pushed into a *quffih* (covered boat) and taken over to the Consulate, where Mírzá Ibráhím Khán castigated and held them. Once again, after a few days, their families came to Bahá'u'lláh to plead for His intercession, and on His word the two men were warned and sent home.

But now the Kurds of Írán (there were some 2,000 in Baghdád) felt aggrieved that one of their leaders had twice suffered punishment and detention, and they made a pact to exterminate the Bábís, of whom, according to Áqá Riḍá, there were no more than thirty to forty, Persian and Arab, then in Baghdád. These gathered round the house* of Bahá'u'lláh to protect it. When Bahá'u'lláh, as was His wont, came out shortly before sunset to go to a coffee-house, He was told what the Kurds intended to do that night. He went on as usual, first to Ṣáliḥ's coffee-house, which was situated at the eastern side of the bridge, and after a while He got up to visit 'Abdu'lláh's coffee-house at the western side, which was frequented by Kurds and Persians. He was accompanied by Mírzá Javád-i-Khurásání, with whom He was talking, while a few of the Bábís walked behind. To Mírzá Javád He said, 'We have been threatened with death. We have no fear, We are ready for them. Here is Our head.' He spoke with such vehemence and authority that all who heard Him were struck dumb. Then He entered the coffee-house and stayed until three hours after sunset, after which He walked home and no one dared approach Him. After this episode, Áqá Riḍá states, there was no further mischief-making or insulting behaviour in the market-place, and all was calm.

Then, 'Umar Páshá, a man high in military command, was appointed Governor of Baghdád (see Addendum V). He had an iron will and governed with an iron hand. He it was who had hordes of resident

* This was the house of Sulaymán-i-Ghannám, in the Karkh quarter of Baghdád, near the western bank of the Tigris.

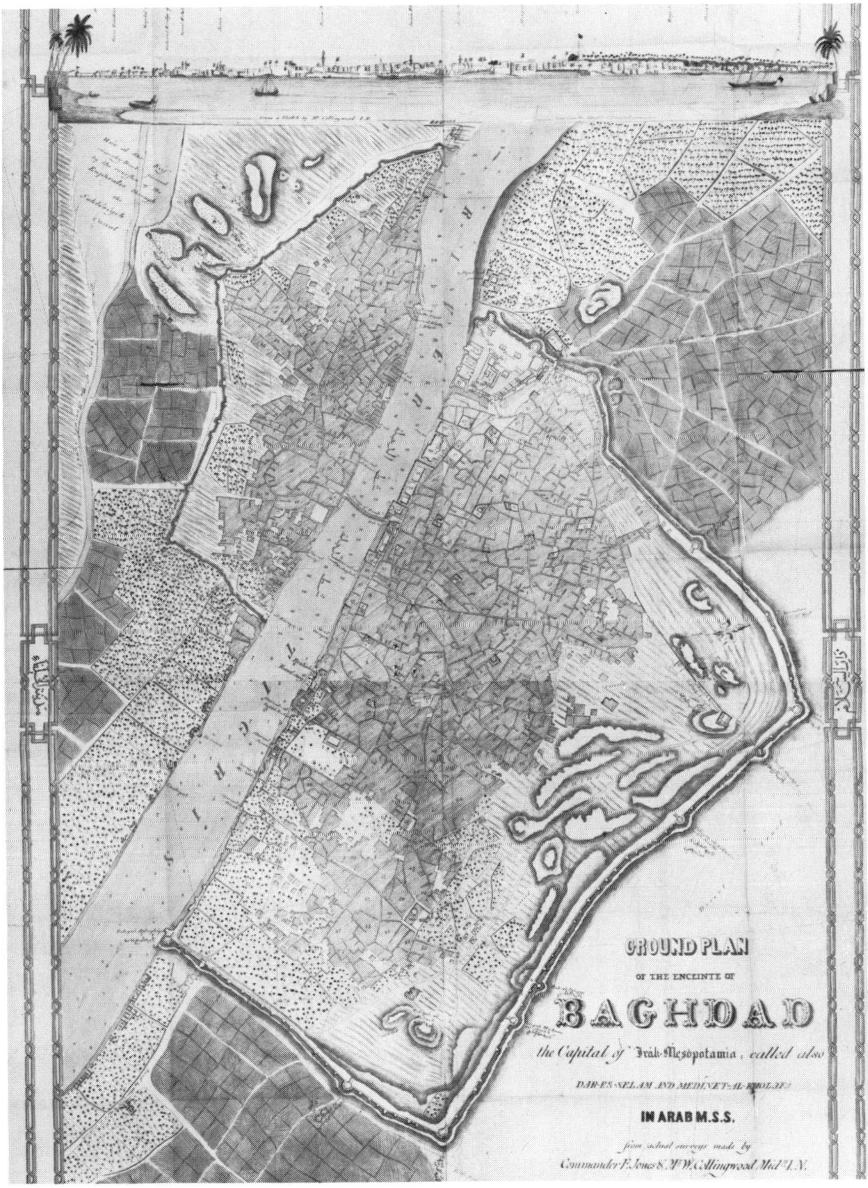

Map of Baghdád, prepared in 1853–54 by Commander James F. Jones and Mr W. Collingwood of the Indian Navy. The district of Karkh where Bahá'u'lláh resided is the part of the town on the western (left-hand) bank of the river. (From Thomas, Memoirs by Commander James Felix Jones, I. N.*)*

Persians in Karbilá detained, hauled to Baghdád and made to wear Ottoman military uniform. To the pleadings and protests of the Íránian envoy this haughty Governor paid not the slightest attention. A good many of these unfortunate people were forced to pay large sums to buy their release.

During the governorship of 'Umar Páshá, a relative of Siyyid Muḥammad-i-Iṣfahání named Mírzá Riḍá, and Mírzá 'Alíy-i-Nayrízí were plotting and conspiring to injure Bahá'u'lláh. Without His knowledge and permission, one or more Bábís set upon them in the bazar. Mírzá Riḍá died on the spot and Mírzá 'Alí, badly wounded, managed to reach the *Seraye* (Government House). 'Umar Páshá, seeing his plight, enquired furiously who was responsible for this outrage. On being told that the perpetrator of the savage assault was a member of the retinue of Bahá'u'lláh, he impetuously ordered that cannons be trained on Bahá'u'lláh's residence. He was advised that it was an impossible task. He then demanded that Bahá'u'lláh come in person before him. Siyyid Dáwúdí, who was present, intervened to say: 'Your Honour must know this, that even ordering one of His servants to come here is not admissible, not to speak of ordering His own presence in this assemblage.' 'Umar Páshá, on hearing these words so bluntly stated as a fact by a prominent member of the Sunní hierarchy, fell silent, and sent Mírzá 'Alí to Bahá'u'lláh's house to obtain justice from His hands.

As remarked previously, Bahá'u'lláh had no more than a few dozen Bábís with and around Him, but His spiritual authority and influence increased so vastly that all those who felt aggrieved and oppressed would flock to His door, begging for His assistance and intercession. Áqá Riḍá mentions a certain Yúsuf Khán, who, when rescued by Bahá'u'lláh from an unjust situation, repeatedly claimed that he had been a believer since the year 1250 – ten years earlier than the advent of the Báb!

Mullá Muḥammad-i-Zarandí, later entitled Nabíl-i-A'ẓam, destined to become the most outstanding chronicler and historian of the Bábí-Bahá'í Faith, and who had himself made certain claims, reached Baghdád at a time when Bahá'u'lláh was at Sulaymáníyyih. By his own admission, he still believed that Mírzá Yaḥyá was a man of consequence and sought a meeting with him. Mírzá Músá, Áqáy-i-

Kalím, whom Nabíl encountered on the bridge, took him home (to the house of 'Alí Madad) to meet the Most Great Branch, then barely ten years old. From Mírzá Músá he learned that Mírzá Yaḥyá did not meet anyone, and so it was, for not only did Mírzá Yaḥyá not show his face, but he sent Nabíl a message, urging him to quit Baghdád and seek the safety of Karbilá where Siyyid Muḥammad-i-Iṣfahání had stationed himself.

In Karbilá, Nabíl carefully watched Siyyid Muḥammad's riotous behaviour and childish pranks, and eventually recorded them. He was unhappy. He had dared to claim leadership; he had not found in Mírzá Yaḥyá a 'shepherd' of a battered and mutilated flock. He writes very movingly of his spiritual odyssey – of Bahá'u'lláh's return from Sulaymáníyyih, attainment to His presence, finding in Him all that he desired, doing penance at His door, coming upon Áqá Muḥammad-Ibráhím-i-Amír-i-Nayrízí (see Addendum V) sweeping the roadway and taking the broom from him to do likewise (the act of a humble penitent), performing a ceremonial ablution in the Tigris (symbolic of washing away all the stains of the past), divesting himself of the robes of a would-be priest. With his rebirth, Nabíl composed a translucent poem, which Bahá'u'lláh lovingly and graciously acknowledged, assuring Nabíl that that poem had set the seal on and completely redeemed the past. Now, at long last, Mullá Muḥammad-i-Zarandí was at peace with himself and with the world. When Bahá'u'lláh was told that Mullá Muḥammad, whom He eventually honoured with the designation of Nabíl-i-A'ẓam, had been sweeping the roadway outside His house, He administered a gentle reproof to His attendant for having allowed it, and said, 'This makes Me feel ashamed', which, when Nabíl heard of it, brought to his mind the famous lines of the poet Sa'dí (the reflection of a verse in the Qur'án):[3]

> 'Consider the generosity and the kindliness of the Lord;
> Sinned the servant has, but ashamed is He.'

Áqá Muḥammad-Karím, a veteran of the Faith from Shíráz, who had been in the presence of the glorious Báb and had known His powers, was another bewildered soul, stranded in 'Iráq. Nabíl found him and led him into the presence of Bahá'u'lláh. He too received that which his whole being longed for: the assurance that the Cause of God was not lost, and that it was in safe hands.

Ḥájí Muḥammad-Taqí of Nayríz, who had stood heroically and proudly under the banner of the erudite, the peerless Vaḥíd, and had suffered immeasurably, was another well-tested veteran of the Faith, come to seek solace and asylum in 'Iráq; he found both, on attaining the presence of Bahá'u'lláh. The story of Ḥájí Muḥammad-Taqí, whom Bahá'u'lláh later honoured with the designation of Ayyúb (Job), is both moving and awe-inspiring. He survived the holocaust of Nayríz and fell into the clutches of Zaynu'l-'Ábidín Khán, the sadistic and greedy governor of that town, who had helped himself copiously to the riches of the wealthy Ḥájí. Every day, as the Governor sat watching and mocking him, he was thrown into an ice-cold pool, battered on the head every time he surfaced, then dragged out and mercilessly lashed (to the accompaniment of the Governor's evident enjoyment and laughter) until blood poured out of his wounds. In response to Zaynu'l-'Ábidín Khán's jeers, Ḥájí Muḥammad-Taqí praised God for the bounty of suffering in His path. At last, the Governor tired of his satanic pleasures and decided to get rid of the Ḥájí. But the Governor's men proved more God-fearing. They let Ḥájí Muḥammad-Taqí go, and told him to take himself away as soon and as far as he could, lest he should be discovered alive by their master.

Ḥájí Muḥammad-Taqí, covered with wounds, was left alone in the wilderness. With that superb patience which would earn him the designation of Ayyúb from the Most Sublime Pen, he managed to reach a village in the neighbourhood, with the headman of which he had been on very friendly terms in the past. That excellent man harboured the Ḥájí for a month, hiding him from all and nursing him with care. But Ḥájí Muḥammad-Taqí knew that before long he must put a safe distance between himself and the town of Nayríz. As soon as he could walk, he bade farewell to the kind headman and joined a caravan wending its way to the holy cities of 'Iráq. In that caravan there were many pilgrims trudging on foot, and Ḥájí Muḥammad-Taqí kept them company, although after all he had gone through he was weak and enfeebled. However, out of a tent emerged a man, obviously well provided for the long journey, who had a good look at Ḥájí Muḥammad-Taqí, and then invited him to be his guest as far as Karbilá. 'In my dream last night,' the man said, 'the Prince of the Martyrs, himself, commanded me to take you as my guest.' In this miraculous way Ḥájí Muḥammad-Taqí reached 'Iráq and the presence of Bahá'u'lláh. The *Lawḥ-i-Ayyúb* (Tablet of Ayyúb), revealed by Bahá'u'lláh, has immortalized the name of Ḥájí Muḥammad-Taqí of Nayríz.

Another claimant to spiritual authority, who came penitent to the door of Bahá'u'lláh, was Ḥájí Mírzá Músá of Qum. He was also a veteran of the Faith of the Báb, who had turned away from Mírzá Yaḥyá because he had found him totally wanting. Considering himself in every way more competent and more accomplished, more daring and more independent than Mírzá Yaḥyá, and viewing with despair the sorry plight of the once renowned community of the Báb, he made a bold attempt to assume authority, but, hearing of the fame of Bahá'u'lláh, he soon became conscious of his gross error, hurried to Baghdád and laid his head on the threshold of that true Redeemer. So pure in heart was he, and so devoid of egotism, that Bahá'u'lláh observed that, should the Ḥájí have persisted with his claim, 'We would have endorsed it'. For penance, Ḥájí Mírzá Músá decided to fast unto death. But Bahá'u'lláh prevented it. Ḥájí Mírzá Músá stayed on in Baghdád until, three days after Bahá'u'lláh's departure for Istanbul, he passed out of this world.

The last claimant whom we shall take note of (although he was not the least of them), was Ḥájí Mullá Háshim, who had been a Shí'ih divine possessed of considerable authority. But he too, having seen the error into which he had fallen, turned to Bahá'u'lláh for forgiveness and rehabilitation, and was amply rewarded.

After recounting in his enchanting chronicle the stories of these devoted followers and faithful friends, Nabíl-i-A'ẓam tells us that, having been three months in Baghdád, he was directed by Bahá'u'lláh to travel to Qazvín and teach the Faith there. 'Outside the gates of Baghdád,' Nabíl writes, 'Áqá Muḥammad-Ibráhím-i-Amír overtook me, and brought me money, the expenses of my journey granted by the Blessed Perfection, that I might be able to hire a steed and join a caravan. I told Amír that when I had first reached His blessed presence, He had graciously granted me the means of living that I should not again suffer want; and I asked Amír to beg at the threshold of His bounty to keep secure that which above everything else He had given me . . . However, as Amír insisted, I took some of the money which he had brought, and we bade farewell. Every instant a new door would fling open before me. It was as if I had wings to soar in the Heaven of the Beloved. I felt no need to have a companion on the road and I had no fear of highwaymen.' Thus he graphically describes his ecstasy and elation as he made his way to Qazvín, over the high peaks and plains of Western Írán. He rested, he writes, in day-time, and started walking some two hours after sunset. In Kirmanshāh he met Mírzá 'Abdu'lláh-i-Ghawghá, who had, obviously, made some claim because, as Nabíl points out, Darvísh Ṣidq-'Alí (see Addendum V) was with him and attending him. (But Siyyid Mihdíy-i-Dahijí denies, in his *Risálih*, that Mírzá 'Abdu'lláh-i-Ghawghá had ever made any claim.)

Nabíl was once again back in Baghdád. Bahá'u'lláh told him then to go over a manuscript of the *Qayyúmu'l-Asmá'* which Áqá Siyyid Ismá'íl-i-Zavári'í had been copying, to ensure that all was correct. Siyyid Ismá'íl had come from Írán with high hopes and had attained the presence of Bahá'u'lláh. He found all that he expected, all that he craved. He was of noble descent, a learned man and a master of calligraphy. He is also known as Dhabíḥ, but should not be confused with Ḥájí Muḥammad-Ismá'íl-i-Dhabíḥ-i-Káshání, the brother of Ḥájí Mírzá Jání. Nabíl says that it took them eighteen days. When the task was completed, he asked Siyyid Ismá'íl to tell him of his experience. Nabíl knew that Siyyid Ismá'íl went out, every night around midnight, and with his turban swept the street where the house of Bahá'u'lláh was situated, gathering up all the sweepings in his *'abá* to fling them into the Tigris. This earth and this dust, he would say, was hallowed by His blessed feet, and should not be touched by anything unclean. To Nabíl's query, Siyyid Ismá'íl answered, precisely and considerately, while his eyes welled with tears: 'What I have seen cannot be described. After I asked Him for spiritual sustenance, and He said that it had been granted to me, door after door opened upon my heart, and my soul became acquainted with thoughts not of this world. One night, in His *bírúní*, His Blessed Person asked for a candle to peruse a paper, and I, as usual lost in wonderment at my own condition, suddenly thought: "Is it possible that that visage, the sight of which the Chosen Ones and the Messengers of God had longed to behold, could be unveiled in a human temple?" and as soon as this thought passed through my mind, His blessed voice called out to me: "Áqá Siyyid Ismá'íl, look!" and when I gazed at His blessed face, I saw that which no word can ever describe. All that I can say is this: it seemed as if a hundred thousand seas, vast and sunlit, billowed upon that Blessed

Face. What happened then, I do not know. My last word to you is this: never ask for anything like this and be contented with what is given unto you, and always say, "O God! allow it all to end well with us" – and pray for me that my own end shall be well.'

The incident which Siyyid Ismá'íl had described to Nabíl happened thus. One day Bahá'u'lláh was a guest in the house of Áqá Muḥammad-Riḍáy-i-'Aríḍ. In front of Him were laid dishes of fruits and sweets. Siyyid Ismá'íl too was there. When Bahá'u'lláh gave the Siyyid some sweets, the latter expressed his desire for spiritual sustenance, to which Bahá'u'lláh replied, 'That has been given to you'.

Now Siyyid Ismá'íl became afire with the love of Bahá'u'lláh. Poems left by him testify to that all-consuming love.[4]

Hear this from me,
Once again I say, and saying it, burn do I:
'Has anyone ever seen flowers pullulant in fire?'
This I say, and saying it, burn do I.

'Tear apart the veils,
Bring forth the means,
Breathe the breath of love.'
This I say, and saying it, burn do I.

'Behold the garden of the Lord,
The land divine,
All in Him to nothingness reach.'
This I say, and saying it, burn do I.

Suffice thus to end my word:
'My soul alight has He set,
My life in His path shall be shed.'
This I say, and saying it, burn do I.

After that, Siyyid Ismá'íl could be seen sweeping before sunrise the doorway of Bahá'u'lláh's house. One day, early in the morning, he was observed leaving Baghdád and going towards Káẓimayn. There by the roadside he sat down and, facing the direction of the house of Bahá'u'lláh and the holy shrines of the seventh and the ninth Imáms, he cut his throat, and thus he died. By his act he became known as 'Dhabíḥ' – the Sacrifice. And the pen of Bahá'u'lláh extolled him as the 'Beloved and the Pride of the Martyrs'.

Customs men, who had noticed the Siyyid leaving the city, when nothing more was seen of him went to investigate. They found him dead with a razor in his hand. They informed the Persian consul, and took the Siyyid's body to the *Seraye*, whence it was carried to Káẓimayn and buried in Tall-i-Aḥmar (the Red Mount).*

And there was Ḥájí Ḥasan-i-Turk. He had attained the presence of Bahá'u'lláh first in Kirmánsháh, and had been several times to Baghdád. A new life was, indeed, breathed into him. Although devoid of learning, he began to compose a commentary on the Báb's *Qayyúmu'l-Asmá'*. But most of the time he said not a word. When his silence was commented on in the presence of Bahá'u'lláh, He observed that the Ḥájí's turn to speak would come soon. Then one day Ḥájí Ḥasan came to Bahá'u'lláh, arrayed with a dagger, and asked for His permission to go, with dagger drawn, to stand on the bridge and proclaim to all the Cause of God. Bahá'u'lláh told him kindly, but firmly: 'Ḥájí, put aside your dagger. The Faith of God has to be given with amity and love to receptive souls. It does not need daggers and swords.'

* The self-sacrifice of Siyyid Ismá'íl took place during the term of Dabíru'l-Mulk as Persian consul, from 8 June 1859 for about one year. He had succeeded Mírzá Ibráhím Khán who died on 28 December 1858. (Dates from British consular records, FO 195 577 and 624.) Both men were friendly to Bahá'u'lláh and His companions.

23

Baghdád – Final Years

THE case and the conduct of a young student of theology, who had been converted to the Faith of the Báb, led to a fresh crisis in the affairs of the Bábí community.

This young man was named Mullá Báqir. He was the son of the Imám-Jum'ih of Qumshih, a township in the environs of Iṣfahán. His father had sent him to Najaf to study theology. There, at the very heart of the Shí'ih world, he became fully aware of the advent of the Báb and met the celebrated Nabíl-i-Akbar, Mullá Muḥammad (or Áqá Muḥammad) of Qá'in. This Nabíl had been one of the most accomplished and learned students of the famed Shaykh Murtiḍáy-i-Anṣárí, the foremost Shí'ih mujtahid of his day (see Addendum V), and had received a certificate for *Ijtihád* from his hands. Consorting with Áqá Muḥammad-i-Qá'iní led Mullá Báqir to espouse the Faith of the Báb, and he did it with great zeal and ardour. Then he attained the presence of Bahá'u'lláh in Baghdád and became well confirmed. However, his misfortune was acquaintance with a young Shaykhí, a disciple and follower of Ḥájí Muḥammad-Karím Khán-i-Kirmání; he was implacably opposed to the Faith of the Báb and kept abusing the Báb and the Bábís within the hearing of Mullá Báqir. The latter tried very hard to dissuade the young Shaykhí from pursuing this abominable habit, but he failed in his purpose and the Shaykhí antagonist remained abusive. Then came a day when Mullá Báqir could bear his foul language no longer. He told his co-religionists that he felt more and more severely inclined to inflict some injury on his tormentor. They tried to stay his hand, but also failed.

One day in the market-place, Mullá Báqir attacked the Shaykhí youth with a scimitar. Others intervened, stopped Mullá Báqir and took him to the Persian consul, who advised him to leave Baghdád. That same night he took the road to Írán. But bad luck dogged his footsteps. In Hamadán he ran into the same obstinate, foul-mouthed youth, now recovered from his wounds, who promptly denounced him to the Governor. Mullá Báqir was arrested and searched. On him they found a Tablet of Bahá'u'lláh, in which he was reprimanded for his rash deed.

The Governor of Hamadán decreed that Mullá Báqir had disobeyed his Master and deserved imprisonment. He was cast into prison and when, at last, he obtained release, he made his way back to Baghdád. However, Bahá'u'lláh did not give him the same reception as before. His assault on the Shaykhí youth had had repercussions detrimental to the Bábí community, and the detention of Áqá 'Abdu'r-Rasúl and his brother resulted from that rash and foolish deed. Bahá'u'lláh instructed most of the Bábís to leave Baghdád.

Now, Mírzá Buzurg Khán-i-Qazvíní arrived on the scene, in July 1860, as Persian consul. He was a man of consequence and had previously held the post of Consul in Erzeroum. Before his arrival it had been rumoured and passed from mouth to mouth that he was coming to put an end, once and for all, to these troublesome Bábís. To show what an important and distinguished man he was, Mírzá Buzurg Khán went riding or strutting about, preening himself in public, attended by a large number of ruffians whom he had brought with him.

Mírzá Buzurg Khán joined forces with Shaykh 'Abdu'l-Ḥusayn-i-Ṭihrání, who had already been in 'Iráq for about two years and was an implacable enemy of Bahá'u'lláh. Shaykh 'Abdu'l-Ḥusayn, entitled Shaykhu'l-'Iráqayn (see Addendum V), had been sent to Karbilá by Náṣiri'd-Dín Sháh, commissioned to supervise the much needed repairs in the holy shrines.

The new Persian consul went to the Ottoman authorities with a strange statement, saying that he intended to lay hands on a number of rascally men who had fled from Írán. Muṣṭafá Núrí Páshá, the Válí (see Addendum V), who had come a few months before the Consul (in March 1860), was a just man and had heard 'Abdu'lláh Páshá of Sulaymáníyyih speak very highly of Bahá'u'lláh. He was also well aware of the purpose of Mírzá Buzurg Khán. But he pretended ignorance and told the Consul to go ahead and make his arrests. To do this, replied Mírzá Buzurg Khán, he would need help from the Government, at which the Válí expressed his surprise that the Persian consul required so much help just to lay hands on a few men. Perforce,

Mírzá Buzurg Khán had to reveal the identity of those Persians whom he wanted to arrest. Muṣṭafá Núrí Páshá showed even greater astonishment that the Consul should speak in such coarse terms of persons whom all the residents of Baghdád, high and low alike, held in great esteem. He refused to have anything to do with Mírzá Buzurg Khán's nefarious designs. The Consul's lame response was: 'But they are enemies of our Faith and yours', to which he received this crushing reply from the Válí: 'Do we then follow different Faiths?'

Nabíl writes that from time to time Bahá'u'lláh would send Áqáy-i-Kalím to visit Mírzá Buzurg Khán. One day the foolish Consul, in all haughtiness, told Áqáy-i-Kalím that he could do whatever he liked about Bahá'u'lláh. Áqáy-i-Kalím replied: 'Why is it that I come occasionally to visit you? Do you think I come to ask you for a post, an office, an allowance? It is only to show you our friendly intent. By God! Should His favour towards you cease, these very men who are close to you would assuredly destroy you.' Then Áqáy-i-Kalím went on to recount all the Consul's intrigues and evil actions, so precisely and effectively that all he could reply was: 'The past is past. Should He [Bahá'u'lláh] consider me with favour in future, I shall be of service to Him.' But, as Nabíl points out, Mírzá Buzurg Khán was incorrigible, and he never ceased concocting plots with Shaykh 'Abdu'l-Ḥusayn.

The opposition of the Consul went to the length of offering rich rewards to a ruffian named Riḍá Turk, should he seek out Bahá'u'lláh and murder Him. This ruthless man, who never knew fear and dared anything for gain, himself related in after years that he kept watch for a suitable opportunity to carry out the wishes of the Persian consul. One day, knowing that Bahá'u'lláh was visiting the bath, he found an opportunity when Bahá'u'lláh's attendant, Áqá Muḥammad-Ibráhím-i-Amír, had gone for a short while on an errand. Riḍá Turk entered the bath but, on his own admission, when he found himself in the presence of Bahá'u'lláh, he was so struck by awe and remorse that he turned on his heel and fled.

Now began a campaign by Mírzá Buzurg Khán for the removal of Bahá'u'lláh from Baghdád. The shrewd Ambassador of Írán at Istanbul, Ḥájí Mírzá Ḥusayn Khán, the Mushíru'd-Dawlih, wrote to Mírzá Sa'íd Khán, the Minister of Foreign Affairs in Ṭihrán (see Addendum V for both men), that the Consul's ardour in clamouring for this was not due to zeal in the service of his country, but to ulterior motives. He wished to marry the daughter of Ḥájí Mírzá Hádíy-i-Javáhirí for her money, and considered Bahá'u'lláh to be standing in his way. Mírzá Sa'íd Khán replied that he was well aware of that fact; nevertheless, it was imperative to press for the banishment of Bahá'u'lláh from the vicinity of the frontiers of Írán.

As to Shaykh 'Abdu'l-Ḥusayn, sheer fanaticism combined with native ambition to achieve greater fame and reputation motivated him to take the course he did, in agitating against Bahá'u'lláh. Decades later, Fáḍil-i-Ṭihrání, the grandson of this inveterate enemy of Bahá'u'lláh, ardently embraced His Faith, which his wayward grandfather had spurned and despised, and achieved well-deserved fame as a teacher and propagator of the Cause of Bahá'u'lláh.

This Válí of Baghdád, Muṣṭafá Núrí Páshá, prior to his appointment to the governorship of 'Iráq, stood very close to the person of Sulṭán 'Abdu'l-Majíd. Because of that, he managed to have a certain Riḍá Páshá dismissed from his post in the court of the Sulṭán. But later, Riḍá Páshá was returned to favour and a new position. Once well established, Riḍá Páshá began plotting to take his revenge. He arranged for a military adviser, named Aḥmad Tawfíq Páshá, to be sent to Baghdád, and instructed him to draw up such charges against Muṣṭafá Núrí Páshá as would cause his dismissal. He told Aḥmad Páshá that should he succeed, the governorship of 'Iráq would be his. Thus primed, Aḥmad Páshá worked his way steadily into the confidence of some of the notables of Baghdád, who, knowing of his close friendship with Riḍá Páshá and the latter's immense influence in the inner circles around Sulṭán 'Abdu'l-Majíd, lent themselves to his designs, and a list of charges of embezzlement and acceptance of bribes was secretly prepared and signed by some of the notables and despatched to Istanbul. As soon as Riḍá Páshá received this document, he had a cable sent to Baghdád, conveying the news of the dismissal of Muṣṭafá Núrí Páshá and his house arrest, pending proper investigation.

Aḥmad Páshá, the military man, got his governorship in March 1861 (though it had to be fully confirmed later) and proceeded to post sentries round the residence of poor Muṣṭafá Núrí Páshá, cutting him off from all association with anyone outside. 'Abdu'lláh Páshá of Sulaymáníyyih, who was a personal friend of the dismissed Válí, found himself prevented from meeting him. As he, too, was threatened, he realized that he stood in great danger. He had no one to turn to but Bahá'u'lláh, Who received him graciously and kindly, advising him not to grieve. 'Go and tell the Válí from Us,' He told 'Abdu'lláh Páshá, 'to put his trust wholly in God, and repeat every day, nineteen times, these two verses: "He who puts his trust in God, God will suffice him" and "He who fears God, God will send him relief."' When 'Abdu'lláh Páshá mentioned that no one was allowed to visit the Válí, Bahá'u'lláh advised him to make a direct appeal to Aḥmad Páshá. 'When he sees you appealing to him in the right way,' Bahá'u'lláh said, 'he will grant you permission to visit your friend.' 'Abdu'lláh Páshá took this advice; Aḥmad Páshá was greatly impressed by his fidelity and allowed him to visit the dismissed Válí as often as he wished. Thus, 'Abdu'lláh Páshá was enabled to visit Muṣṭafá Núrí Páshá and give him the message of Bahá'u'lláh. Within a few days, the news came of the death of Sulṭán 'Abdu'l-Majíd and the accession of Sulṭán 'Abdu'l-'Azíz to the throne, on 14 August 1861, followed by the expulsion of Riḍá Páshá, once again, from the Court, and the receipt of a cable reinstating Muṣṭafá Núrí Páshá. And now it was the turn of Aḥmad Páshá to appeal for help, reminding 'Abdu'lláh Páshá that he had acceded to his request and that the latter should intervene to save him from the Válí's anger. The Páshá of Sulaymáníyyih readily complied and took Aḥmad Páshá to meet the Válí, when a reconciliation was effected. After a while, the Válí's son-in-law arrived from Istanbul, with full powers to make a proper investigation. Muṣṭafá Núrí Páshá's total innocence was proved, to everyone's amazement. And it was left to 'Abdu'lláh Páshá to tell them to Whom the Governor should be grateful for his deliverance.

Muṣṭafá Núrí Páshá, who owed his rescue from disgrace to Bahá'u'lláh, remained firmly devoted to Him to the end of his life, although in Baghdád he had not been able to attain His presence. When Bahá'u'lláh reached Constantinople in 1863, Muṣṭafá Núrí Páshá was also there. Ignoring all restraints, he had his respects conveyed to Bahá'u'lláh, Who sent the Most Great Branch and Áqáy-i-Kalím to meet the Páshá. After that, Muṣṭafá Núrí Páshá himself came several times, and his heart's desire was fulfilled.

As to 'Abdu'lláh Páshá of Sulaymáníyyih, who had always been a faithful friend to Bahá'u'lláh, he was even more confirmed when he read *The Seven Valleys*. He was given the governorship of Ván, but was loath to go because it meant separation from Bahá'u'lláh. Later, he attempted to reach Adrianople to meet Him, but it was not to be. In the year AH 1304 (1886–7), he travelled to Beirut for medical treatment and passed away in that city.

Two distinguished and wealthy Persian residents of Baghdád had become so attracted to Bahá'u'lláh that not only did they espouse the Faith of the Báb, but in their wills they made the settlement of their estates dependent on the wishes of Bahá'u'lláh. One was Ḥájí Mírzá Hádíy-i-Javáhirí and the other Ḥájí Háshim-i-'Aṭṭár. Ḥájí Mírzá Hádí's son, Mírzá Músá, had been for years the despair of his father, who was rightly apprehensive about his future. It was the change in Mírzá Músá, through his attachment to Bahá'u'lláh, which moved his father to follow the way of his son, and to make his will in the terms he did. Nabíl says that the news of the actions taken by these two prominent Persians so inflamed Shaykh 'Abdu'l-Ḥusayn and Mírzá Buzurg Khán, that they began to agitate afresh against Bahá'u'lláh. But, as already noted, the Mushíru'd-Dawlih was astute enough to see through the Consul's stratagems.

Next, Ḥájí Háshim-i-'Aṭṭar organized a feast that it might be honoured with the presence of Bahá'u'lláh. Nabíl states that it was so magnificent an occasion that the people of Baghdád affirmed they had never seen the like of it, and it was particularly reported to Náṣiri'd-Dín Sháh and the Sulṭán of Turkey. On the day of the feast, Ḥájí Háshim himself, despite his advanced years, was continuously on his feet and serving. When it was over, greatly honoured as it had been by the presence of Bahá'u'lláh, Ḥájí Háshim felt that he had nothing more to live for, and soon after he died. Despite the provisions of his will, his sons-in-law, allied with mischief-makers, began to help themselves indiscriminately to his bequest. Some of the upright men of Baghdád came to Bahá'u'lláh and requested Him to intervene, since everyone knew the terms of Ḥájí Háshim's will. But Bahá'u'lláh responded: 'What was ours was the blessed person of the Ḥájí, who has now gone from this world. As for his wealth, let those who set store by the riches of this world go on purveying it.' However, when those sons-in-law began to rob the widow and minor children of the Ḥájí, Bahá'u'lláh intervened, summoned some of those who were behaving so unjustly, and counselled them to mend their ways. They submitted to His authority. The share of the young was separated and given to their mother, and Bahá'u'lláh appointed a trustworthy person to take charge of their inheritance and trade on their behalf.

Likewise, in the case of the bequest of Ḥájí Mírzá Hádíy-i-Javáhirí, Bahá'u'lláh took steps to ensure that no one was treated unjustly. He directed the Most Great Branch and Áqáy-i-Kalím to attend to the matter. Nabíl states that 30,000 *túmáns* (an appreciable sum in those days) was a tenth* of what Ḥájí Mírzá Hádí had left, and that Bahá'u'lláh announced his intention in these words: 'I shall give these 30,000 *túmáns* to Mírzá Músá [the son of Ḥájí Mírzá Hádí] so that he may be at peace with his sisters.'

Nabíl stresses the fact that these increasing evidences of Bahá'u'lláh's authority were galling to Shaykh 'Abdu'l-Ḥusayn, who, although a mujtahid, and honoured and invested with special powers by Náṣiri'd-Dín Sháh, could never command a moiety of that authority. Instead, he took refuge in bragging. 'I had a dream,' he said, 'that I was standing with the Sháh under a dome, and there was a tablet swinging above the head of the Sháh on which verses of the Qur'án were inscribed in Latin characters. It seemed that this was the doing of the Bábís, and the Sháh, sighting the tablet, informed me that the Bábís were responsible for this outrage; "but wait and see," the Sháh continued; "soon, with this very sword I am wearing, I shall demolish these people."' On another occasion, the Shaykh related mendaciously a second dream. 'I dreamt', he said, 'that I was on my way to Ṭihrán, on horseback, with a number of others. One of the Bábís of Baghdád caught up with me near Khániqayn. He had a bottle in his hand, filled with blood, and sprinkled some of the blood over me. It means', he interpreted, 'that my efforts at overthrowing these people will receive royal acclamation and I shall be called to Ṭihrán. But the Bábís will murder me, and my death at their hands will so enrage the government and people of Írán that they will combine to wipe them out.'

One who was close to Shaykh 'Abdu'l-Ḥusayn, and who frequented the house of Bahá'u'lláh in the vain hope of securing the secret of the elixir so eagerly sought by alchemists, reported these dreams to Bahá'u'lláh. He replied with a smile that the Shaykh's first dream was indicative of the fact that the Source of the Báb's Revelation was the same as that of the Qur'án, but renewed and restated; and as to the

* A tenth (*ushr*) was the customary share given to the executor of a will.

second dream, Shaykh 'Abdu'l-Ḥusayn could rest assured that no Bábí would murder him, nor would he be summoned for investiture with fresh honours. All that he heard from Bahá'u'lláh was reported by this man to the Shaykh, with the advice to put aside his extravagant language and seek a meeting with Bahá'u'lláh, to see for himself how genuine were the powers and how wonderful the mien and the speech of the Head of the Bábí community. It seemed that Shaykh 'Abdu'l-Ḥusayn was pleased with the suggestion; Bahá'u'lláh agreed to receive him, but at the last moment the Shaykh failed to come, and continued his plots and intrigues.

Mírzá Buzurg Khán had been shaken and disappointed by the ill-success of his efforts to procure the co-operation of the Válí against the Bábís, and he started to look for chinks in the armour of total integrity surrounding Bahá'u'lláh, in order to effect a grievous injury on Him, but there, too, he was bitterly disappointed because he could find none. Well-wishers of Bahá'u'lláh, aware of the Persian consul's hatred and hostility, were constantly begging Him to take steps for His own protection. His response to all their pleas was always the same: He had placed His trust in God, and 'God is the best of Protectors'. Mullá 'Alí-Mardán, a native of Karkúk, offered Him the use of a very comfortable house which he owned in that city, hoping that Bahá'u'lláh would absent Himself for a while, far from the venomous Consul and his associates.

The failure of the villainous Riḍá Turk to carry out his wishes and murder Bahá'u'lláh must also have been particularly galling to the Consul. Áqá Riḍá writes that the Bábís had gradually become aware of Mírzá Buzurg Khán's wretched designs and his alliance with Shaykh 'Abdu'l-Ḥusayn, and some were quietly keeping a vigilant eye on the house of Bahá'u'lláh.

Decades later, in August 1919, 'Abdu'l-Bahá was relating to the Bahá'ís gathered in His drawing-room in Haifa the events of past times. One evening He spoke of the plots of Shaykh 'Abdu'l-Ḥusayn and Mírzá Buzurg Khán. Dr Luṭfu'lláh Ḥakím took down what the Master was saying, and although his record could not have been word for word, it reflects fairly accurately the Master's recollections of those far-off days. Here is the gist of 'Abdu'l-Bahá's account:*

* What follows is not an exact translation, but is a faithful rendering.

When the mujtahids and Náṣiri'd-Dín Sháh sent Shaykh 'Abdu'l-Ḥusayn to 'Iráq, and he began agitating against the Blessed Perfection [Bahá'u'lláh], the mujtahids gathered at Káẓimayn to talk of waging a holy war, and they appealed to the Válí for help. When the Válí replied that he could not intervene, they sent letters to Baghdád, and a very large number of Persians and Shí'ih Arabs congregated there. Feelings in Baghdád came to the boil; they even sent for Shaykh Murtiḍá to come from Karbilá, on the grounds that the welfare of their Faith was threatened. On his way to Baghdád, Shaykh Murtiḍá met with an accident; he held himself apart then and asked to be left alone. Because he had not personally investigated the matter, he refused to intervene. Through Zaynu'l-'Ábidín Khán, the Fakhru'd-Dawlih, the Shaykh sent this message to the Blessed Perfection: 'I did not know; had I done so, I would not have come. Now I will pray for you.'

Those gathered in Káẓimayn then arranged to come two days later and attack us. We were only forty-six in all, and our strong man was Áqá Asadu'lláh-i-Káshí (Káshání), whose dagger, even when worn above his *shál* [the cloth used as a girdle], would dangle and touch the ground. Now there was a certain Siyyid Ḥasan from Shíráz. He was not a believer, but he was a very good man. One morning, when the Blessed Perfection had been up and about, this Áqá Siyyid Ḥasan came knocking at our door. Our black maid opened the door, Áqá Siyyid Ḥasan came in and, much agitated, asked, 'Where is the Áqá [Bahá'u'lláh]?' I said, 'He has gone to the riverside.' 'What is it that you say?' he responded. I offered him tea and said, 'He will come back.' He replied, 'Áqá! The world has been turned upside down . . . It has become turbulent . . . Do you know that last night they held a council in the presence of Shaykh 'Abdu'l-Ḥusayn and the Consul? They have also reached some sort of agreement with the Válí. How is it that the Blessed Perfection has gone to the riverside? They have decided to start their attack tomorrow.' Whilst he was telling me what had happened, the Blessed Perfection came in. Áqá Siyyid Ḥasan wanted immediately to express his anxiety. But the Blessed Perfection said, 'Let us talk of other matters', and went on speaking. Later, Áqá Siyyid Ḥasan insisted on unburdening himself. However, the Blessed Perfection told him, 'It is of no consequence.' So Áqá Siyyid Ḥasan stayed to lunch and then went home.

Late in the afternoon, the Blessed Perfection came out. The friends gathered round Him. Amongst them were two who were double-faced: Ḥájí 'Abdu'l-Ḥamíd and Áqá Muḥammad-Javád-i-Iṣfahání. The Blessed Perfection was walking up and down. Then He turned to the Friends and said, 'Have you heard the news? The mujtahids and the Consul have come together and gathered ten to twenty thousand people round them to wage *jihád* against Us.' Then He addressed the two double-faced men, 'Go and tell them, by the One God, the Lord of all, I will send two men to drive them away, all the way to Káẓimayn. If they are capable of accepting a challenge, let them come.' The two hurried away and repeated what they had heard. And do you know, they dispersed!

Áqá Riḍá writes that during all that time Bahá'u'lláh did not cease His daily visits to the coffee-houses. He went out alone, except for His two attendants, Áqá Najaf-'Alí and Áqá Muḥammad-Ibráhím-i-Amír-i-Nayrízí, and even then, there were days, Áqá Riḍá reports, when Bahá'u'lláh would leave His house without asking them to accompany Him. He never showed fear, nor displayed anxiety. In contradistinction to Him, Mírzá Yaḥyá went about disguised and never showed his face. At one time he was Ḥájí 'Alíy-i-Lás-Furúsh (silk merchant), at another a dealer in shoes and slippers in Baṣrah, ever afraid, ever apprehensive.

And then Mullá Ḥasan-i-'Amú came to visit Bahá'u'lláh. Let us have his story from 'Abdu'l-Bahá:

> It often happened that in Baghdád certain Muḥammadan 'ulamá, Jewish rabbis, and Christians, met together with some European scholars, in a blessed reunion:* each one had some question to propose, and although they were possessed of varying degrees of culture, they each heard a sufficient and convincing reply, and retired satisfied. Even the Persian 'ulamá who were at Karbilá and Najaf chose a wise man whom they sent on a mission to him; his name was Mullá Ḥasan-i-'Amú. He came into the Holy Presence, and proposed a number of questions on behalf of the 'ulamá, to which Bahá'u'lláh replied. Then Ḥasan-i-'Amú said: 'The 'ulamá recognize without hesitation and confess the knowledge and virtue of Bahá'u'lláh, and they are unanimously convinced that in all learning he has no peer or equal; and it is also evident that he has never studied or acquired this learning'; but still the 'ulamá said: 'We are not contented with this, we do not acknowledge the reality of his mission by virtue of his wisdom and righteousness. Therefore we ask him to show us a miracle in order to satisfy and tranquillize our hearts.'
>
> Bahá'u'lláh replied: 'Although you have no right to ask this, for God should test His creatures, and they should not test God, still I allow and accept this request. But the Cause of God is not a theatrical display that is presented every hour, of which some new diversion may be asked for every day. If it were thus, the Cause of God would become mere child's play.
>
> 'The 'ulamá must therefore assemble and with one accord choose one miracle, and write that after the performance of this miracle they will no longer entertain doubts about me, and that all will acknowledge and confess the truth of my Cause. Let them seal this paper and bring it to me. This must be the accepted criterion: If the miracle is performed, no doubt

* A reunion with Bahá'u'lláh.

will remain for them; and if not, we shall be convicted of imposture.' The learned man, Ḥasan-i-'Amú, rose and replied, 'There is no more to be said'; he then kissed the knee of the Blessed One although he was not a believer, and went. He gathered the 'ulamá and gave them the sacred message. They consulted together and said, 'This man is an enchanter: perhaps he will perform an enchantment, and then we shall have nothing more to say.' Acting on this belief, they did not dare to push the matter further.

This man, Ḥasan-i-'Amú, mentioned this fact at many meetings. After leaving Karbilá he went to Kirmánsháh and Ṭihrán, and spread a detailed account of it everywhere, laying emphasis on the fear and the withdrawal of the 'ulamá.

Briefly, all his adversaries in the Orient acknowledged his greatness, grandeur, knowledge, and virtue; and though they were his enemies, they always spoke of him as 'the renowned Bahá'u'lláh'.[1]

Mullá Ḥasan was so abashed that he felt he could not face Bahá'u'lláh again; he sent a message instead, through Zaynu'l-'Ábidín Khán, the Fakhru'd-Dawlih: 'I am ashamed of the behaviour of my colleagues'.

Amongst this group of mujtahids, the one who stood head and shoulders above them, the most pious, the most learned, the greatest of all, was Shaykh Murtiḍáy-i-Anṣárí. He was truly peerless and matchless in his day, and he categorically refused to lend his weighty support to those who had arisen to oppose Bahá'u'lláh. Whenever anyone asked him what to think of Bahá'u'lláh and the Bábís, he would reply, 'Go and investigate for yourself'.

At the opposite pole, Shaykh 'Abdu'l-Ḥusayn-i-Ṭihrání had viciously placed himself, and as the Guardian of the Bahá'í Faith writes:

> Balked in his repeated attempts to achieve his malevolent purpose, Shaykh 'Abdu'l-Ḥusayn now diverted his energies into a new channel. He promised his accomplice [Mírzá Buzurg Khán] he would raise him to the rank of a minister of the crown, if he succeeded in inducing the government to recall Bahá'u'lláh to Ṭihrán, and cast Him again into prison. He despatched lengthy and almost daily reports to the immediate entourage of the Sháh. He painted extravagant pictures of the ascendancy enjoyed by Bahá'u'lláh by representing Him as having won the allegiance of the nomadic tribes of 'Iráq. He claimed that He was in a position to muster, in a day, fully one hundred thousand men ready to take up arms at His bidding. He accused Him of meditating, in conjunction with various leaders in Persia, an insurrection against the sovereign.[2]

Shaykh Murtiḍáy-i-Anṣárí, the leading mujtahid of the Shí'ih world until his death in 1864

Shaykh 'Abdu'l-Ḥusayn had gathered, as we have already noted in 'Abdu'l-Bahá's account, a company of turbaned heads round himself, to declare a holy war and launch an attack on the Bábís, but, as the Guardian of the Bahá'í Faith comments:

> To their amazement and disappointment, however, they found that the leading mujtahid amongst them, the celebrated Shaykh Murtiḍáy-i-Anṣárí, a man renowned for his tolerance, his wisdom, his undeviating justice, his piety and nobility of character, refused, when apprized of their designs, to pronounce the necessary sentence against the Bábís. He it was whom Bahá'u'lláh later extolled in the 'Lawḥ-i-Sulṭán' [the Tablet addressed to Náṣiri'd-Dín Sháh], and numbered among '*those doctors who have indeed drunk of the cup of renunciation,*' and '*never interfered with Him,*' and to whom 'Abdu'l-Bahá referred as '*the illustrious and erudite doctor, the noble and celebrated scholar, the seal of seekers after truth.*' Pleading insufficient knowledge of the tenets of this community, and claiming to have witnessed no act on the part of its members at variance with the Qur'án, he, disregarding the remonstrances of his colleagues, abruptly left the gathering, and returned to Najaf, after having expressed, through a messenger, his regret to Bahá'u'lláh for what had happened, and his devout wish for His protection.[2]

It seems that so repelled was Shaykh Murtiḍá by the course which Shaykh 'Abdu'l-Ḥusayn and his accomplices were advocating that he felt moved to present his regret and his prayers for the deliverance of Bahá'u'lláh from the evil and venom of those men, through two messengers; one was, as noted before, Zaynu'l-'Ábidín Khán, the Fakhru'd-Dawlih, and the other, Mírzá Ḥasan-i-Gul-i-Guláb.

Two years later, when Bahá'u'lláh was about to leave Baghdád, one of the same squad of turbaned men came up to Him to say: 'We do not yet know what to do or say about you'. Bahá'u'lláh, relating the effrontery of this man to Nabíl, said: 'We told him: for years Shaykh Murtiḍá, when asked about Us, replied, this is a matter for investigation, not imitation;* go and find out for yourself. You did not follow his advice, but at this late hour, when We are on the point of departing, you come to us with your query. What shall we do, you say! Indeed, go away and read your commentaries.' And Bahá'u'lláh added, to Nabíl: 'We had never spoken to anyone in that manner, but the man was transparently insincere.'

Throughout His exile in Baghdád, Bahá'u'lláh stood ready to meet the religious leaders, as He Himself has testified:

* Imitation of a fully-qualified mujtahid is a cardinal point of the Shí'ih doctrine.

For twelve years We tarried in Baghdád. Much as We desired that a large gathering of divines and fair-minded men be convened, so that truth might be distinguished from falsehood, and be fully demonstrated, no action was taken. . . . we wished to come together with the divines of Persia. No sooner did they hear of this, than they fled and said: 'He indeed is a manifest sorcerer!' This is the word that proceeded aforetime out of the mouths of such as were like them. These (divines) *objected to what they said, and yet, they themselves repeat, in this day, what was said before them, and understand not. By My life! They are even as ashes in the sight of thy Lord.*[3]

The praiseworthy attitude of Shaykh Murtiḍáy-i-Anṣárí caused dismay and despondency in Shaykh 'Abdu'l-Ḥusayn's circle. Next, the failure of this group to respond to the efforts of Mullá Ḥasan-i-'Amú exposed the futility of their contentions. But mischief was still rearing its head, and mischief-makers would not keep their peace. Nevertheless, Bahá'u'lláh went on, totally disregarding the perils which beset Him. Many a night He went out, alone and unaccompanied, to the banks of the Tigris, to coffee-houses which He had always frequented during the years of His sojourn in Baghdád. Nabíl remarks that no one would know, at times, where He had gone, except the Most Great Branch and Áqáy-i-Kalím. He would go to places where enemies lurked to harm Him, utterly fearless and unconcerned. Whenever He came face to face with them, He would converse and even joke with them, making it plain that He was well aware of their intentions. Whilst Bahá'u'lláh was standing His ground with such serenity and confidence, Mírzá Yaḥyá was in Baṣrah, disguised, selling slippers and shoes. Riḍá Turk, the same man who had burst into the bath to assassinate Bahá'u'lláh, but had fled trembling, also related in later years that one day, pistol in hand, he was keeping watch at a vantage point. Bahá'u'lláh appeared in the distance, attended by Áqáy-i-Kalím. Riḍá Turk, on his own admission, became so perplexed, as soon as he saw Bahá'u'lláh, that he dropped his pistol and was unable to move. When Bahá'u'lláh came level with him, He said to Áqáy-i-Kalím: 'Pick up his pistol and give it to him, and show him the way to his house; he seems to have lost his way.'

Nabíl states that the companions were on the alert, night after night, patrolling outside the house of Bahá'u'lláh, to ward off the enemy should he dare to attack. A certain Siyyid Ḥusayn-i-Rawḍih-Khán – a Reciter of the sufferings of the House of the Prophet – who had come on pilgrimage to 'Iráq from Ṭihrán and was devoted to Bahá'u'lláh, made his way to His house one night, in disguise, to report that His adversaries had incited more than a hundred Kurds to come the next night as mourners, and mount an assault on His house. Arab Bábís, hearing of the plot, gathered in full force, prepared to offer defence. Bahá'u'lláh assured them that there was no need for action of any kind. And when the next night, about four hours after sunset, the mourners appeared in the street, beating their breasts, Bahá'u'lláh requested His attendants to open the door and let them come in. 'They are our guests', He said, and He had rose-water sherbet and then tea served to them. They came as enemies and went away as friends, readily admitting that they had had evil intents but, on beholding the majesty and the kindliness of Bahá'u'lláh, had a change of heart. As they departed, they were shouting: 'May God curse your enemies.'

Nabíl tells us that even Mírzá Ḥusayn-i-Mutavallí of Qum had written to beseech Bahá'u'lláh not to leave His house for a while. In reply, Bahá'u'lláh revealed a Tablet for him which opens with two lines of an ode by Ḥáfiẓ:

> Warblers, mellifluous-toned, all the parrots of Ind shall be,
> Because of this Pársí sugar-cone which to Bengal goes.*

In this Tablet, Bahá'u'lláh fearlessly declares that He would never waver, never submit to threats, never be daunted by the turmoil of this world. 'We are incandescent as a candle. . . . We have burnt all the veils, We have lighted the fire of love. . . . We shall not run away, We shall not endeavour to repel the stranger, We pray for calamity. . . . What doth a soul celestial care if the physical frame is destroyed; indeed, this body is for it a prison. . . . Until the time ordained cometh no one hath power over Us, and when the ordained time cometh it will find Our whole being longing for it. . . .' Nabíl says that when the mujtahids of Karbilá and Najaf read this Tablet, they were mightily astonished.

Áqáy-i-Kalím, speaking once with Nabíl about those days, recalled that he had felt certain that soon they would all be arrested and turned over in manacles to the Persian authorities, because he knew only too well the motives of the populace of Baghdád and their notables. However, he had not wished to report such matters to Bahá'u'lláh, lest

* This Tablet, which is known as *Shikkar-Shikan-Shavand*, was long supposed to have been addressed to Mírzá Sa'íd Khán, the Foreign Minister of Náṣiri'd-Dín Sháh. But Nabíl's statement makes it clear that it was the fickle Mutavallí of Qum who was honoured by receiving it.

they should cause Him sorrow. 'One night,' he related, 'sleep departed from my eyes. I kept pacing up and down the courtyard, wondering what would happen to our wives and children, once we were apprehended. Then I heard a knock and, going to the door, I was told that a number of people had been detailed to keep watch and patrol outside in the street. . . . When I heard that, I knew that all would be well . . . and went to sleep.'

Then, Bahá'u'lláh decided that the companions should apply for Ottoman nationality, that they might receive the protection of the Ottoman authorities. Námiq Páshá, the Governor of Baghdád, was delighted to hear of it. Nabíl relates that Áqá Muḥammad-Riḍáy-i-Kurd, who was well versed in legal matters, took each day a number of the companions, two by two, to the Government House, and obtained for them Turkish passports. Nabíl himself, with Áqá Muḥammad-Ismá'íl-i-Káshání, was among them. These visits went on for nearly three weeks, until all the Persians were naturalized. Great was the consternation of Shaykh 'Abdu'l-Ḥusayn and Mírzá Buzurg Khán when they came to know that the companions had obtained Ottoman nationality.

Nabíl writes that in those days Bahá'u'lláh visited oftentimes the Mazra'iy-i-Vashshásh, a farm in the environs of Baghdád. Most evenings, when He returned at sunset, Nabíl himself would wait upon Him until He neared the door of His house. Occasionally, Nabíl reports, Bahá'u'lláh would visit a dwelling known as the house of Nabúkí, situated in the same street as His own house, but on the opposite side. A number of the companions, including Nabíl, lived in this house. Áqá Muḥammad-Zamán, a merchant of Shíráz, and Ustád 'Alí-Akbar-i-Najjár (carpenter) also lived there. Sháṭir-Riḍá (see Addendum V) and his brother had a house in the same street, and had set up a grinding-mill and a bakery. Bahá'u'lláh owned this bakery, which supplied all the companions, without charge, with the bread they required. The father of the two bakers, the ninety-year-old Áqá Muḥammad-Ṣádiq, came to Baghdád from Ardakán, near Yazd. He had many stories to tell of the behaviour of the ecclesiastics, and of his own conversion to the Faith of the Báb, which, Nabíl says, evoked smiles from Bahá'u'lláh. This made the old man very happy. Raising his hands in thanksgiving for the privilege of making Bahá'u'lláh smile, he would quote the Prophet: Whoever caused a believer to laugh, he would have made Me happy, and whoever made Me happy, God would be contented with him.

Nabíl relates that one of those Persian ecclesiastics, well-fed and corpulent, came one day into the presence of Bahá'u'lláh, and announced that his title was 'Khátamu'l-Mujtahidín' (the Seal of the Mujtahids), to which Bahá'u'lláh replied: '*Inshá'alláh*' – God willing.

This 'Seal of the Mujtahids' was a humorous man, who amused Bahá'u'lláh greatly with his stories. To him Bahá'u'lláh showed much kindliness. Indeed, everyone received an ample share of His generosity – companions, visitors, neighbours, passers-by alike. Nabíl tells us that in the district where Bahá'u'lláh lived, people of the entire neighbourhood, particularly the poor, the disabled and the orphans, were sent gifts by Him. And as He went about, whenever He came upon the needy, He showered His bounties on them. There was an old woman, eighty years of age, who lived in a ruined house. Every day, at the time when Bahá'u'lláh was going to the coffee-house by the bridge, she would be standing in the roadway awaiting Him. Bahá'u'lláh would stop, enquire after her health and give her some money. She would kiss His hands, and sometimes wanted to kiss His face but, being short of stature, she could not reach Him, and He would bend down His face towards her. He used to say, 'She knows that I like her, that is why she likes Me.' When He left Baghdád, He arranged a daily allowance to be given to her, to the end of her days. Whichever coffee-house He visited, Nabíl comments, would become so thronged with the notables of the city that the owner would find himself greatly prospering. One coffee-house that He frequented belonged to Siyyid Ḥabíb, a white-bearded man of imposing appearance, who presided over his quarter. Every day, Bahá'u'lláh would send for him and give him tea. Any day that passed without attaining the presence of Bahá'u'lláh, Siyyid Ḥabíb felt deprived and considered that day to have been wasted. After Bahá'u'lláh's departure from Baghdád, no one ever saw him again in his coffee-house, and he gave up drinking tea. Such was also the case with Ḥamd, another coffee-house owner. He abandoned his occupation.

Late in 1861, Mírzá Malkam Khán (later Prince, and invested with the title of Náẓimu'd-Dawlih) reached Baghdád, much concerned for his safety. His activities in Ṭihrán, and particularly the founding of a Masonic lodge called Farámúsh-Khánih (the House of Forgetfulness), had angered Náṣiri'd-Dín Sháh, who ordered him out of the country. However, Mírzá Buzurg Khán gave out that he had been charged by his superiors to have Malkam Khán detained and returned to Írán. Alarmed, Malkam Khán came to Bahá'u'lláh. Nabíl states that Bahá'u'lláh judged it wiser for him to lodge elsewhere. He sent him to the *Seraye*, and put him in the care of the Válí, who had him sent safely to Istanbul.

Another who sought out Bahá'u'lláh in those days was Mírzá Muḥammad-Ḥusayn-i-Kirmání, known as Mírzá Muḥíṭ, he who had vied for the leadership of the Shaykhí movement after Siyyid Káẓim's death. This was the man who had been overwhelmed when the Báb challenged him with a declaration of His Mission by the Ka'bah at Mecca, and in answer to whose questions, the Báb revealed the *Ṣaḥífiy-i-Baynu'l-Ḥaramayn*. But despite this, Mírzá Muḥíṭ had turned away from the Báb and had lived on in Karbilá until, more than two decades later, he now sought a secret meeting with Bahá'u'lláh.

Nabíl writes:

> Nearing the end of his days, whilst residing in 'Iráq, he, feigning submission to Bahá'u'lláh, expressed, through one of the Persian princes who dwelt in Baghdád, a desire to meet Him. He requested that his proposed interview be regarded as strictly confidential. 'Tell him,' was Bahá'u'lláh's reply, 'that in the days of My retirement in the mountain of Sulaymáníyyih, I, in a certain ode which I composed, set forth the essential requirements from every wayfarer who treads the path of search in his quest of Truth. Share with him this verse from that ode: "If thine aim be to cherish thy life, approach not our court; but if sacrifice be thy heart's desire, come and let others come with thee. For such is the way of Faith, if in thy heart thou seekest reunion with Bahá; shouldst thou refuse to tread this path, why trouble us? Begone!" If he is willing, he will openly and unreservedly hasten to meet Me; if not, I refuse to see him.' Bahá'u'lláh's unequivocal answer disconcerted Mírzá Muḥíṭ. Unable to resist and unwilling to comply, he departed for his home in Karbilá the very day he received that message. As soon as he arrived, he sickened, and, three days later, he died.[4]

At long last, Mírzá Buzurg Khán, without having achieved his purpose, was recalled to Írán, where he continued his vendetta against Bahá'u'lláh, and 'Iráq had another governor, as well. Námiq Páshá (see Addendum V) replaced Muṣṭafá Núrí Páshá. This change took place in 1862. Námiq, who had once before governed 'Iráq, was, like the previous Válí, a just and disinterested man.

The Guardian of the Bahá'í Faith writes of these final years in Ba<u>gh</u>dád:

Persians of high eminence, living in exile, rejecting, in the face of the mounting prestige of Bahá'u'lláh, the dictates of moderation and prudence, sat, forgetful of their pride, at His feet, and imbibed, each according to his capacity, a measure of His spirit and wisdom. Some of the more ambitious among them, such as 'Abbás Mírzá, a son of Muḥammad <u>Sh</u>áh, the Vazír-Niẓám,* and Mírzá Malkam <u>Kh</u>án, as well as certain functionaries of foreign governments, attempted, in their short-sightedness, to secure His support and assistance for the furtherance of the designs they cherished, designs which He unhesitatingly and severely condemned. Nor was the then representative of the British government, Colonel Sir Arnold Burrows Kemball, consul-general in Ba<u>gh</u>dád, insensible of the position which Bahá'u'lláh now occupied. Entering into friendly correspondence with Him, he, as testified by Bahá'u'lláh Himself, offered Him the protection of British citizenship, called on Him in person, and undertook to transmit to Queen Victoria any communication He might wish to forward to her. He even expressed his readiness to arrange for the transfer of His residence to India, or to any place agreeable to Him. This suggestion Bahá'u'lláh declined, choosing to abide in the dominions of the Sulṭán of Turkey. And finally, during the last year of His sojourn in Ba<u>gh</u>dád the governor Námiq-Pá<u>sh</u>á, impressed by the many signs of esteem and veneration in which He was held, called upon Him to pay his personal tribute to One Who had already achieved so conspicuous a victory over the hearts and souls of those who had met Him. . . . On one occasion, when 'Abdu'l-Bahá and Áqáy i Kalím had been delegated by Bahá'u'lláh to visit him, he entertained them with such elaborate ceremonial that the Deputy-Governor stated that so far as he knew no notable of the city had ever been accorded by any governor so warm and courteous a reception. So struck, indeed, had the Sulṭán 'Abdu'l-Majíd been by the favorable reports received about Bahá'u'lláh from successive governors of Ba<u>gh</u>dád (this is the personal testimony given by the Governor's deputy to Bahá'u'lláh Himself) that he consistently refused to countenance the requests of the Persian government either to deliver Him to their representative or to order His expulsion from Turkish territory.

On no previous occasion, since the inception of the Faith, not even during the days when the Báb in Iṣfahán, in Tabríz and in <u>Ch</u>ihríq was acclaimed by the ovations of an enthusiastic populace, had any of its exponents risen to such high eminence in the public mind, or exercised over so diversified a circle of admirers an influence so far reaching and so potent.[5]

---

* This was Mírzá Faḍlu'lláh-i-Núrí, who was the elder brother of Mírzá Áqá <u>Kh</u>án-i-Núrí, the Prime Minister. When the latter fell from power in 1858, Mírzá Faḍlu'lláh also lost his position. It was at this time that he came to Ba<u>gh</u>dád and met Bahá'u'lláh. He died in Ṭihrán in AH 1279 (AD 1862–3).

The Government of Náṣiri'd-Dín Sháh now began to press hard for the removal of Bahá'u'lláh from the vicinity of its frontiers. Mírzá Ḥusayn Khán, the Mushíru'd-Dawlih, the Sháh's ambassador in Istanbul, in concert with some other foreign envoys, notably the French, was moving heaven and earth to bring about Bahá'u'lláh's banishment. The Grand Vizier of Turkey, 'Álí Páshá, and Fu'ád Páshá, the Foreign Minister (see Addendum V for both men), who were close associates in the governance of the Ottoman Empire and were noted for their reforming radical tendencies, finally gave way to the growing, incessant demands of Mushíru'd-Dawlih, and directed Námiq Páshá to invite Bahá'u'lláh to visit Istanbul.

Námiq Páshá, who was fully cognizant of all the intrigues and conspiracies, the agitations and plottings, the undercurrents, falsities, fears and fanaticism involved, was at a loss as to how to transmit this invitation to Bahá'u'lláh.

The Guardian of the Bahá'í Faith writes:

> So profound was the respect the governor entertained for Him, Whom he regarded as one of the Lights of the Age, that it was not until the end of three months, during which he had received five successive commands from 'Álí Páshá, that he could bring himself to inform Bahá'u'lláh that it was the wish of the Turkish government that He should proceed to the capital.[6]

Bahá'u'lláh celebrated the Festival of Naw-Rúz (1863) at the Mazra'iy-i-Vashsháṣh. It was a happy occasion, until from His Pen – the Most Sublime Pen – flowed the *Tablet of the Holy Mariner*, 'whose gloomy prognostications', in the words of Shoghi Effendi, 'had aroused the grave apprehensions of His companions'. On the fifth day after Naw-Rúz, a message reached Bahá'u'lláh from the Válí, couched most courteously, requesting Him to visit the *Seraye*. Bahá'u'lláh replied that He had never set foot there but, should the Válí wish, He would meet Him in the mosque, opposite the Government House. Námiq Páshá was agreeable, but as Áqá Riḍá describes it, now the flood-gates of hearsay, rumour (false and true) and accusation opened wide. Some of the enemies put it about that Bahá'u'lláh would not stand by His word, would not go to the mosque; others remarked that all the Bábís would be banded together and handed to the Persian authorities at the frontier; still others maintained that they would all be drowned in the Tigris.

One day, late in the afternoon as arranged, Bahá'u'lláh came out of His house attended by Áqá Muḥammad-Riḍá, a Kurdish youth well versed in Turkish, to visit the Válí in the mosque. He permitted no one else to accompany Him. The news was conveyed to Námiq Páshá, who was delighted, but at the last minute he changed his mind and sent his deputy instead, armed with all the communications he had received from Istanbul.

It was an invitation to come to Istanbul that was presented to Bahá'u'lláh, definitely not a command, and He accepted in the spirit and the way it was offered.

When He returned home, He let it be known that He would go alone. Not only His Family, but all the Bábís in Baghdád were greatly distressed when they heard of His intention. But the authorities expressed the hope that the members of His Family, His brothers and a number of attendants would accompany Him.

Everything happened exactly in reverse to what the adversaries had hoped. The reverence shown Bahá'u'lláh by the authorities was truly exemplary. The sum of money offered to Him, as expenses of the journey, He gave that same day, in its entirety, to the poor. When the Most Great Branch and Áqáy-i-Kalím visited the *Seraye* to meet Námiq Páshá, as instructed to do by Bahá'u'lláh, they were accorded a reception truly regal. As the Most Great Branch wrote at the time: 'Such hath been the interposition of God that the joy evinced by them [the adversaries] hath been turned to chagrin and sorrow, so much so that the Persian consul-general in Baghdád regrets exceedingly the plans and plots the schemers had devised. Námiq Páshá himself, on the day he called on Him (Bahá'u'lláh) stated: "Formerly they insisted upon your departure. Now, however, they are even more insistent that you should remain."'[7] They plotted and God plotted, and God is the best of plotters.

Áqá Riḍá writes that on that first night, after Bahá'u'lláh's meeting with the Deputy-Governor and His return from the mosque, when the news of the migration to Istanbul spread, the Bábís of Baghdád were so stricken by sorrow and the thought of their impending separation from Bahá'u'lláh that sleep departed from all eyes. Many of them, Áqá Riḍá says, made up their minds to die rather than suffer the disaster of separation. Gradually, with His counsel and tender care, Bahá'u'lláh calmed their fears, assuaged the pain of their bruised hearts and imbued them with strength to face the unknown future with hope and determination. Throughout those weeks, until the time of departure, Áqá Riḍa reports, meetings were held in the homes of the companions which Bahá'u'lláh attended, and there He spoke to them with love, compassion and authority. Not only were the Bábís sad, anxious and forlorn, but, according to Áqá Riḍá, the whole populace of Baghdád were feeling the pangs of separation.

At last, preparations for the journey were put in hand. Ustád Báqir and Ustád Aḥmad, two brothers, carpenters from Káshán, got down to constructing *kajávihs* (howdahs); and the two brothers, Ustád Báqir and Ustád Muḥammad-Ismá'íl, tailors, also of Káshán, were busy making suitable garments for the journey.

Nabíl-i-A'ẓam supplies, in his chronicle, a list of twenty men, other than His Family and brothers, whom Bahá'u'lláh chose to migrate with Him. They were:

Ustád Báqir and Ustád Muḥammad-Ismá'íl-i-Khayyáṭ of Káshán, the tailors
Ustád Muḥammad-'Alíy-i-Salmání, the bath-attendant and barber
Mírzá Áqá Ján, the personal attendant and amanuensis of Bahá'u'lláh, who was at a later time given the designation of Khádimu'lláh – the Servant of God
Áqá Muḥammad-Ibráhím-i-Amír-i-Nayrízí
Áqá Riḍáy-i-Qannád-i-Shírází, the confectioner of Shíráz
Mírzá Maḥmúd-i-Káshání
Darvísh Ṣidq-'Alíy-i-Qazvíní
Áqá Najaf-'Alíy-i-Zanjání
Áqá Muḥammad-Báqir, Qahvih-chíy-i-Maḥallátí, the coffee-man of Maḥallát
Áqá Muḥammad-Ṣádiq-i-Iṣfahání
Áqá Muḥammad-'Alí, Jilawdár-i-Yazdí, the horseman of Yazd, who was also known as Ṣabbágh-i-Yazdí, the dyer of Yazd
Áqá Muḥammad-'Alíy-i-Iṣfahání
Áqá Mírzá Ja'far-i-Yazdí
Áqá Siyyid Ḥusayn-i-Káshání
Khayyáṭ-i-Káshání, the tailor of Káshán
Áqá Muḥammad-Báqir-i-Káshání
Áqá Muḥammad-Ibráhím-i-Náẓir-i-Káshání
Ḥájí Ibráhím-i-Káshání

Mírzá Áqá, Munír-i-Káshání, entitled Ismu'lláhu'l-Muníb, the Name of God, the Patron

Although Nabíl does not list the following names as having migrated with Bahá'u'lláh, they did in fact travel with him, the second person named below joining the caravan probably on the second stage of the journey:

Áqá 'Abdu'l-Ghaffár-i-Iṣfahání
Áqá Ḥusayn-i-Áshchí
Áqá Muḥammad-Ḥasan

Two others, Siyyid Muḥammad-i-Iṣfahání and Ḥájí Mírzá Aḥmad-i-Káshání, despite their known fickleness, were also included for different reasons in that entourage of Bahá'u'lláh. Ḥájí Mírzá Aḥmad, apart from being unstable so far as his faith was concerned, had a fiery temper and would easily flare up. Once in the bazar in Baghdád, where he kept a shop, he had been abusive to a lady of high birth, who had spoken imperiously to him. Nabíl-i-A'ẓam identifies that lady as a member of the royal family, mother of 'Aynu'l-Mulk (later I'tiḍádi'd-Dawlih).* That incident led to the apprehension of Ḥájí Mírzá Aḥmad by Mírzá Buzurg Khán, the Persian envoy, but he was saved by Bahá'u'lláh. Nabíl states that it was this episode which led to the dismissal of Mírzá Buzurg Khán, because the plaintive letter he wrote to his superiors in Ṭihrán clearly indicated his incapacity, and he was recalled. Now Bahá'u'lláh decided to take Ḥájí Mírzá Aḥmad with His party to Istanbul, lest that kind of incident be repeated in His absence. But this Káshání merchant was not of the same mettle as his illustrious martyred brother, Ḥájí Mírzá Jání, and another brother of whom we shall hear later, Ḥájí Muḥammad-Ismá'íl-i-Dhabíḥ. Although later in Adrianople he was honoured with a Tablet from the pen of Bahá'u'lláh – the Persian Tablet of Aḥmad (*Lawḥ-i-Aḥmad-i-Fársí*) – a Tablet of soaring power and unsurpassed eloquence, he persisted in his waywardness, sided with Mírzá Yaḥyá, and eventually returned to Baghdád where he met a violent death.

As to Siyyid Muḥammad-i-Iṣfahání, he had to be kept under observation after his idiotic activities in Karbilá, which had brought enough ill-fame to the Faith of the Báb, although Bahá'u'lláh had

* He was Shír Khán, son of Sulaymán Khán-i-Qájár (maternal uncle of Náṣiri'd-Dín-Sháh), and the third husband of 'Izzatu'd-Dawlih, the sister of the Sháh. Shír Khán became the Ílkhání of the Qájárs, and was in charge of the royal kitchen.

intended that he remain in Baghdád. (According to Áqá Riḍá, he appealed to 'Abdu'l-Bahá to be allowed to join the caravan.) He was included in Bahá'u'lláh's retinue, and in future would achieve notoriety as the Antichrist of the Bahá'í Revelation. Both he and Mullá Muḥammad-Ja'far-i-Naráqí, a man of the same ilk, had been named by Mírzá Yaḥyá as 'Witnesses of the Bayán'; yet they considered themselves superior to Mírzá Yaḥyá in talent, knowledge and intelligence. Nabíl-i-A'ẓam, who knew them well, comments that each expected to become the 'King of the Bayán', and they were fantastically busy dividing the palatial homes of the nobility of Ṭihrán between themselves. Indeed, Mullá Muḥammad-Ja'far, when speaking of the advent of 'Him Whom God shall make manifest', would sometimes point a finger at himself.

At this hour of crisis, when Bahá'u'lláh was calmly and confidently preparing to start on His long journey to Istanbul, Mírzá Yaḥyá, panic-stricken, fled Baghdád, without informing his 'Witness' of his whereabouts (according to Siyyid Mihdíy-i-Dahijí). When Mullá Muḥammad-Ja'far arrived from Írán, he had to look here and there in 'Iráq for Mírzá Yaḥyá.

The Guardian of the Bahá'í Faith writes:

> Seven years of uninterrupted, of patient and eminently successful consolidation were now drawing to a close. A shepherdless community, subjected to a prolonged and tremendous strain, from both within and without, and threatened with obliteration, had been resuscitated, and risen to an ascendancy without example in the course of its twenty years' history. Its foundations reinforced, its spirit exalted, its outlook transformed, its leadership safeguarded, its fundamentals restated, its prestige enhanced, its enemies discomfited, the Hand of Destiny was gradually preparing to launch it on a new phase in its checkered career, in which weal and woe alike were to carry it through yet another stage in its evolution. The Deliverer, the sole hope, and the virtually recognized leader of this community, Who had consistently overawed the authors of so many plots to assassinate Him, Who had scornfully rejected all the timid advice that He should flee from the scene of danger, Who had firmly declined repeated and generous offers made by friends and supporters to insure His personal safety, Who had won so conspicuous a victory over His antagonists – He was, at this auspicious hour, being impelled by the resistless processes of His unfolding Mission, to transfer His residence to the center of still greater preeminence, the capital city of the Ottoman Empire, the seat of the Caliphate, the administrative center of Sunní Islám, the abode of the most powerful potentate in the Islamic world.[8]

24

From the Most Exalted Pen

DURING the years of His sojourn in Ba<u>gh</u>dád, Bahá'u'lláh revealed three of His best-known Writings: *The Hidden Words* (about AD 1858), *The Seven Valleys,* and the *Kitáb-i-Íqán* or *The Book of Certitude* (AD 1862). *The Four Valleys* was also revealed during the same period.

Walking on the banks of the Tigris, Bahá'u'lláh reflected on the nearness of God ('We are nearer to him than the jugular vein'*) and the remoteness of man, on the outpourings of God's Grace and Love and man's wayward, obstinate refusal to drink of that never-ceasing, never-ending fountain. From His meditations came *The Hidden Words (Kalimát-i-Maknúnih)* – also known as *Ṣaḥífiy-i-Fáṭimíyyih*, the Book of Fáṭimih – in both Arabic and Persian, written in a lucid, captivating prose, presenting those never-changing, eternal verities that stand at the core of every revealed religion. Their sweeping range, the exquisite tenderness of their imagery and description, the majesty – the overwhelming majesty – of their conception, uplift the soul and disclose to the inner eye endless vistas of God's Love and Mercy, His Justice and His Power – an All-Pervading, All-Embracing, All-Conquering Power. *The Hidden Words* show in their crystal clarity the very structure of faith and religion:

> *This is that which hath descended from the realm of glory, uttered by the tongue of power and might, and revealed unto the Prophets of old. We have taken the inner essence thereof and clothed it in the garment of brevity, as a token of grace unto the righteous, that they may stand faithful unto the Covenant of God, may fulfil in their lives His trust, and in the realm of spirit obtain the gem of Divine virtue.*

> *O Son of Man!* Veiled in My immemorial being and in the ancient eternity of My essence, I knew My love for thee; therefore I created thee, have engraved on thee Mine image and revealed to thee My beauty.

* Qur'án: 50, 15

O Son of Man! If thou lovest Me, turn away from thyself; and if thou seekest My pleasure, regard not thine own; that thou mayest die in Me and I may eternally live in thee.

O Son of Being! With the hands of power I made thee and with the fingers of strength I created thee; and within thee have I placed the essence of My light. Be thou content with it and seek naught else, for My work is perfect and My command is binding. Question it not, nor have a doubt thereof.

O Son of Man! Thou art My dominion and My dominion perisheth not, wherefore fearest thou thy perishing? Thou art My light and My light shall never be extinguished, why dost thou dread extinction? Thou art My glory and My glory fadeth not; thou art My robe and My robe shall never be outworn. Abide then in thy love for Me, that thou mayest find Me in the realm of glory.

O Son of Spirit! Noble have I created thee, yet thou hast abased thyself. Rise then unto that for which thou wast created.

O Companion of My Throne! Hear no evil, and see no evil, abase not thyself, neither sigh and weep. Speak no evil, that thou mayest not hear it spoken unto thee, and magnify not the faults of others that thine own faults may not appear great; and wish not the abasement of anyone, that thine own abasement be not exposed. Live then the days of thy life, that are less than a fleeting moment, with thy mind stainless, thy heart unsullied, thy thoughts pure, and thy nature sanctified, so that, free and content, thou mayest put away this mortal frame, and repair unto the mystic paradise, and abide in the eternal kingdom for evermore.

O Son of Justice! Whither can a lover go but to the land of his beloved? And what seeker findeth rest away from his heart's desire? To the true lover reunion is life, and separation is death. His breast is void of patience and his heart hath no peace. A myriad lives he would forsake to hasten to the abode of his beloved.

O Children of Desire! Put away the garment of vainglory, and divest yourselves of the attire of haughtiness.

O Brethren! Be forbearing one with another and set not your affection on things below. Pride not yourselves in your glory, and be not ashamed of abasement. By My beauty! I have created all things from dust, and to dust will I return them again.

O Children of Dust! Tell the rich of the midnight sighing of the poor, lest heedlessness lead them into the path of destruction, and deprive them of

Calligraphy of Mishkín-Qalam. This is the closing portion of the Arabic Hidden Words *showing three styles of Mishkín-Qalam's calligraphy. The top line is in the* Nasta'líq *style and consists of the closing line of no. 70 '. . . that which I have desired for My Self. Be then content with My pleasure and thankful unto Me', and 'O Son of Man!' beginning the last verse, in the* Naskh *style. The middle line is in the* Shikastih *style and is the whole of the last verse (no. 71). The last line is in the* Naskh *style and is the calligraphist's famous signature: 'The servant at the Gate of Bahá, Mishkín-Qalam,' together with the date '99 (AH 1299, AD 1881–2).*

the Tree of Wealth. To give and to be generous are attributes of Mine; well is it with him that adornest himself with My virtues.

O Oppressors of Earth! Withdraw your hands from tyranny, for I have pledged Myself not to forgive any man's injustice. This is My covenant which I have irrevocably decreed in the preserved tablet and sealed it with My seal of glory.

Such is the range of the counsel of *The Hidden Words.*[1]

The Seven Valleys was composed in answer to the questions of Shaykh Muḥyi'd-Dín, the Qáḍí of Khániqayn.* It is a gem of mystical prose, matchless in its beauty, simplicity and profundity. In this small book Bahá'u'lláh describes the stages that the seeker must needs traverse in his spiritual quest. The end of all search is to know God, and that knowledge can only be attained through His Manifestation.

* A township in 'Iráq, close to the Íránian frontier.

These seven valleys or stages are the Valleys of Search, Love, Knowledge, Unity, Contentment, Wonderment, True Poverty and Absolute Nothingness.

The Valley of Search

In this Valley, the wayfarer rides the steed of patience. Without patience the wayfarer in this journey will reach nowhere and attain no goal. . . . Were he to strive for ages, without beholding the beauty of the Friend, he should not become dejected . . . In this journey the seeker reaches a stage wherein he finds all beings madly in search of the Friend. . . .

The Valley of Love

In this Valley, the wayfarer rides the steed of pain; for without pain this journey will never end . . . Every moment he would joyfully offer a hundred lives in the way of the Beloved and at every step he would throw a thousand heads on the path of the Friend . . . Love admits of no life and seeks no existence. In death it sees life and in abasement seeks glory. . . .

The Valley of Knowledge

In this valley the wayfarer, in his pure insight, finds no contradiction or difference in the creation of God, . . . Many a knowledge he will find concealed in ignorance and hosts of wisdom manifest in knowledge. . . .

The Valley of Unity

After traversing the Valley of Knowledge, which is the last plane of limitation, the wayfarer attains the first stage of the Valley of Unity, whereupon he quaffs the chalice of abstraction and witnesses the Manifestations of Oneness. . . . He hears with the ears of God and sees the mysteries of divine creation with the eyes of God. . . . He will gaze upon all things with the eye of oneness and will find the Divine Sun, from the Heavenly Day-Spring, shedding the same light and splendour upon all beings and will see the lights of singleness reflected and visible upon all creation. . . .

The Valley of Contentment

In this Valley, he will feel the breezes of divine contentment wafting from the plane of the spirit; he will burn the veils of want; and with inward and outward eyes, he will witness, within and without all things, the meaning of the verse: 'In that Day, God will make all independent out of His abundance.' His sorrow will be changed into joy, and his grief be replaced by happiness; and his dejection and melancholy will yield to gladness and exultation. . . .

The Valley of Wonderment

Now he sees the temple of wealth as want itself, and the essence of independence as sheer impotence. Now he is astonished at the beauty of the All-Glorious One, and now he wearies of his own existence. . . . For, in this Valley, the wayfarer is thrown into utter confusion; . . . He witnesses a wondrous world and a new creation at every instant, and adds wonderment to wonderment; and he is astonished at the works of the Lord of Oneness. . . .

The Valley of True Poverty and Absolute Nothingness

This state is that of dying from self and living in God, and being poor in self and becoming rich in the Desired One. . . . And when you have attained this lofty plane and reached this mighty state, you will find the Friend and forget all else. . . . In this city, even the veils of light vanish. . . . Ecstasy alone can comprehend this theme, not discussion or argument. . . . The seven stages of this journey which have no visible end in the world of time, may be traversed by the detached wayfarer in seven steps, if not in seven breaths, nay in one breath – if, God willing, invisible assistance favour him. . . .[2]

The Four Valleys, another gem of mystical prose, was also revealed in Baghdád. It was a letter addressed to Shaykh 'Abdu'r-Raḥmán-i-Karkútí, a man of erudition and understanding. It is much shorter than *The Seven Valleys*, but partakes abundantly of its high qualities.

The *Kitáb-i-Íqán* or *The Book of Certitude* was written in answer to questions presented by Ḥájí Mírzá Siyyid Muḥammad, a maternal uncle of the Báb, entitled Khál-i-Akbar (the Greatest Uncle). He and his brother, Ḥájí Mírzá Ḥasan-'Alí, entitled Khál-i-Aṣghar (the Younger or the Junior Uncle) were visiting the holy shrines of 'Iráq, in the year 1862. Both of them, during the six short eventful years of the ministry of their Nephew, had stood firm and steadfast in His support and defence, but neither of them had given Him his allegiance. Bahá'u'lláh, Himself, relates in a Tablet that Ḥájí Siyyid Javád-i-Karbilá'í spoke to Him of the presence of these two uncles of the Báb in 'Iráq.

Bahá'u'lláh then enquired from Ḥájí Siyyid Javád whether he had reminded them of the Cause of the Báb. Ḥájí Siyyid Javád had not, and Bahá'u'lláh related in the Tablet that He wished such close relatives of the Primal Point not to remain deprived of the bounties conferred by the Faith of their glorious Nephew, and He directed Ḥájí Siyyid Javád to bring one or both of them to meet Him. Already in Shíráz Ḥájí Mírzá Siyyid Muḥammad had been prompted by a relative, Áqá Mírzá Áqá, Núri'd-Dín, to travel to 'Iráq, outwardly on pilgrimage to the holy shrines, but in truth with the aim of attaining the presence of Bahá'u'lláh. (As a youth, Áqá Mírzá Áqá had been converted to the Bábí Faith by his aunt, Khadíjih Bigum, the wife of the Báb.) Now, when Ḥájí Siyyid Javád-i-Karbilá'í, whom he had known well for many years, brought Ḥájí Mírzá Siyyid Muḥammad this invitation from Bahá'u'lláh, he gladly and readily responded. Bahá'u'lláh mentions in the same Tablet that when He asked Ḥájí Mírzá Siyyid Muḥammad what it was that stood in his way, the latter replied that there were some questions which had caused him great concern. Bahá'u'lláh advised him to write down those questions that they might be answered. In recent years, amongst the papers left by Ḥájí Mírzá Siyyid Muḥammad, the questions he presented to Bahá'u'lláh have come to light. These, which we can read today in the handwriting of Ḥájí Mírzá Siyyid Muḥammad himself, are related to the Shí'ih expectations of the advent of the Qá'im of the House of Muḥammad.

Ḥájí Mírzá Siyyid Muḥammad worded his questions under four headings, namely:

1. The Day of Resurrection. Is there to be corporeal resurrection? The world is replete with injustice. How are the just to be requited and the unjust punished?
2. The twelfth Imám was born at a certain time and lives on. There are traditions, all supporting the belief. How can this be explained?
3. Interpretation of holy texts. This Cause does not seem to conform with beliefs held throughout the years. One cannot ignore the literal meaning of holy texts and scripture. How can this be explained?
4. Certain events, according to the traditions that have come down from the Imáms, must occur at the advent of the Qá'im. Some of

these are mentioned. But none of these has happened. How can this be explained?

This is the gist of the questions presented to Bahá'u'lláh, by the uncle of the Báb.

Bahá'u'lláh revealed the *Kitáb-i-Íqán*, answering the questions posed by this uncle of the Báb, within forty-eight hours. The original manuscript, in the handwriting of 'Abdu'l-Bahá, with marginal additions made by Bahá'u'lláh Himself, is now preserved in the International Bahá'í Archives on Mount Carmel.

Fáṭimih Khánum Afnán, a great-granddaughter of Ḥájí Mírzá Siyyid Muḥammad, had inherited this manuscript and she presented it to the Guardian of the Bahá'í Faith. A copy, which must have been transcribed for Ḥájí Mírzá Ḥasan-'Alí, the junior uncle of the Báb (who, although he did not accompany his brother into the presence of Bahá'u'lláh, before long gave Him his allegiance), bears a date only one year after its revelation; it is now in the possession of one of Ḥájí Mírzá Ḥasan-'Alí's great-great-grandsons. The present writer has in his possession a fine copy in the handwriting of Áqá Mírzá Áqáy-i-Rikáb-Sáz, the first martyr of Shíráz, bearing the date 1871. (See frontispiece.)

The Book of Certitude was perhaps the earliest of the Writings of Bahá'u'lláh to appear in print. A beautifully lithographed copy, which does not bear a date and must have been printed in Bombay, is known to have been in circulation in the early eighties of the last century. In this book, which the Guardian of the Bahá'í Faith has described as 'of unsurpassed pre-eminence among the writings of the Author of the Bahá'í Revelation', Bahá'u'lláh offers a logical, illuminating and irrefutable explanation of the symbolism and the enigmatic texts of the Scriptures of the past, establishes the fact of progressive revelation, and adduces proofs to substantiate the divine mission of the Báb. Shoghi Effendi says furthermore, of *The Book of Certitude*, 'Well may it be claimed that of all the books revealed by the Author of the Bahá'í Revelation, this Book alone, by sweeping away the age-long barriers that have so insurmountably separated the great religions of the world, has laid down a broad and unassailable foundation for the complete and permanent reconciliation of their followers.'[3] No single quotation can adequately present a picture of the vast field covered by the contents of this momentous book. Speaking of the powers and the signs of God manifest in the entire realm of creation, Bahá'u'lláh says:

> . . . whatever is in the heavens and whatever is on the earth is a direct evidence of the revelation within it of the attributes and names of God, inasmuch as within every atom are enshrined the signs that bear eloquent testimony to the revelation of that most great Light. Methinks, but for the potency of that revelation, no being could ever exist. How resplendent the luminaries of knowledge that shine in an atom, and how vast the oceans of wisdom that surge within a drop! To a supreme degree is this true of man, who, among all created things, hath been invested with the robe of such gifts, and hath been singled out for the glory of such distinction. For in him are potentially revealed all the attributes and names of God to a degree that no other created being hath excelled or surpassed. All these names and attributes are applicable to him. Even as He hath said: 'Man is My mystery, and I am his mystery.' . . .
>
> . . Man, the noblest and most perfect of all created things, excelleth them all in the intensity of this revelation, and is a fuller expression of its glory. And of all men, the most accomplished, the most distinguished and the most excellent are the Manifestations of the Sun of Truth. Nay, all else besides these Manifestations, live by the operation of their Will, and move and have their being through the outpourings of their grace. . . . These Tabernacles of holiness, these primal Mirrors which reflect the light of unfading glory, are but expressions of Him Who is the Invisible of the Invisibles. By the revelation of these gems of divine virtue all the names and attributes of God, such as knowledge and power, sovereignty and dominion, mercy and wisdom, glory, bounty and grace, are made manifest.[4]

The Manifestations of God, the Founders of the world's religions, are the Bearers of God's will and purpose to mankind. They are the *logos* – the Word of God. In them nothing can be seen but the Reality and the Light of God.

> The door of the knowledge of the Ancient of Days being thus closed in the face of all beings, the Source of infinite grace . . . hath caused those luminous Gems of Holiness to appear out of the realm of the spirit, in the noble form of the human temple, and be made manifest unto all men, that they may impart unto the world the mysteries of the unchangeable Being, and tell of the subtleties of His imperishable Essence. These sanctified Mirrors, these Day-springs of ancient glory are one and all the Exponents on earth of Him Who is the central Orb of the universe, its Essence and ultimate Purpose. From Him proceed their knowledge and power; from Him is derived their sovereignty. The beauty of their countenance is but a reflection of His image, and their revelation a sign of His deathless glory. They are the Treasuries of divine knowledge, and the Repositories of

celestial wisdom. Through them is transmitted a grace that is infinite, and by them is revealed the light that can never fade.[5]

This is only one aspect of the great theme that *The Book of Certitude* unfolds.

There was a time, during His sojourn in Baghdád, when Bahá'u'lláh would order Mírzá Áqá Ján to let the Tigris carry away the outpourings of His Pen. In a Tablet, revealed long after in 'Akká, Bahá'u'lláh mentions this fact. Nabíl recalls that some of those writings were saved, because of the pleading of Mírzá Áqá Ján, and these included the Tablet of the *Munáját-i-Ḥúríyyih* (the Prayer of the Maid of Heaven).

25

The March of the King of Glory

THE sun was westering on 22 April 1863 (the thirty-second day after Naw-Rúz) when Bahá'u'lláh walked, for the last time, out of the house that, for many years, had been His home in the city of the 'Abbásids, and made His way to the bank of the Tigris, where a *quffih* awaited to take Him to the further bank, to the garden of Najíb Pásh͟há (known as the Najíbíyyih). The thoroughfare to the riverside brimmed with people, men and women, young and old, from all walks of life, who had gathered to see Him go and bewail His departure.

Bahá'u'lláh, as he walked to the bank of the Tigris, gave generously to the poor and the deprived, and consoled and comforted the people who were never to see Him again. But they were now so acutely conscious of their evident and grievous loss that words failed to console them. And it must be remembered that the vast majority of them were men and women not in any way connected with the Faith of the Báb. Ibn-Álúsí, a leading cleric of the Sunní community, was seen weeping over their plight, and he was heard to heap imprecations on Náṣiri'd-Dín S͟háh, who was generally held responsible for Bahá'u'lláh's exile from Bag͟hdád. 'This man is not Náṣiri'd-Dín – the Helper of Religion; he is Muk͟hd͟hili'd-Dín – the Abaser of Religion.' Such being the reaction of men in high position not affiliated to the Faith of the Báb, one can better imagine the feelings of those Bábís who, perforce, had to remain in Bag͟hdád. Áqá Riḍá writes that so disconsolate were they that those who were to accompany Bahá'u'lláh sorrowed with them. 'God alone knows', he writes, 'how those believers who were not to come fared on that day.'

It was springtime and the garden of Najíb Pásh͟há, henceforth to become known to the Bahá'ís as the Garden of Riḍván (Paradise), was aflame with the brilliant hues of roses, and their bloom was superabundant on that day. Those who have written of that April 22nd in the Garden of Riḍván linger particularly over the beauty of the roses and the bounties and blessings of nature. It was fitting for such a day, when nature was so gladsome and the hearts of men so weighed with sadness, that it should also bring the joyous tiding of the Divine Springtime. The Pen of Bahá'u'lláh wrote of that day:

'The Divine Springtime is come, O Most Exalted Pen, for the Festival of the All-Merciful is fast approaching. Bestir thyself, and magnify, before the entire creation, the name of God, and celebrate His praise, in such wise that all created things may be regenerated and made new. Speak, and hold not thy peace. The day star of blissfulness shineth above the horizon of Our name, the Blissful, inasmuch as the kingdom of the name of God hath been adorned with the ornament of the name of thy Lord, the Creator of the heavens. Arise before the nations of the earth, and arm thyself with the power of this Most Great Name, and be not of those who tarry.

'Methinks that thou hast halted and movest not upon My Tablet. Could the brightness of the Divine Countenance have bewildered thee, or the idle talk of the froward filled thee with grief and paralyzed thy movement? Take heed lest anything deter thee from extolling the greatness of this Day – the Day whereon the Finger of majesty and power hath opened the seal of the Wine of Reunion, and called all who are in the heavens and all who are on the earth. Preferrest thou to tarry when the breeze announcing the Day of God hath already breathed over thee, or art thou of them that are shut out as by a veil from Him?

'No veil whatever have I allowed, O Lord of all names and Creator of the heavens, to shut me from the recognition of the glories of Thy Day – the Day which is the lamp of guidance unto the whole world, and the sign of the Ancient of Days unto all them that dwell therein. My silence is by reason of the veils that have blinded Thy creatures' eyes to Thee, and my muteness is because of the impediments that have hindered Thy people from recognizing Thy truth. Thou knowest what is in me, but I know not what is in Thee. Thou art the All-Knowing, the All-Informed. By Thy name that excelleth all other names! If Thy overruling and all-compelling behest should ever reach me, it would empower me to revive the souls of all men, through Thy most exalted Word, which I have heard uttered by Thy Tongue of power in Thy Kingdom of glory. It would enable me to announce the revelation of Thy effulgent countenance wherethrough that which lay hidden from the eyes of men hath been manifested in Thy name, the Perspicuous, the sovereign Protector, the Self-Subsisting.

'Canst thou discover any one but Me, O Pen, in this Day? What hath become of the creation and the manifestations thereof? What of the names and their kingdom? Whither are gone all created things, whether seen or unseen? What of the hidden secrets of the universe and its revelations? Lo, the entire creation hath passed away! Nothing remaineth except My Face, the Ever-Abiding, the Resplendent, the All-Glorious.

'This is the Day whereon naught can be seen except the splendours of the Light that shineth from the face of Thy Lord, the Gracious, the Most Bountiful. Verily, We have caused every soul to expire by virtue of Our irresistible and all-subduing sovereignty. We have, then, called into being a new creation, as a token of Our grace unto men. I am, verily, the All-Bountiful, the Ancient of Days.

'This is the Day whereon the unseen world crieth out: "Great is thy blessedness, O earth, for thou hast been made the foot-stool of thy God, and been chosen as the seat of His mighty throne." The realm of glory exclaimeth: "Would that my life could be sacrificed for thee, for He Who is the Beloved of the All-Merciful hath established His sovereignty upon thee, through the power of His Name that hath been promised unto all things, whether of the past or of the future." This is the Day whereon every sweet-smelling thing hath derived its fragrance from the smell of My garment – a garment that hath shed its perfume upon the whole of creation. This is the Day whereon the rushing waters of everlasting life have gushed out of the Will of the All-Merciful. Haste ye, with your hearts and souls, and quaff your fill, O Concourse of the realms above!

'Say: He it is Who is the Manifestation of Him Who is the Unknowable, the Invisible of the Invisibles, could ye but perceive it. He it is Who hath laid bare before you the hidden and treasured Gem, were ye to seek it. He it is Who is the one Beloved of all things, whether of the past or of the future. Would that ye might set your hearts and hopes upon Him!

'We have heard the voice of thy pleading, O Pen, and excuse thy silence. What is it that hath so sorely bewildered thee?

'The inebriation of Thy presence, O Well-Beloved of all worlds, hath seized and possessed me.

'Arise, and proclaim unto the entire creation the tidings that He Who is the All-Merciful hath directed His steps towards the Riḍván and entered it. Guide, then, the people unto the garden of delight which God hath made the Throne of His Paradise. We have chosen thee to be our most mighty Trumpet, whose blast is to signalize the resurrection of all mankind.

'Say: This is the Paradise on whose foliage the wine of utterance hath imprinted the testimony: "He that was hidden from the eyes of men is revealed, girded with sovereignty and power!" This is the Paradise, the rustling of whose leaves proclaims: "O ye that inhabit the heavens and the earth! There hath appeared what hath never previously appeared. He Who, from everlasting, had concealed His Face from the sight of creation is now come." From the whispering breeze that wafteth amidst its branches there cometh the cry: "He Who is the sovereign Lord of all is made manifest. The Kingdom is God's," while from its streaming waters can be heard the murmur: "All eyes are gladdened, for He Whom none hath beheld, Whose secret no one hath discovered, hath lifted the veil of glory, and uncovered the countenance of Beauty."

'Within this Paradise, and from the heights of its loftiest chambers, the Maids of Heaven have cried out and shouted: "Rejoice, ye dwellers of the realms above, for the fingers of Him Who is the Ancient of Days are ringing, in the name of the All-Glorious, the Most Great Bell, in the midmost heart of the heavens. The hands of bounty have borne round the cup of everlasting life. Approach, and quaff your fill. Drink with healthy relish, O ye that are the very incarnations of longing, ye who are the embodiments of vehement desire!"

'This is the Day whereon He Who is the Revealer of the names of God hath stepped out of the Tabernacle of glory, and proclaimed unto all who are in the heavens and all who are on the earth: "Put away the cups of Paradise and all the life-giving waters they contain, for lo, the people of Bahá have entered the blissful abode of the Divine Presence, and quaffed the wine of reunion, from the chalice of the beauty of their Lord, the All-Possessing, the Most High."

'Forget the world of creation, O Pen, and turn thou towards the face of thy Lord, the Lord of all names. Adorn, then, the world with the ornament of the favours of thy Lord, the King of everlasting days. For We perceive the fragrance of the Day whereon He Who is the Desire of all nations hath shed upon the kingdoms of the unseen and of the seen the splendour of the light of His most excellent names, and enveloped them with the radiance of the luminaries of His most gracious favours – favours which none can reckon except Him, Who is the omnipotent Protector of the entire creation.

'Look not upon the creatures of God except with the eye of kindliness and of mercy, for Our loving providence hath pervaded all created things, and Our grace encompassed the earth and the heavens. This is the Day whereon the true servants of God partake of the life-giving waters of reunion, the Day whereon those that are nigh unto Him are able to drink of the soft-flowing river of immortality, and they who believe in His unity, the wine of His Presence, through their recognition of Him Who is the Highest and Last End of all, in Whom the Tongue of Majesty and Glory voiceth the call: "The Kingdom is Mine. I, Myself, am, of Mine own right, its Ruler."

'Attract the hearts of men, through the call of Him, the one alone Beloved. Say: This is the Voice of God, if ye do but hearken. This is the Day-Spring of the Revelation of God, did ye but know it. This is the Dawning-Place of the Cause of God, were ye to recognize it. This is the Source of the commandment of God, did ye but judge it fairly. This is the manifest and hidden Secret; would that ye might perceive it. O peoples of the world! Cast away, in My name that transcendeth all other names, the things ye possess, and immerse yourselves in this Ocean in whose depths lay hidden the pearls of wisdom and of utterance, an ocean that surgeth in My name, the All-Merciful. Thus instructeth you He with Whom is the Mother Book.

'The Best-Beloved is come. In His right hand is the sealed Wine of His name. Happy is the man that turneth unto Him, and drinketh his fill, and exclaimeth: "Praise be to Thee, O Revealer of the signs of God!" By the righteousness of the Almighty! Every hidden thing hath been manifested through the power of truth. All the favours of God have been sent down, as a token of His grace. The waters of everlasting life have, in their fullness, been proffered unto men. Every single cup hath been borne round by the hand of the Well-Beloved. Draw near, and tarry not, though it be for one short moment.

'Blessed are they that have soared on the wings of detachment and attained the station which, as ordained by God, overshadoweth the entire creation, whom neither the vain imaginations of the learned, nor the multitude of the hosts of the earth have succeeded in deflecting from His Cause. Who is there among you, O people, who will renounce the world, and draw nigh unto God, the Lord of all names? Where is he to be found who, through the power of My name that transcendeth all created things, will cast away the things that men possess, and cling, with all his might, to the things which God, the Knower of the unseen and of the seen, hath bidden him observe? Thus hath His bounty been sent down unto men, His testimony fulfilled, and His proof shone forth above the Horizon of mercy. Rich is the prize that shall be won by him who hath believed and exclaimed: "Lauded art Thou, O Beloved of all worlds! Magnified be Thy name, O Thou the Desire of every understanding heart!"

'Rejoice with exceeding gladness, O people of Bahá, as ye call to remembrance the Day of supreme felicity, the Day whereon the Tongue of the Ancient of Days hath spoken, as He departed from His House, proceeding to the Spot from which He shed upon the whole of creation the splendours of His name, the All-Merciful. God is Our witness. Were We to reveal the hidden secrets of that Day, all they that dwell on earth and in the heavens would swoon away and die, except such as will be preserved by God, the Almighty, the All-Knowing, the All-Wise.

'Such is the inebriating effect of the words of God upon Him Who is the Revealer of His undoubted proofs, that His Pen can move no longer. With these words He concludeth His Tablet: "No God is there but Me, the Most Exalted, the Most Powerful, the Most Excellent, the All-Knowing."'[1]

While writers and chroniclers have left copious accounts of the throngs of people, their expression of sorrow, the excellence of the skilled work of the gardeners, nothing is said of how Bahá'u'lláh made His long-awaited Declaration. In the words of the Guardian of the Bahá'í Faith:

'Of the exact circumstances attending that epoch-making Declaration we, alas, are but scantily informed. The words Bahá'u'lláh actually uttered on that occasion, the manner of His Declaration, the reaction it produced, its impact on Mírzá Yaḥyá, the identity of those who were privileged to hear Him, are shrouded in an obscurity which future historians will find it difficult to penetrate. The fragmentary description left to posterity by His chronicler Nabíl is one of the very few authentic records we possess of the memorable days He spent in that garden. "Every day," Nabíl has related, "ere the hour of dawn, the gardeners would pick the roses which lined the four avenues of the garden, and would pile them in the center of the floor of His blessed tent. So great would be the heap that when His companions gathered to drink their morning tea in His presence, they would be unable to see each other across it. All these roses Bahá'u'lláh would, with His own hands, entrust to those whom He dismissed from His presence every morning to be delivered, on His behalf, to His Arab and Persian friends in the city." "One night," he continues, "the ninth night of the waxing moon, I happened to be one of those who watched beside His blessed tent. As the hour of midnight approached, I saw Him issue from His tent, pass by the places where some of His companions were sleeping, and begin to pace up and down the moonlit, flower-bordered avenues of the garden. So loud was the singing of the nightingales on every side that only those who were near Him could hear distinctly His voice. He continued to walk until, pausing in the midst of one of these avenues, He observed: 'Consider these nightingales. So great is their love for these roses, that sleepless from dusk till dawn, they warble their melodies and commune with burning passion with the object of their adoration. How then can those who claim to be afire with the rose-like beauty of the Beloved choose to sleep?' For three successive nights I watched and circled round His blessed tent. Every time I passed by the couch whereon He lay, I would find Him wakeful, and every day, from morn till eventide, I would see Him ceaselessly engaged in conversing with the stream of visitors who kept flowing in from Baghdád. Not once could I discover in the words He spoke any trace of dissimulation."'[2]

Áqá Riḍá also describes the constant stream of people who came each day from Baghdád to visit Bahá'u'lláh, who could not tolerate being parted from Him. Food, according to Áqá Riḍá, was brought from the house of Bahá'u'lláh in Baghdád, where His family was still in residence, and also from the house of Mírzá Músáy-i-Javáhirí.

Námiq Páshá himself came one day and offered to provide Bahá'u'lláh with whatever He required for the journey, and asked to be forgiven for what had occurred. Bahá'u'lláh assured him that they had all they needed, and as Námiq Páshá insisted on being of some service, Bahá'u'lláh said: 'Be considerate to My friends and treat them kindly'. The Válí gave his word to this, and he also wrote a letter addressed to the officials on the way to Istanbul, instructing them to provide the travellers with all necessities, and entrusted this document to the officer who was detailed to accompany them. But, Áqá Riḍá states, all along the route Bahá'u'lláh never permitted them to accept such exactions, and they always bought their provisions and paid for them. Námiq Pá<u>sh</u>á had one more request to make: he had a very beautiful horse which he wanted to send to Constantinople, and he asked to be allowed to leave the horse with Bahá'u'lláh's men to look after. His request was granted. Áqá Ḥusayn-i-Á<u>sh</u><u>ch</u>í has related that this horse, which was to be delivered to Námiq Pá<u>sh</u>á's son in Istanbul, was left in the care of Siyyid Ḥusayn-i-Ká<u>sh</u>í (Ká<u>sh</u>ání). He must have been particularly instructed to tend it well. Siyyid Ḥusayn was a simple soul and a man full of jest and humour. He always longed to be able to do and say something to amuse Bahá'u'lláh and make Him smile. Á<u>sh</u><u>ch</u>í says that he used to dance and caper in front of Bahá'u'lláh's own horse, 'a red roan stallion of the finest breed' named Sa'údí. One day along the route, he went to Bahá'u'lláh's tent to complain that the Greatest Branch gave out sufficient barley and fodder to feed the other animals, but did not give him any for his horse, but noticing 'Abdu'l-Bahá come into the tent, he took to his heels and ran off into the desert. Siyyid Ḥusayn, Á<u>sh</u><u>ch</u>í says, was in the retinue of Bahá'u'lláh until they were to move to Adirnih (Adrianople). Then, Bahá'u'lláh told him and a number of others who had joined them *en route* to return home. Still longing to offer Bahá'u'lláh some amusement, he implored the Bahá'ís who were to remain with Him not to forget to mention some of his comic doings that Bahá'u'lláh might smile, should at any time his name come up.

On the ninth day the family of Bahá'u'lláh also moved to the Najíbiyyih, and the twelfth day was appointed for departure. Thus the Festival of Riḍván comprises twelve days. Throughout the twelfth day, people poured into the garden for their final farewells. At last the mules were loaded, the *kajávihs* (howdahs) were settled on them, the ladies and children took their seats in the *kajávihs*, and towards sunset the red roan stallion was brought out for Bahá'u'lláh to mount. All those whose narratives have come down to us state that seeing Bahá'u'lláh in the saddle, and about to depart, evoked from the vast crowd heart-rending, unbearable cries of distress. The call: 'Alláh-u-

Akbar' – 'God is the Greatest' – rang out time and again. People threw themselves in the path of His horse, and as Áqá Riḍá expresses it, 'it seemed as if that heavenly steed was passing over sanctified bodies and pure hearts'. On that day for the first time they witnessed Bahá'u'lláh's splendid horsemanship. During all those years in Baghdád, although horses were never unavailable, Áqá Riḍá states that Bahá'u'lláh had always chosen to ride a donkey. Another symbolic sign of the divine authority that He now visibly wielded was the change of His headgear, on the first day of the Festival of Riḍván – the day He left His house in Baghdád for the last time, to take His residence in the Najíbíyyih prior to His departure for the capital of the Turkish Empire. It was then seen that He was wearing a *táj* (crown), finely embroidered. A number of these tall felt headgears have been preserved: red, green, yellow and white, beautifully adorned with embroidery of the highest quality and skill.

The sun was about to set when they reached Firayját, three miles away, on the bank of the Tigris. Here too there was a verdant garden which contained a considerable mansion, and here the caravan halted for seven days. While Mírzá Músá, the brother of Bahá'u'lláh, was busy tidying their affairs in Baghdád and seeing to the packing and loading of the rest of their goods, Bahá'u'lláh resided in that mansion. In Firayját horses were made to run a course to test them, and once again Bahá'u'lláh's masterly horsemanship was witnessed. He had two other horses besides the stallion, Sa'údí, one called Farangí and the other Sa'íd. There were also two donkeys for the younger sons of Bahá'u'lláh to ride occasionally. At Firayját people were still coming daily from Baghdád. They could not bear to be wrenched from the presence of Bahá'u'lláh.

Bahá'u'lláh would, while on the move, take His seat in a *kajávih*, but would mount His horse when approaching a village or a town, to meet the officials and notables who would invariably come out to greet Him. A man named Ḥájí Maḥmúd walked in front, holding the reins of the mule which bore His *kajávih*, and Mírzá Áqá Ján, Mírzá Áqáy-i-Munír, surnamed Ismu'lláhu'l-Muníb, and Áqá Muḥammad-Ibráhím-i-Amír-i-Nayrízí walked on either side.

'Abdu'l-Bahá has given a vivid and delightful account of the spirit of that journey, in His memoir of Mírzá Áqáy-i-Munír (Jináb-i-Muníb; see Addendum V): 'At the time when, with all pomp and

Drawing of a kajávih *(howdah)*

ceremony, Bahá'u'lláh and His retinue departed from Ba<u>gh</u>dád, Jináb-i-Munib accompanied the party on foot. The young man had been known in Persia for his easy and agreeable life and his love of pleasure; also for being somewhat soft and delicate, and used to having his own way. It is obvious what a person of this type endured, going on foot from Ba<u>gh</u>dád to Constantinople. Still, he gladly measured out the desert miles, and he spent his days and nights chanting prayers, communing with God and calling upon Him.

'He was a close companion of mine on that journey. There were nights when we would walk, one to either side of the howdah of Bahá'u'lláh, and the joy we had defies description. Some of those nights he would sing poems; among them he would chant the odes of Ḥáfiẓ, like the one that begins, "*Come, let us scatter these roses, let us pour out this wine,*" and that other:

> "*To our King though we bow the knee,*
> *We are kings of the morning star.*
> *No changeable colors have we –*
> *Red lions, black dragons we are!*"'[3]

On the seventh day, the caravan set its face in earnest towards Constantinople. Keeping to the bank of the Tigris, Judaydah was reached in late afternoon. There was no garden to be found there and tents were raised. And here at Judaydah they halted for another three days.

At Judaydah, Sẖáṭir-Riḍá reached the caravan, bringing with him Áqá Muḥammad-Ḥasan, a young boy whose father, Áqá 'Abdu'r-Rasúl-i-Qumí, was then a prisoner in Ṭihrán, and was to suffer martyrdom in Bagẖdád. This Áqá Muḥammad-Ḥasan grew up in the household of Bahá'u'lláh and served Him faithfully. In later years he was put in charge of the Pilgrim House in 'Akká. The present writer well remembers Áqá Muḥammad-Ḥasan, in his extreme old age, in 'Akká in the mid-twenties. When no longer able to serve in the Pilgrim House, Áqá Muḥammad-Ḥasan lived in Bayt-i-'Abbúd (Bahá'u'lláh's house in 'Akká) and looked after the place. The old man possessed a veritable treasure – many specimens of the handwriting of Bahá'u'lláh, kept in a trunk, which gave him great pleasure to show to visitors. Ḥájí Muḥammad-Taqí, the Náyibu'l-Iyálih, also came to Judaydah from Bagẖdád. But when the caravan broke camp to proceed on the journey, Bahá'u'lláh instructed him, Sẖáṭir-Riḍá, Sẖaykẖ Ṣádiq-i-Yazdí and Ustád 'Abdu'l-Karím to return to Bagẖdád. Sẖaykẖ Ṣádiq was an old man greatly devoted to the person of Bahá'u'lláh. He felt so acutely the pangs of separation from Him that he could not rest, and not long after, started, a solitary figure, to walk to Istanbul. But he never finished the journey and died on the way, at Ma'dan-i-Nuqrih. (See p. 192)

Áqá Riḍá who himself, together with Mírzá Maḥmúd-i-Kásẖání (see Addendum V), was responsible for the culinary arrangements and for the preparing and dispensing of meals, gives a long and interesting list of other duties and the men who discharged them: Áqá Muḥammad-Báqir-i-Maḥallátí saw to providing coffee and water-pipes. The two brothers: Ustád Báqir and Ustád Muḥammad-Ismá'íl, natives of Kásẖán, were in charge of the tea and the samovar. Áqá Muḥammad-Ibráhím-i-Amír and Áqá Najaf-'Alí were responsible for pitching the tents and for the security of the camp. Mírzá Áqá Ján and Áqáy-i-Munír served the person of Bahá'u'lláh. Darvísẖ Ṣidq-'Alí, Siyyid Ḥusayn-i-Kásẖání and Ḥájí Ibráhím groomed the horses. Áqá Muḥammad-'Alíy-i-Jilawdár (see Addendum V) had charge of the fodder and barley for the animals. Áqá Muḥammad-Ibráhím-i-Náẓir and Mírzá Ja'far saw to the purchase of necessities on the way. Ustád

Muḥammad-'Alíy-i-Salmání (see Addendum V), in addition to carrying on with his calling, kept watch over the tents and the chattels of the journey. Áqá 'Abdu'l-Ghaffár (Áqá 'Abdu'lláh; see Addendum V), who was conversant with Turkish, made himself useful in contacts with the people the caravan met *en route*. The two boys, Áqá Muḥammad-Ḥasan and Áqá Ḥusayn (later known as Áshchí), served the ladies. According to Áqá Riḍá, others in Bahá'u'lláh's retinue were Áqá Muḥammad-'Alíy-i-Iṣfahání, Áqá Muḥammad-Ṣádiq, Siyyid Muḥammad-i-Iṣfahání, and Ḥájí Mírzá Aḥmad-i-Káshání.

The services of Áqá Riḍá himself, with Mírzá Maḥmúd-i-Káshání, were described by 'Abdu'l-Bahá to his secretary:

> . . . [they] rested not for a moment. After our arrival they would immediately become engaged in cooking for this party of nearly seventy-two people – and this after their arduous work of guiding all day or all night the horses which carried the palanquin of the Blessed Perfection. When the meal was cooked and made ready all those who had slept would wake, eat and go to sleep again. These two men would then wash all the dishes and pack them up. By this time they would be so tired that they could have slept on even a hard boulder.
>
> During the journey when they became utterly weary they would sleep while walking. Now and again I would see one of them take a bound and leap from one point to another. It would then become apparent that he was asleep and had dreamed that he had reached a wide creek – hence the jump.
>
> In a word, from Baghdád to Sámsún they served with rare faithfulness. Indeed no human being had the fortitude to bear cheerfully all this heavy labour. But, because they were kindled (by the spirit of God) they performed all these services with greatest happiness. I remember how, in the early morning, when we wanted to start for another caravanserai, we often saw these two men fast asleep. We would go and shake them and they would wake with much difficulty. While walking they always chanted communes and supplications.[4]

'Abdu'l-Bahá, in this same account, explained in brief but telling words the nature of the journey which lay ahead of them. 'Often, by day or by night we covered a distance of from twenty-five to thirty miles. No sooner would we reach a caravanserai than from sheer fatigue everyone would lie down and go to sleep: utter exhaustion having overtaken everybody they would be unable even to move.' But He, Himself, often had little or no rest during these stops, for His was the duty to see that the large party, including the animals, were supplied with food and daily necessities.[4]

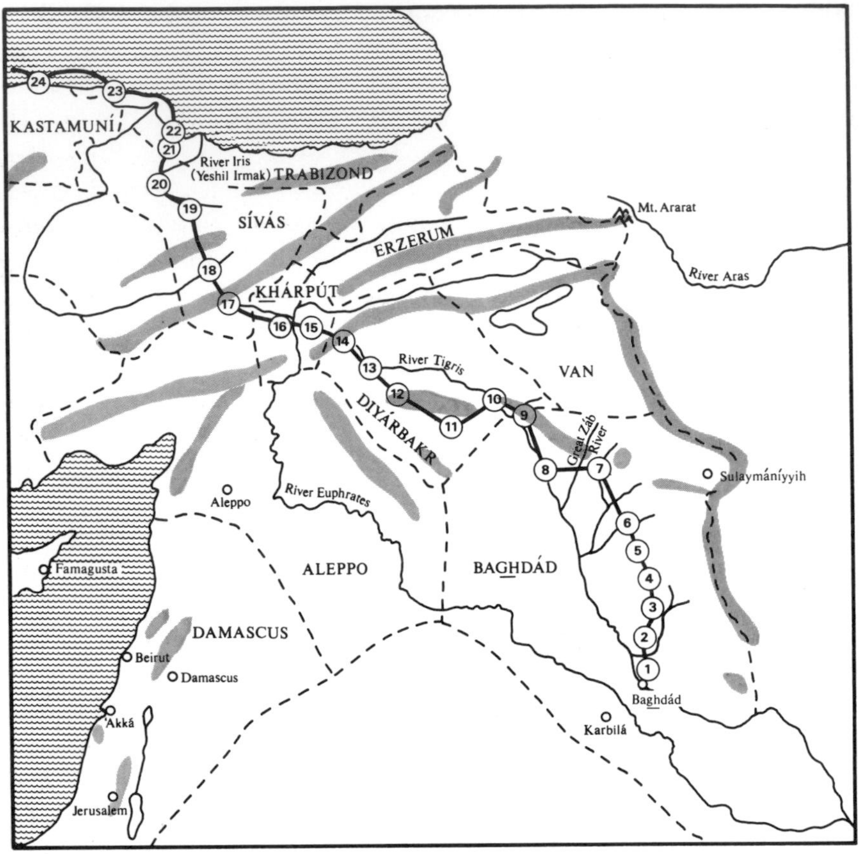

1	Judaydah	9	Zákhú	17	Dilík-Tásh
2	Dilí-'Abbás	10	Jazírih	18	Sívás
3	Qarih-Tapih	11	Niṣíbín	19	Túqát
4	Ṣaláḥíyyih	12	Márdín	20	Amásíyá
5	Dúst-Khurmátú	13	Diyárbakr	21	Iláhíyyih
6	Karkúk	14	Ma'dan-i-Mis	22	Sámsún
7	Irbíl	15	Khárpút	23	Sinope
8	Mosul	16	Ma'dan-i-Nuqrih	24	Anyábulí

The March of the King of Glory. Bahá'u'lláh's journey from Baghdád to Constantinople.

From Judaydah the caravan wended its way to Dilí-'Abbás, situated in a verdant plain by the river. Here again tents were pitched. However, because of the heat of the day it was customary to travel by night, and at midnight the caravan moved on and reached Qarih-Tapih the next day. The following stage was Ṣaláḥíyyih, a small town beside a mountain, situated on a tributary of the river Diyáláh, which was the seat of a qá'im-maqám. The Qá'im-Maqám and the notables of the place came out to greet the caravan, and offer their respects. But they went well beyond formal greetings and held a festival in honour of their guests. The caravan halted at Ṣaláḥíyyih for two nights, and the officials provided nightly watches against the incursion of highwaymen. The third night the caravan was once again on the move, despite intense darkness and winds of hurricane force. Áqá Riḍá, himself, had a frightening experience that night. He would sleep intermittently as he walked; at one time, noticing that Áqa Muḥammad-Ibráhím-i-Amír had sat down, because the *kajávih* carrying Bahá'u'lláh needed some repair, he did likewise and promptly fell asleep again. He slept for five hours and when he awoke there was no sign of the caravan. In the intense darkness of the night his absence had gone unnoticed. What had awakened him was the noise made by some men riding and driving donkeys. Thinking it was his own caravan, he hurried in their direction. But they were too fast for him. Anxious and afraid he plodded on. Suddenly he noticed the glare of a fire in the distance. This must be Áqá Muḥammad-Báqir and his brazier, Áqá Riḍá told himself, and so it proved to be. It was the hour of dawn and of the morning prayer. They had halted Bahá'u'lláh's *kajávih*. When Áqá Riḍá regained his caravan, the first person he met was Mírzá Músá, Áqáy-i-Kalím, who informed him that his absence had just been noticed, and that they were about to send some men in search of him.

Áqá Ḥusayn-i-Á<u>sh</u>chí reports similar incidents, and it must have been a common experience for travellers to lose their way at night.

That morning the caravan reached Dúst-<u>Kh</u>urmátú (shown on maps as Tuz-<u>Kh</u>urmátú) and camped in a copse. The next night's march brought them to Táwuq by a hillside, where a small river flowed. Thence, they made their way to Karkúk, where they stayed for two days in an orchard outside the city. They were now in the homeland of the Kurds, where lived the dervish leader of some 50,000 disciples scattered throughout Mesopotamia. Notables of the town came out, as usual, to pay their respects. And there was a man, in a state of exaltation, who came along shouting. Members of Bahá'u'lláh's retinue wanted to stop him, but Bahá'u'lláh, Who had sojourned for two years among these people, told them to let him be. Karkúk was the largest town in Lower Kurdistán, situated on the Khazá-chai river, and a high bridge crossed the ravine at this stage. The water was cold and the current swift, but a local man, to show his ability, dived from the bridge into the river. This feat pleased Bahá'u'lláh, and when the diver came into His presence, He gave him a sum of money. Some high officials put in an appearance here, who had come to visit Bahá'u'lláh while on their way to Mosul to transact their business. Seeing them made Siyyid Muḥammad-i-Iṣfahání and a few others greatly anxious and perplexed.

And so, on to Irbíl (Arbil), a historic town, near which Alexander fought a great battle with the Persians in October 331 BC. It is located on the ethnological frontier between the Arab and Kurd domains, although little more than a ruin compared to its former greatness. The plain on which it stands opens westward to the Great Záb river, a tributary of the Tigris, and southwards to the valley of the Little Záb. Overlooked by a hill-top castle, it was the market town of the Kurds of that area, and the seat of a qá'im-maqám.

When the caravan arrived, it was the day of al-'Íd al-Aḍḥá – one of the two great Muslim festivals, celebrating Abraham's offer of sacrifice, and on which the faithful throng Mecca to perform the rites of pilgrimage. The prominent men of the town, who came to greet Bahá'u'lláh, brought food prepared with meat of the sacrificial beasts as their offering. Their wondrous attachment to the person of Bahá'u'lláh was evident and unmistakable.

Leaving Irbíl behind, the caravan came upon the great waters of the Záb. This swift-running river, by the banks of which battles famed in history have been fought,* was crossed by boats. Two mules were carried away and nothing could save them. The first part of the night they remained encamped on the bank which they had gained, and at midnight, as they were making ready to resume their journey towards Mosul, high winds began to blow. They halted for a short while at a village named Baraṭallih, whose inhabitants were Christians, reaching

* The fate of the Umayyads was decided here in January AD 750. (See Balyuzi, *Muḥammad and the Course of Islám*, p. 218.)

Mosul an hour or two after sunrise, where a camp was set up on the east bank of the Tigris, the same side of the river as Nabíyu'lláh-Yúnis is situated. Both Muslims and Christians believe that the prophet Jonah is buried in the mound of this settlement, and hence its name. Most of ancient Nineveh lay on this east bank, but Mosul was built on the opposite bank on the site of a western suburb. Though much decayed, Mosul was still a handsome city on the slope of the Jabal-Jubilah, its houses forming an amphitheatre six miles in circumference.

Mírzá Yaḥyá had already reached Mosul in disguise, in the company of an Arab named Ẓáhir. Áqá Riḍá remarks that his behaviour had already lowered him in the eyes of his companion, who was supposed to be his servant, and when he showed his face he was bitter about Ẓáhir's conduct towards himself. 'He lolls about,' complained Mírzá Yaḥyá, 'and although he knows how much I detest the smell of tobacco, he keeps filling his pipe, letting out swirls of smoke.' Furthermore, Áqá Riḍá reports Mírzá Yaḥyá as saying: 'I did not come away from Baghdád with you, because I feared you would be handed over to the Persian authorities, and so I disguised myself and left, to escape that eventuality.' Áqá Riḍá goes on to recount that Bahá'u'lláh had told Mírzá Yaḥyá in Baghdád: 'If you wish to come I will inform Námiq Páshá accordingly; but come in the open', but Mírzá Yaḥyá had turned down the invitation. At Mosul, however, which was a good distance from the Íránian frontier, Mírzá Yaḥya became bold enough to show his face, although still in disguise; apart from Mírzá Áqá Ján and Siyyid Muḥammad-i-Iṣfahání who knew him, others did not know who he was, and some took him for a travelling Jew, who had joined their caravan to travel in safety, and so they were kind to him. Sometimes, according to Áqá Riḍá, he would come into the tent which was common to all of the men, but would not reveal his identity.

In a Tablet addressed to the Bahá'ís of Shíráz, 'Abdu'l-Bahá gives a detailed account of the life of Mírzá Yaḥyá: his craven fears, his incompetence, his uxoriousness, his constant flights from danger, real or imaginary, his failure to promote the Cause of the Báb. He writes: 'When we reached Mosul, and a camp was set up on the bank of the Tigris, where the notables of the town flocked group after group to come into His blessed presence [Bahá'u'lláh's], on a midnight that

View of Mosul across the Tigris (from Geary, Through Asiatic Turkey*)*

aforementioned Arab, Ẓáhir, came to say that his Honour [Mírzá Yaḥyá] was staying at an inn outside the city, and wished to meet someone. My uncle, Mírzá Músá, went there at midnight and met him. Mírzá Yaḥyá asked about his family, and was told that they were there and had their own tent and he could visit them. He said that he did not at all consider it advisable to do so, but he would accompany the caravan with which his family too would be travelling. Thus he continued to Diyárbakr, a black cord round his head, and a begging-bowl in his hand, consorting only with the Arabs and the Turks in the caravan. At Diyárbakr, he sent word that he would visit his family at night and join the main body of the caravan in the morning. That was done. Since Ḥájí Siyyid Muḥammad knew him, he gave out that he was a Persian dervish, an acquaintance of his, and visited him, but other friends because they had never seen him [Mírzá Yaḥyá], did not recognize him.'[5] 'Abdu'l-Bahá then relates how Mírzá Yaḥyá picked a quarrel with Siyyid Muḥammad, the man who in years to come was to become his chief advocate and his evil genius, and then ran complaining to Bahá'u'lláh. After hearing Siyyid Muḥammad's explanation, Bahá'u'lláh upbraided him for causing controversy.

The caravan halted for three days in Mosul, and Bahá'u'lláh and the members of his retinue visited the public bath there. On the third day towards sunset they broke camp and started for Zákhú which was three stages away. At the last stage the Yazídí Kurds inhabiting the region were hostile. The caravan had halted at the foot of a mountain; the Kurds refused them sentinels, would not sell them food, were abusive and threw stones at them. They, themselves, provided the watch, one group intoning aloud, 'Whose is the dominion?' and another group answering: 'God's – the All-Powerful, the All-Mighty.' As dawn broke, the caravan, no doubt tired because of the night's experience, stirred to move on. The road lay now over stony mountain passes and through narrow defiles, shaded by an abundance of leafy trees. Áqá Riḍá states that their progress was necessarily very slow, as it was a difficult manœuvre to get the *kajávihs* through. In the vicinity of Zákhú, the Qá'im-Maqám of the place sent a large body of men to help with the progress of the journey, particularly with the movement of the *kajávihs*. Each *kajávih* was held in position and guided along by four men. Thus they went on, and when they neared Zákhú they found the Qá'im-Maqám himself with the notables of the town waiting by the roadside to greet them and pay their respects to Bahá'u'lláh. It was a very warm and joyous welcome they gave the travellers, and they had already prepared a feast for them, which Bahá'u'lláh graciously accepted. The Muftí, in particular, stressed the delight of the people to be thus honoured. Bahá'u'lláh told the Qá'im-Maqám: 'Whenever on our way they wanted to treat us as their guests and provide us with a feast, We did not accept, just as Noah's Ark rested nowhere but on the peak of Ararat.' Áqá Riḍá remarks that Zákhú was not far from Mount Ararat. The caravan now crossed the river which Áqá Riḍá particularly remembered for its cold, refreshing waters. Tents were pitched opposite the town. Áqá Riḍá recalled the Muftí saying that should Bahá'u'lláh have stayed a few days in their town, all the inhabitants would have become devoted to Him. But the day soon passed, and when night fell, the caravan resumed its journey towards Jazírih. The Qá'im-Maqám had sent various gifts, including snow, and had had the insubordinate, unruly Kurds of the previous night brought in for punishment. Zákhú's river joined another river on the route, and once more the Qá'im-Maqám provided an escort to see the caravan across, and give added protection to the *kajávihs*.

The next day Jazírih was gained. It had an old castle, near which, on the bank of the river, the caravan encamped. Centuries earlier, in the days of the Kurdish Ayyúbid dynasty founded by the celebrated Ṣaláḥi'd-Dín (Saladin), Jazírih, peopled by Kurds, had been a flourishing town, but now it had dwindled in significance. In the fourteenth century a large Jewish colony dwelt there, and at the opening of the nineteenth century it was a stronghold of the Yazídís, until most were put to the sword during a Turkish attack. Thereafter the populace of Jazírih remained chiefly Kurdish.

After sunset the caravan went on its way towards Niṣíbín, also once a historic city – residence of Tigranes of Armenia, a Roman bulwark against the Parthians, and at one time having several thousand inhabitants – but it was now fallen on evil days, being the seat only of a mudír. Here their tents were pitched in a delightful spot by the torrential Jakhjakh stream which rushed swiftly to the Khabur river.

From Niṣíbín, the caravan continued towards Márdín, two or three stages away, one of which was a place called Ḥasan-Ághá, situated in a barren plain devoid of verdure and pasturage. Uthmán, the muleteer, complained that his animals could not get enough to eat. That night, Áqá Riḍá writes, Bahá'u'lláh came out of His tent to visit the members of His retinue and see to their welfare.

'Abdu'l-Bahá has related of that time:

> In those days a famine raged all along the road. When we reached a station Mírzá Jaf'ar and I would ride from one village to another, from one Arab or Kurdish tent to another trying to get food, straw, barley, etc., for men and animals. Many a time we were out till midnight.
>
> One day we happened to call on a Turk who was harvesting. Seeing his large pile of straw we thought we had come to the end of our search. I approached the Turk politely, and said, 'We are your guests and one of the conditions of (religious) Faith is to honour the newly arrived guests. I have heard that you are a very liberal people, very generous, and that whenever you entertain a guest you kill and cook for him a whole sheep. Now, we desire such and such a thing, and are ready to pay any price that you demand. We hope this is sufficiently reasonable.'
>
> He thought for a moment, and then said, 'Open your sack.'
>
> Mírzá Jaf'ar opened it and he put into it a few handfuls of straw.
>
> I was amused, and said, 'Oh, my friend! What can we do with this straw? We have thirty-six animals and we want feed for every one of them!'
>
> In brief, everywhere we encountered many difficulties, until we arrived in Khárpút. Here, we saw that our animals had become lean, and walked with great difficulty. But we could not get straw and barley for them.[6]

From Ḥasan-Ágh̲á, the caravan moved to a village at the foot of Mount Márdín, a limestone crag surmounted by a fortress deemed impregnable. There, during the night, two mules, belonging to an Arab travelling with the caravan, were stolen. The owner was beside himself with grief. Bahá'u'lláh asked the official who accompanied the caravan to try and find the missing animals. Other officials were called in, but no animal was forthcoming. As the caravan was on the point of departing, the poor Arab went crying to Bahá'u'lláh. 'You are leaving,' he moaned, 'and I shall never get back my beasts.' Bahá'u'lláh immediately called off the resumption of the journey. 'We will go to Firdaws and stay there', He said, 'until this man's mules are found and restored to him.' Firdaws (Paradise), Áqá Riḍá explains, was a magnificent mansion standing within an orchard on the mountain-top, adjoining the city of Márdín, which is situated at an altitude of nearly 4,000 feet. Firdaws was indeed a beautiful place with running brooks. The *kajávihs* were led up there, and the part of the caravan that had gone ahead turned back. The Mutaṣarrif of Márdín together with other officials and the notables of the town hurried to greet Bahá'u'lláh. Men were sent to tidy and clean the mansion, and let water through the brooks and sprinklers. Now, there was a constant stream of prominent people of the town, passing through the gates of

Márdín (from Geary, Through Asiatic Turkey*)*

Firdaws, coming to pay their respects. Nearly half the population was Christian – Armenians, Chaldeans, Jacobites, Syrians – who had fled to the mountains before orthodox Christian and Muslim assaults.

The Mutaṣarrif threatened the headman of the village, where the mules had been stolen, with imprisonment if the animals were not found. The headman offered a sum of money in lieu of the mules. But Bahá'u'lláh insisted that the Arab was entitled to have his beasts restored to him. On the second day the headman came with a promissory note guaranteed by higher officials, offering to pay 60 pounds within a month, the value of the two mules. But Bahá'u'lláh refused this offer too. Then the headman realized that the game was up, sent for the animals and gave them to their distraught owner. People were amazed, for such a thing had never happened before. No stolen property had ever been retrieved, nor restitution made to the rightful owner. Áqá Ḥusayn-i-Á<u>sh</u><u>ch</u>í, in his reminiscences some four decades later, recalled that various officials went to Bahá'u'lláh to speak of the part they had played in retrieving the beasts and received suitable rewards. The Mutaṣarrif was given a costly cashmere shawl, the Muftí an illuminated copy of the Qur'án, the head of the horsemen a sword with bejewelled scabbard.

The purpose of the halt at Firdaws achieved, Bahá'u'lláh ordered the resumption of the journey on the third day. And what was seen then was also an event of rare splendour. The road lay through the main street of the city of Márdín. Government cavalry with flags flying and drums beating preceded the caravan; then came the caravan escorted by the Mutaṣarrif himself with other high officials and notables. And the whole town had come out, thronging the streets to hail and see the passage of the caravan. It was a slow descent from the mountain-top, and then Bahá'u'lláh bade farewell to the escort and told the men to go back to their town; while the caravan went on its way, moving all day long through copses and over lush meadows, until a halt was called at the end of the day, in a verdant spot beside running water. Tents were pitched there for the night. There were two more stages until another historic city was reached within three days: Diyárbakr, in the heartland of Kurdistán.

Diyárbakr, in the extreme north of Mesopotamia, stands on the site of ancient Ámid, at the strategic confluence of the main routes between the Euphrates and Tigris basins, where Turkish, Armenian,

Kurd and Arab ethnical territories converge. At an altitude of 2,000 feet, it overlooks an immense and fertile plain, throughout history the granary of Western Asia. Although its climate is mild, within its black basalt walls the city was unhealthy and dank, its streets narrow and muddy, perhaps sufficient to account for the unpleasant reception accorded the travellers.

In any case, for some reason the Válí of Diyárbakr, Ḥájí Kíyámilí Pá_sh_á, unlike his colleagues in the service of the Government, was not friendly. He did not, would not, co-operate to find the caravan a suitable place for encampment. The official who accompanied the caravan had hastened into the town, long before its arrival, to find where they could stay. And when the caravan arrived outside the gates of the city, they had to wait a long while for the official to return. He had been kept waiting for two hours before being told that the caravan should go to 'Alí-Páríb, at the southern side of Diyárbakr. As it happened they had stopped at the wrong side, and now, with some difficulty, they had to turn round, and skirt the town to get to 'Alí-Páríb, which was an extensive orchard encircling a lovely mansion. But they were refused entry on the plea that the silk cocoons there would be disturbed by the smell of cooking. It was useless to carry on arguing, equally useless to go back to the recalcitrant Válí, and Bahá'u'lláh told His retinue to set up tents outside the orchard. These manœuvres took the whole day, and it was about sunset before the caravan could settle down.

This Válí, who showed such rank discourtesy, had his meed before long. There was a shortage of bread in Diyárbakr, and prices rose abnormally. People cast their eyes around and rightly or wrongly concluded that the Válí himself was responsible for their misfortune. They rioted and inflicted such humiliations on him that the Government had no choice but to dismiss him from his post.*

* In a dispatch dated 1 July 1863, Mr I. G. Taylor, the British consul at Diyárbakr, reported to the British minister at Istanbul as follows:

'I regret I am not able to report favorably on the condition of this Pashalik for the last six months. Disorder prevails everywhere, . . . and the Government seems to have lost all hold and influence over the people, outside as well as in the towns . . .'

Less than two months before, 11 May 1863, Mr Taylor had reported the chaotic state of affairs in these terms: 'The administration of Government and justice in the town is in keeping with the confusion and tyranny outside. Just and fictitious complaints and claims are either swamped or carried by secret intimidation or unblushing perjury.' The same dispatch mentions some twenty murders that had recently occurred in the province. 'In no single case have the murderers been captured and the most perfect indifference seems to prevail if they are or not . . .' (FO 195 752)

As to the food riots, he reported in his July 1st dispatch:

The caravan halted for three days outside Diyárbakr. Now, a long way from the frontiers of Írán, Mírzá Yaḥyá made himself known to all. He even began to take part in the life of the caravan, according to Áqá Riḍá, going into the town with some of the companions to make purchases. It must be noted that there were a few men travelling with the caravan who had no connection with the Bábí community, but had chosen to travel in that fashion because of the greater safety it provided, and also because of the hospitality they received. Among these was a dervish and also a Kurd named Shaykh Maḥmúd. That was the reason Mírzá Yaḥyá's inclusion in the caravan at Mosul had not aroused any particular interest. As mentioned before, some took him to be a Jew who had come to obtain protection.

From Diyárbakr the caravan continued on its way to Ma'dan-i-Mis (Copper Mine). The first day out they halted at the foot of a mountain. They could see a town and a castle on the peak, but the mountain road leading to the top was not an easy one and nobody went there. At this

---

'In Diarbekr [*sic*] itself the effects of the wretched and corrupt Government of the last eighteen months have resulted in disgraceful riots ostensibly caused by the high price of grain – I say ostensibly, for the actual price, stock on hand or state of the crops, do not warrant such an unseemly demonstration, which must be attributed to other causes. The Pasha sees this himself, and has consequently imprisonned [*sic*] several influential men, of the party supposed to be unfavorable to him, altho' he has not scrupled on several occasions to borrow large sums from them.

'The financial state of the Province is also far from favorable. The Salt and Tobacco dues have – as compared with the large sums expected from them – proved miserable failures; nor, with the country in its present state, can any change for the better be expected.' (FO 195 752)

The background to the riots was given in his semi-annual trade report, also dated 1 July 1863, from which these extracts come:

'The state of the crops, owing to our severe winter and late spring, are poor in comparison with the last three years – tho' not below the average – and causes apprehension among the poorer classes. There is not, nor do I in the least apprehend any serious scarcity – considering the large stocks of old wheat still on hand – but as the whole are in the hands of capitalists, who have been induced by the state of the crops to buy up and store all available grain the country is entirely at their mercy and they have already proved this by closing their magazines from time to time to suit their own purposes. These combinations; ravages committed by the locusts – most unduly magnified by unprincipled men who hope to obtain the government tithes on grain at a much lower rate than last year –; and large exportations of grain to Kharput; have caused a serious rise and wheat which I quoted in December at Ninety Piastres a Kilo . . . is now One Hundred and Fifty Piastres . . . Serious riots in which women however alone participated took place in consequence; magazines were broken open, loads forcibly discharged and plundered and well known corn dealers and the Pasha and other Government Officers insulted. To calm the rioters – against whom it was hardly possible to bring physical force – His Excellency forbad the export of grain and imposed a fixed rate. These measures have temporarily lowered prices – tho' still high – and I am afraid no great reduction will take place as long as they are in force.'

On receipt of the British consul's dispatch of 11 May 1863, Sir Henry Bulwer, British minister at Istanbul, gave instructions that it be translated and sent to the Porte, with a note recommending that a severe example should be made of the murderers, and the Válí replaced. In December 1863, Ḥájí Kíyámilí Páshá was dismissed, his successor arriving early in January 1864. (FO 195 752 and 799)

halting-place, towards sunset, Nabíl-i-A'ẓam, Áqá Ḥusayn-i-Naráqí and another person joined the caravan.

At Ma'dan-i-Mis they found a Persian imprisoned, who managed to reach the *kajávih* in which Bahá'u'lláh was sitting to beg for His intercession. Bahá'u'lláh promised to approach, in Istanbul, the Persian envoy, Mírzá Ḥusayn K͟hán, the Mus͟híru'd-Dawlih, on his behalf, which He did when they reached the Ottoman capital. He sent word to Mus͟híru'd-Dawlih to bring about the poor man's release, and it was done.

It would seem, from dispatches of the British consul in Diyárbakr to the British minister in Istanbul, that the Qá'im-Maqám of Ma'dan-i-Mis was given to incidents of this kind, as, shortly before Bahá'u'lláh's arrival there, a British-protected Ionian Christian had been set upon by a rabble led by the Qá'im-Maqám's men, who had thrown him out of his house and plundered his property. It was nearly a year before the British consul could bring the affair to a satisfactory close. Ma'dan's population was about equally Muslim and Christian, but the power lay with the Muslims who, in the words of the Consul, 'domineer most insolently over the latter and have them entirely at their mercy'. It was an appeal to religion which had roused the populace to their attack on the Ionian Christian. (FO 195 752)

And here at Ma'dan-i-Mis, a mishap nearly brought very serious consequences. Áqá Riḍá gives a graphic description of how Bahá'u'lláh's life was endangered and how that calamity was averted. In a mountain pass on a narrow road, Ḥájí Maḥmúd lost his hold on the rein of the mule which bore Bahá'u'lláh's *kajávih*; the animal slipped, lost its balance and started to slide down the precipice. It all happened in an instant, and no one could do anything but watch in horror for what seemed inevitable: the animal hurtling down into the abyss. But then, miraculously, the mule regained its balance and slowly came to a stop. Áqá Riḍá writes that the peril was indescribable and one had to be a witness to understand how miraculous was the deliverance. Because of the sheer joy of realization that the Blessed Perfection was safe, tears welled from their eyes.

This averted calamity was followed by the breaking of a carboy of rose-water which made the whole plain fragrant. Towards sunset the caravan came upon another mountain pass with many poplar trees and a running rivulet, the waters of which Áqá Riḍá describes as 'delicious'. Here they halted for the night, although there were no dwellings around. The following day's march brought them to a village the inhabitants of which were Christian. Here also was an abundance of trees, and tents were pitched under them.

The next day they reached the fortified city of Khárpút, which overlooks a cultivated and fruitful plain. According to Áqá Riḍá, it was then called Ma'múrati'l-'Azízah (the Glorious City). Within three miles of the town, officials and notables were awaiting their arrival to greet them and bid them welcome. Later, when they had pitched their tents, the Válí himself, accompanied by a number of high officials, came to pay his respects to Bahá'u'lláh, and on his return to the town sent presents of a sheep, meat, rice, cooking fat, cherries and other items of food. Here is 'Abdu'l-Bahá's account of this most welcome event, and the days that followed, as told to his secretary:

> At Khárpút the Acting Governor-General came to call on us – and with him brought ten car-loads of rice, ten sacks of barley, ten sheep, several baskets of rice, several bags of sugar, many pounds of butter, etc. These were sent as gifts by the Governor-General, 'Izzat Páshá, to the Blessed Perfection.
>
> After our experiences, and knowing how difficult it was to get anything from the farmers along the way – when I looked at these things I knew that they were sent from God, and they were gladly accepted.
>
> At that time Áqá Ḥusayn Áshchí was the assistant cook. He worked day and night and had no time to sleep.
>
> We stayed at Khárpút one week and had a good rest. For two days and nights I did nothing but sleep.
>
> The Governor-General, 'Izzat Páshá, called on the Blessed Perfection. He was a very good man and showed much love and service.[7]

Mírzá Muḥammad-'Alí, Ghuṣn-i-Akbar (Greater Branch), a younger son of Bahá'u'lláh, was taken ill here, and so the caravan halted until he recovered. In the meantime, Bahá'u'lláh and some members of His retinue visited the public bath. The original town of Khárpút, possessing a fortified castle, is situated at the top of a peak. A number, including Mírzá Ja'far, climbed the mountain to have a look at the old town, and reported back, according to Áqá Riḍá, that it was not attractive.

After a few days the caravan moved on to Ma'dan-i-Nuqrih (Silver Mine). It was here that Shaykh Ṣádiq-i-Yazdí died, he who, two months after being sent back to Baghdád, had found separation from

Bahá'u'lláh unbearable and had started to walk to Istanbul. Now, they had gained the upper reaches of the Euphrates, which they crossed, and set up their tents on the opposite bank.

Here Bahá'u'lláh's anger was aroused by the behaviour of some members of His retinue, who had fallen on some mulberry trees, of which there were many, and were eating the fruit voraciously. He spoke sternly to His brother, Mírzá Muḥammad-Qulí, and then entered His tent. In the late afternoon, when He was expected to come out of the tent, all the members of His retinue, including Mírzá Yaḥyá, were waiting outside, and as Bahá'u'lláh emerged, they, one and all, bowed their heads. Bahá'u'lláh said, smiling: 'Today, Divine anger nearly seized all, as you witnessed'. There was absolute silence. Then Bahá'u'lláh sat down, and had tea served to them.

There were four stages from Ma'dan-i-Nuqrih to Sívás, the next large town on their route. Áqá Riḍá remarks how very cold it was in these uplands of Anatolia. And at all of these stages notables never failed to come out to make the travellers welcome. One of these stops was at a place called Dilík-Tá<u>sh</u>. Another was by the banks of a river where Bahá'u'lláh underwent blood-letting. Áqá Riḍá comments that Bahá'u'lláh's blood was spilled into this river.

Then they reached Sívás, about 4,000 feet above sea-level on the Kizil-Irmak river, and encamped at its northern side. As the point where caravan routes between the Euxine, Euphrates and the Mediterranean met, it was a large and flourishing town. Yet, Áqá Riḍá remarks, it did not possess orchards, and the fruit yield of its trees was meagre; vegetables were brought from Túqát. Towards sunset the Válí came, attended by some officials and notables, to pay his respects. While in Sívás, Bahá'u'lláh visited the public bath.

And now the caravan made its way to Túqát in three stages, and the weather, Áqá Riḍá remarks, was very cold. At one of these stages they found that all the houses were subterranean. The people living there told them that during the winter months they had, perforce, to go underground. At another stage they came upon a very large orchard, and pitched their tents beside it. Mírzá Yaḥyá was also helping to raise a tent, holding a rope; noticing him thus engaged, Nabíl-i-A'ẓam composed a couplet, describing his condition.

At Túqát, which they found blessed with an abundance of apples and pears of excellent flavour, they encamped on the bank of the

Yeshil Irmak (or Iris) river that flows in the direction of Amásíyá. Túqát was an important town on the road between Upper Mesopotamia and Constantinople, but despite available marble and stone in the adjacent hills, and a busy copper foundry which exported to Persia, Turkistán and Egypt, most of the town dwellings were adobe hovels. The suburbs of Túqát, however, with their fertile gardens, extended far into the hillside valleys.

Proceeding to Amásíyá, the caravan stopped for two days outside the town, which was described as the 'Oxford of Anatolia' because of its eighteen theological colleges with their 2,000 Muslim students. Although it was a stronghold of Muslim orthodoxy, Greeks and Armenians made up about a quarter of the population. The town lay in a narrow valley of the Iris, overhung by mountain crags to the west and less precipitous slopes to the east where terraces of vines were planted and houses built. Strabo was born in Amásíyá, and the citadel described by him still surmounted a western height. With its handsome mosque, fountains, old houses and relative cleanliness, the town held its attractions. As usual, the Governor and his officials came to pay their respects. Bahá'u'lláh visited the public bath, and the travellers

Amásíyá (from Reclus, The Universal Geography*)*

found good supplies of fruit. But by this time they had exhausted their resources, Áqá Riḍá tells us, and some had to sell their horses – that of Áqá Muḥammad-'Alíy-i-Yazdí fetching an excellent price.

From Amásíyá they moved to Iláhíyyih, a small town of pleasing aspect, which was the seat of a qá'im-maqám. He and his officials came out, well in advance, to greet the travellers, and finding that the tents had arrived but not the men, got down to pitching the tents for them, later going into the presence of Bahá'u'lláh to pay their respects. Some rain fell here, and Áqá Riḍá remarks that they had a wonderful time at Iláhíyyih, for its people were kindness itself.

Then the caravan set out on the last lap of its long overland journey, and moved on towards Sámsún, on the shores of the Black Sea. The road lay now through wooded mountains and thick forests. A mule carrying trunks was lost in these woods. 'Abdu'l-Bahá, accompanied by Áqá Muḥammad 'Alíy-i-Jilawdár and another, went in search of it, found it and rejoined the caravan the next day, in the vicinity of the Black Sea port. That night the caravan halted at a large coffee-house *en route*. There was just one stage more to Sámsún, and at long last they came within sight of the sea.[8] To mark the occasion, Mírzá Áqá Ján begged Bahá'u'lláh to honour it with the revelation of a Tablet.

Mírzá Áqá Ján brought writing material. And Bahá'u'lláh's hand moved over the paper, as He sat in His *kajávih*, reciting aloud what flowed from His creative Pen. That was how the stirring verses of the *Súriy-i-Hawdaj* (the Súrih of Howdah) were revealed, while drawing close to the shore of the Black Sea and within sight of it. It was the end of a journey which had lasted one hundred and ten days – through the flat northern regions of 'Iráq and the homeland of the Kurds, and finally across the uplands, mountains and valleys of Anatolia. When Bahá'u'lláh left His house in Baghdád for the last time, signalling the first day of the most memorable, the greatest of all festivals – the Festival of Riḍván – the *Súriy-i-Ṣabr* (Patience) had flowed from the Supreme Pen, as now did the *Súriy-i-Hawdaj*, on the last day of this toilsome but triumphant journey which had taken ten days short of four months to accomplish. Áqá Riḍá has recorded the full text of the *Súriy-i-Hawdaj* in his narrative, and writes movingly of the power and the majesty of that wondrous occasion. It was a fitting end to an exodus, intended by its instigators to be fraught with humiliation, but which became the march of a king.

The overland travel was over, but a short sea trip was yet to come. Bahá'u'lláh and His retinue stayed for a week at Sámsún, waiting the arrival of an Ottoman steamer. An Inspector of Roads had also arrived at Sámsún from Istanbul. Once in the presence of Bahá'u'lláh, he became captivated by His charm and graciousness. He had various Turkish dishes cooked to present to Him, and horses brought to take Him to view some construction work which was going on under his supervision. And at last the Ottoman steamer arrived. After their trunks and goods and horses were put on the steamer, two boats took them to the ship, in one of which Bahá'u'lláh sat with the members of His family, and in another the members of His retinue. At sunset, on the day of their embarkation, the steamer cast off anchor, and the next day, about noon, it appeared before Sinope, continuing after a few hours to Anyábulí, which it gained the following day. On the third day, Sunday, 16 August 1863 (1 Rabí'u'l-Avval AH 1280), the steamer dropped anchor at Istanbul. And thus ended the remarkable journey of the King of Glory, from one city of ancient renown: the city of the 'Abbásids, to another city of equal renown: the city of Constantine the Great.

26

In the City of Constantine

WHEN the steamer had dropped anchor, the official who had accompanied the travellers went ashore to find out what arrangements had been made for their reception. He learned that the house of Shamsí Big was appointed as their residence and Shamsí Big himself was to be their host. And carriages were ready to take them there. The house, near the Mosque of Khirqiy-i-Sharíf,* consisting of two storeys, was spacious, but not sufficient. It soon became evident that larger premises had to be acquired. They stayed for one month, in cramped conditions, in the house of Shamsí Big, who was fulfilling his task as host with promptitude and to the best of his ability. He had engaged two cooks, and the travellers themselves, Áqá Riḍá states, were also helping to prepare the meals.

The day after Bahá'u'lláh's arrival at Constantinople, a representative came on behalf of the Persian envoy, Ḥájí Mírzá Ḥusayn Khán, the Mushíru'd-Dawlih, to present his respects and compliments, and state that because of the circumstances he could not come in person and must forgo the pleasure of a visit. That day, about noon, Bahá'u'lláh went out to visit the mosque. And He did that regularly, as had been His wont in the Baghdád days. Actually the only places He visited in Istanbul were public baths and mosques. Many came to visit Him and pay their respects. But He never went to anyone's house, except His brother's. His visitors – men in high places – told Him that it was customary for a distinguished person visiting the capital to call on the

* The Mosque of the Exalted Cloak, so called because the cloak of Muḥammad is said to be preserved therein. It is one of the traditions of Islám that on hearing Ka'b Ibn Zuhayr's poem, the Prophet Muḥammad gave him the cloak (*burda*) that He was wearing. This cloak was bought from the son of the poet by the Caliph Mu'áwíyah and later was kept in the treasury of the 'Abbásid caliphs. It is said to have been burned by Húlágú Khán at the capture of Baghdád, but others maintain that it was saved and transferred to Egypt where it was used to shore up the claims of the puppet 'Abbásid Caliphate in Mamlúk Egypt. When he conquered Egypt in 1517, Selim I removed this cloak to Istanbul where it is still preserved in this mosque. Thus this *burda* or *khirqiy-i-sharíf* became a symbol of the authority of the caliph.

Istanbul – Constantinople – in the nineteenth century (from Pardoe, Beauties of the Bosphorus*)*

Foreign Minister after three days, through him meet the Grand Vizier, and through the Grand Vizier ask to be received by the Sulṭán; they advised Him to do likewise. He countered their advice by saying that He had no design or project to further, and no favour to solicit and gain, that He had come to Istanbul by the invitation of the Ottoman Government and for no other reason; therefore, let them seek Him if they had anything to convey to Him.

Áqá Riḍá recounts the delicious tale of a dream he had in those early days in Istanbul. He says he dreamt that Bahá'u'lláh had written a book, which was held by someone in a public square. And there was a mill which people wanted to set going, but the mill would only move in jerks — stop, then move, then stop again. Someone told Bahá'u'lláh of Áqá Riḍá's dream. That day, towards sunset, when Bahá'u'lláh was about to leave the house and visit the mosque, Áqá Riḍá went into His presence. Bahá'u'lláh told him, smiling, that he should endeavour to set the mill going. And Áqá Riḍá relates that for some time (even in the days of Adrianople) Bahá'u'lláh would occasionally turn to him and say 'the mill did not get started'.

One of the visitors who often came was Ḥájí Mírzá Ṣafá (see

Addendum V), a man with pretensions to mur<u>sh</u>idship amongst some of the Ṣúfís, and a close confidant of the Persian ambassador, Ḥájí Mírzá Ḥusayn <u>Kh</u>án. Bahá'u'lláh spoke to him so authoritatively at times, Áqá Riḍá states, that he was at a loss for words to respond. One day when he was in the presence of Bahá'u'lláh, His voice addressing him in tones of power could be heard ringing even in the ground floor of the house. We shall meet this man, who was not always sincere and straightforward, again and again in the course of this narrative.

As already mentioned, the house of <u>Sh</u>amsí Big was inadequate and too small for a large number of people. <u>Sh</u>amsí Big saw to his duties as the official host, and was always courteous and attentive. But transfer to a larger residence was becoming imperative, and after a month's stay the house of Vísí Pá<u>sh</u>á, in proximity to the Mosque of Sulṭán Muḥammad-i-Fátiḥ (the Conqueror of Constantinople) was secured. This was a palatial residence, having both a '*bírúní*' (outer, i.e. men's quarters), and an '*andarúní*' (inner, i.e. ladies' quarters); both buildings were three-storeyed and provided with all appurtenances. The house had a Turkish bath of its own, and the *bírúní* had a vast garden. There were facilities for storing the rain-water.

As stated earlier, the only other place apart from mosques and public baths which Bahá'u'lláh visited from time to time, was the house of Mírzá Músá, Áqáy-i-Kalím, to meet various officials who had come with messages from the Government. On these occasions He was attended by Áqá 'Abdu'l-<u>Gh</u>affár, who was conversant with Turkish and acted as interpreter.

One day as Mírzá Músá approached the Big-Ú<u>gh</u>lí bazar, a photographer came up and said that he wished to photograph him, without charge, and would present a number of copies to him. Nabíl, who relates this incident, writes that Mírzá Músá responded to the photographer's request: 'He wants to earn something by photographing us. This is his means of livelihood. We will not deprive him of it.' According to Nabíl, they were then all photographed. (See p. 200).

Then came a day when <u>Sh</u>amsí Big brought news of the possibility of transfer to Adrianople. And it was apparent that this transfer was of the nature of banishment, ordained by Sulṭán 'Abdu'l-'Azíz and his chief ministers,* on the insistence of Mu<u>sh</u>íru'd-Dawlih. Bahá'u'lláh was angry and refused to comply. He had done nothing to deserve

* They were 'Álí Pá<u>sh</u>á, the Grand Vizier, and Fu'ad Pá<u>sh</u>á, the Minister of Foreign Affairs.

Group photograph taken in Constantinople. Seated (L. to R.): Ḥájí Mírzá Aḥmad-i-Káshání, Mírzá Músá (Áqáy-i-Kalím), Siyyid Muḥammad-i-Iṣfahání. Standing (L. to R.): Áqá Muḥammad-Ṣádiq-i-Iṣfahání, Nabíl-i-A'ẓam.

such curt treatment. Ever since His arrival at Istanbul He had kept aloof from the cross-currents of the capital. Several of the dignitaries of Istanbul had called upon Him. And none had heard from Him one word of complaint or denunciation.

Around an oriental court, in the last century, there were droves of intriguers and malcontents, with axes to grind. While living in Baghdád, Bahá'u'lláh had been approached by a number of such persons, who had hoped to win the support and the affection of the Bábís in Írán. Some He had refused to meet, and those who were honoured with admittance to His presence received no encouragement, much less any promise of support. In the capital of the Ottoman Empire, Bahá'u'lláh adhered strictly to the same rule, refusing to endorse or advocate their nefarious designs. His Cause had not the remotest connection with treason and sedition. And this was exactly the same course which Christ had followed eighteen hundred years before.

To Ḥájí Mírzá Ṣafá, who was one of the conspirators endeavouring to bring about the removal of the Bábís from Constantinople and their banishment to a remote corner of the European continent, and who had now dared to show his face, Bahá'u'lláh, as attested by Áqá Riḍá, spoke sternly and reprovingly, telling him: 'We, few that we are, will stand our ground, until every one of us meets a martyr's death'. Ḥájí Mírzá Ṣafá replied, with obvious duplicity, 'But it is not possible to withstand a government'. Bahá'u'lláh said in answer to him, as reported by Áqá Riḍá: 'Are you intimidating Me with the power of the government? Whenever I find the whole world assailing Me with drawn swords, all alone and engulfed as I may be, I see Myself seated on the throne of Might and Authority. It has always been the fate of the Manifestations of God to meet such injustice and oppression, but repressive measures have never hindered Them from delivering what has been entrusted to Them by God, neither has Their purpose been thwarted.' He then spoke of that believer in the household of Pharaoh whose story is related in the Qur'án, and of his arguments with the monarch of Egypt, telling Ḥájí Mírzá Ṣafá to call the Persian envoy's attention to that text. Áqá Riḍá writes that Ḥájí Mírzá Ṣafá was thunderstruck, and asked leave to depart. Then Bahá'u'lláh turned to His followers: 'What would you say? Do you wish Me to cause your deaths? Do you wish to drain the cup of martyrdom? No better time

Ḥájí Mírzá Ṣafá

can there be than now to offer your lives in the path of your Lord. Our innocence is manifestly evident, and they have no alternative but to declare their injustice.' Words to that effect are reported by Áqá Riḍá, who adds: 'Truly, at that time, all of us, with the utmost joy, fidelity, unity and detachment, were eager to attain to that high station; and God is my witness that we were blissfully expecting martyrdom.'

But then, Mírzá Yaḥyá, poltroon as he always was, together with a few others of his kind, began to waver and show signs of alarm and perplexity. They made Mírzá Yaḥyá their spokesman to go to Bahá'u'lláh and entreat Him to accept this banishment. Their plea was: 'We have our wives and our children with us and they will perish too.' Bahá'u'lláh assured them: 'To offer all that one has in the path of God is an act of highest merit.' And as to the wives and children, He said, they could be sent to the houses of the foreign envoys, who would look after them. Áqá Riḍá quotes Ustád Muḥammad-'Alíy-i-Salmání that he himself witnessed Mírzá Yaḥyá, Siyyid Muḥammad-i-Iṣfahání and Ḥájí Mírzá Aḥmad-i-Ká<u>sh</u>ání putting their heads together to contrive some means by which to save their lives. And Bahá'u'lláh, perceiving the possibility of a rift in the ranks of the Bábís which would be damaging to the Cause of God, reluctantly agreed to leave Istanbul. But He commented that a golden opportunity, which would have redounded to the glory of the Cause, had been missed. 'They called us here, as their guests,' He is reported to have said, 'and innocent as we are, they turned on us with vengeance. If we, few as we are, had stood our ground to fall martyrs in the midmost heart of the world, the effect of that martyrdom would have been felt in all the worlds of God. And possibly nothing would have happened to us.'

It was the cowardice of Mírzá Yaḥyá, who had always fled from danger, eking out his days incognito, over the course of years risking nothing, that stayed the hand of Bahá'u'lláh.

It must not be thought that now Bahá'u'lláh chose complete seclusion and shut Himself away from all contact with the outside world. On the contrary, the comings and goings of people were as constant as before. Notables of the capital, including even the ministers (some anonymously, according to Áqá Riḍá), still came to call on Bahá'u-lláh. Shujá'u'd-Dawlih was one such frequent visitor.* Even Ḥájí Mírzá Ṣafá came, as he had done in earlier days. Bahá'u'lláh met them all with composure and detachment, refusing to be bowed, refusing to be a suppliant. Áqá Riḍá hints that Mírzá Yaḥyá and his associates wished Bahá'u'lláh to beg for favours, to bend His knee before the oppressor. But in future years, he writes, the very people who had had a hand in bringing about Bahá'u'lláh's banishment confessed to the pride they had felt in His independent stand, His total disdain of mendacity, His refusal to grovel for favours. Mushíru'd-Dawlih is reported to have said in Ṭihrán that Bahá'u'lláh's mien and conduct brought His compatriots prestige and saved their reputations, at a time when Qájár princes and princelings were clamouring at the Sublime Porte, asking for money and pensions. The authorities of the Ottoman Government, he averred, came to realize that Írán had men who would not demean themselves.

About this time, a daughter of Bahá'u'lláh named Sádhijíyyih, eighteen months old, died. She was buried in a plot of land outside the Adirnih Gate of Istanbul.

Now, additional Bábís came to Constantinople, including Darvísh Muḥammad, whom Siyyid Ismá'íl-i-Zavári'í had converted to the

* Prince Shujá'u'd-Dawlih was a son of 'Alí-Sháh, the Ẓillu's-Sulṭán, and a grandson of Fatḥ-'Alí Sháh. His father, Ẓillu's-Sulṭán, rebelled against Muḥammad Sháh (who was his nephew), but his assumption of power was short-lived.

Faith. But their arrival was contrary to the wishes of Bahá'u'lláh, for He did not want more Bábís in Istanbul. Áqá Ḥusayn-i-Qaṣṣáb (the butcher) was one of those newly-arrived, who, with Darvísh Muḥammad, went one day into the presence of Bahá'u'lláh, when He was about to leave the house and visit a mosque. He received them, but with sorrow. Both these men, Áqá Riḍá states, came in future years to the Holy Land and attained joyfully the presence of Bahá'u'lláh.

When all arrangements had been made for departure to Adrianople, Bahá'u'lláh sent a number of His followers away, including Mírzá Áqáy-i-Muníb (who had walked beside His *kajávih* all the way from Baghdád), Nabíl-i-A'ẓam, Áqá 'Abdu'r-Raḥím-i-Misgar (the coppersmith), Siyyid Ḥusayn-i-Káshí (who groomed the horses during the journey from Baghdád), Khayyáṭ-Báshí and Ḥájí Báqir-i-Káshání (Makhmal-Báf, the weaver of velvet, and one of those who had come later to Istanbul). They were all given their travelling expenses. Áqá Muḥammad-'Alíy-i-Jilawdár was told to stay in Istanbul, but eventually he rejoined the others in Adrianople. All went their several ways, except Khayyáṭ-Báshí, who, disobeying, travelled independently to Adrianople and arrived there a day or two later than the rest.

It was now the heart of winter, which can be very severe in those eastern parts of Europe. Although carriages, wagons and pack animals were provided, as well as ox-carts for their belongings, it was a hard journey, taxing the strength of all, and it lasted twelve days. Snow was falling as they left Istanbul and they were not clad for freezing weather. Recalling their sufferings, Bahá'u'lláh declared, 'The eyes of Our enemies wept over Us, and beyond them those of every discerning person.' 'They expelled us . . . with an abasement with which no abasement on earth can compare.'[1]

Mírzá Muṣṭafáy-i-Naráqí arrived just as Bahá'u'lláh's carriage was starting. Having heard of Bahá'u'lláh's imminent departure, he had left his family on the quayside, and had hurried to Bahá'u'lláh's residence, but could only see Him for a few brief moments. Knowing that Mírzá Yaḥyá was there too, Mírzá Muṣṭafá now hastened to meet him, but Siyyid Muḥammad-i-Iṣfahání and Ḥájí Mírzá Aḥmad-i-Káshání hid him behind themselves in the carriage. What danger could possibly have touched Mírzá Yaḥyá had he spoken to Mírzá Muṣṭafáy-i-Naráqí is beyond conjecture, but the cowardly Yaḥyá had always to seek cover. Áqáy-i-Kalím, who as usual was bringing up the rear, attending to all the requirements of the journey, met Mírzá Muṣṭafá, a brave and heroic soul destined to die a martyr's death in the city of Tabríz.

In the late afternoon of the first day the travellers reached Kúchik-Chakmachih, about three hours' journey from Istanbul. An official named 'Alí Big, with the rank of Yúz-Báshí (Centurion, commander of a hundred men), who accompanied them, found lodgings for Bahá'u'lláh. The next day, they left at dawn and arrived towards noon at Búyúk-Chakmachih, where they were housed in the home of a Christian. It was night-time when they took to the road again, to reach Salvarí. Here too they were lodged in the house of a Christian. But, Áqá Riḍá states, some had to be taken elsewhere with all the cooking utensils. At midnight, in pouring rain and intense cold, they moved out of Salvarí, and reached Birkás the next day. The last halting-place before arrival at Adrianople was Bábá-Iskí. Apart from the inconveniences of the extreme cold, Áqá Riḍá had nothing in particular to record of the events of the journey. But he says that everywhere, the owners of the houses where they lodged were liberally remunerated, to their satisfaction.

Bridge at Búyúk-Chakmachih over which Bahá'u'lláh and His entourage passed

'Álí Pá<u>sh</u>á, grand vizier of Sulṭán 'Abdu'l-'Azíz. It was to him that the Súriy-i-Ra'ís *was addressed.*

It was Saturday, 12 December 1863 (1 Rajab AH 1280), when they arrived at Adrianople, a city characterized by Bahá'u'lláh as 'the place which none entereth except such as have rebelled against the authority of the sovereign'.[2] Bahá'u'lláh was now virtually a prisoner of the Ottoman government.

During His four-month sojourn in the city of Constantine the Great, Bahá'u'lláh, in addition to the Tablet of *Subḥánika-Yá-Hú*, revealed *Lawḥ-i-'Abdu'l-'Azíz-Va-Vukalá* – a Tablet addressed to the Sulṭán. It was revealed on the very day that the brother-in-law of the Grand Vizier came to inform Bahá'u'lláh of the edict which had been issued against Him. Refusing to meet the envoy, Bahá'u'lláh delegated 'Abdu'l-Bahá and Áqáy-i-Kalím to receive it, and promised to reply within three days. Next morning the Tablet was delivered by <u>Sh</u>amsí Big directly to 'Álí Pá<u>sh</u>á, with a message from its Author that 'it was sent down from God'. The Guardian of the Bahá'í Faith gives a vivid description of this occasion, as well as a summary of the contents of the Tablet:

> 'I know not what that letter contained,' Shamsí Big subsequently informed Áqáy-i-Kalím, 'for no sooner had the Grand Vizir perused it than he turned the color of a corpse, and remarked: "It is as if the King of Kings were issuing his behest to his humblest vassal king and regulating his conduct." So grievous was his condition that I backed out of his presence.' '*Whatever action,*' Bahá'u'lláh, commenting on the effect that Tablet had produced, is reported to have stated, '*the ministers of the Sulṭán took against Us, after having become acquainted with its contents, cannot be regarded as unjustifiable. The acts they committed before its perusal, however, can have no justification.*'
>
> That Tablet, according to Nabíl, was of considerable length, opened with words directed to the sovereign himself, severely censured his ministers, exposed their immaturity and incompetence, and included passages in which the ministers themselves were addressed, in which they were boldly challenged, and sternly admonished not to pride themselves on their worldly possessions, nor foolishly seek the riches of which time would inexorably rob them.[3]

Unfortunately, the text of this Tablet is not available, but its tenor may be realized from these paragraphs which Bahá'u'lláh revealed in Adrianople at a later date for Sulṭán 'Abdu'l-'Azíz, in His Tablet to the concourse of monarchs, known as *Súriy-i-Mulúk*:

'Hearken, O King, to the speech of Him that speaketh the truth, Him that doth not ask thee to recompense Him with the things God hath chosen to bestow upon thee, Him who unerringly treadeth the straight Path. He it is Who summoneth thee unto God, thy Lord, Who showeth thee the right course, the way that leadeth to true felicity, that haply thou mayest be of them with whom it shall be well.

'Beware, O King, that thou gather not around thee such ministers as follow the desires of a corrupt inclination, as have cast behind their backs that which hath been committed into their hands and manifestly betrayed their trust. Be bounteous to others as God hath been bounteous to thee, and abandon not the interests of thy people to the mercy of such ministers as these. Lay not aside the fear of God, and be thou of them that act uprightly. Gather around thee those ministers from whom thou canst perceive the fragrance of faith and of justice, and take thou counsel with them, and choose whatever is best in thy sight, and be of them that act generously.

'Know thou for a certainty that whoso disbelieveth in God is neither trustworthy nor truthful. This, indeed, is the truth, the undoubted truth. He that acteth treacherously towards God will, also, act treacherously towards his king. Nothing whatever can deter such a man from evil, nothing can hinder him from betraying his neighbour, nothing can induce him to walk uprightly.

'Take heed that thou resign not the reins of the affairs of thy state into the hands of others, and repose not thy confidence in ministers unworthy of thy trust, and be not of them that live in heedlessness. . . . Beware that thou allow not the wolf to become the shepherd of God's flock, and surrender not the fate of His loved ones to the mercy of the malicious. . . . He that giveth up himself wholly to God, God shall, assuredly, be with him; and he that placeth his complete trust in God, God shall, verily, protect him from whatsoever may harm him, and shield him from the wickedness of every evil plotter.

'Wert thou to incline thine ear unto My speech and observe My counsel, God would exalt thee to so eminent a position that the designs of no man on the whole earth could ever touch or hurt thee. . . . Seize thou, and hold firmly within the grasp of thy might, the reins of the affairs of thy people, and examine in person whatever pertaineth unto them. Let nothing escape thee, for therein lieth the highest good.

'Render thanks unto God for having chosen thee out of the whole world, and made thee king over them that profess thy faith. . . . Thou canst best praise Him if thou lovest His loved ones, and dost safeguard and protect His servants from the mischief of the treacherous, that none may any longer oppress them. . . .

'Shouldst thou cause rivers of justice to spread their waters amongst thy subjects, God would surely aid thee with the hosts of the unseen and of the seen and would strengthen thee in thine affairs. . . .

'Place not thy reliance on thy treasures. Put thy whole confidence in the grace of God, thy Lord. Let Him be thy trust in whatever thou doest, and be of them that have submitted themselves to His Will. . . .

'Overstep not the bounds of moderation, and deal justly with them that serve thee. Bestow upon them according to their needs and not to the extent that will enable them to lay up riches for themselves, to deck their persons, to embellish their homes, to acquire the things that are of no benefit unto them, and to be numbered with the extravagant. Deal with them with undeviating justice, so that none among them may either suffer want, or be pampered with luxuries. This is but manifest justice.

Sulṭán 'Abdu'l-'Azíz (from the Bettmann Archive)

'Allow not the abject to rule over and dominate them who are noble and worthy of honour, and suffer not the high-minded to be at the mercy of the contemptible and worthless, for this is what We observed upon Our arrival in the City (Constantinople), and to it We bear witness. We found among its inhabitants some who are possessed of an affluent fortune and lived in the midst of excessive riches, whilst others were in dire want and abject poverty. This ill beseemeth thy sovereignty, and is unworthy of thy rank.

'. . . Beware lest thou aggrandize thy ministers at the expense of thy subjects. Fear the sighs of the poor and of the upright in heart who, at every break of day, bewail their plight, and be unto them a benignant sovereign. They, verily, are thy treasures on earth. It behoveth thee, therefore, to safeguard thy treasures from the assaults of them who wish to rob thee. . . .

'Set before thine eyes God's unerring Balance and, as one standing in His Presence, weigh in that Balance thine actions every day, every moment of thy life. Bring thyself to account ere thou art summoned to a reckoning, on the Day when no man shall have strength to stand for fear of God, the Day when the hearts of the heedless ones shall be made to tremble.

'It behoveth every king to be as bountiful as the sun, which fostereth the growth of all beings, and giveth to each its due, whose benefits are not inherent in itself, but are ordained by Him Who is the Most Powerful, the Almighty. The king should be as generous, as liberal in his mercy as the clouds, the outpourings of whose bounty are showered upon every land, by the behest of Him Who is the Supreme Ordainer, the All-Knowing.

'Have a care not to entrust thine affairs of state entirely into another's hands. None can discharge thy functions better than thine own self. Thus do We make clear unto thee Our words of wisdom, and send down upon thee that which can enable thee to pass over from the left hand of oppression to the right hand of justice, and approach the resplendent ocean of His favours. Such is the path which the kings that were before thee have trodden, they that acted equitably towards their subjects, and walked in the ways of undeviating justice.

'Thou art God's shadow on earth. Strive, therefore, to act in such a manner as befitteth so eminent, so august a station. If thou dost depart from following the things We have caused to descend upon thee and taught thee, thou wilt, assuredly, be derogating from that great and priceless honour. Return, then, and cleave wholly unto God, and cleanse thine heart from the world and all its vanities, and suffer not the love of any stranger to enter and dwell therein. Not until thou dost purify thine heart from every trace of such love can the brightness of the light of God shed its radiance upon it, for to none hath God given more than one heart. This, verily, hath been decreed and written down in His ancient Book. And as the human heart, as fashioned by God, is one and undivided, it behoveth thee to take heed that its affections be, also, one and undivided. . . . God is My witness. My sole purpose in revealing to thee these words is to sanctify thee from the transitory things of the earth, and aid thee to enter the realm of everlasting glory, that thou mayest, by the leave of God, be of them that abide and rule therein. . . .

'Let thine ear be attentive, O King, to the words We have addressed to thee. Let the oppressor desist from his tyranny, and cut off the perpetrators of injustice from among them that profess thy faith. By the righteousness of God! The tribulations We have sustained are such that any pen that recounteth them cannot but be overwhelmed with anguish. No one of them that truly believe and uphold the unity of God can bear the burden of their recital. So great have been Our sufferings that even the eyes of Our enemies have wept over Us, and beyond them those of every discerning person. . . .

'Have I, O King, ever disobeyed thee? Have I, at any time, transgressed any of thy laws? Can any of thy ministers that represented thee in 'Iráq produce any proof that can establish My disloyalty to thee? No, by Him Who is the Lord of all worlds! Not for one short moment did We rebel against thee, or against any of thy ministers. Never, God willing, shall We revolt against thee, though We be exposed to trials more severe than any We suffered in the past.

'In the day-time and in the night season, at even and at morn, We pray to God on thy behalf, that He may graciously aid thee to be obedient unto Him and to observe His commandment, that He may shield thee from the hosts of the evil ones. Do, therefore, as it pleaseth thee, and treat Us as befitteth thy station and beseemeth thy sovereignty. Be not forgetful of the law of God in whatever thou desirest to achieve, now or in the days to come. Say: Praise be to God, the Lord of all worlds!'[4]

But Sulṭán 'Abdu'l-'Azíz failed to respond to the twice-repeated call of Bahá'u'lláh and brought doom and destruction upon himself.

Ḥájí Mírzá Ḥusayn Khán, the Mushíru'd-Dawlih, the Persian envoy who over the course of several years had been the focal point of opposition to Bahá'u'lláh in the capital of the Ottoman Empire, had received from Him, ere He left Constantinople, these startling words of admonition and prophecy.

> What did it profit thee, and such as are like thee, to slay, year after year, so many of the oppressed, and to inflict upon them manifold afflictions, when they have increased a hundredfold, and ye find yourselves in complete bewilderment, knowing not how to relieve your minds of this oppressive thought. . . . His Cause transcends any and every plan ye devise. Know this much: were all the governments on earth to unite and take My life and the lives of all who bear this name, this Divine Fire would never be quenched.[5]

Ḥájí Mírzá Ḥusayn Khán-i-Qazvíní, Mushíru'd-Dawlih, later Sipahsálár-i-A'ẓam. Persian minister at Istanbul and later grand vizier to Náṣiri'd-Dín Sháh.

And later, from Adrianople, Bahá'u'lláh addressed to him this further reproof, in the *Súriy-i-Mulúk* (Tablet of the Kings):

> Dost thou imagine, O Minister of the Sháh in the City (Constantinople), that I hold within My grasp the ultimate destiny of the Cause of God? Thinkest thou that My imprisonment, or the shame I have been made to suffer, or even My death and utter annihilation, can deflect its course? Wretched is what thou hast imagined in thine heart! Thou art indeed of them that walk after the vain imaginings which their hearts devise. No God is there but Him. Powerful is He to manifest His Cause, and to exalt His testimony, and to establish whatsoever is His Will, and to elevate it to so eminent a position that neither thine own hands, nor the hands of them that have turned away from Him, can ever touch or harm it.
>
> Dost thou believe thou hast the power to frustrate His Will, to hinder Him from executing His judgment, or to deter Him from exercising His sovereignty? Pretendest thou that aught in the heavens or in the earth can resist His Faith? No, by Him Who is the Eternal Truth! Nothing whatsoever in the whole of creation can thwart His Purpose. Cast away, therefore, the mere conceit thou dost follow, for mere conceit can never take the place of truth. Be thou of them that have truly repented and returned to God, the God Who hath created thee, Who hath nourished thee, and made thee a minister among them that profess thy faith.[6]

But happily for Mushíru'd-Dawlih his story does not end there. In the *Lawḥ-i-Ibn-i-Dhi'b* (*Epistle to the Son of the Wolf*), which Bahá'u'lláh revealed in the evening of His life, an Ever-Forgiving Lord said this of him:

'His Excellency, the late Mírzá Ḥusayn Khán, Mushíru'd-Dawlih – may God forgive him – hath known this Wronged One, and he, no doubt, must have given to the Authorities a circumstantial account of the arrival of this Wronged One at the Sublime Porte, and of the things which He said and did. On the day of Our arrival the Government Official, whose duty it was to receive and entertain official visitors, met Us and escorted Us to the place he had been bidden to take Us. In truth, the Government showed these wronged ones the utmost kindness and consideration. The following day Prince Shujá'u'd-Dawlih, accompanied by Mírzá Ṣafá, acting as the representatives of the late Mushíru'd-Dawlih, the Minister, . . . came to visit Us. Others, among whom were several Ministers of the Imperial Government, and including the late Kamál Páshá [see Addendum V], likewise called on Us. Wholly reliant on God, and without any reference to any need He might have had, or to any other matter, this Wronged One sojourned for a period of four months in that city. His actions were known and evident unto all, and none can deny them except such as hate Him, and speak not the truth. He that hath recognized God, recognizeth none other but Him. We have never liked, nor like We, to make mention of such things.

'Whenever high dignitaries of Persia came to that city (Constantinople) they would exert themselves to the utmost soliciting at every door such allowances and gifts as they might obtain. This Wronged One, however, if He hath done nothing that would redound to the glory of Persia, hath at least acted in a manner that could in no wise disgrace it. That which was done by his late Excellency (Mushíru'd-Dawlih) – may God exalt his station – was not actuated by his friendship towards this Wronged One, but rather was prompted by his own sagacious judgment, and by his desire to accomplish the service he secretly contemplated rendering his Government. I testify that he was so faithful in his service to his Government that dishonesty played no part, and was held in contempt, in the domain of his activities. It was he who was responsible for the arrival of these wronged ones in the Most Great Prison ('Akká). As he was faithful, however, in the discharge of his duty, he deserveth Our commendation. This Wronged One hath, at all times, aimed and striven to exalt and advance the interests of both the government and the people, not to elevate His own station.'[7]

And in a Tablet, addressed to one named Mihdí, Bahá'u'lláh specifically mentions that in later years Ḥájí Mírzá Ḥusayn Khán said or did nothing to cause sorrow, and even spoke words that were commendable; and moreover, because he was closely related to a believer, nothing derogatory should be said about him, perchance this relationship would cause the past to be forgiven.*

Thus writes the Ever-Forgiving Lord.

Bahá'u'lláh's four-month sojourn in Constantinople has been characterized by the Guardian of the Bahá'í Faith as the 'opening scene of one of the most dramatic episodes in the ministry of Bahá'u'lláh'. Its significance, in the course of His ministry of nearly forty

* Mullá Káẓim-i-Samandar (a native of Qazvín), one of the nineteen apostles of Bahá'u'lláh, so designated by the Guardian of the Bahá'í Faith, mentions in his history that that close relative of Ḥájí Mírzá Ḥusayn Khán, the Mushíru'd-Dawlih, was named Mírzá Muḥammad-'Alí, known as Kad-khudá (Headman). See pp. 441–8 for additional information about Mushíru'd-Dawlih.

years' duration, is summarized in so masterly a fashion by the Guardian as to call for repetition at this critical point in our narrative.

'With the arrival of Bahá'u'lláh at Constantinople, the capital of the Ottoman Empire and seat of the Caliphate . . . the grimmest and most calamitous and yet the most glorious chapter in the history of the first Bahá'í century may be said to have opened. A period in which untold privations and unprecedented trials were mingled with the noblest spiritual triumphs was now commencing. The day-star of Bahá'u'lláh's ministry was about to reach its zenith. The most momentous years of the Heroic Age of His Dispensation were at hand. The catastrophic process, foreshadowed as far back as the year sixty [AH 1260] by His Forerunner in the Qayyúmu'l-Asmá', was beginning to be set in motion.

'Exactly two decades earlier the Bábí Revelation had been born in darkest Persia, in the city of Shíráz. Despite the cruel captivity to which its Author had been subjected, the stupendous claims He had voiced had been proclaimed by Him before a distinguished assemblage in Tabríz, the capital of Ádhirbáyján. In the hamlet of Badasht the Dispensation which His Faith had ushered in had been fearlessly inaugurated by the champions of His Cause. In the midst of the hopelessness and agony of the Síyáh-Chál of Ṭihrán, nine years later, that Revelation had, swiftly and mysteriously been brought to sudden fruition. The process of rapid deterioration in the fortunes of that Faith, which had gradually set in, and was alarmingly accelerated during the years of Bahá'u'lláh's withdrawal to Kurdistán, had, in a masterly fashion after His return from Sulaymáníyyih, been arrested and reversed. The ethical, the moral and doctrinal foundations of a nascent community had been subsequently, in the course of His sojourn in Baghdád, unassailably established. And finally, in the Garden of Riḍván, on the eve of His banishment to Constantinople, the ten-year delay, ordained by an inscrutable Providence, had been terminated through the Declaration of His Mission and the visible emergence of what was to become the nucleus of a world-embracing Fellowship. What now remained to be achieved was the proclamation, in the city of Adrianople, of that same Mission to the world's secular and ecclesiastical leaders, to be followed, in successive decades, by a further unfoldment, in the prison-fortress of 'Akká, of the principles and precepts constituting the bedrock of that Faith, by the formulation of the laws and ordinances designed to safeguard its integrity, by the establishment, immediately after His ascension, of the Covenant designed to preserve its unity and perpetuate its influence . . .

'The initial phase of that Proclamation may be said to have opened in Constantinople with the communication (the text of which we, alas, do not possess) addressed by Bahá'u'lláh to Sulṭán 'Abdu'l-'Azíz himself, the self-styled vicar of the Prophet of Islám and the absolute ruler of a mighty empire. So potent, so august a personage was the first among the sovereigns of the world to receive the Divine Summons, and the first among Oriental monarchs to sustain the impact of God's retributive justice. The occasion for this communication was provided by the infamous edict the Sulṭán had promulgated, less than four months after the arrival of the exiles in his capital, . . .

'. . . an edict which envinced a virtual coalition of the Turkish and Persian imperial governments against a common adversary, and which in the end brought such tragic consequences upon the Sultanate, the Caliphate and the Qájár dynasty. . . .

'Thus closes the opening scene of one of the most dramatic episodes in the ministry of Bahá'u'lláh. The curtain now rises on what is admittedly the most turbulent and critical period of the first Bahá'í century – a period that was destined to precede the most glorious phase of that ministry, the proclamation of His Message to the world and its rulers.'[8]

27

Adrianople, the Remote Prison

O Aḥmad! Forget not My bounties while I am absent. Remember My days during thy days, and My distress and banishment in this remote prison.

– *Bahá'u'lláh*

IN the well-known Arabic Tablet of Aḥmad, revealed for a native of Yazd, Bahá'u'lláh refers to Adrianople as the 'remote prison'.[1] This historic city, in a far corner of the European continent, was the furthest place from His native land that Bahá'u'lláh was ever to reach in the course of His ministry. And it was the first time in the known history of religion that a Manifestation of God had come to dwell on the European continent.

Adrianople, now known as Edirne, is situated inside a bend of the river Tunja (Tunca) just before its junction with the Maritsa. Its strategic position on the main route between Asia Minor and the Balkans has made it an important city from ancient times. The city was captured from the Thracian tribes by the Macedonians, who named it Orestias. It was rebuilt by the Emperor Hadrian in the second century AD and named after him Hadrianopolis or Adrianople. It thereafter had a turbulent history, being the scene of many battles between the Byzantines and other nations until its capture by the Ottoman Turks in 1362. From 1413 to 1458, Adrianople was the capital of the rapidly expanding Ottoman Empire, and even after the capital had been transferred to Istanbul, it continued to be an important administrative and commercial centre frequently visited by sulṭáns and princes. During the eighteenth and nineteenth centuries, a series of incidents such as a fire in 1745, an earthquake in 1751, brief occupation by the Russians in 1828–9 and 1878–9, and several mutinies, began to affect

A view of Adrianople in 1835 (from the Radio Times Hulton Picture Library)

the city's fortunes. At the time of Bahá'u'lláh's sojourn there, Adrianople's population was 100,000 and it was the capital of an important province of the Turkish Empire.

At first sight, Adrianople appeared to Áqá Riḍá to be a delightful place; but it was very cold. He comments that for them, who were used to the warm climate of 'Iráq, the cold weather of Rumelia was trying – and particularly so that first year because of the exceptional severity of the winter, and because they lacked adequate clothing.

On their arrival the travellers were all huddled together in a caravanserai called Khán-i-'Arab, where accommodation was poor and restricted. Bahá'u'lláh stayed there for three nights. Then a house in the Murádíyyih quarter, in the north-eastern part of the city, was procured for Him and His family, which Áshchí recalls was on high ground, with a good view of the whole of Adrianople. (This quarter is centred on the Murádíyyih mosque, which was built by Sulṭán Murád II.) Others remained at the inn, where their meals were brought to them from the house of Bahá'u'lláh. Áshchí, too, has something to say about the extreme severity of that winter. On the road from Constantinople to Adrianople he had seen a number of people frozen to death. In Adrianople it was said that they had not experienced such a hard winter for forty years, and there were frequent snowfalls well into the spring. For several days the public baths had to shut their doors, and springs were blocked with ice so that people had to light huge fires by them and wait a long time before any water would flow. In Bahá'u'lláh's own room, despite the stove, a carafe of water froze one night. The suffering of Bahá'u'lláh and His people, ill-provided as they were, is obvious.

After a short stay in that house in the Murádíyyih quarter, which was too small, another house in the same quarter but more spacious, close to the *Takyih* of the Mawlavís,* was obtained for Bahá'u'lláh. Others, who were still in the caravanserai, moved to the first house which Bahá'u'lláh had just vacated. Next door to the second residence in the Murádíyyih quarter, a third house was rented for Áqáy-i-Kalím and Mírzá Yaḥyá and their families. All these houses, Áqá Riḍá remarks, were old, draughty and badly constructed, and keeping out the cold was a constant problem.

Áqá Riḍá recounts the story of 'Alí Big, the centurion, who had accompanied Bahá'u'lláh and His party from Constantinople. When he came to take his leave, he begged Bahá'u'lláh for promotion. He had been a centurion too long and was no longer young; to gain the rank of Big-Bá<u>sh</u>í and to be posted to Adrianople was his dearest wish. Bahá'u'lláh assured him that all would be well with him, and indeed, before long he turned up at Adrianople, a Big-Bá<u>sh</u>í. He sought Bahá'u'lláh's presence to express his gratitude, telling everyone that it was by the bounty of Bahá'u'lláh that he had obtained his remarkable promotion. After a while, however, he began to long for another step up the ladder. Once again he begged Bahá'u'lláh that his desideratum be granted to him, and once again he was assured that he would be given the higher rank. And so, one day, he appeared with the badge of a Mír-Áláy. He himself could not believe his luck in having attained such a high military rank, and never ceased to declare openly that he owed it all to Bahá'u'lláh. And he consorted with His followers wherever and whenever he could. But as he had come such a long way, would it be unreasonable to desire and attain the rank of a Pá<u>sh</u>á? 'How long do you want to live?' Bahá'u'lláh asked him. And not long after, he was dead – Mír-Áláy 'Alí Big.

Life was indeed hard in that first winter in Adrianople. Before long, financial difficulties too began to be felt. By this time Áqá Ḥusayn,

* The meeting-place of members of a mystic order, going back to the great Ṣúfí poet, Jaláli'd-Dín-i-Rúmí. It is adjacent to the Murádíyyih mosque.

himself, was working in the kitchen; hence his name of Á<u>sh</u><u>ch</u>í (maker of broth, in other words, cook). He recalls that there were days when the only fare available for the luncheon spread was bread and cheese; yet he effected economies enabling him to prepare, every now and then, a feast for Bahá'u'lláh, and managed to buy two cows and a goat to provide the household with milk and yoghurt.

Áqá Riḍá brings to mind the unravelling of the mysteries of the 'year 80' (1280 AH) in that house in the Murádíyyih quarter. From the creative Pen of Bahá'u'lláh, Tablets were now unceasingly flowing, vibrant with power and authority, and carrying open and public announcement of His Revelation – Tablets such as *Lawḥ-i-Sayyáḥ* and *Lawḥ-i-Nuqṭih.* And the Bábís everywhere, except for a few dissident voices, rallied to His Cause and submitted to His God-given mandate. Mírzá Yaḥyá, however, though outwardly subdued, was, with a number of the self-seeking around him – men such as Siyyid Muḥammad-i-Iṣfahání and Ḥájí Mírzá Aḥmad-i-Ká<u>sh</u>ání – secretly concerting plans for subversion and opposition. The account of his base intrigues, to which we shall come presently, makes sorry reading.

But, first, to the supreme joy and bliss of those loyal companions of Bahá'u'lláh, which Áqá Riḍá's and Á<u>sh</u><u>ch</u>í's narratives depict. No matter how hard the winter, no matter how straitened the circumstances, no matter how poorly clad and badly housed, how dire the dark look of an uncertain future, they had attained their heart's desire and were happy. They lived in close proximity to their Lord and served Him with utter devotion. They heard by day and by night, from His own lips, verses – majestic, commanding, compassionate – which betokened the sunrise of the Day of Days, and they basked continuously in the life-giving rays of that Sun. Áqá Riḍá relates that Bahá'u'lláh visited them oftentimes, in that first house of the Murádíyyih quarter, and also visited the house of Áqáy-i-Kalím, His brother, next door to His own house, where those few of His followers who were in Adrianople forgathered.

It happened one day at sunset, when He was out in the open, that He turned to His companions and said: 'A bird perching on a branch of this tree (pointing to one) uttered these words three times, "Muḥammad came and calamity came"'. Áqá Riḍá comments that some of the companions thought that Bahá'u'lláh was referring to Mullá Muḥammad-i-Zarandí, Nabíl-i-A'ẓam, as it was rumoured that he had returned to Constantinople. Others put different interpretations on those words of Bahá'u'lláh. But, before very long, it became apparent that He was referring to Ḥájí Siyyid Muḥammad-i-Iṣfahání – the Antichrist of the Bahá'í Revelation.

Bahá'u'lláh, according to Áqá Riḍá, stayed about ten months in that second house in the Murádíyyih quarter. But since its accommodation was inadequate, and its situation made it lonely and difficult of access, He wished to obtain another residence, more commodious and easier to reach. One day, Áqá Riḍá relates, Bahá'u'lláh said to Mírzá Maḥmúd-i-Káshání: 'You are a tall man and nearer to God. Pray that He may give Us a better house', and within a few days a house was found, right in the heart of the city, to the north of the Mosque of Sulṭán Salím and close to it. This mosque, the glory of Adrianople, was built in the sixteenth century by the architect Sinán, with a great dome which is higher by six cubits than that of Saint Sophia in Istanbul. As to the house, it was a spacious and magnificent mansion, called the house of Amru'lláh, which means 'the Cause of God'.* Bahá'u'lláh, Áqá Riḍá says, personally went to view it, and it met with His approval. Mírzá Yaḥyá was also present. Bahá'u'lláh observed: 'God answers the prayer of Áqá Mírzá Maḥmúd. He prayed that God may give us a house; his prayer was answered and this house was found.' Its *andarúní* (inner quarter) of three storeys had thirty rooms. Bahá'u'lláh and His family occupied the upper floor, Mírzá Muḥammad-Qulí and his family the middle one, and some of the attendants were housed in the ground floor. This vast house had a Turkish bath of its own, with running water in the kitchen and also a place for the storage of water. Áqá Riḍa writes: 'The house could not be faulted'. The *bírúní* (outer quarter) had four or five beautiful rooms on its upper floor for reception, as well as accommodation for preparing and serving refreshments. The rest of the companions occupied the middle floor of the *bírúní*. Two other houses were found in the same quarter, one for Áqáy-i-Kalím and his family, and one for Mírzá Yaḥyá and his. All meals were prepared in the house of Amru'lláh and distributed from there.

Bahá'u'lláh had advised His companions that it was now the op-

* Shoghi Effendi, in *God Passes By*, p. 162, translates the 'house of Amru'lláh' as 'House of God's Command'.

portune time for them to engage in some trade. Áqá Riḍá says that he himself had no desire but to serve Bahá'u'lláh personally, and thought that plying a trade might stand in the way of the fulfilment of that desire. But, as it happened, it did not. One day, when they were all in the presence of Bahá'u'lláh, He told them: 'We commanded you to follow a trade so that you may be usefully occupied and not get bored, and may earn money and invite Us to feasts.'

In this house of Amru'lláh, Áqá Riḍá comments, they were all together at night, and in the daytime, some went about their trades, while others served in the house. Áqá Muḥammad-Báqir-i-Qahvih-chí and Ustád Muḥammad-'Alíy-i-Salmání saw to the preparation and serving of tea, coffee and other refreshments. Áqá Ḥusayn-i-Áshchí (now grown up) was in charge of the kitchen and did the cooking. Áqá Muḥammad-Ḥasan, still a young lad, served in the *andarúní*. Áqá Muḥammad-Ibráhím-i-Amír (Nayrízí) and Áqá Najaf-Qulí saw to the purchase of provisions and other necessities in the bazar. Mírzá Áqá Ján was the amanuensis of Bahá'u'lláh. Ḥájí Siyyid Muḥammad-i-Iṣfahání and Ḥájí Mírzá Aḥmad-i-Káshání had no particular employment in the house, nor did they have a trade or manage a shop. Áqá Muḥammad-Ibráhím-i-Náẓir (see Addendum V) was engaged in the weaving of silk. Áqá Riḍá himself together with Mírzá Maḥmúd-i-Káshání kept a confectioner's shop. Áqá Muḥammad-'Alí and Áqá 'Abdu'l-Ghaffár became tobacconists. Ustád Báqir, Áqá Muḥammad-Ismá'íl and Khayyáṭ-Báshí did tailoring. Mírzá Ja'far and Áqá Muḥammad-Ṣádiq (see Addendum V) also opened shops.

It was in the house of Amru'lláh, on the night of 12 Rabí'u'l-Avval AH 1281 (15 August 1864), that Mírzá Ḍíyá'u'lláh, a son of Bahá'u'lláh, was born, according to Áqá Riḍá. 'We were all very happy together in that house of Amru'lláh', he comments, 'and no thought of separation ever crossed anyone's mind.' This state of affairs lasted for about a year.

In the second year of their stay in that house, Áqá Riḍá states, Siyyid Muḥammad-i-Iṣfahání and Ḥájí Mírzá Aḥmad-i-Káshání began openly to show their true natures, compounded of treachery and insubordination. It will be recalled that Bahá'u'lláh had brought Ḥájí Mírzá Aḥmad with Himself from Baghdád, lest he might again fall foul of the Persian consul-general because of his uncontrollable tongue, as a result of which he had been detained and jailed. The

Persian Tablet of Aḥmad, resonant with power and authority, is addressed to this Ḥájí Mírzá Aḥmad:*

> Thine eye is My trust, suffer not the dust of vain desires to becloud its lustre. Thine ear is a sign of My bounty, let not the tumult of unseemly motives turn it away from My Word that encompasseth all creation. Thine heart is My treasury, allow not the treacherous hand of self to rob thee of the pearls which I have treasured therein. Thine hand is a symbol of My loving-kindness, hinder it not from holding fast unto My guarded and hidden Tablets. . . . Unasked, I have showered upon thee My grace. Unpetitioned, I have fulfilled thy wish. In spite of thy undeserving, I have singled thee out for My richest, My incalculable favours. . . . O My servants! Be as resigned and submissive as the earth, that from the soil of your being there may blossom the fragrant, the holy and multi-coloured hyacinths of My knowledge. Be ablaze as the fire, that ye may burn away the veils of heedlessness and set aglow, through the quickening energies of the love of God, the chilled and wayward heart. Be light and untrammelled as the breeze, that ye may obtain admittance into the precincts of My court, My inviolable Sanctuary.[2]

During that time, writes Áqá Riḍá, the companions gathered every night in the large room in the outer quarters of the house of Amru'lláh, to read prayers of the Báb, because signs of Mírzá Yaḥyá's defection were appearing. But it was all still under cover. At times, he and Siyyid Muḥammad were closeted together, concerting their plans. For a while, matters thus rested, until all at once a chasm gaped open, wide and unbridgeable. It was caused by the open rebellion of Mírzá Yaḥyá and the titanic upheaval which resulted from it.

The Guardian of the Bahá'í Faith has thus described the rebellion against Bahá'u'lláh of His half-brother, its origin, nature and threat to the newly-born Faith:

> A twenty-year-old Faith had just begun to recover from a series of successive blows when a crisis of the first magnitude overtook it and shook it to its roots. Neither the tragic martyrdom of the Báb nor the ignominious attempt on the life of the sovereign, nor its bloody aftermath, nor Bahá'u'lláh's humiliating banishment from His native land, nor even His two-year withdrawal to Kurdistán, devastating though they were in their consequences, could compare in gravity with this first major internal convulsion which seized a newly re-arisen community, and which threatened to cause an irreparable breach in the ranks of its members. . . . the monstrous

* See Balyuzi, *Edward Granville Browne and the Bahá'í Faith*, pp. 64–5, for further details about him.

behavior of Mírzá Yaḥyá, one of the half-brothers of Bahá'u'lláh, the nominee of the Báb, and recognized chief of the Bábí community, brought in its wake a period of travail which left its mark on the fortunes of the Faith for no less than half a century. This supreme crisis Bahá'u'lláh Himself designated as the Ayyám-i-S̲h̲idád (Days of Stress), during which '*the most grievous veil*' was torn asunder, and the '*most great separation*' was irrevocably effected. It immensely gratified and emboldened its external enemies, both civil and ecclesiastical, played into their hands, and evoked their unconcealed derision. It perplexed and confused the friends and supporters of Bahá'u'lláh, and seriously damaged the prestige of the Faith in the eyes of its western admirers.* It had been brewing ever since the early days of Bahá'u'lláh's sojourn in Bag̲h̲dád, was temporarily suppressed by the creative forces which, under His as yet unproclaimed leadership, reanimated a disintegrating community, and finally broke out, in all its violence, in the years immediately preceding the proclamation of His Message. It brought incalculable sorrow to Bahá'u'lláh, visibly aged Him, and inflicted, through its repercussions, the heaviest blow ever sustained by Him in His lifetime. It was engineered throughout by the tortuous intrigues and incessant machinations of that same diabolical Siyyid Muḥammad, that vile whisperer who, disregarding Bahá'u'lláh's advice, had insisted on accompanying Him to Constantinople and Adrianople, and was now redoubling his efforts, with unrelaxing vigilance, to bring it to a head.

Mírzá Yaḥyá had, ever since the return of Bahá'u'lláh from Sulaymáníyyih, either chosen to maintain himself in an inglorious seclusion in his own house, or had withdrawn, whenever danger threatened, to such places of safety as Ḥillih and Basra. To the latter town he had fled, disguised as a Bag̲h̲dád Jew, and become a shoe merchant. So great was his terror that he is reported to have said on one occasion: 'Whoever claims to have seen me, or to have heard my voice, I pronounce an infidel.' On being informed of Bahá'u'lláh's impending departure for Constantinople, he at first hid himself in the garden of Huvaydar, in the vicinity of Bag̲h̲dád, meditating meanwhile on the advisability of fleeing either to Abyssinia, India or some other country. Refusing to heed Bahá'u'lláh's advice to proceed to Persia, and there disseminate the writings of the Báb, he sent a certain Ḥájí Muḥammad Káẓim, who resembled him, to the government-house to procure for him a passport in the name of Mírzá 'Alíy-i-Kirmáns̲h̲áhí, and left Bag̲h̲dád, abandoning the writings there, and proceeded in disguise, accompanied by an Arab Bábí, named Ẓáhir, to Mosul, where he joined the exiles who were on their way to Constantinople.

. . . allowing himself to be duped by the enticing prospects of unfettered leadership held out to him by Siyyid Muḥammad, the Antichrist of the Bahá'í Revelation, even as Muḥammad S̲h̲áh had been misled by the Antichrist of the Bábí Revelation, Ḥájí Mírzá Áqásí; refusing to be ad-

---

* Such as Nicolas and Edward Granville Browne. (H M B)

monished by prominent members of the community who advised him, in writing, to exercise wisdom and restraint; forgetful of the kindness and counsels of Bahá'u'lláh, Who, thirteen years his senior, had watched over his early youth and manhood; emboldened by the sin-covering eye of his Brother, Who, on so many occasions, had drawn a veil over his many crimes and follies, this arch-breaker of the Covenant of the Báb, spurred on by his mounting jealousy and impelled by his passionate love of leadership. was driven to perpetrate such acts as defied either concealment or toleration. . . .

Desperate designs to poison Bahá'u'lláh and His companions, and thereby reanimate his own defunct leadership, began, approximately a year after their arrival in Adrianople, to agitate his mind. Well aware of the erudition of his half-brother, Áqáy-i-Kalím, in matters pertaining to medicine, he, under various pretexts, sought enlightenment from him regarding the effects of certain herbs and poisons, and then began, contrary to his wont, to invite Bahá'u'lláh to his home, where, one day, having smeared His tea-cup with a substance he had concocted, he succeeded in poisoning Him sufficiently to produce a serious illness which lasted no less than a month, and which was accompanied by severe pains and high fever, the aftermath of which left Bahá'u'lláh with a shaking hand till the end of His life.* So grave was His condition that a foreign doctor, named Shíshmán, was called in to attend Him. The doctor was so appalled by His livid hue that he deemed His case hopeless, and, after having fallen at His feet, retired from His presence without prescribing a remedy. A few days later that doctor fell ill and died. Prior to his death Bahá'u'lláh had intimated that doctor Shíshmán had sacrificed his life for Him. To Mírzá Áqá Ján, sent by Bahá'u'lláh to visit him, the doctor had stated that God had answered his prayers, and that after his death a certain Dr Chúpán, whom he knew to be reliable, should, whenever necessary, be called in his stead.

On another occasion this same Mírzá Yaḥyá had, according to the testimony of one of his wives, who had temporarily deserted him and revealed the details of the above-mentioned act, poisoned the well which provided water for the family and companions of Bahá'u'lláh, in consequence of which the exiles manifested strange symptoms of illness.†[3]

Bahá'u'lláh had done His utmost to save His brother from the consequences of his 'crimes' and 'follies'; but His kindness and generosity had met with more venom and hatred. Time, that unfaltering test of right and wrong, eventually showed the true stature of

* In the International Archives of the Bahá'í Faith, on Mount Carmel, a blood-stained handkerchief is preserved with which Bahá'u'lláh used to wipe His mouth on the night He fell ill, as a result of poisoning.

† Áqá Riḍá states that Dr Shíshmán was Christian. That wife of Mírzá Yaḥyá, who revealed the poisoning of the well, according to Áqá Riḍá, was the woman from Tafrish, Badrí-Ján, sister of Mírzá Naṣru'lláh and Mírzá Riḍá-Qulí (see Balyuzi, *Edward Granville Browne and the Bahá'í Faith*, pp. 36–7).

Mírzá Yaḥyá, the hollowness of his contentions and the misery of his purpose. Having failed in his dastardly attempt of poisoning, Mírzá Yaḥyá turned round and pointed an accusing finger at Bahá'u'lláh. It was his Brother, he alleged, Who had poisoned the food, and then accidentally partaken of it. Today, at the remove of a century, we can pity the malefactor, and see in perspective how puny and insignificant he was, matched against the overwhelming majesty of Bahá'u'lláh. We can even feel amused by the calumnies and presumption of Mírzá Yaḥyá; but at the time, such vile conduct served to increase the rigours of Bahá'u'lláh's life.

Narrating the circumstances of Bahá'u'lláh's prolonged illness, Áqá Riḍá says that for weeks the companions were bereft of attaining the presence of Bahá'u'lláh. They were heart-broken, but certainly would not be so bold as to ask to be permitted to visit Him. Then, one night during His convalescence, when most of them (including 'Abdu'l-Bahá and His half-brother, Mírzá Muḥammad-'Alí) had been invited to dinner in the house of Áqáy-i-Kalím, and Áqá Riḍá and two others had remained to carry wood for heating, Bahá'u'lláh, sitting up in His bed, called them in and bade them be seated. He spoke to them and told them how weak He felt. After that, as soon as He was able to walk unaided, He came to visit the companions. In the vicinity of the Murádíyyih quarter there was a piece of land, dotted with trees. Mírzá Muḥammad-Qulí rented it, and Mírzá Maḥmúd-i-Ká<u>sh</u>ání planted flowers there. In the late afternoon Bahá'u'lláh would repair to that shaded spot, and the companions, returning from their day's work, knew where to find Him and attain His presence. One such day, Bahá'u'lláh enquired how <u>Kh</u>ayyáṭ-Bá<u>sh</u>í was, for the man had been ill. When Áqá Riḍá said that he had no news of his progress, Bahá'u'lláh replied that he should have gone first to visit <u>Kh</u>ayyáṭ-Bá<u>sh</u>í, before coming to this garden. 'This I tell you,' He said, 'that you all should learn to care for one another at all times, and look after each other.' The house of Áqáy-i-Kalím was close by this orchard, and Bahá'u'lláh would, at times, visit His brother's home before returning to His own.

Áqá Riḍá relates the circumstances of an embarrassing moment for Mírzá Yaḥyá in that house of Áqáy-i-Kalím. The well-famed courier, <u>Sh</u>ay<u>kh</u> Salmán, who came from Persia with letters and petitions and went back with Tablets and letters, had asked Mírzá Yaḥyá to explain for him the meaning of these famous lines from the poetry of Sa‘dí:

> The Friend is nearer to me than myself.
> Even more astonishing is my remoteness from Him.

Mírzá Yaḥyá's answer was nonsensical. Siyyid Muḥammad-i-Iṣfahání and Ḥájí Mírzá Aḥmad-i-Káshání (the very people who became his lieutenants, when he rebelled against his Brother) joined forces to show him how mistaken he was, and that Sa‘dí was expressing in poetical lines the sentiment conveyed by this verse of the Qur'án: 'We are nearer to him than his jugular vein' (50:15). When his ignorance was shown up, Mírzá Yaḥyá tried to confuse the issue. It will be recalled that on the way to Istanbul, Siyyid Muḥammad so routed Mírzá Yaḥyá in argument that the latter went to Bahá'u'lláh, bitterly complaining. Áqá Riḍá adds that Siyyid Muḥammad always mocked Mírzá Yaḥyá and laughed at him. Then came a day when Siyyid Muḥammad pretended that he had been insulted and went away to lodge in the Mawlaví-Khánih. Áqáy-i-Kalím sought him out and took him to his own home and gave him sound counsel and advice, but, Áqá Riḍá says, the man was wedded to mischief and again the same thing happened. He ran away for a second time to the Mawlaví-Khánih.

Áqá Riḍá gives his witness that Mírzá Yaḥyá had for a long time nurtured enmity towards Bahá'u'lláh, designing to bring about His death. One episode of the kind is described by Ustád Muḥammad-‘Alíy-i-Salmání, the barber, in his autobiography from which this extract is taken:

'One day, while I was attending at the bath, waiting for the Blessed Perfection to arrive, Azal came in, washed himself and began to apply henna. I sat down to serve him and he began to talk to me. He mentioned a former governor of Nayríz who had killed the believers and had been an inveterate enemy of the Cause. Then Azal went on to praise courage and bravery and said that some were brave by nature and at the right time it showed in their conduct. He again mentioned Nayríz and said that at one time there was left of the children of the believers only one boy, of ten or eleven years. One day, when the Governor was in the bath, this boy went in with a knife, and as the Governor came out of the water, he stabbed him in the belly and ripped him open. The Governor cried out and his servants rushed into

Ustád Muḥammad-'Alíy-i-Salmání

the bath, saw the boy with the knife in his hand and attacked him. Then they went to see how their master was, and the boy, although wounded, rose up and stabbed him again. Azal again began to praise bravery and to say how wonderful it is to be courageous. He then said, "See what they are doing to the Cause; everybody has risen up against me, even my Brother, and in my wretched state I know nothing of comfort." His tone and implication were that he, being the successor of the Báb, was the wronged one and his Brother a usurper and aggressor. (I take refuge in God!) Then he again said that bravery is praiseworthy, and the Cause of God needs help. In all this talk, relating the story of the Governor of Nayríz and praising bravery and encouraging me, he was really urging me to kill Bahá'u'lláh.

'The effect of all this upon me was so disturbing that I had never felt so shattered in my life. I felt as if the building were tumbling about me. I said nothing, but in a very agitated state of mind went out to the anteroom and sat upon the bench there. I told myself that I would go back to the bath and cut off his head, no matter what the consequences. Then I reflected that to kill him was not an easy matter and perhaps I would offend Bahá'u'lláh. Suppose I kill this man, I said to myself, and then go into the presence of the Blessed Perfection and He asks me why I killed him, what answer could I give? This thought prevented me from carrying out my intention. I returned to the bath and being very angry told Azal to "clear off". [In Persian "*Gum Shaw*" is highly insulting.] Azal began to whimper and tremble and asked me to pour water over his head to wash off the henna. I complied and he washed and went out of the bath in a state of great trepidation and I have never met him since.

'My condition was such that nothing could calm me. As it happened the Blessed Perfection did not come to the bath that day, but Mírzá Músá came, and I told him that Azal had set me on fire with his fearful suggestion. Mírzá Músá said, "He has been thinking of this for years; take no notice of him. He has always been thinking in this way." No one else came to the bath; so I closed it. I then went to the Master ['Abdu'l-Bahá, the Most Great Branch] and told Him that Mírzá Yaḥyá had spoken words which had infuriated me and that I had wanted to kill him, but did not. The Master said this was something which people did not realize and told me not to speak of it but to keep it secret. I then went to Mírzá Áqá Ján and reported the whole incident to him and asked him to tell Bahá'u'lláh. Mírzá Áqá Ján returned and said: "Bahá'u'lláh says to tell Ustád Muḥammad-'Alí not to mention this to anyone."

'That night I collected all the writings of Azal and went to the coffee-room of Bahá'u'lláh's house and burnt them in the brazier. Before doing this I showed them to seven or eight of the believers present, saying "These are the writings of Azal". They all protested and asked me why I did it. I answered that until today I esteemed Azal highly, but now he was less than a dog in my sight.'

Mírzá Yaḥyá's attempt to subvert and induce the barber was, according to Áqá Riḍá, of long standing, covering a period of at least three months until he was emboldened to speak so openly to the barber. As we have seen, it put Ustád Muḥammad-'Alí in such a rage that he nearly did away with Mírzá Yaḥyá himself, on the spot.

Referring to this episode, the Guardian of the Bahá'í Faith writes, 'Though ordered subsequently by Bahá'u'lláh not to divulge this occurrence to any one, the barber was unable to hold his peace and betrayed the secret, plunging thereby the community into great consternation. "*When the secret nursed in his* (Mírzá Yaḥyá's) *bosom was revealed by God,*" Bahá'u'lláh Himself affirms, "*he disclaimed such an intention, and imputed it to that same servant* (Ustád Muḥammad-'Alí).""[4]

The same Ustád Muḥammad-'Alí relates that Mírzá Yaḥyá, in his craven fear lest he be recognized, told Shamsí Big, who had been their official host in Istanbul, that he was a servant of Bahá'u'lláh. And to the same end, the concealment of his identity, he oftentimes betook himself to the quarters of the attendants, although he had a home of his own.

The actions of Mírzá Yaḥyá, in his vain attempt to 'reanimate his own defunct leadership', led to events of great significance which are described by Shoghi Effendi, as he continues his narrative of this 'first major internal convulsion':

> The moment had now arrived for Him Who had so recently, both verbally and in numerous Tablets, revealed the implications of the claims He had advanced, to acquaint formally the one who was the nominee of the Báb with the character of His Mission. Mírzá Áqá Ján was accordingly commissioned to bear to Mírzá Yaḥyá the newly revealed Súriy-i-Amr, which unmistakably affirmed those claims, to read aloud to him its contents, and demand an unequivocal and conclusive reply. Mírzá Yaḥyá's request for a one-day respite, during which he could meditate his answer, was granted. The only reply, however, that was forthcoming was a counter-declaration, specifying the hour and the minute in which he had been made the recipient of an independent Revelation, necessitating the unqualified submission to him of the peoples of the earth in both the East and the West.
>
> So presumptuous an assertion, made by so perfidious an adversary to the envoy of the Bearer of so momentous a Revelation was the signal for the open and final rupture between Bahá'u'lláh and Mírzá Yaḥyá – a rupture that marks one of the darkest dates in Bahá'í history. Wishing to allay the fierce animosity that blazed in the bosom of His enemies, and to assure to each one of the exiles a complete freedom to choose between Him and them, Bahá'u'lláh withdrew with His family to the house of Riḍá Big (Shavvál 22, 1282 AH),* which was rented by His order, and refused, for two months, to associate with either friend or stranger, including His own companions. He instructed Áqáy-i-Kalím to divide all the furniture, bedding, clothing and utensils that were to be found in His home, and send half to the house of Mírzá Yaḥyá; to deliver to him certain relics he had long coveted, such as the seals, rings, and manuscripts in the handwriting

* 10 March 1866. This house was in another quarter of the town. (HMB)

of the Báb; and to insure that he received his full share of the allowance fixed by the government for the maintenance of the exiles and their families. He, moreover, directed Áqáy-i-Kalím to order to attend to Mírzá Yaḥyá's shopping, for several hours a day, any one of the companions whom he himself might select, and to assure him that whatever would henceforth be received in his name from Persia would be delivered into his own hands.[5]

Áqá Riḍá writes of the great distress which Bahá'u'lláh's seclusion caused amongst the companions. Ḥájí Mírzá Aḥmad-i-Káshání, although leagued with Mírzá Yaḥyá, did not tarry in Adrianople, but asked for a passport and left. He made his way back to Baghdád, where he was murdered by an Arab, who was supposed to have been a Bahá'í. Bahá'u'lláh was still in Adrianople when the news came of Ḥájí Mírzá Aḥmad's foul murder, and the news grieved Him. Áqá Muḥammad-Ṣádiq and Mírzá Ja'far also preferred to leave Adrianople. Mírzá Muḥammad-Qulí, another half-brother of Bahá'u'lláh, and Mírzá Áqá Ján, His personal attendant and amanuensis, moved with Him to the house of Riḍá Big, and Áqá Ḥusayn also went there to cook for the household. The rest of the companions, heart-broken and distressed, were one and all forbidden access to the house of Riḍá Big, except for one day, soon after the move from the house of Amru'lláh. On that day, early in the afternoon, they were bidden to the presence of Bahá'u'lláh. He gave them tea and then addressed them: 'This restraint has an ordained time; you should all turn to God. Such must be your conduct as to see all under your shadow. Do not let anything deflect you from turning to God. Put your trust in Him, look up to Him. Be patient and forbearing. Do not seek conflict with anyone.' Áqá Riḍá, recalling the counsel of Bahá'u'lláh, says that such was the power of His utterance that they felt it in the very marrow of their bones, and tears welled from their eyes. Then Bahá'u'lláh bade them leave Him, instructing Darvísh Ṣidq-'Alí to visit Mírzá Yaḥyá's house every day and make necessary purchases for him and his family. Darvísh Ṣidq-'Alí hated it, but since he was bidden by Bahá'u'lláh, he obeyed, until the time when Mírzá Yaḥyá moved away to the Murádíyyih quarter, and told the Darvísh that he no longer needed his services.

When Bahá'u'lláh decreed that Mírzá Yaḥyá and his family should receive their ample share of the monthly allowance which the Ottoman Government gave to the exiles, all of the companions were given their share of the money and also of the utensils in use, copper and otherwise.

Áqá Riḍá states that they were all stunned by the intensity and the ferocity of ill-feeling displayed by Mírzá Yaḥyá and those near to him. One of those won to the side of Mírzá Yaḥyá was a certain Ḥájí Ibráhím-i-Ká<u>sh</u>í, who was treated with extreme kindness, was given letters to Persia, and was instructed what to say, wherever he went. But Ḥájí Ibráhím saw the shabbiness of their arguments, repented and rejoined the companions. 'I thought at first', Ḥájí Ibráhím is reported to have said, 'that their aim was to bring about reform and reconciliation. However, on second thought, I found that they had nothing but hatred and calumny to impart.' Áqá Riḍá states that he and others had a look at some of the writings given to Ḥájí Ibráhím, and were greatly astonished by the measure of falsehood which these writings contained.

Next, having failed to achieve their ends by enticements offered to Ḥájí Ibráhím-i-Ká<u>sh</u>í, Mírzá Yaḥyá and his infamous crew resorted to another shameful act. One of Mírzá Yaḥyá's wives, the mother of his son, Mírzá Aḥmad,* was sent to the Governor's house, moaning and bewailing. She told the authorities that they were hungry and had nothing to eat, because Bahá'u'lláh had withheld funds from them. And this was at a time, says Áqá Riḍá, when two thousand *túmáns*, recently sent from Qazvín, had all been handed over to Mírzá Yaḥyá. There was never a time, he repeats, when the needs of Mírzá Yaḥyá and those who were with him were neglected. Even when Siyyid Muḥammad-i-Iṣfahání had gone to lodge at the Mawlaví-<u>Kh</u>ánih he was provided with tea and sugar and other necessities. At this point in his diary, Áqá Riḍá, after relating these odious deeds of Mírzá Yaḥyá and his lieutenant, puts in a prayer of his own:

'O God! Thou knowest that mentioning these events has only one purpose: to state the truth and explain the situation. That which happened and of which we were witnesses is mentioned so that it would become clear and evident to all. We have never entertained

* This Mírzá Aḥmad, several decades later, turned to 'Abdu'l-Bahá, penitent and in need of care. The present writer well remembers him, in the twenties of this century, leading a very quiet life in his old age, in the Pilgrim House on Mount Carmel. When a number of students from the American University of Beirut were in Haifa, staying in the same Pilgrim House (the present writer was in that group), the Guardian of the Bahá'í Faith particularly counselled them not to hurt the feelings of that old, silent man, by referring, in any manner, to the aberrations and misdeeds of his notorious father, while in his presence.

hatred towards anyone. We put our trust in Thy grace and bounty to preserve us from falsehood, so that we should never deviate from the path of justice and equity and trustworthiness and loyalty, that we should never speak but the truth. Thou confirmest all, Thou art the All-Knowing, the All-Powerful.'

Then Áqá Riḍá relates a tale even more strange. The supporters of Mírzá Yaḥyá, when in 'Iráq, were asked why he had sent his wife a-begging to the Government House, when they knew full well that they were not in need of anything. They had replied that this was the work of Siyyid Muḥammad, and it had been done without the knowledge of Mírzá Yaḥyá. The excuse offered was even worse than the deed!

In those days of turmoil Khurshíd Páshá (see Addendum V) had just been appointed to the governorship of Adrianople, and had taken up his duties in March 1866, according to British consular records (FO 195 794). His deputy was 'Azíz Páshá. Both were capable administrators, whose integrity was beyond reproach. One day, 'Azíz Páshá called to visit Bahá'u'lláh, showing remarkable humility and reverence. He became particularly attached to 'Abdu'l-Bahá, and was eager to drink deeply from His fount of knowledge, although Ghuṣn-i-A'ẓam (the Most Great Branch) was a young man in His early twenties. Many years later, when Bahá'u'lláh had been exiled to 'Akká, 'Azíz Páshá became the Válí of Beirut. He visited 'Akká twice to pay his respects to Bahá'u'lláh and renew his friendship with Bahá'u'lláh's eldest Son, Whom he greatly admired.

Mírzá Yaḥyá now appealed to Khurshíd Páshá obsequiously, as well as to 'Azíz Páshá. Khurshíd Páshá and his deputy showed Mírzá Yaḥyá's letters, replete with fulsome flattery, to Ghuṣn-i-A'ẓam. Áqá Riḍá writes that when Bahá'u'lláh was apprised of Mírzá Yaḥyá's action, He knew that the time had come to end His seclusion; the 'ordained time' was over. 'We secluded ourselves', He said, 'that perchance the fire of hostility might be quenched, and such disgraceful acts be averted, but they have resorted to measures more extreme than before.'

It was now springtime. 'We had rented a house in another quarter,' writes Áqá Riḍá; 'we were all together there, and prayed together by day and by night. We read from the sacred Writings and implored God that this night of separation might end, and the dawn of nearness

'Abdu'l-Bahá in Adrianople

break; that the door might be opened once again unto His presence. And when our prayers were answered, and the gates of bounty were flung open, we rented another house in the vicinity of the house of Riḍá Big and all took our abode there. That house had a well with good water, and the courtyard was vast with plenty of flower-beds, well planted. We took it in turns, every day, for one to stay in the house and do all the housework: draw water, sweep, cook, prepare tea, tend the flower-beds, as if all the rest were his guests for the day, and he himself was the host. When dinner was over he would wash up and hand over the plates and utensils to the one whose turn it was, the next day, to act as host. Most days, the Branches [sons of Bahá'u'lláh] came to this house, and occasionally the Blessed Beauty would come too. It was a good, pleasant house.'

There were visitors now, who had travelled to Adrianople to attain the presence of Bahá'u'lláh, such as Áqá 'Alí-Akbar-i-Khurásání and Shaykh Salmán, the courier. They all stayed with evident joy at the house which Áqá Riḍá has described. Some Tablets were revealed in that house, and verses would flow from the tongue of Bahá'u'lláh as He sat with His companions. One day, Áqá Riḍá has recorded, He said: 'This is a fine place and a fine province. But I do not wish that we stay here. Before long all will be changed.' Áqá Riḍá adds that henceforth Bahá'u'lláh spoke frequently of the change which was to come, although outwardly there was no sign of it. Áqáy-i-Kalím had also taken a house in that neighbourhood.

The house of Riḍá Big had both a *bírúní* and an *andarúní* (outer and inner quarters), the former being smaller then the latter. The *bírúní* had a vast courtyard with a variety of trees and bushes and flowers, and Bahá'u'lláh would occasionally come to the outer quarters, usually late in the afternoon, to pace up and down this garden and speak to the companions. Áqá Riḍá mentions one day in particular, when Bahá'u'lláh spoke of those who had opposed the Cause of God, tried to harm it, and persecuted the believers, naming them one by one, and saying how they had been brought low. Before long, He said (and Áqá Riḍá has recorded), 'you shall see all the tyrants and enemies and opponents of the Cause of God vanquished, and the Word of God triumphant.' Then He added: 'It must be evident to all that We did not accept calamities and did not become captive except for the glorification of the Cause of God and bearing witness to the truth of His Word.'

House of Riḍá Big in Adrianople (by Ted Cardell)

Abundant and prolific was the revelation of Tablets and verses in those days at Adrianople. Áqá Riḍá tells us that such was the outpouring that the Aghṣán, sons of Bahá'u'lláh, and Mírzá Áqá Ján, His attendant and amanuensis, spent long days and nights copying and recording.

Bahá'u'lláh was still living in the house of Riḍá Big, and would, at times, come to spend an hour or two in the orchard and meadow near the Murádíyyih quarter. Then the house of Amru'lláh (which had been rented by 'Azíz Páshá) fell vacant again, and Bahá'u'lláh moved to it once more. The companions moved at the same time to a house close by, which had been previously occupied by Mírzá Yaḥyá and his family. Áqáy-i-Kalím also moved to another house at this time.

Amongst the new arrivals now were Ḥájí 'Alí-'Askar-i-Tabrízí and the brothers Ḥájí Ja'far and Ḥájí Taqí (see Addendum V), who lodged at an inn. Siyyid Ashraf of Zanján (later to be martyred; see p. 471) together with his sister; and Ḥájí Mírzá Ḥaydar-'Alí, accompanied by Ḥájí Mírzá Ḥusayn-i-Shírází (both soon to be arrested in Egypt and banished to the Súdán) also came to Adrianople and stayed in the house which the companions occupied. Mírzá Riḍá-Qulí and Mírzá

Naṣru'lláh, two brothers of Tafrish, whose sister, Badrí-Ján, was married to Mírzá Yaḥyá but estranged from him,[7] came about this time from Ṭihrán, and took a house of their own. Both in the house of Amru'lláh (which was now the residence of Bahá'u'lláh) and in the house rented by the companions, meetings were held regularly, to which Bahá'u'lláh came and spoke. And they, the companions, thus highly honoured, were privileged witnesses of how revelation came and how divine verses flowed from His tongue. It was in the house of Amru'lláh that the answer to 'Alí-Muḥammad-i-Sarráj (the leather-maker, who was a partisan of Mírzá Yaḥyá) was revealed. It has the proportions of a book.

Shaykh Salmán, the courier, Ustád 'Abdu'l-Karím, Áqá 'Alí-Akbar, and Áqá Muḥammad-Ḥasan and his sister were now advised to depart for 'Iráq. They were sorrowful, being wrenched from their Beloved, but they obeyed. Áqá Riḍá records that the day of their departure was unique, for when they had gone, Bahá'u'lláh received him in the *andarúní*, where the lamp had just been lit, and asked him whether he had written anything to anyone. Then Bahá'u'lláh said, 'Now write this' – and He spoke with tremendous power and authority – 'write this'. He continued: 'By the truth of God, from the horizon of My visage a Sun hath dawned, on which the Supreme Pen of God hath inscribed: "This day, sovereignty is God's, the All-Powerful, the All-Encompassing, the Most Exalted, the Most Glorious." Like a sword, when it smiteth the back of Satan, he and his hosts are put to flight; they flee to the lowest depths of hell. Thus hath emanated the command of God.' The Most Great Branch ('Abdu'l-Bahá), who was present, remarked that this verse ought to be recorded at once. Pen and paper were produced and that admonition was written down, to appear at the head of a Tablet addressed to Siyyid 'Alíy-i-'Arab, who lived in Tabríz.

The partisans of Mírzá Yaḥyá, the Azalís, have maintained that this man was murdered by Shaykh Aḥmad-i-Khurásání. The report of the British consular agent in Tabríz confirms their statement, and further confirmation is found in an unpublished history of the Bahá'í Faith in the province of Ádharbáyján, written by Mírzá Ḥaydar-'Alí Uskú'í and supplemented by Áqá Muḥammad-Ḥusayn-i-Mílání. They state that in the days when Bahá'u'lláh was still in Adrianople, Shaykh Aḥmad-i-Khurásání, Mírzá Muṣṭafáy-i-Naráqí and a dervish named

'Alí Naqí arrived at Tabríz, on their way to the Ottoman domain to attain the presence of Bahá'u'lláh. One night they chanced to meet Siyyid 'Alíy-i-'Arab. In the course of conversation, Siyyid 'Alí became abusive, and referred to Bahá'u'lláh in vile terms. This so stung his visitors and so taxed their patience that they rushed him and tied around his neck the shawl he wore round his waist, which led to his death. The next day, when Siyyid 'Alí's body was found, the three were arrested and later beheaded in public.* According to the British consular report, Shaykh Aḥmad-i-Khurásání made no attempt to deny the deed and readily admitted that Siyyid 'Alí had died at his hand. Ḥájí Mu'ínu's-Salṭanih of Tabríz, author of a detailed chronicle-history of the Bábí Faith, personally witnessed the execution of the three Bahá'ís. It ought to be remarked, however, that those three were not beheaded because of the murder of Siyyid 'Alíy-i-'Arab, which was incidental in the eyes of the authorities who sought them, but because they were Bahá'ís.

That deplorable and tragic episode had a sequel, even more tragic. In the pockets of the martyrs of Tabríz a petition was found, addressed to Bahá'u'lláh, which was written by Mírzá Muḥammad-'Alí, a well-known physician of Zanján. The authorities in Tabríz sent this letter to Ṭihrán. When Náṣiri'd-Dín Sháh was apprised of it, he wrote to the Governor of Zanján, ordering him to put Mírzá Muḥammad-'Alí to death. One night the physician was summoned to the Governor's house to attend the sick. On his arrival there, the executioner was waiting for him. A tub was brought in, and the innocent physician was pitilessly decapitated. However, it was witnessing the execution of the three martyrs in Tabríz, who showed no fear at all of death and died joyously, that converted a high official, Shírzád Khán-i-Sartíp. Strange indeed are the decrees of Providence.

Áqá Riḍá relates that another night, about that time, all of the visitors and most of the companions were in the presence of Bahá'u'lláh in the *andarúní*. He spoke to them of the events occurring in 'Iráq (where the partisans of Mírzá Yaḥyá were active), of the behaviour of Mullá Muḥammad-Ja'far-i-Naráqí, and of miracles and supernatural feats. The natural ordering of matters, He said, is not to be trifled with; but if a group of people make a particular event the touchstone

* The reports of the Russian consul in Tabríz state that they were arrested in December 1866 and executed the following January.

of their faith, and promise to abide by the outcome, God will, from His grace, bring that event to pass for them. For example, said Bahá'u'lláh, Mullá Muḥammad-Ja'far is crippled and lame; let him make his cure the test of his faith. The choice is his: let him first turn to Mírzá Yaḥyá, but if he does not find satisfaction, then let him turn to this exalted Threshold.

Bahá'u'lláh's challenge was conveyed to Mullá Muḥammad-Ja'far, but he was irredeemable. The Shí'ih divines of 'Iráq had, some years before, run away in like manner, not daring to heed His challenge.

Bahá'u'lláh was still residing in the house of Amru'lláh, when Mírzá Áqá Ján and Áqá 'Abdu'l-Ghaffár were sent to Istanbul to counter the mischief of Siyyid Muḥammad-i-Iṣfahání. But His second stay in that house was of short duration, for within six months the owner of the house sold it, and Bahá'u'lláh then rented the house of 'Izzat Áqá in another quarter of the city – the last of His residences in Adrianople. The Guardian of the Bahá'í Faith has described a decisive event which took place at this time:

> It was in this house, in the month of Jamádíyu'l-Avval 1284 AH (Sept. 1867) that an event of the utmost significance occurred, which completely discomfited Mírzá Yaḥyá and his supporters, and proclaimed to friend and foe alike Bahá'u'lláh's triumph over them. A certain Mír Muḥammad,* a Bábí of Shíráz, greatly resenting alike the claims and the cowardly seclusion of Mírzá Yaḥyá, succeeded in forcing Siyyid Muḥammad to induce him to meet Bahá'u'lláh face to face, so that a discrimination might be publicly effected between the true and the false. Foolishly assuming that his illustrious Brother would never countenance such a proposition, Mírzá Yaḥyá appointed the mosque of Sulṭán Salím as the place for their encounter. No sooner had Bahá'u'lláh been informed of this arrangement than He set forth, on foot, in the heat of midday, and accompanied by this same Mír Muḥammad,† for the afore-mentioned mosque, which was situated in a distant part of the city, reciting, as He walked, through the streets and markets, verses, in a voice and in a manner that greatly astonished those who saw and heard Him.
>
> '*O Muḥammad!*', are some of the words He uttered on that memorable occasion, as testified by Himself in a Tablet, '*He Who is the Spirit hath, verily, issued from His habitation, and with Him have come forth the souls of God's chosen ones and the realities of His Messengers. Behold, then, the*

* This man, with his pack animals, was in the caravan of the exiles, from Baghdád to Sámsún. (HMB)

† Mírzá Áqá Ján and Áqá Muḥammad-Ibráhím-i-Amír also accompanied Him. (HMB)

dwellers of the realms on high above Mine head, and all the testimonies of the Prophets in My grasp. Say: Were all the divines, all the wise men, all the kings and rulers on earth to gather together, I, in very truth, would confront them, and would proclaim the verses of God, the Sovereign, the Almighty, the All-Wise. I am He Who feareth no one, though all who are in heaven and all who are on earth rise up against me. . . . This is Mine hand which God hath turned white for all the worlds to behold. This is My staff;* were We to cast it down, it would, of a truth, swallow up all created things.*' Mír Muḥammad, who had been sent ahead to announce Bahá'u'lláh's arrival, soon returned, and informed Him that he who had challenged His authority wished, owing to unforeseen circumstances, to postpone for a day or two the interview. Upon His return to His house Bahá'u'lláh revealed a Tablet, wherein He recounted what had happened, fixed the time for the postponed interview, sealed the Tablet with His seal, entrusted it to Nabíl,† and instructed him to deliver it to one of the new believers, Mullá Muḥammad-i-Tabrízí, for the information of Siyyid Muḥammad, who was in the habit of frequenting that believer's shop. It was arranged to demand from Siyyid Muḥammad, ere the delivery of that Tablet, a sealed note pledging Mírzá Yaḥyá, in the event of failing to appear at the trysting-place, to affirm in writing that his claims were false. Siyyid Muḥammad promised that he would produce the next day the document required, and though Nabíl, for three successive days, waited in that shop for the reply, neither did the Siyyid appear, nor was such a note sent by him. That undelivered Tablet, Nabíl, recording twenty-three years later this historic episode in his chronicle, affirms was still in his possession, 'as fresh as the day on which the Most Great Branch had penned it, and the seal of the Ancient Beauty had sealed and adorned it,' a tangible and irrefutable testimony to Bahá'u'lláh's established ascendancy over a routed opponent.

Bahá'u'lláh's reaction to this most distressful episode in His ministry was, as already observed, characterized by acute anguish. '*He who for months and years,*' He laments, '*I reared with the hand of loving-kindness hath risen to take My life.*' '*The cruelties inflicted by My oppressors,*' He wrote, in allusion to these perfidious enemies, '*have bowed Me down, and turned My hair white. Shouldst thou present thyself before My throne, thou wouldst fail to recognize the Ancient Beauty, for the freshness of His countenance is altered, and its brightness hath faded, by reason of the oppression of the infidels.*' '*By God!*' He cries out, '*No spot is left on My body that hath not been touched by the spears of thy machinations.*' And again: '*Thou hast perpetrated against thy Brother what no man hath perpetrated against another.*' '*What hath proceeded from thy pen,*' He, furthermore, has af-

* References to Moses and His staff. (HMB)

† Nabíl, Muḥammad-Javád-i-Qazvíní and Mis͟hkín-Qalam, the celebrated calligraphist, had come to Adrianople not long before and lodged with the companions. Áqá Muḥammad-Javád-i-Qazvíní had been arrested in Tabríz, at the same time as the three martyrs, but had effected his release. (HMB)

> firmed, '*hath caused the Countenances of Glory to be prostrated upon the dust, hath rent in twain the Veil of Grandeur in the Sublime Paradise, and lacerated the hearts of the favored ones established upon the loftiest seats.*' And yet, in the Kitáb-i-Aqdas, a forgiving Lord assures this same brother, this '*source of perversion,*' '*from whose own soul the winds of passion had risen and blown upon him,*' to '*fear not because of thy deeds,*' bids him '*return unto God, humble, submissive and lowly,*' and affirms that '*He will put away from thee thy sins,*' and that '*thy Lord is the Forgiving, the Mighty, the All-Merciful.*' . . .
>
> A temporary breach had admittedly been made in the ranks of its [the Faith of God's] supporters. Its glory had been eclipsed, and its annals stained forever. Its name, however, could not be obliterated, its spirit was far from broken, nor could this so-called schism tear its fabric asunder. The Covenant of the Báb, to which reference has already been made, with its immutable truths, incontrovertible prophecies, and repeated warnings, stood guard over that Faith, insuring its integrity, demonstrating its incorruptibility, and perpetuating its influence.[8]

Áqá Riḍá, writing of this episode, mentions a Persian tobacconist, Ḥasan Áqáy-i-Salmásí, who was not a believer but was well aware of the turn of events; he witnessed all that was happening, as Bahá'u'lláh passed by his shop. Yet, subsequently, Mírzá Yaḥyá had the temerity to write to his partisans that it was Bahá'u'lláh who did not come to meet him face to face, and that he himself had kept the tryst; and for good measure, he added another untruth to his false statement, that none had seen him all the way from Baghdád to Adrianople, whereas from Mosul onwards he had travelled in the retinue of Bahá'u'lláh.

The house of 'Izzat Áqá was newly built and possessed a fine view of the river and the southern orchards of the city. Its rooms were spacious, and although the *bírúní* was smaller than the *andarúní*, both had ample space and large courtyards planted with a variety of trees. Mírzá Maḥmúd-i-Káshání did the gardening and kept the flower-beds well stocked. The companions moved to another house in the same neighbourhood, large enough for them all and provided with a Turkish bath. Visitors also lodged in this house, amongst them Mírzá Báqir-i-Shírází (see Addendum V), whose sister was married to Mírzá Yaḥyá. He arrived in the company of Áqá 'Abdu'lláh-i-'Arab. Mírzá Báqir deplored the insubordination and defection of Mírzá Yaḥyá and had written a treatise in refutation of his claims and vanities. He was an excellent calligraphist, and stayed for a time in Adrianople, copying and transcribing Tablets.

'Abdu'l-Bahá in Adrianople with His brothers and companions of Bahá'u'lláh. Standing (L. to R.): Áqá Muḥammad-Qulíy-i-Iṣfahání, Mírzá Naṣru'lláh-i-Tafrishí, Nabíl-i-A'ẓam, Mírzá Áqá Ján (Khádimu'lláh), Mishkín-Qalam, Mírzá 'Alíy-i-Sayyáḥ, Áqá Ḥusayn-i-Áshchí, and Áqá 'Abdu'l-Ghaffár-i-Iṣfahání. Seated (L. to R.): Mírzá Muḥammad-Javád-i-Qazvíní, Mírzá Mihdí (the Purest Branch), 'Abdu'l-Bahá, Mírzá Muḥammad-Qulí (with, presumably, one of his children), and Siyyid Mihdíy-i-Dahijí. Seated on the ground (L. to R.): Majdi'd-Dín (son of Mírzá Músá, Áqáy-i-Kalím) and Mírzá Muḥammad-'Alí (half-brother of 'Abdu'l-Bahá).

We have already noted the high esteem in which Khurshíd Páshá, the Válí of Adrianople, held Bahá'u'lláh. Áqá Ḥusayn-i-Áshchí relates that he was most eager to entertain Bahá'u'lláh at Government House, but at first He did not accept to call on Khurshíd Páshá. But one day in the month of Ramaḍán, when the Governor had invited the divines and the leading men of the city to break their fast at his house, he entreated 'Abdu'l-Bahá to beg Bahá'u'lláh to honour that great feast and glittering assemblage with His presence. Bahá'u'lláh accepted that invitation. Áshchí relates how the guests, amongst whom were both men of substance and men of high learning, sat spellbound, captivated and exhilarated by Bahá'u'lláh's utterance. Humbly and courteously they asked Him questions which He answered with overwhelming power and authority, to their marvel and complete satisfaction. And when, Áshchí remarks, the Sulṭán decreed Bahá'u'lláh's removal from Adrianople, these men were sorely aggrieved and felt acutely their loss. Being signally honoured by Bahá'u'lláh, Khurshíd Páshá requested 'Abdu'l-Bahá to spend as many evenings as He could in Government House, during that month of Ramaḍán, which, Áshchí says, the Most Great Branch granted him.

More visitors were now coming to Adrianople. Two brothers, Áqá Muḥammad-Ismá'íl and Áqá Naṣru'lláh came and stayed for a while. They were followed by Siyyid Mihdíy-i-Dahijí, Áqá Jamshíd-i-Gurjí (see Addendum V), Mírzá 'Alíy-i-Sayyáḥ-i-Mará̲gh̲i'í and Ḥusayn-i-Bag̲h̲dádí. They were lodged in the *bírúní* of the house of 'Izzat Áqá. We have already noted the arrival of Nabíl-i-A'ẓam, Muḥammad-Javád-i-Qazvíní and the renowned calligraphist, Mishkín-Qalam. Another visitor was Ḥájí Abu'l-Qásim-i-Shírází, who came from Egypt. He was soon, because of his wealth, to be embroiled in the intrigues of Ḥájí Mírzá Ḥasan Khán, the Persian consul in Cairo. As before, meetings were held regularly in the house of the companions, for the recital of Tablets and verses, to which Bahá'u'lláh came many a time. Then a house was rented for Mishkín-Qalam so that he could practise his art unhindered. Nabíl and Áqá Jamshíd joined him there at a later date. This house too Bahá'u'lláh honoured several times with His visits. Áqáy-i-Kalím also moved to a house near the house of 'Izzat Áqá.

The remaining months in the house of 'Izzat Áqá constituted the most fecund period in the whole course of the ministry of Bahá'u'lláh:

Tablets and verses flowed continuously from His pen and His tongue. One day, Áqá Riḍá relates, Bahá'u'lláh said to His companions and the visitors, as He paced the courtyard of the *bírúní*: 'Today in the bath We wrote something to Náṣiri'd-Dín Sháh; it is not transcribed yet, but who will "bell the cat"?' There were many, Áqá Riḍá says, who coveted that distinction, but the great task, which would call forth such heroism and immolation, was specified, as we shall see, for a youth, as yet impervious to the power emanating from Bahá'u'lláh.

It was during His testing years in Adrianople that Bahá'u'lláh proclaimed the Revelation with which God had entrusted Him. No better description of those fruitful years could be given, than that from the pen of the Guardian of the Bahá'í Faith, as he writes in *God Passes By*:

> Though He Himself was bent with sorrow, and still suffered from the effects of the attempt on His life, and though He was well aware a further banishment was probably impending, yet, undaunted by the blow which His Cause had sustained, and the perils with which it was encompassed, Bahá'u'lláh arose with matchless power, even before the ordeal was overpast, to proclaim the Mission with which He had been entrusted to those who, in East and West, had the reins of supreme temporal authority in their grasp. The day-star of His Revelation was, through this very Proclamation, destined to shine in its meridian glory, and His Faith manifest the plenitude of its divine power.
>
> A period of prodigious activity ensued which, in its repercussions, outshone the vernal years of Bahá'u'lláh's ministry. 'Day and night,' an eyewitness has written, 'the Divine verses were raining down in such number that it was impossible to record them. Mírzá Áqá Ján wrote them as they were dictated, while the Most Great Branch was continually occupied in transcribing them. There was not a moment to spare.' . . . Bahá'u'lláh, Himself, referring to the verses revealed by Him, has written: '*Such are the outpourings . . . from the clouds of Divine Bounty that within the space of an hour the equivalent of a thousand verses hath been revealed.*' '*So great is the grace vouchsafed in this day that in a single day and night, were an amanuensis capable of accomplishing it to be found, the equivalent of the Persian Bayán would be sent down from the heaven of Divine holiness.*' '*I swear by God!*' He, in another connection has affirmed, '*In those days the equivalent of all that hath been sent down aforetime unto the Prophets hath been revealed.*' '*That which hath already been revealed in this land* (Adrianople),' He, furthermore, referring to the copiousness of His writings, has declared, '*secretaries are incapable of transcribing. It has, therefore, remained for the most part untranscribed.*'
>
> Already in the very midst of that grievous crisis, and even before it came

to a head, Tablets unnumbered were streaming from the pen of Bahá'u'lláh, in which the implications of His newly-asserted claims were fully expounded. The Súriy-i-Amr [Command], the Lawḥ-i-Nuqṭih [Tablet of the Point], the Lawḥ-i-Aḥmad [The Tablet of Aḥmad], the Súriy-i-Aṣḥáb [The Tablet of the Companions], the Lawḥ-i-Sayyáḥ, the Súriy-i-Damm [The Tablet of Blood], the Súriy-i-Ḥajj [The Tablet of Pilgrimage], the Lawḥu'r-Rúḥ [The Tablet of Spirit], the Lawḥu'r-Riḍván [The Tablet of Riḍván], the Lawḥu't-Tuqá [The Tablet of Piety or The Fear of God] were among the Tablets which His pen had already set down when He transferred His residence to the house of 'Izzat Áqá. Almost immediately after the 'Most Great Separation' had been effected, the weightiest Tablets associated with His sojourn in Adrianople were revealed. The Súriy-i-Mulúk, the most momentous Tablet revealed by Bahá'u'lláh (Súrih of Kings) in which He, for the first time, directs His words collectively to the entire company of the monarchs of East and West, and in which the Sulṭán of Turkey, and his ministers, the kings of Christendom, the French and Persian Ambassadors accredited to the Sublime Porte, the Muslim ecclesiastical leaders in Constantinople, its wise men and inhabitants, the people of Persia and the philosophers of the world are separately addressed; the Kitáb-i-Badí', His apologia, written to refute the accusations levelled against Him by Mírzá Mihdíy-i-Ras͟htí,* corresponding to the Kitáb-i-Íqán, revealed in defense of the Bábí Revelation; the Munáját͟háy-i-Ṣíyám (Prayers for Fasting), written in anticipation of the Book of His Laws; the first Tablet to Napoleon III, in which the Emperor of the French is addressed and the sincerity of his professions put to the test; the Lawḥ-i-Sulṭán, His detailed epistle to Náṣiri'd Dín S͟háh, in which the aims, purposes and principles of His Faith are expounded and the validity of His Mission demonstrated; the Súriy-i-Ra'ís [Chieftain], begun in the village of Kás͟hánih on His way to Gallipoli, and completed shortly after at Gyáwur-Kyuy – these may be regarded not only as the most outstanding among the innumerable Tablets revealed in Adrianople, but as occupying a foremost position among all the writings of the Author of the Bahá'í Revelation.[9]

* This man was a judge in Constantinople. *Kitab-i-Badí'* is written as though it were Áqá Muḥammad-'Alí Tambákú-Furús͟h-i-Iṣfahání who is replying to Mírzá Mihdíy-i-Ras͟htí. *Badí'* means 'Unique'.

28

Adrianople – the Last Years

At the time when Mírzá Yaḥyá failed to abide by his promise and did not appear at the mosque to face Bahá'u'lláh, we learn from Áqá Riḍá that Bahá'u'lláh's faithful brother, Áqáy-i-Kalím, was in Anatolia. By way of Salonica he had gone to Smyrna, to which town Mír Muḥammad also repaired at a later date, relating to him the full account of Mírzá Yaḥyá's cowardice and failure to keep the tryst. After a while, Bahá'u'lláh sent Nabíl-i-A'ẓam to ask Áqáy-i-Kalím to return to Adrianople, and he instantly obeyed.

About this time (1867), a powerful Tablet, in which reference is made to a vision, was revealed for Siyyid Ḥusayn-'Alí, a Bábí who resided in Baghdád, and on that same night the Siyyid broke away completely from the company of the partisans of Mírzá Yaḥyá. When the Tablet reached Baghdád, and the circumstances became known, a number of other Bábís did likewise. This Tablet is not the same as the *Lawḥ-i-Ru'yá* (The Tablet of the Vision) which was revealed, at a later date, in the Holy Land.

The Azalís who were in Baghdád now wished to have a confrontation and debate with the Bahá'ís, in the presence of Jewish, Christian and Muslim divines who were to act as arbiters. The Bahá'ís considered the proposal to be ludicrous, but finally it was agreed that a few from each side should meet with two men: Ḥájí Muḥammad-Ḥusayn – Ḥakím-i-Qazvíní (physician of Qazvín; see Addendum V) – and Áqá Mírzá Aḥmad-i-Hindí (the Indian), who had accepted neither the claim of Bahá'u'lláh, nor the position of Ṣubḥ-i-Azal. Just about then, *Lawḥ-i-Qamíṣ* (The Tablet of the Shirt or Robe) had reached them from Adrianople, and Mírzá Mihdíy-i-Káshání read portions of it in that gathering. The partisans of Mírzá Yaḥyá totally ignored it. Instead, they produced the *Dalá'il-i-Sab'ih* (The Seven Proofs) by the Báb, completely misinterpreting what they read, and the meeting broke up inconclusively. But the two arbiters, the physician of Qazvín and the Indian Bábí, who had hitherto kept aloof and apart, became convinced of the truth of the claim of Bahá'u'lláh and gave Him their unreserved allegiance. At a later period, when troubles arose in Baghdád, Ḥájí Muḥammad-Ḥusayn stepped forth to defend the Bahá'ís. A vociferous official of the Persian Consulate challenged him arrogantly: 'Who art thou?' to which he retorted, 'Who art thou?' 'I am the dragoman of the government', the official said. Unabashed, the physician replied boldly: 'And I am the dragoman of the nation.'

It was also in 1867 that Mírzá Badí'u'lláh, the youngest son of Bahá'u'lláh, was born.

Mírzá 'Alíy-i-Sayyáḥ (Mullá Ádí Guzal), who had been the courier of the Báb and at one time His personal attendant, together with Mishkín-Qalam and Áqá Jamshíd-i-Gurjí (or Bukhárá'í) left Adrianople and went to Istanbul. It is not known exactly why they did so. Ustád Muḥammad-'Alíy-i-Salmání seems to suggest that Mishkín-Qalam wished to earn money with his splendid and almost unrivalled (at the time) calligraphy and that Bahá'u'lláh was not pleased. Be that as it may, that journey had incalculable consequences for the three of them. About the same time, Ḥájí 'Alí-'Askar (see Addendum V), who had attained the presence of the Báb in Tabríz, and his family took up residence in the house which Mishkín-Qalam and his two companions had vacated. Other arrivals included Áqá Mírzá Zaynu'l-'Ábidín, Mírzá 'Alí-Akbar-i-Bujnurdí and Abu'l-Qásim Khán (who came with a lady whom Áqá Riḍá calls the Princess). They had apparently first gone on pilgrimage to Mecca. Then, the arrival of the widow of Mírzá Muṣṭafáy-i-Naráqí (who had recently been put to death in Tabríz) and her child, also named Muṣṭafá, and Áqá Luṭfu'lláh together with his young son, further increased the number of the Bahá'ís in Adrianople. But Siyyid Mihdíy-i-Dahijí, honoured by Bahá'u'lláh with the designation 'Ismu'lláhu'l-Mihdí'* (who, several decades later, broke the Covenant of Bahá'u'lláh) left for Baghdád, and, on the road, encountered the Bahá'ís who had been rounded up in Baghdád and were being taken to Mosul. Bahá'u'lláh refers to this outrage perpetrated against His people, in His Letter to Náṣiri'd-Dín Sháh. The arrest and transportation of these Bahá'ís was preceded by the brutal murder in Baghdád of Áqá 'Abdu'r-Rasúl-i-Qumí, whose task it was to carry

* 'The Name of God Who Guides Aright'.

water in sheepskins from the river to the house of Bahá'u'lláh. One morning, by the riverside, enemies were waiting for him. They set upon him and with daggers tore open his bowels. He staggered on, clinging with one hand to his load of water, holding back with the other his entrails, until he reached the house. Then he collapsed and died. Áqá Ḥusayn-i-Áshchí gives a graphic and moving account of the day when the letter conveying the news of the martyrdom of Áqá 'Abdu'r-Rasúl reached Bahá'u'lláh. Those who were present and heard Bahá'u'lláh read the account wept unrestrainedly. Bahá'u'lláh assured them that they were lamenting the cruel death of Áqá 'Abdu'r-Rasúl, but he had attained what he had always desired – the station of martyrdom.

The increase in the number of Bahá'ís in Adrianople was apparently causing concern in the ranks of the Ottoman officials, especially since Siyyid Muḥammad-i-Iṣfahání, who had also gone to Istanbul, together with Áqá Ján Big-i-Kaj-Kuláh, like him a partisan of Mírzá Yaḥyá and a former officer in the Ottoman artillery, were constantly feeding false information to the authorities. Mishkín-Qalam, as expected, had obtained wide fame as a calligraphist and was close to the person of Ḥájí Mírzá Ḥusayn Khán, the Persian ambassador. Mírzá 'Alíy-i-Sayyáḥ had, likewise, won the esteem of Ḥájí Mírzá Ḥusayn Khán. But both of them, according to Áqá Riḍá (and Ustád Muḥammad-'Alí as well) were not sufficiently circumspect, talking unwisely in the circles to which they had found access, particularly in the presence of the Persian ambassador. The Guardian of the Bahá'í Faith refers thus to their overstepping of the bounds of wisdom: 'The indiscretion committed by some of its [the Faith of Bahá'u'lláh's] overzealous followers, who had arrived in Constantinople, no doubt, aggravated an already acute situation.'[1]

Then came news of Ḥájí Mírzá Ḥaydar-'Alí's detention and banishment to the Súdán, when he had gone to Egypt at the bidding of Bahá'u'lláh. However, the news reaching Adrianople was far from clear, and Bahá'u'lláh sent Nabíl to Egypt to make proper enquiries. Nabíl composed a poem in *mathnaví* style, addressed to Ismá'íl Páshá, the Khedive of Egypt, and sent a copy to Adrianople, but he too was detained and kept in prison in Alexandria. We shall come to the story of his Alexandrian imprisonment in the next chapter.

The outrages in Baghdád; the martyrdoms in Írán; the extortions of

Áqá Ḥusayn-i-Iṣfahání, Mis͟hkín-Qalam

the Persian consul-general in Cairo which had led to the arrest, the barbarous treatment and the banishment of Ḥájí Mírzá Ḥaydar-'Alí and his companions to Khartúm; the totally unexpected detention of Nabíl-i-A'ẓam in Alexandria; the arrests and imprisonments in the capital of the moribund Ottoman Empire (which we are about to witness), were all preludes to a far greater dénouement bringing to a close the episode of Adrianople. To this event Bahá'u'lláh alluded with increasing frequency, for it was near at hand.

The closing years at Adrianople were also marked by significant internal developments. The appellations 'Bábí' and 'the people of the Bayán' gave way to 'Bahá'í' and 'the people of Bahá'; the greeting '*Alláh-u-Akbar*' (God is the Greatest) was replaced by '*Alláh-u-Abhá*' (God is the Most Glorious), although it ought to be noted that both of these greetings as well as another, '*Alláh-u-Ajmal*' (God is the Most Beauteous), were sanctioned by the Báb. The *Súriy-i-Ghuṣn (The Tablet of the Branch)*,[2] revealed for Mírzá 'Alí-Riḍá, a prominent Bahá'í of Khurásán, envisaged the station of Ghuṣnu'lláhu'l-A'ẓam (the Most Great, or Mighty, Branch), the eldest Son of Bahá'u'lláh, Who in future years, known by the name 'Abdu'l-Bahá, was to be the Centre of Bahá'u'lláh's peerless Covenant. The significant journey of Nabíl-i-A'ẓam to Shíráz and then to Baghdád – prior to his mission in Egypt – bearing with him the two Tablets of the Pilgrimage (*Súriy-i-Ḥajj* I and II) recently revealed, which he recited whilst visiting those hallowed cities, must be particularly noted. Nabíl carried gifts with him, as well, for the wife of the Báb. Mullá Báqir-i-Tabrízí, one of the Báb's Letters of the Living, who had lived on into this seventh decade of the nineteenth century, and Mullá Ṣádiq-i-Muqaddas-i-Khurásání,[3] on whom the honorific title of Ismu'lláhu'l-Aṣdaq (the Name of God the Most Truthful) was later conferred by Bahá'u'lláh, one of the very few survivors of the heroic company of Shaykh Ṭabarsí, gave their allegiance joyously to Bahá'u'lláh. A martyr of the same period, Áqá Najaf-'Alí, was also a survivor of a holocaust of the past: the episode of Zanján;[4] at the moment of death, he gave his gold to the executioner and died with the name of Bahá'u'lláh on his lips.

Mírzá Músáy-i-Javáhirí had sent three horses from Baghdád as a gift to Bahá'u'lláh. Feeling that the expense of keeping a stable was difficult to meet, He ordered their removal to Istanbul to be sold. Darvísh Ṣidq-'Alí, Áqá Muḥammad-Báqir-i-Qahvih-chí and Ustád

هو البهی الأبهی
هذا ما نزّل من جبروت العزّة بلسان القدرة والقوّة على
النبيين من قبل وانّا اخذنا جواهره واقمصناه قميص الاختصار
فضلاً على الاحبار ليوفوا بعهد الله ويؤدّوا اماناته
فی انفسهم وليكوننّ بجوهر التّقى فی ارض الرّوح من الفائزين
يا ابن الرّوح
فی اوّل القول املك قلباً جيّداً حسناً منيراً لتملك ملكاً

Opening passage of The Hidden Words *in the Calligraphy of Mishkín-Qalam. This page consists of the whole of the preamble to* The Hidden Words *beginning: 'He is the Glory of Glories! This is that which hath descended . . .' The first of the Hidden Words: 'O Son of Spirit!' begins on the penultimate line.*

Muḥammad-'Alíy-i-Salmání set out for the Ottoman capital with the horses. Áqá 'Abdu'l-Ghaffár had also gone on an errand to Istanbul (to sell some goods, according to Áqá Riḍá). No sooner had they set foot in the capital than they were detained. Their detention was preceded by the arrest of Mishkín-Qalam and his companions, whose outspokenness and the intrigues of their enemies had borne fruit. But in the process, the mischief-makers, too, were entrapped. Both Siyyid Muḥammad-i-Iṣfahání and Áqá Ján Big-i-Kaj-Kuláh were apprehended, and the latter was divested of his rank and Ottoman decorations. Áqá Riḍá relates that unsigned letters, purporting to have emanated from the Bahá'ís and boasting of their numbers and their resolution, were thrown into the houses of the notables of Istanbul. This ploy (or something like it), which recoiled upon its perpetrators, was adopted in Ṭihrán, decades later, with exactly similar results. Ustád Muḥammad-'Alí writes of the interrogations to which they were subjected. Officials wanted to know whether Bahá'u'lláh had claimed to be the Mahdí. The Bahá'ís answered in the negative, which was of course true because that claim belonged to the Báb, but apparently this reply much dismayed the interrogators. Both Áqá Riḍá and Ustád Muḥammad-'Alí mention that the officials impounded whatever they could find of books and papers in the possession of the prisoners, but did not find anything seditious. The head of the police was greatly impressed by the prayers which Áqá Muḥammad-Báqir carried and made him recite them.

At first Mishkín-Qalam and his companions, and Ustád Muḥammad-'Alí and his, were kept apart in separate prisons, neither group knowing of the detention of the other. But before long they were all brought together. Ustád Muḥammad-'Alí relates that Mishkín-Qalam was particularly distraught, because he had no pen or paper with which to exercise his craft. But at last, the officials succumbed to his loud expostulations and, to obtain some peace, provided him with all the writing material he needed, which greatly pacified him. (Today those excellent specimens of calligraphy which his pen inscribed will fetch hundreds, if not thousands, in sale rooms.)

Meanwhile matters were coming to a head in Adrianople. Bahá'ís there were called several times to the administrative quarters of the government. They were counted one by one and their names were recorded, to their total puzzlement. Áqá Riḍá states that each time they were called away they had no hope of being returned to their houses. They did not know what was happening nor what was to happen. But Bahá'u'lláh knew. He told some of his companions to leave Adrianople. 'Why should all be imprisoned,' He said, 'and no one be left to teach the Cause of God?' Ḥájí Muḥammad-Ismá'íl-i-Dhabíḥ, brother of Ḥájí Mírzá Aḥmad-i-Káshání, Mírzá 'Alí-Akbar-i-Naráqí and a siyyid from Shíráz all reached Adrianople as the storm broke. Bahá'u'lláh did not allow them to stay and bade them go to Gallipoli instantly.

When the ministers of Sulṭán 'Abdu'l-'Azíz decided to banish Bahá'u'lláh to 'Akká and Mírzá Yaḥyá to Cyprus, Khurshíd Páshá, the Válí of Adrianople, who was devoted to the person of Bahá'u'lláh, refused to be associated in any way with the enforcement of the imperial rescript. He informed Bahá'u'lláh accordingly, expressed his regret and disgust, packed his bags, ostensibly to go to some distant place on urgent business, but moved quietly to a locality nearby to

Family and Companions of Bahá'u'lláh: this photograph was probably taken towards the close of Bahá'u'lláh's exile in Adrianople. Seated (L. to R.): possibly Ḍiyá'u'lláh (half-brother of 'Abdu'l-Bahá), Mírzá Muḥammad-Qulí (half-brother of Bahá'u'lláh), Mírzá Muḥammad-'Alí (half-brother of 'Abdu'l-Bahá), Mírzá Músá (Áqáy-i-Kalím). Standing: Mírzá Áqá Ján (Khádimu'lláh) behind Mírzá Muḥammad-'Alí.

watch the course of events. Now it was the function of his deputy to carry out the odious task, which was done with utmost harshness and insensibility. It ought to be noted that Khurshíd Páshá's predecessors, Muḥammad Páshá-i-Qibrisí (the Cypriot), who had once been the Grand Vizier of the Ottoman Empire, and Sulaymán Páshá (a Ṣúfí of the Qádiríyyih Order) had evinced no less admiration and esteem for Bahá'u'lláh.*

Áshchí maintains that 'Izzat Áqá, the Páshá who owned the house where Bahá'u'lláh resided, had become a government spy, dropping in at odd times to note who was there, and how many were the residents and visitors. As already mentioned, the arrival of a few Bahá'ís (their numbers greatly exaggerated by the mischief-makers) had caused alarm in high places. Those mischief-makers had implanted seeds of doubt in the besotted minds of the ministers of the Sulṭán; Fu'ád Páshá, the Minister of Foreign Affairs, was particularly alarmed by the suggestion of Bahá'u'lláh's possible entanglement with Bulgarian revolutionaries. It sounds laughable at this distance of time, but in its day the frightened Minister, already prejudiced, took it seriously.

Then the storm broke.

* According to British consular records (FO 195 794), Muḥammad Páshá-i-Qibrisí was Governor of Adrianople until April 1864, and was followed by Sulaymán Páshá who died in December 1864; he was succeeded by 'Árif Páshá (d. December 1865).

Fu'ád Páshá (from Farley, Turkey*)*

29

Banishment to 'Akká

ONE day, early in the morning, soldiers surrounded the house of Bahá'u'lláh, and would let no one enter or depart. Those Bahá'ís who kept shops or had trading centres were all arrested and removed to the *Seraye*.

Áqá Riḍá states that before nightfall they were called, one by one, to the presence of the Ottoman officials and were interrogated to make them admit that they were Bahá'ís. They were told that their goods would be sold or auctioned, which the officials proceeded to do the next day. Great commotion ensued amongst the populace, who were bewildered and aghast. 'What has happened', they queried, 'that these people are thus treated? We never saw anything in them but truthfulness, trustworthiness and piety . . . Why should they be subjected to such injustice and atrocity?' Some tried to console the Bahá'ís, to express their sympathy, Áqá Riḍá states, and some wept openly.

Then 'a number of the consuls of foreign powers came,' Áqá Riḍá writes, 'were admitted to the presence [of Bahá'u'lláh] and requested that He should bid them render Him the utmost of assistance. "We will then inform our governments and stop such behaviour." ' But Bahá'u'lláh replied, according to Áqá Riḍá, 'In such matters We have not turned, We will not turn, to anyone at all.' 'He was gracious to them,' Áqá Riḍá states, 'and they left.'

Áqá Ḥusayn-i-Á<u>sh</u><u>ch</u>í, recollecting those events many decades later, says exactly the same, that Bahá'u'lláh did not accept the offer of assistance and intervention by the consuls of the foreign powers. His account is more detailed since, being cook in the household, he was free to come and go as he liked, and could see at close quarters all that went on around Bahá'u'lláh. He relates the circumstances of the siege of the house of Bahá'u'lláh by the troops; the insistence of <u>Kh</u>ur<u>sh</u>íd Pá<u>sh</u>á's deputies that Bahá'u'lláh leave Adrianople at the earliest moment; and His refusal to do this and embark on yet another exile, because His steward owed a substantial sum of money in the bazars and could not pay these debts until His men in Istanbul were freed to sell their horses.

Á<u>sh</u><u>ch</u>í continues his account: '. . . all of a sudden the consuls of the foreign powers became aware of what was happening and together they sought the presence of Bahá'u'lláh. The soldiers stationed around the house, blocking the way to everyone, could not prevent the consuls from entering. After paying their homage, they said they had come as a body, and any one of them whom Bahá'u'lláh might command would take up the issue with the Turks and ward off this evil.' Á<u>sh</u><u>ch</u>í states that Bahá'u'lláh declined categorically their oft-repeated offer of assistance and intervention, saying: 'You wish me to give you the word to bring Me relief, but My relief lies in the hands of God. My focus is God, and to Him alone do I turn.' Then Á<u>sh</u><u>ch</u>í relates that the consuls continued to call and no one was able to prevent them. He himself took them to the presence of the Most Great Branch. And he adds that some of the high Turkish officials were scandalized and infuriated by the preferential treatment of those foreign representatives. The easy access they had to the person of the eldest Son of Bahá'u'lláh riled them, particularly as the Ottoman officials were usually put off on some pretext. Áqá Ḥusayn writes that when he heard the Big-Bá<u>sh</u>í threaten to punish the troops on the morrow, should they again fail to prevent the consuls entering the house, he reported this to Bahá'u'lláh, Who smiled and, turning to His eldest Son, asked, 'Did you hear what Ḥusayn has said?' Nor did the matter rest there, Á<u>sh</u><u>ch</u>í reports, for the following day the consuls came as usual, and the guards did not, could not stop them. The Most Great Branch told them of the Ottoman officer's threats, which highly amused them, and one jestingly suggested that they might ask the British consul to lead the way next time, to receive the beating from the Big-Bá<u>sh</u>í. As to the officer himself, Áqá Ḥusayn says, his superiors were displeased when they heard of his rash threats and reprimanded him, for they realized their impotence to prevent the visits of the foreign representatives, who continued to come and go whenever they wished.

The Guardian of the Bahá'í Faith thus writes of the closing stage of Bahá'u'lláh's sojourn in Adrianople:

> Suddenly, one morning, the house of Bahá'u'lláh was surrounded by soldiers, sentinels were posted at its gates, His followers were again summoned by the authorities, interrogated, and ordered to make ready for their departure. '*The loved ones of God and His kindred,*' is Bahá'u'lláh's

testimony in the Súriy-i-Ra'ís, '*were left on the first night without food . . . The people surrounded the house, and Muslims and Christians wept over Us . . . We perceived that the weeping of the people of the Son* (Christians) *exceeded the weeping of others – a sign for such as ponder.*' 'A great tumult seized the people,' writes Áqá Riḍá, one of the stoutest supporters of Bahá'u'lláh, exiled with him all the way from Baghdád to 'Akká. 'All were perplexed and full of regret . . . Some expressed their sympathy, others consoled us, and wept over us . . . Most of our possessions were auctioned at half their value.' Some of the consuls of foreign powers called on Bahá'u'lláh, and expressed their readiness to intervene with their respective governments on His behalf – suggestions for which He expressed appreciation, but which He firmly declined. '*The consuls of that city* (Adrianople) *gathered in the presence of this Youth at the hour of His departure,*' He Himself has written, '*and expressed their desire to aid Him. They, verily, evinced towards Us manifest affection.*'

The Persian Ambassador promptly informed the Persian consuls in 'Iráq and Egypt that the Turkish government had withdrawn its protection from the Bábís, and that they were free to treat them as they pleased.[1]

The present writer is well aware of the existence in governmental archives of certain documents which suggest that Bahá'u'lláh Himself petitioned foreign consuls and asked for their aid and protection (see Addendum II). He cannot (at the moment) satisfactorily resolve and deal with this problem. But he must point out a number of valid facts in this respect. As we have seen, Bahá'u'lláh Himself and the people who were there at the time – Áqá Riḍá and Áqá Ḥusayn-i-Áshchí – recollecting, decades apart, the events of Adrianople, declare emphatically that the consuls themselves came with offers of aid and protection which were courteously and graciously declined. In the Ottoman Archives, there is a letter purportedly from Bahá'u'lláh, which is written in Persian, and yet the document in the French Archives is in Turkish, and in poor Turkish. How was it, one might ask, that Bahá'u'lláh would write to the Turks in Persian, and to the French in a language which was not His own? Expert opinion on documents in Turkish states that they 'were written by non-Turks and contain numerous mistakes of grammar and spelling. Some misspellings are of Arabic words, and this suggests that the scribes were non-Muslim, possibly Armenians.' Would such errors originate from the same Pen from which came the *Kitáb-i-Íqán*, *The Hidden Words*, *The Seven Valleys*, the *Kitáb-i-Badí'*, and numberless Tablets in Arabic? It is impossible.

And the handwriting of the Turkish documents is certainly not that of Bahá'u'lláh, nor of any one of His amanuenses, from whom innumerable specimens exist.

Áqá Riḍá writes: 'In brief, there was tremendous commotion. Most of our goods were sold at half-price. The stock of tobacco belonging to Ḥájí 'Alí-'Askar was purchased at a very low price. They gave a promissory note to pay the money within a few months, but eventually failed to make the payment. Áqá Muḥammad-'Alíy-i-Jilawdár and Áqá Muḥammad-'Alíy-i-Iṣfahání [see Addendum V], who were married, were forced to divorce their wives because relatives would not allow them to accompany their husbands . . . And it was rumoured in those days that whoever had his name recorded in a register would be allowed to go, but those whose names were not there would not be permitted to leave.

'The two brothers, Ḥájí Ja'far and Ḥájí Taqí, resided in the inn. They were not molested nor imprisoned. It was therefore assumed that they would be left behind. But they were most of the time in the *bírúní*, and they came and went without hindrance. One night after sunset, we were all in the *bírúní*, and Ḥájí Ja'far and his brother were both there. Ḥájí Ja'far got up and went over to the window which overlooked the street. Soon, we heard a hissing noise and, going to investigate, we found that the Ḥájí had cut his throat, and blood was gushing out. We were greatly perplexed. Should he die, we said, how could we prove that he had committed suicide? And so we hurried to convey the news to the Most Great Branch. He came out to the *bírúní*, and since the house of the Cadi (*Qáḍí*) was near, He sent for him and also for a surgeon, named Muḥammad Effendi, who lived in the neighbourhood. Then a crowd gathered. The surgeon took hold of the Ḥájí's throat, cut as it was. This action revived the Ḥájí, who began to speak. The Cadi asked him, "You did this to yourself?" "I myself", he replied. "But why?" the Cadi asked. "Because", he answered, "I saw that I was about to be deprived of accompanying my Lord, of the bounty of His presence. So I did not wish to live." "With what instrument did you cut your throat?" the Cadi asked. "With a razor, such as is used by barbers, which I bought in the bazar", the Ḥájí replied. They instituted a search, found the razor [in the street] and brought it. The Ḥájí was repeatedly questioned, and he stoutly stood by his answer that he found the thought of life unbearable in separation, and wished to die. All these questions and answers were put down in writing.'

The surgeon expertly attended to Ḥájí Ja'far's self-inflicted wound and eventually he recovered. Áqá Riḍá comments on the astonishment of the onlookers, who said: 'These people know that banishment entails imprisonment and much hardship, yet they prefer it to being left behind, and choose death rather than separation; what is this evident attraction that has seized them?' Some of them, Áqá Riḍá says, burst into tears over Ḥájí Ja'far's plight, and some tried to comfort him. Referring to this attempt at suicide by Ḥájí Ja'far-i-Tabrízí, the Guardian of the Bahá'í Faith comments that it was 'an act which Bahá'u' lláh, in the Súriy-i-Ra'ís, characterizes as "*unheard of in bygone centuries,*" and which "*God hath set apart for this Revelation, as an evidence of the power of His Might.*"'[2] The *Súriy-i-Ra'ís* was revealed at Ká<u>sh</u>ánih on the way to Gallipoli.

Ḥájí Ja'far had to be put to bed in the *bírúní* of the house of Bahá'u'lláh. There Bahá'u'lláh visited him, sat by his bedside, consoled him, and advised him: 'Look up to God and be content with His will.'

Áqá Riḍá writes: 'Then, all made ready for emigration. Firstly, they brought several carts for the transportation of the luggage, and a number of the companions went with them. On the same day, Mírzá Yaḥyá and his family, together with Siyyid Muḥammad, were sent ahead. After a week, arrangements were completed for the journey of the Blessed Perfection. In the morning, horse-drawn wagons drew up, and by the time the remainder of the luggage was gathered and loaded, and the members of the family had taken their seats, it was about noon. Then the Blessed Perfection came out. Firstly, He showered His bounties on the Ḥájí and his brother, and recommended them to the care of the landlord and Muḥammad Effendi, the surgeon. Next, He turned to the neighbours and the people of the quarter, who had gathered to bid Him farewell. They came, one by one, sorrow-stricken, to kiss His hands and the hem of His garment, to express their grief at His departure and this deprivation. Indeed that day was a strange day. Methinks the city, its very walls and gates bemoaned their separation from Him. Close to noontide we were on our way. When night approached, we set up tents within three hours of Adrianople. We covered the distance between Adrianople and Gallipoli in five stages. The second stage was a place called Úzún-Kúprí, and the next was Ká<u>sh</u>ánih.'

A view of Gallipoli where Bahá'u'lláh and His family and companions spent a few days in August 1868, before leaving for 'Akká.

It was on 12 August 1868 (22 Rabí'u'th-Thání AH 1285) that Bahá'u'lláh and His companions left the city which He had called 'the Remote Prison' and 'the Land of Mystery'. A Turkish captain named Ḥasan Effendi and a number of soldiers accompanied them. On the fifth day, Gallipoli was reached. A house had been appointed for their reception. Bahá'u'lláh and His family and the womenfolk took residence on the upper floor. Some of the companions were lodged on the floor below. Others were taken to a *khán*. Mírzá 'Alíy-i-Sayyáḥ, Mishkín-Qalam, and other Bahá'ís brought from Istanbul, who had arrived the previous day, had been placed in the same inn. But Mírzá Yaḥyá and his dependents, as well as Siyyid Muḥammad and Áqá Ján-i-Kaj-Kuláh, had been housed in another *khán*. Ustád Muḥammad-'Alíy-i-Salmání and Áqá Jamshíd-i-Gurjí had been singled out by the authorities to be expelled to Írán. They were taken to the frontier and handed to the Kurds, who promptly set them free. Eventually, by different routes, they made their way to 'Akká.

Ustád Muḥammad-'Alí has related their story in his short autobiography. Whilst in Írán Ustád Muḥammad-'Alí met Ḥájí Muḥammad-Ismá'íl-i-Dhabíḥ, whom Bahá'u'lláh refers to as Anís in the *Súriy-i-Ra'ís*, and who attained His presence at Gallipoli. Two others,

Mírzá 'Alí-Akbar-i-Naráqí and his friend (a Shírází siyyid) also shared that bounty of reaching the presence of Bahá'u'lláh in the public bath. Ustád Muḥammad-'Alí has recorded how displeased and upset Ḥájí Muḥammad-Ismá'íl was, when told of the defection of his brother, the fickle Ḥájí Mírzá Aḥmad-i-Káshání, who had been murdered in Baghdád; neither Ustád Muḥammad-'Alí nor Ḥájí Muḥammad-Ismá'íl had until then any knowledge of it. Mírzá Fatḥ-'Alí of Ardistán (see Addendum V), whom Bahá'u'lláh had honoured with the surname Fatḥ-i-A'ẓam (the Most Great Victory) was another prominent Bahá'í whom Ustád Muḥammad-'Alí met in his wanderings in Írán, before he reached the Holy Land. Mírzá Fatḥ-'Alí received Ustád Muḥammad-'Alí with great kindness and took him to his home. Bahá'u'lláh has said of Fatḥ-i-A'ẓam that, all the way from Baghdád to Constantinople, he was with Him in spirit, though not corporeally.

Áqá Riḍá writes of Gallipoli: 'We were there for a few days. God knows how we fared in that time. Once it was rumoured that the Blessed Perfection and His brothers would be sent to one place, and that others would be scattered and banished to a number of localities. Then it was said that all of the companions would be sent to Írán. There was also talk of extermination. It was the thought of separation and dispersal which caused us the most anxiety. The captain who had accompanied us from Adrianople came one night to take his leave. And as he stood humbly, expressing his regrets, the Blessed Perfection addressed him: "Tell the king that this territory will pass out of his hands, and his affairs will be thrown into confusion. Not I speak these words, but God speaketh them." In those moments He was uttering verses which we, who were downstairs, could overhear. They were spoken with such vehemence and power that, methinks, the foundations of the house itself trembled.[3] That man stood silent and submissive. Then the Blessed Perfection said to him: "It would have been meet for His Majesty the Sulṭán to have gathered an assembly and called Us to be present, that he should have investigated the matter, and had he then found any portent of sedition, any sign of anything contrary to the Will of God, to have meted out this treatment to which he hath now resorted. He should have asked Us to present him proofs of what We profess. Should he have found Us wanting, then he could have subjected Us to whatever he wished. He should not have allowed such wrong-doing, such enmity, such injuries, without reason, solely by following the behest of authors of mischief." The captain, listening intently, promised to report what he had heard.'

Indeed, as Áqá Riḍá remarks, all that Bahá'u'lláh foretold in the *Súriy-i-Ra'ís* did come to pass, exactly as He said it would: 'The day is approaching when the Land of Mystery (Adrianople) and what is beside it shall be changed, and shall pass out of the hands of the king, and commotions shall appear, and the voice of lamentation shall be raised, and the evidences of mischief shall be revealed on all sides, and confusion shall spread by reason of that which hath befallen these captives at the hands of the hosts of oppression. The course of things shall be altered, and conditions shall wax so grievous, that the very sands on the desolate hills will moan, and the trees on the mountain will weep, and blood will flow out of all things. Then wilt thou behold the people in sore distress.'[4]

It took exactly a decade, but it came to pass. 'Álí Pá<u>sh</u>á, to whom the *Súriy-i-Ra'ís* was addressed, was swept into oblivion within this decade. 'Abdu'l-'Azíz was toppled from his throne in 1876, losing not only his throne but his life as well. The disastrous war of 1877–8 with Russia followed, which brought the Russians and their Bulgarian allies to the gates of the city of Constantine the Great. Adrianople was occupied by a relentless enemy, and the sufferings of the people were great. Áqá Riḍá, writing as he did in later years, quotes a Turkish captain, who had been in the territory where battles had raged, and who described most vividly the magnitude of the calamity which overtook the Ottoman power. 'May God never again make it the lot of a people', the Turkish captain had said, 'to witness such times and such days. Truly, blood flowed beneath the trees and beneath the stones. The whole plain was bathed in blood, and consternation was such as no one had ever known.'*

In far-off Írán, there was one man, struggling to attain certitude, who waited, waited anxiously to see if Bahá'u'lláh's look into the future would come true. And when it happened and nemesis descended upon 'Abdu'l-'Azíz and his ramshackle realm, he made doubly sure that the report of the downfall of the Sulṭán was correct. Then he dedicated his life, his powerful pen and his vast, unsurpassed erudition to the service of Bahá'u'lláh. That man was Mírzá Abu'l-Faḍl of Gulpáygán.

* See Addendum III concerning the terrible retreat of Turkish troops after the siege of Plevna.

Sulṭán 'Abdu'l-'Azíz

The siege of Plevna and the heroic stand of the Turkish commander, Osman ('Uthmán) Páshá, against terrible odds, and the fall of that fortress which opened the gates of hell, so fired the zeal and evoked the sympathy of an English public-school boy, the son of a wealthy shipbuilder of Newcastle-on-Tyne, that he set his face towards the East and eventually attained high eminence as one of the greatest orientalists of all time. That young Etonian was Edward Granville Browne, whose oriental interest brought him at a later date into close contact with the Faith of Bahá'u'lláh.

After three harrowing days in Gallipoli, when all was uncertain, 'Umar Effendi, the Big-Báshí who had been sent from Constantinople to accompany the exiles, announced that they would be kept together and not dispersed, that they would all be sent to the same destination. However, he stated, only those whose names were on the register qualified for the sea journey at the government's expense; others would be voluntary exiles and would have to pay their own fares. To the amazement of 'Umar Effendi and other officials, Ḥájí 'Alí-Askar, a veteran of the days of the Báb, and a few others who were not included in the list, joyfully bought their tickets for the steamship, an Austrian-Lloyd liner. What kind of people were these, the officials wondered, who would buy their own passages to be transported to an unknown prison in an unknown land?

At last the steamer arrived and dropped anchor. Áqá Riḍá writes: 'On an evening our luggage was taken to the ship, and the next morning boats took us aboard. The sea was very rough. In the same boat where the Blessed Perfection was to sit, I and another one of the companions had the bounty of being in His presence. Jináb-i-Anís and his friends were at the quayside. Tears of deep sorrow welled from their eyes. The Blessed Perfection bade them farewell with great kindness, then took His seat in the boat and told us to be seated. Verses flowed from His lips, . . . and He spoke to us words of consolation. He then said jestingly, "Would it not be a treat if the liner should sink?" but added with utmost power and authority, "But it will not sink, even if it is battered by all the waves." Thus He spoke to us until we reached the steamer, which was very crowded. Amongst the passengers was the Persian consul, newly-appointed to serve in Izmír (Smyrna), with his retinue. But the Blessed Perfection spoke to no one. He went to the upper deck, which was cloistered and very spacious. It was the second day of Jamádíyu'l-Avval AH 1285 – 21 August 1868.

The Guardian of the Bahá'í Faith writes:

> So grievous were the dangers and trials confronting Bahá'u'lláh at the hour of His departure from Gallipoli that He warned His companions that '*this journey will be unlike any of the previous journeys,*' and that whoever did not feel himself '*man enough to face the future*' had best '*depart to whatever place he pleaseth, and be preserved from tests, for hereafter he will find himself unable to leave*' – a warning which His companions unanimously chose to disregard.[5]

Towards sunset of the first day of the journey, the liner appeared before Madellí, where she stopped for a few hours, and the same night proceeded to Smyrna, which she reached soon after sunrise. She remained anchored at Smyrna for two days. Persians resident there came on board to escort their Consul, and seemed to be unaware of the presence of the exiles. Here the grave illness of Mírzá Áqáy-i-Ká<u>sh</u>ání (Jináb-i-Munír), whom Bahá'u'lláh had honoured with the surname

Ismu'lláhu'l-Muníb (the Name of God, the Overlord), necessitated his removal to the local hospital, to his and everyone's distress. The Most Great Branch took him ashore, and stayed with him as long as was possible. He passed away very soon and lies buried in Izmír. Jináb-i-Munír it was who walked with a lantern, in front of Bahá'u'lláh's *kajávih* or steed, all the way from Baghdád to the Black Sea. He was a comely youth, exceedingly handsome, with a sweet, enchanting voice. And he sang and chanted as he walked. When he became a Bábí, his fanatical father took him out into the fields, threw him down and sat on his chest, prepared to cut his throat. But his life was saved to attain the presence of Bahá'u'lláh and serve Him with utter devotion. Áqá Riḍá writes: 'In truth, the very moment he threw himself at the feet of the Blessed Perfection, weeping at his separation, he had already yielded his life and was gazing at the horizon of separation.'

On the second night, the liner cast off anchor to continue the journey to Alexandria, which she gained on a morning two days later. Here the exiles changed ship. This liner, set for Haifa, was also an Austrian-Lloyd. A number of Persians came aboard at Alexandria to pay their respects to Bahá'u'lláh. Among them was Ḥájí Muḥammad-'Alí Pírzádih (usually known as Ḥájí Pírzádih), a celebrated Ṣúfí seer. Unbeknown to the exiles, Nabíl-i-A'ẓam was in the prison-house of Alexandria. He had been sent to Egypt by Bahá'u'lláh to appeal to the Khedive on behalf of Mírzá Haydar-'Alí and six other believers. The fact of his detention in Egypt was known, but not the location of his imprisonment. Several of the exiles went ashore in Alexandria to make purchases; one of them, Áqá Muḥammad-Ibráhím-i-Náẓir (the steward) passed by the prison-house, and Nabíl-i-A'ẓam, looking out, noticed him, and surprised, called him. But let Nabíl himself, that excellent narrator, tell the circumstances of his arrest and imprisonment, and of his unexpected contact with Bahá'u'lláh and His party in Alexandria:

> I went to Manṣúriyyah by the railway [after arriving from Adrianople], searched for Áqá Siyyid Ḥusayn [of Ká<u>sh</u>án], found him and told him why I was there. He said that Mírzá Ḥasan <u>Kh</u>án, the [Persian] Consul, from the day he managed to send those seven to the Súdán, feared for his life, and had placed spies everywhere that they might inform him whenever a stranger arrived in Egypt. 'It is best that you leave your *Ma<u>th</u>naví* with me, carry nothing of the sacred writings with you, and go to Cairo. There

take lodgings at the Takyiy-i-Mawlaví with Shaykh Ibráhím-i-Hamadání, who receives a stipend from Ismá'íl Páshá, and stay until the Khedive returns, when we can find means to send him your *Mathnaví*. I went to Cairo, and lodged with Shaykh Ibráhím, not knowing that he was also a spy. One night, in the early hours of the morning, I saw the Blessed Perfection in the world of dreams. He said: 'Some people have come, asking for permission to harm Mírzá Ḥasan Khán; what sayest thou?' When I awoke I knew that something would happen that day. I went to Sayyid-ná Ḥusayn Square, and walked about for an hour or two. Then I found myself surrounded by a number of people who said, 'They have asked for you at the *Seraye*.' But instead they took me to the house of Mírzá Ḥasan Khán. Then I realized that they had duped me by mentioning the *Seraye*, so that I should give myself up, and not say that I was not a Persian subject. After long talks with the Consul, I was handed over to an official, who put me in chains. Several times they sent for me. At one time, a number of Persian merchants, such as Mírzá Siyyid Javád-i-Shírází, who was a British subject but presided over the Persians, Ḥájí Muḥammad-Taqíy-i-Namází and Ḥájí Muḥammad-Ḥasan-i-Kázirúní, were there, seated on chairs, and they made me sit down with them. However, I was feverish and weakened. They brought a photograph of the Most Great Branch, and asked me whether I knew who He was. I said: 'Yes, that is the eldest Son of Bahá'u'lláh, Who is known as 'Abbás Effendi. I have seen Him many times in the drawing-room of Khurshíd Páshá, the Válí of Adrianople.' They then produced the *Kitáb-i-Íqán*, and told me to read to them. I said, 'I have fever and I can't read.' The Consul said, 'He fears to be mocked, should he read.' I replied, 'Let someone else read and I shall have my share of the good deed of mocking.' The book was passed to Ḥájí Muḥammad-Taqíy-i-Namází. He read the account of the detachment and self-sacrifice of the followers of the Point of the Bayán [the Báb]; if they were not in the right [it asks], then by what proofs could one demonstrate the rightness of the cause of the people of Karbilá. He read on and they kept laughing. Then Mírzá Javád turned to me and asked, 'Why did you become a Bábí? Had the Cause of the Báb been true, I should have become a Bábí, because I am both a siyyid and a Shírází.' I answered, 'But neither has it been proved that I am a Bábí, nor that you are not one. As the poet, Ḥáfiẓ, has it:

> From Baṣrah comes Ḥasan, from Ḥabash comes Bilál,
> From Shám comes Ṣuhayb; but from the soil of Mecca
> arises Abú-Jahl; how strange!*

* The references in this sentence are to Ḥasan al-Baṣrí, a leading seer and pietist of the early days of Islám (see Balyuzi, *Muḥammad and the Course of Islám*, p. 227); Ḥabash, or Ethiopia; Bilál Ibn Ribáḥ, one of the early Muslims, the first mu'adhdhin (muezzin) of Islám, appointed by the Prophet; Shám, or Damascus; Ṣuhayb, a companion of Muḥammad, noted for his abstemiousness; and Abú-Jahl, arch-enemy of the Prophet. (HMB)

At that all the people present burst out laughing, and Mírzá Javád became crestfallen. The Consul noticed that the people there had no cause to rejoice, and sent me back to the prison. And I beseeched God never to see him again. That same day he was called to Alexandria on some business. And I had another dream, in which the Blessed Perfection was telling me: 'Within the next eighty-one days, to thee will come some cause of rejoicing.' Then Mírzá Ṣafá arrived from Mecca, and was told that Mírzá Ḥasan Khán had imprisoned a traveller in a dark and dismal . . . place. 'Tell him', they said, 'for God's sake to free this innocent man.' Mírzá Ṣafá expostulated with him, and telegraphed to have me handed over to the Egyptian authorities and sent to Alexandria. When I was taken there, the late Siyyid Ḥusayn petitioned Sharíf Páshá, and wrote that this traveller was an Ottoman subject whom the Persian consul had unlawfully imprisoned and tortured. Whereupon, I was transferred from the lower to the higher prison. And it was arranged to take the Persian consul to task. A physician was there in that prison. He tried to convert me to the Protestant Faith. We had long talks and he became a Bahá'í.

On the eighty-first day of my dream, from the roof-top of the prison-house, I caught sight of Áqá Muḥammad-Ibráhím-i-Náẓir, passing through the street. I called out to him and he came up. I asked him what he was doing there, and he told me that the Blessed Perfection and the companions were being taken to 'Akká . . . and that he had come ashore in the company of a policeman to make some purchases. The policeman, he said, 'will not allow me to stop here much longer. I will go and report your presence here to the Áqá [the Most Great Branch]. Should the ship stay here longer, I shall perhaps come and see you again.' He set my being on fire and went away. The physician was not there at the time. When he came, he found me shedding tears, and reciting these lines: 'The Beloved is by my side and I am far away from Him; I am on the shore of the waters of proximity and yet deprived I am. O Friend! Lift me, lift me to a seat on the ship of nearness; I am helpless, I am vanquished, a prisoner am I.' It was in the evening that Fáris (that was the name of the physician) came, and saw my distress. He said, 'You were telling me that on the eighty-first day of your dream, you must receive some cause of rejoicing, and that today was that eighty-first day. Now, on the contrary, I find you greatly disturbed.' I replied, 'Truly that cause for rejoicing has come, but alas! "The date is on the palm-tree and our hands cannot reach it"'. He said, 'Tell me what has happened, perhaps I could do something about it.' And so I told him that the Blessed Perfection was on that boat. He too, like me, was greatly disturbed, and said, 'Were the next day not a Friday, and the *Seraye* closed, we could, both of us, have got permission to board the ship and attain His presence. But still, something can be done. You write whatever you wish. I will also write. Tomorrow, one of my acquaintances is coming here. We will get these letters to him to take to the liner.' I wrote my story and gathered together all the poems I had composed in the prison. Fáris, the physician, also wrote a letter and stated his great sorrow. It was very touching. All of these he put in an envelope, which he gave to a young watch-maker named Constantine, to deliver early in the morning. I gave him the name of Khádim [Mírzá Áqá Ján] and some others of the companions, told him how to identify them, and impressed on him not to deliver the envelope until he had found one of them. He went out in the morning. We were looking from the roof-top. We first heard the signal, and then the noise of the movement of the ship, and were perplexed, lest he had not made it. Then the ship stopped, and started again after a quarter of an hour. We were on tenterhooks, when suddenly Constantine arrived. He handed me an envelope and a package in a handerchief, and exclaimed, 'By God! I saw the Father of Christ.' Fáris, the physician, kissed his eyes and said, 'Our lot was the fire of separation, yours was the bounty of gazing upon the Beloved of the World.' In answer to our petitions, there was a Tablet, in the script* of Revelation, a Letter from the Most Great Branch, and a paper filled by almond *nuql* [a sweet] sent by the Purest Branch. In the Tablet, Fáris, the physician, had been particularly honoured. One of the attendants had written: 'Several times I have witnessed evidences of power which I can never forget. And so it was today. The ship was on the move, when we saw a boat far away. The captain stopped the ship, and this young watch-maker reached us, and called aloud my name. We went to him and he gave us your envelope. All eyes were on us and we are exiles. Yet no one questioned the action of the captain.'[6]

The next port of call was Port Sa'íd, which was reached the following morning. The liner anchored there the rest of the day, and at nightfall journeyed on. The next day, at sunset, she stood before Jaffa, and at midnight left for her destination – Haifa.

* Mírzá Áqá Ján's quick script to take down verses as Bahá'u'lláh spoke them.

30

Arrival at 'Akká

WHEN the Austrian-Lloyd liner stood before Haifa, the authorities set about preparing for the journey of Mírzá Yaḥyá and his dependents to Cyprus. This move entailed the separation of the four Bahá'ís, whom they had decreed should accompany Mírzá Yaḥyá to his place of exile, from the compact body of the companions of Bahá'u'lláh. These four, all arrested at Constantinople, as we have seen, were Mishkín-Qalam, the noted calligraphist, Mírzá 'Alíy-i-Sayyáḥ (of Marághih in Ádharbáyján), Áqá Muḥammad-Báqir-i-Qahvih-chí and Áqá 'Abdu'l-Ghaffár. Naturally, they and all the companions were greatly distressed when the hour of separation came. The Guardian of the Bahá'í Faith writes:

> It was at the moment when Bahá'u'lláh had stepped into the boat which was to carry Him to the landing-stage in Haifa that 'Abdu'l-Ghaffár, . . . whose '*detachment, love and trust in God*' Bahá'u'lláh had greatly praised, cast himself, in his despair, into the sea, shouting 'Yá Bahá'u'l-Abhá', and was subsequently rescued and resuscitated with the greatest difficulty, only to be forced by adamant officials to continue his voyage, with Mírzá Yaḥyá's party, to the destination originally appointed for him.[1]

Áqá 'Abdu'l-Ghaffár was saved from death, as Ḥájí Ja'far-i-Tabrízí had been at Adrianople, and in the end they both attained their desideratum – nearness to Bahá'u'lláh. Ḥájí Ja'far, when recovered from his self-inflicted wound, was taken to 'Akká, in the company of his brother. Áqá 'Abdu'l-Ghaffár managed to escape from Cyprus and reached Syria. He changed his name, and as Áqá 'Abdu'lláh remained secure.

A sailing-boat took the exiles from Haifa, across the bay to 'Akká. Wild rumours had preceded them, and the inhabitants of the town were puzzled, curious, and certainly prejudiced, hostile and even contemptuous. Some of them were at the quayside to gape at 'The God of the Persians', and to jeer. It was the afternoon of 31 August 1868,

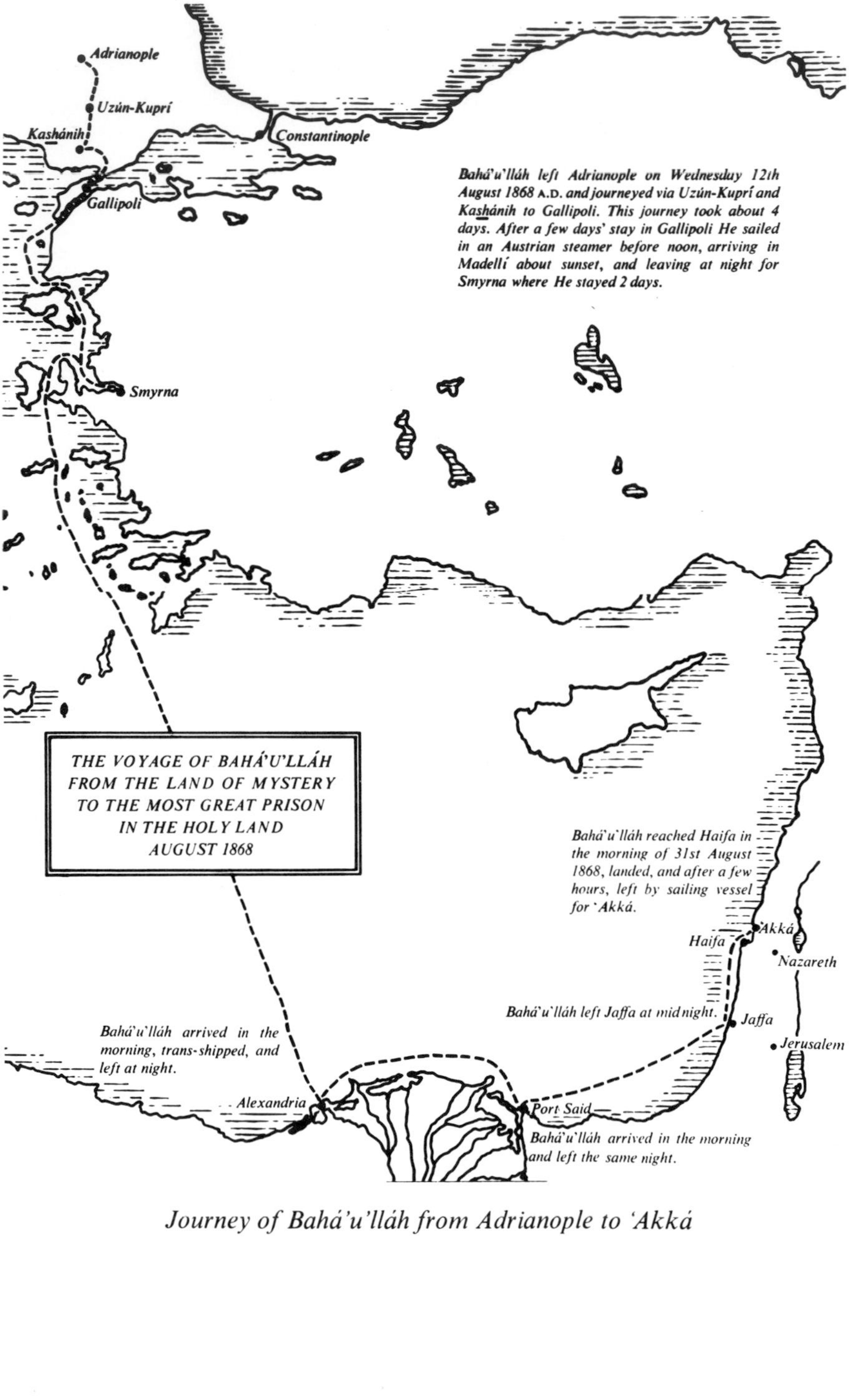
Adrianople
Uzún-Kuprí
Kashánih
Constantinople
Gallipoli
Bahá'u'lláh left Adrianople on Wednesday 12th August 1868 A.D. and journeyed via Uzún-Kuprí and Kashánih to Gallipoli. This journey took about 4 days. After a few days' stay in Gallipoli He sailed in an Austrian steamer before noon, arriving in Madellí about sunset, and leaving at night for Smyrna where He stayed 2 days.
Smyrna
THE VOYAGE OF BAHÁ'U'LLÁH FROM THE LAND OF MYSTERY TO THE MOST GREAT PRISON IN THE HOLY LAND AUGUST 1868
Bahá'u'lláh reached Haifa in the morning of 31st August 1868, landed, and after a few hours, left by sailing vessel for 'Akká.
'Akká
Haifa
Nazareth
Bahá'u'lláh left Jaffa at midnight.
Jaffa
Jerusalem
Bahá'u'lláh arrived in the morning, trans-shipped, and left at night.
Alexandria
Port Said
Bahá'u'lláh arrived in the morning and left the same night.

Journey of Bahá'u'lláh from Adrianople to 'Akká

corresponding to the twelfth day of Jamádíyu'l-Avval AH 1285, that Bahá'u'lláh, with His family and companions, entered the 'Most Great Prison' and were incarcerated in the strongly-fortified citadel.

'Akká is one of the oldest continuously-inhabited cities in the world, as well as one of the most fought-over. This is not surprising considering that it is situated on the best natural harbour of the eastern Mediterranean coastline and on the route between Egypt and Mesopotamia, two cradles of civilization. It is first mentioned on two Egyptian figures, almost 4,000 years old. It was then a Canaanite/Phoenician city under Egyptian control, but it passed in and out of Egyptian control for several centuries, then passed successively to the Assyrians, the Persians, the Greeks, the Romans, the Arabs and the Crusaders. During the thirteenth century, 'Akká became the capital of the Crusader kingdom and was the last significant stronghold to remain in the hands of the Crusaders, holding out until 1291 when it was taken by the Mamlúk army and laid waste.

For a time 'Akká became an insignificant village under the control of the Turkish Empire. Then in the sixteenth century French merchants rediscovered its natural advantages. The Druse leader, Fakhru'd-Dín, rebuilt a few of the Crusader ruins at the end of the sixteenth century; but the real revival of 'Akká's fortunes occurred under Ẓáhiru'l-'Umar, a local notable of Tiberias who succeeded in carving a principality for himself out of the declining Turkish Empire and made 'Akká its capital in 1749. The Ottoman government recognized Ẓáhiru'l-'Umar's *de facto* authority by making him governor of the province of 'Akká, but when he gave assistance to the rebellious 'Alí Bey of Egypt, a Turkish army was sent to besiege 'Akká in 1775. Through treachery the town was taken and Ẓáhiru'l-'Umar killed. One of the leaders of the besieging army, Aḥmad Pásha, al-Jazzár (the Butcher), an Albanian adventurer, was named the new governor in 1776.

The work that Ẓáhiru'l-'Umar had begun in rebuilding and fortifying 'Akká was pursued energetically by Aḥmad Pásha. Al-Jazzár's rule was severe and his influence was paramount in most of Syria and Palestine, and 'Akká prospered. In 1799, the city turned back the army of Napoleon Bonaparte and brought an end to his eastern adventure.

Al-Jazzár died in 1803 and was succeeded by his *mamlúk* and adopted son Sulaymán Pásha, who also built several important

The Bay of Haifa in the early nineteenth century showing the town of Haifa on the near side and 'Akká on the far side of the Bay. (from Wilson, Picturesque Palestine*)*

Haifa in the nineteenth century with Mount Carmel in the background (from Wilson, Picturesque Palestine*)*

edifices in 'Akká. On his death in 1818 he was succeeded by 'Abdu'lláh Pá<u>sh</u>á, the son of 'Alí Pá<u>sh</u>á, who had been another *mamlúk* and adopted son of al-Jazzár.* 'Abdu'lláh Pá<u>sh</u>á was the fourth successive governor of 'Akká to be a prolific builder both within and without the city. However, events were occurring in Egypt that were soon to have repercussions for 'Akká. Muḥammad-'Alí Pá<u>sh</u>á, an Albanian adventurer who had seized control of Egypt, was in revolt against the Ottomans. 'Abdu'lláh Pá<u>sh</u>á sided with the Sulṭán, and in 1831 an Egyptian army led by Muḥammad-'Alí's son, Ibráhím Pá<u>sh</u>á, besieged 'Akká. The bombardment was severe and no help was forthcoming from Istanbul; so eventually 'Abdu'lláh Pá<u>sh</u>á had no course but to surrender. He was treated generously and sent to Egypt where he was received with honour. He later proceeded to Istanbul and, after living there a while, he journeyed to Medina, where he spent the rest of his life and is buried. Ibráhím Pá<u>sh</u>á, foreseeing that the Egyptian presence in Syria would be challenged, rebuilt many of the edifices that had been damaged by his bombardment and strengthened 'Akká's defences so as to make it the Egyptian bulwark in Syria.

Following Ibráhím Pá<u>sh</u>á's spectacular successes in Syria and in Anatolia itself, the European powers, fearing the disintegration of the Turkish Empire, decided to intervene. In 1840, a predominantly British fleet appeared before 'Akká under Admiral Sir Robert Stopford and began a bombardment of the town. After four and a half hours of bombardment, there was a sudden loud explosion and a thick pall of smoke arose from the town. The principal powder magazine had been hit and had exploded, killing two companies of Ibráhím Pá<u>sh</u>á's best soldiers. To this day, the effects of that explosion may be seen, in that the inner land wall (Ẓáhiru'l-'Umar's wall) is missing on the eastern side of the site where the near-by explosion destroyed it. On the following day, the allied fleet found that Ibráhím Pá<u>sh</u>á had abandoned the town and was retreating to Egypt.

The departure of the Egyptians marks a turning point in 'Akká's fortunes. From being the capital of an important province it was henceforth reduced to being the administrative centre of a subprovince subordinate to Damascus and Beirut. Ẓáhiru'l-'Umar, who

* A *mamlúk* was a slave who was bought at a young age and given military training. On completion of his training, he was usually given his freedom and became an adopted son of his master. Such persons frequently rose to high office, and indeed, Egypt was ruled for several centuries by a series of Mamlúk Sulṭáns.

View of 'Akká from the south

had founded 'Akká's renewed prosperity, had also begun the process that would eventually lead to its decline. For he had re-sited and fortified the small town of Haifa across the bay from 'Akká. As the nineteenth century progressed, it became evident that 'Akká's port, which was silting in, could no longer cope with the larger draught of steamships. 'Akká's trade and prosperity declined, as much of its mercantile activity was transferred to Haifa.*

By the time of Bahá'u'lláh's arrival, 'Akká's principal importance to the Turkish Empire was that it acted as a prison-city for criminals and political prisoners – the 'Bastille of the Middle East', as it is referred to by one writer. The citadel where Bahá'u'lláh was imprisoned is among the most interesting buildings in 'Akká. It occupies the site of the citadel or *Grand Maneir* of the Knights of St John of the Hospital. Their refectory ('the Crypt of St John') has been excavated almost intact beneath the present building, and Crusader masonry is evident in the lower courses of the building itself. When, in the sixteenth century, the Druse leader Fakhru'd-Dín started to build on the Crusader ruins, he made the ruins of the Hospitaller's building the basis of his palace and citadel. Ẓáhiru'l-'Umar and Aḥmad al-Jazzár also built their palaces on this site, but the present building dates from al-Jazzár's successor, Sulaymán Páshá, and was completed by

* In contrast to 'Akká's decline, Haifa's progress was uninterrupted. The German Templars, who arrived there a few months after Bahá'u'lláh Himself, added to the prosperity of the town by their industry and technical knowledge. By the end of the nineteenth century, Haifa was an important port with a large colony of merchants; it was connected to Damascus by railway and most of the important foreign powers had established consular representation there.

'Abdu'lláh Pá<u>sh</u>á in 1819. It was used as both barracks and prison by the Turks and continued to serve the latter function during the British Mandate. The walls of the building have embedded in them cannon-balls from the bombardment by the Allied fleet under Admiral Sir Robert Stopford in 1840.

Áqá Riḍá depicts 'Akká as 'a town, with narrow and mean streets, dark and dirty, gloomy and tortuous; without a single dwelling-place worth looking at.' He also describes the citadel:

'It was built in the days of Jazzár Pá<u>sh</u>á for troops. It is very high and spacious, with a pool of water in the middle, and palms and fig-trees. To the north-west, the upper floor, well-built, contained four or five good rooms with an *ayván*, and there was also a *bírúní*: one large room with verandah and other rooms. The Blessed Perfection and His family occupied that section. Áqá Mírzá Muḥammad-Qulí and his family lodged on the lower floor. To the north, there were rooms on three floors. Ḥájí 'Alí-'Askar, Amír and Áqá Muḥammad-Javád occupied these rooms. In the north-west corner, there were rooms in which we lodged, . . . to the west, there was a very good bath. And to the south and east, there was a set of good spacious rooms. One of them was occupied by Jináb-i-Kalím; in another, others of the companions were housed, and most of them remained empty. Siyyid Muḥammad

The Sea Gate of 'Akká through which Bahá'u'lláh entered the city

Aerial View showing the Citadel of 'Akká. At the bottom left of the picture is the counterscarp from which those pilgrims excluded from the city could catch a glimpse of Bahá'u'lláh. In the foreground is the Mansion of 'Abdu'lláh Pá<u>sh</u>á. Behind the citadel may be seen the large dome of the Mosque of al-Jazzár. Between the mosque and the citadel is the Seraye *(the Governorate), and next to it, behind the citadel, is the small dome of the Hammám (the public baths).*

and Kaj-Kuláh [Áqá-Ján Big] resided here for two or three days, and then asked the government to move them. They were given a room over the second city gate [of 'Akká].

'The first night of our arrival we suffered because of lack of water. The water in the pool had become malodorous. We wanted to go out and procure fresh water, but they would not permit us. From the house of 'Abdu'l-Hádí Pá<u>sh</u>á, the Mutaṣarrif of 'Akká, they brought some cooked rice, but it was not enough. The next day, officials came to see what was happening to us. They went into the presence of the Blessed Perfection, and to them He spoke such words of knowledge and wisdom that, in that very first meeting, they realized that here were people endowed with erudition, wisdom and rare understanding. One of them had said, there and then, that never before had such pure and sanctified souls set foot in 'Akká. Some days later they brought Ḥájí Ja'far and his brother, Ḥájí Taqí.'

The ration for each person, according to Áqá Riḍá and Áqá Ḥusayn-i-Áshchí, was three loaves of black bread, salty and inedible. So revolting was this ration that Áqá Ḥusayn, young and headstrong as he was, made rude and insulting remarks about it in Turkish, directed to the Mutaṣarrif. This earned him a sharp slap in the face from the Most Great Branch. But it also caused the Mutaṣarrif, Áqá Ḥusayn says, to take note of the situation. Soon the officials discontinued this ration; instead they gave the exiles a sum of money each day, which was shared by all the companions.

Before long, autumn set in with its attendant ailments and maladies, because of the insalubrious conditions of 'Akká. Within the prison walls, the exiles suffered greatly.

Here is a list of the exiles who entered the Most Great Prison on the afternoon of 31 August 1868. The list was originally compiled with the help of Mírzá 'Abdu'r-Ra'úf, the son of Mírzá Muḥammad-Qulí, brother of Bahá'u'lláh. But the present writer has made certain alterations where he found inaccuracies. For example, Mírzá 'Abdu'r-Ra'úf had included in the list a number of people who reached 'Akká at a later date.

1. Bahá'u'lláh
2. Buyúk Khánum,* the mother of the Most Great Branch
3. 'Abdu'l-Bahá (the Most Great Branch)
4. Bahá'íyyih Khánum (the Greatest Holy Leaf)
5. Mírzá Mihdí (the Purest Branch)
6. Mahd-i-'Ulyá, the mother of Mírzá Muḥammad-'Alí
7. Mírzá Muḥammad-'Alí
8. Mírzá Badí'u'lláh, son of Mahd-i-'Ulyá
9. Mírzá Ḍíyá'u'lláh, son of Mahd-i-'Ulyá
10. Ṣamadíyyih Khánum, sister of Mírzá Muḥammad-'Alí and wife of Mírzá Majdi'd-Dín
11. Mírzá Músá – Jináb-i-Kalím, brother of Bahá'u'lláh
12. Fáṭimih-Sulṭán Khánum, daughter of Shaykh Sulṭán-i-'Arab and wife of Mírzá Músá
13. Ḥavvá Khánum, second wife of Mírzá Músá
14. Mírzá Majdi'd-Dín, son of Mírzá Músá and Fáṭimih-Sulṭán Khánum

* Ásíyih Khánum

15. Liqá Khánum, wife of Mírzá Muḥammad-'Alí
16. Mírzá 'Alí-Riḍá, son of Mírzá Músá
17. Mírzá Muḥammad-Qulí, brother of Bahá'u'lláh
18. Khánum Ján, wife of Mírzá Muḥammad-Qulí
19. Nash'ih Khánum, second wife of Mírzá Muḥammad-Qulí
20. Mírzá 'Abdu'r-Ra'úf, son of Mírzá Muḥammad-Qulí
21. Mírzá Dhikru'lláh, son of Mírzá Muḥammad-Qulí
22. Mírzá Vaḥíd, son of Mírzá Muḥammad-Qulí
23. Qudsíyyih Khánum, daughter of Mírzá Muḥammad-Qulí and Nash'ih Khánum
24. Ábájí Qazvíní, a maid-servant
25. Badrí-Ján, wife of Mírzá Yaḥyá, Ṣubḥ-i-Azal
26. Mírzá Riḍá-Qulíy-i-Tafrishí, brother of Badrí-Ján
27. Mírzá Faḍlu'lláh, nephew of Mírzá Riḍá-Qulí, son of Mírzá Naṣru'lláh (d. Adrianople)
28. Áqá 'Aẓím-i-Tafrishí, attendant to Mírzá Naṣru'lláh and Mírzá Riḍá-Qulí
29. Áqá Riḍáy-i-Shírází, Qannád
30. Gawhar Khánum, wife of Áqá Riḍá, mother of 'Aynu'l-Mulk
31. Mírzá Maḥmúd-i-Káshání
32. Salṭanat Khánum, wife of Mírzá Maḥmúd-i-Káshání, sister to Gawhar Khánum
33. Ḥájí Áqáy-i-Tabrízí, brother of Gawhar Khánum and Salṭanat Khánum
34. Zahrá Khánum, mother of Ḥájí Áqáy-i-Tabrízí
35. Áqá Riḍá, brother of Ḥájí Áqá
36. Ḥájí 'Alí-'Askar-i-Tabrízí
37. Ḥusayn-Áqá Qahvih-chí, son of Ḥájí 'Alí-'Askar
38. Khánum Ján, wife of Ḥájí 'Alí-'Askar
39. Ma'ṣúmih, daughter of Ḥájí 'Alí-'Askar
40. Fáṭimih, daughter of Ḥájí 'Alí-'Askar
41. Ḥusníyyih, daughter of Ḥájí 'Alí-'Askar and wife of Áqá Muḥammad-Javád-i-Qazvíní
42. Áqá Muḥammad-Javád-i-Qazvíní
43. Mashhadí Faṭṭáḥ, brother of Ḥájí 'Alí-'Askar-i-Tabrízí
44. Áqá Muḥammad-'Alíy-i-Yazdí
45. Áqá Abu'l-Qásim-i-Sulṭánábádí (d. in the citadel)
46. Áqá Faraj, cousin to Áqá Abu'l-Qásim

47. Áqá Muḥammad-Ismá'íl*
48. Áqá Muḥammad-Báqir*
49. Mírzá Ja'far-i-Yazdí
50. Za'farán Khánum, wife of Mírzá Ja'far
51. Áqá Muḥammad-Ibráhím-i-Nayrízí, known as Amír; he was of the company of the Bábís who were with Vaḥíd at Nayríz
52. Ḥabíbih Khánum, wife of Amír and a maid-servant in the household of Bahá'u'lláh
53. Badí'ih Khánum, daughter of Amír and Ḥabíbih, married to Ḥusayn Áqá Qahvih-chí
54. Ṣáḥib-Ján Khánum, a maid-servant
55. Mírzá Muṣṭafá, son of Ṣáḥib-Ján; he was known as Abú-Hurayrih
56. Darvísh Ṣidq-'Alí
57. Mírzá Áqá Ján, amanuensis and attendant to Bahá'u'lláh
58. Ḥájí Faraju'lláh-i-Tafrishí
59. Áqá Ḥusayn-i-Áshchí
60. Áqá Muḥammad-'Alíy-i-Iṣfahání
61. Ustád Aḥmad-i-Najjár
62. Áqá Mírzá Ḥusayn-i-Najjár
63. Áqá Muḥammad-Ibráhím-i-Náẓir
64. Khayyáṭ-Báshí
65. Mírzá Asadu'lláh
66. Siyyid Muḥammad-i-Iṣfahání†
67. Áqá Ján Big, known as Kaj-Kuláh†

* These two brothers died in the citadel; their brother Pahlaván Riḍá was a Bábí of Káshán.
† Azalis.

31

The Lord of Hosts

> Lift up your heads, O ye gates; even lift them up, ye everlasting doors; and the King of glory shall come in. Who is this King of glory? The Lord of hosts, he is the King of glory.[1]

THE Guardian of the Bahá'í Faith writes:

'The arrival of Bahá'u'lláh in 'Akká marks the opening of the last phase of His forty-year-long ministry, the final stage, and indeed the climax, of the banishment in which the whole of that ministry was spent. A banishment that had, at first, brought Him to the immediate vicinity of the strongholds of Shí'ah orthodoxy . . . and which, at a later period, had carried Him to the capital of the Ottoman empire, and led Him to address His epoch-making pronouncements to the Sulṭán, to his ministers and to the ecclesiastical leaders of Sunní Islám, had now been instrumental in landing Him upon the shores of the Holy Land – the Land promised by God to Abraham, sanctified by the Revelation of Moses, honored by the lives and labors of the Hebrew patriarchs, judges, kings and prophets, revered as the cradle of Christianity, and as the place where Zoroaster, according to 'Abdu'l-Bahá's testimony, had "*held converse with some of the Prophets of Israel,*" and associated by Islám with the Apostle's night-journey, through the seven heavens, to the throne of the Almighty. Within the confines of this holy and enviable country, "*the nest of all the Prophets of God,*" "*the Vale of God's unsearchable Decree, the snow-white Spot, the Land of unfading splendor*" was the Exile of Baghdád, of Constantinople and Adrianople, condemned to spend no less than a third of the allotted span of His life, and over half of the total period of His Mission.'[2]

'Akká – Ptolemais of the ancient world, St Jean d'Acre of the Crusaders and their last stronghold, which refused to bow to the might of Napoleon, a city that gathered renown throughout the centuries – had indeed fallen into disrepute at this period of its chequered history. Its air and water were foul and pestilential. Proverb had it that a bird flying over 'Akká would fall dead. To its forbidding barracks were consigned the rebels, the desperadoes, the unredeemable criminals of the Ottoman domains – sent there to perish.

This was also the city of which David had spoken as 'The Strong City', which Hosea had extolled as a 'door of hope', of which Ezekiel had said, 'Afterward he brought me to the gate, even the gate that looketh toward the east: And, behold, the glory of the God of Israel came from the way of the east: and his voice was like a noise of many waters: and the earth shined with his glory. . . . And the glory of the Lord came into the house by the way of the gate whose prospect is toward the east.'[3] And the Founder of Islám had thus eulogized this very city, 'Blessed the man that hath visited 'Akká, and blessed he that hath visited the visitor of 'Akká. . . . And he that raiseth therein the call to prayer, his voice will be lifted up unto Paradise.'[4]

The 'Akká which opened its gates to receive as a Prisoner the Redeemer of the world, was a city that had fathomed the depths of misery. And Bahá'u'lláh's exile to the Holy Land, His incarceration in the grim citadel of 'Akká, was intended by His adversaries to be the final blow which, in their calculations, would shatter His Faith and fortune. How significant and momentous will this exile seem, if we recall certain prophecies uttered in the past. 'Abdu'l-Bahá, the Centre of the Covenant of Bahá'u'lláh, and the Expounder of His Message, thus speaks of this stupendous event:

> When Bahá'u'lláh came to this prison in the Holy Land, the wise men realized that the glad tidings which God gave through the tongue of the Prophets two or three thousand years before, were again manifested, and that God was faithful to His promise; for to some of the Prophets He had revealed and given the good news that 'The Lord of Hosts should be manifested in the Holy Land.' All these promises were fulfilled; and it is difficult to understand how Bahá'u'lláh could have been obliged to leave Persia, and to pitch His tent in this Holy Land, but for the persecution of His enemies, His banishment and exile.[5]

David had so majestically announced: 'and the King of glory shall come in. Who is this King of glory? The Lord of hosts, he is the King of glory.'

'The wilderness and the solitary place shall be glad for them' Isaiah had said, 'and the desert shall rejoice, and blossom as the rose. It shall blossom abundantly, and rejoice even with joy and singing: the glory of Lebanon shall be given unto it, the excellency of Carmel and Sharon; they shall see the glory of the Lord, and the excellency of our God.'[6]

'The Lord will roar from Zion' had been Amos's testimony, 'and utter his voice from Jerusalem; and the habitations of the shepherds shall mourn, and the top of Carmel shall wither.'[7]

And Micah had thus foreseen,[8] '. . . from Assyria, and from the fortified cities, and from the fortress even to the river, and from sea to sea, and from mountain to mountain', he shall come.

32

Life in the Barracks

LIFE was indeed hard and onerous in the barracks of 'Akká, and particularly so when the exiles fell victim to maladies, such as malaria and dysentery, that the autumn brought in its wake. Áqá Riḍá says that they had never known such fevers as afflicted them, and states that the Most Great Branch, being very careful of what He ate or drank, did 'not go down' like the rest, but was always up and about, tending the sick and nursing them. Áqáy-i-Kalím and Áqá Riḍá himself were able to help with the nursing. But three of the exiles died. Áqá Abu'l-Qásim-i-Sulṭánábádí was the first to go, and then Ustád Báqir and his brother Ustád Ismá'íl-i-Khayyáṭ, who died the same night, in the words of Bahá'u'lláh, 'locked in each other's arms'. The guards would not allow the exiles to see to the funeral of their dead. Bahá'u'lláh had to give a carpet on which He Himself slept, to be sold to defray the expenses demanded by the guards. However, the guards pocketed the money, and had the corpses interred in their clothes – unwashed, unshrouded and without coffins. Bahá'u'lláh has attested that the money given to the guards was twice the amount normally required for a decent burial. Recounting His sufferings in this period, He has written regarding Himself: 'He hath, during the greater part of His life, been sore-tried in the clutches of His enemies. His sufferings have now reached their culmination in this afflictive Prison, into which His oppressors have so unjustly thrown Him.'[1]

The Guardian of the Bahá'í Faith writes:

> Explicit orders had been issued by the Sulṭán and his ministers to subject the exiles, who were accused of having grievously erred and led others far astray, to the strictest confinement. Hopes were confidently expressed that the sentence of life-long imprisonment pronounced against them would lead to their eventual extermination. The farmán of Sulṭán 'Abdu'l-'Azíz, dated the fifth of Rabí'u'th-Thání 1285 AH (July 26, 1868), not only condemned them to perpetual banishment, but stipulated

Text of the Farmán *issued by Sulṭán 'Abdu'l-'Azíz banishing Bahá'u'lláh to 'Akká.*

their strict incarceration, and forbade them to associate either with each other or with the local inhabitants. The text of the farmán itself was read publicly, soon after the arrival of the exiles, in the principal mosque of the city as a warning to the population.[2]

The Ottoman official archives reveal the fact that the promulgation of such a sentence was recommended and demanded by the officials in charge of the interrogation of the Bahá'ís and the two Azalís arrested in Istanbul. These documents also denote the fact that Khurshíd Páshá, the Válí of Adrianople, had defended the Bahá'ís and repudiated the accusations levelled against them.

In a Tablet addressed to Áqá Mírzá Áqáy-i-Afnán, Núri'd-Dín, over the signature of Khádim (Mírzá Áqá Ján, the amanuensis), Bahá'u'lláh recounts that such was the surveillance exercised by the authorities that even when a barber or bath-attendant was required, he was brought to the citadel accompanied by a member of the police force, who stood by all the time. For that reason Bahá'u'lláh did not use the bath for a while. It will be recalled that Ustád Muḥammad-'Alíy-i-Salmání, who had served Bahá'u'lláh as a bath-attendant (and would serve Him in that capacity in future), was at this date in Írán, having been expelled by the Ottoman authorities. This Tablet, revealed two decades later, particularly points out the change that had taken place over the years. At the beginning of their imprisonment in 'Akká the rules were harshly applied, whereas at the time this Tablet

The Citadel of 'Akká. The room in which Bahá'u'lláh was confined can be seen on the upper floor at the extreme right.

Bahá'u'lláh's Room in the Citadel

was revealed, anyone could go wherever he wished, in or out of 'Akká, without hindrance.

The Guardian of the Bahá'í Faith writes further:

> The Persian Ambassador, accredited to the Sublime Porte, had thus assured his government, in a letter, written a little over a year after their [the Bahá'ís] banishment to 'Akká: 'I have issued telegraphic and written instructions, forbidding that He (Bahá'u'lláh) associate with any one except His wives and children, or leave under any circumstances, the house wherein He is imprisoned. 'Abbás-Qulí Khán, the Consul-General in Damascus . . . I have, three days ago, sent back, instructing him to proceed direct to 'Akká . . . confer with its governor regarding all necessary measures for the strict maintenance of their imprisonment . . . and appoint, before his return to Damascus, a representative on the spot to insure that the orders issued by the Sublime Porte will, in no wise, be disobeyed. I have, likewise, instructed him that once every three months he should proceed from Damascus to 'Akká, and personally watch over them, and submit his report to the Legation.' Such was the isolation imposed upon them that the Bahá'ís of Persia, perturbed by the rumors set afloat by the Azalís of Iṣfahán that Bahá'u'lláh had been drowned, induced the British Telegraph Office in Julfá to ascertain on their behalf the truth of the matter.[3]

However, despite this high-handed action on the part of the Persian ambassador, more than a year after the arrival of the exiles in ‘Akká, which was tantamount to unabashed interference with the internal administration of the Turkish realm, and despite the fact that nothing had been changed by a jot or tittle in the original edict of Sulṭán ‘Abdu’l-‘Azíz, the Ottoman officials on the spot, as we shall see, found themselves more and more disinclined, even unable, to resort to harsh measures in their treatment of the prisoners; and the townspeople, exceedingly hostile at the start, had been slowly and gradually won over to respect and reverence towards the inmates of the citadel. It was chiefly the mien and the bearing of Bahá’u’lláh’s eldest Son that wrought this amazing transformation.

Áqá Riḍá and Áqá Ḥusayn have both put on record a short prayer, revealed by Bahá’u’lláh subsequent to the death of the three companions, which the exiles recited for their protection. Here is its text:

> In the Name of God, the Forgiver! Although this evil state in which I am, O my God, maketh me deserving of Thy wrath and punishment, Thy good-pleasure and Thy bounties demand Thy forgiveness to encompass Thy servants and Thy good favour to reach them. I ask Thee by Thy Name which Thou hast made the King of all names to protect me by Thy power and Thine Omnipotence from all calamity and all that is repugnant to Thee and all that is contrary to Thy Will. Thou art Supreme over all things.[4]

Although illness was still rife, there were no more fatalities. Áqá Riḍá states that for four months a huge cauldron of broth was prepared for the sick, and at night plain rice, which the Most Great Branch doled out personally for each, according to his needs. And then, Áqá Riḍá says, the Most Great Branch Himself fell sick, and so ill was He that the companions were greatly concerned and perturbed. But that passed too, and gradually all were restored to health.

Áqá Ḥusayn-i-Á<u>sh</u><u>ch</u>í gives more detail of the care and supervision which the Most Great Branch exercised in attending to the welfare and health of the companions. Every day He would stand by the gates of the citadel, awaiting the return of those who had gone into the town, accompanied by guards, to make necessary purchases, and would inspect all they had bought and even their pockets, to see that nothing injurious to the health of the inmates was brought in. Whatever He considered unsuitable for their consumption He would throw away.

There was one more case of very severe illness, then miraculous recovery. Mírzá Ja'far-i-Yazdí was almost given up for dead. A Christian physician, named Butrus (Peter), was called in. On feeling the pulse of the patient, he rose up angrily, protesting that he had been brought to attend a dead man. 'I am not Christ', he said and departed. Áqáy-i-Kalím went to Bahá'u'lláh and reported Mírzá Ja'far's plight. Bahá'u'lláh, Áqá Riḍá recounts, revealed a prayer and told Áqáy-i-Kalím not to give up hope but continue nursing him. As Áqá Riḍá puts it, a new life was breathed into Mírzá Ja'far, and he recovered. Hence Bahá'u'lláh called him Badí'u'l-Ḥayát (Wondrous Life).

Bahá'ís in Írán had, at last, learned that Bahá'u'lláh was incarcerated in the citadel of 'Akká. A number of them came that perchance they might gain admittance to the presence of their Lord. However, the two Azalís, lodged as they were over the gateway, were keeping a keen watch and reporting to the authorities the arrival of any Bahá'í whom they recognized. And the officials would immediately take action to expel the Bahá'í who had managed to come within the city walls. There were some who had walked all the way, over the high mountains of western Írán and the deserts of 'Iráq and Syria, to reach 'Akká. Foiled, at the end, by the machinations of enemies, the only solace left for them was to stand beyond the second moat, facing the citadel, to obtain a momentary glimpse of the figure of their Lord, as He stood behind the bars. Only a wave of His blessed hand, from afar, was their reward after months of toil and travel. Then, most of them turned homewards, grateful for that bounty bestowed upon them. It was enough to kindle a more vigorous flame in their hearts, enough to intensify their dedication. Others came in their wake and took back the memory of that figure, appearing at the window behind iron bars – a memory which they treasured above everything else in their lives. However, there were some, such as Badí', whose story is told in the next chapter, and Nabíl-i-A'ẓam (at the second attempt), who had the supreme bounty of attaining the presence of Bahá'u'lláh.

The Guardian of the Bahá'í Faith writes:

> The very few who succeeded in penetrating into the city had, to their great distress, to retrace their steps without even beholding His countenance. The first among them, the self-denying Ḥájí Abu'l-Ḥasan-i-Ardikání, surnamed Amín-i-Iláhí (Trusted of God), to enter His presence was only able to do so in a public bath, where it had been arranged that he should see Bahá'u'lláh without approaching Him or giving any sign of recognition.

Hammám al-Páshá. The Public Bath where Bahá'u'lláh met Ḥájí Abu'l-Ḥasan-i-Ardikání, the first pilgrim to be able to enter 'Akká and meet Bahá'u'lláh. The building is now the Municipal Museum.

Another pilgrim, Ustád Ismá'íl-i-Káshí, arriving from Mosul, posted himself on the far side of the moat, and, gazing for hours, in rapt adoration, at the window of his Beloved, failed in the end, owing to the feebleness of his sight, to discern His face, and had to turn back to the cave which served as his dwelling-place on Mt Carmel – an episode that moved to tears the Holy Family who had been anxiously watching from afar the frustration of his hopes.

Ustád Ismá'íl was the maternal uncle of Áqá Ḥusayn-i-Áshchí. He had been a master-builder and had seen service with Farrukh Khán-i-Ghaffárí, the Amínu'd-Dawlih* of Káshán, one of the first envoys ever appointed by the Persian government to the courts of Europe, who had negotiated and signed the peace treaty of Paris, with Britain, in 1856.

Áqá Ḥusayn thus recalled his uncle's arrival and the months which followed: 'When he arrived by way of Mosul, and could not attain [the presence of Bahá'u'lláh], he went to stay in Haifa, with Khalíl Manṣúr, the copper-smith of Káshán [see Addendum V]. Khalíl Manṣúr was the first person [Bahá'í] to settle down in Haifa. There, he looked after the pilgrims, who kept arriving from various places. Under instructions which he received from 'Akká and through secret intermediaries, he reported the case of each pilgrim. Then, they did as they were commanded. Khalíl Manṣúr came, occasionally, into 'Akká, to sell copper ware, reported how the pilgrims fared, and took away letters to post from Haifa.'

Áqá Ḥusayn was in the presence of Bahá'u'lláh the day his uncle came to keep vigil and failed to recognize the figure of his Lord. He recounts how bitterly he himself wept, and how kind and gracious Bahá'u'lláh was, as He spoke of the sorely disappointed master-builder of Káshán. And He said on that occasion, Áqá Ḥusayn recalled, that soon, God willing, the gates would be opened to the faces of the pilgrims, and they would come, safe and secure, into His presence. According to Áqá Ḥusayn, besides his uncle and Áqá Muḥammad-Ibráhím-i-Khalíl-i-Manṣúr, Áqá 'Abdu'lláh, a brother of the latter, and Pidar-Ján-i-Qazvíní also dwelt in Haifa.

Nabíl-i-A'ẓam, whom we last met in an Egyptian prison, was freed and banished to Anatolia, not long after the ship which carried

* During the ministry of 'Abdu'l-Bahá, a son of Amínu'd-Dawlih, Mihdí Khán-i-Ghaffárí, the Vazír Humáyún and Qá'im-Maqám, who had served under Náṣiri'd-Dín Sháh, and had occupied ministerial posts in the early days of the constitution, became a Bahá'í, much to the consternation of his family, and visited 'Abdu'l-Bahá, at Ramlih, Alexandria, in Egypt.

Bahá'u'lláh left Alexandria for Haifa. Thence he went to Cyprus, learnt what was happening to the Bahá'ís there, and then made his way to 'Akká, but due to the machinations of the Azalís he was deprived of gaining admittance to the presence of Bahá'u'lláh. Áqá Ḥusayn recounts that the first time Nabíl made his way into 'Akká he was spotted, intercepted and hauled before the authorities, who wanted to know what he was doing there. He said that he had come to buy provisions. But the officials forbade him to make any purchases and expelled him from the city. However, outside the citadel, around the district of 'Izzi'd-Dín, to the north of 'Akká, he stood one day gazing at the fortress. Bahá'u'lláh appeared at the window, behind the bars, and with the movement of His hands recognized Nabíl's presence there. The same day, a prayer was revealed by the Supreme Pen in his honour. Nabíl, thereafter, spent his days roaming over Mount Carmel and the Galilee, alternating his residence between Haifa and Nazareth. The Guardian of the Bahá'í Faith mentions that he also lived for a while in Hebron. Then he was summoned to 'Akká and stayed eighty-one days in the citadel.

Áqá Muḥammad-'Alíy-i-Qá'iní was another who established his residence in Nazareth. He was at one time a confidant of the Amír of Qá'inát in the province of Khurásán and frequently visited the capital. There he met Bahá'u'lláh in early days and they became friends. As soon as he heard of the claim of Bahá'u'lláh, he, without any hesitation, gave Him his allegiance, and became instrumental in leading a number of prominent people to the Faith which he himself had zealously and ardently embraced. Having become well known as a Bábí he was forced to leave his native land and set out for the prison-city. Arriving there he succeeded in gaining admittance to the presence of Bahá'u'lláh. Thereafter, as Áqá Ḥusayn-i-Áshchí relates, he settled in Nazareth, where he guided a Christian youth, named 'Abdu'lláh Effendi Maríní, to become a Bahá'í. This 'Abdu'lláh Effendi, according to Áqá Ḥusayn, rose high in the service of the government, and also compiled a book, based on Jewish and Christian Scriptures, portending the advent of Bahá'u'lláh, but during the ministry of 'Abdu'l-Bahá (the Most Great Branch), he was tempted by a malpractice, only too common amongst government officials, which caused 'Abdu'l-Bahá great sorrow. Realizing that, 'Abdu'lláh Effendi could not outlive his disgrace and took his own life.

Á<u>sh</u><u>ch</u>í also relates that one day Áqá Muḥammad-'Alíy-i-Qá'iní went to the Most Great Branch and said that he wished to become a partner with Him, asking for a loan of seven paltry piastres. With these as his capital, he bought some reels of cotton and packets of needles and went about peddling in and around Nazareth. A man of consequence, who had known great luxury in the service of the Amír of Qá'inát, he was now happy to ply the trade of a poor pedlar, because he was living in proximity to his Lord and was engaged in a trade.

The same was true of the uncle of Áqá Ḥusayn, the master-builder, who had enjoyed prosperity in the employment of Amínu'd-Dawlih. He too had become a pedlar, going about with a tray of small items, and making his home in a cave on Mount Carmel.

33

The Story of Badí'

FROM Adrianople, the Remote Prison, and later from 'Akká, the Most Great Prison, Bahá'u'lláh addressed the rulers of the world in a series of Letters. To them He declared His divine Mission, and called them to serve the cause of peace and justice and righteousness. The majestic sweep of His counsel and admonition, revealed in these Letters, arrests the deepest attention of every earnest student of the Bahá'í Faith.

Here we see a Prisoner wronged by the world, judged and condemned by a conspiracy of tyrants, facing the concourse of sovereigns, nay, the generality of mankind. He stands in judgement upon the values of human society and, undaunted, throws a bold challenge, not alone to His oppressors, not alone to ephemeral shadows of earthly might and dominion, but principally to those dark passions and motives and imaginings which dare to intervene between man and the goal destined for him by his Maker. Here, the Exile rejected and betrayed, incarcerated and held in odium, is seen to be the true and only Judge – the King of Glory.

'Never since the beginning of the world,' is Bahá'u'lláh's own testimony, 'hath the Message been so openly proclaimed.' 'Each one of them [the Tablets addressed by Him to the sovereigns of the earth] hath been designated by a special name. The first hath been named "The Rumbling," the second "The Blow," the third "The Inevitable," the fourth "The Plain," the fifth "The Catastrophe," and the others "The Stunning Trumpet-Blast," "The Near Event," "The Great Terror," "The Trumpet," "The Bugle," and the like, so that all the peoples of the earth may know, of a certainty, and may witness, with outward and inner eyes, that He Who is the Lord of Names hath prevailed, and will continue to prevail, under all conditions, over all men.'[1]

One of the earliest of these momentous Letters was addressed to

Náṣiri'd-Dín Sháh. It was revealed in Adrianople, but its dispatch to the ruler of Írán had to await the lapse of some years. The story of the bearer of that Tablet, of how he carried it to Ṭihrán, and of what happened to him after he delivered his trust, is thrilling and soul-stirring, appalling as well. Here it is, together with extracts from that Tablet, translated by the Guardian of the Bahá'í Faith.

Mullá Muḥammad-i-Zarandí, Nabíl-i-A'ẓam, in the course of his travels (prior to his Egyptian episode, his imprisonment in Alexandria and his subsequent sojourn in the Holy Land) came to Níshábúr (or Níshápúr), in the province of Khurásán. There he met Ḥájí 'Abdu'l-Majíd-i-Shálfurúsh (dealer in shawls), a noted merchant and a survivor of Shaykh Ṭabarsí, and as Nabíl himself says, 'an old acquaintance'. Ḥájí 'Abdu'l-Majíd took him to his home. There, Nabíl met Shaykh Muḥammad-i-Ma'múrí, the uncle of the martyr, Shaykh Aḥmad-i-Khurásání, engaged in copying Tablets of Bahá'u'lláh. And to his surprise, Nabíl found Ḥájí 'Abdu'l-Majíd attending personally to everything. He asked the Ḥájí whether he did not have a son old enough to assist him. Ḥájí 'Abdu'l-Majíd replied that he had, but his son did not obey him. Indeed, his son, Áqá Buzurg, a youth in his teens, led a wild life, was unruly, and took no interest at all in his father's preoccupations; in a word, he was the despair of his family. To see what followed, let Nabíl, that inimitable narrator, tell us himself:

'I said, "Send for him to come, I wish to see him." He was sent for and he came. I saw a tall, gangling youth, who, instead of physical perfections, had merely a simple heart, and I told his father to make him my host and leave his case to God . . . Then, I mentioned matters, very moving, which would melt a heart of stone.' Nabíl-i-A'ẓam here quotes a number of verses from the long poem by Bahá'u'lláh – *Qaṣídiy-i-'Izz-i-Varqá'íyyih*, which he composed in Sulaymáníyyih. In these verses quoted by Nabíl, Bahá'u'lláh speaks of His own sufferings and tribulations.

'Hearing these divine themes, the colour of the visage of that youth reddened, his eyes welled with tears, and the sound of his lamentation rose high. I calmed his agitation, but throughout that night, his enamourment and attraction kept sleep away from the eyes of Shaykh Muḥammad and myself. Until the light broke we read and recited from the holy script. In the morning, when he prepared the samovar

Áqá Buzurg-i-Nís͟hápúrí, Badí'

for tea, and went out to fetch milk, his father came and said: "I had never heard my son weep. I thought that nothing could move him. Now, what is the spell cast on him to make his tears flow and to cause him to cry out, to make him afire with the love of God?" I said: "In any case he is no longer in command of himself, and you must give him up." And his father said: "This manner of losing one's self is exactly what I desired. If he remains firm in the Cause of God, I myself shall serve him."

'Áqá Buzurg was insistent that he should accompany me to Mashhad. But his father said: "I brought Shaykh Muḥammad here, specifically to be his tutor, so that he might learn reading and writing within a short time, and study the *Íqán* under Shaykh Muḥammad's tuition, and make a copy of the book. Should he do these, then I undertake to provide him with a steed and all his expenses."

'Subsequent to my departure from Khurásán and arrival at Ṭihrán, Shaykh Fání* reached Níshábúr and mentioned that he was on his way to Bandar-i-'Abbás, so as to go to Baghdád, and ultimately to the Land of Mystery [Adrianople], and was permitted to take one person with himself. Jináb-i-Abá-Badí' [the Father of Badí'] provided his dear son with a steed and money, so that he might catch up with me at Baghdád, and we might travel together to the abode of the Beloved.

'Badí' had accompanied the Shaykh up to Yazd, and there had parted company with him, and giving the Shaykh all that he possessed, and all alone, had set out on foot to walk all the way to the Dáru's-Salám – the Abode of Peace [Baghdád].

'After his arrival at Baghdád, Áqá 'Abdu'r-Rasúl was martyred, and he stepped in to replace the martyr, carrying Áqá 'Abdu'r-Rasúl's water-skin over his shoulders, and served as the water-carrier of the companions there. And when the companions were rounded up, to be taken to Mosul, that illumined youth, although wounded in several places by rascally men, betook himself to Mosul, and reached that city before the arrival of the captives, where, once again, he engaged in carrying water for them. Later he set his steps towards the Holy Land, and attained the presence of the Abhá Beauty.'[2]

The day had come in the life of this seventeen-year-old youth when he felt that he had to turn to Bahá'u'lláh. And he began to walk – to

* In one source he is identified as Shaykh Aḥmad-i-Khurásání, who met a martyr's death in Tabríz.

walk all the way from Mosul to the waters of the Mediterranean, to the foot of the citadel of 'Akká, where, he knew, his Lord was incarcerated.

He arrived in 'Akká early in 1869 and, since he was still wearing the garb of a simple water-carrier, he had no trouble slipping past the vigilant guards at the city gates. Once inside the city, however, he was at a loss, for he had no idea how to contact his fellow-believers and could not risk betraying himself by making enquiries. Uncertain as to the course he should follow, he repaired to a mosque in order to pray. Towards evening, a group of Persians entered the mosque and, to his delight, Badí' recognized 'Abdu'l-Bahá among them. He wrote a few words on a piece of paper and managed to slip this to 'Abdu'l-Bahá. The same night, arrangements were made to enable him to enter the citadel and go into the presence of Bahá'u'lláh.

Badí' had the honour of two interviews with Bahá'u'lláh. During the course of these, Bahá'u'lláh made reference to the Tablet that He had already revealed, addressed to Náṣiri'd-Dín Sháh – the Letter which opens thus:

'O King of the Earth! Hearken to the call of this Vassal: verily, I am a Servant Who believed in God, and in His Signs and sacrificed Myself in His path. To this testifieth the calamity that surroundeth Me: such calamity as none of the creatures of God hath borne. My Lord, the All-Knowing, is witness unto what I say. I have summoned the people unto naught save Thy Lord and the Lord of the worlds, and for His love I have encountered that, the like of which the eyes of creation have not seen.'[3]

Many were the men, veterans, who had longed for the honour to be entrusted with that Letter. But Bahá'u'lláh had made no move and waited. He had waited a long time until the forlorn, the weary youth, who had come to receive the gift of second birth from His hands, reached the gates of 'Akká, and entered the citadel. At those two interviews Áqá Buzurg of Khurásán came face to face with his Lord, and became Badí' – the Wonderful. Bahá'u'lláh wrote that in him 'the spirit of might and power was breathed'.[4]

We know that to him was given the task which others, much older, much more tried and experienced than he, had hoped to perform, that Badí' asked for the honour of delivering the Tablet to the Sháh and that it was bestowed upon him. Since it would have entailed risks to have carried the Tablet out of 'Akká, Badí' was instructed to go to

Haifa and wait there, and that on his way back to Persia he must travel alone and not contact the believers.

Ḥájí Mírzá Ḥaydar-'Alí has recorded in his history *Bihjatu'ṣ-Ṣudúr* an account he heard from Ḥájí Sháh-Muḥammad-i-Amín: 'I was given a small box, the length of which was one and a half spans, its width was less than one span and its thickness was one-quarter of a span, and I was told to deliver it to him [Badí'] in Haifa together with a few pounds. I did not know what was in the box. I met him in Haifa and gave him the good news that a favour had been bestowed upon him and I was entrusted with its delivery. And so we went outside the town, onto Mount Carmel, and I delivered the box to him. He held it with both hands and kissed it, then he prostrated himself. There was also a sealed envelope for him which he took from me. He walked some twenty or thirty paces away from me and, turning towards the place of Bahá'u'lláh's imprisonment, he sat down and read it. He then prostrated himself again and his face was radiant with joy and ecstasy. I asked him whether I could also have the honour of reading the Tablet which he had received but he replied: "There is no time." I understood that it was a matter which could not be divulged. What was it? I had no idea at all of the significance of what was happening, nor of the importance of the task with which he had been commissioned.

'I said to him, "Come with me into Haifa for I have been instructed to deliver a sum of money to you." He replied, "I won't come into the town with you, you go and bring the money." I went and returned but could not find him anywhere – he had departed. I wrote to Beirut that they should give him the money there but they had not seen him. I had no further news of him until I heard reports of his martyrdom from Ṭihrán. Then I realized that in that box had been the *Lawḥ-i-Sulṭán*, and in the envelope had been a Tablet bearing tidings of the martyrdom of that essence of steadfastness and constancy.'[5]

In one of the Appendices to *A Traveller's Narrative*, Edward Granville Browne has translated the words addressed to the bearer (Badí') of the Tablet to Náṣiri'd-Dín Sháh. The text of these words as well as the Tablet itself had been obtained by Russian consular officials in Persia and sent to St Petersburg, where they were deposited in the Collection of the Institute of Oriental Languages by the head of that Institute, Gamazov. Baron Rosen had sent Browne a copy of his catalogue of this Collection in which this Tablet is fully described.

These then are the words addressed by Bahá’u’lláh to Badí‘:

He is God, exalted is He.

We ask God to send one of His servants, and to detach him from Contingent Being, and to adorn his heart with the decoration of strength and composure, that he may help his Lord amidst the concourse of creatures, and, when he becometh aware of what hath been revealed for His Majesty the King, that he may arise and take the Letter, by the permission of his Lord, the Mighty, the Bounteous, and go with speed to the abode of the King. And when he shall arrive at the place of his throne, let him alight in the inn, and let him hold converse with none till he goeth forth one day and standeth where he [i.e. the King] shall pass by. And when the Royal harbingers shall appear, let him raise up the Letter with the utmost humility and courtesy, and say, ‘It hath been sent on the part of the Prisoner.’ And it is incumbent upon him to be in such a mood that, should the King decree his death, he shall not be troubled within himself, and shall hasten to the place of sacrifice saying, ‘O Lord, praise be to Thee because that Thou hast made me a helper to Thy religion, and hast decreed unto me martyrdom in Thy way! By Thy Glory, I would not exchange this cup for [all] the cups in the worlds, for Thou hast not ordained any equivalent to this, neither do Kawthar and Salsabíl* rival it!’ But if he [i.e. the King] letteth him [i.e. the messenger] go, and interfereth not with him, let him say, ‘To Thee be praise, O Lord of the worlds! Verily I am content with Thy good pleasure and what Thou hast predestined unto me in Thy way, even though I did desire that the earth might be dyed with my blood for Thy love. But what Thou willest is best for me: verily Thou knowest what is in my soul, while I know not what is in Thy soul; and Thou art the All-knowing, the Informed.’[6]

Ḥájí Sháh-Muḥammad-i-Amín has further related: ‘The late Ḥájí ‘Alí, brother of Ḥájí Aḥmad of Port Sa‘íd, used to recount:[7] “From Trebizond to Tabríz I was in his [Badí‘’s] company for some of the stages of the journey. He was full of joy, laughter, gratitude and forbearance. And I only knew that he had been in the presence of Bahá’u’lláh and was now returning to his home in Khurásán. Time and again I observed that, having walked a little more or less than one hundred paces, he would leave the road and, turning to face ‘Akká, would prostrate himself and could be heard to say: ‘O God, that which you have bestowed upon me through Your bounty, do not take back through Your justice; rather grant me strength to safeguard it.’”’

* The names of two rivers in Paradise. (EGB)

Badí' plodded on, a solitary figure, over deserts and mountain peaks, for four months, never seeking a companion, never choosing a friend with whom he could share his great secret. His father had no knowledge of his return. In Ṭihrán, as bidden by Bahá'u'lláh, Badí' did not go in search of his fellow Bahá'ís, but spent three days in fasting while he made certain where the Sháh's summer camp was, and went straight there, sitting on a hillock, all day long, so that he might be seen and taken to the Sháh. The hour came when the Sháh set out on a hunting expedition; Badí' approached him calmly, addressing the monarch with respect: 'O King! I have come to thee from Sheba with a weighty message'.[4] Náṣiri'd-Dín Sháh may have been taken aback, but the confident tone of that youth had already impressed on his consciousness that this message had come to him from Bahá'u'lláh. In the words of Shoghi Effendi, 'at the Sovereign's order, the Tablet was taken from him and delivered to the mujtahids of Ṭihrán who were commanded to reply to that Epistle – a command which they evaded, recommending instead that the messenger should be put to death. That Tablet was subsequently forwarded by the Sháh to the Persian Ambassador in Constantinople, in the hope that its perusal by the Sulṭán's ministers might serve to further inflame their animosity.'[4]

We have known that Badí' was tortured and that he remained undaunted and steadfast to the very end. We have known that the pen of Bahá'u'lláh, for the space of three years, lauded his valour and constancy. We have known that to him was given the title of Fakhru'sh-Shuhadá' – The Pride of Martyrs, and that Bahá'u'lláh characterized His references to his 'sublime sacrifice' as 'the Salt of My Tablets'. But it was left to the strange ways of Providence to bring to light the full story of the last days of Badí', his ordeal and his immolation. It is a horrific story, but moving, a story of which every Bahá'í cannot but be proud. The fiendish cruelty which it discloses, sickens, but the unassailable integrity, the never-wavering faith, the invincible courage of that wonderful youth of seventeen ennoble the soul.

To see how it happened, how Providence intervened, we have to move swiftly with the years – more than four decades – in fact, to the year 1913.

Early in 1913, Muḥammad-Valí Khán-i-Tunukábuní, Naṣru's-Salṭanih and the Sipahdár-i-A'ẓam (later Sipahsálár-i-A'ẓam) was in

Paris. Tunukábun, the home town of this grandee of Írán, of which he was himself the governor over a period of years, is situated in the province of Mázindarán. Núr and Kujúr and Tákur, where Bahá'u'-lláh's forbears lived, also belong to this lush Caspian province. Sipahdár-i-A‘ẓam was one of the two Nationalist leaders, who, in 1909, marched on Ṭihrán, at the head of their men, to restore the Constitution which Muḥammad-‘Alí Sháh had wantonly destroyed. He converged on the capital from the north, and the other leader, the Bakhtíyárí chieftain Ḥájí ‘Alí-Qulí Khán, the Sardár-i-As‘ad, from the south.

When Muḥammad-‘Alí Sháh had staged his *coup*, in June 1908, relying heavily on Russian support, and had sent his Cossack Brigade, under Colonel Liakhoff, to storm the Baháristán, the Parliament building, and arrest those deputies who had incurred his wrath, Sipahdár-i-A‘ẓam not only did not challenge the autocracy of Muḥammad-‘Alí Sháh, but gave him his active support and led the

Muḥammad-Valí Khán-i-Tunukábuní, Naṣru's-Salṭanih, Sipahdár-i-A‘ẓam, and later Sipahsálár-i-A‘ẓam

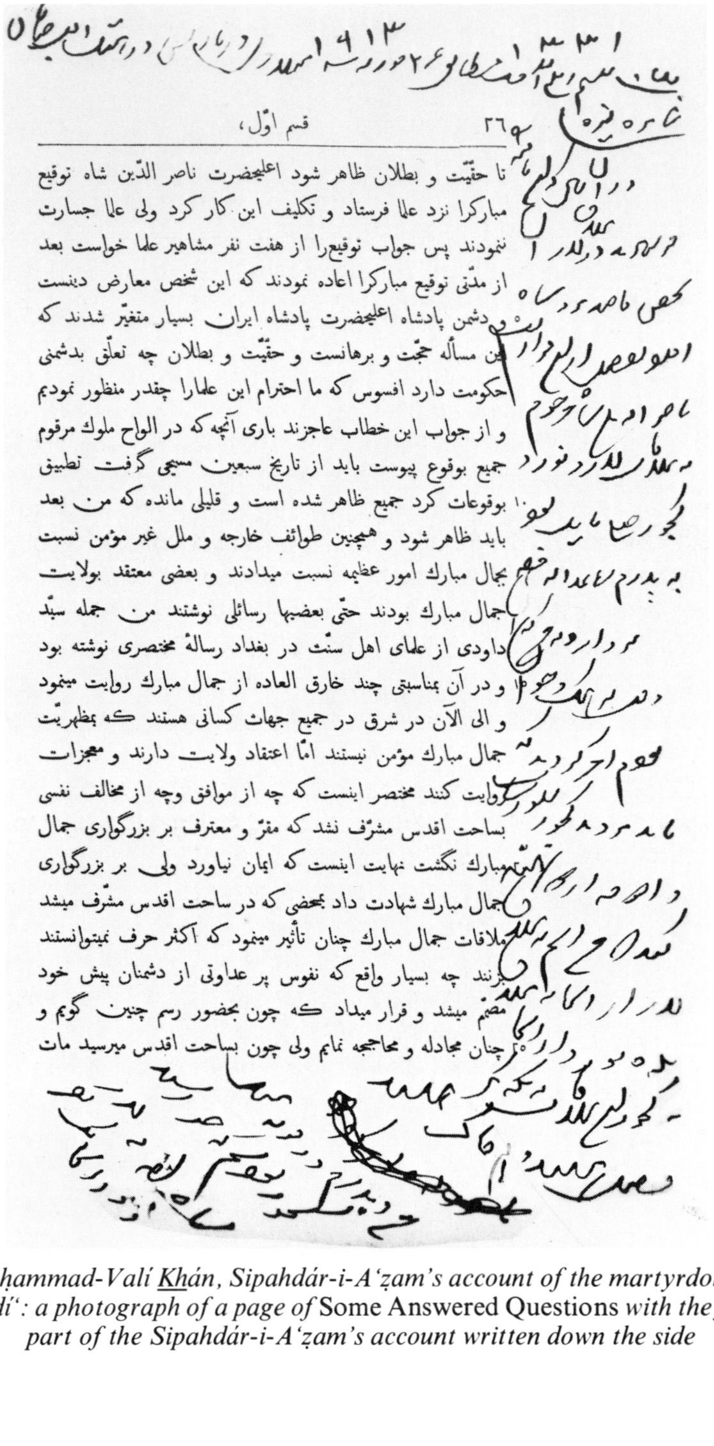

قسم اوّل، ٢٦

تا حقیّت و بطلان ظاهر شود اعلیحضرت ناصر الدّین شاه توقیع مبارکرا نزد علما فرستاد و تکلیف این کار کرد ولی علما جسارت ننمودند پس جواب توقیعرا از هفت نفر مشاهیر علما خواست بعد از مدّتی توقیع مبارکرا اعاده نمودند که این شخص معارض دینست دشمن پادشاه اعلیحضرت پادشاه ایران بسیار متغیّر شدند که این مسأله حجّت و برهانست و حقیّت و بطلان چه تعلّق بدشمنی حکومت دارد افسوس که ما احترام این علمارا چقدر منظور نمودیم و از جواب این خطاب عاجزند باری آنچه که در الواح ملوك مرقوم جمیع بوقوع پیوست باید از تاریخ سبعین مسیحی گرفت تطبیق بوقوعات کرد جمیع ظاهر شده است و قلیلی مانده که من بعد باید ظاهر شود و همچنین طوائف خارجه و ملل غیر مؤمن نسبت بجمال مبارك امور عظیمه نسبت میدادند و بعضی معتقد بولایت جمال مبارك بودند حتّی بعضیها رسائلی نوشتند من جمله سیّد داودی از علمای اهل سنّت در بغداد رسالهٔ مختصری نوشته بود و در آن بمناسبتی چند خارق العاده از جمال مبارك روایت مینمود و الی الآن در شرق در جمیع جهات کسانی هستند که بمظهریّت جمال مبارك مؤمن نیستند امّا اعتقاد ولایت دارند و معجزات روایت کنند مختصر اینست که چه از موافق وچه از مخالف نفسی بساحت اقدس مشرّف نشد که مقرّ و معترف بر بزرگواری جمال مبارك نگشت نهایت اینست که ایمان نیاورد ولی بر بزرگواری جمال مبارك شهادت داد بمحضی که در ساحت اقدس مشرّف میشد ملاقات جمال مبارك چنان تأثیر مینمود که اکثر حرف نمیتوانستند بزنند چه بسیار واقع که نفوس پر عداوتی از دشمنان پیش خود مصمّم میشد و قرار میداد که چون بحضور رسم چنین گویم و چنان مجادله و محاجّه نمایم ولی چون بساحت اقدس میرسید مات

Muḥammad-Valí Khán, Sipahdár-i-A'ẓam's account of the martyrdom of Badí': a photograph of a page of Some Answered Questions *with the first part of the Sipahdár-i-A'ẓam's account written down the side*

royal forces to invest the city of Tabríz that had risen in revolt. However, he was soon disillusioned and drifted away from the side of Muḥammad-‘Alí Sháh to the ranks of his opponents. In Rasht, he became a member of the Revolutionary Council and there he planned his march on Ṭihrán.

In the meantime, the powerful Bakhtíyárí tribe, with a few dissidents, declared for the Constitution, and Ḥájí ‘Alí-Qulí Khán, the Sardár-i-As‘ad, whose father had died in the prison of the notorious Ẓillu's-Sulṭán,* hurried from Europe to assist his elder brother, Ṣamṣámu's-Salṭanih, who had taken possession of Iṣfahán.

Russian officials, in concert with the British, tried to dissuade Sipahdár-i-A‘ẓam and Sardár-i-As‘ad from carrying out their plans. They failed, the Nationalist forces occupied Ṭihrán in mid-July, Muḥammad-‘Alí Sháh took refuge in the Russian Legation and was deposed. His eldest son, Sulṭán-Aḥmad Mírzá, twelve years old, was put on the throne with a regent: the venerable ‘Aḍudu'l-Mulk, chief of the Qájár notables; and Sipahdár-i-A‘ẓam became the first prime minister of the restored constitutional régime. But despite his signal service to the cause of the Constitution, Sipahdár-i-A‘ẓam was suspected of being a reactionary at heart, sympathetic to the ex-Sháh and Russian schemes. In truth, he was aloof and imperious, much of a grandee, totally lacking the arts of the demagogue. In the summer of 1911, while he was once again the Prime Minister, Muḥammad-‘Alí Sháh made an abortive attempt to win back his throne, and Sipahdár-i-A‘ẓam was forced to resign. It was thought that he would not act promptly and energetically to foil the designs of the ex-Sháh. He has stated that he went to France, in 1913, for medical treatment. Howbeit, he was in Paris in March, at the time when ‘Abdu'l-Bahá was still visiting the French capital. Either then, or possibly sometime earlier, Mme Laura Dreyfus-Barney had presented to him a copy of the Persian version of *Some Answered Questions*† by ‘Abdu'l-Bahá. One day Sipahdár-i-A‘ẓam opened the book to read the story of Badí‘, and as he read he recalled an incident of his early youth, and wrote his recollections in the margin. This is what he wrote:‡

* Mas‘úd Mírzá, the Ẓillu's-Sulṭán, was the eldest surviving son of Náṣiri'd-Dín Sháh, but he could not come to the throne, because his mother was not of the royal family. His life was embittered and he was always intriguing to gain the throne, which he considered to be rightly his.
† For details regarding this remarkable book see Balyuzi, *'Abdu'l-Bahá*, pp. 82–3.
‡ The recollections are in Persian and are translated by the author.

'6 Rabí'u'l-Avval 1331
26 February AD 1913
Paris, Hôtel d'Albe, Avenue Champs Elysée

'That year, when this letter [Bahá'u'lláh's Tablet] was sent, the messenger came to the Sháh in the summer resort of Lár, and this is the full account of what happened.

'The late Náṣiri'd-Dín Sháh was very fond of the summer resorts of Lár, Núr and Kujúr. He ordered my father, Sá'idu'd-Dawlih the Sardár [Sirdar], and myself (then a youth with the rank of Sarhang [Colonel]) to go to Kujúr and find provisions and victuals for the royal camp. "I am coming", he said, "to the summer resort of Lár and from there to the resort of Baladih of Núr and thence to Kujúr." These resorts adjoin each other and are contiguous. My father and I were in the environs of Manjíl-i-Kujúr when news reached us that the Sháh had arrived at Lár, and that there he had put someone to death, by having him strangled. Then it was reported that this man [who was put to death] was a messenger of the Bábís. At that time the word "Bahá'í" was not known and we had never heard it. All the people rejoiced over the slaying of that messenger. Then the Sháh came to Baladih of Núr. My father and I went forth to greet him. Near the village of Baladih, where a large river flows, they had set up the Sháh's pavilion, but the Sháh had not yet arrived. Káẓim Khán-i-Turk, the Farrásh-Báshí of the Sháh, had brought the advance equipage. We wanted to pass by. My father, who had the rank of Mír-Panj [General] and had not yet received the title of Sá'idu'd-Dawlih, was acquainted with this Káẓim Khán. He told me, "Let us go and visit this Farrásh-Báshí." We rode up to the pavilion and dismounted. Káẓim Khán was seated with much pomp in his tent. We entered the tent. He received my father respectfully and showed me great kindness. We sat down and tea was served. The talk was about the journey. Then my father said, "Your Honour the Farrásh-Báshí, who was this Bábí and how was he put to death?" He replied, "O Mír-Panj! let me tell you a tale. This man was a strange creature. At Safíd-Áb-i-Lár, the Sháh mounted to go hunting. As it happened I had not mounted. Suddenly I saw two cavalrymen galloping towards me. The Sháh had sent for me. I immediately mounted, and when I reached the Sháh, he told me that a Bábí had brought a letter. 'I ordered his arrest,' the Sháh said, 'and he is now in the custody of Kishikchí-Báshí [Head of the Sentries]. Go and take him to the Farrásh-Khánih. Deal with him gently at first, but if not successful use every manner of force to make him confess and reveal who his friends are and where they are to be found – until I return from the hunt.' I went, took him from the Kishikchí-Báshí and brought him away, hands and arms tied. But let me tell you something of the sagacity and the alertness of the Sháh. This man was unmounted in that plain and as soon as he raised his paper to say that he had a letter to deliver, the Sháh sensed that he must be a Bábí and ordered his arrest and the removal of any letter he had. He was then detained but had not given his letter to anyone and had it in his pocket. I took this messenger home. At first I spoke to him kindly and gently; 'Give me a full account of all this. Who gave you this letter? From where have you brought it? How long ago was it? Who are your comrades?' He said, 'This letter was given to me in 'Akká by Ḥaḍrat-i-Bahá'u'lláh.* He told me: "You will have to go to Írán, all alone, and somehow deliver this letter to the Sháh of Írán. But your life may be endangered. If you accept that, go; otherwise I will send another messenger." I accepted the task. It is now three months since I left. I have been looking for an opportunity to give this letter into the hands of the Sháh and bring it to his notice. And thanks be to God that today I rendered my service. If you want Bahá'ís, they are numerous in Írán, and if you want my comrades, I was all alone and have none.' I pressed him to tell me the names of his comrades and the names of the Bahá'ís of Írán, particularly those of Ṭihrán. And he persisted with his denial: 'I have no comrade and I do not know the Bahá'ís of Írán.' I swore to him: 'If you tell me these names I will obtain your release from the Sháh and save you from death.' His reply to me was: 'I am longing to be put to death. Do you think that you frighten me?' Then I sent for the bastinado, and *farráshes* (six at a time) started to beat him. No matter how much he was beaten he never cried out, nor did he implore. When I saw how it was I had him released from the bastinado and brought him to sit beside me and told him once again: 'Give me the names of your comrades.' He did not answer me at all and began to laugh. It seemed as if all that beating had not harmed him in any way. This made me angry. I ordered a branding-iron to be brought and a lighted brazier. While they were preparing the brazier I said: 'Come and speak the truth, else I will have you branded'; and at that I noticed that his

* His Holiness Bahá'u'lláh. (H M B)

Badí' after his arrest while he was being tortured

laughter increased. Then I had him bastinadoed again. Beating him that much tired out the *farráshes*. I myself was also tired out. So I had him untied and taken to the back of another tent, and told the *farráshes* that by dint of branding they ought to get a confession from him. They applied red-hot iron several times to his back and chest. I could hear the sizzling noise of the burning flesh amd smell it too. But no matter how hard we tried we could get nothing out of him. It was about sunset that the Sháh returned from hunting and summoned me. I went to him and related all that had happened. The Sháh insisted that I should make him confess and then put him to death. So I went back and had him branded once again. He laughed under the impact of the red-hot iron and never implored. I even consented that this fellow should say that what he had brought was a petition and make no mention of a letter. Even to that he did not consent. Then I lost my temper and ordered a plank to be brought. A *farrásh*, who wielded a pounder used for ramming in iron pegs, put this man's head on the plank, and stood over him with the raised pounder. I told him: 'If you divulge the names of your comrades you will be released, otherwise I will order them to bring that pounder down on your head.' He began to laugh and give thanks for having gained his object. I consented that he should say it was a petition he had brought, not a letter. He even would not say that. And all those red-hot rods applied to his flesh caused him no anguish. So, in the end, I gave a sign to the *farrá<u>sh</u>*, and he brought down the pounder on this fellow's head. His skull was smashed and his brain oozed through his nostrils. Then I went myself and reported it all to the <u>Sh</u>áh."

'This Káẓim <u>Kh</u>án-i-Farrá<u>sh</u>-Bá<u>sh</u>í was astounded by that man's behaviour and endurance, astonished that all the beatings and application of red-hot metal to his body had no effect on him, causing him no distress. He said, "I went and told the <u>Sh</u>áh and was rewarded with a *sardárí* [an outer garment], which was the <u>Sh</u>áh's own. We interred the corpse in the same place – Safíd-Áb – and no one knows where it is." But now the Bahá'ís have discovered the place, and for them it is a place of pilgrimage.

'These utterances of Káẓim <u>Kh</u>án-i-Farrá<u>sh</u>-Bá<u>sh</u>í I heard with my own ears. He related it all to us. I was very young and I was astonished. That same letter the <u>Sh</u>áh sent to Ṭihrán for Ḥájí Mullá 'Alíy-i-Kaní and other mullás to read and to answer. But they said that there was nothing to answer; and Ḥájí Mullá 'Alí wrote to Mustawfíyu'l-Mamálik (who was the Premier at the time) to tell the <u>Sh</u>áh that, "If, God forbid, you should have any doubts regarding Islám and your belief is not firm enough, I ought to take action to dispel your doubts. Otherwise such letters have no answer. The answer was exactly what you did to his messenger. Now you must write to the Ottoman Sulṭán to be very strict with him and prevent all communications." Sulṭán 'Abdu'l-'Azíz was living then. It was during his reign.'

'27 Rabí'u'l-Avval 1331, 2 March AD 1913
Written at the Hôtel d'Albe in Paris.

'Tonight I could not sleep. Mme Dreyfus had sent me this book and I had not yet read it. It is early morning. I opened the book and read on till I reached the theme of Letters to the Kings, and to Náṣiri'd-Dín <u>Sh</u>áh. Because I had been there on that journey and had heard this

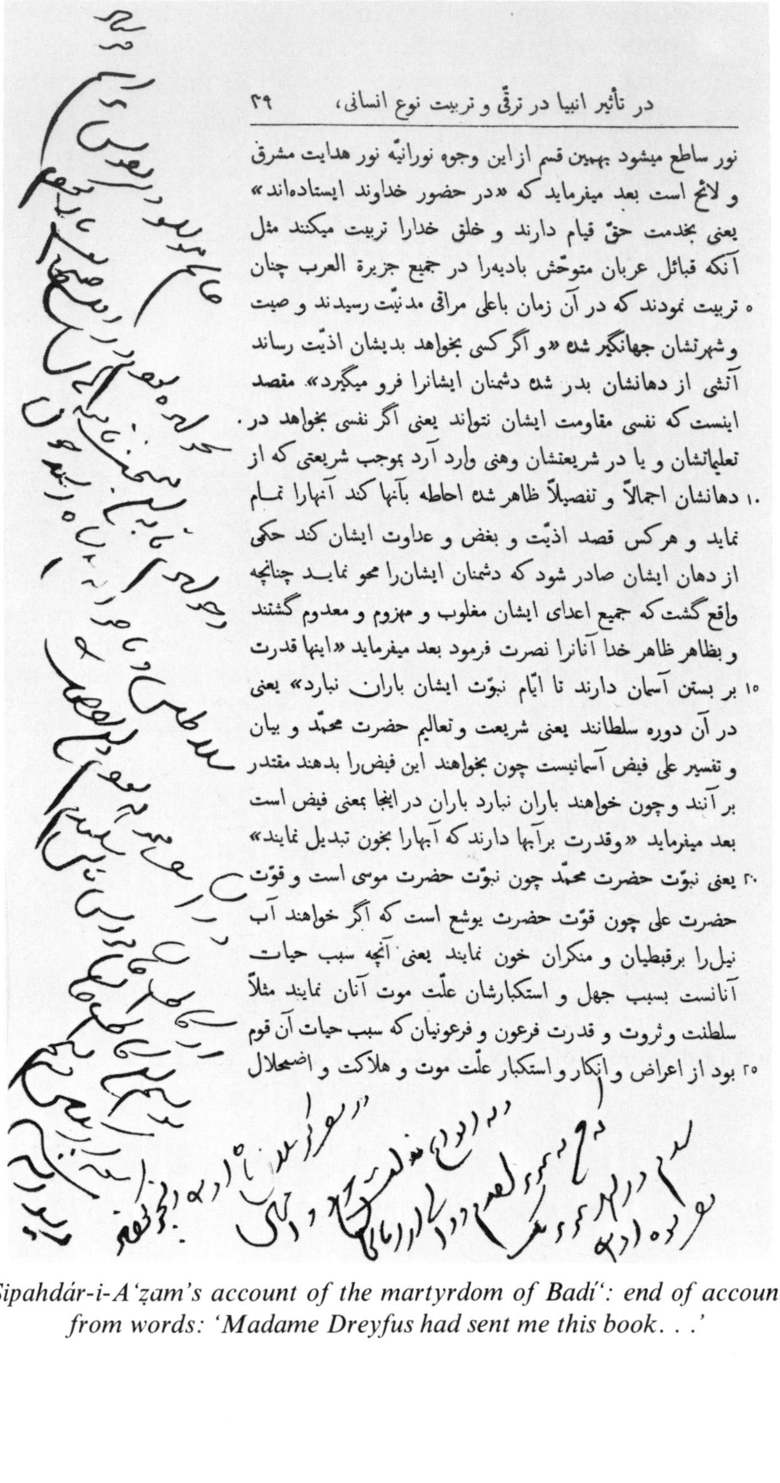

در تأثیر انبیا در ترقّی و تربیت نوع انسانی، ۴۹

نور ساطع میشود بهمین قسم ازاین وجوه نورانیّه نور هدایت مشرق و لائح است بعد میفرماید که «در حضور خداوند ایستاده‌اند» یعنی بخدمت حقّ قیام دارند و خلق خدارا تربیت میکنند مثل آنکه قبائل عربان متوحّش بادیه‌را در جمیع جزیرة العرب چنان تربیت نمودند که در آن زمان باعلی مراقی مدنیّت رسیدند و صیت وشهرتشان جهانگیر شد «و اگر کسی بخواهد بدیشان اذیّت رساند آتشی از دهانشان بدر شد دشمنان ایشانرا فرو میگیرد» مقصد اینست که نفسی مقاومت ایشان نتواند یعنی اگر نفسی بخواهد در تعلیماتشان و یا در شریعتشان وهنی وارد آرد بموجب شریعتی که از دهانشان اجمالاً و تفصیلاً ظاهر شد احاطه بآنها کند آنهارا تمام نماید و هرکس قصد اذیّت و بغض و عداوت ایشان کند حکمی از دهان ایشان صادر شود که دشمنان ایشان‌را محو نماید چنانچه واقع گشت که جمیع اعدای ایشان مغلوب و مهزوم و معدوم گشتند و بظاهر ظاهر خدا آنانرا نصرت فرمود بعد میفرماید «اینها قدرت بر بستن آسمان دارند تا ایّام نبوّت ایشان باران نبارد» یعنی در آن دوره سلطانند یعنی شریعت وتعالیم حضرت محمّد و بیان وتفسیر علی فیض آسمانیست چون بخواهند این فیض‌را بدهند مقتدر بر آنند وچون خواهند باران نبارد باران در اینجا بمعنی فیض است بعد میفرماید «وقدرت برآبها دارند که آبهارا بخون تبدیل نمایند» یعنی نبوّت حضرت محمّد چون نبوّت حضرت موسی است و قوّت حضرت علی چون قوّت حضرت یوشع است که اگر خواهند آب نیل‌را برقبطیان و منکران خون نمایند یعنی آنچه سبب حیات آنانست بسبب جهل و استکبارشان علّت موت آنان نمایند مثلاً سلطنت وثروت و قدرت فرعون و فرعونیان که سبب حیات آن قوم بود از اعراض وانکار واستکبار علّت موت و هلاکت و اضمحلال

Sipahdár-i-A'ẓam's account of the martyrdom of Badí': end of account from words: 'Madame Dreyfus had sent me this book. . .'

account personally from Kázim K͟hán-i-Farrá͟sh-Bá͟shí, I wrote it down.

'A year and a half later, on the journey to Karbilá, this Kázim K͟hán went mad. The S͟háh had him chained and he died miserably. The year I went to Tabríz, as the Governor-General of Ád͟harbáyján, I found a grandson of his, begging. "Take heed, O people of insight and understanding".

Muḥammad-Valí, Sipahdár-i-A'ẓam.'

The call of Bahá'u'lláh in the Tablet to the Qájár monarch resounds down the years:

> O King! I was but a man like others, asleep upon My couch, when lo, the breezes of the All-Glorious were wafted over Me, and taught Me the knowledge of all that hath been. This thing is not from Me, but from One Who is Almighty and All-Knowing. And He bade Me lift up My voice between earth and heaven, and for this there befell Me what hath caused the tears of every man of understanding to flow. The learning current amongst men I studied not; their schools I entered not. Ask of the city wherein I dwelt, that thou mayest be well assured that I am not of them who speak falsely. This is but a leaf which the winds of the will of thy Lord, the Almighty, the All-Praised, have stirred. Can it be still when the tempestuous winds are blowing? Nay, by Him Who is the Lord of all Names and Attributes! They move it as they list. The evanescent is as nothing before Him Who is the Ever-Abiding. His all-compelling summons hath reached Me, and caused Me to speak His praise amidst all people. I was indeed as one dead when His behest was uttered. The hand of the will of thy Lord, the Compassionate, the Merciful, transformed Me. Can any one speak forth of his own accord that for which all men, both high and low, will protest against him? Nay, by Him Who taught the Pen the eternal mysteries, save him whom the grace of the Almighty, the All-Powerful, hath strengthened. . . .
>
> I have seen, O S͟háh, in the path of God what eye hath not seen nor ear heard . . . How numerous the tribulations which have rained, and will soon rain, upon Me! I advance with My face set towards Him Who is the Almighty, the All-Bounteous, whilst behind Me glideth the serpent. Mine eyes have rained down tears until My bed is drenched. I sorrow not for Myself, however. By God! Mine head yearneth for the spear out of love for its Lord. I never passed a tree, but Mine heart addressed it saying: 'O would that thou wert cut down in My name, and My body crucified upon thee, in the path of My Lord!' . . . By God! Though weariness lay Me low, and hunger consume Me, and the bare rock be My bed, and My fellows the beasts of the field, I will not complain, but will endure patiently as those endued with constancy and firmness have endured patiently, through the

> power of God, the Eternal King and Creator of the nations, and will render thanks unto God under all conditions. We pray that, out of His bounty – exalted be He – He may release, through this imprisonment, the necks of men from chains and fetters, and cause them to turn, with sincere faces, towards His Face, Who is the Mighty, the Bounteous. Ready is He to answer whosoever calleth upon Him, and nigh is He unto such as commune with Him.[8]

This Letter, vibrant with power and endued with authority, which the indomitable Badí' had brought and which he had stoutly refused to designate as a mere petition, was certainly disturbing to the capricious tyrant, who had banished Bahá'u'lláh from His native land and envisaged His further exile to far-off Rumelia. He was thus prompted to order the destruction of the fearless messenger. Yet, at least, he had the desire to have an answer sent to Bahá'u'lláh. But the spiritual mentors on whom Náṣiri'd-Dín Sháh relied – Ḥájí Mullá 'Alíy-i-Kaní and his peers and associates – lacked the grace to acknowledge the challenge. And theirs were not those qualities of mind and spirit which would enable them to meet it. In the end theirs was the great loss and everlasting infamy, whilst the memory of the heroism and the sacrifice of that seventeen-year-old youth shines with fadeless splendour, across the centuries, not to be obscured by the passage of time.

34

The Great Sacrifice

AND now occurred the great tragedy of the death of the Purest Branch – Mírzá Mihdí, a son of Bahá'u'lláh. Mírzá Mihdí, designated Ghuṣnu'lláhu'l-Aṭhar (The Purest Branch) by his Father, was the second surviving son of Bahá'u'lláh. He was the full brother of 'Abdu'l-Bahá (Ghuṣnu'lláhu'l-A'ẓam: The Most Great Branch) having the same mother, Navvábih Khánum. In 1870, he was twenty-two years old. It was his wont to go in the evening to the roof-top of the citadel to pray and meditate. There one gets a wonderful view of the pellucid blue of the Mediterranean, with the silhouette of Mount Carmel beyond the seascape; and to the other side lies stretched the plain of 'Akká with the majestic peak of Mount Hermon in the background. One evening, Mírzá Mihdí, pacing up and down that roof-top engrossed with his thoughts and meditations, did not notice an open skylight and plunged through it to the floor below, falling upon a crate which pierced his chest. The injury proved fatal.

Áqá Ḥusayn-i-Áshchí recalled that the sound of his fall and the rush of the companions towards him brought Bahá'u'lláh from His room. He anxiously enquired what had happened. The Purest Branch said that he had always counted his steps to that skylight but on that evening had forgotten to do so. An Italian physician was called in, but his treatment was of no avail. Although obviously suffering, the Purest Branch remained attentive to his visitors, the companions who came to stand or sit at his bedside and to attend to his needs. Áqá Ḥusayn remembered that he would express his unease at having to lie down in their presence. Within twenty-two hours of his fall he breathed his last. Áqá Ḥusayn recalled hearing Bahá'u'lláh lamenting aloud: 'Mihdí! O Mihdí!' He also recalled that before death overtook the Purest Branch, Bahá'u'lláh asked him: 'Áqá, what do you wish, tell Me', to which His son replied: 'I wish the people of Bahá to be able to attain Your presence.' 'And so it shall be,' Bahá'u'lláh said; 'God will grant your

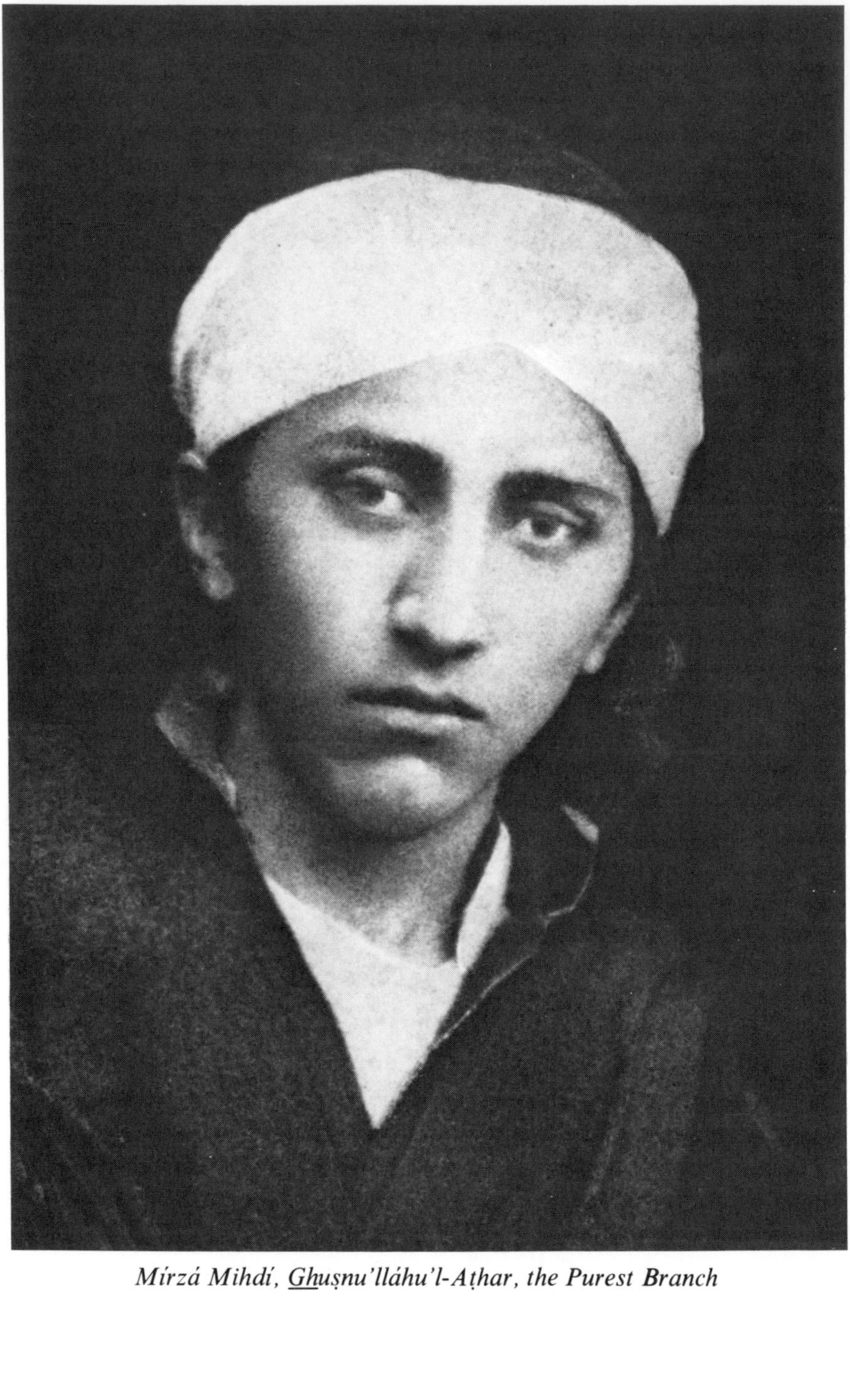

Mírzá Mihdí, Ghuṣnu'lláhu'l-Aṭhar, the Purest Branch

wish.' The day of his death was 23 June 1870 (23 Rabí'u'l-Avval AH 1287).

The Guardian of the Bahá'í Faith writes:

> His dying supplication to a grieving Father was that his life might be accepted as a ransom for those who were prevented from attaining the presence of their Beloved.
>
> In a highly significant prayer, revealed by Bahá'u'lláh in memory of His son – a prayer that exalts his death to the rank of those great acts of atonement associated with Abraham's intended sacrifice of His son, with the crucifixion of Jesus Christ and the martyrdom of the Imám Ḥusayn – we read the following: '*I have, O my Lord, offered up that which Thou hast given Me, that Thy servants may be quickened, and all that dwell on earth be united.*' And, likewise, these prophetic words, addressed to His martyred son: '*Thou art the Trust of God and His Treasure in this Land. Erelong will God reveal through thee that which He hath desired.*'[1]

Áqá Ḥusayn related that Shaykh Maḥmúd (whose wondrous story we shall shortly come by) told the Most Great Branch that he desired the honour of washing and shrouding the body of the Purest Branch, so that the guards should not lay their hands on that which was holy, and his offer was accepted; whereupon a tent was pitched in the yard, inside which the body of Mírzá Mihdí was laid, and with the aid of some of the companions (one of whom was Áshchí himself), who brought water and other accessories, Shaykh Maḥmúd prepared the body of the martyred son of Bahá'u'lláh for interment. The Most Great Branch, sorely stricken by the death of His dearly-loved brother, His grief, Áshchí remarks, imprinted on His visage, was during that period walking outside the tent with rapid paces, keeping watch. And Áqá Riḍá says that the notables of 'Akká joined the funeral procession. The Guardian of the Bahá'í Faith further writes:

> After he had been washed in the presence of Bahá'u'lláh, he '*that was created of the light of Bahá*', to whose '*meekness*' the Supreme Pen had testified, and of the '*mysteries*' of whose ascension that same Pen had made mention, was borne forth, escorted by the fortress guards, and laid to rest, beyond the city walls, in a spot adjacent to the shrine of Nabí Ṣáliḥ [the Prophet Ṣáliḥ], from whence, seventy years later, his remains, simultaneously with those of his illustrious mother, were to be translated [in December 1939] to the slopes of Mt Carmel, in the precincts of the grave of his sister, and under the shadow of the Báb's holy sepulcher.

During the few years of his adult life, Mírzá Mihdí had acted as an amanuensis of his Father, and Bahá'u'lláh's Tablets in his distinguished handwriting are extant. According to Áqá Riḍá's testimony, who had seen him grow up to young manhood, he was a pillar of strength amongst the companions, from the days they came out of Ba<u>gh</u>dád to the day a tragic mishap brought his short and unsullied life to its conclusion, sitting with them at their gatherings, reading to them of that which flowed from the Supreme Pen, teaching them the lessons of courtesy and patience, of dignity and radiant submission to the will of God.

35

The Gates Open

AT last came a day, four months after the death of the Purest Branch, when the movement of troops in the Ottoman domain compelled the authorities to have access to and make use of the barracks of 'Akká. The gates were flung open and the exiles were sent to other accommodation within the city walls.

Bahá'u'lláh and His family were moved to the house of Malik, in the Fákhúrah quarter, in the western part of the prison-city. The majority of the companions were lodged in a caravanserai, called Khán-i-'Avámíd, close to the sea-shore. But a number of them found separate homes. Áqáy-i-Kalím and his family went to live in a house within the compound of the caravanserai. The Khán-i-'Avámíd or Khán al-'Umdán was built by Aḥmad al-Jazzár using pillars brought from Caesarea. Its clock tower is a more modern structure, having been built to commemorate the jubilee of Sulṭán 'Abdu'l-Ḥamid. It served as the first pilgrim house of the Holy Land and many eminent Bahá'ís, including Mishkín-Qalam, Zaynu'l-Muqarrabín and Ḥájí Mírzá Ḥaydar-'Alí, resided there. 'Abdu'l-Bahá frequently entertained the pilgrims there and it is probable that Bahá'u'llah also visited it.

Bahá'u'lláh's sojourn in the house of Malik lasted three months. Then He took residence in the house of Manṣúr Khavvám, which was situated opposite the previous house. Here too His stay was short. His next residence was the house of Rábi'ih. But after another four months He had to move once again, this time to the house of 'Údí Khammár, which in the words of the Guardian of the Bahá'í Faith 'was so insufficient to their needs that in one of its rooms no less than thirteen persons of both sexes had to accommodate themselves'.[1]

'Údí Khammár was a notable of 'Akká, a Christian of the Roman Catholic (Maronite) denomination. He and his nephew, Ilyás 'Abbúd, who was of the same persuasion and lived next door, were partners. 'Údí Khammár, in whose house Bahá'u'lláh and His family finally took their abode, was noted for his parsimony. However, about the time the exiles were condemned to banishment and incarceration in 'Akká, it was seen, to the astonishment of the populace, that he was planning to have a palatial home built for himself in the vicinity of Bahjí, which was the palace* of 'Abdu'lláh Pá<u>sh</u>á. Bahjí was within half an hour's ride from the city; it was richly designed and equipped, surrounded by a delightful grove of lemon and orange trees, and with a large pond which was particularly inviting. With the passage of time 'Abdu'lláh Pá<u>sh</u>á's palace passed into the possession of the Bayḍúns, a prominent Muslim family of 'Akká, who always remained antagonistic to the Faith of Bahá'u'lláh. In the opening years of this century, when a highly-placed commission of inquiry came from Istanbul with the sole aim of inculpating 'Abdu'l-Bahá, 'Abdu'l-<u>Gh</u>aní Bayḍún invited its members to stay in his mansion.

* Today it is a government centre for the handicapped.

<u>Kh</u>an-i-'Avámíd or <u>Kh</u>án al-'Umdán where many of the companions of Bahá'u'lláh resided

'Údí Khammár went ahead with the construction of his palace, but Ilyás 'Abbúd considered it a madcap scheme and did not follow suit. However, some members of his family thought otherwise and had a number of houses built for themselves close to the mansion of 'Údí Khammár. When Khammár moved out of 'Akká to reside in his newly-built palace, he leased his house in the city to Bahá'u'lláh. Ilyás 'Abbúd was greatly displeased and tried to prevent the transaction. He failed, but took steps to avoid all contact with the exiles, whom he reckoned to be in every way undesirable as neighbours. Then occurred a shameful and horrendous, but inevitable, event which outwardly justified Ilyás 'Abbúd's worst fears. This was the murder of three Azalís at the hands of seven Bahá'ís, an appalling incident which added immeasurably to the rigours and burdens of Bahá'u'lláh's life, and wrung from His heart the cry:

> My captivity cannot harm Me. That which can harm Me is the conduct of those who love Me, who claim to be related to Me, and yet perpetrate what causeth My heart and My pen to groan. . . . My captivity can bring on Me no shame. Nay, by My life, it conferreth on Me glory. That which can make Me ashamed is the conduct of such of My followers as profess to love Me, yet in fact follow the Evil One.[2]

It will be recalled that two Azalís, partisans of Mírzá Yaḥyá, had been sent to 'Akká by the authorities to be confined there together with the Bahá'ís. Those two, Siyyid Muḥammad-i-Iṣfahání (the Antichrist of the Bahá'í Revelation) and Áqá Ján-i-Kaj-Kuláh (of Salmás in Ádharbáyján), on arrival at the citadel had asked to be accommodated elsewhere. Over the city gates and the jail, called Límán, into which desperadoes were cast, a room was found to suit them. It was a vantage-point from which they could spy and keep strict watch on all who came into 'Akká. Thus they reported immediately to the authorities the arrival of anyone whom they recognized as a follower of Bahá'u'lláh. Through their machinations Nabíl-i-A'ẓam and Áqá Muḥammad-'Alíy-i-Qá'iní were expelled from 'Akká as soon as they passed through the gates. They even went further and beguiled a local man, who represented the Íránian consular service, with promises of rich rewards and decorations, should he join hands with them to foil and frustrate the Bahá'ís. This man was responsible for the immediate removal of Áqá 'Abdu'r-Rasúl-i-Zanjání and those who were with him. Then came Na'ím Effendi from Cyprus. He had learned of the

Aerial View of 'Akká

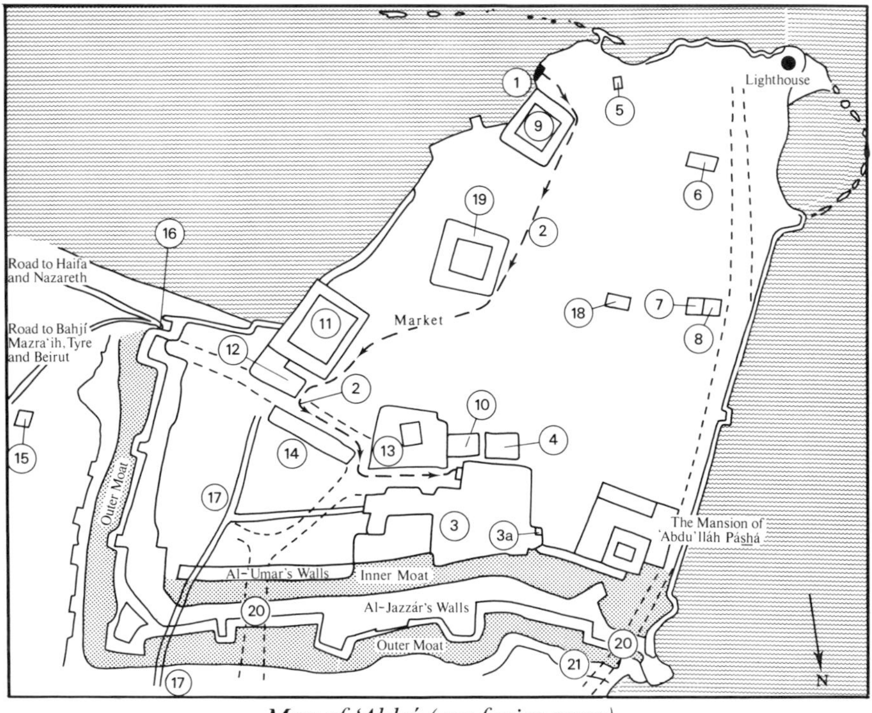

Map of 'Akká (see facing page)

Places in 'Akká Associated with Bahá'u'lláh

1. Sea Gate, through which Bahá'u'lláh entered 'Akká on 31 August 1868.
2. Route by which Bahá'u'lláh was taken from the Sea Gate to the eastern entrance of the Citadel, on 31 August 1868, according to oral tradition.
3. Citadel and barracks where Bahá'u'lláh and His companions were imprisoned for two years, two months and five days.

3a. Bahá'u'lláh's cell in the Citadel.

4. Public bath visited weekly by Bahá'u'lláh, this being the only occasion He left the Citadel. It was here that Ḥájí Amín was able to enter Bahá'u'lláh's presence, the first pilgrim to do so.
5. Church of St Andrew's, near which are situated the houses of Malik and Khavvám which Bahá'u'lláh occupied for three months and a few months, respectively, after His release from the Citadel.
6. Shrine of Shaykh Ghánim, near which is situated the house of Rábi'ih which Bahá'u'lláh occupied for four months after leaving the house of Khavvám.
7. House of 'Údí Khammár where Bahá'u'lláh lived for two years. The *Kitáb-i-Aqdas* was revealed here.
8. House of 'Abbúd, adjoining the house of 'Údí Khammár, made available to Bahá'u'lláh and His family in 1873. Bahá'u'lláh lived here for four years in a room overlooking the sea.
9. Khán-i-'Avámíd (Khán al-'Umdán or Khán-i-Juraynī), in the northern and eastern wings of which many of the companions of Bahá'u'lláh took up their residence, and where pilgrims stayed.
10. The Governorate where Bahá'u'lláh was taken to be interrogated after the murder of the three Azalís on 22 January 1872. It is now a school.
11. Khán-i-Shávirdí where Bahá'u'lláh was imprisoned for one night and many of His companions for longer periods, after the murder of the Azalís.
12. The Límán where 'Abdu'l-Bahá was imprisoned for three days after the murder of the Azalís. It was into a room over the building that Bahá'u'lláh was moved after spending one night in the Khán-i-Shávirdí. The seven Bahá'ís responsible for the murders spent several years here.
13. Mosque of Al-Jazzár, where the Sulṭán's firman decreeing the terms of Bahá'u'lláh's exile was publicly read soon after His arrival, inciting the populace to fear and hatred of the exiles. 'Abdu'l-Bahá was later given a room in the theological seminary in the courtyard of the mosque as a mark of the great respect in which He was held.
14. As-Súq al-Abyaḍ (The White Bazar); in its vicinity was the house of Mírzá Músá, Áqáy-i-Kalím, often visited by Bahá'u'lláh.
15. Shrine of Nabí-Ṣáliḥ; in the cemetery around this shrine, the Purest Branch was buried prior to the removal of his remains to Haifa. Other companions of Bahá'u'lláh are also buried here.
16. The Land Gate through which Bahá'u'lláh left 'Akká in June 1877. It was the only land entrance to the city until the period of the British Mandate and was frequently used by Bahá'u'lláh, 'Abdu'l-Bahá, the companions and pilgrims.
17. The aqueduct repaired by Aḥmad Big Tawfíq at Bahá'u'lláh's suggestion. The part of the aqueduct shown on this map can scarcely be seen now, but other parts of it are clearly visible on the road to Bahjí and Mazra'ih.
18. The Church of St George, of which the family of 'Údí Khammár were munificent patrons. The area around this church and extending to the Church of St Andrew's was the Christian quarter of the city.
19. Khán-i-Afranj where a few of the believers such as Áqá 'Abdu'l-Ghaffár-i-Iṣfahání and Mírzá Riḍáy-i-Qannad took up their residence.
20. Breeches in the town walls made during the British Mandate. Dotted lines show the present course of principal roads.

Bahá'í Faith from the celebrated calligraphist, Mishkín-Qalam, who was exiled in that island. Na'ím Effendi embraced the Faith zealously, attained the presence of Bahá'u'lláh, and was entrusted by the Most Great Branch with letters to take away with him. The Azalís and the Persian consular agent found out what had occurred and had Na'ím Effendi detained when he was on his way to Haifa. The letters he had with him were confiscated and he himself was taken to Beirut and cast into prison, where he languished for six months. The Most Great Branch tried hard to dissuade the Persian agent from following his nefarious designs, but he had fallen too deeply under the influence of the Azalís. According to Nabíl-i-A'ẓam, even Caesar Catafago, who had become a follower of Bahá'u'lláh – and whose father, Khájih Louis, was the French consular agent in 'Akká* and had dispatched the Tablet addressed to Napoleon III – was for a while thoroughly beguiled by Siyyid Muḥammad-i-Iṣfahání, although at a later date he saw the error of his ways and returned to his former allegiance. Na'ím Effendi, when released, went back to Cyprus, where he prospered greatly and, according to Áqá Riḍá, after the annexation of that island by the British, was given a high position. Áqá Riḍá also relates that Na'ím Effendi came to 'Akká a second time, with his two sons whom he was taking to Istanbul to receive higher education. On being asked whether he knew what had befallen the one who had once caused him so much suffering, he replied that he bore no grudge against him; the evil-doer, in truth, harms himself, he said, and God deals with him justly. That Persian consular agent had indeed fallen on evil days, for he had lost his family, his trade, his property, and almost his reason. Full of penitence, he would sometimes come to see the Bahá'ís to express his sorrow and remorse for the injuries he had, when at the height of power and influence, inflicted upon them.

Siyyid Muḥammad and Kaj-Kuláh had, by the time the prison gates were opened to the exiles, been joined by Mírzá Riḍá-Qulí, the brother-in-law of Mírzá Yaḥyá, whom Bahá'u'lláh had expelled from the company of His followers for his oft-repeated misdeeds. Time and

* Louis Catafago was the French consular agent for 'Akká and Haifa for a number of years. Mary Rogers, in her book *Domestic Life in Palestine*, describes him as he appeared in 1858: 'One of our neighbours, Signor Luïs Catafago, a widower, was the wealthiest and most influential of the Christian Arabs of Hâifa, and more learned in Arabic literature than anyone in the Pashalic. He was well acquainted with Italian and French, and lived in semi-European style. His sons were brought up at college, and dressed like Europeans, though his little girls were quite Oriental.' (pp. 384–5)

The House of 'Abbúd. The house of 'Údí Khammár is at the back of the building and that of 'Abbúd at the front. Bahá'u'lláh lived in both houses, latterly in the room with the balcony.

again, he had broken his solemn promises, until his actions could no longer be tolerated or condoned. With the addition of this recruit, the Azalís intensified their mischief-making. As they waxed bolder and bolder, Bahá'u'lláh increased His counsel to the companions to be patient and forbearing. On the other hand, with the freedom now gained, the Azalís were all the while seeking new allies to harm the Bahá'ís.

Then, Bahá'u'lláh revealed the Tablet which has become known in English as *The Fire Tablet*, so designated from its opening verse: 'Indeed the hearts of the sincere are consumed in the fire of separation'. This Tablet is unique amongst the Writings of the Author of the Bahá'í Faith and immediately brings to mind that intense mystical communion which Jesus Christ experienced, during the last night of His life, in the Garden of Gethsemane, and also the cry which He uttered the next day on the Cross: 'My God, my God, why hast thou forsaken me?' In reading *The Fire Tablet* one is moved to the depths of one's being by the agony of the Supreme Manifestation of God:

> Bahá is drowning in a sea of tribulation: Where is the Ark of Thy salvation, O Saviour of the worlds? . . . The branches of the Divine Lote-Tree lie broken by the onrushing gales of destiny: Where are the banners of Thy succour, O Champion of the worlds? . . . The leaves are yellowed by the poisoning winds of sedition: Where is the downpour of the clouds of Thy bounty, O Giver of the worlds? . . .

And then comes the response:

> O Supreme Pen, We have heard Thy most sweet call in the eternal realm: Give Thou ear unto what the Tongue of Grandeur uttereth, O Wronged One of the worlds! Were it not for the cold, How would the heat of Thy words prevail, O Expounder of the worlds? Were it not for calamity, How would the sun of Thy patience shine, O Light of the worlds? Lament not because of the wicked. Thou wert created to bear and endure, O Patience of the worlds. . . . By Thee the banner of independence was planted on the highest peaks, And the sea of bounty surged, O Rapture of the worlds. By Thine aloneness the Sun of Oneness shone, and by Thy banishment the land of Unity was adorned. Be patient, O Thou Exile of the worlds. We have made abasement the garment of glory, And affliction the adornment of Thy temple, O Pride of the worlds. Thou seest the hearts are filled with hate, And to overlook is Thine, O Thou Concealer of the sins of the worlds. . . .

And then, once again, the Supreme Manifestation of Almighty God speaks:

> Verily, I have heard Thy Call, O All-Glorious Beloved; And now is the face of Bahá flaming with the heat of tribulation and with the fire of Thy shining word, and He hath risen up in faithfulness at the place of sacrifice, looking toward Thy pleasure, O Ordainer of the worlds.[3]

Let no one belittle and underestimate the dangers and hazards, the extreme gravity of the situation which the activities of the Azalís and their associates had engendered for the Bahá'ís within the enclave of 'Akká. Harassment was wearying, unbroken and ever-increasing. The life of Bahá'u'lláh was indeed imperilled by the venom of their hostility.

According to Áqá Riḍá, the fact that the views and attitudes of officials and notables, whose minds the Azalís had poisoned, were time and again changed by meeting the Most Great Branch, aroused in these evil-doers even more defiance and fury. Driven by boundless, consuming hate and jealousy, they strove the harder to injure Bahá'u'lláh and bring Him, His Cause and His followers into disrepute. Moreover, since their break with Mírzá Yaḥyá, we learn from Áqá Riḍá that Mírzá Riḍá-Qulí and his sister Badrí-Ján expected to have their own way at all times and to receive the best of everything. Mírzá Faḍlu'lláh, the son of Mírzá Naṣru'lláh (who had died in Adrianople), and Áqá 'Aẓím-i-Tafrishí, who had come from Ṭihrán with the two brothers, Naṣru'lláh and Riḍá-Qulí, as their servants, took themselves away and ceased to associate with Mírzá Riḍá-Qulí and Badrí-Ján. This separation so incensed Mírzá Ridá-Qulí that he went to the length of making a collection of some of the Writings of Bahá'u'lláh, corrupting the text with alterations and interpolations to make them sound heretical, anti-social and provocative. These forgeries were widely circulated to incite the public.

It was then that some of the followers of Bahá'u'lláh began to think of putting an end to these activities. Apart from Áqá Ḥusayn and Áqá Riḍá, whose accounts have frequently been referred to previously, our sources for this dire episode include two historical tracts, one by Mírzá Áqá Ján, the amanuensis of Bahá'u'lláh, and the other by Áqá Muḥammad-Javád-i-Qazvíní. Both men were eye-witnesses and both broke the Covenant of Bahá'u'lláh after His ascension.

An Arab believer named Náṣir, who was also known as Ḥájí 'Abbás, came to 'Akká from Beirut determined to silence the mischief-makers. In all probability, he was the same Náṣir who was implicated in the murder of Ḥájí Mírzá Aḥmad-i-Káshání, in Baghdád.* Once in 'Akká, his purpose was made clear, and not only would Bahá'u'lláh not countenance it, but He promptly ordered him to return to Beirut, which he did. Muḥammad-Javád quotes a Tablet addressed to Náṣir, which caused his return. The following is Professor Browne's translation of that Tablet:

HE is the Helper.

I bear witness that thou hast helped thy Lord, and art one of the helpers. To [the truth of] my testimony all things testify: this indeed is the root of

* According to Nabíl's Narrative, among the companions of Ṭáhirih as she travelled from Baghdád towards Persia was a certain 'Ábid and his son Náṣir, who later was known as Ḥájí 'Abbás. If this Náṣir is the same man, and there seems little reason to doubt it, then his later actions would seem to reflect something of the fervour and impetuosity of those who surrounded that far-famed Bábí heroine.

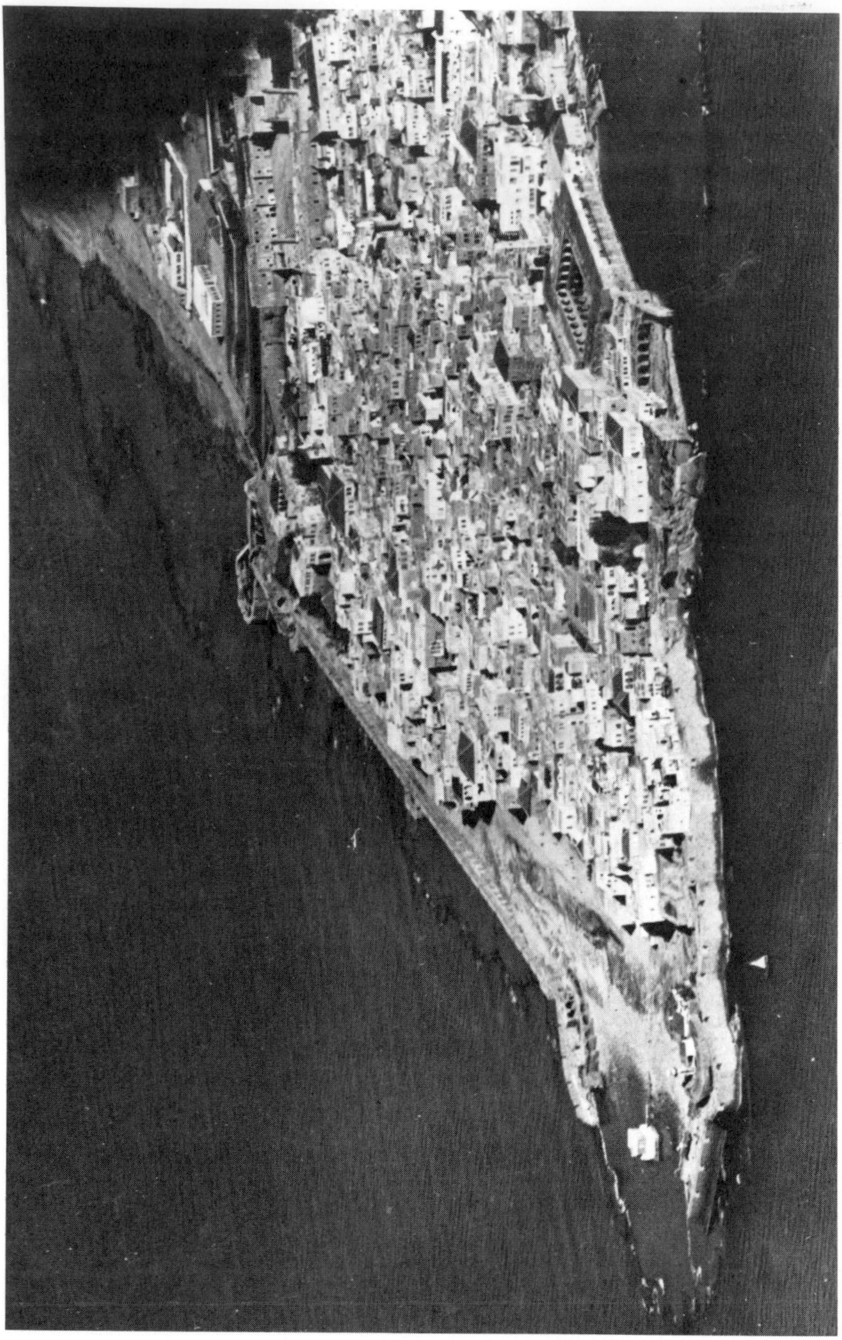

Aerial view of 'Akká in 1914 (by Adolf Kärcher)

the matter, if thou art of those who know. What thou dost by His command and approval is indeed the duty of help in the sight of thy Lord the All-knowing and All-understanding. Go hence and do not perpetrate that wherefrom mischief will result! Put thy trust in God: verily He will take whomsoever He will: verily He hath power over all things. Verily we have accepted what thou didst intend in the Way of God. Return to thy place: then commemorate thy Lord, the Mighty, the Praiseworthy.[4]

After Náṣir's departure, some of the companions, finding this highly-charged situation intolerable, went to Bahá'u'lláh to beg His permission to deal with the authors of mischief in their own way and bring their satanic activities to an end. Bahá'u'lláh, however, not only would not grant them the permission they sought, but counselled them most emphatically to shun all violence and retaliation. It seems that Muḥammad-Javád-i-Qazvíní, himself, was at first in league with those men, but withdrew from their company when bidden to do so by Bahá'u'lláh. Muḥammad-Javád relates that he was present, when Áqá Muḥammad-Ibráhím-i-Ká<u>sh</u>ání was pleading with Bahá'u'lláh for permission to eliminate Siyyid Muḥammad-i-Iṣfahání and his associates. Bahá'u'lláh directed Muḥammad-Javád to go home and stay there, and commanded Mírzá Muḥammad-Qulí, His brother, to eject Áqá Muḥammad-Ibráhím from His presence, which he did.

Seven of the companions, Áqá Muḥammad-Ibráhím-i-Náẓir, Mírzá Ḥusayn-i-Najjár (another native of Ká<u>sh</u>án), Áqá Ḥusayn-i-Á<u>sh</u><u>ch</u>í (also of Ká<u>sh</u>án), Mírzá Ja'far of Yazd, Ustád Aḥmad-i-Najjár, Áqá Muḥammad-'Alíy-i-Salmání and Ustád 'Abdu'l-Karím-i-<u>Kh</u>arráṭ, both of Iṣfahán, chose to disregard Bahá'u'lláh's strong injunction and began plotting to rid 'Akká and the exiles of the incubus of those evil men. There was such commotion afoot throughout the whole community that Bahá'u'lláh secluded Himself from all. He did what He had done in Adrianople at the time the rebellion of Mírzá Yaḥyá was about to come into the open, receiving no one, meeting no one.

Despite all this, these seven men persisted in their plans and committed those foul murders. Thus died Siyyid Muḥammad-i-Iṣfahání, the Antichrist of the Bahá'í Revelation; the irredeemable Áqá Ján-i-Kaj-Kuláh, the right-hand man of Siyyid Muḥammad from the days of Adrianople; and the fickle Mírzá Riḍá-Qulíy-i-Tafri<u>sh</u>í.

Let it be said at once that nothing condones murder. But the pressures to which the Bahá'ís were subjected can be measured by the fact that one of the seven men who murdered the Azalís was Áqá

Ḥusayn-i-Áshchí, whose recollections we have often quoted in these pages. Áqá Ḥusayn, it is true, was headstrong and self-willed, even standing up to the highest among the authorities. But he had grown up in the household of Bahá'u'lláh from the early days in Baghdád, and his devotion was total and hard to match. Yet at this juncture he succumbed to the pressures inflicted on the Bahá'ís by their adversaries.

As it happened, the three Azalís were lodged in a house fronting the *Seraye*. The sound of pistol shots, and of shouts and yelling, brought Ṣáliḥ Páshá, the Mutaṣarrif, from his house. And then pandemonium broke out. Áqá Riḍá writes: 'All, young and old, notables and humble folk, the Governor, the Chief of Police, and troops rose up, as if a powerful state had made an attack on them. Armed with stones and sticks, swords and rifles, they set out towards the house of the Blessed Perfection and the houses of the companions, arresting whomever they met. The Mutaṣarrif and his retinue and troops gathered around the house of the Blessed Perfection. It was now late in the afternoon. . .'

As was His custom at this time of day, Bahá'u'lláh was absorbed in the revelation of verses: 'Verily, the sea of calamity hath surged, and gales have overtaken the Ark of God, the All-Encompassing, the Self-Subsistent. O Mariner! Be not daunted by gales, for He Who is the Breaker of Dawns is with Thee in this darkness which hath enveloped the worlds'.[5]

It was an hour after sunset that an army officer, an official whom Muḥammad-Javád names as Sa'íd Big, and Ilyás 'Abbúd came into the *bírúní*. The Most Great Branch, Áqá Muḥammad-'Alíy-i-Iṣfahání, Ḥusayn-Áqáy-i-Tabrízí and Muḥammad-Javád-i-Qazvíní were there. They were asked by the officials to accompany them to the *Seraye*. Then they requested that Bahá'u'lláh should come as well. The Most Great Branch went into the inner quarters and presented their request to Bahá'u'lláh. He came out of the house, and, as it was quite dark, a man led the way with a lantern.

Áqá Riḍá tells us that all who encountered Him on that walk to the Government House marvelled at the power emanating from His person. One of the inhabitants of 'Akká, who saw Him on that day, instantly came to believe in Him and joined the ranks of the companions.

The Guardian of the Bahá'í Faith writes:

> The consternation that seized an already oppressed community was indescribable. Bahá'u'lláh's indignation knew no bounds. '*Were We,*' He thus voices His emotions, in a Tablet revealed shortly after this act had been committed, '*to make mention of what befell Us, the heavens would be rent asunder and the mountains would crumble.*'[6]

When Bahá'u'lláh entered the *Seraye*, Muḥammad-Javád-i-Qazvíní writes, Ṣáliḥ Páshá, the Mutaṣarrif, Salím Mulkí, the head of the secretariat, and other officials present stood up before Him. Bahá'u'lláh walked in and took a seat at the top end of the room. There was utter silence until, at last, the commandant of the garrison spoke: 'Is it meet that your men should commit such a heinous deed?' To which Bahá'u'lláh replied: 'Should a soldier under your command break a rule, would you be held responsible and punished for it?' Again there was total silence until Bahá'u'lláh rose up, according to Áqá Riḍá, and went into another room.

Then, officials went in search of other companions. Mírzá Muḥammad-Qulí, Mírzá Muḥammad-'Alí, the second surviving son of Bahá'u'lláh, and Mírzá Áqá Ján were brought in. But since Áqáy-i-Kalím was indisposed they let him be. Throughout that night, Muḥammad-Javád-i-Qazvíní writes, the whole town was in great commotion. That same night a Russian steamer cast anchor before 'Akká, and immediately officials banned all entry to or exit from that ship.

Four hours after sunset, they took Bahá'u'lláh away from the office of the Mutaṣarrif and lodged him, together with His son, Mírzá Muḥammad-'Alí, in a room in Khán-i-Shávirdí, while the Most Great Branch was led to the Límán (prison), and Áqá Mírzá Muḥammad-Qulí was taken elsewhere. Mírzá Áqá Ján was allowed to go home and bring all that Bahá'u'lláh required for the night. Then he was placed with a number of other companions in the gaol of the *Seraye*. The Guardian of the Bahá'í Faith writes of these events:

> Bahá'u'lláh was . . . kept in custody the first night, with one of His sons, in a chamber in the Khán-i-Shávirdí,* transferred for the following two

* Khán-i-Shávirdí is one of the caravanserais of 'Akká. Its date of construction is uncertain but it was probably built by al-Jazzár or Sulaymán Páshá. In its south-eastern corner is the Burju's-Sulṭán, the only one still standing of the numerous Crusader towers that once surrounded 'Akká. The eastern wing of this *khán* is adjacent to the Límán and was used as an extension of it. Thus this is probably where Bahá'u'lláh and His son were imprisoned.

Khán-i-Shávirdí: to the right is the Burju's-Sulṭán and behind it is the part of the Khán in which the companions were probably kept.

nights to better quarters in that neighbourhood, and allowed only after the lapse of seventy hours to regain His home. 'Abdu'l-Bahá was thrown into prison and chained during the first night, after which He was permitted to join His Father. Twenty-five of the companions were cast into another prison and shackled . . .[7]

Áqá Riḍá relates the case of Ḥájí 'Alí-'Askar, the same devoted soul who, at Adrianople, voluntarily accepted banishment to 'Akká and incarceration there. This veteran of the Faith had come face to face with the Báb, decades before, and had readily espoused His Cause. Now, not having been out of his house that day, he had not been arrested and taken away. But being informed of the detention of his fellow believers, he could not rest that night, and at dawn hurried to the *Seraye* and knocked at the gate. Although told to go away and not make a nuisance of himself, he continued to knock, insisting that he should share their fate. He would not hold his peace until he was pushed into prison with the rest of the companions. Áqá Riḍá also states that Mírzá Muḥammad-Qulí was detained in the same room with Bahá'u'lláh.

Finally, the Mutaṣarrif cabled all that had occurred to Ṣubḥí

Páshá,* the Válí of Syria, who took exception at once to the way Bahá'u'lláh had been treated and reprimanded the Mutaṣarrif. The next day, He was moved to the rooms above the Límán. In the afternoon of the third day, Muḥammad-Javád writes, Bahá'u'lláh, the Most Great Branch, Mírzá Muḥammad-'Alí and Mírzá Muḥammad-Qulí were led once again to the office of the Mutaṣarrif. Bahá'u'lláh had a slight fever that day, and when He told the Mutaṣarrif and the Muftí that they had not acted according to the edicts of God, the Mutaṣarrif informed Him that He was free to return home; as He rose to go, they all stood up and humbly apologized for their high-handed behaviour. Then He and the Most Great Branch, as well as Mírzá Muḥammad-'Alí, Mírzá Muḥammad-Qulí and Mírzá Áqá Ján, walked home.

The Guardian of the Bahá'í Faith has thus described that occasion:

> When interrogated, He was asked to state His name and that of the country from which He came. '*It is more manifest than the sun,*' He

* According to British consular records, Ṣubḥí Páshá arrived in Damascus 27 October 1871 to take up duties as Governor-General; he remained Governor until January 1873. (FO 195 976 and 1027)

Khán-i-Shávirdí

answered. The same question was put to Him again, to which He gave the following reply: '*I deem it not proper to mention it. Refer to the farmán of the government which is in your possession.*' Once again they, with marked deference, reiterated their request, whereupon Bahá'u'lláh spoke with majesty and power these words: '*My name is Bahá'u'lláh* (Light of God), *and My country is Núr* (Light). *Be ye apprized of it.*' Turning then, to the Muftí, He addressed him words of veiled rebuke, after which He spoke to the entire gathering, in such vehement and exalted language that none made bold to answer Him. Having quoted verses from the Súriy-i-Mulúk, He, afterwards, arose and left the gathering. The Governor, soon after, sent word that He was at liberty to return to His home, and apologized for what had occurred.[8]

The seven who were guilty of committing those murders were consigned to the Límán; their imprisonment lasted seven years. Sixteen others of the companions were moved after six days to Khán-i-Shávirdí, to the same room where Bahá'u'lláh had been held on the first night, and were confined there for six months.

Muḥammad-Javád-i-Qazvíní next records in his tract the murder of two other men, previous to the murder of Siyyid Muḥammad-i-Iṣfahání and his two accomplices. He names them as Ḥusayn-'Alí of Káshán, known as Khayyáṭ-Báshí, and Ḥájí Ibráhím, also of Káshán; but he does not name those who murdered them. Apparently, these two men of Káshán, who had always been fickle, had been in communication with the Azalís, although they lived with the companions in Khán al-'Umdán. Muḥammad-Javád writes that one day, in the bazar, Ḥájí Ibráhím denounced Áqáy-i-Kalím, in his presence, before the Muftí. This reprehensible behaviour roused the ire of the companions, and some of them (unnamed) murdered those two, and buried them in a room in the inn. This happened at a time when Bahá'u'lláh, because of the mounting animosity of the Azalís, had ceased admitting anyone into His presence. However, Siyyid Muḥammad had noted their disappearance and had reported it to the authorities. But, at the time, there was no reason to suspect any crime. After the murder of the three Azalís, during the interrogation of the companions, the murder of the two Káshánís came to light. Again, Muḥammad-Javád does not mention any names, but merely records that the authorities were told that the two had died of cholera, and lest all should be taken away and put into quarantine, they had been immediately and quietly interred in a room of the inn. The authorities exhumed their corpses and had them buried beside the Azalís.

Another point worth noting in the tract by Muḥammad-Javád-i-Qazvíní is that whereas the wife of Mírzá Yaḥyá, sister of Mírzá Riḍá-Qulíy-i-Tafrishí, has been named elsewhere as Badrí-Ján, Muḥammad-Javád calls her Badr-i-Jahán. And the sixteen men detained in the Khán-i-Shávirdí for six months are named as follows: Ḥájí 'Alí-'Askar-i-Tabrízí, his son, Ḥusayn-Áqá, and his brother, Mashhadí Fattáḥ; Ḥájí Ja'far and his brother, Ḥájí Taqí; Muḥammad-Javád-i-Qazvíní, himself; Áqá Faraj-i-Sulṭánábádí; Áqá Riḍáy-i-Shírází; Mírzá Maḥmúd-i-Káshání; Ḥájí Faraju'lláh-i-Tafrishí; Áqá 'Aẓím-i-Tafrishí; Áqá Muḥammad-'Alíy-i-Iṣfahání; Áqá Muḥammad-'Alíy-i-Yazdí; Darvísh Ṣidq-'Alíy-i-Qazvíní; Áqá Muḥammad-Ibráhím-Nayrízí, known as Amír-i-Nayrízí; and Ḥájí Áqáy-i-Tabrízí.

Nabíl-i-A'ẓam and Áqá Muḥammad-Ḥasan, the son of Ustád Báqir-i-Káshání, were also detained for a few days, but since they were not of the company of the exiles they were sent to Tripoli, near Beirut.

The situation in which Bahá'u'lláh and His companions were now placed has been described by the Guardian of the Bahá'í Faith:

> A population, already ill-disposed towards the exiles, was, after such an incident, fired with uncontrollable animosity for all those who bore the name of the Faith which those exiles professed. The charges of impiety, atheism, terrorism and heresy were openly and without restraint flung into their faces . . . Even the children of the imprisoned exiles, whenever they ventured to show themselves in the streets during those days, would be pursued, vilified and pelted with stones.
>
> The cup of Bahá'u'lláh's tribulations was now filled to overflowing . . .[9]

Even Ilyás 'Abbúd was so alarmed and terrified that he took steps to barricade his house against any access from the adjacent house of 'Údí Khammár, in which Bahá'u'lláh dwelt.

Áqá Riḍá gives a graphic account of the days of their detention in the Khán-i-Shávirdí. The artillerymen, stationed there to keep watch over them, were suspicious of any move they made, and treated them with great harshness. The exiles were constantly abused to their faces. However, their behaviour and their gentleness gradually broke down all barriers between them, until their gaolers confessed they had been misled by the lies fed to them. A day came at last, long before their release, when the exiles were allowed to visit other homes, as well as the house of Bahá'u'lláh. In the afternoon they entertained the artillerymen and the policemen to tea. They planted flowers in the yard and kept the old inn tidy. Each day one of them took charge of cooking and cleaning. Eventually their gaolers expressed their disgust at the attitude of those in high places, who remained adamant, refusing to let the exiles go home for good. But release was not far off. The Governor was dismissed, and Aḥmad Big Tawfíq, appointed in his place, was a just man.

36

The Turn of the Tide

AT last, Áqá Riḍá tells us, the men of the artillery revolted against the shilly-shallying of the authorities, took some of the exiles with them, and went to the *Seraye*, saying bluntly: 'We are soldiers, not gaolers. If these men are criminals then take them away and put them in prison. If not, let them go in peace to their homes. We refuse to act any longer as their keepers.' Whereupon the authorities relented. Eventually, the newly-appointed Mutaṣarrif sent for the relevant papers and released the companions who had been confined without cause in the Khán-i-Shávirdí.

The Guardian of the Bahá'í Faith writes:

> The gradual recognition by all elements of the population of Bahá'u'lláh's complete innocence; the slow penetration of the true spirit of His teachings through the hard crust of their indifference and bigotry; the substitution of the sagacious and humane governor, Aḥmad Big Tawfíq, for one whose mind had been hopelessly poisoned against the Faith and its followers; the unremitting labors of 'Abdu'l-Bahá, now in the full flower of His manhood, Who, through His contacts with the rank and file of the population, was increasingly demonstrating His capacity to act as the shield of His Father; the providential dismissal of the officials who had been instrumental in prolonging the confinement of the innocent companions – all paved the way for the reaction that was now setting in . . .[1]

Indeed, Aḥmad Big Tawfíq was so overwhelmed and captivated by the majesty of bearing, the charm of manners, the dignity of behaviour, and the vast knowledge of the Most Great Branch that, in order to show his reverence for Him, he would shed his shoes when in His presence. The writings of Bahá'u'lláh, which the antagonists had collected to turn the authorities against the Faith, also left a deep imprint on the mind of this just man, who was anxious to learn more. The Guardian of the Bahá'í Faith further writes:

> It was even bruited about that his [Aḥmad Big Tawfíq's] favored counselors were those very exiles who were the followers of the Prisoner in his

The town of 'Akká in the second half of the nineteenth century: this view from the north-east shows the Mosque of al-Jazzár on the right, the aqueduct in the foreground, and Mount Carmel in the distance across the Bay of Haifa on the left. (From Wilson, Picturesque Palestine*)*

custody. His own son he was wont to send to 'Abdu'l-Bahá for instruction and enlightenment. It was on the occasion of a long-sought audience with Bahá'u'lláh that, in response to a request for permission to render Him some service, the suggestion was made to him to restore the aqueduct which for thirty years had been allowed to fall into disuse* – a suggestion which he immediately arose to carry out.[2]

Áqá Riḍá states that Aḥmad Big Tawfíq met the Most Great Branch for the first time on the sea-shore, where 'Abdu'l-Bahá had gone for a swim. The Mutaṣarrif came there too and sat down and listened to Him. He was led to seek 'Abdu'l-Bahá's company by his perusal of the writings that had been handed over to the government in order to compromise the Faith. But reading them had the opposite effect on him. He was greatly impressed and felt bewildered. So, finding that the Most Great Branch was by the sea, he went there, and all his doubts were dispelled. Subsequently he requested that all the writings of Bahá'u'lláh which were in his possession should be copied in the best calligraphic style for him.

Even Ilyás 'Abbúd, who had been horrified to find himself a neigh-

* The aqueduct used to run from the spring at Kabrí to the mansion of 'Abdu'lláh Pá<u>sh</u>á at Mazra'ih, from there to Bahjí and thence to 'Akká, entering the city close to the Burj al-Kummandar. The first to build an aqueduct from Kabrí to the city was al-Jazzár, but that aqueduct ran along a course to the east of the present one, which was built by Sulaymán Pá<u>sh</u>á in 1814. It was improved by 'Abdu'lláh Pá<u>sh</u>á who used it to supply his properties at Mazra'ih and Bahjí. It had, however, evidently fallen into disrepair at the time of Bahá'u'lláh's arrival in 'Akká.

bour of Bahá'u'lláh, was now so subdued, so won over, and eventually, so devoted to Bahá'u'lláh and His eldest Son, that he knocked down the barriers he had erected between their two houses, and at last put his own house at the disposal of Bahá'u'lláh. It will be recalled that when 'Údí Khammár moved to his new mansion outside 'Akká, his house became available to Bahá'u'lláh and His family (see p. 317). This was the rear house, away from the sea-front, and Bahá'u'lláh took a room overlooking an open space at the back (the Saḥatu'l-'Abbúd). When, after a few years, Ilyás 'Abbúd made his own house available to Bahá'u'lláh, He moved into a room looking on the sea, and the cramped conditions in which the family had lived were much relieved. Today that whole complex of houses in which Bahá'u'lláh and His family dwelt for six years is named after him alone: Bayt 'Abbúd. It was through his intercession, repeated several times, that Bahá'u'lláh finally agreed to receive the Mutaṣarrif. As Áqá Riḍá puts it, one day, late in the afternoon, he went into the presence of the Blessed Perfection 'humbly and silently'. Ilyás 'Abbúd was beckoning to others who were present to bring a *qalyán* (hookah or water-pipe) for the Governor, but Aḥmad Big motioned them not to do so, for he

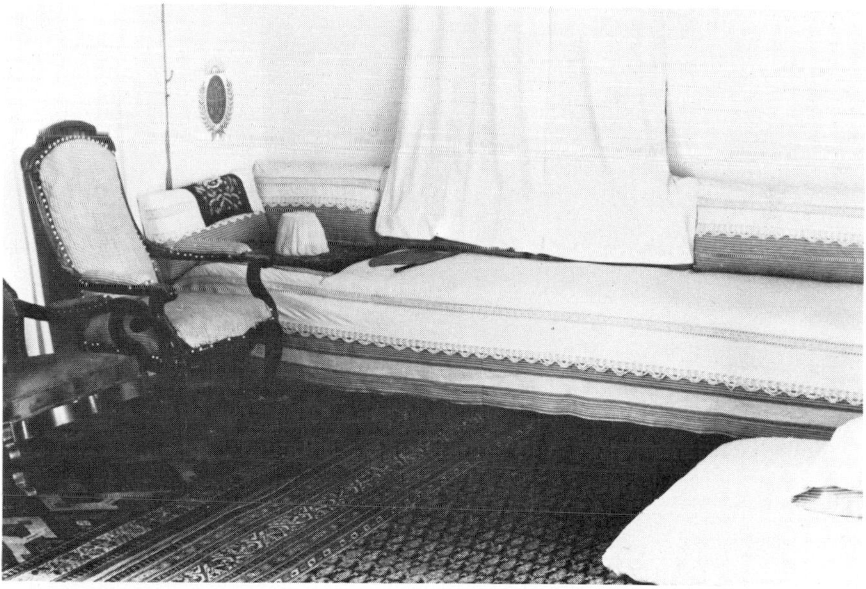

The room of Bahá'u'lláh in the House of 'Abbúd, overlooking the sea. (By Gunther Spank)

would not indulge himself in the presence of his Prisoner. Bahá'u'lláh, Áqá Riḍá states, requested him to review the cases of all who had been detained. This the Mutaṣarrif proceeded to do at once, reviewing each case with care and equity, including the cases of the seven who were incarcerated in the dreaded Límán. Those who knew that the authorities had, in the past, asked for 300 pounds before allowing anyone to leave the Khán-i-Shávirdí, were amazed when he permitted the companions, who had been in custody there for several months, to return to their homes in the other caravanserai. The seven guilty of murder were not released, however, as we have heard.

But Badrí-Ján was still agitating, complaining that her life was in danger, and that the companions would kill her as they had killed her brother, Mírzá Riḍá-Qulí. Therefore, Aḥmad Big Tawfíq decided that she should rejoin her husband, Mírzá Yaḥyá, but she would not consent to go peaceably and had to be taken away forcibly by the police. Once in Cyprus, she again demonstrated her aversion to Mírzá Yaḥyá by giving wide berth to Famagusta and choosing to live instead in another city, apparently Nicosia. From Cyprus, after a year or two, she went to Izmír (Smyrna), and thence to Istanbul, where she dwelt in

View from the room of Bahá'u'lláh in the House of 'Abbúd, 1922

the house of a Persian dealer in tobacco. We know that her daughters were married to Shaykh Aḥmad-i-Rúḥí and Mírzá Áqá Khán-i-Kirmání.[3] Six years later, hearing that the wife of Mírzá Yaḥyá, who was the mother of Mírzá Aḥmad, had died, she returned to Cyprus and joined her husband.

Thus the two years of Aḥmad Big Tawfíq's governorship passed, until he was recalled for another post. During those years no special favour was shown to him by Bahá'u'lláh and His eldest Son. But as soon as it became known that he was to go away, he was offered such hospitality as astonished the populace, until they learned that this could have been misconstrued while he held the reins of power in 'Akká. On the tower by the seaside, close to Bayt 'Abbúd, the Greatest Branch had a tent set up for him, to receive his guests and those coming to bid him farewell. Luncheons and dinners were provided for all during the days that he tarried there, preparing to leave. He asked for a copy of the Greatest Name, which Mírzá Muḥammad-'Alí, the son of Bahá'u'lláh, who was truly a master of calligraphy, penned for him. Until the day of his departure from 'Akká, Aḥmad Big Tawfíq continued to express his sorrow at his coming separation from Bahá'u'lláh and His eldest Son.

Thus did the tide turn, until no less a person than Shaykh Maḥmúd, the Muftí of 'Akká, gave his allegiance to the Prisoner, Who, according to the rescript of the Sulṭán, the Caliph of the House of Ottoman, was still to be kept in close confinement. But no one could ever dream now of enforcing that decree.

And now to the story of Shaykh Maḥmúd. He was a man well known in 'Akká, extremely fanatical, and, to begin with, extremely hostile to the exiles. Years later, after he had given his allegiance to Bahá'u'lláh, he recounted his spiritual odyssey. When he first heard the *farmán** of Sulṭán 'Abdu'l-'Azíz read in the mosque, he recalled, he boiled with rage and, not being able to contain himself, went to the gate of the citadel and demanded entry. He being a prominent figure amongst the citizens of 'Akká, the guards could not refuse his demand and allowed him to enter, but told him that he needed permission to go into the presence of Bahá'u'lláh. He asked for that permission, and the

* This *farmán* was supposed to have been lost, at a time when the *Seraye* was burnt down, but it survived the disaster, and, many years later, it miraculously came into the hands of 'Abdu'l-Bahá.

answer which came from Bahá'u'lláh was to the effect that he should first change his intent (which was to be abusive and insulting) before seeking a meeting. This reply shook him considerably but did not abate his hostility and ire. After a while, he made a second attempt to reach the presence of Bahá'u'lláh. This time he had a weapon hidden about him, intending to use it. Now the answer which came was: let him first divest himself of that which he is carrying. Shaykh Maḥmúd was truly astounded. Who is this man, he asked himself, who knows the secrets of hearts? At his third attempt he was a changed man, and was taken to Bahá'u'lláh's chamber. There and then he threw himself at the feet of Bahá'u'lláh, and declared his belief in Him, whoever He was.

Thus, Shaykh Maḥmúd, the erstwhile bitter foe, became a Bahá'í, ever ready to be of service to his Lord.

Mírzá Núri'd-Dín-i-Zayn (Zeine) states in his most valuable memoirs that Shaykh Maḥmúd used to go out into the countryside at night with a lantern and, whenever he encountered a Bahá'í come from afar and unable to gain entry into the city, he gave him the lantern to carry in front of him, as his servant; and thus he took the pilgrim into 'Akká, and into the citadel. And in the same way he would lead the pilgrim back to the safety of the countryside. And again, according to Mírzá Núri'd-Dín's memoirs, after the ascension of Bahá'u'lláh, until the outer wall of the shrine-chamber was reinforced and strengthened, Shaykh Maḥmúd kept watch in a tent set up next to the wall. That construction work took about a week to complete.

37

The Marriage of the Most Great Branch

Two brothers, natives of Iṣfahán, Mírzá Muḥammad-'Alíy-i-Nahrí and Mírzá Hádíy-i-Nahrí, were guided by the Bábu'l-Báb to espouse most ardently the new Faith which had dawned at Shíráz. A third brother, Mírzá Ibráhím, whose name is immortalized not because of his own attainments, but because of the achievements and the supreme sacrifice of his two sons,* did not go their way and not only held himself aloof, but helped to deprive his brothers of a good share of their patrimony because of their recognition of the Qá'im of the House of Muḥammad when He shed His light upon the world.

Mírzá Muḥammad-'Alí and Mírzá Hádí were the sons of Mírzá Siyyid Mihdíy-i-Nahrí, a man of great wealth, whose father, Siyyid Muḥammad-i-Hindí (the Indian), a native of Zavárih (a small town close to Iṣfahán), had acquired his vast riches in India by marriage to a daughter of an Indian royal house. During his sojourn in India, Siyyid Muḥammad had been assured by a seer that his descendants would, before long, come to witness the advent of the Qá'im; thus he had specified in his will that the bulk of his wealth should be laid at the feet of that 'Lord of the Age'.

After the death of Siyyid Muḥammad-i-Hindí, his son, Ḥájí Siyyid Mihdí, migrated to 'Iráq and resided in Najaf. Both there and in Karbilá he had shops and caravanserais built for the convenience of the public, and a rivulet (canal) dug which greatly benefited the people; hence he came to be known as Nahrí (of the river).

In the days of Siyyid Káẓim-i-Rashtí, Mírzá Muḥammad-'Alí and Mírzá Hádí had seen a young Siyyid of Shíráz in Karbilá, to whom they were greatly attracted by His demeanour, His devotion and His courtesy. And so, when first they heard of the dawning Light in Shíráz,

* These sons were Mírzá Ḥasan and Mírzá Ḥusayn, who gained the crown of martyrdom, and on whom the Most Exalted Pen conferred the designations Sulṭánu'sh-Shuhadá' (the King of the Martyrs) and Maḥbúbu'sh-Shuhadá' (the Beloved of the Martyrs).

their thoughts went back to the memory of that encounter with the young Shírází Siyyid. They were not mistaken, for He was no other than Siyyid 'Alí-Muḥammad – the Báb.

It is related that the wife of Ḥájí Siyyid Mihdí was a woman known for her piety and her observance of the devotions of her Faith. Prior to the birth of her two sons, she dreamt one night that two moons, in the fulness of their splendour, came out of the well in the courtyard of their house and sought repose in the shelter of her garments. So thrilled was she by her dream that the next day at the hour of dawn she betook herself to the house of the celebrated mujtahid, Ḥájí Siyyid Muḥammad-Báqir-i-Shaftí, to ask his interpretation. He told her to be well assured, for her dream denoted that two of her offspring would become shining lights, whose éclat would illumine the annals of their family. Soon after, Mírzá Muḥammad-'Alí and, fifteen months later, Mírzá Hádí were born. As they grew up, the elder showed talent and inclination for theological studies, and the younger chose to seclude himself from the mart, where his father engaged in buying and selling, to devote himself to a life of prayer and meditation. So impressed by his mien and attitude was that same mujtahid that he gave Mírzá Hádí his own niece to be his wife. This lady, who eventually became the mother-in-law of the King of the Martyrs, was honoured by the title of Shamsu'ḍ-Ḍuḥá (the Luminous Orb) from the Most Sublime Pen (Bahá'u'lláh).

After the espousal of the Cause of the Báb by these two brothers, other sons of Ḥájí Siyyid Mihdíy-i-Nahrí rose up to oppose them and mulcted them of the major share of their inheritance. These two presented a box of jewels to Ṭáhirih in Karbilá, which had belonged to their father, Ḥájí Siyyid Mihdí. From the proceeds of their sale, Ṭáhirih was enabled to defray her expenses. Mírzá Muḥammad-'Alí was in Iṣfahán and lived in the theological college, Madrisiy-i-Kásihgarán, while his wife, their marriage being childless, lived and died in Karbilá. It was then that Ḥájí Áqá Muḥammad-i-Nafaqih-Furúsh, another Bábí of Iṣfahán, suggested to Mírzá Muḥammad-'Alí to move from the *Madrisih* to his house and be wedded to his sister, with which Mírzá Muḥammad-'Alí complied. But this marriage too was childless, until the time when the Báb reached Iṣfahán.

The Governor of Iṣfahán, Manúchihr Khán, the Mu'tamidu'd-Dawlih, had asked Mír Siyyid Muḥammad, the Imám-Jum'ih of that city, to receive and lodge the Báb; and the Imám-Jum'ih had appointed Mírzá Ibráhím, the brother of Mírzá Muḥammad-'Alíy-i-Nahrí, who worked for the Imám in the management of his properties, to act as host to the Báb. One night, a number of people were invited to dine with the Báb, and Mírzá Muḥammad-'Alíy-i-Nahrí was one of the guests. The Báb asked him if he had any children, and on hearing that although married twice he had remained childless, the Báb offered a spoonful of His own sweet to Mírzá Muḥammad-'Alí, who ate some and kept the rest for his wife. Not long after, she found herself with child.

But much had happened since those days of the Báb's sojourn in Iṣfahán, and He was now a prisoner in the castle of Máh-Kú in Ádharbáyján, while His followers were experiencing fierce opposition and persecution. In response to the call of the Báb, Mírzá Muḥammad-'Alíy-i-Nahrí, together with twenty-five Bábís of Iṣfahán and its environs, set out for Khurásán, as did many other followers of the Báb, where they gathered in the hamlet of Badasht to take counsel together. Before leaving, he advised his wife, who was expecting their child, that should a daughter be born to them she should be called Fáṭimih. It was this child, the first-born of the marriage of Mírzá Muḥammad-'Alíy-i-Nahrí and the sister of Áqá Muḥammad-i-Nafaqih-Furúsh, who was destined to become the wife of the Most Great Branch, the eldest Son of Bahá'u'lláh.

Mírzá Muḥammad-'Alí has recounted that when the Conference of Badasht had ended, and its participants were set upon by the people of Níyálá, he and his brother, Mírzá Hádí, together with other Bábís, took a particular road to escape their tormentors. Mírzá Hádí was much fatigued and faint and, happening upon an old ruined caravanserai, they all took refuge. In the course of the night Mírzá Hádí died; when morning came, Mírzá Muḥammad-'Alí found that his companions had already gone. His plight seemed hopeless, for how could he find assistance to inter his dead brother? As he stood outside the gates of the caravanserai, gazing blankly at the waste around him, a woman appeared who stopped to ask who he was and what he was doing there. Mírzá Muḥammad-'Alí replied that his dead brother lay within, and that he required help to consign him to his grave. To his amazement and relief the woman replied: 'Have no worry on that account. Last night I dreamt of the Lady, Fáṭimih. She told me, "One of my descendants has just died in that caravanserai; go and help with his interment." That is why I am here.' The woman went back to her village and presently returned with some men. They washed and shrouded the body of Mírzá Hádí, and laid him to rest by the roadside. Mírzá Muḥammad-'Alí, utterly weary, his brother dead and all traces of his sister lost after Badasht, took the road back to Iṣfahán.

Years rolled by. Holocausts decimated the ranks of the Bábís. The Báb, Himself, suffered martyrdom. Then came the attempt on the life of Náṣiri'd-Dín Sháh, and many more of Mírzá Muḥammad-'Alí's co-religionists met the death of martyrs. Jináb-i-Bahá, Whom Mírzá Muḥammad-'Alí had come to know at Badasht, was banished to 'Iráq. And in the meantime, Mírzá Muḥammad-'Alí's nephews, Mírzá Ḥasan and Mírzá Ḥusayn, had embraced the new Faith.

The fame of Jináb-i-Bahá (Mírzá Ḥusayn-'Alíy-i-Núrí) was spreading far and wide. The uncle and his nephews decided to travel to 'Iráq to meet Him. On the way the nephews often besought their uncle to be their spokesman when they reached 'Iráq, and Mírzá Muḥammad-'Alí would assure them: 'Do not feel so anxious. At Badasht, Jináb-i-Bahá and myself became great friends. I know Him very well.'

But as soon as they went into the presence of Bahá'u'lláh, Mírzá Muḥammad-'Alíy-i-Nahrí became almost tongue-tied, and his deference knew no bounds. On leaving the presence of Bahá'u'lláh, the nephews were insistent to know what had happened to their uncle, after all his claims of close friendship with Bahá'u'lláh. He could only reply: 'But this is not that Jináb-i-Bahá whom I came to know at Badasht. I swear by the Almighty God that He is no other than the Promised One of the Bayán; this is "He Whom God shall make manifest".'

For His part, Bahá'u'lláh poured out His Divine love abundantly on these dedicated, self-effacing believers from Iṣfahán. And He, Himself, reminded Mírzá Muḥammad-'Alíy-i-Nahrí: 'We, you must remember, were close companions and great friends at Badasht.'

Bahá'u'lláh intended to give His niece, Shahr-Bánú Khánum, the daughter of Mírzá Muḥammad-Ḥasan, in marriage to His eldest Son. That was also the great hope of Mírzá Muḥammad-Ḥasan, who hurried to Baghdád and pleaded with Bahá'u'lláh to bring about this union. But he passed away before the Most Great Branch came of age.

And when Bahá'u'lláh sent Áqá Muḥammad-Javád-i-Káshání (the father of Áqá Ḥusayn-i-Áshchí) with a ring and a cashmere shawl (as was the custom of the day) to Ṭihrán, to ask the hand of Shahr-Bánú Khánum for 'Abbás, the Most Great Branch, both Sháh-Sulṭán Khánum (known as Khánum Buzurg – the Great Lady), His half-sister who eventually sided with Mírzá Yaḥyá, and His half-brother, Ḥájí Mírzá Riḍá-Qulí, who after the death of Mírzá Muḥammad-Ḥasan stood as father to Shahr-Bánú, refused to allow her to go to 'Iráq to be wedded to the Most Great Branch. She was eventually married to Mírzá 'Alí Khán, a son of the Grand Vizier, Mírzá Áqá Khán. As her brother, Mírzá Faḍlu'lláh, the Niẓámu'l-Mamálik, a devout follower of Bahá'u'lláh, has recorded, Shahr-Bánú Khánum was never reconciled to this marriage forced upon her by her aunt and uncle and pined all the rest of her young life, until consumption took her away. Ḥájí Mírzá Riḍá-Qulí, it has been said, stood out against the marriage of Shahr-Bánú and the Most Great Branch because he was

Sháh-Sulṭán Khánum (Khánum Buzurg) the half-sister of Bahá'u'lláh

afraid that Náṣiri'd-Dín Sháh and his ministers would frown on this marriage and take him to task.

Naturally, speculation was rife as to whom the Most Great Branch would marry. It is reported that one day Bahá'u'lláh told Siyyid Mihdíy-i-Dahijí of a dream He had had. 'We dreamt', He said, 'that the face of the winsome girl, the daughter of Our brother Mírzá Ḥasan, whom We had asked to be married to the Most Great Branch, became gradually darker and darker, until it vanished, and there appeared another girl, whose face was luminous and whose heart was luminous, and We chose her for the wife of the Most Great Branch.'

In the meantime, in Iṣfahán, Fáṭimih Khánum, the daughter of Mírzá Muḥammad-'Alíy-i-Nahrí, was wedded to her cousin, a younger brother of the King of the Martyrs and the Beloved of the Martyrs. Fáṭimih Khánum consented to this marriage, although she had not wished it. But strangely, on their wedding night, the bridegroom kept apart from the bride, to the utter astonishment of their relatives, and not long after, the young man suddenly passed away. Before long a Tablet addressed to the King of the Martyrs (Sulṭánu'sh-Shuhadá') reached Iṣfahán, in which Bahá'u'lláh told him: 'We have considered you as related to Us', which rather made him wonder whether one of his relatives had sent a supplication to Bahá'u'lláh. He made enquiries and was assured that no one had. He advised them all not to breathe a word to anyone, but await what might follow that blessed Tablet. A few months passed, until Shaykh Salmán, the courier, came to Iṣfahán. He told Sulṭánu'sh-Shuhadá': 'I have brought you tidings of a wonderful bounty. I am commissioned to take your cousin, the daughter of the late Mírzá Muḥammad-'Alí, to the Holy Land, going by way of Mecca as pilgrims on *ḥajj*. You must make arrangements for us to leave Iṣfahán in time for the pilgrimage, to travel to Shíráz and Búshihr. These preparations must be done quietly, and no one should know of our journey until a few days before our departure.' When the time came, Fáṭimih Khánum and her brother, Siyyid Yaḥyá, accompanied by Shaykh Salmán and a servant, left for Shíráz. On arrival there, they first took lodgings in a caravanserai, but the Afnáns came soon and led them to the house of Ḥájí Mírzá Siyyid Muḥammad, the maternal uncle of the Báb. This was in the year 1872.

The next day, Khadíjih-Bigum, the wife of the Báb, called on Fáṭimih Khánum, and took her to the house of Ḥájí Mírzá Siyyid 'Alí,

Fáṭimih, Munírih Khánum, the wife of 'Abdu'l-Bahá

the martyred uncle of the Báb, where Khadíjih-Bigum herself lived. These houses were close to each other. Fáṭimih Khánum, herself, writes in her short autobiography:[1]

> The wife of the uncle [of the Báb] was a lady of great probity, always occupied with her devotions, but she was not confirmed in this wondrous Cause. [She was a half-sister of the wife of the Báb.] She used to say: 'What an uproar did this Mírzá 'Alí-Muḥammad of ours cause in this world! How many precious souls perished! How much blood was shed!' I would tell her politely: 'My dear Lady, this Mírzá 'Alí-Muḥammad of yours was the Qá'im of the House of Muḥammad, the Promised One of all the Scriptures. Every time and in every age when the Call of God was sounded, the same uproar was caused in this world, and streams of blood flowed. It has ever been the same. You read the Qur'án, by day and by night. Do you not read there these verses: " . . . and whensoever there came to you a Messenger with that your souls had not desire for, did you become arrogant, and some cry lies to, and some slay?" and "Ah, woe for those servants! Never comes unto them a Messenger, but they mock at Him." '[2] Then I read a few more verses from the Qur'án. She said: 'No one knows the true meaning of what is in the Qur'án, except God, and the people confirmed in learning.' I said: 'Very well, be it so, with your view and your inclination! We will leave the Qur'án aside, and read from the *Mathnaví* [the great poetical work of Jaláli'd-Dín-i-Rúmí]. What did Pharaoh do with Moses? What did the people of Palestine do with Jesus? What did the people of Ḥijáz do with the Messenger of God?' . . . We spent a good deal of time reading from the *Mathnaví*. . . . After our departure from Shíráz, she accepted the Faith.

Fáṭimih Khánum, whom we shall soon know as Munírih Khánum, the name given to her by Bahá'u'lláh, then relates in her autobiography some of what she heard from the wife of the Báb about herself. Khadíjih-Bigum told her:

> One night, I dreamt that Fáṭimih [the daughter of the Prophet] had come to our house, to ask for my hand. My sisters and I went to her presence with great joy and eagerness. She rose up and kissed me on my forehead. In my dream, I felt that she had approved of me. In the morning, I got up very elated, but modesty stopped me telling anyone of my dream. The same day, in the afternoon, the mother of that Blessed Being [the Báb] came to our house. My sister and myself went to meet her, and exactly as I had seen in my dream she rose up and, embracing me, kissed me on my forehead. When she had gone, I was told by my elder sister that she had come to ask for my hand. I said: 'How fortunate I am', and then, I related my dream of the previous night . . .

The stay in Shíráz greatly delighted Fáṭimih Khánum, particularly by reason of consorting with the wife of the Báb. But, too soon for her, the time came when Shaykh Salmán expedited departure on the next stage of their journey. He told Fáṭimih Khánum and Siyyid Yaḥyá that Bahá'u'lláh specifically wanted them to travel with the caravan of pilgrims going to Mecca. They were eighteen days at sea before reaching Jiddah (Jaddih), and then went on to Mecca to perform the rites of the pilgrimage, in February 1873. There they met Siyyid 'Alí-Akbar-i-Dahijí (nephew of Siyyid Mihdí) and his wife, who had come from the Holy Land to perform the *ḥajj*. From them they learned to their consternation that, because of certain recent events (the murder of the Azalís), the companions had been, once again, thrown into gaol, and no one was allowed to enter 'Akká. But Shaykh Salmán was certain that because it had been the wish of Bahá'u'lláh, a way would be found for them to go into 'Akká. Returning from Mecca, they found at Jiddah a letter from Mírzá Áqá Ján awaiting them. It instructed them to remain in that sea-town until all the pilgrims had gone home, and then proceed to Alexandria and await there a cable from the Holy Land. Fáṭimih Khánum writes that there were seventeen of them (Bahá'ís) thus gathered in Alexandria. At last, a cable came from Bahá'u'lláh, directing them all to disperse except their party of four – Fáṭimih Khánum, Siyyid Yaḥyá, Shaykh Salmán and their servant – who were to take the Austrian boat to 'Akká, where they would be met by 'Abdu'l-Aḥad. This 'Abdu'l-Aḥad, a native of Shíráz, had been directed by Bahá'u'lláh, when it had become apparent that He would be banished to 'Akká, to go there and establish himself. Being free and under no restraint, 'Abdu'l-Aḥad could thus be of service to the companions, who did as they were bidden; but when the steamer anchored before 'Akká, there was no sign of 'Abdu'l-Aḥad. All the passengers disembarked, the ship was emptied, night came on, and the gangway was raised. Shaykh Salmán was calling aloud, all the while, Fáṭimih Khánum recalls, until, at the very last minute, 'Abdu'l-Aḥad came in a boat; once again the steps were lowered and they left the steamer. It was very dark, Fáṭimih Khánum writes, and she saw no one on the landing-stage except Áqáy-i-Kalím and Ilyás 'Abbúd. But later the Greatest Holy Leaf told her that the Most Great Branch had also been on the quayside, at the behest of Bahá'u'lláh, although she had failed to see Him. Áqáy-i-Kalím took them to the Khán-i-Juraynı́ (also known as Khán al-'Umdán), where he and his family lodged. The next day, members of the family of Bahá'u'lláh called to conduct those who had newly arrived to His presence. Fáṭimih Khánum writes, 'His very first words were: "We brought you into the prison-city, at a time when the prison-gates were closed in the face of all, to make clear and evident to all the power of God."' Fáṭimih Khánum lived for five months in the home of Áqáy-i-Kalím. She attained the presence of Bahá'u'lláh every now and then, and whenever Áqáy-i-Kalím came from the presence of Bahá'u'lláh, he had with him a gift for her. And then, she writes:

> One day, Áqáy-i-Kalím told me: 'I have brought you a wonderful gift from the Blessed Perfection. He has given you a new name: Munírih [Luminous].' Hearing that, I immediately recalled the dream of which the Blessed Perfection had spoken to Áqá Siyyid Mihdí, who had related it to us: 'In the world of dreams, I saw that the daughter of My brother, Mírzá Ḥasan, fell ill, the colour of her visage changed, and gradually she became more and more slender and weak, until she departed from this world; and in her place stood a girl with a luminous face and a luminous heart, and We chose her for the Most Great Branch.' Because of the lack of a house, I lived in the house of Áqáy-i-Kalím, and whenever Khájih 'Abbúd, the landlord, asked the reason, no definite answer was given to him, until he himself realized that it was the lack of space. Thereupon, he immediately opened up a room in his own house to the quarters where the members of the Holy Family lived, and had it beautifully decorated.

Khájih 'Abbúd presented this room to Bahá'u'lláh, saying, 'I have had this room prepared for the Master.' Bahá'u'lláh accepted it, and there was no longer any hindrance to the wedding of the Most Great Branch. Bahá'íyyih Khánum, the Greatest Holy Leaf, gave Munírih Khánum a white dress to wear, and at three hours after sunset she was led into the presence of Bahá'u'lláh, Who was then resting, as Munírih Khánum writes, under a mosquito net. Then the Tongue of Grandeur thus addressed her:

> O My Leaf and My Handmaiden, verily We chose thee and accepted thee to serve My Most Great Branch, and this is by My grace which is not equalled by all the treasures of Earth and Heaven. Many maidens, in Baghdád, in Adirnih, in this Most Great Prison, hoped for this bounty, but it was not given to them. You must render thanks unto God for this great bounty, and this exalted bestowal given unto you. May God be with you.

Bahá'íyyih Khánum, the Greatest Holy Leaf, the sister of 'Abdu'l-Bahá

The room in which the Kitáb-i-Aqdas was revealed, in the back portion of the House of 'Abbúd (the house of 'Údí Khammár) where Bahá'u'lláh lived at first; later, Bahá'u'lláh moved to the front of the house and 'Abdu'l-Bahá occupied this room. The furnishings are from 'Abdu'l-Bahá's time.

38

Last Years within the City Walls

IT was in Bayt 'Abbúd, in the year 1873, during the governorship of Aḥmad Big Tawfíq, that Bahá'u'lláh completed the revelation of the *Kitáb-i-Aqdas* – the Most Holy Book – containing the laws and ordinances of His Dispensation, and much else besides. He had but recently taken His residence in this house belonging to 'Údí Khammár, and the troubles inflicted upon Him by enemies and even His own companions still surged about Him. The *Kitáb-i-Aqdas* superseded the *Kitáb-i-Bayán* revealed by the Báb, and its 'promulgation', in the words of the Guardian of the Bahá'í Faith, 'may well rank as the most signal act of His ministry . . .'

In his exposition of the range and significance of this unique Book, some lines of which are quoted below, the Guardian discloses a vision of the central and majestic part the *Kitáb-i-Aqdas* is destined to take in the unfoldment of world society.

> Alluded to in the Kitáb-i-Íqán; the principal repository of that Law which the Prophet Isaiah had anticipated, and which the writer of the Apocalypse had described as the '*new heaven*' and the '*new earth,*' as '*the Tabernacle of God,*' as the '*Holy City,*' as the '*Bride,*' the '*New Jerusalem coming down from God,*' this '*Most Holy Book,*' whose provisions must remain inviolate for no less than a thousand years, and whose system will embrace the entire planet, may well be regarded as the brightest emanation of the mind of Bahá'u'lláh, as the Mother Book of His Dispensation, and the Charter of His New World Order.
>
> . . . this Book, this treasury enshrining the priceless gems of His Revelation, stands out, by virtue of the principles it inculcates, the administrative institutions it ordains and the function with which it invests the appointed Successor of its Author, unique and incomparable among the world's sacred Scriptures. . . . the Kitáb-i-Aqdas, revealed from first to last by the Author of the Dispensation Himself, not only preserves for posterity the basic laws and ordinances on which the fabric of His future World Order must rest, but ordains, in addition to the function of interpretation

which it confers upon His Successor, the necessary institutions through which the integrity and unity of His Faith can alone be safeguarded.

In this Charter of the future world civilization its Author – at once the Judge, the Lawgiver, the Unifier and Redeemer of mankind – announces to the kings of the earth the promulgation of the '*Most Great Law*'; pronounces them to be His vassals; proclaims Himself the '*King of Kings*'; disclaims any intention of laying hands on their kingdoms; reserves for Himself the right to '*seize and possess the hearts of men*'; warns the world's ecclesiastical leaders not to weigh the '*Book of God*' with such standards as are current amongst them; and affirms that the Book itself is the '*Unerring Balance*' established amongst men. In it He formally ordains the institution of the '*House of Justice,*' defines its functions, fixes its revenues, and designates its members as the '*Men of Justice,*' the '*Deputies of God,*' the '*Trustees of the All-Merciful,*' alludes to the future Center of His Covenant, and invests Him with the right of interpreting His holy Writ; anticipates by implication the institution of Guardianship; bears witness to the revolutionizing effect of His World Order; enunciates the doctrine of the '*Most Great Infallibility*' of the Manifestation of God; asserts this infallibility to be the inherent and exclusive right of the Prophet; and rules out the possibility of the appearance of another Manifestation ere the lapse of at least one thousand years . . .

The significant summons issued to the Presidents of the Republics of the American continent to seize their opportunity in the Day of God and to champion the cause of justice; the injunction to the members of parliaments throughout the world, urging the adoption of a universal script and language; His warnings to William I, the conqueror of Napoleon III; the reproof He administers to Francis Joseph, the Emperor of Austria; His reference to '*the lamentations of Berlin*' in His apostrophe to '*the banks of the Rhine*'; His condemnation of '*the throne of tyranny*' established in Constantinople, and His prediction of the extinction of its '*outward splendor*' and of the tribulations destined to overtake its inhabitants; the words of cheer and comfort He addresses to His native city, assuring her that God had chosen her to be '*the source of the joy of all mankind*'; His prophecy that '*the voice of the heroes of Khurásán*' will be raised in glorification of their Lord; His assertion that men '*endued with mighty valor*' will be raised up in Kirmán who will make mention of Him; and finally, His magnanimous assurance to a perfidious brother who had afflicted Him with such anguish, that an '*ever-forgiving, all-bounteous*' God would forgive him his iniquities were he only to repent – all these further enrich the contents of a Book designated by its Author as '*the source of true felicity,*' as the '*Unerring Balance,*' as the '*Straight Path*' and as the '*quickener of mankind.*'[1]

'So vast is its range', was Bahá'u'lláh's own testimony, 'that it hath encompassed all men ere their recognition of it. Erelong will its sovereign power, its pervasive influence and the greatness of its might be manifested on earth.'[2]

Aḥmad Big Tawfíq, the benevolent governor, was succeeded by 'Abdu'r-Raḥmán Pá<u>sh</u>á, a man double-faced, who began his game of duplicity soon after his arrival. Outwardly, he was all friendliness, and when meeting the Most Great Branch on several occasions, he would display both amity and respect. But, in stealth, he was keeping in close touch with the adversaries of the Faith amongst the inhabitants of 'Akká. Together they planned a systematic campaign against the Bahá'ís. Report after report to higher authorities pressed the complaint that these exiles, who had been sent to 'Akká to be segregated lest they contaminate others, had gained a high measure of freedom, met with anyone they liked, went unhindered wherever they pleased, had profitable shops, conducted remunerative businesses. At last, an order came, stating that as the Bahá'ís were prisoners they had no right to keep shops and engage in business. 'Abdu'r-Raḥmán Pá<u>sh</u>á was greatly delighted with these fresh instructions from his superiors and decided to put them into effect in a dramatic way. As it was the month of Ramaḍán, the Muslim month of fasting, he planned to walk into the bazar with his men, and order the Bahá'ís to close and abandon their shops. Such a public act by the governor of the city would, undoubtedly, have been highly damaging to the reputation of the Bahá'ís.

The Most Great Branch was cognizant of these trickeries of the Mutaṣarrif, and Bahá'u'lláh instructed the companions to keep their shops closed. When the day came and 'Abdu'r-Raḥmán Pá<u>sh</u>á walked into the bazar, all haughtiness and pomposity, attended by a circle of fawning officials as well as some of the adversaries of the Faith, he found the first shop owned by a companion shut, then the next, the third, and the fourth. 'It is the month of Ramaḍán,' he commented, 'and they have not opened their shops early. But they are certain to come before long and open them.' So he waited in the house of the sentry for an hour or two, but still there was no sign of any Bahá'í coming to open his shop. Just then, into the midst of that company walked the Muftí, an expression of concern on his face and holding a sheet of paper which he passed to the Governor. It was a cable from Raf'at Big, in Damascus, announcing the dismissal of 'Abdu'r-Raḥmán Pá<u>sh</u>á, and the temporary appointment of As'ad Effendi in his place; he also asked that his greetings be conveyed to His Eminence 'Abbás Effendi. 'Abdu'r-Raḥmán Pá<u>sh</u>á was aghast, and the adversaries of the Faith dumbfounded. In the meantime, the head of the telegraph office had hurried with a copy of the cable to show it to 'Abdu'l-Bahá. Had 'Abbás Effendi, an official queried, been in communication with high authorities? No, the Most Great Branch replied, He had not made any complaint to anyone; He had only turned to the Concourse on high. The official, Áqá Riḍá tells us, affirmed that what had occurred was unprecedented, indeed, a miracle.

As'ad Effendi had been commissioned to investigate in 'Akká the reports concerning the Bahá'ís, prior to the appointment of another governor. The well-wishers of the Faith had warned him against hasty action or any display of power; these exiles, they had told him, were people who should receive every consideration. He had well understood the situation, and when he reached 'Akká all he said was that his superiors had laid on him the duty of investigation. That was why he wished to go into the presence of Bahá'u'lláh. Although informed that Bahá'u'lláh did not receive visitors, he repeated his request, for it had been stated in the reports drawn up by the adversaries of the Faith that Bahá'u'lláh could not be seen because He was not there; He had managed to take Himself away. Once again Ilyás 'Abbúd interceded, Bahá'u'lláh granted the request, and As'ad Effendi came. He entered the presence of Bahá'u'lláh with humility and reverence, knelt down and kissed the hem of His garment, and begged for His blessings and confirmation.

As'ad Effendi remained acting mutaṣarrif for a time, until Fayḍí Pá<u>sh</u>á came. During the new Governor's short tenure of office he did a great deal to further the cause of education in 'Akká, and also to secure for the city a good supply of fresh water. Towards the exiles he displayed a very friendly manner. And now another miracle was witnessed by all in 'Akká, when, from deep wells that had carried only brackish water, fresh water suitable for human consumption gushed out. Describing this period, the Guardian of the Bahá'í Faith has written:

> Though Bahá'u'lláh Himself practically never granted personal interviews, as He had been used to do in Ba<u>gh</u>dád, yet such was the influence He now wielded that the inhabitants openly asserted that the noticeable improvement in the climate and water of their city was directly attributable to

His continued presence in their midst. The very designations by which they chose to refer to him, such as the 'august leader,' and 'his highness' bespoke the reverence with which He inspired them.[3]

After nearly two months Fayḍí Pá<u>sh</u>á was called back to Istanbul, and was replaced by Ibráhím Pá<u>sh</u>á Ḥaqqí, who also acted with great rectitude and friendliness. Muṣṭafá Ḍíyá Pá<u>sh</u>á, who followed him, and stayed as Mutaṣarrif of 'Akká for some years, showed even more goodwill than his predecessors and went so far as to indicate that Bahá'u'lláh could at any time leave the boundary of the city walls and establish His residence in the countryside; but Bahá'u'lláh did not accede to that invitation. Indeed, we are told by the Guardian of the Bahá'í Faith, 'for almost a decade, [Bahá'u'lláh] had not set foot beyond the city walls, and [His] sole exercise had been to pace, in monotonous repetition, the floor of His bed-chamber.'[4]

But now, let us read in the words of 'Abdu'l-Bahá how it happened that His Father left for ever the confines of the city walls.

The Land Gate of 'Akká in the nineteenth century, through which Bahá'u'lláh left the prison-city (from Wilson, Picturesque Palestine*)*

The Land Gate of 'Akká, from a recent photograph (by Hooper Dunbar)

Bahá'u'lláh loved the beauty and verdure of the country. One day He passed the remark: 'I have not gazed on verdure for nine years. The country is the world of the soul, the city is the world of bodies.' When I heard indirectly of this saying I realized that He was longing for the country, and I was sure that whatever I could do towards the carrying out of His wish would be successful. There was in 'Akká at that time a man called Muḥammad Pás͟há Ṣafwat [a great-nephew of 'Abdu'lláh Pás͟há], who was very much opposed to us. He had a palace called Mazra'ih, about four miles north of the city, a lovely place, surrounded by gardens and with a stream of running water. I went and called on this Pás͟há at his home. I said: 'Pás͟há, you have left the palace empty, and are living in 'Akká.' He replied: 'I am an invalid and cannot leave the city. If I go there it is lonely and I am cut off from my friends.' I said: 'While you are not living there and the place is empty, let it to us.' He was amazed at the proposal, but soon consented. I got the house at a very low rent, about five pounds per annum, paid him for five years and made a contract. I sent laborers to repair the place and put the garden in order and had a bath built. I also had a carriage prepared for the use of the Blessed Beauty [Jamál-i-Mubárak]. One day I determined to go and see the place for myself. Notwithstanding the repeated injunctions given in successive firmans that we were on no account to pass the limits of the city walls, I walked out through the City

The Mansion of Mazra'ih where Bahá'u'lláh resided when He first left the prison-city of 'Akká

The Mansion of Mazra'ih as it is today

Gate. Gendarmes were on guard, but they made no objection, so I proceeded straight to the palace. The next day I again went out, with some friends and officials, unmolested and unopposed, although the guards and sentinels stood on both sides of the city gates. Another day I arranged a banquet, spread a table under the pine trees of Bahjí, and gathered round it the notables and officials of the town. In the evening we all returned to the town together.

One day I went to the Holy Presence of the Blessed Beauty and said: 'The palace at Mazra'ih is ready for You, and a carriage to drive You there.' (At that time there were no carriages in 'Akká or Haifa.) He refused to go, saying: 'I am a prisoner.' Later I requested Him again, but got the same answer. I went so far as to ask Him a third time, but He still said 'No!' and I did not dare to insist further. There was, however, in 'Akká a certain Muḥammadan Shaykh, a well-known man with considerable influence, who loved Bahá'u'lláh and was greatly favored by Him. I called this Shaykh and explained the position to him. I said, 'You are daring. Go tonight to His Holy Presence, fall on your knees before Him, take hold of His hands and do not let go until He promises to leave the city!' He was an Arab. . . . He went directly to Bahá'u'lláh and sat down close to His knees. He took hold of the hands of the Blessed Beauty and kissed them and asked: 'Why do you not leave the city?' He said: 'I am a prisoner.' The Shaykh replied: 'God forbid! Who has the power to make you a prisoner? You have kept yourself in prison. It was your own will to be imprisoned, and now I beg you to come out and go to the palace. It is beautiful and verdant. The trees are lovely, and the oranges like balls of fire!' As often as the Blessed Beauty said: 'I am a prisoner, it cannot be,' the Shaykh took His hands and kissed them. For a whole hour he kept on pleading. At last Bahá'u'lláh said, 'Khaylí khúb (very good)' and the Shaykh's patience and persistence were rewarded.* . . . In spite of the strict firman of 'Abdu'l-'Azíz which prohibited my meeting or having any intercourse with the Blessed Perfection, I took the carriage the next day and drove with Him to the palace. No one made any objection. I left Him there and returned myself to the city.[5]

Mazra'ih was a very pleasant place, far away from the turmoil of 'Akká. It had been the property of 'Abdu'lláh Páshá, a summer lodge which he had built on land owned by his father. A complex of houses inside 'Akká, where, in later times, 'Abdu'l-Bahá resided for a number of years, and where Shoghi Effendi, the Guardian of the Bahá'í Faith, was born, had likewise belonged to 'Abdu'lláh Páshá. Today, apart from his palace at Bahjí (which has considerably changed its character

* *'Khaylí khúb'* is Persian. Shaykh 'Alíy-i-Mírí was Muftí of 'Akká. (HMB)

The Garden of Riḍván near 'Akká. Bahá'u'lláh rested beneath these mulberry trees; one of His seats is on the right.

The Garden of Riḍván with the small house where Bahá'u'lláh sometimes stayed

and has lost its old designation), all the other residences of 'Abdu'lláh Pá<u>sh</u>á, both inside and outside 'Akká, are in the possession of the World Centre of the Bahá'í Faith.

Now, at long last, Bahá'u'lláh was freed from the oppressive atmosphere of 'Akká and of those who still opposed Him, and Mazra'ih, set in such charming countryside, with its eastern view of valley and near hills, the sea not far to the west, offered Him the first surcease for many a year from the constant assaults to eye and ear of His confinement within the crowded city walls. In the words of the Guardian of the Bahá'í Faith, this residence and the 'garden of Na'mayn, a small island, situated in the middle of a river to the east of the city, honoured with the appellation of Riḍván, and designated by Him the "*New Jerusalem*" and "*Our Verdant Isle*",' became His 'favourite retreats'.[6]

At the height of the stringencies of incarceration, Bahá'u'lláh had written: 'Fear not. These doors shall be opened, My tent shall be pitched on Mount Carmel, and the utmost joy shall be realized.'[7]

Viewing the circumstances of the exile and the imprisonment of Bahá'u'lláh – the strict and harsh edicts of the Sulṭán of Turkey, who was also recognized as the Caliph, the supreme Pontiff of Islám; the character, the deviousness, and the vagaries of the Ottoman despotism and its officialdom; the relentless persecution engineered by the Íránian authorities, dogging the footsteps of the exiles right into the prison-city and its grim citadel; and the added tribulations caused by the foul murder of the partisans of Mírzá Yaḥyá – who would have thought that within only nine years of the arrival of the exiles in 'Akká, no less a person than Shaykh 'Alíy-i-Mírí, the muftí of that city, would go down on his knees before Bahá'u'lláh, to beg Him to leave the confines of the city walls and establish His residence in the countryside?

And yet all that Bahá'u'lláh had foretold in the darkest days had come to pass; all the gates were opened, He had moved out of 'Akká, unhindered, and His tent would be raised on Mount Carmel.

The Garden of Riḍván

39

The Years at Bahjí

Two years after Bahá'u'lláh took His residence in Mazra'ih, the mansion which today is known as Bahjí (Delight), and which 'Údí Khammár had built for himself and his family in proximity to 'Abdu'lláh Páshá's old palace, fell vacant. An epidemic raged in the countryside, people fled, 'Údí Khammár died in 1879 and was buried by the wall of his mansion. Then, the Most Great Branch moved to secure the mansion of 'Údí Khammár for His Father. It was rented at first and then purchased, and Bahá'u'lláh moved there in September 1879. This majestic Mansion of Bahjí remained the residence of Bahá'u'lláh for the rest of His life, and it was here that His ascension occurred in 1892. Bahjí was not far from the seashore, but it was far enough from the bleak and drab surroundings of 'Akká to possess rural beauty, the charm of the countryside. The pine trees that grew close to it, and can be seen there right to the pesent day, added to its charm. From the windows of His room Bahá'u'lláh could see the blue waters of the Mediterranean, the high minarets of 'Akká, and, beyond the bay, the dim outline of the gentle slope of Mount Carmel. The Mansion, in all its beauty and splendour, stands guard today over the adjoining Shrine, which for the Bahá'ís is the most sacred spot on the face of the earth, for it harbours the mortal remains of Bahá'u'lláh. In its radius one can experience that peace for which one's soul has ever yearned.*

* Bahjí is the name of a beautiful garden planted by Sulaymán Páshá for his daughter, Fáṭimih. 'Abdu'lláh Páshá, whose father, 'Alí Páshá, had owned the area, further beautified it and built a mansion on the site for his harem. When Ibráhím Páshá besieged 'Akká in 1831, he used this mansion as his headquarters. The property, which had become famous for its beautiful gardens and cool, refreshing pond fed by the water of the aqueduct, passed in Bahá'u'lláh's time into the possession of the al-Jamáls, a Christian family who were later to become enemies of 'Abdu'l-Bahá. Later still, it came into the possession of the Bayḍún family, who were also enemies of the Faith. The mansion is now a government institution for the handicapped.

The Mansion of Bahá'u'lláh at Bahjí was built by 'Údí Khammár, close to 'Abdu'lláh Páshá's mansion and on land bought from the Jamáls. Old accounts and maps indicate that a building existed on this site, on the foundations of which 'Údí Khammár built; according to the inscription on the Mansion, it was completed in 1870. Presumably, it was 'Údí Khammár's son, Andrávís Khammár, who later rented it to 'Abdu'l-Bahá for Bahá'u'lláh's residence.

The Mansion of Bahá'u'lláh at Bahjí: an old view from the south before the present gardens were planted

Dr J. E. Esslemont, the immortal author of *Bahá'u'lláh and the New Era*, thus describes the life at Bahjí:

> Having in His earlier years of hardship shown how to glorify God in a state of poverty and ignominy, Bahá'u'lláh in His later years at Bahjí showed how to glorify God in a state of honour and affluence. The offerings of hundreds of thousands of devoted followers placed at His disposal large funds which He was called upon to administer. Although His life at Bahjí has been described as truly regal, in the highest sense of the word, yet it must not be imagined that it was characterized by material splendour or extravagance. The Blessed Perfection and His family lived in very simple and modest fashion, and expenditure on selfish luxury was a thing unknown in that household. Near His home the believers prepared a beautiful garden called Riḍván, in which He often spent many consecutive days or even weeks, sleeping at night in a little cottage in the garden. Occasionally He went further afield. He made several visits to 'Akká and Haifa, and on more than one occasion pitched His tent on Mount Carmel, as He had predicted when imprisoned in the barracks at 'Akká. . . .[1]

Bahá'u'lláh visited the homes of the companions in 'Akká from time to time, and frequently went over, by day and night, to the homes of His two brothers: Mírzá Muḥammad-Qulí, who had lodgings overlooking Khán-i-Shávirdí, and Áqáy-i-Kalím, who once lodged in Khán al-'Umdán and then in premises above Khán-i-Pahlaván, which was on the right of the entrance of the *Súq al-Abyaḍ* (oriental market). There were several gardens in the vicinity of Mazra'ih and the Mansion of Bahjí, such as the Garden of Riḍván, the garden of Firdaws, the gardens of Junaynih and Bustán-i-Kabír at Mazra'ih. He also visited nearby villages, such as Yirkih and Abú-Sinán. At Yirkih, He had His tent pitched on the top of a hill, spending the day in the tent and the night in the village itself. Then there were hills nearer to 'Akká, such as Tall-i-Fakhkhár, which is also known as Napoleon's Hill, and is situated near the Garden of Riḍván; recent archeological work has demonstrated that it is the site of the ancient Phoenician/Canaanite city of 'Akká. And the hill named Samaríyyih, which overlooks Bahjí, and where red flowers grew in abundance, was called Buq'atu'l-Ḥamrá' – the Crimson Spot; today it is occupied by the army. In the springtime when the hill was verdant and covered with red flowers such as poppies and anemones, Bahá'u'lláh would have His tent pitched there. Many years later, when 'Abdu'l-Bahá was again incarcerated within the city walls of 'Akká, He would wistfully ask those who had gone to visit the Shrine of His Father: 'Were red, red flowers blooming on Buq'atu'l-Ḥamrá'?'

Although from time to time there came to 'Akká and its environs governors, deputies and officials of various ranks, who were either malevolent and avaricious, or highly fanatical and therefore unfriendly towards the Faith of Bahá'u'lláh, gone for good were the days when all officialdom opposed and denigrated the Faith; and after the storms and stresses of earlier years, the years at Bahjí were calm and peaceful.

Mention was made earlier of Muṣṭafá Ḍíyá Páshá, the Mutaṣarrif of 'Akká, who had made it known that should Bahá'u'lláh wish to leave the confines of the city walls of 'Akká, He would not be prevented. Áqá Riḍá states that this just and benevolent Governor, throughout his time in 'Akká, evinced the utmost goodwill and, when sent to occupy the post of Governor in Tripoli, continued to write and express his warm sentiment. And any Bahá'í whom he met he treated with the utmost consideration. When 'Abdu'l-Bahá visited Beirut, Muṣṭafá Ḍíyá Páshá was there and put himself at His service.

After him, Zívar Páshá came to govern 'Akká. He was an Istanbuli and very proud, keeping himself to himself. None of the notables dared approach him without his prior permission. But, meeting the Most Great Branch just once, he became so devoted to Him that for most of the time he consorted with no one else. His governorship lasted a year. Áqá Riḍá states that during his period of office, the Khavvám, in their entirety, rose up to oppose the Faith and the

The balcony outside Bahá'u'lláh's room at Bahjí. Above the windows and door may be seen some of the paintings which embellish the walls.

Bahá'ís. Manṣúr, the head of that family, was a member of the town council and a man of great influence, who always received much kindness at the hands of the Most Great Branch. He became, however, vainglorious and proud. One day he and his friends visited Bahjí and were most hospitably welcomed. They then retired to the shade of the pine trees, in pursuit of their own pleasures. There they set upon an Arab, who had gone near them while engaged in carrying water for the Mansion. A Bahá'í went to rescue the poor water-carrier from their clutches. Him they castigated too, beating him mercilessly. But realizing the enormity of their deed, they went to the Mansion to apologize. Once back in 'Akká, they changed their tune and went about claiming that they had been attacked at Bahjí with daggers and swords. It all recoiled on them, for Manṣúr lost his official position and, despite every effort, never regained the position and respect that he had erstwhile enjoyed. He had to go into the market-place to ply the trade of a money-changer.

It was during the governorship of Zívar Pá͟shá that Furú͟ghíyyih K͟hánum, a daughter of Bahá'u'lláh, was given in marriage to Siyyid 'Alí Afnán. Áqá Riḍá has recorded that the Mutaṣarrif and all the high officials and notables of 'Akká attended the wedding feast. This was in the year 1885. And when Zívar Pá͟shá was recalled he left with great regret, and his letters came without fail after his departure, indicating the measure of his devotion.

General Gordon of K͟harṭúm fame was in the Holy Land throughout 1883 (see Addendum IV). He certainly knew Laurence Oliphant and visited him, the latter a noted figure of his time who lived on Mount Carmel, where his first wife is buried. (He himself died in London.) Gordon also certainly knew of the Bahá'í Faith. He it was who had liberated Ḥájí Mírzá Ḥaydar-'Alí and his companion from detention in K͟harṭúm, in the year 1877, and for whom Ḥájí Mírzá Ḥaydar-'Alí had done some etching on glass. It is known that a European general visited Bahá'u'lláh, but his name is not recorded. The Guardian of the Bahá'í Faith has thus written of him: 'On one occasion, a European general who, together with the governor, was granted an audience by Him, was so impressed that he "remained kneeling on the ground near the door."'[2] Could Gordon have been that general? This is just a conjecture, but it is possible. Both Laurence Oliphant and Sir Valentine Chirol wrote about Gordon's visits to

Haifa and 'Akká (see Addendum IV). In the year 1885, Chirol – a celebrated publicist and correspondent of *The Times* of London – was in the Holy Land. He had become an authority on the affairs of the Middle East and Central Asia, wrote extensively on them, and was a confidant of Lord Curzon. In a chapter headed 'The Revival of Babiism', in his book *The Middle Eastern Question and Some Political Problems of Indian Defence*, he wrote: 'It was as Oliphant's guest that in 1885 I enjoyed the favour of Beha'ullah's hospitality . . .' (p. 122)

As it happened, after the departure of Zívar Pás͟há, a mutaṣarrif was sent to 'Akká who had been there previously, and he was both avaricious and fanatical. He was a Kurd, named Muḥammad-Yúsuf, a pás͟há of Damascus, who had, on the previous occasion, cause to learn of the erudition and immensity of knowledge of the Most Great Branch, and he was full of admiration. One evening during his earlier tenure of office, a number of Christians were having a parley, in his presence, with a number of Muslims. All were learned men. The Christian side was gaining ground, and the Kurdish mutaṣarrif felt distressed that his fellow Muslims were unable to cope with them. Knowing of the intellectual brilliance of the eldest Son of Bahá'u'lláh, he quietly sent word and requested Him to come. At this time the Most Great Branch was still within the citadel. When He arrived at the Governor's residence, the latter greeted Him warmly, but as if he had no idea that He would be calling. Once coffee was served the arguments were resumed. 'Abdu'l-Bahá dealt with them all authoritatively and convincingly. Then He posed a question to the Christians which they were reluctant to answer, nor would they commit themselves in any way, until one of them, a man very acute, named As'ad Sayqal, said: 'You know what this city is like, and you know what Damascus is like – yet we prefer to live in this city.' He implied that their Christian Faith was like their native town, no matter what the glories and splendours of Islám might be, which he compared to Damascus. Then the Most Great Branch said, 'After your statement I have no more to say.' The Mutaṣarrif and his friends were greatly impressed.

The second time that the Kurdish pás͟há came to 'Akká, he found himself without a residence. The Government had sold the spacious governor's residence to the S͟hád͟hilí Order to pull down, and build for themselves a *takyih* in its place. As soon as Zívar Pás͟há had gone, the S͟hád͟hilís claimed the governor's residence and proceeded with their project. The new mutaṣarrif had perforce to rent a house near Bayt 'Abbúd.

Bahá'u'lláh was then residing at Bahjí, but the Most Great Branch and His family lived in 'Akká. Just at this time, the Válí* came for a visit from Damascus and stayed with the Mutaṣarrif. As it happened, Shaykh Yúsuf, the Muftí of Nazareth, a man highly esteemed both because of his office and his personal merits, had come to 'Akká shortly before the arrival of the Kurdish mutaṣarrif. He had been received and lodged by the Most Great Branch in Bayt 'Abbúd. Close by were other good houses occupied by the Bahá'ís. The hospitality extended to Shaykh Yúsuf was particularly galling to the adversaries of the Faith. In the future, so they reasoned, nothing they might do would have any éclat, as compared with the treatment that the Muftí of Nazareth was receiving from the Bahá'ís. They were beside themselves with jealousy, and began to work on the fickle mind of the new mutaṣarrif. Why should these people have the use of some of the best houses in the town, they asked him, while you must content yourself with an insignificant rented house?

The Muftí of Nazareth had visited 'Akká previously, and it was then that he had fallen under the spell of the wonderful charm, knowledge, eloquence, and the majestic mien of the eldest Son of Bahá'u'lláh. Since then he had kept up a correspondence with 'Abdu'l-Bahá, sent Him as a gift a noble horse, and invited Him to visit Nazareth. The Guardian of the Bahá'í Faith writes about this visit, and the succeeding visit of Shaykh Yúsuf to 'Akká:

> The splendid welcome accorded him by . . . Shaykh Yúsuf, the Muftí of Nazareth, who acted as host to the válís of Beirut, and who had despatched all the notables of the community several miles on the road to meet Him as He approached the town, accompanied by His brother and the Muftí of 'Akká, as well as the magnificent reception given by 'Abdu'l-Bahá to that same Shaykh Yúsuf when the latter visited Him in 'Akká, were such as to arouse the envy of those who, only a few years before, had treated Him and His fellow-exiles with feelings compounded of condescension and scorn.[3]

Now, Muḥammad-Yúsuf Páshá, under the baneful influence of men hostile to Bahá'u'lláh and His followers, began to make incessant demands. He wanted to take possession of the house in which the

* Probably he was Nashíd Páshá who, according to British consular records, was Governor-General of Damascus from October 1885 until 1888. (FO 195 1510 and 1613.)

Most Great Branch and His family resided. He pretended that the Válí required it, but when the Válí was apprised of the approaches made by the Mutaṣarrif, he strongly denied that he was in any way connected with the demand, nor had he any need of a house. However, this statement did not daunt the avaricious Governor, who continued his demand, and this at a time when the mother of 'Abdu'l-Bahá, who was living in 'Akká, was desperately ill.

Nonetheless, the Most Great Branch said that as soon as He had found another house, He would let the Mutaṣarrif have the large house he claimed to require. All through this time when 'Abdu'l-Bahá was much concerned and occupied with the worsening condition of His mother, Muḥammad-Yúsuf Pás͟há was constantly demanding the occupation of Bayt 'Abbúd. Then, in 1886, Ásíyih K͟hánum passed away. Notables of 'Akká, as well as Muslim and Christian divines, came to follow the funeral cortège which was preceded by muezzins and reciters of the Qur'án. Schoolchildren joined the procession chanting verses and poems expressing their grief. Overwhelming was the sorrow of 'Abdu'l-Bahá, and yet the Mutaṣarrif lacked the grace to desist from pressing his demand. As soon as He could, the Most Great Branch vacated the house and handed it over to him. The following year, the Bahá'í community sustained a great loss in the death of Mírzá Músá, Áqáy-i-Kalím. He had been indeed a pillar of the Faith, always standing ready to serve his Brother, in any capacity.

The avarice of Muḥammad-Yúsuf was not easily abated, however. In the face of his demands and aggressive attitude, 'Abdu'l-Bahá remained calm and composed, did not utter a word of complaint and secluded Himself from the people. In the meantime, the Mutaṣarrif, with the aid of a few accomplices as corrupt as himself, was busy with embezzlement. A certain As'ad Effendi, the Qá'im-Maqám of Nazareth, was, however, keeping a watchful eye on all that was happening in 'Akká and recording it to send to higher authorities. There was in 'Akká a merchant who presided over the Chamber of Commerce, outwardly a friend of the exiles but in truth double-faced, who assured the Most Great Branch that he knew how to deal with the Mutaṣarrif. Hypocritically sympathizing, talking with scorn of the infidelity and avarice of men like the Mutaṣarrif, he stated at last that with the gift of a sum of money Muḥammad-Yúsuf Pás͟há could be made to behave in a friendly way in future.

Áqá Riḍá writes that the Most Great Branch replied that if it were only the matter of a gift it could be arranged, and left the hypocrite. He retired to pray. The merchant sat waiting and hoping that at any moment purses laden with coins would be brought to him. When 'Abdu'l-Bahá returned, He said only that all that was required had been sent and that the merchant should go and find out for himself. At the *Seraye* he found only profound gloom, and learned to his amazement that a cable had just arrived, announcing the dismissal of the Kurdish pá<u>sh</u>á and his accomplices, because of their embezzlement of government funds. A board of investigators was already on its way. Then the merchant understood what 'Abdu'l-Bahá had meant, and astonishment was written large on his face.

The crestfallen Muḥammad-Yúsuf felt pangs of remorse when he learned what had occurred, and he assured the merchant that the exiles were in no way involved or concerned with the action of his superiors. It was their prayer which had brought about his downfall. After writing a letter, he rode out next day to the Garden of Riḍván, hoping to find 'Abdu'l-Bahá there to offer his apologies. But 'Abdu'l-Bahá was not there. The dismissed mutaṣarrif then appealed to Áqá Riḍá to convey to the Most Great Branch the expression of his regret and remorse.

Within a few days the officials appointed to investigate the malefactions of Muḥammad-Yúsuf Pá<u>sh</u>á arrived from Beirut. One of them was Aḥmad Fá'iq Effendi. Both he and his brother were followers of Bahá'u'lláh. Those who knew this wondered why a Bahá'í had been commissioned to investigate the misdeeds of persons so unfriendly to the exiles. The head of the secretariat at the *Seraye* in 'Akká had, in particular, shown extreme malevolence. He, and others like him, now turned to Bahá'u'lláh and His eldest Son for help and forgiveness. And while Aḥmad Fá'iq was engaged in examining the irregularities in the administration of government funds, Bahá'u'lláh and the Most Great Branch would not receive him.

To the amazement of the inhabitants of 'Akká, the malefactors, who had through their own deeds fallen on evil days, received from Bahá'u'lláh and His Son a full share of Their liberal generosity. The head of the secretariat had fled to Damascus and left his family behind. 'Abdu'l-Bahá provided them with all their needs and sent them away in the safe company of two Bahá'ís. Bahá'u'lláh, in a

Tablet addressed to Ḥájí Mírzá Buzurg-i-Afnán, a cousin of the Báb, who lived and traded in Hong Kong, mentions this Kurdish pá͟shá, his hostility and his downfall. In the same Tablet, He instructed the Afnán to send Him a few pairs of good spectacles mounted in silver or gold and in suitable cases, which He wished to send as gifts to the válís of Beirut and Damascus.

Aḥmad Pá͟shá was the next mutaṣarrif of 'Akká. He had been particularly instructed to show due respect and consideration towards Bahá'u'lláh. For some two years he governed 'Akká well, and spent his time often in the company of 'Abdu'l-Bahá. During his tenure of office, the Válí of Beirut* came by boat to Haifa, and all the high officials went there to meet him. 'Abdu'l-Bahá did likewise. The Válí especially requested Him to offer Bahá'u'lláh his respects and beg for His blessings and bounteous regard. And he gave a melon (rare at the time in those parts), which was brought from his cabin, to an official, Nuṣúhí Big, to present to Bahá'u'lláh.

The next Mutaṣarrif of 'Akká was 'Árif Effendi. His father had come to know the Most Great Branch in Adrianople and had learned to hold Him in high esteem. During 'Árif Effendi's governorship Bahá'u'lláh visited Haifa, and stayed there for nearly three months.

In the spring of 1890, Edward Granville Browne, Fellow of Pembroke College, Cambridge, and the eminent orientalist of future years, reached 'Akká. He had come to visit Bahá'u'lláh. For the full story of that truly historic visit, the reader is directed to the book, *Edward Granville Browne and the Bahá'í Faith* (by the present writer). But this work will be incomplete without the inclusion of the unique, unparalleled pen-portrait of Bahá'u'lláh, which Edward Browne has bequeathed to posterity. Indeed, it is the only one of its kind in existence. Today a visitor to Bahjí may read this document, affixed to the wall, before venturing into Bahá'u'lláh's chamber, and thus try to re-create in imagination the interview granted to the English orientalist:

> . . . my conductor paused for a moment while I removed my shoes. Then, with a quick movement of the hand, he withdrew, and, as I passed, replaced the curtain; and I found myself in a large apartment, along the

* The Viláyat of Beirut was separated from the Viláyat of Damascus in March 1888, chiefly through the efforts of the Grand Vizier Kiyámil Pá͟shá, who had formerly been Mutaṣarrif of Beirut, according to British consular records. (FO 195 1613)

The Room of Bahá'u'lláh at Bahjí. Here in 1890 He received Edward Granville Browne, and in 1892 His ascension occurred in this room.

upper end of which ran a low divan, while on the side opposite to the door were placed two or three chairs. Though I dimly suspected whither I was going and whom I was to behold (for no distinct intimation had been given to me), a second or two elapsed ere, with a throb of wonder and awe, I became definitely conscious that the room was not untenanted. In the corner where the divan met the wall sat a wondrous and venerable figure, crowned with a felt head-dress of the kind called *táj* by dervishes (but of unusual height and make), round the base of which was wound a small white turban. The face of him on whom I gazed I can never forget, though I cannot describe it. Those piercing eyes seemed to read one's very soul; power and authority sat on that ample brow; while the deep lines on the forehead and face implied an age which the jet-black hair and beard flowing down in indistinguishable luxuriance almost to the waist seemed to belie. No need to ask in whose presence I stood, as I bowed myself before one who is the object of a devotion and love which kings might envy and emperors sigh for in vain!

A mild dignified voice bade me be seated, and then continued: – 'Praise be to God that thou hast attained! . . . Thou hast come to see a prisoner and an exile . . . We desire but the good of the world and the happiness of the nations; yet they deem us a stirrer up of strife and sedition worthy of bondage and banishment . . . That all nations should become one in faith and all men as brothers; that the bonds of affection and unity between the sons of men should be strengthened; that diversity of religion should cease, and differences of race be annulled – what harm is there in this? . . . Yet so it shall be; these fruitless strifes, these ruinous wars shall pass away, and the 'Most Great Peace' shall come . . . Do not you in Europe need this also? Is not this that which Christ foretold? . . . Yet do we see your kings and rulers lavishing their treasures more freely on means for the destruction of the human race than on that which would conduce to the happiness of mankind . . . These strifes and this bloodshed and discord must cease, and all men be as one kindred and one family . . . Let not a man glory in this, that he loves his country; let him rather glory in this, that he loves his kind . . .'

Such, so far as I can recall them, were the words which, besides many others, I heard from Behá. Let those who read them consider well with themselves whether such doctrines merit death and bonds, and whether the world is more likely to gain or lose by their diffusion.[4]

The Guardian of the Bahá'í Faith states that Bahá'u'lláh visited Haifa four times. The first visit was of short duration, when He disembarked in 1868 from the Lloyd-Triestino steamer. The second

The Táj of Bahá'u'lláh placed on the divan in the corner of His room where He was wont to sit

visit was for just a few days, and He stayed in Bayt-i-Fanduq, a house in the German colony, part of which still stands today. There is a dated Tablet, in the handwriting of Mírzá Áqá Ján, which indicates that Bahá'u'lláh was in Haifa in August 1883, probably the date of this second visit. The third visit was in 1890, and when Edward Granville Browne reached 'Akká, Bahá'u'lláh was in Haifa. In the course of this visit, He stayed, at first, near Bayt-i-Zahlán, near the town, and then He moved to a house in the German colony which was known as the Oliphant house. His tent was pitched on a piece of land opposite that house. His fourth and last visit was in the year 1891. This sojourn was the longest, and it was here in Haifa that members of the Afnán family met him when they came in July, as described in a later chapter. Bahá'u'lláh was then in Haifa for three months, staying in the house of Ilyás Abyaḍ near the German colony, and His tent stood near by.

One day, when standing by the side of some lone cypress trees nearly half-way up the slopes of Mount Carmel, Bahá'u'lláh pointed to an expanse of rock immediately below Him, telling His eldest Son that on that spot should be built the mausoleum to enshrine the remains of the Martyr-Prophet, the glorious Herald of His own advent: remains that had been kept in hiding and moved from place to place, since the second night after 9 July 1850, the day on which the Báb was shot in the public square of Tabríz. More than a decade had to elapse before

The German Templar Colony in 1877 at the foot of Mount Carmel near Haifa, where Bahá'u'lláh stayed during two of His visits to Haifa. (A drawing by Jakob Schumacher, who was head of the colony and American Vice-Consul until his death in 1891.)

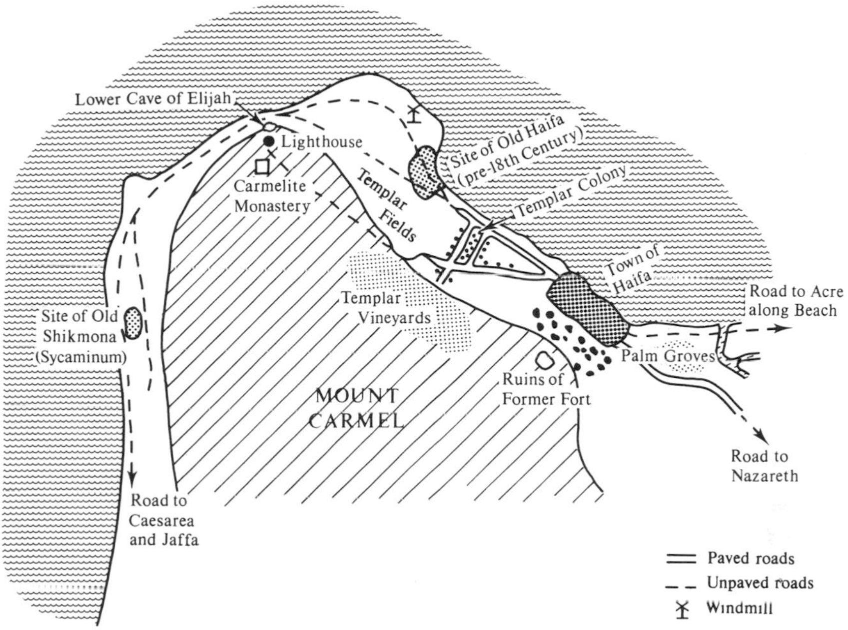

Plan of Haifa in the 1880s

'Abdu'l Bahá could carry through the mandate laid upon Him by His Father. Today, on the very spot indicated by Bahá'u'lláh, stands a mausoleum of entrancing beauty, surmounted by a golden dome reflecting many hues of the sea and sky, and surrounded by gardens of inexpressible beauty that ravish the eyes and enchant the soul. Within that mausoleum, reared with tender care by 'Abdu'l-Bahá and His grandson, Shoghi Effendi, the mangled remains of the Martyr-Prophet and of His disciple, Mírzá Muḥammad-'Alíy-i-Zunúzí, inseparable in death, are laid to rest. That Mausoleum, the Queen of Carmel, conveys the message to the concourse of mankind that evil can never achieve the ultimate victory.

It was also in the course of this three-month-long visit that Bahá'u'lláh went to the cave of Elijah, over which a Christian monastery stands. On a promontory near by, where in years to come a Mashriqu'l-Adhkár – House of Worship – will be raised in its full majesty, He revealed a momentous Tablet: *Lawḥ-i-Karmil* – the Tablet of Carmel. This is its text, as translated by the Guardian of the Bahá'í Faith:

The Shrine of the Báb as built by 'Abdu'l-Bahá; the superstructure was added later by Shoghi Effendi.

All glory be to this Day, the Day in which the fragrances of mercy have been wafted over all created things, a Day so blest that past ages and centuries can never hope to rival it, a Day in which the countenance of the Ancient of Days hath turned towards His holy seat. Thereupon the voices of all created things, and beyond them those of the Concourse on high, were heard calling aloud: 'Haste thee, O Carmel, for lo, the light of the countenance of God, the Ruler of the Kingdom of Names and Fashioner of the heavens, hath been lifted upon thee.'

Seized with transports of joy, and raising high her voice, she thus exclaimed: 'May my life be a sacrifice to Thee, inasmuch as Thou hast fixed Thy gaze upon me, hast bestowed upon me Thy bounty, and hast directed towards me Thy steps. Separation from Thee, O Thou Source of everlasting life, hath well nigh consumed me, and my remoteness from Thy presence hath burned away my soul. All praise be to Thee for having enabled me to hearken to Thy call, for having honoured me with Thy footsteps, and for having quickened my soul through the vitalizing fragrance of Thy Day and the shrilling voice of Thy Pen, a voice Thou didst ordain as Thy trumpet-call amidst Thy people. And when the hour at which Thy resistless Faith was to be made manifest did strike, Thou didst breathe a breath of Thy spirit into Thy Pen, and lo, the entire creation shook to its very foundations, unveiling to mankind such mysteries as lay hidden within the treasuries of Him Who is the Possessor of all created things.'

No sooner had her voice reached that most exalted Spot than We made reply: 'Render thanks unto Thy Lord, O Carmel. The fire of thy separation from Me was fast consuming thee, when the ocean of My presence surged before thy face, cheering thine eyes and those of all creation, and filling with delight all things visible and invisible. Rejoice, for God hath in this Day established upon thee His throne, hath made thee the dawning-place of His signs and the day spring of the evidences of His Revelation. Well is it with him that circleth around thee, that proclaimeth the revelation of thy glory, and recounteth that which the bounty of the Lord thy God hath showered upon thee. Seize thou the Chalice of Immortality in the name of thy Lord, the All-Glorious, and give thanks unto Him, inasmuch as He, in token of His mercy unto thee, hath turned thy sorrow into gladness, and transmuted thy grief into blissful joy. He, verily, loveth the spot which hath been made the seat of His throne, which His footsteps have trodden, which hath been honoured by His presence, from which He raised His call, and upon which He shed His tears.

'Call out to Zion, O Carmel, and announce the joyful tidings: He that was hidden from mortal eyes is come! His all-conquering sovereignty is manifest; His all-encompassing splendour is revealed. Beware lest thou hesitate or halt. Hasten forth and circumambulate the City of God that hath descended from heaven, the celestial Kaaba round which have circled in adoration the favoured of God, the pure in heart, and the company of the most exalted angels. Oh, how I long to announce unto every spot on the surface of the earth, and to carry to each one of its cities, the glad-tidings of this Revelation – a Revelation to which the heart of Sinai hath been attracted, and in whose name the Burning Bush is calling: "Unto God, the Lord of Lords, belong the kingdoms of earth and heaven." Verily this is the Day in which both land and sea rejoice at this announcement, the Day for which have been laid up those things which God, through a bounty beyond the ken of mortal mind or heart, hath destined for revelation. Ere long will God sail His Ark upon thee, and will manifest the people of Bahá who have been mentioned in the Book of Names.'

Sanctified be the Lord of all mankind, at the mention of Whose name all the atoms of the earth have been made to vibrate, and the Tongue of Grandeur hath been moved to disclose that which had been wrapt in His knowledge and lay concealed within the treasury of His might. He, verily, through the potency of His name, the Mighty, the All-Powerful, the Most High, is the ruler of all that is in the heavens and all that is on earth.[5]

It was also during the last years at Bahjí that the range of powers and abilities of 'Abdu'l-Bahá – the Most Great Branch – became

Midḥat Pásh͟há

evident for all, friend and foe, to see. He stood as the shield of His Father against the pressures of the outside world – a fact to which Bahá'u'lláh has testified. For that very purpose the Most Great Branch lived in 'Akká.

Sometime in 1879, 'Abdu'l-Bahá travelled to Beirut at the invitation of Midḥat Pásh͟há, the válí of the province of Syria, who is hailed and revered by the people of Turkey as the 'Father of the Constitution'.* It was a historic journey, unparalleled in the religious annals of mankind, and was thus immortalized by the Most Sublime Pen:

> Praise be to Him Who hath honoured the Land of Bá [Beirut] through the presence of Him round Whom all names revolve. All the atoms of the earth have announced unto all created things that from behind the gate of the Prison-city there hath appeared and above its horizon there hath shone forth the Orb of the beauty of the great, the Most Mighty Branch of God – His ancient and immutable Mystery – proceeding on its way to another land. Sorrow, thereby, hath enveloped this Prison-city, whilst another land rejoiceth. Exalted, immeasurably exalted is our Lord, the Fashioner of the heavens and the Creator of all things, He through Whose sovereignty the

* According to British consular records, Midḥat Pásh͟há was Governor-General in Damascus from November 1878 to August 1880. He visited Haifa and 'Akká in May 1880. (FO 195 1201 and 1306) (See p. 476)

doors of the prison were opened, thereby causing what was promised aforetime in the Tablets to be fulfilled. He is verily potent over what He willeth, and in His grasp is the dominion of the entire creation. He is the All-Powerful, the All-Knowing, the All-Wise.

Blessed, doubly blessed, is the ground which His footsteps have trodden, the eye that hath been cheered by the beauty of His countenance, the ear that hath been honoured by hearkening to His call, the heart that hath tasted the sweetness of His love, the breast that hath dilated through His remembrance, the pen that hath voiced His praise, the scroll that hath borne the testimony of His writings. We beseech God – blessed and exalted be He – that He may honour us with meeting Him soon. He is, in truth, the All-Hearing, the All-Powerful, He Who is ready to answer.[6]

'Abdu'l-Bahá's journey to Beirut had a special significance, because it was undertaken at the invitation of the Válí of the province of Syria, at a time when He was still a prisoner of the Ottoman Empire. The edict of Sulṭán 'Abdu'l-'Azíz, deposed some three years before, which had consigned Bahá'u'lláh and His family to the grim citadel of 'Akká, had never been revoked.

In Beirut, apart from meeting the illustrious Válí, who had played a major part in deposing Sulṭán 'Abdu'l-'Azíz, the Most Great Branch met a number of men eminent in various walks of life, one of whom was Shaykh Muḥammad-'Abduh, the future Grand Muftí of Egypt. This good and righteous man was so thoroughly captivated by the profundity of 'Abdu'l-Bahá's knowledge, by His charm of mien and manner, that he intended to follow Him to 'Akká, but the Most Great Branch stopped him from taking such an irrevocable step. His letters which reached 'Abdu'l-Bahá afterwards, as well as the letters of other outstanding men of the region of Syria, testified to that 'influence and esteem' to which Edward Granville Browne bore witness in the following lines, describing the Most Great Branch as he found Him in April 1890:

Seldom have I seen one whose appearance impressed me more. A tall strongly-built man holding himself straight as an arrow, with white turban and raiment, long black locks reaching almost to the shoulder, broad powerful forehead indicating a strong intellect combined with an unswerving will, eyes keen as a hawk's, and strongly-marked but pleasing features – such was my first impression of 'Abbás Efendí, 'the master' (Áḳá)* as he *par excellence* is called by the Bábís. Subsequent conversation with him

* Áqá. (HMB)

> served only to heighten the respect with which his appearance had from the first inspired me. One more eloquent of speech, more ready of argument, more apt of illustration, more intimately acquainted with the sacred books of the Jews, the Christians, and the Muhammadans, could, I should think, scarcely be found even amongst the eloquent, ready, and subtle race to which he belongs. These qualities, combined with a bearing at once majestic and genial, made me cease to wonder at the influence and esteem which he enjoyed even beyond the circle of his father's followers. About the greatness of this man and his power no one who had seen him could entertain a doubt.[7]

'Abdu'l-Bahá was then in the prime of His manhood. After the ascension of His Father, when the mantle of authority came to rest on His shoulders, the treachery of His half-brothers aged Him too soon.

The last years of Bahá'u'lláh's life were devoted to writing and revealing innumerable Tablets, Epistles and Treatises on many and varied subjects of spiritual and educative purport. He was relieved of such cares as His supreme station entailed by the able and unsurpassed administration of 'Abdu'l-Bahá, Who shielded Him from the interference of the outside world and met and conversed with the officials

Central hall of the Mansion of Bahjí

Aerial view of Bahjí with original buildings

of the government, enquirers and the learned, admitting into the presence of Bahá'u'lláh only those who had genuine problems to resolve.

On the revelations that constantly came from the Most Sublime Pen, the Guardian of the Bahá'í Faith thus comments:

> Indeed, in their scope and volume, His writings, during the years of His confinement in the Most Great Prison, surpassed the outpourings of His pen in either Adrianople or Baghdád. . . . this unprecedented extension in the range of His writings, during His exile in that Prison, must rank as one of the most vitalizing and fruitful stages in the evolution of His Faith.
>
> The tempestuous winds that swept the Faith at the inception of His ministry and the wintry desolation that marked the beginnings of His prophetic career, soon after His banishment from Ṭihrán, were followed during the latter part of His sojourn in Baghdád, by what may be described as the vernal years of His Mission – years which witnessed the bursting into visible activity of the forces inherent in that Divine Seed that had lain dormant since the tragic removal of His Forerunner. With His arrival in Adrianople and the proclamation of His Mission the Orb of His Revelation climbed as it were to its zenith, and shone, as witnessed by the style and tone of His writings, in the plenitude of its summer glory. The period of His incarceration in 'Akká brought with it the ripening of a slowly

> maturing process, and was a period during which the choicest fruits of that mission were ultimately garnered.
>
> The writings of Bahá'u'lláh during this period, as we survey the vast field which they embrace, seem to fall into three distinct categories. The first comprises those writings which constitute the sequel to the proclamation of His Mission in Adrianople. The second includes the laws and ordinances of His Dispensation, which, for the most part, have been recorded in the Kitáb-i-Aqdas, His Most Holy Book. To the third must be assigned those Tablets which partly enunciate and partly reaffirm the fundamental tenets and principles underlying that Dispensation.[8]

Within the extensive range of this third category, mentioned by the Guardian, came such Tablets as *Lawḥ-i-Aqdas* (The Most Holy Tablet), particularly addressed to those professing the Christian Faith; *Bis͟hárát* (Glad Tidings); *Ṭarázát* (Ornaments); *Tajallíyát* (Effulgences); *Is͟hráqát* (Splendours); *Lawḥ-i-Burhán* (Tablet of the Proof), addressed to S͟hayk͟h Muḥammad-Báqir of Iṣfahán, one of the divines responsible for the martyrdom of Sulṭánu's͟h-S͟huhadá' (King of the Martyrs) and Maḥbúbu's͟h-S͟huhadá' (Beloved of the Martyrs); *Lawḥ-i-Dunyá* (Tablet of the World), revealed in honour of Áqá Mírzá Áqá Afnán, subsequent to the martyrdom of the Seven Martyrs of Yazd, who were put to death by the orders of Sulṭán-Ḥusayn Mírzá, Jalálu'd-Dawlih, the son of Sulṭán-Mas'úd Mírzá, Ẓillu's-Sulṭán; *Lawḥ-i-Ḥikmat* (Tablet of Wisdom), revealed in honour of Áqá Muḥammad, known as Nabíl-i-Akbar or Nabíl-i-Qá'iní, who had been a pupil of the celebrated S͟hayk͟h Murtiḍáy-i-Anṣárí; and *Kalimát-i-Firdawsíyyih* (Words of Paradise).

The last book which flowed from the creative pen of Bahá'u'lláh was the *Epistle to the Son of the Wolf.* It was revealed in the year 1891 and is addressed to S͟hayk͟h Muḥammad-Taqí, commonly known as S͟hayk͟h Najafí, or Áqá Najafí, the son of S͟hayk͟h Muḥammad-Báqir, a clergyman of Iṣfahán who was stigmatized by Bahá'u'lláh as 'D͟hi'b' (Wolf). Together with Mír Muḥammad-Ḥusayn, the Imám-Jum'ih of that city, S͟hayk͟h Muḥammad-Báqir had conspired with Sulṭán-Mas'úd Mírzá, the Ẓillu's-Sulṭán, and brought about the martyrdom of the two brothers, Mírzá Ḥasan, Sulṭánu's͟h-S͟huhadá', and Mírzá Ḥusayn, Maḥbúbu's͟h-S͟huhadá'. Mír Muḥammad-Ḥusayn, the Imám-Jum'ih, stigmatized by Bahá'u'lláh as 'Raqs͟há' (She-Serpent), died a horrible death in 1881. The disease which took him away caused his body to become so loathsome that no one would go near him. A few

Shaykh Muḥammad-Taqí, 'The Son of the Wolf', to whom Bahá'u'lláh addressed His last book

porters buried him in all haste in an unknown grave. His accomplice, 'The Wolf', died some three years later in 'Iráq, abandoned and deserted by all. In the *Epistle*, addressed to his son, who was also an inveterate and notorious enemy of the Faith and whose greed and schemings resulted in murder and cruel persecution, Bahá'u'lláh reiterates His challenge to His detractors. His call is from God, His trust is in God, and no earthly power can deter Him in His purpose. In this book, His 'last outstanding Tablet',[9] is also a representative selection from the vast volume of His Writings, culled and presented by Himself. An important aspect of the *Epistle* is Bahá'u'lláh's own narration of the dire events engineered by the supporters of Mírzá Yaḥyá, which occurred in Constantinople, and which had a most tragic outcome. To the details of these events and Bahá'u'lláh's statements about them in *Epistle to the Son of the Wolf*, the next chapter is devoted, for these unhappy events cast a dark shadow over Bahá'u'lláh's closing years.

In their range, their scope and their depth, the Writings of Bahá'u'lláh remain unequalled and unmatched amongst the Scriptures of mankind. That erudite Bahá'í teacher and scholar, Mírzá Abu'l-Faḍl of Gulpáygán, classifies them into four categories, namely: laws and ordinances; meditations, communes and prayers; interpretations of the sacred Scriptures of the past; and discourses and exordiums. Of the first category he writes: 'Some of them contain laws and regulations whereby the rights and interests of all the nations of the world can be perpetuated, for these statutes are so enacted that they meet the necessities of every land and country and are acceptable to every man of intelligence. In this universality they resemble the laws of Nature, which secure the progress and development of all peoples; and they will bring about universal union and harmony.'[10]

Bahá'u'lláh states that the volume of His revealed Word totals the Scriptures of the Manifestations of God preceding Him. We ought to remember the incalculable advantage which the Writings of Bahá'u'lláh possess in relation to the Holy Books of former times. Their originals are extant and well preserved, and future generations will be spared the crushing responsibility of deciding the authenticity of the Works ascribed to the Prophet. Oral tradition finds no place in the Scriptures of the Bahá'í Faith.

40

The Activities of the Azalís in Constantinople

In the late eighties and the early nineties of the nineteenth century Constantinople had become a centre of activity for the followers of Mírzá Yaḥyá. They were doing their utmost to inflict as much harm and injury as they could on the Bahá'ís. Shaykh Aḥmad-i-Rúḥí and 'Abdu'l-Ḥusayn Khán-i-Bardsírí, generally known as Mírzá Áqá Khán-i-Kirmání, both married to daughters of Ṣubḥ-i-Azal, lived at Constantinople. They were men accomplished in many respects, who wielded fluent pens. And both were inveterate enemies of Bahá'u'lláh. That stormy petrel of Eastern politics and exponent of Pan-Islamism, Siyyid Jamálu'd-Dín-i-Asadábádí,* known as Afghání, who was also hostile to the Faith proclaimed by Bahá'u'lláh, was in Istanbul as well. Shaykh Aḥmad and Mírzá Áqá Khán attached themselves to Siyyid Jamálu'd-Dín, although that subtle schemer's hostility had the Faith of the Báb also within its orbit. When Mírzá Áqá Khán had visited 'Akká, ostensibly to investigate truth, Bahá'u'lláh had remarked that his purpose was not to discover what was true, but solely to cause confusion and mischief. And it happened exactly as Bahá'u'lláh had stated, for Mírzá Áqá Khán gave out, on leaving 'Akká, that what he had found there was duplicity and falsehood.

Áqá Muḥammad-Ṭáhir of Tabríz had established in 1875 a newspaper in Constantinople, bearing the title of *Akhtar* (Star), which was published for twenty years and was looked upon with great disfavour by Náṣiri'd-Dín Sháh. Before long it fell under the influence of the supporters of Mírzá Yaḥyá, and particularly of Mírzá Áqá Khán, who regularly contributed to it. In the *Epistle to the Son of the Wolf*, Bahá'u'lláh refers to the activities of the Azalís in Istanbul:

* Asadábád is in the environs of Hamadán, in western Írán.

Mírzá Áqá Khán-i-Kirmání (left) and Shaykh Aḥmad-i-Rúḥí (right) (from Browne, The Persian Revolution of 1905–1909*)*

In the Great City (Constantinople) they have roused a considerable number of people to oppose this Wronged One. Things have come to such a pass that the officials in that city have acted in a manner which hath brought shame to both the government and the people. A distinguished siyyid,* whose well-known integrity, acceptable conduct, and commercial reputation, were recognized by the majority of fair-minded men, and who was regarded by all as a highly honored merchant, once visited Beirut. In view of his friendship for this Wronged One they telegraphed the Persian Dragoman informing him that this siyyid, assisted by his servant, had stolen a sum of money and other things and gone to 'Akká. Their design in this matter was to dishonor this Wronged One.

. . . Briefly, they have incited a great many such as Akhtar [the newspaper] and others, and are busying themselves in spreading calumnies. It is clear and evident that they will surround with their swords of hatred and their shafts of enmity the one whom they knew to be an outcast among men

* Ḥájí Mírzá Siyyid Ḥasan, Afnán-i-Kabír (the Great Afnán), a brother of the wife of the Báb. (HMB)

and to have been banished from one country to another. This is not the first time that such iniquity hath been perpetrated, nor the first goblet that hath been dashed to the ground, nor the first veil that hath been rent in twain in the path of God, the Lord of the worlds. This Wronged One, however, remained calm and silent in the Most Great Prison, busying Himself with His own affairs, and completely detached from all else but God. Iniquity waxed so grievous that the pens of the world are powerless to record it.

In this connection it is necessary to mention the following occurrence, that haply men may take fast hold of the cord of justice and truthfulness. Ḥájí Shaykh Muḥammad-'Alí – upon him be the glory of God, the Ever-Abiding – was a merchant of high repute, well-known unto most of the inhabitants of the Great City (Constantinople). Not long ago, when the Persian Embassy in Constantinople was secretly engaged in stirring up mischief, it was noticed that this believing and sincere soul was greatly distressed. Finally, one night he threw himself into the sea, but was rescued by some passers-by who chanced to come upon him at that moment. His act was widely commented upon and given varied interpretations by different people. Following this, one night he repaired to a mosque, and, as reported by the guardian of that place, kept vigil the whole night, and was occupied until the morning in offering, ardently and with tearful eyes, his prayers and supplications. Upon hearing him suddenly cease his devotions, the guardian went to him, and found that he had already surrendered his soul. An empty bottle was found by his side, indicating that he had poisoned himself. Briefly, the guardian, while greatly astonished, broke the news to the people. It was found out that he had left two testaments. In the first he recognized and confessed the unity of God, that His Exalted Being had neither peer nor equal, and that His Essence was exalted above all praise, all glorification and description. He also testified to the Revelation of the Prophets and the holy ones, and recognized what had been written down in the Books of God, the Lord of all men. On another page, in which he had set down a prayer, he wrote these words in conclusion: 'This servant and the loved ones of God are perplexed. On the one hand the Pen of the Most High hath forbidden all men to engage in sedition, contention or conflict, and on the other that same Pen hath sent down these most sublime words: "Should anyone, in the presence of the Manifestation, discover an evil intention on the part of any soul, he must not oppose him, but must leave him to God." Considering that on the one hand this binding command is clear and firmly established, and that on the other calumnies, beyond human strength to bear or endure, have been uttered, this servant hath chosen to commit this most grievous sin. I turn suppliantly unto the ocean of God's bounty and the heaven of Divine mercy, and hope that He will blot out with the pen of His grace and bounteousness the misdeeds of this servant. Though my transgressions be manifold, and unnumbered my evil-doings, yet do I cleave tenaciously to the cord of His bounty, and cling unto the hem of His generosity. God is witness, and they that are nigh unto His Threshold know full well, that this servant could not bear to hear the tales related by the perfidious. I, therefore, have committed this act. If He chastise me, He verily is to be praised for what He doeth; and if He forgive me, His behest shall be obeyed.'

. . . We beseech God – blessed and glorified be He – to forgive the aforementioned person (Ḥájí Shaykh Muḥammad-'Alí), and change his evil deeds into good ones. He, verily, is the All-Powerful, the Almighty, the All-Bounteous.[1]

Ḥájí Shaykh Muḥammad-'Alí, known as Nabíl Ibn Nabíl, was a brother of Shaykh Káẓim of Qazvín, to whom Bahá'u'lláh gave the surname Samandar (Salamander). Both brothers were merchants of high repute. Their father, Shaykh Muḥammad, known as Nabíl, espoused the Faith of the Báb in early days, and passed away in Baghdád, one year before the Declaration of Bahá'u'lláh. What caused Ḥájí Shaykh Muḥammad-'Alí, Nabíl Ibn Nabíl, to commit suicide were the intrigues of the followers of Mírzá Yaḥyá in Constantinople, and here is the story (as much as the present writer has been able, with documentary evidence, to construct it) of their disgraceful proceedings.

The Afnáns, relatives of the Báb, had extensive commercial interests. Ḥájí Mírzá Muḥammad-'Alí, a son of Ḥájí Mírzá Siyyid Muḥammad (a maternal uncle of the Báb), was resident in Hong Kong; his brother, Ḥájí Mírzá Muḥammad-Taqí, the Vakílu'd-Dawlih, resided in Yazd (later in 'Ishqábád). There were also always one or two of the Afnáns in Bombay, where they managed a prosperous publishing house and printing press, from which the first Bahá'í books ever to be printed were issued, such as *Kitáb-i-Iqtidárát** and *Kitáb-i-Mubín*,* in the handwriting of Mishkín-Qalam. Áqá Mírzá Áqá, Núri'd-Dín, was in Port Sa'íd, trading under the name of Núri'd-Dín Ḥasan; Ḥájí Mírzá Siyyid Ḥasan, Afnán-i-Kabír (the Great Afnán), a brother of the wife of the Báb, and his son Ḥájí Siyyid 'Alí, married to Furúghíyyih Khánum, a daughter of Bahá'u'lláh, were in Beirut.

In addition, the Afnáns had partners or agents in a number of other commercial centres. Áqá 'Alí-Ḥaydar-i-Shirvání (before he moved to Ṭihrán) was a partner in Caucasia; Ḥájí Shaykh Muḥammad-'Alí,

* The contents of these books were Tablets of Bahá'u'lláh.

another partner in Istanbul. A third partner in the Ottoman capital was Áqá Muḥammad-'Alíy-i-Iṣfahání. This man gradually fell under the influence of the supporters of Ṣubḥ-i-Azal. Shaykh Aḥmad-i-Rúḥí and Mírzá Áqá Khán-i-Kirmání were the most prominent of these followers of Mírzá Yaḥyá. But there were others, equally as active and mischief-making, such as Shaykh Muḥammad-i-Yazdí, Áqá Muḥammad-'Alíy-i-Tabrízí (who had been expelled by Bahá'u'lláh, because of his continuously-repeated misdeeds), and Najaf-'Alí Khán, who had connections with the Persian Embassy. Allied with Shaykh Aḥmad-i-Rúḥí and Mírzá Áqá Khán-i-Kirmání, in furthering the aims of Siyyid Jamálu'd-Dín-i-Asadábádí (Afghání), was Ḥájí Mírzá Ḥasan Khán, the Khabíru'l-Mulk (sometime the Persian consul-general in Istanbul), but it cannot be ascertained whether he too was an Azalí or not. Eventually all the three suffered the same fate together. They were beheaded in Tabríz, in the year 1896, in the presence and on the orders of Muḥammad-'Alí Mírzá (later Sháh), the Crown-Prince of Persia.

Ḥájí Mírzá Ḥasan Khán, the Khabíru'l-Mulk (from Browne, The Persian Revolution of 1905–1909*)*

Although, before long, there came a break between Mírzá Áqá Khán and Áqá Muḥammad-Ṭáhir, the founder and owner of the newspaper *Akhtar*, at the height of the crisis resulting from the activities of the Azalís this paper was completely dominated by Mírzá Áqá Khán and his associates. Strangely enough, it seems that the break was caused by the marriage of a daughter of Áqá Muḥammad-Ṭáhir with Mírzá Ḥusayn-i-Sharíf-i-Káshání, a son of Mullá Muḥammad-Ja'far-i-Naráqí, one of the ardent supporters of Ṣubḥ-i-Azal in earlier times. Mullá Muḥammad-Ja'far (author of a book entitled *Tadhkiratu'l-Ghháfilín* – A Reminder to the Heedless – which he wrote in refutation of Bahá'u'lláh), after roving round 'Iráq in search of Mírzá Yaḥyá, who had not bothered to inform his zealous champion of his departure, had taken refuge in Káẓimayn. But this township, adjacent to Baghdád, was always teeming with pilgrims, and because Mullá Muḥammad-Ja'far was known to be a Bábí, Káẓimayn was not, in the estimation of Mírzá Buzurg Khán, the Persian consul-general, a safe place for Mullá Muḥammad-Ja'far. Therefore, in the year 1869, when Mírzá Buzurg Khán was returning to Írán, he took with him Mullá Muḥammad-Ja'far together with his son, Mírzá Ḥusayn, then a boy young in years, as well as Mírzá Núru'lláh,* a son of Mírzá Yaḥyá then stranded in 'Iráq. In Kirmánsháh, Mullá Muḥammad-Ja'far fell ill and was unable to travel. Mírzá Buzurg Khán was forced to abandon him and the two boys, and leave them in charge of Prince Imám-Qulí Mírzá, the 'Imádu'd-Dawlih, Governor of Kirmánsháh. When Mullá Muḥammad-Ja'far had recovered, 'Imádu'd-Dawlih sent the three, under escort, to Ṭihrán, where they were taken to the Síyáh-Chál. Mullá Muḥammad-Ja'far was poisoned in the gaol and the boys were set free. Later we shall return to the story of Ḥájí Mírzá Ḥusayn-i-Sharíf-i-Káshání, this son of Mullá Muḥammad-Ja'far.

In the thirty-sixth issue of the newspaper *Akhtar*, dated 12 August 1886, a letter appeared over the signature of Áqá Muḥammad-'Alíy-i-Iṣfahání, accusing Ḥájí Mírzá Siyyid Ḥasan, the Afnán-i-Kabír, and his sons of double-dealing, of conspiracy to mulct him of his riches, and almost of theft. His sweeping statement imputed trickery, treachery, bad faith, and duplicity to all the co-religionists of Afnán-i-

* Mírzá Núru'lláh became, eventually, a physician, resident in Rasht, in the Caspian province of Gílán.

Kabír. His purpose at the moment, he wrote, was to expose falsehoods as a warning to his compatriots, and to declare as null and void some documents which, he alleged, Ḥájí Mírzá Siyyid Ḥasan had obtained from him by misrepresentation. He had, he stated, broken away from Afnán-i-Kabír and his sons, the partnership had ended, and they owed him a huge sum of money. Later, he wrote, he would take his case, supported by ample evidence, to the Persian Consulate-General in Constantinople; and the evidence which he had, he affirmed, included writings of the Spiritual Guide of Ḥájí Mírzá Siyyid Ḥasan.

Bahá'u'lláh states categorically, in the *Epistle to the Son of the Wolf*, that:

> For years no untoward incident hath occurred in Persia. The reins of the stirrers of sedition among various sects were held firmly in the grasp of power. None hath transgressed his limits. By God! This people have never been, nor are they now, inclined to mischief. Their hearts are illumined with the light of the fear of God, and adorned with the adornment of His love. Their concern hath ever been and now is for the betterment of the world. . . .
>
> On the other hand, the officials of the Persian Embassy in the Great City (Constantinople) are energetically and assiduously seeking to exterminate these wronged ones. They desire one thing, and God desireth another. Consider now what hath befallen the trusted ones of God in every land. At one time they have been accused of theft and larceny; at another they have been calumniated in a manner without parallel in this world. Answer thou fairly. What could be the results and consequences, in foreign countries, of the accusation of theft brought by the Persian Embassy against its own subjects? If this Wronged One was ashamed, it was not because of the humiliation it brought this servant, but rather because of the shame of its becoming known to the Ambassadors of foreign countries how incompetent and lacking in understanding are several eminent officials of the Persian Embassy. . . . Briefly, instead of seeking, as they should, through Him Who occupieth this sublime station, to attain unto the most exalted ranks, and to obtain His advice, they have exerted themselves and are striving their utmost to put out His light. However, according to what hath been reported, His Excellency the Ambassador Mu'ínu'l-Mulk, Mírzá Muḥsin Khán* – may God assist him – was, at that time, absent from Constantinople. Such things have happened because it was believed that His Majesty the Sháh of Persia – may the All-Merciful assist him – was angry with them that have attained and revolve round the Sanctuary of Wisdom. God well knoweth and testifieth that this Wronged One hath, at

* Later, Mushíru'd-Dawlih and the Foreign Minister of Írán. (HMB)

all times, been cleaving fast unto whatever would be conducive to the glory of both the government and the people. God, verily, is sufficient Witness.

Describing the people of Bahá, the Most Sublime Pen hath sent down these words: 'These, verily, are men who if they come to cities of pure gold will consider them not; and if they meet the fairest and most comely of women will turn aside.' Thus hath it been sent down by the Most Sublime Pen for the people of Bahá, on the part of Him Who is the Counsellor, the Omniscient. In the concluding passages of the Tablet to His Majesty the Emperor of Paris (Napoleon III) these exalted words have been revealed: 'Exultest thou over the treasures thou dost possess, knowing they shall perish? Rejoicest thou in that thou rulest a span of earth, when the whole world, in the estimation of the people of Bahá, is worth as much as the black in the eye of a dead ant? Abandon it unto such as have set their affections upon it, and turn thou unto Him Who is the Desire of the world.'

God alone – exalted be His glory – is cognizant of the things which befell this Wronged One. Every day bringeth a fresh report of stories current against Us at the Embassy in Constantinople. Gracious God! The sole aim of their machinations is to bring about the extermination of this servant. They are, however, oblivious of the fact that abasement in the path of God is My true glory. In the newspapers the following hath been recorded: 'Touching the fraudulent dealings of some of the exiles of 'Akká, and the excesses committed by them against several people, etc. . . .' Unto them who are the exponents of justice and the daysprings of equity the intention of the writer is evident and his purpose clear. Briefly, he arose and inflicted upon Me divers tribulations, and treated Me with injustice and cruelty. By God! This Wronged One would not barter this place of exile for the Most Sublime Habitation. In the estimation of men of insight whatsoever befalleth in the path of God is manifest glory and a supreme attainment. . . .

. . . This Wronged One, however, cleaveth to seemly patience. Would that His Majesty the Sháh of Persia would ask for a report of the things which befell Us in Constantinople, that he might become fully acquainted with the true facts. . . . Is there to be found a just man who will judge in this day according to that which God hath sent down in His Book? Where is the fair-minded person who will equitably consider what hath been perpetrated against Us without any clear token or proof?[2]

In other Tablets, such as one addressed to Áqá Mírzá Áqá, Núri'd-Dín, and another addressed to Karbilá'í Ḥájí-Bábá, a Bahá'í of Zarqán (in the province of Fárs, near Shíráz), Bahá'u'lláh speaks in particular of the accusations levelled against Afnán-i-Kabír. Unfortunately, the present writer could find no access anywhere to a complete set of the newspaper *Akhtar*, and the issues of this paper that belonged to Edward Granville Browne, and are deposited in the University

Library at Cambridge, do not carry any reference to the intrigues of the Azalís in Constantinople. Perhaps there nowhere exists a complete set of *Akhtar*. At the time, when it was strongly under the influence of Mírzá Áqá Khán-i-Kirmání, Náṣiri'd-Dín Sháh had banned its circulation in Írán. However, a time came when Mírzá Áqá Khán was estranged from Áqá Muḥammad-Ṭáhir, and the latter found it more and more difficult to go on producing his newspaper, in great measure because of financial stringency. 'Alá'u'l-Mulk, the Persian ambassador in Constantinople, then intervened and requested his government for a subsidy, to be given to Áqá Muḥammad-Ṭáhir so that he could continue to publish *Akhtar*, as a counterweight to the newspaper, *Qánún*, which Mírzá Malkam Khán, the Náẓimu'd-Dawlih, was editing and publishing in London, severely criticizing the Government of Írán, and mounting vicious attacks, in particular, on Mírzá 'Alí-Aṣghar Khán, the Amínu's-Sulṭán,* Náṣiri'd-Dín Sháh's capable and astute, if unscrupulous, Ṣadr-i-A'ẓam. A document exists, bearing the

* At the time of the assassination of Náṣiri'd-Dín Sháh in 1896, Amínu's-Sulṭán was the Ṣadr-i-A'ẓam or Grand Vizier. It was his stratagem which saved the day and prevented the outbreak of disorder. Some modern writers have made the ridiculous suggestion that Amínu's-Sulṭán, himself, was implicated in the murder of Náṣiri'd-Dín Sháh. In the year 1898, Sulaymán Khán, known as Jamál Effendi, came from 'Akká. It was a part of his mission to meet Amínu's-Sulṭán in the city of Qum, to which he had retired after his dismissal by Muẓaffari'd-Dín Sháh. The fallen Minister had once spoken in favour of the oppressed Bahá'ís. But, restored to office again, he soon forgot his promises.

Mírzá 'Alí-Aṣghar Khán, the Amínu's-Sulṭán (from Browne, The Persian Revolution of 1905–9*)*

Sháh's own handwriting, which gives approval to subsidizing Áqá Muḥammad-Ṭáhir and his newspaper. However, the éclat of previous years could not be retrieved and *Akhtar* died out.

The story of the intrigues in Istanbul is rather complicated as all plottings are. It can be divided into several episodes. That which concerns Ḥájí Shaykh Muḥammad-'Alí, Nabíl Ibn Nabíl, is fully described in a tract written by his nephew, Mírzá 'Abdu'l-Ḥusayn, a son of Shaykh Káẓim-i-Samandar. But, unfortunately, that which concerns the Afnáns is nowhere put into a continuous narrative. There are gaps which require bridging.

As stated before, the Afnáns had a string of commercial interests which stretched from Hong Kong to Istanbul. About the year 1882, Ḥájí Shaykh Muḥammad-'Alí of Qazvín, who had for years been engaged in trade in his native land, moved to Istanbul at the bidding of Bahá'u'lláh. He was there for seven years, until 1889, managing a trading-house. Whether he began outright in partnership with the Afnáns, or that partnership came about later, is not known. Neither is it known which of the sons of Ḥájí Mírzá Siyyid Ḥasan, the Afnán-i-Kabír, was in Istanbul for any length of time, during those seven years. But it is certain that Ḥájí Shaykh Muḥammad-'Alí was personally directing and managing a trading-house there for the whole of those seven years. Thus, he became a well-known figure in the Ottoman capital, dealing equally with people of all Faiths: Jewish, Christian and Muslim. Pilgrims too, of all Faiths, bound for Mecca, Jerusalem, or 'Akká, called on Ḥájí Shaykh Muḥammad-'Alí to obtain advice, guidance or assistance. However, his well-deserved fame caused the supporters of Ṣubḥ-i-Azal in Constantinople – men such as Shaykh Muḥammad-i-Yazdí, Shaykh Aḥmad-i-Rúḥí and Mírzá Áqá Khán-i-Kirmání – to mark him for close observation. On the other hand, the Most Great Branch maintained communications with eminent Ottoman officials, such as Núrí Big, through Ḥájí Shaykh Muḥammad-'Alí and, probably, Azalís became aware of this fact.

Now, Mírzá Áqá Khán began to frequent the business premises of Ḥájí Shaykh Muḥammad-'Alí, coming every day with a fresh lot of questions, and eventually expressing his desire to embrace the Bahá'í Faith. But he wished first, he said, to visit 'Akká and witness the truth of what he had been told. He asked Ḥájí Shaykh Muḥammad-'Alí to obtain permission for him, from Bahá'u'lláh, to go to 'Akká. Two years before, Mírzá Yaḥyá of Qazvín, whose father was a supporter of Ṣubḥ-i-Azal, had been guided to see the error of his ways and became a confirmed believer in the Faith of Bahá'u'lláh. Ḥájí Shaykh Muḥammad-'Alí hoped that Mírzá Áqá Khán would go the same way. But it was not to be; Mírzá Áqá Khán was a dissembler, a fact which soon became apparent.

Áqá Muḥammad-'Alíy-i-Iṣfahání had also been in Constantinople for a number of years. Nothing has been recorded of his antecedents, at least not to the knowledge of the present writer. He traded on a small scale, and took commissions on deals which he put through. Although receiving nothing but kindness from Ḥájí Shaykh Muḥammad-'Alí, he was moved by jealousy of the unqualified success of the Qazvíní merchant to send adverse reports regarding him to some of his clients, and to spread false rumours about him. Then it was that Ḥájí Shaykh Muḥammad-'Alí thought of a plan to counter the malevolence of Áqá Muḥammad-'Alí. He proposed a business partnership between the Afnáns, himself and this Iṣfahání, to which the Afnáns agreed. This partnership, which lasted several years, flourished and the Iṣfahání gained huge profits by it. But gradually he fell under the spell of Áqá Muḥammad-'Alíy-i-Tabrízí (whom Bahá'u'lláh had expelled), and the supporters of Ṣubḥ-i-Azal. In point of time that was also the period when Mírzá Áqá Khán had established ascendancy over Áqá Muḥammad-Ṭáhir, the founder and editor of *Akhtar*. So persistent became the malicious rumours spread by the two Muḥammad-'Alís, one of Tabríz and the other of Iṣfahán, that Bahá'u'lláh sent Ḥájí Siyyid Javád-i-Yazdí to investigate and find out the truth of the matter. That venerable siyyid stayed for a while in Istanbul and realized what a pack of calculated lies the adversaries of the Faith were concocting in the Ottoman capital. However, a time came when Ḥájí Shaykh Muḥammad-'Alí could no longer bear the weight of false rumours, libels and innuendoes. Apart from his nephew, Mírzá 'Abdu'l-Ḥusayn, who was very young, he was all alone. One night, he threw himself into the sea, but was rescued by some boatmen. The customs officials and others around, who knew him well, were astounded by what they witnessed. Ḥájí Shaykh Muḥammad-'Alí lived to see another day, but the thought of having attempted suicide, and the reporting of his attempt by newspapers, particularly *Akhtar*, weighed heavily on his mind.

In the midst of it all, Ḥájí Mírzá Abu'l-Qásim-i-Náẓir, a native of Iṣfahán, reached Constantinople from the Holy Land, bound for 'Ishqábád. Áqá Muḥammad-'Alí had not yet come out in the open, and since he too was a native of Iṣfahán, for his own nefarious ends he prevailed on Náẓir to stay in Constantinople. But before long, he was convinced that Náẓir would not lend him support and become a tool in his hands. Then it came to his ears that some of the Afnáns would shortly be visiting Istanbul, and that they might possibly effect some changes in the trading-house, owned jointly by all of them. So, one day, he gave out that there had been a theft of 400 pounds from their coffers in the trading-house, and he acted the part of accuser so well that his false assertion was believed. He had a poor siyyid, also an Iṣfahání, in his service, to whom he owed 60 pounds in unpaid wages, and suspicion rested on him. Through the influence of the Persian Consulate-General, where the Azalís could exert some pressure, this Siyyid Muḥammad, who was a Muslim and an honest man, was turned over to the police, and remained chained in custody for two months. But in the end he managed to clear himself, and stated truthfully that Áqá Muḥammad-'Alí was a liar and a cheat, who owed him 60 pounds, and, having heard of the coming of the Shírází siyyids (the Afnáns), had resorted to this ruse to help himself to 400 pounds of their money.

In the meantime, the news of Ḥájí Shaykh Muḥammad-'Alí's attempted suicide having reached the Holy Land, Bahá'u'lláh bade him leave Constantinople after his seven years there, and come to 'Akká. Mírzá Muḥsin, a younger son of Afnán-i-Kabír, was directed by Bahá'u'lláh to Constantinople to relieve him of his onerous duties. It was also arranged that his nephew, Mírzá 'Abdu'l-Ḥusayn, who knew the ins and outs of the trading-concern, should remain to help Mírzá Muḥsin. Ḥájí Shaykh Muḥammad-'Alí left the Ottoman capital in March 1889, recording in his notebook his happiness at being relieved at last of all the cares and anxieties which enemies had inflicted upon him in that city.

On the eve of Ḥájí Shaykh Muḥammad-'Alí's departure, Náẓir had found, in a public lavatory in Qárshí, the sum of 125 pounds secreted away, and to Ḥájí Shaykh's regret he mentioned this to Áqá Muḥammad-'Alí. The supporters of Mírzá Yaḥyá in Istanbul joined forces and invited Áqá Muḥammad-'Alí to build a case against Náẓir. Despite the fact that it was Áqá Muḥammad-'Alí himself who had begged Náẓir to stay in Istanbul, and although it was fully two months after Náẓir had discovered the money and had made no attempt to conceal the fact, Áqá Muḥammad-'Alí pointed a finger at him and shamelessly accused him of stealing the 400 pounds from the coffers of the trading-house. He had also the temerity to pen a supplication to Bahá'u'lláh, defaming Náẓir. An answer came from the Holy Land, over the signature of Khádimu'lláh, to the effect that should Áqá Muḥammad-'Alí be able to prove his charge against Náẓir, he should receive from Áqá Mírzá Muḥsin-i-Afnán the sum he claimed had been stolen, together with the interest due.

Apart from Muḥammad-'Alíy-i-Tabrízí and the prominent Azalís of Constantinople, a son of Mírzá Yaḥyá was also at that time in the Ottoman capital. From them, and from *Akhtar*, then a tool in the hands of Mírzá Áqá Khán, went up a chorus of condemnation. When he had embarked on his journey to 'Ishqábád, Ḥájí Mírzá Abu'l-Qásim-i-Náẓir had left his family in the Holy Land, and his sojourn in Istanbul having lengthened, and because he had permission from Bahá'u'lláh to go back to the Holy Land to see his family, faced now with Áqá Muḥammad-'Alí's monstrous slander he decided to leave at once. But he was brought back. In the Persian Embassy, Mu'ínu'l-Mulk, the Ambassador, who knew him personally, conducted the case brought against him, found in his favour, and completely exonerated him. Notwithstanding that clear verdict, Áqá Muḥammad-'Alí, goaded by his Tabrízí namesake and by Shaykh Muḥammad-i-Yazdí, dragged Náẓir to the Ottoman courts, where once again his innocence was irrefutably established.

Then it was that Áqá Muḥammad-'Alí, smarting under the defeat he had suffered in the presence of Shaykh Muḥsin Khán, the Mu'ínu'l-Mulk, as well as in the Ottoman courts, threw all pretence aside and showed his true colours by writing the notorious letter to the newspaper *Akhtar* (already cited), in which he maliciously accused Ḥájí Mírzá Siyyid Ḥasan, the Afnán-i-Kabír, his sons, and by implication all his co-religionists, of duplicity and crooked practices. He even dared to make mention of Bahá'u'lláh. In the meantime, Mírzá Muḥsin-i-Afnán and Mírzá 'Abdu'l-Ḥusayn had wound up the affairs of the trading-house in Constantinople, even to selling the office furniture, and had left for the Holy Land.

The present writer has in his possession a letter written by Áqá Mírzá Muḥsin, in which he states that Bahá'u'lláh had bidden Áqá Siyyid Aḥmad, another son of the Afnán-i-Kabír, to go to Istanbul and rebut the serious and impudent charges made by Áqá Muḥammad-'Alí of Iṣfahán. Ḥájí Mírzá Abu'l-Qásim-i-Náẓir and Ḥájí Abu'l-Ḥasan-i-Amín were also directed to proceed to the Ottoman capital: the former, to settle his own affairs; the latter, to lend a hand to Áqá Siyyid Aḥmad. Mírzá 'Abdu'l-Ḥusayn states that, as a matter of fact, Áqá Muḥammad-'Alí owed the Afnáns and Ḥájí Amín a considerable sum of money. Despite his behaviour, Áqá Siyyid Aḥmad and Ḥájí Amín tried to come to terms with him amicably, but it was of no avail. Once again, the presence in Istanbul of Ḥájí Shaykh Muḥammad-'Alí became urgently necessary. In September 1889, accompanied by his nephew and Áqá Muḥammad, their servant, he sailed for Istanbul with a heavy heart. He had been instructed by Bahá'u'lláh not to prolong his stay there, and to go on to Persia. But that was not to be.

As Mírzá 'Abdu'l-Ḥusayn and Fáḍil-i-Mázindarání have both recorded, Ḥájí Shaykh Muḥammad-'Alí, with the evidence based on ledgers and account books, proved in the Ottoman courts of law and also before the Persian ambassador the total falsity of the claims of Muḥammad-'Alíy-i-Iṣfahání. Leading merchants of Constantinople, Persian and non-Persian alike, readily signed a document stating their conviction that the Iṣfahání, who had maligned his erstwhile partners, had lied, grossly misled others, and, in fact, owed the Bahá'ís a considerable sum of money.

Despite this outstanding success achieved by Ḥájí Shaykh Muḥammad-'Alí and the rout of the Iṣfahání renegade, the adversaries of the Bahá'í Faith in Constantinople waxed bolder in manufacturing fresh lies and giving them wide currency. They gave out as a fact that the Ottoman authorities had decided to set fire to the Mansion of Bahjí, and to destroy the very source and centre of the new Faith. Ḥájí Shaykh Muḥammad-'Alí, while doing his duty loyally and faithfully, was constantly subjected to the grinding effect of such falsehoods and to the jibes of the ignorant, until he could bear it no longer. And so he committed suicide. Áqá Siyyid Aḥmad held a memorial meeting for him which was attended by Mu'ínu'l-Mulk, the Persian ambassador, who had been greatly moved by the tragic death of Ḥájí Shaykh, and was seen to shed tears. He is reported to have said: 'We had one merchant, wise, sagacious, a man of high integrity; and now we have lost him.'

Ḥájí Shaykh Muḥammad-'Alí had gone from the reach of plotters and ill-wishers, but the story of the intrigues against the Bahá'ís in Constantinople does not end with his decease. Áqá Siyyid Aḥmad-i-Afnán was still there, the very sight of whom was hated by the two Muḥammad-'Alís: the Iṣfahání and the Tabrízí. But he was much needed elsewhere, and Bahá'u'lláh bade Áqá 'Azízu'lláh-i-Jadhdháb, a convert from the Jewish fold in Mashhad, to go to Constantinople and expedite Áqá Siyyid Aḥmad's departure. Moreover, he was to take charge of the Afnáns' commercial interests. Ḥájí Siyyid Mírzá, an elder brother of Siyyid Aḥmad, who resided in Yazd, owed 12,000 *túmáns* to Áqá 'Alí-Ḥaydar-i-Shírvání, a merchant of high repute who attended to the transference of Ḥuqúqu'lláh* from Ḥájí Abu'l-Ḥasan-i-Amín to the Holy Land. Áqá 'Alí-Ḥaydar had, at one time, been an agent for the Afnáns in the Caucasus, but had now resided for some years in Ṭihrán, where Edward Granville Browne met him in 1888. In the mid-eighties of the nineteenth century, there were those who, having failed commercially, were dogging the steps of some of the Afnáns. It appears that Ḥájí Siyyid Mírzá was somewhat dilatory in the matter of settling his debts. In a Tablet addressed to him, Bahá'u'lláh tells him sternly to pay his debts and not to delay longer.

Now it was Bahá'u'lláh's wish that Áqá Siyyid Aḥmad should first visit the Holy Land, then go to 'Ishqábád and sell some of the land which the Afnáns had purchased in earlier years, to settle their accounts with Áqá 'Alí-Ḥaydar. By this time, Ḥájí Abu'l-Ḥasan-i-Amín, together with Ḥájí Mullá 'Alí-Akbar-i-Shahmírzádí – a Hand of the Cause of God who was known as Ḥájí Ákhund – were languishing in the prison of Qazvín. (Bahá'u'lláh refers to this in the Tablet of the World – *Lawḥ-i-Dunyá* – revealed in honour of Áqá Mírzá Áqá, Núri'd-Dín.) Bahá'u'lláh requested Áqá 'Azízu'lláh-i-Jadhdháb to convey this message to Áqá Siyyid Aḥmad: We command you not to tarry any longer in Constantinople, not for a moment, and to leave at once. Jadhdháb, who had been trading for a time in Transcaucasia and held a passport from the Emir (Amír) of Bukhárá – which was tantamount to a Russian passport – travelled in a Khedival steamer and

* The 'Right of God' – a payment by believers instituted in the *Kitáb-i-Aqdas*.

betook himself to Constantinople as quickly as possible. When he reached the Ottoman capital in the opening days of August 1891, the sacred month of Muḥarram had come on, and Áqá Siyyid Aḥmad was delaying his departure. But Jadhdháb, carrying as he did a command of Bahá'u'lláh, pressed on Áqá Siyyid Aḥmad the urgency of his departure until it was arranged that he should leave in the afternoon of 'Áshúrá (the tenth of Muḥarram), the very day of the martyrdom of Imám Ḥusayn. There was in Istanbul at this time a merchant, native of Iṣfahán, named Áqá Ḥusayn-'Alí, who consorted with Muslims, Bahá'ís and Azalís alike. On the eve of 'Áshúrá he invited Áqá Siyyid Aḥmad, Áqá 'Azízu'lláh-i-Jadhdháb, and many others to a meeting in the inn of Khán-i-Válidih, in commemoration of the martyrdom of the third Imám, after which, as was customary, dinner was to be served. Khán-i-Válidih was well known as a haunt of the Persians, and many Persians had offices and homes in that inn. When they sat down to dinner, it was seen that Shaykh Aḥmad-i-Rúḥí, Muḥammad-'Alíy-i-Tabrízí and Muḥammad-'Alíy-i-Iṣfahání were also present. They kept stealthily eyeing Áqá Siyyid Aḥmad and Áqá 'Azízu'lláh. Later, these two, accompanied by Mírzá Ismá'íl Khán, the official in charge of passports in the Persian Embassy (a native of Rasht), and a broker named Ḥájí Muḥammad-Javád-i-Iṣfahání, both of whom were Bahá'ís, repaired to the home and office of Afnán in the inn of Áyinih-Lí. In the vestibule which led into the inn they came upon Áqá Naṣru'lláh-i-Ardakání, the servant of Áqá Siyyid Aḥmad, seated there with the caretaker of the caravanserai and a number of porters. The Afnán enquired of his servant, 'Why didn't you come to Khán-i-Válidih as I told you?' to which Naṣru'lláh replied that the police had prevented his entering. The following morning early, Jadhdháb, with Áqá Naṣru'lláh as guide, visited the grave of Ḥájí Shaykh Muḥammad-'Alí. Bahá'u'lláh had bidden him have that grave repaired and a marble tombstone laid upon it. Naṣru'lláh, having taken Jadhdháb to the spot where Ḥájí Shaykh was buried, left him to his task and quickly returned to the city. At midday of 'Áshúrá, having finished the work entrusted to him, Jadhdháb also returned, to find Siyyid Aḥmad, Mírzá Ismá'íl Khán and Ḥájí Muḥammad-Javád sunk in gloom. That morning, after he had gone, the police had arrived with information from the Persian Embassy concerning a case lodged by the two Muḥammad-'Alís – the Tabrízí and the Iṣfahání. It was to the effect that the previous night, whilst they were guests of Áqá Ḥusayn-'Alíy-i-Iṣfahání in the inn of Khán-i-Válidih, the servant of Siyyid Aḥmad, whom they named as Áqá Naṣru'lláh-i-Ardakání, had broken into their premises, smashed the lock of their iron safe, and stolen several thousand pounds and all documents pertaining to the sums which Bahá'ís owed them; and now this thief, in the company of his master, was about to escape to 'Akká and should be stopped. Jadhdháb reminded Áqá Siyyid Aḥmad that he had been warned to quit the Ottoman capital without delay and should leave at once. Within hours he and his servant were on board an Austrian steamer.

When Jadhdháb, having seen them off, came back, he was faced with a summons to the Persian Embassy. As it happened, neither Mu'ínu'l-Mulk, the Ambassador, nor Ḥájí Mírzá Najaf-'Alí Khán, his deputy, both of whom had friendly relations with Jadhdháb, was in Constantinople. The Consul was an Armenian, Ovanes (Uvánis) Khán – in later years, Ovanes Khán Musá'id, the Persian minister in Tokyo – who was not well acquainted with all that had taken place in Istanbul. He was very angry because Áqá Siyyid Aḥmad and Áqá Naṣru'lláh had been spirited away. But Jadhdháb stood up to him, convinced him that the plaintiffs had acted out of malice, and that there was no case to answer.

Mention was made earlier in this chapter of the strained relations between Mírzá Áqá Khán and Áqá Muḥammad-Ṭáhir due to the marriage of the latter's daughter to Mírzá Ḥusayn-i-Sharíf-i-Káshání. In the archives of Mírzá Malkam Khán, presented to the Bibliothèque Nationale of Paris by his widow, there are many letters written to Malkam by Mírzá Áqá Khán. These letters are indeed astonishing. Apart from the reviling of Mírzá Ḥusayn-i-Sharíf, and the denigration of Áqá Muḥammad-Ṭáhir, they include such incredible statements as that the Bábís in Constantinople believed Malkam to be the Christ descended from Heaven, whose second advent must follow the advent of the Mahdí: the Qá'im of the House of Muḥammad. Mírzá Áqá Khán so overreaches the limits of credibility as to say that these Bábís (he must have had Azalís in mind) must have had an intimation to this effect from their leader, and in another letter he actually asserts that this fantastic pronouncement had been made by the leader of the Bábís. Who could this leader have been but Mírzá Yaḥyá, Ṣubḥ-i-Azal? But is it possible that Mírzá Yaḥyá, no matter how stupid, would have made so ridiculous a statement? Did Mírzá Áqá Khán, astute as he was, not know Mírzá Malkam Khán better, when he wrote in that vein to him to ingratiate himself? Again, to blacken the name of Mírzá Ḥusayn-i-Sharíf, Mírzá Áqá Khán tells Malkam that this 'beastly' son-in-law of Áqá Muḥammad-Ṭáhir had asked him to compose a book about the Báb and the Bábís, since he had extensive knowledge of them, promising in return a not inconsiderable remuneration. He had taken great pains and written the book,* Mírzá Áqá Khán writes, but Mírzá Ḥusayn not only did not pay for it, but was showing it to all and sundry in Istanbul as proof that Mírzá Áqá Khán was a Bábí. (It was, of course, well known that Mírzá Áqá Khán and Shaykh Aḥmad-i-Rúḥí had married daughters of Ṣubḥ-i-Azal.) These letters of Mírzá Áqá Khán to Mírzá Malkam Khán indicate clearly his scheming nature.

As to Mírzá Ḥusayn-i-Sharíf, he entered the service of the government of India, retired as a very rich man, and was knighted. Sir Mírzá Ḥusayn ended his days in Cairo, where he lived in noteworthy affluence. He died without issue; and when his brother, Shaykh Mihdíy-i-Sharíf-i-Káshání, who was a schoolmaster in Ṭihrán, hurried to Cairo, he found to his chagrin that the Persian Consulate-General in Egypt had appropriated all the wealth of Sir Mírzá Ḥusayn.

The eventual fate of Shaykh Aḥmad-i-Rúḥí and Mírzá Áqá Khán-i-Kirmání is known – they were imprisoned and executed in 1896† – but of what happened to the two treacherous Muḥammad-'Alís, one of Tabríz and the other of Iṣfahán, nothing is known. The intrigues and the mischief-making of the supporters of Ṣubḥ-i-Azal in Constantinople brought much sorrow to Bahá'u'lláh in His closing years, resulted in the destruction of a precious life, held up to ridicule and contempt, although only for a while, men of high integrity whose probity and trustworthiness were widely and generally acknowledged. But they left no indelible mark in the annals of the Faith of Bahá'u'lláh. That Ark of Salvation surmounted all the storms and the stresses of the time.

* This must have been the tome entitled *Khuláṣatu'l-Bayán* – Summary of the *Bayán*.
† See p. 389. Their story is more fully told in Balyuzi, *Edward Granville Browne and the Bahá'í Faith*.

41

Pages of an Autobiography

THESE are some pages of the autobiography of Ḥájí Mírzá Ḥabíbu'-lláh Afnán. He was a son of Áqá Mírzá Áqá, whom Bahá'u'lláh honoured with the designation of Núri'd-Dín – the Light of Faith. Áqá Mírzá Áqá's father was Ḥájí Mírzá Zaynu'l-'Ábidín, a cousin of Siyyid Muḥammad-Riḍá, the father of the Báb. Another cousin of the Báb's father was Mírzá Maḥmúd-i-Khushnivís (Calligraphist), whose son, Ḥájí Mírzá Muḥammad-Ḥasan (1815–95), generally known as Mírzáy-i-Shírází, became the most eminent Shí'ih mujtahid of his day. Ḥájí Siyyid Javád, the Imám-Jum'ih of Kirmán, also a distinguished personage of his day, was another cousin of the father of the Báb. Both he and Mírzáy-i-Shírází were secretly believers in the Faith of their glorious Kinsman, Whom they believed to be the Qá'im of the House of Muḥammad. No one ever heard from their mouths one word condemnatory of the Faith of the Báb, and they gave protection, whenever possible, to the followers of that Faith. The most signal example was the respect and consideration which Quddús received from the Imám-Jum'ih of Kirmán.

Áqá Mírzá Áqá's mother, named Zahrá Bigum, was a sister of Khadíjih Bigum, the wife of the Báb, both being daughters of Mírzá 'Alí, a merchant of Shíráz. And the mother of Ḥájí Mírzá Ḥabíbu'lláh (see Addendum V) was Maryam-Sulṭán Bigum, a daughter of Ḥájí Mírzá Abu'l-Qásim, one of the two brothers of the wife of the Báb. The other brother was Ḥájí Mírzá Siyyid Ḥasan, known as Afnán-i-Kabír – the Great Afnán.

The first member of the family to espouse zealously the Cause of their Kinsman, the Báb, was His wife, and the second was Ḥájí Mírzá Siyyid 'Alí, a maternal uncle known as Khál-i-A'ẓam – the Most Great Uncle – who had become His guardian when He was orphaned, and was one of the Seven Martyrs of Ṭihrán. Áqá Mírzá Áqá, Núri'd-Dín, was the third member of the family to do so. It was his maternal aunt,

The Paternal Genealogy of the Báb

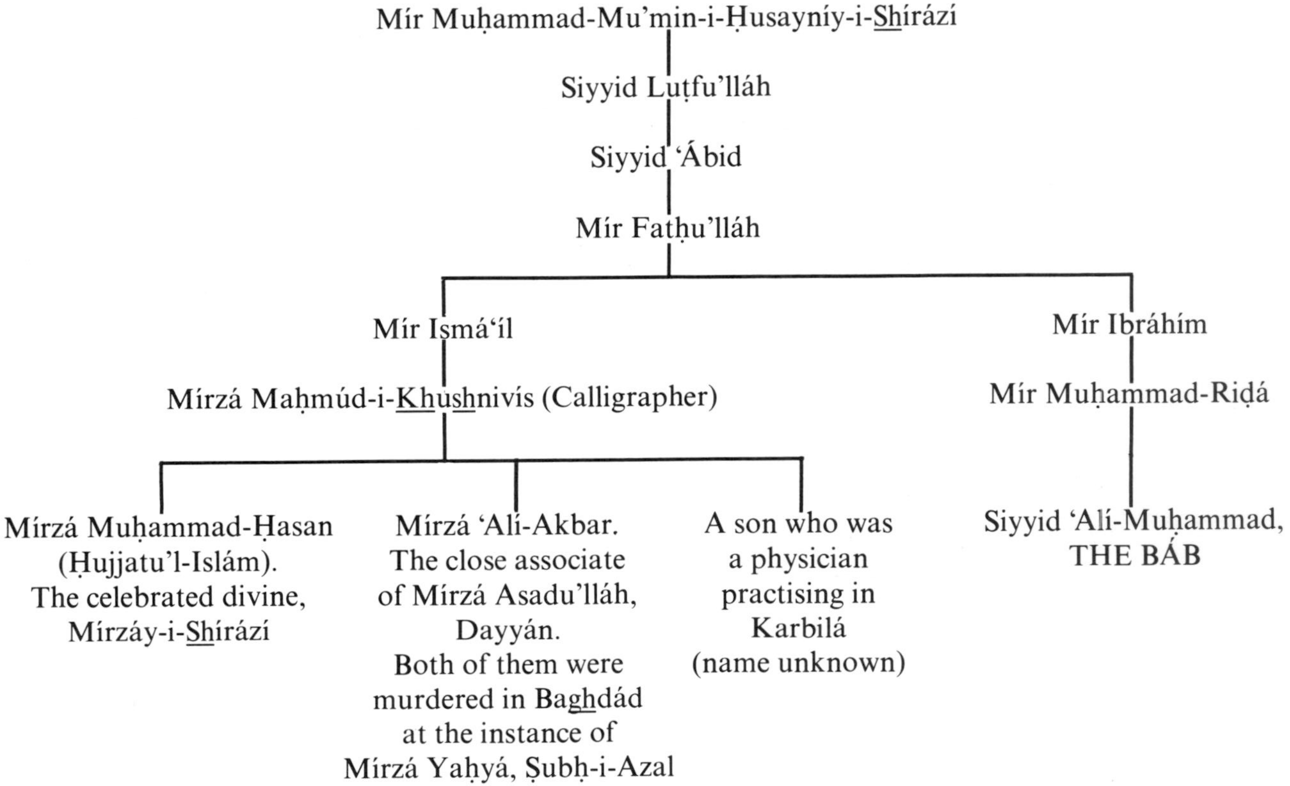
Mír Muḥammad-Mu'min-i-Ḥusayníy-i-Shírází
Siyyid Luṭfu'lláh
Siyyid 'Ábid
Mír Fatḥu'lláh
Mír Ismá'íl
Mírzá Maḥmúd-i-Khushnivís (Calligrapher)
Mírzá Muḥammad-Ḥasan (Ḥujjatu'l-Islám). The celebrated divine, Mírzáy-i-Shírází
Mírzá 'Alí-Akbar. The close associate of Mírzá Asadu'lláh, Dayyán. Both of them were murdered in Baghdád at the instance of Mírzá Yaḥyá, Ṣubḥ-i-Azal
A son who was a physician practising in Karbilá (name unknown)
Mír Ibráhím
Mír Muḥammad-Riḍá
Siyyid 'Alí-Muḥammad, THE BÁB

Áqá Mírzá Áqá Afnán, Núri'd-Dín

the wife of the Báb, who led him to the Faith of the Báb and helped him to understand and accept it. And Áqá Mírzá Áqá, in his turn, persuaded Ḥájí Mírzá Siyyid Muḥammad, known as Khál-i-Akbar – the Greater Uncle, another maternal uncle of the Báb – to travel to 'Iráq as a pilgrim to the holy cities there, in order to attain the presence of Bahá'u'lláh.

Áqá Mírzá Áqá, Núri'd-Dín, became so well known as a faithful and fervent follower of Bahá'u'lláh, throughout the city of Shíráz and beyond, that his life was in jeopardy, and particularly so in the wake of the martyrdoms, in Iṣfahán, of the King of the Martyrs and the Beloved of the Martyrs (Sulṭánu'sh-Shuhadá' and Maḥbúbu'sh-Shuhadá').* The older members of the family, headed by Ḥájí Mírzá Abu'l-Qásim, the father-in-law of Áqá Mírzá Áqá, Núri'd-Dín, thought it advisable that he should leave Shíráz at once. As his son, Ḥájí Mírzá Ḥabíbu'lláh, records, within twenty-four hours he was out of Shíráz and on his way to Bombay, where he established himself for a

* The full story of their martyrdoms and the part played by Sulṭán-Mas'úd Mírzá, the Ẓillu's-Sulṭán, son of Náṣiri'd-Dín Sháh, will be featured in a forthcoming volume.

time. Later, he moved to Port Sa'íd, where his trading-house was known as Núri'd-Dín Ḥasan.

Zahrá Bigum, the mother of Áqá Mírzá Áqá, passed away in October 1889, and within a few months, Ḥájí Mírzá Ḥabíbu'lláh writes, Bahá'u'lláh called the whole family of Áqá Mírzá Áqá to visit the Holy Land. Mírzá Jalál, the eldest son, was left in Shíráz as custodian of the House of the Báb. Ḥájí Mírzá Ḥabíbu'lláh was then fourteen years old. He, together with his mother, Maryam-Sulṭán Bigum, his sister, Ṭúbá Khánum, his brothers, Mírzá Buzurg and Mírzá Ḍíyá'u'lláh, and a servant (a Bahá'í of Káshán), accompanied also by Zívar-Sulṭán Khánum – whose son, Áqá Mírzá Hádí, was to become the father of Shoghi Effendi, the future Guardian of the Bahá'í Faith – left Shíráz bound for the Holy Land. Their journey over the mountain passes on the road to Búshihr – the very road which the Báb had traversed four times – was exceedingly toilsome. Búshihr was extremely hot, and all suffered illness. 'In Búshihr,' Ḥájí Mírzá Ḥabíbu'lláh writes, 'we stayed in the house of Ḥájí Mírzá 'Abdu'lláh Khán, uncle of Muvaqqari'd-Dawlih, who was related to us. At the time when Muḥammad Khán-i-Balúch was detained in Shíráz, he managed to have him freed. . . . I met this Muḥammad Khán, in the days of the Blessed Perfection, in 'Akká. He had become a shepherd.'

After a sojourn in Búshihr of more than a month, the party continued by sea, through the Persian Gulf, the Arabian Sea and the Red Sea, a journey not without its hazards. Near the town of Lingih, around Aden, the ship was battered by a terrific storm, a hole appeared in the hulk, and further on in the Red Sea the engine caught fire. After these frightening adventures they reached Port Sa'íd, where they were greeted by their father, Áqá Siyyid Áqá, and an elder brother. 'We stayed in Port Sa'íd for seven months,' writes Ḥájí Mírzá Ḥabíbu'lláh, 'and then my father supplicated the Blessed Perfection to permit us to attain His presence. Permission was granted.'

Travelling by boat, they reached Haifa at the end of July 1891. where Bahá'u'lláh was then staying. 'The late Jináb-i-Manshádí', writes Ḥájí Mírzá Ḥabíbu'lláh, 'met us on the boat, on the instructions of the Blessed Perfection, arranged for our landing, took us through the customs, and led us to the tent of Bahá'u'lláh which was pitched at the foot of Mount Carmel. I well remember that day. It was early morning, the sun was not yet well up over the crest of the mountain,

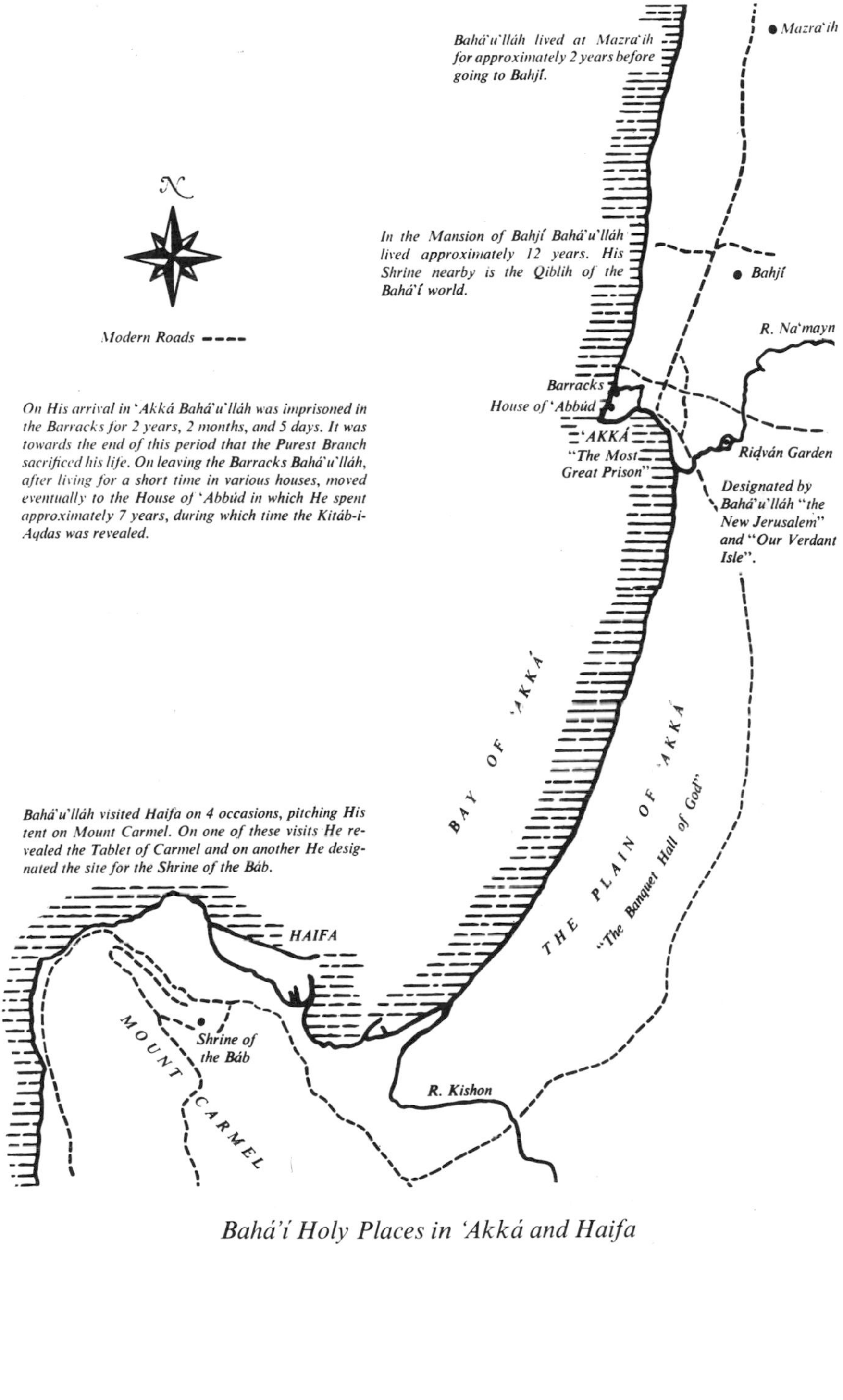
Bahá'u'lláh lived at Mazra'ih for approximately 2 years before going to Bahjí.
Mazra'ih
N
Modern Roads
In the Mansion of Bahjí Bahá'u'lláh lived approximately 12 years. His Shrine nearby is the Qiblih of the Bahá'í world.
Bahjí
R. Na'mayn
Barracks
House of 'Abbúd
'AKKÁ
"The Most Great Prison"
Riḍván Garden
Designated by Bahá'u'lláh "the New Jerusalem" and "Our Verdant Isle".
On His arrival in 'Akká Bahá'u'lláh was imprisoned in the Barracks for 2 years, 2 months, and 5 days. It was towards the end of this period that the Purest Branch sacrificed his life. On leaving the Barracks Bahá'u'lláh, after living for a short time in various houses, moved eventually to the House of 'Abbúd in which He spent approximately 7 years, during which time the Kitáb-i-Aqdas was revealed.
BAY OF 'AKKÁ
THE PLAIN OF 'AKKÁ
"The Banquet Hall of God"
Bahá'u'lláh visited Haifa on 4 occasions, pitching His tent on Mount Carmel. On one of these visits He revealed the Tablet of Carmel and on another He designated the site for the Shrine of the Báb.
HAIFA
MOUNT CARMEL
Shrine of the Báb
R. Kishon

Bahá'í Holy Places in 'Akká and Haifa

and the air was very fresh and truly vivifying. Within the tent, Jináb-i-Manshádí was talking to us, enquiring after the Friends in Shíráz, when suddenly Mírzá Muṣṭafá – known as Abú-Hurayrih (after a fickle follower of Muḥammad) – who was an attendant of the Blessed Perfection, and in later years broke the Covenant, entered and led us to the house and the presence of the Blessed Perfection.* He held aside the curtain. All our hopes and earnest wishes were now fulfilled. The Abhá Beauty was standing in the middle of the room. Beholding His blessed Figure and His luminous Visage overwhelmed us. . . . Our tears were out of control. As they flowed, we were circumambulating His blessed Person. He sat down on the divan and invited us to sit. We four brothers sat on the floor. On our right, Mírzá Áqá Ján was seated with the samovar and tea things in front of him. The Blessed Perfection said: "Pour tea for the young Afnáns; they have just come ashore"; and then He spoke to us: "O flowers of the rose-garden of his honour the Afnán! You are welcome, you are welcome. Your departure from Shíráz was very difficult and toilsome. The will of God and the resolution of Jináb-i-Afnán brought you to this sacred threshold. During your sea journey dangers beset you and God protected you. Consider, this very day several thousand are treading the ground between Ṣafá and Marwih [on one foot].† The Beloved of the world of being resides in this Land, but they are all negligent; all are heedless, all unaware, all uninformed. You are the real pilgrims." Thrice He said: "You are the real *ḥájís* [pilgrims]." At that moment, when I was lost in wonderment and hearkening to the words of the Beloved of the worlds, these lines of Mawlavís‡ came to my mind:[1]

> O *Ḥájís!* Ye who have performed the *ḥájj*, where are ye,
> where are ye?
> The Beloved is here, come hither ye, come hither ye.

* Bahá'u'lláh had His tent pitched on the slopes of Mount Carmel. The exact position is known and has, for years, been in the possession of the World Centre of the Bahá'í Faith. But during these sojourns in Haifa, He rented houses in the neighbouring German colony. As to Mírzá Muṣṭafá, whose father died a martyr in Tabríz (see index concerning Mírzá Muṣṭafáy-i-Naráqí), he became a follower of Mírzá Muḥammad-'Alí and lived towards the end of his life near Tiberias, on property belonging to Mírzá Majdi'd-Dín.

† The tenth day of Dhu'l-Ḥijjih – 'Íd al-Aḍḥá or 'Íd-i-Qurbán (The Festival of Sacrifice) – the day of pilgrimage at Mecca. Part of the rites of pilgrimage include traversing seven times the distance between these two mounds where, according to tradition, Hagar ran back and forth seven times, seeking a spring to quench her son's thirst.

‡ Jaláli'd-Dín-i-Rúmí, the greatest of all the mystic poets of Persia.

The Beloved is your neighbour, wall by wall;
Why in the wilderness lost are ye all?

And at that very moment, the Blessed Perfection turned to me and said: "The mystics had something to say on this account." Then He asked Mírzá Áqá Ján to pour us tea again. After that, we left His presence.

'The house next door to His was rented for us. We dwelt in close proximity to the abode of the Abhá Beauty. Attaining His blessed threshold, meeting the veterans of the Faith and those resident in the Holy Land had blotted everything else from our minds. The sweetness of living and the spiritual ecstasies that we experienced in those days lie beyond description. . . . Haifa was hot during this period and we, who were unaccustomed to it, oftentimes fell ill. But the bounties of our beloved Lord were measureless. The sea of His grace and bounty was ever billowing. I remember well one day when we were summoned to His presence, at three o'clock in the afternoon.' Mírzá Ḥabíbu'lláh was very feverish that day and his eldest brother tried to stop him from accompanying them, but he went just the same. He writes; 'The Blessed Perfection, turning to me, said: "You are with fever," at which I bowed my head, and He continued: "Fever is a product of this land. Whoever comes here must have it." Then He ordered tea to be given to us. Immediately I started to perspire, so much so that my clothes were drenched. Then the Blessed Perfection said: "Go and change your clothes. Fever will not trouble you again." During the rest of the nine months we spent in the Holy Land I did not suffer from fever at all.'

After fifteen days, the eldest of the four brothers returned to Port Sa'íd, and their father came to the Holy Land. When news of the death of the Seven Martyrs of Yazd reached them,* it brought great sorrow to Bahá'u'lláh. Ḥájí Mírzá Ḥabíbu'lláh writes that for nine days all revelation ceased and no one was admitted into His presence, until on the ninth day they were all summoned. The deep sorrow that surrounded Him, Ḥájí Mírzá Ḥabíbu'lláh says, was indescribable. 'He spoke extensively about the Qájárs and their deeds. Afterwards, He mentioned the events of Yazd; thus sternly did the Tongue of Grandeur speak of Jalálu'd-Dawlih and Ẓillu's-Sulṭán: "Ẓillu's-Sulṭán

* The full story of this tragic event, brought about by Ẓillu's-Sulṭán and his son, Jalálu'd-Dawlih, which occurred in the spring of 1891, will be related in a forthcoming volume.

wrote Me a letter which was in his own handwriting, and gave it to Ḥájí Sayyáḥ [Ḥájí Muḥammad-'Alíy-i-Sayyáḥ] to bring. He requested Me to aid him with the Bábís to destroy his Sháh-Bábá [his father, the Sháh]. Should You do this, he wrote, 'I will give you freedom, I will give you official recognition, I will help and support you, I will make amends for the past; whatever Sháh-Bábá did, I will do just the opposite.' The entire letter is full of such statements. The answer which was given to him was this: 'Praying for the Sháh is obligatory for both: you and Us. Never again write in this vein to Us. Never again put such requests to this Wronged One. We have arisen to improve the morals of a number of people, wronged in this world. Were we after leadership, what leadership could have been better than occupying the post of a vizier in Írán?' Having received this answer from Us, he has despaired of Us, and is now behaving in this manner. Were We to send his letter to Náṣiri'd-Dín Sháh, he would skin him alive. But God is the Veiler, He draws veils over the deeds of His servants." Then He said: "Do not be sad, do not be downcast, do not let your hearts bleed. The sacred tree of the Cause of God is watered by the blood of the martyrs. A tree, unless watered, does not grow and bear fruit. Before long, you will see the name of the Qájárs obliterated, and the land of Írán cleansed of them." Regarding Jalálu'd-Dawlih, the Blessed Perfection said: "This ingrate has done what has caused the eyes of the denizens of the Supreme Concourse to shed tears of blood." Only thirty-two years from that date, the rule of the Qájárs came to an end and they were overthrown.' The first Tablet revealed after nine days, Ḥájí Mírzá Ḥabíbu'lláh writes, was *Lawḥ-i-Dunyá* (Tablet of the World), with which Áqá Mírzá Áqá was honoured. That reference to Jalálu'd-Dawlih can be read also in this Tablet: 'The tyrant of the land of Yá [Yazd], committed that which hath caused the Concourse on high to shed tears of blood.'[2] A copy of the *Tablet of the World*, in the handwriting of Zaynu'l-Muqarrabín, was given by Bahá'u'lláh, Himself, to Ḥájí Mírzá Buzurg, an elder brother of Ḥájí Mírzá Ḥabíbu'lláh.

The writer continues: 'Fifteen days had passed since the arrival of my father, and the days of our attainment were drawing to their close, when an epidemic of cholera broke out in Syria and Lebanon. The government set up quarantine around the frontiers. My father asked for permission to leave, but it was not granted; not while the epidemic

The Mansion of Bahjí as it appeared before the present gardens were planted

raged. For us this was supreme felicity. Autumn came on, the air of Haifa and 'Akká improved. The Blessed Perfection moved from Haifa to the Mansion of Bahjí. We were provided with a small house, next to the Mansion. . . . Our house was so situated that we could see from it His blessed chamber. Getting up at dawn to say our prayers, we could see most of the time that His chamber was lighted, and Tablets were being revealed. The Blessed Perfection was pacing in the room and the amanuensis was busy writing. I do not remember anyone other than Mírzá Áqá Ján taking down the revealed Word. In those days the late Mírzá Yúsuf Khán-i-Vujdání and the late Áqá Siyyid Asadu'lláh-i-Qumí were tutoring the Branches in the Mansion. The Blessed Perfection instructed my brothers, Ḥájí Mírzá Buzurg, Ḥájí Mírzá Ḍíyá', and myself to attend their lessons. Every day we went to the room, in the ground floor of the Mansion, set aside as a classroom, to receive tuition. The late Mishkín-Qalam taught us calligraphy . . .

'On the first day of Muḥarram 1309 [7 August 1891],* the Blessed Perfection was celebrating the festival. My father was corpulent and

* The anniversary of the birth of the Báb. Because of the lunar calendar, the Christian date varies.

The Mansion of Bahjí

suffered from rheumatism. He could not sit on the floor. The Blessed Perfection said: "Bring a chair for the Afnán," and then: "Bring chairs for his sons as well," and so we all were seated on chairs. . . . The Blessed Perfection, Himself, distributed *báqlavá* [a sweetmeat] to the believers present. Then He said: "This is the day on which Ḥaḍrat-i-Mubashshir [the Herald] set foot in this world and illumined it with His light. There is every reason for rejoicing. . . ." The next day, the second day of Muḥarram, was the day of the birth of the Master of Days and of the World of Being [Bahá'u'lláh]. In the morning, all of the pilgrims and residents were summoned to His blessed Presence. He spoke about the sublimity of His advent, the power of the Most Exalted Pen, the circumstances of His exile, and the arrival at the Most Great Prison. Then He spoke extensively about the aggression and transgressions on the part of the tyrants and divines. He said, "Náṣiri'd-Dín Sh̲áh and 'Abdu'l-'Azíz both transgressed against Us and harmed the body of the Cause of God, but the tyranny of 'Abdu'l-'Azíz was by far the more severe, because he banished, without any reason, the Wronged One of the worlds to the Most Great Prison. But, Náṣiri'd-Dín Sh̲áh, because of the ill-advised action of the believers in the early days of the Cause, whenever he stroked his limbs and felt the pellets under his skin, would be roused in anger to commit these harsh deeds and adopt tyrannical measures against the believers, spilling the blood of innocent people. Notwithstanding all these injuries inflicted upon them by the Sh̲áh and the Government, the Friends do not cease to demonstrate their Faith openly and do not observe caution. You cannot blame them, because two great festivals have been joined into one, auguring a brilliant future." Then the Blessed Perfection spoke these two lines [which are by Ḥáfiẓ]:[3]

These times more bitter than venom shall pass away,
And once again, times as sweet as sugar shall come this way.

He then gave us sweetmeats and we left His presence.

'. . . I have already mentioned that our house was adjacent to the Mansion. We usually got up at dawn to engage in our devotionals. One morning, before sunrise, an attendant came with the tidings that the Blessed Perfection was coming to our house. He placed this crown of honour everlasting upon the heads of these servants. This tiding given to us made us weep with joy and we hastened out. His blessed Person we beheld, coming with all power and glory towards our house. We all prostrated ourselves and kissed His feet. We made the earth trodden by His blessed feet the kohl of our eyes. . . . He entered our house and conferred on us this ever-abiding honour. I offered Him a cup of tea. He drank half of it and gave the rest back to me. He also gave me a black rosary, made of olive wood, which He was carrying. I kissed His hands. That rosary, which was as dear to me as life, is now placed in the archives of the House in Sh̲íráz [The House of the Báb].

'Again, I have mentioned that His blessed chamber was visible from our house. We saw Him several times at dawn and early morning, while He was speaking the revealed Word and Mírzá Áqá Ján was writing it down as He spoke it. Mírzá Áqá Ján used to have several pens [reed pens they would be] well cut and pointed, with ink and paper ready. The flow of verses from the heaven of Revelation was swift. It was indeed like unto a fast-billowing ocean. Mírzá Áqá Ján wrote as quickly as he could – so quickly that the pen at times jumped out of his hand. He would immediately take up another pen. There were times when he could not keep up and would say: "I am incapable of writing." Then the Blessed Perfection would repeat what He had spoken.'

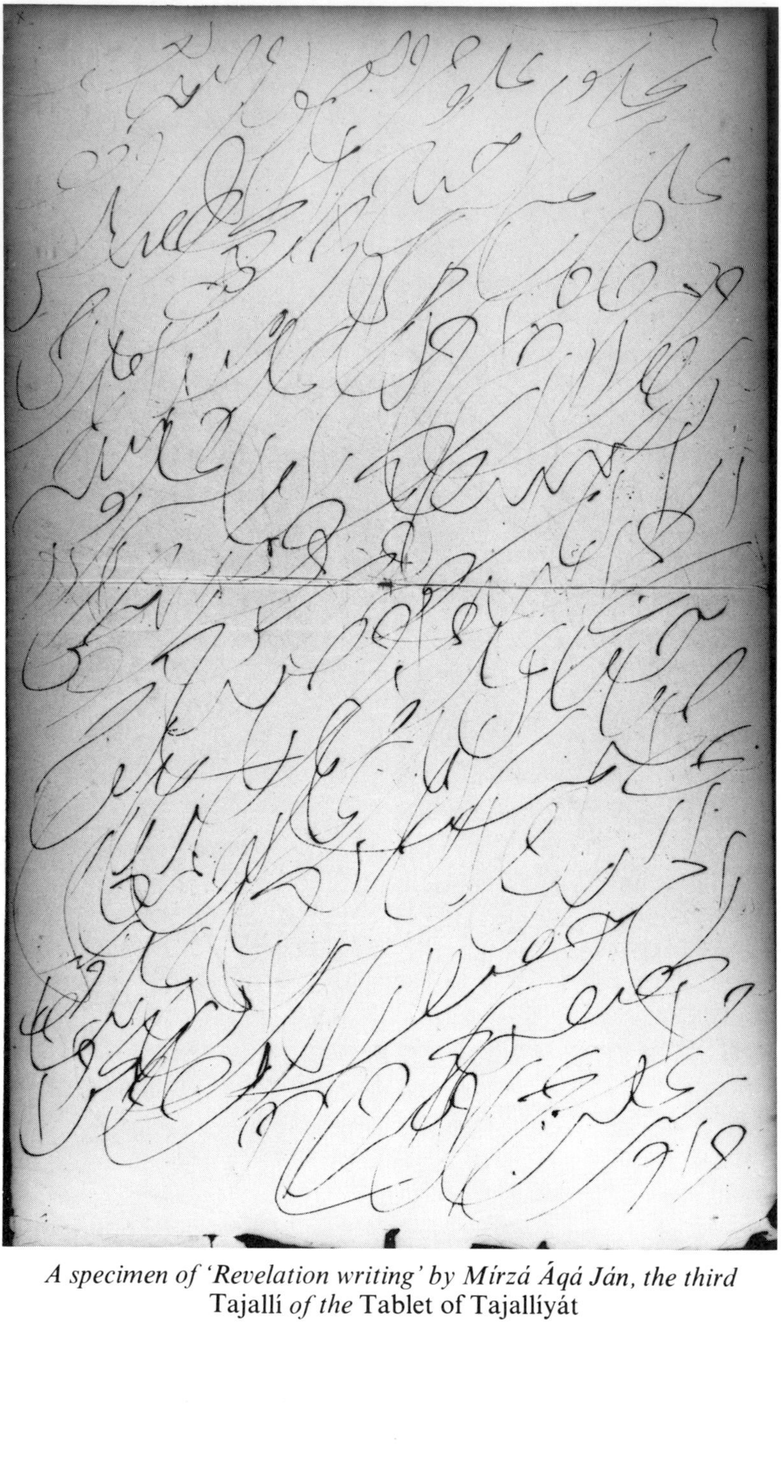

A specimen of 'Revelation writing' by Mírzá Áqá Ján, the third Tajallí *of the* Tablet of Tajallíyát

Ḥájí Mírzá Ḥabíbu'lláh relates that Bahá'u'lláh instructed Ḥájí Mírzá Buzurg to make a copy of *Qaṣídiy-i-'Izz-i-Varqá'íyyih*, the poem which He Himself had composed in Sulaymáníyyih. When Ḥájí Mírzá Buzurg had finished the task allotted to him, Bahá'u'lláh gave him a pen-case made in Iṣfahán which held a silver ink-stand. That pen-case is now deposited in the archives of the House of the Báb. On another occasion, Ḥájí Mírzá Ḥabíbu'lláh relates, Bahá'u'lláh summoned him and said that He had bidden Mírzá Yúsuf K͟hán and Áqá Siyyid Asadu'lláh to pay particular attention to his instruction, and then gave him a bottle of rose-water, saying: 'This rose-water comes from Qamṣar of Kás͟hán. It has taken forty days for it to reach this land. God has created this rose-water for such a day as this, which is the Lord of days.' Ḥájí Mírzá Ḥabíbu'lláh regrets that he did not keep some of that rose-water but let it all go, over the years, to friends who used it.

Then, Ḥájí Mírzá Ḥabíbu'lláh gives a graphic description of a day in the Garden of Junaynih, in the presence of Bahá'u'lláh. Abú-Hurayrih, he writes, came one evening to announce that the next day Bahá'u'lláh would be visiting Junaynih, and had bidden all, pilgrims and residents, to be there. That night, Ḥájí Mírzá Ḥabíbu'lláh says, the joy of anticipating a whole day spent in the presence of the Blessed Perfection kept them awake. Before sunrise, they were all gathered outside the gates of the Mansion. An hour later, Bahá'u'lláh came out. A white donkey was brought for Him to ride. This donkey was the offering of Áqá G͟hulám-'Alí and Áqá Muḥammad-Hás͟him, both natives of Kás͟hán. It was a beautiful morning, says Ḥájí Mírzá Ḥabíbu'lláh; the air was fresh and invigorating, as they walked to the Garden of Junaynih, where all had been made ready for the arrival of Bahá'u'lláh. Ḥájí K͟hávar, a resident for years in the Holy Land, who was fairly tall, held an umbrella over the head of Bahá'u'lláh, against the sun. Thus they reached the garden. Following the luncheon, 'Abdu'l-Bahá arrived from 'Akká. Bahá'u'lláh told them all: 'Áqá is coming; hasten to attend Him.' Ḥájí Mírzá Ḥabíbu'lláh writes that he was present on several occasions when, as 'Abdu'l-Bahá approached the place where people were gathered in the presence of Bahá'u'lláh, He would say: 'Áqá is coming; hasten to attend Him.' And now, 'Abdu'l-Bahá, attended by all, came with great humility into the presence of the Blessed Perfection, reports Ḥájí Mírzá Ḥabíbu'lláh,

Site of the Garden of Junaynih to the north of 'Akká

and Bahá'u'lláh said: 'The garden was not pleasant enough this morning, but now with the arrival of Áqá it has become most pleasant.' Then turning towards 'Abdu'l-Bahá, He observed: 'It would have been so good, if you had come this morning', and 'Abdu'l-Bahá replied: 'The Mutaṣarrif and a number of others had sent word that they were coming. I had to receive them and offer them hospitality.' Ḥájí Mírzá Ḥabíbu'lláh writes, 'the Blessed Perfection smiled, and said: "Áqá is Our shield and the shield of everyone else; all live at ease, all know utmost comfort and tranquillity. Consorting with men such as these is very, very difficult. It is Áqá who stands up to everything and supplies the means for the well-being and peace of all. May God preserve Him from the evil of all the envious and the inimical." "One day in Baghdád," Bahá'u'lláh continued, "a beggar asked for alms. One *majídí* was given to him, and he told Me: 'Go in peace, young man; may Ḥaḍrat-i-'Abbás* give you support.' He prayed for Us – it was a good prayer."' Ḥájí Mírzá Ḥabíbu'lláh continues: 'About an hour before sunset, the Blessed Perfection rode back to the Mansion, and, as in the morning, we all walked there and at the gates we left His presence.'

* 'Abbás, a brother of Imám Ḥusayn, the third Imám, suffered martyrdom with him at Karbilá; he is greatly revered and extolled by the Shí'ihs. 'Abdu'l-Bahá was named 'Abbás.

Another incident is related in this autobiography: 'The Garden of Jamál is one of the gardens [see p. 363], remote from 'Akká, but near the Mansion of Bahjí. Passing by this garden, one comes within full view of the Mansion. The door of the chamber of the Blessed Perfection opened this way, and whenever 'Abdu'l-Bahá approached by this route, as soon as the Mansion became visible, He would dismount and walk the rest of the way with utmost humility and reverence. One day which I well remember, we were in the presence of the Blessed Perfection. The Aghsán were there, and among others also the following: Nabíl-i-A'ẓam, Afnán-i-Kabír, Áqá Riḍáy-i-Shírází, Ustád Muḥammad-'Alíy-i-Salmání, Mishkín-Qalam, my father, and Áqá Muḥammad-Ḥasan of the Pilgrim House. Suddenly, the Blessed Perfection turned round to look at the plain, and seeing 'Abdu'l-Bahá approaching the Mansion, He said: "Áqá is coming, go and attend Him." We all hastened out, and with "Him round Whom all Names revolve" ['Abdu'l-Bahá] went back to the presence of the Blessed Perfection.'* Ḥájí Mírzá Ḥabíbu'lláh mentions also a number of others who were there that day and witnessed all that happened, and yet, in later years, broke the Covenant. The writer stresses particularly the fact that in those days Bahá'u'lláh oftentimes warned the believers to remain steadfast and loyal to the Covenant. Once, Ḥájí Mírzá Ḥabíbu'lláh tells us, He pointed to Mírzá Muḥammad-'Alí, Mírzá Ḍíyá'u'lláh and Mírzá Badí'u'lláh and said: 'Should one of our Aghsán ever for a moment pass out from the shadow of the Cause he shall cease to be of any consequence.' On another occasion, when they were in the presence of Bahá'u'lláh, Mírzá Ḍíyá'u'lláh came in to say: 'Áqá supplicates for permission that we all may go with the Friends to the Garden of Junaynih.' 'Who has said so?' Bahá'u'lláh enquired, to which Mírzá Ḍíyá'u'lláh replied: 'Áqáy-i-Ghuṣn-i-Akbar' (the Greater Branch). Angrily, Bahá'u'lláh spoke: 'There is only one Áqá [Master, without specification], all the others have names; that one Áqá is "He round Whom all Names revolve", the Ghuṣn-i-A'ẓam' (the Most Great Branch).

Ḥájí Mírzá Ḥabíbu'lláh recalls one late afternoon in the Garden of Riḍván, when they were there in the presence of Bahá'u'lláh. The air was fresh, pure and redolent, he writes, and it was raining slightly.

* See Balyuzi, *'Abdu'l-Bahá*, pp. 43–4, for a similar incident.

Bahá'u'lláh spoke to them on that day about Mírzá Yaḥyá and his crew, during the Baghdád period; how Mírzá Yaḥyá took as his wife the sister of Mullá Rajab-'Alí, the second wife of the Báb, and then gave her to Siyyid Muḥammad-i-Iṣfahání, despite the injunction of the Báb. This shameful deed, Bahá'u'lláh said, had prevented the mother of the Báb from giving her allegiance to the Faith. Ḥájí Mírzá Ḥabíbu'-lláh states that traces of sorrow appeared on the face of Bahá'u'lláh, as He spoke of those days in Baghdád. His father, Áqá Mírzá Áqá, was greatly affected, but Bahá'u'lláh said, 'Do not grieve. Praise be to God, the mother of that Blessed Being came to believe, at the end.' That same afternoon in the Garden of Riḍván, Ḥájí Mírzá Ḥabíbu'lláh records, Bahá'u'lláh spoke about some of the Shí'ih divines of Náṣiri'd-Dín Sháh and Sulṭán 'Abdu'l-'Azíz, of their total failure, despite their great exertions, to extinguish the light of the Faith of God. 'Before long,' He said, 'you shall see people of all the nations of the world gathered under the shade of the tent of the Cause of God.'

On another day, Ḥájí Mírzá Ḥabíbu'lláh recalls, Bahá'u'lláh spoke of Mullá 'Alíy-i-Sabzivárí, the martyr. He it was who, when led to the scaffold, instructed the executioner to open one of his veins, and, when a bit of his throat was cut, filled his hand with his blood and dyed his white beard red with it. Then, turning to the crowd, he called out: 'O people! On the day of his martyrdom, Ḥusayn Ibn 'Alí [the third Imám, martyred at Karbilá] uttered these words: "Is there anyone, truly capable of dispensing victory, to come to aid me?" and I say to you, O people, is there anyone truly capable of beholding, to come to behold me?' Ḥájí Mírzá Ḥabíbu'lláh records that Bahá'u'lláh, in relating this story, several times repeated: 'What weighty words did that man speak, and how, with his precious blood, did he bear witness to the truth of his faith! People witnessed it, but were not moved, and heartlessly put to death that innocent soul. All these strange events support the greatness of this blessed Cause. They will all be recorded in the pages of history and future generations will feel proud of them.'

One of those present that day, Ḥájí Mírzá Ḥabíbu'lláh writes, was Ḥájí Abu'l-Ḥasan of Shíráz, the father of Mírzá Muḥammad-Báqir Khán Dihqán (usually written as Dehkan). He had travelled on the same boat with the Báb, when both were going as pilgrims to Mecca, and now asked Bahá'u'lláh: 'How was it that all those long years after the martyrdom of the Primal Point, Náṣiri'd-Dín Sháh was still ruling

The Garden of Riḍván

the land with full powers, inflicting so much injury on the Faith and the believers, and God spared him, whereas, after the martyrdom of Imám Ḥusayn, Yazíd had no more than three years given to him?' Bahá'u'lláh replied: 'Because of the wrong action of some of the believers in the early days, and their attempt on his life, God has given him this grace; but he too will have his day, you shall see.'

Nine months had now passed since the arrival of the party from Egypt, the cholera epidemic was over, and the hour for their departure had come. The autobiography of Ḥájí Mírzá Ḥabíbu'lláh poignantly describes that last time when they entered the presence of Bahá'u'lláh. It was after this that, at the bidding of Bahá'u'lláh, his mother received from Bahá'íyyih Khánum, the Greatest Holy Leaf, a ring that Bahá'u'lláh had worn. Today that ring is preserved in the archives of the House of the Báb.

42

The Ascension of Bahá'u'lláh

It was only a few brief weeks after the departure of the Afnáns that Bahá'u'lláh left His human temple in the early hours of the morning of 29th of May 1892. A telegram bore the news to Sulṭán 'Abdu'l-Ḥamíd, the despot of Turkey: 'The Sun of Bahá has set.' It was sent by 'Abdu'l-Bahá.

'Abdu'l-Ḥamíd of Turkey and Náṣiri'd-Dín Sháh of Írán were jubilant, unmindful of the fact that the Sun of Bahá will continue to shine dazzlingly in the full meridian. Its energizing and life-bestowing rays will continue to revivify the hearts and minds of men, to penetrate the dark and dense clouds of superstition, bigotry and prejudice, to disperse the heavy and oppressive fogs of despair and disillusionment, to shed revealing light upon the baffling problems which bewilder a wayward, fatigued and storm-tossed humanity. Man – ungrateful Man – has essayed to dim Its brilliance, to deny Its potency, to abjure Its gifts, to disparage Its claims – futile and bootless attempts, for the signal proof of the Sun remains the Sun itself.

Almost a century separates us from the days when Bahá'u'lláh lived amongst men. The Faith which He proclaimed has encircled the globe and marches from triumph to triumph, and the resplendent edifice which He raised stands to offer certitude and peace to a disordered world.

In His Will and Testament, Bahá'u'lláh appointed His eldest Son – Whom we know as 'Abdu'l-Bahá (the Servant of Glory) – the Centre of His Covenant with all men, and the sole Expounder of His revealed Word. His name was 'Abbás. His Father referred to Him as Ghuṣnu'lláhu'l-A'ẓam – the Greatest Branch, and spoke of Him as Sirru'lláh – the Mystery of God. Bahá'u'lláh referred to Him also as Áqá – the Master, and so did the Bahá'ís. 'Abdu'l-Bahá was the designation which He, the Mystery of God, chose for Himself after His Father's ascension.

'Abdu'l-Bahá, the Centre of the Covenant of Bahá'u'lláh

The Will and Testament of Bahá'u'lláh is indeed a unique document. Never before had a Manifestation of God so explicitly established a Covenant to be the shield and the buttress of His Faith, or so clearly and indubitably named Him Who was to be His authorized successor with power to ward off the machinations of self-seekers, to keep pure and unsullied His Word, to preserve and watch over the unity of His followers, to bar sectarianism and banish corruption. Indeed, the Covenant of Bahá'u'lláh is, in the words of 'Abdu'l-Bahá, '*the "Sure Handle" mentioned from the foundation of the world in the Books, the Tablets and the Scriptures of old.*' '. . . *the pivot of the oneness of mankind is nothing else but the power of the Covenant.*' Furthermore, 'Abdu'l-Bahá has stated, '*The lamp of the Covenant is the light of the world, and the words traced by the Pen of the Most High a limitless ocean.*' And again, '*The power of the Covenant is as the heat of the sun which quickeneth and promoteth the development of all created things on earth. The light of the Covenant, in like manner, is the educator of the minds, the spirits, the hearts and souls of men.*'[1]

The Guardian of the Bahá'í Faith writes: 'Extolled by the writer of the Apocalypse as "the Ark of His (God's) Testament"; associated with the gathering beneath the "*Tree of Anísá*" (Tree of Life) mentioned by Bahá'u'lláh in the Hidden Words; glorified by Him, in other passages of His writings, as the "*Ark of Salvation*" and as "*the Cord stretched betwixt the earth and the Abhá Kingdom*", this Covenant has been bequeathed to posterity in a Will and Testament which, together with the Kitáb-i-Aqdas and several Tablets, in which the rank and station of 'Abdu'l-Bahá are unequivocally disclosed, constitute the chief buttresses designed by the Lord of the Covenant Himself to shield and support, after His ascension, the appointed Center of His Faith . . .'[2]

It is on this rock – the rock of the Covenant – that the edifice of the World Order is built. It is this ark, the ark of the Covenant, that has brought the Cause of Bahá'u'lláh safely through storms and hurricanes of unsurpassed intensity. Many a Judas has tried to pierce this shield, the shield of the Covenant, only to find himself in grievous loss.

Bahá'u'lláh wrote in His Will and Testament:*

> Although the Realm of Glory hath none of the vanities of the world, yet

* *Kitáb-i-'Ahd* (Book of the Covenant).

within the treasury of trust and resignation we have bequeathed to Our heirs an excellent and priceless heritage. Earthly treasures We have not bequeathed, nor have We added such cares as they entail. . . .

The aim of this Wronged One in sustaining woes and tribulations, in revealing the Holy Verses and in demonstrating proofs hath been naught but to quench the flame of hate and enmity, that the horizon of the hearts of men may be illumined with the light of concord and attain real peace and tranquillity. . . . Verily I say, the tongue is for mentioning what is good, defile it not with unseemly talk. . . . Lofty is the station of man! . . . Great and blessed is this Day – the Day in which all that lay latent in man hath been and will be made manifest. Lofty is the station of man, were he to hold fast to righteousness and truth and to remain firm and steadfast in the Cause. . . .

O ye that dwell on earth! The religion of God is for love and unity; make it not the cause of enmity or dissension. In the eyes of men of insight and the beholders of the Most Sublime Vision, whatsoever are the effective means for safeguarding and promoting the happiness and welfare of the children of men hath already been revealed by the Pen of Glory. . . .

. . . Let not the means of order be made the cause of confusion and the instrument of union an occasion for discord. We fain would hope that the people of Bahá may be guided by the blessed words: 'Say: all things are of God.' This exalted utterance is like unto water for quenching the fire of hate and enmity which smouldereth within the hearts and breasts of men. By this single utterance contending peoples and kindreds will attain the light of true unity. Verily He speaketh the truth and leadeth the way. He is the All-Powerful, the Exalted, the Gracious.[3]

The Guardian of the Bahá'í Faith writes:

'In this weighty and incomparable Document its Author discloses the character of that "*excellent and priceless heritage*" bequeathed by Him to His "*heirs*"; proclaims afresh the fundamental purpose of His Revelation; enjoins the "*peoples of the world*" to hold fast to that which will "*elevate*" their "*station*"; announces to them that "*God hath forgiven what is past*"; stresses the sublimity of man's station; discloses the primary aim of the Faith of God; directs the faithful to pray for the welfare of the kings of the earth, "*the manifestations of the power, and the daysprings of the might and riches, of God*"; invests them with the rulership of the earth; singles out as His special domain the hearts of men; forbids categorically strife and contention; commands His followers to aid those rulers who are "*adorned with the ornament of equity and justice*"; and directs, in particular, the Aghṣán (His sons) to ponder the "*mighty force and the consummate power that lieth concealed in the world of being*". He bids them, moreover, together

Mansion of Bahjí: aerial view taken in May 1979

with the Afnán (the Báb's kindred) and His own relatives, to "*turn, one and all, unto the Most Great Branch* ('Abdu'l-Bahá)"; identifies Him with "*the One Whom God hath purposed*", "*Who hath branched from this pre-existent Root*", referred to in the Kitáb-i-Aqdas; ordains the station of the "*Greater Branch*" (Mírzá Muḥammad-'Alí) to be beneath that of the "*Most Great Branch*" ('Abdu'l-Bahá); exhorts the believers to treat the Aghṣán with consideration and affection; counsels them to respect His family and relatives, as well as the kindred of the Báb; denies His sons "*any right to the property of others*"; enjoins on them, on His kindred and on that of the Báb to "*fear God, to do that which is meet and seemly*" and to follow the things that will "*exalt*" their station; warns all men not to allow "*the means of order to be made the cause of confusion, and the instrument of union an occasion for discord*"; and concludes with an exhortation calling upon the faithful to "*serve all nations*", and to strive for the "*betterment of the world*".'[4]

Bahá'u'lláh had left the mortal plane. Many there were who came to mourn Him. They did not bear allegiance to Him, they could not see in Him the Redeemer of Mankind, yet they knew that a great Being had gone from their midst. They were from diverse backgrounds and sects and Faiths and nations – officials and leading figures and priests, learned men and poets and men of letters, rich and poor, Druses, Sunní and Shí'ih Muslims, Christians of diverse denominations, and Jews. From other cities renowned in the history of the world, such as Damascus and Aleppo and Cairo, they sent their eulogies and poems and panegyrics and tributes. And Bahá'u'lláh, at the time of His ascension, was still a prisoner of the Turkish government. No imperial edict of the Sulṭán had set Him free.

How different was this day of His ascension, when the plain stretching between the city of 'Akká and the Mansion of Bahjí teemed with crowds who came to pay Him homage and lament their loss, from that far-off day nearly twenty-four summers before when hordes of misinformed people had gathered at the sea-shore of 'Akká, awaiting His arrival to deride and insult Him. Total, unrelieved, unmitigated defeat seemed to be His fate then, and now all triumph was His.

How strange, indeed, and awe-inspiring had been the contrasts of His sojourn among men, particularly in the Holy Land.

Brutally insulted in His native province, shorn of all earthly possessions, which He had in abundance, twice consigned to a foul prison of thieves and desperadoes, four times set on the road to exile, basely betrayed by a brother whom He had endeavoured to protect, forced to seek the solitude of bare and bleak mountains, venomously and ferociously assailed and denounced and opposed by hosts of the mighty and the powerful and hordes of the insignificant alike, He had stood His ground with a certitude and a constancy which no adversity could shake and no cataclysm could thwart. And upon a swelling number of faithful adherents He conferred that supreme gift which Jesus had spoken of to Nicodemus when the Jewish nobleman sought Him in the dead of night – the gift of second birth. He touched the hearts of men, and He won their allegiance by His Divine power. His followers were not alone in feeling its sweep and its command. Many who had denied Him and reviled Him and openly contended with Him, were eventually subdued by the charm, the majesty, the kindliness, the radiance of His Being. Indeed there were many amongst those erstwhile adversaries who, without enrolling in the ranks of His followers, bore testimony to His supremacy, and lent their support to His defence.

And on this summer's day where was the proud 'Abdu'l-'Azíz of Turkey, the Sulṭán who had decreed His exile and incarceration? Where was the overbearing Napoleon, Emperor of the French who had disdained His summons? Beaten, forgotten. Náṣiri'd-Dín, the 'tyrant' of Persia, who had cast Him out of His native land and forced Him to take the road to exile twice, fell only four years after the ascension of Bahá'u'lláh before the bullets of an avenger, on the very eve of his golden jubilee. The records of history amply show that great was the fall of anyone, mighty or low alike, who dared to challenge Bahá'u'lláh and gainsay His sovereignty. Mírzá Yaḥyá, the brother who repudiated His authority and plotted His death, died in the obscurity of Cyprus, more than three decades after regaining his freedom in 1878. In all those forlorn years, although free to act and to move, he remained a man incapable of exercising his freedom. He was so abandoned by all at the end that, according to the written testimony of his son, at his death in 1912, there was no one of the 'people of the Bayán' near him to consign him to his grave according to the prescriptions of the Bábí Faith.

No one has opposed Bahá'u'lláh and raised his hand to injure His

Cause and His followers, and has escaped shame, doom and degradation.

The same cable which bore the news of the ascension of Bahá'u'lláh, also informed the Sulṭán that His earthly temple would be laid to rest in a house next to the Mansion of Bahjí. 'Abdu'l-Ḥamíd gave his consent.

The Guardian of the Bahá'í Faith writes: 'Bahá'u'lláh was accordingly laid to rest in the northernmost room of the house which served as a dwelling-place for His son-in-law,* the most northerly of the three houses lying to the west of, and adjacent to, the Mansion. His interment took place shortly after sunset, on the very day of His ascension.

'The inconsolable Nabíl, who had had the privilege of a private audience with Bahá'u'lláh during the days of His illness; whom 'Abdu'l-Bahá had chosen to select those passages which constitute the text of the Tablet of Visitation now recited in the Most Holy Tomb; and who, in his uncontrollable grief, drowned himself in the sea

* Ḥájí Siyyid 'Alí Afnán, a son of Ḥájí Mírzá Siyyid Ḥasan – Afnán-i-Kabír (the Great Afnán).

The Shrine of Bahá'u'lláh is in the centre of this photograph taken circa 1919, with the Mansion and the other buildings then at Bahjí behind and at each side.

shortly after the passing of his Beloved, thus describes the agony of those days: "Methinks, the spiritual commotion set up in the world of dust had caused all the worlds of God to tremble. . . . My inner and outer tongue are powerless to portray the condition we were in. . . . In the midst of the prevailing confusion a multitude of the inhabitants of 'Akká and of neighboring villages, that had thronged the fields surrounding the Mansion, could be seen weeping, beating upon their heads, and crying aloud their grief."

'For a full week a vast number of mourners, rich and poor alike, tarried to grieve with the bereaved family, partaking day and night of the food that was lavishly dispensed by its members. . . .

'. . . these effusive manifestations of sorrow and expressions of praise and of admiration, which the ascension of Bahá'u'lláh had spontaneously evoked among the unbelievers in the Holy Land and the adjoining countries, were but a drop when compared with the ocean of grief and the innumerable evidences of unbounded devotion which, at the hour of the setting of the Sun of Truth, poured forth from the hearts of the countless thousands who had espoused His Cause, and were determined to carry aloft its banner in Persia, India, Russia, 'Iráq, Turkey, Palestine, Egypt and Syria.

'With the ascension of Bahá'u'lláh draws to a close a period which, in many ways, is unparalleled in the world's religious history. The first century of the Bahá'í Era had by now run half its course. An epoch, unsurpassed in its sublimity, its fecundity and duration by any previous Dispensation, and characterized, except for a short interval of three years, by half a century of continuous and progressive Revelation, had terminated. The Message proclaimed by the Báb had yielded its golden fruit. . . .'[5]

This book is an attempt to catch the ocean in a diminutive cup, to gaze at the orb through plain glass. Far, very far from man's effort must be an adequate portrayal of a Manifestation of the qualities and attributes of Almighty God. And here we deal with the life of One Whose advent implies the 'coming of age of the entire human race', and under Whose dominion the earth will become one fatherland.

Entrance to the Shrine of Bahá'u'lláh

Addendum I

The Disastrous Reign of Náṣiri'd-Dín Sháh

QÁJÁRS were the Umayyads of Írán. They were usurpers. They were treacherous. They did not, would not keep their word.

By the year 1795, when the revolutionary ardour of France had subsided, Robespierre and his works and the rump of the National Convention were all of the past, and Catherine the Great, the Tsarina of Russia, had only one more year to live, the founder of the Qájár dynasty, the despicable Agha Muḥammad Khán, was well established as the undisputed monarch of Írán. And thus began for Írán a long nightmare, a period of unmitigated disaster. The Qájárs were in turn cruel, sensuous, spineless, obscurantist and tyrannical. Under their yoke, Írán steadily declined from one infamy to another.

Írán has had a past – a brilliant past – of which she can justly be proud. She has had great kings, outstanding ministers and administrators; great divines and mystics; great poets and men of letters; great and eminent men of arts and builders. But, under the Qájárs she touched the very depths of degradation in the course of the disastrous reign of Náṣiri'd-Dín Sháh (1848–96), which brought to Írán misery upon misery and shame upon shame. Corruption crept into her vitals: intellectually starved, spiritually moribund, morally decrepit, she ceased to be of any consequence in the counsels of the nations. The rapid fall of a nation that has known high pinnacles of achievement is always most piteous, noticeable, and tragic.

'Abbás Mírzá, the Mulk-Árá, the half-brother of Náṣiri'd-Dín Sháh, who, throughout his life, suffered greatly at the hands of this avaricious, vindictive monarch, writes this epitaph on him in his autobiography:

> Better is it for a man to leave a good name behind:
>
> (Living is the happy name of Núshíraván* with justice coupled,
> Though long years have gone with no Núshíraván in the world)

* Chosroes I, the Sásánid monarch. These lines are Sa'dí's. (HMB)

Unlike Náṣiri'd-Dín Sháh, who in the course of forty-nine years of reign [lunar years] left no trace behind, save ignorance, folly, ruination of the land, no care for the proper education of the official and the subject; who ruined and despoiled Írán beyond the possibility of reform and redemption; who displayed folly to such a high degree as both the tongue and the pen are unable adequately to describe.[1]

The Guardian of the Bahá'í Faith thus refers to this ruler, who brought Írán so low:

Náṣiri'd-Dín Sháh, stigmatized by Bahá'u'lláh as the '*Prince of Oppressors,*' as one who had '*perpetrated what hath caused the denizens of the cities of justice and equity to lament,*' was, during the period under review, in the full tide of his manhood and had reached the plenitude of his despotic power. The sole arbiter of the fortunes of a country 'firmly stereotyped in the immemorial traditions of the East'; . . . the head of an administration in which 'every actor was, in different aspects, both the briber and the bribed'; allied, in his opposition to the Faith, with a sacerdotal order which constituted a veritable 'church-state'; . . . this capricious monarch, no longer able to lay hands upon the person of Bahá'u'lláh, had to content himself with the task of attempting to stamp out in his own dominions the remnants of a much-feared and newly resuscitated community. Next to him in rank and power were his three eldest sons, to whom, for purposes of internal administration, he had practically delegated his authority, and in whom he had invested the governorship of all the provinces of his kingdom. The province of Ádhirbáyján he had entrusted to the weak and timid Muẓaffari'd-Dín Mírzá, the heir to his throne, who had fallen under the influence of the Shaykhí sect, and was showing a marked respect to the mullás. To the stern and savage rule of the astute Mas'úd Mírzá, commonly known as Ẓillu's-Sulṭán, his eldest surviving son, whose mother had been of plebeian origin, he had committed over two-fifths of his kingdom, including the provinces of Yazd and Iṣfáhán, whilst upon Kámrán Mírzá, his favorite son, commonly called by his title the Náyibu's-Salṭanih, he had bestowed the rulership of Gílán and Mázindarán, and made him governor of Ṭihrán, his minister of war and the commander-in-chief of his army. Such was the rivalry between the last two princes,* who vied with each other in courting the favor of their father, that each endeavored, with the support of the leading mujtahids within his

* On the day that Náṣiri'd-Dín Sháh was assassinated, Ẓillu's-Sulṭán was at Iṣfahán; he immediately offered his submission and loyalty to the brother whom he despised and in the past had attempted to supplant, knowing that he had no chance whatsoever of gaining the throne. Kámrán Mírzá, the Náyibu's-Salṭanih, was in Ṭihrán. But he, the Minister of War and the Governor of the capital, was such a coward that he went into hiding and nothing could persuade him to come out and attend to his duties. He was not present at the ceremony of preparing the corpse of his father for interment. (HMB)

> jurisdiction, to outshine the other in the meritorious task of hunting, plundering and exterminating the members of a defenseless community, who, at the bidding of Bahá'u'lláh, had ceased to offer armed resistance even in self-defense, and were carrying out His injunction that '*it is better to be killed than kill.*' Nor were the clerical firebrands, Ḥájí Mullá 'Alíy-i-Kaní and Siyyid Ṣádiq-i-Ṭabáṭabá'í, the two leading mujtahids of Ṭihrán, together with Shaykh Muḥammad-Báqir, their colleague in Iṣfáhán, and Mír Muḥammad-Ḥusayn, the Imám-Jum'ih of that city, willing to allow the slightest opportunity to pass without striking, with all the force and authority they wielded, at an adversary whose liberalizing influences they had even more reason to fear than the sovereign himself.[2]

The same 'Abbás Mírzá, the Mulk-Ará, relates how appalled he was by what he saw and experienced when he was sent, against his own wishes, to govern the city of Zanján and its environs. Three decades after the holocaust which enveloped the intrepid Ḥujjat and his brave companions, large areas of the city still lay devastated; the city swarmed with plaintiffs, carrying contradictory edicts and judicial rulings issued by various officials and divines; governmental finances were in total disarray; tribal heads and chieftains were laws unto themselves; the common people had no one to whom they could turn to seek redress against extortions which weighed so heavily upon them. Mulk-Ará had been an exile for twenty-seven years in 'Iráq. Because of what he had suffered himself at the hands of Náṣiri'd-Dín Sháh his criticisms could not be totally disinterested. But no matter how uncharitable his sentiments might have been regarding Náṣiri'd-Dín Sháh and the ramshackle government of Írán, his observations receive ample confirmation from other sources. Muḥammad-Ḥasan Khán, a son of Ḥájí 'Alí Khán, the Ḥájibu'd-Dawlih – who had at first the title of Ṣaní'u'd-Dawlih, and then of I'timádu's-Salṭanih, and served faithfully at the court of Náṣiri'd-Dín Sháh for many years, ending his days as the Minister of Publications – left behind a voluminous diary. A cursory glance through this diary, which covers nearly two decades, suffices to show the basic corruption of Náṣiri'd-Dín Sháh and of many of those who were near and dear to him, the restlessness which pervaded his daily life, the detestable and even horrific practices which flourished under his rule. Muḥammad-Ḥasan Khán, who knew French, was well acquainted with the ways and thoughts of Europeans, and is credited with a variety of translations as well as original writings, died only shortly before the assassination of his royal master. We shall come back to his remarkably frank diary later on.

But let us at first turn to the evidence provided by Valentine Chirol (later knighted), a noted journalist of Victorian and Edwardian times, who visited Persia in 1884 on behalf of Nordenfelt, a Swede resident in Britain, who had put a new type of machine-gun on the market, and wished to do business with the government of Írán. Nordenfelt at first approached Mírzá Malkam Khán, the Náẓimu'd-Dawlih, the Persian minister in London, who 'gave him every encouragement' and advised him to pave the way with the presentation of a model to the person of Náṣiri'd-Dín Sháh, 'so as to enlist His Majesty's personal interest in the matter'.

Valentine Chirol writes:[3]

'Nordenfelt, knowing my *Wanderlust* and trusting to the experience I had already gained of Eastern ways and customs, asked me whether I would undertake that mission. Persia was still for me a name to conjure with, and I accepted the offer. The first question was how to convey the gun to Teheran. The shortest and most convenient route in those days would have been through Russia and across the Caspian to the Persian port of Enzeli [Anzálí] and thence by road, if it could be called a road, to the Persian capital. But the Russian Government, being unwilling to encourage the introduction of modern weapons of war into Persia, the only available route was by the Persian Gulf to Bushire, where I was to take charge of it and see to its safe conveyance by land through Shiraz and Isfahan to Teheran.'

Chirol describes graphically the ascent on to the Íránian Plateau, through the most difficult mountain passes between Búshihr and Shíráz, which today can be done through long tunnels that are marvels of engineering. In Iṣfahán, Ẓillu's-Sulṭán insisted on having a look at the machine-gun and seeing it at practice, which rather disconcerted Chirol. But there was no way out, and it had to be done. Ẓillu's-Sulṭán was greatly pleased. Chirol goes on to say:

'Once on a particularly desolate stage with the sun beating down out of a cloudless sky, I happened on to one of the sights which bring home to one the primitive methods by which law and order are apt to be maintained in truly Oriental countries. Some way ahead on the broad level track worn by countless caravans, which had of course no milestones or signposts, I descried a big post about man high, and as I rode up to it I saw what had been a human face and shoulders rising out of it. The wretched man, who may or may not have been, as I was afterwards told, a notorious brigand, had been forced down into a hollow column built up of closely-piled stones into which cement had been afterwards poured up to nearly his shoulders. There he had been left to live for another few hours, until myriads of flies settling down upon his face or the swifter mercies of birds of prey put an end to his torture. . . .

'Meanwhile I had plenty of time to explore the sights of Isfahan itself, though of the splendid city which excited the wonder and admiration of European travellers in the days when Elizabeth reigned in England and Akbar at Delhi only enough had survived to mark the contrast between the Persia of the sixteenth and of the nineteenth century. Whole quarters of the city were deserted and in ruins; of the bazaars, which were once the finest and most thriving marts of Western Asia, many were entirely abandoned, and but few more than partially tenanted. The *Chehar Bagh* [Chihár Bágh] still existed, but its avenues of giant plane trees had been grievously thinned; water no longer flowed down them through a succession of marble channels and ornamental basins. In spite of the neglect with which the Kajar [Qájár] dynasty seemed deliberately to treat every remainder of the greatness of their Sefavi [Ṣafaví] predecessors, the superb mosque erected by Shah Abbas on the Meidan [Maydán] still remained unique, but not unscathed, in the glory of its green-and-blue tiles, but in the ancient palace of the Sefavi princes, where the Zill-es-Sultan resided as Prince-Governor, some clumsy attempts at restoration had done more to mar the artistic beauty of the building than the ravages of deliberate vandalism. The entire population of the city, with the villages of the surrounding plains, was not reckoned at more than a quarter of a million, whereas two and a half centuries ago the estimates for the city alone varied between 600,000 and 1,100,000, and within ten leagues of its walls Chardin counted 1,500 villages. The days are indeed past when it was the proud boast of its people that Isfahan was half the world – *Isfahan nusf-el-jehan* [Niṣf-i-Jahán]. . . .

'. . . Then I went on to Sultanabad [Sulṭánábád], the centre of the carpet-making industry, where I had an entertaining illustration of the huge sham that called itself a Government. On the doors of the chief workshop in which the best craftsmen were employed on the merest pittance weaving carpets for the Shah himself, a Royal ordinance was nailed up conspicuously, forbidding under the severest penalties the use of all aniline dyes which 'wicked people were trying to import from the land of the Infidels.' But inside scarcely a single carpet for the Shah's palaces was shown me for which aniline dyes had not been used. During the rest of my slow and rather wearisome journey to Teheran, I continued to meet with the same contrast between profession and observance in the slipshod methods of government, between the abject misery of the many and the unwholesome luxury of the few, between small oases of fertile vegetation and vast waste spaces of untenanted desert.

'It was high summer before I reached Teheran, and I was thankful to accept the friendly hospitality of the French Minister, M. de Ballois, in his summer retreat at Tejrish [Tajrísh] . . . The Russian Legation was near by, and the British Legation not much farther off in another direction at Gulahek [Qulhak]. Germany was not even represented,* as Bismarck had no desire to launch out into a 'world-policy.' England and Russia were the only powers that counted, and British ascendancy in Teheran itself was for the time being scarcely challenged. For five and twenty years Great Britain had been represented by three Ministers† in succession whose diplomatic experience had been chiefly confined to Persia, and for whom Teheran had become the Hub of the Universe, and the Shah the one potentate that mattered in their narrow world. . . . I have never seen pettier jealousies and more storms in a teacup than those that then raged between the different European Legations at Teheran, and sometimes within the walls of each Legation. . . . In Persia itself Anglo-Russian antagonism was for the moment quiescent. It was the year after Russian troops had occupied Merv, and Russia was busy consolidating the new position she had just acquired on the road to Herat, and pushing her frontier forward along the borders of Afghanistan. Nasr-ed-Din Shah had twice visited Europe, and had imported a few Europeans who were supposed to be engaged on administrative reforms. Of these General Schindler, an Austrian by birth, alone did any lasting work, mainly in the fields of

* During his second visit to Europe, Náṣiri'd-Dín Sháh had talks with Kaiser Wilhelm I and Prince Bismarck. That was in 1878. In 1883 he approached Bismarck for an exchange of envoys. In 1885, Mírzá Riḍá Khán Giránmáyih, the Mu'ayyidu's-Salṭánih, was appointed the Persian envoy in Berlin and Bismarck sent Graf von Braunschweig to Ṭihrán. (HMB)

† Charles Alison (died in Ṭihrán), W. Taylour Thomson, Sir Ronald Thomson. (HMB)

science and natural history, which lay outside his official functions, whilst the others merely excited general hilarity by the splendour of their uniforms and their adroitness in playing upon the weaknesses of their Persian employers. One of them who was organizing an international postal service was wont when warmed with wine to talk of the King of Kings familiarly as *Ma vache à lait*, and he was credited with having invented a practice afterwards widely adopted in the Central American Republics for adding to his official stipend, by making fresh issues of postage stamps almost at once withdrawn from circulation and then sold with great profit to European philatelists. The scandals of the Shah's own court and his immense *anderouns* [*andarúns*] – the Persian equivalent of the *hareem* – were only less disreputable than those of his sons' and other relatives who filled the highest offices of state. The most notorious was Naib-es-Sultaneh [Náyibu's-Salṭanih], who was Minister of War, and was said to 'eat a hundred rations,' i.e. their equivalent in cash, for every ration that reached the tattered rabble which did duty for the Persian army.

'Corruption was rampant everywhere, as I soon discovered to my own cost. For though my Nordenfelt gun arrived in due course safely and I at first received affable messages from the Shah promising to fix a day for its presentation, I never had occasion to unpack it, but ultimately sent it off on its long homeward journey again *via* Bushire, as I found that the road for it to the Palace would have had to be paved with gold tomans to satisfy the greed of a whole chain of officials great and small, with no prospect of any serious business at the end of it. The British Minister was far too Olympian to concern himself with my affairs, and the French Minister could obviously not give me any official assistance.

'As France had few political interests in Persia, M. de Ballois was a detached and somewhat cynical observer of Persian ways, and soon after my arrival, he had warned me that '*dans ce pays-ci il n'y a rien à faire pour les honnêtes gens*'. Nordenfelt with his unfailing good humour was even more amused than disgusted, and rather enjoyed cabling me to come home and *send the Shah to Jericho*. The Zill would have liked to detain the gun at Isfahan on its way back to Bushire, but was afraid of giving offence to his father who, I was told, flew into a passion when he ultimately learnt that I had left – but it was too late.'

Chirol returned home by way of Russia. He had hoped, as any

journalist would, to see something of the Trans-Caspian railway which the Russians had begun laying in Central Asia. The Russian Legation gave him support and 'letters of recommendation' from the Russian Ministry of Foreign Affairs. However, when he reached Khrasnovodsk, on the eastern shores of the Caspian, a young ADC of the Governor came aboard the ship and conducted him to Government House, where he was held, virtually a prisoner, for thirty-six hours, and then conducted back to the same ship to go to the opposite shore of the Caspian. The Governor told him in plain language that he could not be allowed to go anywhere near the railway, and that he would be his guest, until the boat was ready to sail away. Chirol writes: 'My host, who was himself, of course, a general, explained to me as the evening advanced and an abundant consumption of vodka loosened his tongue, that only the consciousness of the tremendous responsibility vested in him as Warden of the Central Asian Marches for his august master, the Tsar, made it possible for him to endure so *morne* a place of residence, after having enjoyed for many years the amenities of court life in the capital. I learned, it is true, from the captain of my steamer that the pickings of the office were more than commensurate with its responsibilities. But in any case I had seen enough to convince me that a far-reaching policy of Central Asian expansion which would sooner or later spell Russian domination at Teheran could alone account for the secrecy with which Russia was pushing on in so desolate a region the construction of a great railway along the whole Russo-Persian borderline east of the Caspian.'

Russians first descended in force upon Khrasnovdosk in 1869, and moved on, shortly after, to Chíkíshlíyár, close to the mouth of the River Atrak. It evoked strong protest from Persia which Russians did not heed. The predatory Turkomans had been a thorn in the flesh, both of Írán and Russia. From time to time they would venture deep into Persian territory and carry off men and women and children, whom they sold in their slave-markets. Russians received the same treatment. Persian efforts to subdue the Turkomans failed, but the Russian efforts succeeded.

Sulṭán-Murád Mírzá, the Ḥisámu's-Salṭanih, the Governor-General of Khurásán who had captured Hirát, subsequent to the unhappy settlement of affairs in the eastern part of the territory which he governed, then turned to the north. In 1857 he asked eighty prominent Turkomans to visit him in Mashhad; whereupon, true to form, this double-dealing uncle of Náṣiri'd-Dín Sháh arrested them and threw them into his gaol. Having momentarily overcome the Turkomans in this dastardly manner, Ḥisámu's-Salṭanih next led an army to Marv which he easily occupied. Marv, like Hirát, had always been an integral part of Khurásán. But alas, three years later, the next Governor-General of Khurásán, Ḥamzih Mírzá, the Ḥishmatu'd-Dawlih – also an uncle of Náṣiri'd-Dín Sháh – although able to recapture Hirát, was soundly beaten, indeed ignominiously, by the Turkomans, and Marv was lost, to fall prey to the Russians. Poor Ḥamzih Mírzá had no luck. At one time he was worsted by Sálár, at another, by the Turkomans. It should be said to his credit that, when Governor-General of Ádharbáyján, he bravely defied the orders received from Ṭihrán, telling him to have the Báb executed, and Mírzá Taqí Khán had to hand over the arrangement and supervision of that unjust task to his own brother, Vazír-Niẓám.

Ḥishmatu'd-Dawlih's rout took place in the battle with the Takkih Turkomans, close to Marv. He even lost his guns to the victorious Turkomans. Of course he also lost his governorship. So disgusted was Náṣiri'd-Dín Sháh by his uncle's failure (which to a considerable extent was due to the incompetence of the Vizier of Khurásán) that on a photograph of that hapless uncle he wrote the word '*najis*' – the foul Ḥishmatu'd-Dawlih. Some of the guns that had fallen to the Turkomans were later recaptured when another expedition was sent against them from Sarakhs, which became a frontier post. Incidentally, the victorious Turkomans took so many prisoners that their victory was followed by a serious slump in the prices of their slave markets.

Next, Russia commenced its advance into Transoxania. The Khánate of Khívih, over which Írán had a just claim but was unable to exercise authority, was easily overrun and the Yamút Turkomans were decisively subdued. But General Lomakin's move against the Takkih Turkomans was foredoomed to failure, because of lack of sufficient preparations. Although the Turkomans were glaringly savaged by the Russian artillery at Gi'uk Tappih (Geok Teppe) – the Blue Hill – it was the failure of the Russians to dislodge and bring them to their knees which stood out prominently in General Lomakin's campaign. And this was a terrible blow to Russian prestige. Very soon, General

Skobelev took over from General Lomakin and in January 1881, despite the desperate resistance offered by the Turkomans, their position at the Blue Hill was overwhelmed and, as a consequence, the historic city of Marv, an undoubted adjunct of Khurásán, passed into the possession of Russia. True, the victory of the Russians brought relief to Persia from the depredations of the Turkomans (the Gawkaláns, the Yamúts and the Tikkihs), but it was sad and humiliating for her to lose the city of Marv.

Another loss which Persia incurred in the second half of the nineteenth century, during the reign of Náṣiri'd-Dín Sháh, was in the area of Balúchistán. That province had suffered from disorder for a long time. Sir Frederic Goldsmid, the first Director of Telegraphs in Persia, came up against seemingly insurmountable obstacles in the year 1864, in Balúchistán, as there was no one west of Gwadur (Gúwádur), a small sea-town on the Gulf of Oman ('Ummán), whom he could confidently deal with. The Khán of Kalát exercised only a shadowy authority.

> Persia had lately been pursuing a forward policy in Makran and Baluchistan, which had probably been in contemplation in 1856, when the treaty with Muscat [Masqaṭ] was concluded, and which accounted for inclusion in the treaty of the article requiring the Sultan to assist the passage of Persian troops eastwards through Bandar 'Abbas and its districts. From the Sudaij River eastwards to Chahbar [Cháhbahár], about 150 miles, the land was ruled by a powerful Baluchi chieftain, Mir 'Abdullah ibn Murad Muhammad. Twelve years previously he had acknowledged Persian suzerainty, but according to some Baluchi chiefs . . . he would welcome an opportunity to shake off that allegiance. The dilemma . . . was to judge whether Mir 'Abdullah could act on his own authority, under his obligations to Persia, or whether it would be unfair to him and to other Baluchi chiefs similarly placed, to apply to Persia for permission to construct the telegraph through territory which they considered their own, although control of it had been temporarily wrested from them by Persia. Further, if Persian sovereignty over the coast were recognized, the local chiefs might retaliate by impeding the construction of the telegraph.
>
> Chahbar was a small coastal town subject to Muscat, whose jurisdiction extended along the coast eastwards to Gwatar [Gúwátar]. Gwatar town and Jiwani, on the other side of Gwatar Bay, were ruled by independent, petty Baluchi chiefs. Beyond Jiwani lay Gwadur, which . . . had been given to Saiyid Sultan ibn Ahmad of Muscat by a former Khan of Kalat in perpetuity . . . The Khan of Kalat already controlled the coast for eighty miles

> to the east of Gwadur, and from that point to the Sind frontier the land was under the authority of the Jam of Las Bailah, who was both related to the Khan and subject to him. Neither of them . . . would object to the laying of the telegraph through his territory, and both were capable of protecting it.[4]

The lonely, barren and inhospitable wastelands of the Makrán coast, where the army of Alexander of Macedonia suffered incredibly when returning from India, were not worth concern and contention, had it not been for their strategic position and the fact that their fortunes were linked with the fortunes of the hinterland of Balúchistán and Sístán. Considerable headway had been made in extending the area of Íránian jurisdiction over the Makrán coast, during the reign of Muḥammad Sháh, but when the time came for the construction of the telegraph line, troubles and disputes arose, culminating in the appointment of a commission to draw a frontier line. This commission itself ran into difficulties. Then, Goldsmid went on to Gwadur (Gúwádur) and Major Lovett, who, according to Sir Percy Sykes, 'had made a survey of the proposed frontier line and was able to complete the information previously collected' (p. 361), met him there, and the British commissioner opted for a frontier line east of Gúwátar, which was finally accepted by Náṣiri'd-Dín Sháh. Sykes comments that although the Qájár monarch would, at first, have none of it, the decision was favourable to Írán.

Next came the thorny problem of Sístán, to be settled between Írán and Afghánistán. The latter was in a chronic state of disorder, fomented partly by the fears of Britain. That was prior to the well-ordered times of Amír 'Abdu'r-Raḥmán Khán. In any case, not without reason, the Persian authorities entertained the notion that Britain could, if she wished, put an end to the inroads made by the Afgháns within the area which was undoubtedly Persian. Sir Frederic Goldsmid together with General Pollock – delegated by the Viceroy, Lord Mayo – and Dr Bellew, an orientalist of note, worked out a settlement between Írán and Afghánistán. Mír 'Alam Khán, the Amír of Qá'inát, was not at all co-operative, as his domain was contiguous to Sístán. But Náṣiri'd-Dín Sháh agreed to the settlement made by Goldsmid.

The frontier line between Írán and the Ottoman Empire remained in the arena of conflict and contention until the very eve of the entry of Turkey into the First World War. However, in 1851, Lord Palmerston made an effort to bring matters to a conclusion.

In the year 1870, Náṣiri'd-Dín Sháh decided to visit the holy cities of 'Iráq. To make the requisite arrangements, Ḥájí Mírzá Ḥusayn Khán, the Mushíru'd-Dawlih, was summoned from Istanbul. Náṣiri'd-Dín Sháh was the first monarch to go to Karbilá and Najaf and the other shrines in 'Iráq as a pilgrim. His predecessors had made the journey always as warriors and conquerors, while he himself wrote a journal of his pilgrimage which was published in his lifetime.

The Válí of Baghdád, during Náṣiri'd-Dín Sháh's pilgrimage, was Midḥat Páshá, the celebrated Turkish Constitutionalist and reformer. He journeyed as far as Kháníqayn to receive and bid welcome to the Sháh. Almost a decade later, when Válí of Beirut, at his invitation the Most Great Branch, 'Abdu'l-Bahá, visited that city.

Ḥájí Mírzá Ḥaydar-'Alí, the veteran teacher and promulgator of the Faith, who in his declining years was known to Bahá'í pilgrims from the West as the Angel of Mount Carmel, writes, in his unpublished biography of Mírzá Abu'l-Faḍl of Gulpáygán, about Mushíru'd-Dawlih and events at this time:[5]

'When . . . Náṣiri'd-Dín Sháh left Ṭihrán, on pilgrimage to the Holy Shrines, [Mushíru'd-Dawlih] engineered the banishment of the Bahá'ís to Mosul. The Ambassador had left Istanbul, by way of Aleppo, to be in Baghdád for the reception of the royalty. In Aleppo he put Shaykh Salmán, who was well known, and had two to three hundred petitions [to Bahá'u'lláh] with him, under arrest. He also confiscated all the goods and offerings that Shaykh Salmán had with him, and had the Shaykh locked up in a derelict room in the same house where he [Mushíru'd-Dawlih] lodged. I was told by Shaykh Salmán: "On an evening, he [Mushíru'd-Dawlih] and the consuls with their entourage were pacing up and down the courtyard. I saw him and heard him say: 'We believed and were certain that the Cause of Bahá'u'lláh was a political cause, and that His aim was to obtain power and sovereignty and amass riches to make a name for Himself. Therefore we tried hard to put Him down and made plans accordingly. No matter how much we harmed Him, no matter how many times we banished Him – and we contended with Him backed by the full powers of two states – indeed, no matter what we did, His power and authority and fame, His greatness and grandeur were enhanced. We were much amazed, lost in wonderment trying to find the reason. Now I see that this man [Salmán] has something like three hundred petitions with him. In these, there is no mention at all of politics, government, state and nation. Notwithstanding all the injuries, notwithstanding imprisonments, banishments, executions, and pillages inflicted on the Bahá'ís all this time, no mention is made of them and there is no complaint. These petitions he carries all consist of supplications, and are confined entirely to spiritual matters such as: "O God! keep me safe from the evil of selfish and carnal desires, give me constancy, make me steadfast in Thy love, bestow on me the bounty of servitude, confirm me in service to Thy Cause, make me free of all else save Thee, confirm us that we may serve the people of all the world, kiss the hand of the executioner and hands clapping, feet dancing, hurry to the scaffold."' Then he called for two or three of those petitions, and had them read aloud. They all admired the eloquence and the excellence of style and composition. Then he [Mushíru'd-Dawlih] said: 'Why should we repress such people who love God, seek God and speak of God? In His Book, the Qur'án, God has related the story of the believer in the household of Pharaoh, so as to warn us, remind us, and make us remember that should there be falsehood, the one who is false will not endure, but if the one whom we are contending with is the bearer of truth, it will all rebound upon us and will finish us; we shall be the losers and pay a heavy penalty. Nothing detrimental to the nation and to the state has been witnessed in their deeds, or reflected in their words. Whatever has been heard has come either from their enemies, from those who deny them, or from those bereft of knowledge. Moreover, we have all seen, and it has been our experience, that the more we tried to repress them, the more we insulted and denigrated them, the more we encompassed their death and extermination, the greater became their number, and the more their strength and power, their might and fame. Now they are living in the utmost of health, of glory, of bliss.' Mushíru'd-Dawlih was speaking in this manner, and others were saying that they agreed with him, quoting instances. The next morning he sent for me, apologized to me, and said: 'We had been misled. I am very grateful to you, because you have made me see the truth of the matter. Government ought not to interfere in spiritual affairs, in matters connected with faith and conscience.' He restored to me all the petitions, and told his men to bring all the merchandise and other articles which had been confiscated, and in his own presence they were given back to me. And he wrote a letter of recommendation to the vice-consul in Beirut, telling him: 'Give the Shaykh the utmost consideration and protection, and see that he reaches 'Akká with all that he has with him, to the presence of Ḥaḍrat-i-'Abbás Effendi.' Then he said to me: 'Kiss His hands on my behalf, offer Him my apologies, ask for His forgiveness, and beg for confirmation that I may be enabled to make redress for the past.' " '

And Ḥájí Mírzá Ḥaydar-'Alí continues:

'And so, when he [Mushíru'd-Dawlih] went to Ṭihrán, and ministers, grandees and notables came to visit him, amongst them was the late Ḥájí Mírzá Riḍá-Qulí . . . half-brother of the Blessed Perfection. Someone introduced [this visitor] as the brother of Bahá'u'lláh. This introduction frightened him and he protested: "I have had a well-known father, why do you not introduce me as his son?" That remark angered Mushíru'd-Dawlih. He reprimanded [Ḥájí Mírzá Riḍá-Qulí], saying: "You ought to be proud of being the brother of Ḥaḍrat-i-Bahá'u'lláh, and glory in it. It is much, very much, the cause of pride for Írán and the Íránians and to their honour that Bahá'u'lláh is Írání. Any prince or vizier or amír who ever came to Istanbul, on many accounts, brought abasement and belittlement to the people and the government of Írán. Day after day, they went a-begging, abjectly and full of flattery, to the house of this vizier or that páshá, to complain of and abuse the Sháh of Írán and the notables of Írán, asking for allowances and annuities. As exponents of the characteristics of the people of this land, they displayed barbarism, bestiality, venality and impoverishment. Whereas, Bahá'u'lláh, although exiled by the State, bore Himself with such constancy, repose, assurance and dignity, with such sublimity and detachment, as to revivify Írán and the Íránians and gladden their eyes. He did not frequent anyone's house, He did not seek to meet anyone. Whoever went to visit Him was received with the utmost kindliness. He spoke to them of the ancient civilization of Írán, and of the better ways and the humanity of her people. He behaved in such a way that all bore witness to His greatness and nobility. They came to see and understand that Írán has men, cultured, civilized and humane." '

Mírzá Ḥusayn Khán, the Mushíru'd-Dawlih, had left Istanbul for good, and soon accompanied Náṣiri'd-Dín Sháh back to Ṭihrán, where they arrived in the first days of February 1871. In November of the same year, he was elevated to the position of Ṣadr-i-A'ẓam (Grand Vizier), which had remained vacant since the downfall and dismissal of Mírzá Áqá Khán-i-Núrí, on the last day of August 1858. (Incidentally, the fall from office of Mírzá Áqá Khán was followed by the disgrace of his relatives in Shíráz: men who had been responsible for the atrocities in Nayríz – his cousins, Mírzá Na'ím and Shujá'u'l-Mulk, whose name was Mihr-'Alí Khán, as well as Ḥájí Háshim Khán, an official hitherto highly respected as the Head of the Department of Justice.)

Ḥájí Mírzá Ḥaydar-'Alí goes on to say of Mushíru'd-Dawlih:

'Time and again, in many a gathering where notables and grandees were present, he would say: "With the power of two states, with the political planning of two governments, I tried to withstand Bahá'u'lláh and to contend with Him; the more I tried, the greater became His power and authority." And he would relate that story of the detention of Shaykh Salmán and his own perusal of the petitions that the Shaykh carried with him, by which "I came to realize that the powers of this world are unable to withstand this Cause". He also made the Sháh see that opposing these people was greatly to the detriment of the state. On many occasions when, in various towns and cities of Persia, at the instigation of evil men, or because of the avarice of the authorities, the friends had been seized, this outstanding, wise, just and kindly man brought about their release. In the Council of the State, he declared that the Government of Írán committed a gross error by encompassing the expulsion and banishment of Bahá'u'lláh, since His Cause was all-conquering and would spread over the world. Were He a Prisoner in Írán, people would in future have come from all parts on pilgrimage to His Shrine, and that would have added to the wealth of the nation. Just as now Persians spend their money going on pilgrimage to Mecca and Medina and the Holy Shrines outside Írán, hereafter people would have spent their money to visit the Shrine of Bahá'u'lláh and the tombs of His companions and those banished from this country.

'This man [Mushíru'd-Dawlih] served the people and the government of Persia with utter truthfulness and perspicacity, and after the untold harm and oppression he inflicted on this Cause, he came to judge the matter rightly and justly, and rendered services as much as he could.'

Soon Mushíru'd-Dawlih persuaded Náṣiri'd-Dín Sháh to visit

Europe. He wanted his sovereign to see for himself the advances that Europe and the Europeans had made. This tour took place in the spring of 1873. At Windsor, Queen Victoria invested the Sháh with the Order of the Garter. It was a signal gesture of amicable relations.

The previous year, on 25 July, Náṣiri'd-Dín Sháh had granted to Baron Julius de Reuter, the founder of the world-famed news agency, a concession which had many ramifications. This significant step was taken as planned and directed by the new Grand Vizier. The Reuter Concession included such projects as the construction of a railway line from the Caspian Sea to the Persian Gulf, a tramway line in Ṭihrán, and the working of all the mineral resources of the country. Reuter had by this time taken British nationality; therefore Russia became apprehensive. But despite these fears and suspicions, Náṣiri'd-Dín Sháh was given a warm reception in St Petersburg by Tsar Alexander II (1855–81).

In the absence of the Sháh, one of his uncles, Ḥájí Farhád Mírzá, the Mu'tamidu'd-Dawlih, was acting as regent, and a court party had been formed, headed by the Minister of Foreign Affairs, Mírzá Sa'íd Khán, the Mu'taminu'l-Mulk, in opposition to the Ṣadr-i-A'ẓam. So strong had grown this opposition that on reaching Persian soil, at the port of Anzalí, Náṣiri'd-Dín Sháh was constrained to take away the office of Grand Vizier from Mushíru'd-Dawlih. It has been claimed that Russians acted in concert with Mírzá Sa'íd Khán to bring about the dismissal of Mushíru'd-Dawlih, who had now the additional title of Sipahsálár-i-A'ẓam. Whatever the case, Náṣiri'd Dín Sháh was now in one of his very angry moods, and as soon as he gained his capital he went into action, broke up the court party, and dispersed all those who were in the plot. The Ministry of Foreign Affairs was taken away from Mírzá Sa'íd Khán and given to Mushíru'd-Dawlih, and Mírzá Sa'íd Khán was sent away to Mashhad to be custodian of the Shrine of Imám Riḍá. But the office of the Ṣadr-i-A'ẓam remained, once again, unfilled until it was forced on Mírzá Yúsuf, the Mustawfíyu'l-Mamálik, in June 1884. And the Reuter Concession died a natural death.* Also involved in that plot against Mushíru'd-Dawlih were Ḥájí Mullá 'Alíy-i-Kaní and Siyyid Ṣáliḥ-i-'Arab, two of the most influential divines of the capital, who, in their obscurantism, de-

* For details and the eventual fate of this Concession which opened a new epoch, the reader is referred to Kazemzadeh, *Russia and Britain in Persia, 1864–1914*, pp. 100–147.

nounced and castigated the Ṣadr-i-A'ẓam as a renegade and irreligious. Some writers have alleged that Mu'tamidu'd-Dawlih, the Sháh's uncle, was the prime mover in that plot.

Mírzá Sa'íd Khán had been an old hand at the Ministry of Foreign Affairs, and had stepped into that office after the death of its previous occupant, Mírzá Muḥammad-'Alí Khán-i-Shírází, in February 1852, first as deputy and then as full Minister. He and Mírzá Káẓim Khán, the Niẓámu'l-Mulk, the eldest son of the Núrí Ṣadr-i-A'ẓam, took part in the execution of the Bábís in 1852. They fired the first shots at Mullá Ḥusayn-i-Khurásání. He also bore a considerable measure of responsibility for the banishment of Bahá'u'lláh from 'Iráq, urging Mushíru'd-Dawlih in Istanbul to persuade the Ottoman authorities to remove Bahá'u'lláh from the vicinity of the Íránian territories. At times, however, Mírzá Sa'íd Khán had made friendly gestures towards the Bahá'ís, so much so that for a long time they believed that the Tablet known as *Shikkar-Shikan Shavand* was addressed to him. (See p. 149n.) In May 1880, Mírzá Sa'íd Khán was brought back from Mashhad and installed once again in the Foreign Office. He died in the spring of 1884.

Mírzá Yúsuf, the Mustawfíyu'l-Mamálik, whose grand-vizierate was of short duration – he died within two years of his appointment – was one of the most remarkable men of his day. Thoroughly upright, incorruptible, fearless, he was generally called 'Áqá' or 'Jináb-i-Áqá', even by Náṣiri'd-Dín Sháh. Although it was imputed to him that he had participated in the execution of the Bábís in 1852, having been first to fire at Mullá Zaynu'l-'Ábidín-i-Yazdí, he stoutly denied it and sent a message to this effect to Bahá'u'lláh, Who favoured him with a gracious reply. (See Addendum V)

Although no longer the Ṣadr-i-A'ẓam, Mushíru'd-Dawlih prevailed on Náṣiri'd-Dín Sháh to visit Europe once again. This second visit took place in 1878. It was the year of the Congress of Berlin, and Europe was in an unsettled state. Russia, despite being directly involved in the conflict, again accorded Náṣiri'd-Dín Sháh a warm reception. A military manœuvre on a grand scale was held in his honour, and he became so enamoured of the uniform, arms and bearing of the Russian Cossacks that he asked Tsar Alexander to make available to him the services of a number of Russian officers and instructors, that they might organize for him a similar force. Such were

Mírzá Yúsuf-i-Ashtíyání, the Mustawfíyu'l-Mamálik

the beginnings of the Persian Cossack Brigade (later, Division), a military unit which was to play a significant part in the destinies of Írán and remained under Russian command until the autumn of 1920. Colonel de Mantovitch (the first commander and organizer of this unit) and his staff reached Ṭihrán in January 1879. In Vienna, too, Náṣiri'd Dín Sháh engaged a number of Austrian officers, who arrived at the Persian capital a month earlier than the Russians. At their head was also a colonel, named Schynovsky. However, theirs was a hopeless task, faced as they were with Russian rivalry. It is alleged that the restoration of Mírzá Sa'íd Khán to his former post was done under pressure from Russia, which looked askance at the policies of Mushíru'd-Dawlih. In December 1881, Mírzá Sa'íd Khán signed with the Russian envoy a treaty known as the Treaty of Ákhál, by virtue of which Írán forewent all her frontier claims regarding Transoxania. Mushíru'd-Dawlih was first given the governorship of his native city, Qazvín, and next, subsequent to the assassination of Tsar Alexander II, he was sent at the head of a mission to St Petersburg to convey the condolences of Náṣiri'd-Dín S͟háh to Alexander III. On his return, he was sent to Mas͟hhad to assume the custodianship of the Shrine of Imám Riḍá and govern the province of K͟hurásán as well. There he died in November 1881. It is generally agreed that he was poisoned on the order of Náṣiri'd-Dín S͟háh.

I'timádu's-Salṭanih, in his diary, writes that the S͟háh was openly displaying his delight on hearing that Mus͟híru'd-Dawlih was dead, as were also the uncles of the S͟háh: Mu'tamidu'd-Dawlih and Ḥisámu's-Salṭanih. It had become Náṣiri'd-Dín S͟hah's wont to help himself liberally to the riches of any notable and well-known person in his realm who died a wealthy man. Mus͟híru'd-Dawlih, the Sipahsálár-i-A'ẓam, was no exception, although his wife was a daughter of Fatḥ-'Alí S͟háh. According to the diary of I'timádu's-Salṭanih: 'Within the last two days, all the ministers have been busy, in the Council, preparing a list of the writings and the jewelry of the late Sipahsálár. His will and bank statements have not been produced as yet.' Another entry in the same diary reads: 'Ḥakímu'l-Mulk [Mírzá 'Alí-Naqí] has been commissioned by the S͟háh to negotiate with Qamaru's-Salṭanih, the widow of the late Sipahsálár, and obtain cash for the S͟háh from the estate . . .'*[6]

The title of Mus͟híru'd-Dawlih was now given to Yaḥyá K͟hán, the Mu'tamidu'l-Mulk, the brother of Mírzá Ḥusayn K͟hán, who is also generally known as Sipahsálár. That is the name applied to the magnificent mosque and theological college which he had built in Ṭihrán and richly endowed. Both the mosque and the college (which owns and houses one of the best libraries in Persia) feature largely in the subsequent history of the nation. Adjacent to the mosque is Baháristán, the seat of the Persian Lower House of Parliament, a building which (although rebuilt after being bombarded to ruins, as a result of Muḥammad-'Alí S͟háh's *coup d'état*[7] in 1908) shows well its original splendour. Baháristán was also a creation of Sipahsálár-i-A'ẓam, which Náṣiri'd-Dín S͟háh had purloined. It was given to the nation to be the home of its Parliament, by Muẓaffarí'd-Dín S͟háh, the son of Náṣiri'd-Dín, when a constitution was promulgated.

---

* A similar case was that of 'Imádu'd-Dawlih, a Qájár prince and Governor of Kirmáns͟háh. When he died, it was mooted that I'timádu's-Salṭanih, who was his son-in-law, should hasten to that city to collect jewelry and other riches left by him, chiefly for the benefit of Náṣiri'd-Din S͟háh – an honour which he declined.

The new Mushíru'd-Dawlih also held the portfolio of foreign affairs, for a while, and it was during his tenure of office that, in the winter of 1882–3, S. G. W. Benjamin was appointed by President Arthur to represent the United States in Ṭihrán: the first American envoy to Persia. In January 1885, Náṣiri'd-Dín Sháh purchased a 600-ton vessel from Germany, which he named *Persepolis*, for service in the Persian Gulf, as well as a smaller vessel, named *Shúsh*. Both were navigated by Germans. The first German minister, Graf von Braunschweig, established a German school in Ṭihrán and students were sent for higher studies to Germany. It was rumoured that a concession for the construction of a railway line was to be given to the Germans. Navigation by Germans in the Persian Gulf alarmed Britain, and the construction of a railway line in the north alarmed Russia. Náṣiri'd-Dín Sháh found himself forced, in the year 1887, to promise Russia that under no circumstances would he ever grant concessions for the construction of railway lines to any foreigner without the consent of the government of the Tsar. A year later, because of the insistence of the British, free passage for all foreign merchantmen along the river Kárún, in the (now oil-producing) province of Khúzistán, was officially notified to the diplomatic representatives in Ṭihrán. Immediately in the wake of this announcement a British firm, Lynch Brothers, started operating on the Kárún. Russia had to be compensated for what it considered to be a British victory, and was given the right to make use of the coastal waters at the port of Anzalí on the Caspian Sea.

In that same year 1888, Náṣiri'd-Dín Sháh, who had left the office of Ṣadr-i-A'ẓam vacant after the death of Mustawfíyu'l-Mamálik, elevated Mírzá 'Alí-Aṣghar Khán, the Amínu's-Sulṭán, to that exalted office. Amínu's-Sulṭán, like his opponent, Mírzá Malkam Khán, the Náẓimu'd-Dawlih, who was at the time the Persian envoy at the Court of St James's, is a controversial figure in the history of Persia. He has had his admirers and violent detractors. There is no doubt that he was astute and capable, as his prompt action at the moment of the assassination of Náṣiri'd-Dín Sháh amply proved. But he was a totally different man from Sipahsálár and Mustawfíyu'l-Mamálik. It was he who now persuaded Náṣiri'd-Dín Sháh to visit Europe a third time. The Sháh and his large entourage – which included both the Ṣadr-i-A'ẓam and our diarist, I'timádu's-Salṭanih (bitterly opposed to and

Náṣiri'd-Dín Sháh in Paris, 1889

critical of Amínu's-Sulṭán) – left Ṭihrán in April 1889, and via Caucasia travelled to St Petersburg, where Tsar Alexander III, like his predecessor, gave Náṣiri'd-Dín <u>Sh</u>áh an impressive welcome. Britain had also extended a specific invitation to Náṣiri'd-Dín <u>Sh</u>áh. Queen Victoria, the Prince of Wales (later Edward VII), and Lord Salisbury, the Prime Minister, offered the <u>Sh</u>áh a remarkably friendly reception. He stayed in Britain for a month, but this long visit which was seemingly eminently successful bore bitter fruits which we shall presently see. Another outcome of this third European tour was a meeting in Munich with Siyyid Jamálu'd-Dín-i-Asadábádí (reputed as Afg<u>h</u>ání), and an invitation to him to visit the country of his forefathers for a second time. His previous visit in 1886 had ended in near disaster; this time it ended in total disaster.

Siyyid Jamálu'd-Dín was truly the stormy petrel of Eastern politics, and was the supreme advocate of Pan-Islamism. And let it be said, at once, that he was by no means friendly towards the Faith of Bahá'u'lláh.[8] But, undoubtedly, Siyyid Jamálu'd-Dín was a very remarkable man, highly talented, eloquent, learned, possessed of both a fiery

Siyyid Jamálu'd-Dín-i-Asadábádí, known as Afg<u>h</u>ání (from Browne, The Persian Revolution of 1905–1909*)*

tongue and a fiery pen. He could be both gentle* and unswerving. Professor Elie Kedourie, of the London School of Economics and Political Science, writes of him: 'The actual career of the Sage of the East is then seen to be quite unlike his legend.What this career portended, political activism and the transformation of religion into a political ideology, has now come to pass and its consequences are visible all around us. What is also worth noticing is that this man and his followers who, on any reckoning, must be considered subverters of Islam as the orthodox have considered and practised it, have seldom if at all had their doctrines criticized, let alone refuted, by the representatives of orthodoxy.'[9] A discerning, well-informed Persian biographer of Siyyid Jamálu'd-Dín writes: 'One point should be brought up, in this preface, which will help to understand Siyyid Jamálu'd-Dín and his thought: whoever and whatever Siyyid Jamálu'd-Dín was, he strongly believed in what he knew and did, and he was a strong man of action. More than anyone else he detested the tyrant. One of his bright ideas which he always mentioned was this: "I am opposed to both the tyrant, and to the subject of tyranny. The tyrant, I hold as an enemy, because he commits tyranny, and the subject of tyranny, I dislike, because he allows it, thus making the tyrant wax bold." '[10] Mr Halabí also draws a very interesting parallel between Midhat Páshá and Siyyid Jamálu'd-Dín. Both suffered greatly at the hands of two implacable tyrants. The former was gravely wronged by Sulṭán 'Abdu'l-Ḥamíd, and the latter by Náṣiri'd-Dín Sháh. When Midhat Páshá was released and reached Europe, he did not engage in violent abuse of the Sulṭán; whereas Siyyid Jamálu'd-Dín, as soon as he was free of Persian soil, opened a vituperative campaign against the Sháh which, in the end, destroyed that wilful monarch. The Siyyid was in full cry when Edward Browne encountered him in London. Browne writes: '. . . I met him by invitation of the late Prince Malkom Khán at the house in Holland Park, which until that eminent diplomatist's quarrel with the Sháh in 1889, was the Persian Legation. . . . During his stay in London

* The diary of the father of the present writer reads, under the date, Sunday, 3 October 1886: 'Went to visit Siyyid Jamálu'd-Dín this morning. He has lodged near us. He is a man, very meek and kind, dressed in Arab garments, a small black turban wound round his head. He is corpulent, olive-skinned. May be he is more than fifty years old, has a black, closely-cropped beard. He told me that though he signs his name as Afghání, he is a native of Hamadán. Early in life he had gone to further his studies in the holy cities of 'Iráq. Thither he had gone to Afghánistán. It is now nearly thirty years later. He has been travelling here and there, all this while, residing for a while in Egypt. He is a very erudite, talented man. I enjoyed his talk.'

Sulṭán 'Abdu'l-Ḥamíd II

he addressed several meetings and wrote sundry articles on "The Reign of Terror in Persia," attacking the Sháh's character, and even his sanity, with great violence.'[11]

The alienation of Mírzá (or Prince) Malkam Khán was another direct result of the Sháh's third visit to Europe. In a dubious deal of concession-snatching, regarding a state lottery, Malkam (who like Siyyid Jamálu'd-Dín commanded a very fluent pen) felt that he had been badly let down and humiliated by Náṣiri'd-Dín Sháh and his Ṣadr-i-A'ẓam; and the avaricious monarch felt that he had been tricked. Consequently relations between them became strained and finally snapped. Malkam had been a protégé of Mírzá Ḥusayn Khán, the Mushíru'd-Dawlih, who rescued him from the political wilderness when he first fell foul of Náṣiri'd-Dín Sháh. It will also be recalled that Bahá'u'lláh saved him in Baghdád from the clutches of Mírzá Buzurg Khán.

Now, Malkam instituted a journal in London, which he named *Qánún* (Law), publishing forty-one issues all told. And this organ of attack was apart from political and social tracts which constantly flowed from Malkam's pen. Amínu's-Sulṭán was the particular butt of Malkam's fierce criticism. The entry of *Qánún* into Írán was prohibited by royal edict, but it reached many highly influential people despite the ban. And Náṣiri'd-Dín Sháh, led and guided by Amínu's-Sulṭán, continued giving concessions which had vast repercussions. In December 1889 Reuter obtained the concession to establish a bank and issue bank notes; thus the Imperial Bank of Persia came into being. In January 1890, the Russian government was given the concession to construct roads and railways in the north, and in March of the same year, Major Gerald F. Talbot won the concession to institute a monopoly of the tobacco trade in Persia.* This concession, which came to be known as the Tobacco Régie, aroused the landlords who cultivated tobacco and the large number of merchants whose trade was the buying and selling of tobacco, to such a degree that a public outcry led to the intervention of Mírzáy-i-Shírází, the most influential divine of the time. He totally interdicted the use of tobacco. And Náṣiri'd-Dín Sháh was baffled to see that in his own harem, the hubble-bubble or *qalyán* was cast aside. Only one powerful divine in Ṭihrán, Siyyid 'Abdu'lláh-i-Bihbahání (who played a major part in the Constitutional Movement in later years), dared to defy the ban, and took his *qalyán* with him to the pulpit. In April 1892, Náṣiri'd-Dín Sháh had to borrow £500,000 against the southern customs from the newly-instituted Imperial Bank, pay it as compensation to the British company, and cancel the Régie Concession.

Náṣiri'd-Dín Sháh had already begun to seek out and imprison the partisans of Mírzá Malkam Khán and Siyyid Jamálu'd-Dín. The man before whose bullet he eventually fell, went to prison, with many others, on this occasion. Two prominent Bahá'ís, Ḥájí Abu'l-Ḥasan-i-Ardakání, known as Ḥájí Amín, and Ḥájí Mullá 'Alí-Akbar-i-Shahmírzádí, known as Ḥájí Ákhund, were also detained and imprisoned. (Their story will feature in a forthcoming volume.) Subsequently, Bahá'u'lláh revealed the *Lawḥ-i-Dunyá* (Tablet of the World).

* For the full story of this and other concessions, the reader is directed to Kazemzadeh, *Russia and Britain in Persia, 1864–1914*.

Náṣiri'd-Dín Sháh, after the cancellation of the Régie, had another four years to live. On the eve of his jubilee celebrations, on 19 April 1896, in the innermost shrine of Ḥaḍrat-i-'Abdu'l-'Aẓím, a bullet fired by Mírzá Riḍáy-i-Kirmání, who was a devotee of Siyyid Jamálu'd-Dín, tore open his heart, and he died on the spot. And only the sagacity of Amínu's-Sulṭán and his prompt action, successfully concealing the fact of the assassination of the Sháh, saved the day and prevented the capital from plunging into chaos.

At his interrogation, the assassin, when asked why he had struck down the monarch and not any of the men in high places, including Kámrán Mírzá, the Náyibu's-Salṭanih, a son of the Sháh, at whose hands he had personally suffered, this disciple of Siyyid Jamálu'd-Dín answered with a line from *Mathnaví*, the immortal work of Mawláná Jaláli'd Dín-i-Rúmí: 'A fish goes putrid at its head, not at its tail'.

Addendum II

Representations to Consuls at the Time of Bahá'u'lláh's Banishment to 'Akká

HEREWITH is a brief résumé of the facts relating to certain documents in governmental archives; the reader should refer to pp. 257–8. The author plans to give a fuller account of these documents in a subsequent volume.

On 6 August 1868, Mr John E. Blunt, British consul at Adrianople, sent to Mr Elliot, the British minister at Istanbul, the following dispatch:

'I have the honor to transmit herewith inclosed to Your Excellency the copy of a letter which the Reverend Mr Rosenberg Protestant missionary at this place has addressed to me respecting a certain Shek [Shaykh] Mirza Hussein Ali Effendi [Bahá'u'lláh], chief of a Persian sect called "Babee" who with a party of 40 of his adherents has been undergoing exile at Adrianople during the last six years, and is about to be deported to Gallipoli and thence to the interior of Africa, I believe.

'Yesterday before this letter was addressed to me the Reverend Mr Rosenberg and Boghos Agha, chief of the native protestant community called on me and requested me to endeavour to persuade the local Ottoman authorities not to deport from here this Shek and his adherents, but as they also told me that the measure complained of by the Shek has not originated with these authorities but that it is the result of an imperative order addressed to them by the Sublime Porte, I respectfully declined to comply with their request.

'Mr Rosenberg then said that he should address to me the letter I have inclosed and expressed the hope that I would report the subject to Your Excellency.

'I do not know what the tenets of this "Babee" sect are. The

Reverend Mr Rosenberg and Boghos Agha believe that they are adopted from the Holy Scripture, and this belief has naturally excited their sympathy and zeal on behalf of the Shek.

'All I can say is that the Shek in question has led a most exemplary life in this city; that he is regarded with sympathy, mingled with respect and esteem, by the native Mahomedans and has received good treatment at the hands of the Ottoman authorities; and that the general impression here is that the persecution he is now made the object originates with the Persian Government and the Legation at Constantinople.' (FO 195 901)

The Rev. Rosenberg referred to in this dispatch was a missionary of the British Society for the Propagation of the Gospel among the Jews. As indicated, it was he who had drawn Blunt's attention to the situation that threatened Bahá'u'lláh. A few days later, on 10 August 1868, Blunt sent a further dispatch relative to an appeal that he states had been made to him by Bahá'u'lláh:

'With reference to my despatch No. 54 of the 6 instant relative to the case of Shek Hussein Ali Effendi chief of the Persian sect called "Babee" I have the honor to further report to Your Excellency that I received this morning from the Shek in question the inclosed paper written in Turkish in which he appeals for protection to this Consulate. A similar appeal has been addressed by the Shek to my colleagues in this city.

'Shortly after the appeal in question was put in my hands my Austrian colleague called on me and asked me what I proposed doing in the matter. I replied that in my humble opinion it was not a case in which I could in any way officially interfere on the spot without instructions from the Embassy, and that I had already reported the subject to Your Excellency. Monsieur de Camerloher appeared to be entirely of the same opinion and told me that he had also submitted the case to Baron Prokesh.

'But as Monsieur de Camerloher has strong reasons to think that the Shek and his party are about to be delivered by the Ottoman Government into the power of the Persian authorities; and that by so doing the Ottoman Government will be guilty of a breach of faith towards this unfortunate people dangerous to their lives and at the same time hurtful to its credit, we agreed to address to our respective Embassies the telegram we despatched this morning and of which the following is a copy:

'"Hussein Ali Effendi with seventy others will be sent today to Gallipoli there to be made over to an agent of the Shah. He has addressed a written appeal for protection to Foreign Consular Corps. Undersigned decided to solicit instructions from their respective embassies before acting. My colleague begs present may be communicated to Baron Prokesh."

'I beg leave also to add that my Austrian colleague told me that Baron Prokesh is personally acquainted with the Shek and wrote to the Austrian Consulate here very strongly on his behalf.

'I regret that the early departure of today's mail leaves me no time to prepare a translation of the paper I have inclosed herein.' (FO 195 901)

Unfortunately, the enclosure in Blunt's dispatch is missing from the files of the British Public Record Office. Since, however, Blunt had stated that a similar appeal had been addressed to the other consuls in Adrianople, a search was made through the French Foreign Office Archives. It was found that the acting French consul, Ferdinand Ronzevalle, had indeed, on 14 August 1868, forwarded such an appeal to the French minister, Nicolas Bourée. The text of this appeal consists of eight lines written in Turkish with a signature and seal both reading 'Ḥusayn-'Alí'.

Thus there were at least three ministers of foreign powers making enquiries about Bahá'u'lláh at Istanbul. They all received the same answer from either 'Álí-Pás͟há or Fu'ád-Pás͟há: that this further exile was brought about by the fact that the followers of Bahá'u'lláh were trying to bring about dissension among Muslims by converting them to a new religion, and that the Persian Legation was in no way involved.

On 13 August 1868, Blunt reported:

'I beg leave to report that I have acted in this business in conformity with your Excellency's order.

'Before I received this order Mirza Hussein Ali . . . requested me through the Revd Mr Rosenberg to call on him, but I respectfully declined doing so, as he was confined to his house and vigilantly watched by the police . . .

'The Mirza and his adherents were sent from here to Gallipoli on Monday evening last . . .' (FO 195 901)

Rev. Rosenburg, however, continued his efforts on behalf of Bahá'u'lláh. On 15 August 1868, he sent to Blunt a copy of what is stated to be a letter from Bahá'u'lláh to the Evangelical Alliance of London asking them to intervene with the Ottoman authorities so that religious toleration may be extended to the Bahá'ís. The Evangelical Alliance specialized in obtaining religious toleration for Christians throughout the world.

Addendum III

The Aftermath of the Siege of Plevna

THESE extracts from *The Balkan Volunteers*,[1] a book about the doctors and assistance sent from Britain, during the war of 1877–8, amply bear out the story of the Turkish captain who spoke of 'blood' flowing 'beneath the trees and beneath the stones'. (See p. 262.)

'The condition of the wounded in the Plevna hospitals was more dreadful than anything they [the British doctors] had hitherto witnessed. Ryan, the only British doctor in the besieged fortress, conducted them through the rooms of wounded where he had struggled on with no drugs other than chloroform, no antiseptic dressings, no stores, no soups. Bandages had been made out of the coloured prints from the bazaar, and the dye had been poisonous. Wounds had been plugged with cotton wool. There were cases of smallpox, gangrene, typhoid; and all had lice. The state of the hospitals, claimed *The Times* correspondent, "would dwarf Defoe's description of the lazar house of The Plague". . . .

'Plevna fell and the great retreat began: Turkish troops withdrawing through mud, snow and ice, . . . to Philippopolis, . . . to Varna, . . . from the Serbian border to Gallipoli, to Salonica. With them, trudging along the same bullock tracks, crawling over the same hillsides came the refugees: the trickle of six months earlier had become a torrent, all the Mussulman population of Bulgaria and Roumelia falling before the avenging Muscovites. . . . The retreat became a rout. . . .

'. . . At the Adrianople hospital when the order for evacuation was given, the Turkish populace and the Turkish staff fled, and the Stafford House doctors [British] "went into the fields, caught the oxen, yoked them up, and then carried down the wounded from the wards themselves." At Philippopolis, eight hundred and fifty wounded were placed in empty warehouses alongside the station to await trains that never came. There was panic and uproar in the town, buildings ablaze . . . two days later the Russians entered; by then the number of living wounded in the warehouses had dwindled to one hundred and twenty. . . .

'At Rustchuk the ending was more dramatic. A Russian shell fell on the hospital on 29 December 1877, and even though the two doctors, Stiven and Beresford, rushed out and waved the Red Crescent flag vigorously up and down, more shells followed. The doctors spent the night moving their patients from the destroyed wards into the others. Next day shelling began again. Terrified, all the patients who could walk and all the domestic staff rushed out of the buildings into the snow and so, reported Stiven, "Dr Beresford and myself were quite alone with some eighty patients to do what best we could for their safety." By nightfall some thirty to forty shells had fallen on the hospital; then firing ceased, and the two doctors transported their patients from the ruined building into the town. Next day they took them on by rail to Varna and the hospital there. . . .

'Young Sandwith . . . and Hume, both veterans of the Serbian campaign, joined Baker Pasha's division in the retreat from Tatar Bazardijk to Philippopolis and then over the Rhodope mountains. The telegraph and the railway had ceased to function, and Sandwith was caught up in a precipitous route over icy roads. Hume arrived at Philippopolis more rapidly if no less dangerously, having made the journey down the railway line, first in an engine he had commandeered and then on a trolley manipulated by hand. The retreat south over the mountains was a grim journey: "On every side, upon the ice and in the snow, struggling and falling horses, soldiers and wounded mixed in frightful confusion with women and children fleeing from their burnt houses, all toiling wearily upwards. In the plain below, could be seen the Cossacks advancing to the foot of the hill, and as from there, they fired on the struggling masses. . . ."

'. . . At the railway station at Tatar Bazardijk thousands massed daily in the open wagons, "frozen white, black, and blue," and Bartlett did what he could – there was no means of organizing a system – to bring food and warmth to them. Then the railway line lower down was cut and the waiting had been in vain. He and the thousands were forced to retreat over the Rhodope mountains to the sea.

'Master* had been more fortunate. He had been in Sofia for a

* Robert E. Master, assisting the Turkish Compassionate Fund distribution. (HMB)

month prior to the fall of the town to the Russians. At the cost of 1*d.* per day per person he had kept a soup kitchen going for twenty-five thousand refugees, "each person receiving a pint and a half of good strong soup, and enough firewood to keep them warm." He left by train before the Russians entered, a slow journey of mounting horror. Three days the train took to travel from Adrianople to Constantinople, the open wagons packed tight with women and children and soldiers, huddled together without shelter, warmth or food; many died, some gave birth, others despairing of any future "almost mad with grief, horror and hunger, flinging their children over the bridges as they pass along in the train . . ." At one station between Adrianople and Constantinople Blunt worked without ceasing, handing out bread and clothing; but the numbers were too great, and all that he could do seemed as nothing. Master, sent up from Constantinople with a railway wagon of food, found Blunt exhausted and ill. He took over: "I just managed to feed the people, but I could not keep the cold away. Corpse after corpse came out of the trucks, and was carried away and buried . . . it was an awful sight, and yet how quietly the refugees behaved. I hardly heard a murmur except from the Circassians who threatened to burn the station if the station master did not send on the train at once. These gentlemen also attacked my bread van with knives, but I managed to close the van in time."

'Down the line at Constantinople they waited: for the soldiers, for the wounded, for the refugees, for the Russian army; for England to come to the help of Turkey.'

Addendum IV

General Gordon in Haifa and 'Akká

LAURENCE Oliphant, under the heading 'General Gordon's Last Visit to Haifa', writes:

'It was just twenty-nine years ago since I first met him in the trenches before Sebastopol. He was quite a young and unknown officer at that time, and I should have forgotten the circumstance had we not again come across each other three years afterwards in China . . . I left China before he entered the Chinese service . . . Still, I had seen enough to make me watch his subsequent career with great interest, but our paths had not again crossed until one day, about two years ago [written 10 May 1885], I received a letter from Jaffa signed C. G. Gordon, asking for information in regard to Haifa as a residence, and expressing his intention of possibly paying me a visit. As I have many friends of the name I was puzzled for the moment. . . . It was only accidentally that the same afternoon the vice-consul here asked me if I knew anything of a General Gordon, as some letters had arrived to his care for an individual of that name. I at once perceived who my correspondent must be. I immediately addressed him a cordial invitation to pay me a visit, which he promptly responded to, and we spent a few very pleasant days together. . . .

'General Gordon, after spending a few days at Haifa, returned to Jerusalem, promising to bring his tents two months later and pitch them next to mine at Esfia on the summit of Carmel. I was eagerly looking forward to his companionship in the delightful wilderness of this mountain, and had even marked out in my own mind a spot for his camping-ground within fifty yards of my own, when, to my great disappointment, I received a letter from him saying that he was so deeply interested in biblical studies at the Holy City that he felt it his duty to change his mind, as he might never again have an opportunity of verifying the correctness of the views he entertained in regard to the typical nature of its configuration. . . .

'Towards the end of the year he wrote, saying that he was suddenly summoned to the Congo, and bidding me adieu. Curiously enough, in my reply I said that I did not say good-bye, as I felt sure I should see him again before he left the country. A few days afterwards he once more turned up at Haifa. He had embarked at Jaffa for Port Said in a country sailing craft, and he had been driven by stress of weather so far out of his course that his crew finally ran in here for shelter. . . . He was detained here a week . . . One day I observed him writing notes on a slip of paper. He asked me the Christian names of two friends who were staying with me. I told him, and feeling, I suppose, that my curiosity ought to be gratified, he said, "I am writing them down on my prayer list." Another day, after using some very strong language in regard to a very high personage who shall be nameless, he added quickly, "but I pray for him regularly." All this without a vestige of cant. If there was a thing he detested it was hypocrisy . . . He was full of fun and a most cheery companion with those he knew intimately. He never forced a conversation into a religious channel. . . . He left here on the 18th or 19th of December, 1883, and walked to Acre, twelve miles, to meet the steamer that was to take him direct to Marseilles. He sent his luggage in a carriage.

'His last words as we parted were that he felt sure we should never meet again. I said he had been wrong once when he told me that he should not see me again, and I hoped he was wrong now. He said no, he felt that he had no more work to do for God on this earth, and that he should never return from the Congo. Within a month he was in Upper Egypt.

'It was characteristic of the man that scarcely anyone in Haifa knew who he was. Seeing a very handsome garden belonging to a rich Syrian, near Acre, he strolled into it, and was accosted by the proprietor, who asked him who he was. He replied, "Gordon Pasha," on which my Syrian friend, who told me the story, laughed incredulously, and politely showed him out. Gordon meekly departed without attempting to insist on his identity. The proprietor told me that he felt convinced that he was being imposed upon, because Gordon, when spoken to in English, would answer in bad Arabic, and because, when asked his name, he took his card-case half out of his pocket, as though to give his card, and then, on second thought, put it back again and answered verbally. So my friend lost his chance of entertaining an angel unawares, which he has never ceased to regret, the more especially as his friends take a pleasure in teasing him about it.

'My last letter from Gordon is dated Khartoum, the 6th of March.' (See below for a note on General Gordon's life.)

Sir Valentine Chirol writes, in *Fifty Years in a Changing World*:

'More to the point is my recollection of my meeting with Gordon a few months before his forlorn hope in the Sudan at Laurence Oliphant's house on Mount Carmel. Gordon was at that time living in Jerusalem entirely absorbed in the study of Biblical topography. The French, more than usually jealous and suspicious of all British activities in those parts since our occupation of Egypt, could not for a moment believe that for an Englishman and a General with Gordon's world-wide reputation Biblical topography was anything but a cloak for sinister political activities, and the French Consulate at Jerusalem watched all his movements. He had set out, he told us, on the previous day for one of his usual long walks in the country, and he had soon observed that he was being followed, as was also quite usual, by a Syrian whom he believed to be specially employed by the French to shadow him. So instead of turning back after a few miles' stretch he determined to go on and see how soon he would tire the man out. He walked on for many miles before he did so, and then, as it was getting too late for him to be back in Jerusalem before dark, he decided to push on to Nablous for the night – a matter of 35 or 40 miles – and having slept there he had thought he might as well push on next day to Haifa; and so there he was, and would the Oliphants give him another night's lodging?' (p. 42)

Note

Charles George Gordon (1833–85) was an Englishman who served in the Royal Engineers during the siege of Sebastopol and in the capture of Peking. Later (1863–4), in command of a Chinese force, he crushed a formidable rebellion and was recognized as one of the foremost soldiers of his day. After six years in England, during which he gave his spare time to relief of the poor, feeding and clothing homeless children, and visiting the sick, he accepted employment under the Khedive of Egypt and opened up additional regions of the equatorial Nile. In 1877 he became Governor of Súdán, reconnoitred a vast territory, and gained a world reputation by his achievements in government and engineering. He resigned in 1880 because of poor health, and spent nearly a year in Palestine, after which, at the request of the British government, he undertook to relieve garrisons in rebel territory in Egypt. He reached Kharṭúm, but within a month the Mahdí began a siege which continued for five months. A relief force from England, arriving in January 1885, found Kharṭúm captured and Gordon murdered on the palace steps.

Addendum V

Biographical Notes

THE following brief notes concern some of the persons mentioned in this book, whether followers of Bahá'u'lláh or others. Certain major figures have not been included, since information about them is readily available in various standard works in print, and it is also the author's intention to write more fully about a number of them in a forthcoming volume.

The notes have been written by Dr Moojan Momen, and those about the Bahá'ís have been based, in part, on 'Abdu'l-Bahá's *Memorials of the Faithful*, to which page references are given. The assistance of Mr Sami Doktoroglu, in contributing information about some of the Turkish pá<u>sh</u>ás, is gratefully acknowledged.

'Abdu'l-<u>Gh</u>affár-i-Iṣfahání, Áqá

Áqá 'Abdu'l-<u>Gh</u>affár was a trader of Iṣfahán who became a believer whilst on a journey to Ba<u>gh</u>dád. He was one of the companions of Bahá'u'lláh in His exile to Adrianople. He was sent by Bahá'u'lláh to Istanbul, where he was arrested and sentenced to exile in Cyprus. When the ship carrying Bahá'u'lláh and His fellow-exiles reached Haifa, he threw himself into the sea, unable to bear separation from Bahá'u'lláh, but was rescued and sent on to Cyprus. However, he succeeded in escaping from the island on 29 September 1870 and rejoined Bahá'u'lláh in 'Akká, where he settled down in the <u>Kh</u>án-i-Afranj. In order to conceal his presence from the authorities he changed his name to Áqá 'Abdu'lláh. After the ascension of Bahá'u'-lláh, he went to live in Damascus where he died. (See *Memorials of the Faithful*, pp. 59–61.)

'Abdu'l-Ḥusayn-i-Ṭihrání, <u>Sh</u>aykh

<u>Sh</u>ay<u>kh</u> 'Abdu'l-Ḥusayn-i-Ṭihrání, known as <u>Sh</u>ay<u>kh</u>u'l-'Iráqayn,

was the son of 'Alíy-i-Ṭihrání. He obtained the usual religious education and studied under Ḥájí Siyyid Shafíy-i-Burújirdí. He lived in Ṭihrán and was a close associate of Mírzá Taqí Khán, the Amír Kabír. Shaykh 'Abdu'l-Ḥusayn was named the Amír Kabír's executor and, from the money of this will, he built in Ṭihrán a mosque and a *madrisih* of which he was director. In 1858, Náṣiri'd-Dín Sháh put him in charge of a mission to 'Iráq to regild the dome of the tomb of Ḥusayn at Karbilá. When he had finished this, he was put in charge of the gilding of the dome of the Askaríyayn shrine at Sámarrá. He fell ill at Káẓimayn, died 16 December 1869, and is buried at Karbilá.

Ádí Guzal, Mullá ('Alíy-i-Sayyáḥ, Mírzá)

Mullá Ádí Guzal of Marághih, better known as Mírzá 'Alíy-i-Sayyáḥ, became a Bábí in the very earliest days of the Faith, and was the trustee and courier of the Báb during the days of His imprisonment in Máh-Kú and Chihríq. He was sent by the Báb on several important missions; he was the first to visit the scene of the Shaykh Ṭabarsí upheaval and recite prayers of visitation for the martyrs. During the severest of the Bábí persecutions, Mírzá 'Alí fled to 'Iráq and lived in Karbilá. During Bahá'u'lláh's sojourn in Adrianople, Mírzá 'Alí came to that city and was sent by Bahá'u'lláh to Istanbul. Here he was arrested and interrogated and, when Bahá'u'lláh was exiled from Adrianople to 'Akká in 1868, he was one of His followers who was sent to Cyprus with Mírzá Yaḥyá. He died in Famagusta on 4 August 1871.

'Alí Khán, Ḥájí, Ḥájibu'd-Dawlih

Ḥájí 'Alí Khán was a native of Marághih. He had entered the service of Muḥammad Sháh when the latter had been Governor of Marághih, at a time when his father was Governor of Ádharbáyján. Later, when Muḥammad Sháh acceded to the throne, Ḥájí 'Alí Khán was made Steward of the Household. He fell from favour and was exiled to 'Iráq following rumours of an unsavoury affair between him and Mahd-'Ulyá, the wife of the Sháh. However, through Mahd-'Ulyá's influence, he was able to regain his position, and on Muḥammad Sháh's death resumed his post as Steward of the Royal Household. Early in 1849 Mírzá Taqí Khán appointed him Farrásh-Báshí. It was Ḥájí 'Alí

Khán who repaid Mírzá Taqí Khán for this favour by encompassing his death early in 1852. As a reward, he was given the title Ḥájibu'd-Dawlih. He went on to have a chequered career, falling out of favour once again at the time of Mírzá Áqá Khán's downfall and being restored yet again through the intervention of Mahd-'Ulyá. He died in 1867. His son was Muḥammad-Ḥasan Khán, I'timádu's-Salṭanih. The Guardian of the Bahá'í Faith has written of him:

> Ḥájibu'd-Dawlih, that bloodthirsty fiend, who had strenuously hounded down so many innocent and defenseless Bahá'ís, fell in his turn a victim to the fury of the turbulent Lurs, who, after despoiling him of his property, cut off his beard, and forced him to eat it, saddled and bridled him, and rode him before the eyes of the people, after which they inflicted under his very eyes shameful atrocities upon his womenfolk and children.[1]

'Álí Páshá, Muḥammad Amín

Muḥammad Amín 'Álí Páshá was born in Istanbul in February 1815, the son of a shopkeeper. Because he had acquired a knowledge of French, he was able to obtain a post in the translation bureau of the Ottoman government in 1833. He was sent on several foreign missions and was the Turkish ambassador in London, 1838–9. In 1840, he became Minister of Foreign Affairs for a short time and returned to this position in 1846 under Rashíd Páshá. In 1852 he became Grand Vizier for a few months and then, in 1854, he was again appointed Foreign Minister and, in 1855, Grand Vizier (until the following year). He continued in high office for most of the rest of his life, being Foreign Minister in 1857–8, July 1861 and November 1861 to 1867, and Grand Vizier in 1858–9, 1861 and 1867–71. After Fu'ád Páshá's death in 1869, he combined the posts of Foreign Minister and Grand Vizier. He was a successful diplomat and one of a small group of Turkish statesmen determined to steer Turkey into the nineteenth century, but he tended to be authoritarian and overbearing in his personal manner. He died on 7 September 1871 after three months of illness.

'Alí-'Askar-i-Tabrízí, Ḥájí

Ḥájí 'Alí-'Askar was one of the notable merchants of Tabríz, and a believer from the time of the Báb. At last the persecutions forced him to leave his home town and he emigrated with his brother and family to Adrianople, where he settled down and made a living by peddling small wares. He was arrested and sent with Bahá'u'lláh to 'Akká, where he passed away in AH 1291 (AD 1874). (See *Memorials of the Faithful*, pp. 161–4.)

'Alí-Sháh, Ẓillu's-Sulṭán

'Alí-Sháh was the tenth son of Fatḥ-'Alí Sháh and a consanguineous brother of 'Abbás Mírzá, Muḥammad Sháh's father. He was made Governor of Ṭihrán and, on Fatḥ-'Alí Sháh's death in 1834, made a bid for the throne, styling himself 'Ádil Sháh. Within a short reign of forty days, in an effort to buy himself support, he succeeded in almost emptying the treasury of the hoards amassed by his miserly father. But it proved of no avail and he was brushed aside when Muḥammad Sháh reached Ṭihrán. He was at first imprisoned but managed to escape to Russia; he finally settled down in exile in Baghdád, where he was living when Bahá'u'lláh arrived there. He died in AH 1271 (AD 1854–5).

Ashraf, Áqá Siyyid

Áqá Siyyid Ashraf's father, Mír Jalíl, was one of the companions of Ḥujjat. He married in the early days of the Zanján upheaval, and Áqá Siyyid Ashraf was born during this episode. At its close, Mír Jalíl was taken to Ṭihrán and executed, leaving Umm-i-Ashraf (the mother of Ashraf) to bring up her children alone. In his early twenties, Áqá Siyyid Ashraf came twice to Adrianople and entered the presence of Bahá'u'lláh. Shortly after returning from the second of these journeys, he was arrested and condemned to death as a Bábí. The manner in which he steadfastly refused to renounce his Faith, and the way in which his mother – although brought to him with the idea that she would induce him to recant – urged him to remain firm, were praised in many passages from the pen of Bahá'u'lláh. Siyyid Ashraf's martyrdom occurred in 1870.

Báqir-i-Shírází, Mírzá

Mírzá Báqir remained in Adrianople for a while before returning to Shíráz. There he began to teach the Faith and journeyed from town to town in order to do so. He lived for a while in Hindíyán, then returned to S͟híráz. In AH 1288 (AD 1871–2) he was imprisoned with some of the other believers for four months, and then expelled from the town. He went to Kirmán and began to teach the Faith there, until he was expelled from that town also. He then lived in Sírján, but was arrested again by the Governor of Kirmán and spent another four months in prison, after which he was strangled and his body was thrown outside the city walls.

Fatḥ-'Alí, Mírzá, Fatḥ-i-A'ẓam

Mírzá Fatḥ-'Alí, surnamed Fatḥ-i-A'ẓam by Bahá'u'lláh, was one of the leading Bahá'ís of Ardistán, near Iṣfahán. He had accepted the Báb, with others in Ardistán, when Mullá 'Alí-Akbar-i-Ardistání and Mullá Ṣádiq-i-Muqaddas passed through the town after their persecution in 1845, with Quddús, in S͟híráz. (See Balyuzi, *The Báb*, pp. 76–8.) Later, he was one of the Bábís who early recognized the station of Bahá'u'lláh. The horse on which Bahá'u'lláh was mounted as He set off for Constantinople (see p. 175) was a gift from Mírzá Fatḥ-'Alí, who was not among those accompanying Him. He returned to Ardistán where he served Bahá'u'lláh as a point of contact for the distribution of Tablets to believers in Írán, often having to use his own judgement as to the intended recipient when no names were given on the Tablets. His son was married to the daughter of Mullá 'Alí-Akbar. He died shortly before the ascension of Bahá'u'lláh, Who revealed two Tablets of Visitation in his honour.

Fu'ád Pás͟há (Keçeci-Zádih Muḥammad)

Fu'ád Pás͟há was born in Istanbul in 1815, the son of a famous poet and scholar, 'Izzat Mullá. He studied at the Medical School where he learnt French. He spent three years as an army doctor and then switched to the Translation Bureau in 1837. He was sent on several important diplomatic missions until, in 1852, he was appointed Foreign Minister under 'Álí Pás͟há. He again served as Foreign Minister in 1855–6, 1858–60, 1861 and 1867, and as Grand Vizier in 1861–3 and 1863–6, alternating with 'Álí Pás͟há in these important posts. Fu'ád advocated the modernization of the Ottoman state and was also influential in the development of the Turkish language. He died on 12 February 1869 in Nice, France, of a heart condition.

Ḥabíbu'lláh Afnán, Ḥájí Mírzá

Ḥájí Mírzá Ḥabíbu'lláh was born in Shíráz on 7 February 1875. He was called Muḥammad-'Alí at birth, but his father later changed his name to Ḥabíbu'lláh out of respect for the fact that one of Bahá'u'lláh's children was named Muḥammad-'Alí. Ḥájí Mírzá Ḥabíbu'lláh grew up in Shíráz in constant contact with the wife of the Báb, who was his aunt. In September 1890, he set out with his mother, brothers and sister to join his father in Egypt. From there they proceeded to Haifa where they remained for nine months in the presence of Bahá'u'lláh. The family then returned to Port Sa'íd, where they had a trading establishment. After the ascension of Bahá'u'lláh, Mírzá Ḥabíbu'lláh's father left for Írán, while he himself remained in Egypt. He was often at this time in the company of Mírzá Abu'l-Faḍl who was also then residing in Egypt. He visited 'Abdu'l-Bahá in the Holy Land on several occasions. Then in 1900, he was instructed by 'Abdu'l-Bahá to return to Shíráz to assist with the repair of the House of the Báb, and he was appointed Custodian of that House by 'Abdu'l-Bahá. He died in 1951.

Ḥamzih Mírzá, Ḥishmatu'd-Dawlih

Ḥamzih Mírzá was the twenty-first son of 'Abbás Mírzá, and thus an uncle of Náṣiri'd-Dín Sháh. In 1847, he was appointed Governor of Khurásán but, due to the revolt of the Sálaŕ there, he could exert no authority and, on the death of Muḥammad Sháh, when the Sálár's rebellion became more intense, he was forced to flee to Afghánistán. In 1849, he was appointed Governor of Ádharbáyján, and when in 1850 the order for the Báb's execution came to him, he refused to be associated with it. He was later reappointed Governor of Khurásán, and his forces suffered a crushing defeat at the hands of the Turkomans in 1860–61. After holding several more governorships, he died while campaigning against the rebel Shaykh 'Ubaydu'lláh in 1880.

Ḥusayn Khán, Ḥájí Mírzá, Mushíru'd-Dawlih

Ḥájí Mírzá Ḥusayn Khán, the Mushíru'd-Dawlih and Sipahsálár-i-A'ẓam, eldest son of Mírzá Nabí Khán-i-Qazvíní, was born in AH 1243 (1827–8). He was sent to Europe for his education but did not stay there long. In 1266 (1849–50) he was appointed Persian consul at Bombay by Mírzá Taqí Khán, and in 1271 (1854–5) became Consul-General at Tiflis. He was promoted to Minister at Istanbul in 1275 (1858–9), given the title Mushíru'd-Dawlih in 1282 (1865–6), and raised to the rank of Ambassador in June 1869. In November–December 1870, Náṣiri'd-Dín Sháh performed a pilgrimage to the sacred shrines at Karbilá and Najaf. Mírzá Ḥusayn Khán, as Persian ambassador in Turkey, made all the preparations for this journey and proceeded from Istanbul to meet the Sháh. The Sháh was very favourably impressed by his Ambassador, instructed him to accompany the royal party back to Ṭihrán, and not long after, in September 1871, made him Minister of War with the title Sipahsálár-i-A'ẓam. In November 1871 he was formally appointed Prime Minister. His ministry was marked by a number of reforms but is chiefly remembered for the granting of the Reuter Concession in July 1872. He arranged for, and accompanied the Sháh on, his first European tour in 1873. During their absence, however, opposition to Mírzá Ḥusayn Khán mounted and when the Sháh landed at Anzalí on his return to Persia, he was met by a deluge of demands for Mírzá Ḥusayn Khán's dismissal. The Sháh, although at first inclined to resist this, was eventually forced to relieve Mírzá Ḥusayn Khán of his position in December 1873. He was made Minister of Foreign Affairs, and in the following year Minister for War as well. He accompanied the Sháh on his second European tour in 1878. In 1880, he became Governor of Qazvín and in the following year was sent as the Sháh's personal representative to the coronation of Tsar Alexander III. In 1881, he became Governor of Khurásán, but after only a little more than two months died suddenly on 14 November 1881. It is usually stated that he was poisoned.

Ḥusayn-i-Áshchí, Áqá

Áqá Ḥusayn was a native of Káshán. During the Báb's stay in Káshán, Áqá Ḥusayn's father, Áqá Muḥammad-Javád, had met Him at the house of his uncle, Ḥájí Mírzá Jání, and had become a believer. When Bahá'u'lláh was in Baghdád, Áqá Muḥammad-Javád emigrated to Baghdád and settled there with his son. He was entrusted by Bahá'u'lláh with the mission of going to Ṭihrán to ask for the hand of the daughter of His brother, Mírzá Muḥammad-Ḥasan, in marriage to 'Abdu'l-Bahá. It was as he was returning from this mission that he fell ill at Kirmánsháh, and he died as he reached Baghdád. Áqá Ḥusayn was raised for a time in the care of his uncle, Ustád Ismá'íl, but when Bahá'u'lláh was about to leave Baghdád, Áqá Ḥusayn was honoured by being accepted into His household, initially to serve the womenfolk and later as cook. (Áshchí means cook or maker of broth.) He accompanied Bahá'u'lláh at all stages of His exile until 'Akká was reached. He was involved in the murder of the Azalís and served a term of imprisonment. After this he opened a small shop in 'Akká. He lived throughout the period of 'Abdu'l-Bahá's ministry and into that of the Guardian of the Faith, and died in AH 1346 (1927–8).

Ja'far-i-Tabrízí, Ḥájí, and Taqí-i-Tabrízí, Ḥájí

There were three brothers of Tabríz, pedlars by trade, who had become believers in the time of the Báb. The eldest, Ḥájí Ḥasan, had met Bahá'u'lláh in Baghdád. He became so well known as a believer, and so open in his teaching, that the enemies of the Faith lured him into a garden and killed him. Ḥájí Ja'far and his brother Ḥájí Taqí journeyed to Adrianople and settled there. At the time of Bahá'u'lláh's departure from Adrianople, unable to bear separation from Him, Ḥájí Ja'far cut his throat. Therefore, he and his brother remained there until the wound was healed, when, by Bahá'u'lláh's direction, they proceeded to 'Akká and arrived some two months later. One night, Ḥájí Ja'far fell from the roof of the caravanserai and died. Similarly, his brother Ḥájí Taqí died after a fall from the roof while chanting prayers. (See *Memorials of the Faithful*, pp. 122–5.) Ḥájí Taqí is also referred to in some sources as Karbilá'í Taqí and Mashhadí Taqí.

Jamshíd-i-Gurjí, Áqá

Áqá Jamshíd-i-Gurjí was, as his name implies, from Georgia, but he grew up in Káshán and it was there that he became a believer. He journeyed to Adrianople to meet Bahá'u'lláh, Who, after a time, instructed him to proceed to Istanbul. While there he was arrested through the efforts of the Persian Embassy and sent with Ustád Muḥammad-'Alíy-i-Salmání to Persia, travelling under very harsh conditions. At the Persian frontier they were handed over to Kurdish tribal leaders who freed them, and they were able to make their way to 'Akká and rejoin Bahá'u'lláh. Áqá Jamshíd remained in 'Akká until his death. (See *Memorials of the Faithful*, pp. 120–2.)

Khalíl Manṣúr and 'Abdu'lláh, Áqá

Áqá Muḥammad-Ibráhím, Khalíl Manṣúr, of Káshán was a young man when he first heard of the Báb and became a believer. He succeeded in converting his mother and brothers to the Faith. He travelled to Baghdád and came into the presence of Bahá'u'lláh there. And after a while, he returned to Káshán and brought his family to Baghdád, where they settled. After the departure of Bahá'u'lláh, he and his family were among those exiled to Mosul. But during Bahá'u'lláh's second year of imprisonment in the citadel of 'Akká, he, together with his brother, Áqá 'Abdu'lláh, travelled to the Holy Land and established themselves as copper-smiths in Haifa. Thus these two brothers were able to render many services to the pilgrims who arrived there, as well as purchasing the requisites of the Holy Family in Haifa. (See *Memorials of the Faithful*, pp. 81–2, and Blomfield, *The Chosen Highway*, pp. 119–28.)

Khurshíd Páshá, see *Muḥammad Khurshíd Páshá*

Maḥmúd-i-Káshání, Mírzá

Mírzá Maḥmúd became a believer as a young man in Káshán and emigrated to Baghdád. Here he became a partner in Áqá Muḥammad-Riḍá's confectioner's shop and the two became like brothers, sharing everything. When Bahá'u'lláh left Baghdád, they accompanied Him and continued in His company to 'Akká. After the passing of Bahá'u'lláh they continued to serve 'Abdu'l-Bahá until they died within a short time of each other in about 1912. (See *Memorials of the Faithful*, pp. 39–41.)

Midḥat Páshá

Midḥat Páshá was born in Istanbul in October 1822, the son of a Turkish judge. He held several government appointments before becoming governor of the Danube districts. When in 1864 the decree for the reorganization of the *vilayats* was issued, he was given the task of implementing this for the first time in his area. He was extremely successful and raised the prosperity of the province, administering strict justice among its Muslim and Christian inhabitants. In 1869, he was sent to Baghdád where he once again began to pursue his policies of reform and modernization vigorously, much impressing Náṣiri'd-Dín Sháh who visited the province. In 1872, he was made Grand Vizier, but was soon dismissed. He used his enforced retirement to draw up his plans for a Turkish constitution and, on the accession of Sulṭán 'Abdu'l-Ḥamíd in 1876, he succeeded in having the constitution proclaimed. He himself became Grand Vizier. However, the reactionary and arrogant 'Abdu'l-Ḥamíd could brook no limitations on his power and in 1877 Midḥat was dismissed and exiled. On British insistence he was brought back as Governor of Syria in 1878 and was transferred to Smyrna in 1880. But 'Abdu'l-Ḥamíd could not forgive him; in 1881 he was arrested and charged with the murder of Sulṭán 'Abdu'l-'Azíz. Although the charge was patently false, he was found guilty and the death sentence was only commuted to exile in Ṭá'if in Arabia after much pressure from the European powers. However, 'Abdu'l-Ḥamíd was not to be balked and managed to have his enemy secretly put to death in Ṭá'if on 10 April 1883. He was perhaps the most able administrator of nineteenth-century Turkey.

Muḥammad Khurshíd Páshá (Mehmed Hourshid Paşa)

Muḥammad Khurshíd Páshá was a minister and provincial governor during the reign of Sulṭán 'Abdu'l-'Azíz and the early days of Sulṭán 'Abdu'l-Ḥamíd's reign. He had been a slave of Yaḥyá Páshá and had been trained in the secretariat of the Turkish Foreign Office. He served under Fu'ád Páshá in Syria. He was made Governor of Sidon and then of Erzerum. In 1863 he became Minister of Finance. During his term as Governor of Edirne (Adirnih), he was also Minister of Religious Endowments. He later spent periods of time as Governor of Ma'múratu'l-'Azíz and Sivas, and as Minister of Finance. He died in 1878 in Ankara while he was governor of that city.

Muḥammad-'Alíy-i-Iṣfahání, Áqá

Áqá Muḥammad-'Alí was a close relative of the Imám-Jum'ih of Iṣfahán and had become a believer at the time of the Báb's sojourn in that city. Later he moved to Baghdád, and was one of the companions of Bahá'u'lláh until he died in 'Akká in AH 1305 (AD 1887–8). (See *Memorials of the Faithful*, pp. 23–5.)

Muḥammad-'Alíy-i-Jilawdár-i-Yazdí, Áqá

This man, who was also known as Ṣabbá<u>gh</u>-i-Yazdí, had become a believer in Ba<u>gh</u>dád and accompanied Bahá'u'lláh to Istanbul. When Bahá'u'lláh was exiled to Adrianople, Áqá Muḥammad-'Alí was left in Istanbul to assist the pilgrims on their way to Adrianople. Later he joined Bahá'u'lláh and was exiled with Him to 'Akká. After a time he settled in Sidon where he engaged in trade. After the ascension of Bahá'u'lláh, he returned to 'Akká where he lived until his death. (See *Memorials of the Faithful*, pp. 57–9.)

Muḥammad-Ḥusayn, Ḥájí, Ḥakím-i-Qazvíní

Ḥájí Muḥammad-Ḥusayn, a physician of Qazvín, was a resident of Ba<u>gh</u>dád. He was one of the believers, and was frequently in Bahá'u'-lláh's presence until the latter's departure from Ba<u>gh</u>dád. In 1868, with others of the Bahá'ís, he was exiled to Mosul. After a few years he went to 'Akká and lived there for a time, until going to Persia to teach the Cause. He was arrested in Ṭihrán and spent some time in prison. Upon his release, he left for Ba<u>gh</u>dád, but here he was again arrested. He was sentenced again to exile in Mosul, but Mírzá Músá Javáhirí interceded on his behalf and he was allowed to live out the remainder of his days in Ba<u>gh</u>dád.

Muḥammad-Ibráhím-i-Amír-i-Nayrízí, Áqá

Áqá Muḥammad-Ibráhím was a native of Nayríz, who accepted the Faith of the Báb in his youth. Together with his two brothers, he participated in both the first and second Nayríz upheavals; they managed to escape from the general massacre that followed the second upheaval and, although arrested by several soldiers, Áqá Muḥammad-Ibráhím managed to burst his bonds and release his brothers. He then went to Ba<u>gh</u>dád and settled there. He accompanied Bahá'u'lláh on each stage of His exile from Ba<u>gh</u>dád to 'Akká and settled in the latter city. He married Ḥabíbih who was a servant in the household of Bahá'u'lláh. After the ascension of Bahá'u'lláh, he was for a time the teacher of the Bahá'í children in 'Akká, but his health declined; he died and is buried in 'Akká. (See *Memorials of the Faithful*, pp. 94–5.)

Muḥammad-Ibráhím-i-Náẓir-i-Káshání, Áqá

Áqá Muḥammad-Ibráhím emigrated from Káshán to Baghdád, and then accompanied Bahá'u'lláh on each stage of His exile to Adrianople and 'Akká. He earned his living as a weaver and carpenter. Later, in the 'Akká period, he undertook to guard the house of Bahá'u'lláh, and he was also a bath attendant to Bahá'u'lláh. He died in about 1920, and is buried in 'Akká.

Muḥammad-Riḍáy-i-Qannád-i-Shírází, Áqá

Áqá Riḍá was a native of Shíráz, but was living in Baghdád when he first heard of the Faith and became a believer. He was the owner of a small confectionery shop, and Mírzá Maḥmúd-i-Káshání became his partner. The two are described by 'Abdu'l-Bahá as having become like brothers. He accompanied Bahá'u'lláh in all stages of His exile and served both Bahá'u'lláh and 'Abdu'l-Bahá as steward until his death in about 1912. He is buried in 'Akká. (See *Memorials of the Faithful*, pp. 39–41.)

Muḥammad-Ṣádiq-i-Iṣfahání, Áqá

Áqá Muḥammad-Ṣádiq was one of four brothers who, together with their uncle, lived close by the house of Bahá'u'lláh in Baghdád. Thus it was that they came to know of the Faith and became believers. When Bahá'u'lláh set out from Baghdád, Áqá Muḥammad-Ṣádiq accompanied Him as far as Adrianople, when he received permission to rejoin his family in Baghdád. He was one of the Bahá'ís exiled to Mosul where he died.

Muḥammad-Taqí, Shaykh, 'Allámiy-i-Núrí

Shaykh Muḥammad-Taqí, known as 'Allámiy-i-Núrí, was born in Núr in AD 1787, the son of Mírzá 'Alí-Muḥammad-i-Mustawfí. After completing his religious studies in Karbilá and Najaf, he returned to Núr, where he became one of the eminent mujtahids of his age and the foremost religious authority in Mázindarán. He held his classes at Yálrúd and Sa'ádat-Ábád; a mosque was named for him in the latter place. Mírzá Buzurg, the father of Bahá'u'lláh, made him the executor and trustee of his will. Shaykh Muḥammad-Taqí died in AH 1259 (1843–4).

Munír, Mírzá Áqáy-i-, Jináb-i-Muníb

Mírzá Áqáy-i-Munír was a native of Káshán. His father was a merchant, bitterly opposed to the Faith of the Báb. Mírzá Áqá came into contact with the Bábís shortly after the martyrdom of the Báb and became a believer. At first he kept his new belief hidden from his father, but eventually the fact of his being a Bábí became well known. The 'ulamá of Káshán declared him an unbeliever, and clamoured for his blood. His father, fearing for his own wealth and safety, determined to be rid of this troublesome son and, together with a number of accomplices, captured and bound Mírzá Áqá and took him out of the town, intending to kill him. But Mírzá Áqá managed to escape and fled to Baghdád. Here he settled, occupying himself with transcribing the Holy Writings. Then he undertook a journey on foot throughout Írán, visiting Ṭihrán, Qazvín, Nayríz and other places in order to distribute these texts to the believers. In the journey from Baghdád to Istanbul, he walked before the howdah of Bahá'u'lláh carrying a lantern. From Istanbul, Bahá'u'lláh instructed him to return to 'Iráq and Írán to teach the Cause and confirm the believers. And it was while Mírzá Áqá was in Írán that a Tablet reached him from Bahá'u'lláh in Adrianople, instructing him to inform the Bábís of Írán of His claim to be 'He Whom God will make manifest', the Promised One of the Báb. Thus he was the first to announce this to the Bábís of Ṭihrán and other places. He journeyed to Adrianople shortly before Bahá'u'lláh's further exile to 'Akká. Although he was already ill at the time that the decree of exile came, he insisted on accompanying the exiles. But on board the boat, his condition grew steadily worse until the captain of the boat insisted that he be put ashore at Smyrna. He was taken to the hospital in Smyrna by 'Abdu'l-Bahá, where he died shortly afterwards. Bahá'u'lláh honoured him with the designation Ismu'lláhu'l-Muníb – The Name of God, the Overlord. (See *Memorials of the Faithful*, pp. 145–7.)

Murtiḍáy-i-Anṣárí, Shaykh

Shaykh Murtiḍáy-i-Anṣárí was born at Dizfúl in south-western Írán about 1799. He studied under the greatest mujtahids of the Shí'ih world in 'Iráq and travelled widely through Írán, finally settling in Najaf in 1833. By about 1850, with the death of other prominent mujtahids, he had become recognized as the leading Shí'ih mujtahid, acknowledged throughout 'Iráq, Írán and India. He was famed for his memory, his speedy resolution of difficult problems, and the loftiness of his motives. At the time of his death he is reported to have possessed but seventeen *túmáns* which exactly equalled his debts. This was in marked contrast to other mujtahids such as Shaykh Muḥammad-Báqir, the 'Wolf', and Ḥájí Mullá 'Alíy-i-Kaní, who became extremely wealthy during their lives. He died in Najaf on 18 November 1864.

Muṣṭafá Núrí Páshá

Muṣṭafá Núrí Páshá was the son of Ḥasan Ághá, a resident of Qandílí. His father died when he was young, and he was brought up by Ja'far Ághá, his grandmother's husband. In 1813 he began employment at the royal Court, and went on to the Treasury. He became Kátib-i-Sirr, Private Secretary to the Sulṭán. He held several governorships, including that of Baghdád from 1860 to 1861. He died in 1879, at which time he was one of the oldest of the páshás.

Námiq Páshá (Mehmed Namik Paşa)

Námiq Páshá was born in 1804 in Konya. He entered the new-style army pioneered by the Ottoman Sulṭán Maḥmúd II and was sent to Paris for training. When he returned, he was quickly promoted to the rank of General and later sent as ambassador to London (1834). He was promoted to the rank of *Mushír* (marshal), and he and Ahmed Fevzi Páshá established the first military academy in the Ottoman Empire. He subsequently held many important offices including Governor of Baghdád (1851–2), *Mushír* of the Ṭúpkhánih (1852), Governor of Baṣrah (1854–7), Governor of Arabia (1857–8) and again Governor of Baghdád (1861–8). He then returned for a time to Paris, after which he achieved the highest rank in the army (*Saraskar*). He also held ministerial posts including that of Minister without Portfolio in Muḥammad Rushdí's Government of 1876. He spoke French and English as well as Arabic and, although known as a liberal in his youth, became more conservative in his advanced years. He was one of the oldest páshás of the empire when he died in 1892.

Naẓar-'Alí, Mírzá, Ḥakím-Báshí

Mírzá Naẓar-'Alí was a native of Qazvín who was practising medicine in Hamadán at a time when Muḥammad Mírzá (later Muḥammad S͟háh) became governor of that town. He came to Muḥammad Mírzá's attention when he was able to cure an attack of gout which had afflicted the prince after other physicians had failed. Knowing of the prince's proclivity to Ṣúfism, Mírzá Naẓar-'Alí quickly gave himself the trappings of a Ṣúfí in order to strengthen his influence over the heir-apparent. When the prince became S͟háh, Mírzá Naẓar-'Alí was made Ḥakím-Bás͟hí and continued to be very influential, even contesting the premiership with Ḥájí Mírzá Áqásí. The enmity between these two reached great proportions, until finally the latter succeeded in having Mírzá Naẓar-'Alí exiled (after a plot against the Prime Minister was discovered). Mírzá Naẓar-'Alí took refuge in Qum and remained there until Muḥammad S͟háh's death. At that time he made another attempt to obtain the premiership, but he was sent back to Qum where he died.

Riḍá, Áqá, see *Muḥammad-Riḍáy-i-Qannád-i-S͟hírází, Áqá*

Riḍá, S͟háṭir-

S͟háṭir-Riḍá was a native of Ardikán. He became a believer in the early days of the Bábí Faith and was soon well known as a Bábí. As a result, he met increasing persecution in his home town and was arrested on a number of occasions. Soon he had to leave Ardikán and lived for a while in the wilderness, until eventually making his way to Bag͟hdád. Here he opened a bakery near Bahá'u'lláh's house and supplied the Holy Family and the believers. Following Bahá'u'lláh's departure from Bag͟hdád, he returned to Ardikán where he continued to bake bread for a living. Opposition forced him to move to Yazd for a time; eventually he died in Ardikán at an advanced age.

Ṣafá, Ḥájí Mírzá

Riḍá-Qulí, also called Qanbar-'Alí and best known as Ḥájí Mírzá Ṣafá, came from the family of Savád-Kúh in Mázindarán. He was born in AH 1212 (AD 1797–8) and, after studying under the great mujtahids of 'Iráq, donned the garb of a *darvís͟h* of the Ni'matu'lláhí Order and travelled throughout the Middle East and North Africa, performing the pilgrimage to Mecca during the course of his wanderings. His travels took him to Istanbul where he became the *murs͟hid* (spiritual guide) of Mírzá Ḥusayn Khán (then Persian ambassador at Istanbul). Later, when Mírzá Ḥusayn Khán became Prime Minister, Ḥájí Mírzá Ṣafá came to Ṭihrán and stayed in his house, continuing to exert a powerful influence over the Prime Minister. He died in 1874 and Mírzá Ḥusayn Khán caused a shrine and gardens to be built around his grave.

Sa'íd Khán-i-Anṣárí, Mírzá, Mu'taminu'l-Mulk

Mírzá Sa'íd Khán-i-Anṣárí was born in AH 1231 (AD 1815–16), the son of the Shaykhu'l-Islám of Garmrúd. He himself was educated as one of the 'ulamá, and would probably have remained thus were it not for a meeting with Mírzá Taqí Khán, the Amír-Niẓám. Mírzá Taqí Khán took Mírzá Sa'íd Khán as his private secretary and in early 1852 he was made Foreign Minister. He remained in this post until 1873 when he was succeeded by Mírzá Ḥusayn Khán, and was then appointed Mutavallí-Báshí of the Shrine of Imám Riḍá in Mashhad. In 1880, he returned as Foreign Minister and retained this post until his death on 5 March 1884. Some three years after his death, his son brought to the Court about one thousand letters sent to his father over the years, from various Persian diplomats abroad and European diplomats in Ṭihrán, all unopened and unread. Thus was Persia's Foreign Ministry administered over a quarter of a century.

Ṣidq-'Alíy-i-Qazvíní, Darvísh

Darvísh Ṣidq-'Alí was a resident of Qazvín when he heard of the Faith and left Persia to visit Baghdád. He became one of the companions of Bahá'u'lláh and accompanied Him in all stages of His exile. Bahá'u'lláh honoured him by setting aside a special day every year, dedicated to him, on which all dervishes should gather. He died in AH 1299 (AD 1880–81) and is buried in 'Akká. (See *Memorials of the Faithful*, pp. 36–8.)

'Umar Lütfí Páshá

'Umar Lüṭfí Páshá was an Austrian Croat, born in Plaski in 1806. His name was originally Michel Lattas. Following political upheavals in Hungary, he fled to Turkey in 1828, and having adopted Islám and changed his name, he went on to become one of the principal dignitaries of the Ottoman Empire. He became Sardár Akram, Commander-in-Chief of Turkish armies, in 1855, and was Governor-General of 'Iráq, 1858–9. His period of governorship in Baghdád was marked by severe treatment of dissident tribesmen, and is described by Dr Josef Koetschet, a Swiss physician who accompanied him (*Erinnerungen aus dem Leben des Serdar Ekrem Omer Pascha (Michael Lattas)*, Sarajevo, 1885). He died in Istanbul, in 1871.

Ustád Muḥammad-'Alíy-i-Salmání

Ustád Muḥammad-'Alí had been a believer from the time of the Báb, and in the persecution of 1852 his ear was cut off. After this he came to Baghdád and was a companion of Bahá'u'lláh on the way from Baghdád to Adrianople. The events that befell him in Adrianople, his arrest and deportation to Írán, his release from captivity by the Kurds, and his return to 'Akká are dealt with in this book. (See Index.) In 'Akká, he would carry water to the town in waterskins from a good distance away so that the Holy Family and the companions would not have to drink the dirty, unhealthy water of 'Akká. He was involved in the episode of the murder of the Azalís and, after his release from prison, set up a small shop in the bazar of the town where he would perform minor surgical procedures. After the ascension of Bahá'u'lláh, he proceeded to 'Ishqábád where he lived for a time until his death.

Yúsuf-i-Ashtíyání, Mírzá, Mustawfíyu'l-Mamálik

Mírzá Yúsuf-i-Ashtíyání was born in 1812. His father, Mírzá Ḥasan, the Mustawfíyu'l-Mamálik, was in charge of the Treasury and, on his father's death in 1845, Mírzá Yúsuf inherited his father's position and title. He held great enmity towards Mírzá Áqá Khán-i-Núrí and, during the latter's premiership, Mírzá Yúsuf was out of office and in retirement at Ashtíyán. After Mírzá Áqá Khán's fall, however, he resumed his position and over the ensuing years held many important government positions, although always retaining the prestigious and lucrative post of being in charge of the Treasury. From 1867 to 1871, he was the Sháh's principal minister, but when Mírzá Ḥusayn Khán came to power in 1871, he retired once more and did not re-emerge until Mírzá Ḥusayn Khán's downfall in 1873, when he took up his former post. In 1877, he was given the title Vazír-i-A'ẓam and was in effect Prime Minister, although he did not in fact receive the designation of Ṣadr-i-A'ẓam until 1881. He died in 1886.

Yúsuf Kamál Pá<u>sh</u>á

Yúsuf Kamál Pá<u>sh</u>á was born in the year AD 1808 (AH 1223). He was orphaned at an early age, and was brought up under the care of his uncle 'U<u>th</u>mán Pá<u>sh</u>á, one of the renowned ministers of his time. Yúsuf Kamál entered the service of the state as a secretary in 1829. He gradually progressed to higher positions and duties, held ministerial posts on several occasions, and became a member of the Council of State. In the year 1861, he was appointed deputy to Fu'ád Pá<u>sh</u>á, the Grand Vizier, and took the place of Fu'ád Pá<u>sh</u>á when the latter resigned. Kamál Pá<u>sh</u>á died in Istanbul, in the year AD 1876 (AH 1293).

Glossary

'Abá Cloak or mantle.
Aghṣán 'Branches'. Sons and male descendants of Bahá'u'lláh.
Ájúdán-Báshí Chief Adjutant.
Amír-i-Dívan Head of the Court.
Andarúní Inner or ladies' quarters.
Ayván Verandah, portico.
Azalí Follower of Mírzá Yaḥyá, Ṣubḥ-i-Azal.
Bábá Father.
Bast Sanctuary. A *bastí* is one who takes refuge.
Big-Báshí Major in the Turkish army.
Bírúní Outer or men's quarters.
Cadi (Qáḍí) Judge.
Caravanserai Inn for caravans.
Darvísh Dervish. A Ṣúfí vowed to poverty.
Farmán Order or royal decree.
Farmán-Farmá Commander.
Farrásh Footman, lictor or attendant.
Farrásh-Báshí Head footman or chamberlain.
Farrásh-Khánih Establishment of the Farrásh-Báshí.
Ghuṣnu'lláhu'l-A'ẓam (Ghuṣn-i-A'ẓam) The Most Great Branch.
Ḥájí Muslim who has performed the pilgrimage to Mecca, or *Ḥajj*.
Ḥuqúqu'lláh 'Right of God', payment by believers instituted in the *Kitáb-i-Aqdas*.
Ijtihád The power of the Shí'ih divine to issue *ex cathedra* decrees and judgments.
Ílkhání Chief of the Clans.
Imám Applied particularly by Shí'ihs to one of the twelve Apostolic successors of Muḥammad. An *imám* is also one who leads a congregation in prayer.
Imám-Jum'ih Member of the 'ulamá who leads the Friday prayers.

Jihád Holy War.
Kad-khudá Headman of a village or a quarter of a town.
Kajávih A kind of pannier, howdah, or litter.
Kalántar Mayor.
Kashkúl Begging-bowl used by dervishes.
Khán Prince or chieftain. A khán is also an inn.
Límán Prison.
Madrisih School or religious college.
Mahdí The Manifestation expected by the Muslims at the end of time.
Mír-Áláy Colonel in the Turkish army.
Mírzá Prince when after a name, or simply 'mister' when prefixed to a name.
Mu'adhdhin Muezzin, one who sounds the call to prayer.
Mudír Local governor, under the Qá'im-Maqám.
Mujtahid Doctor of Law.
Mullá One who has had a theological education.
Murshid Ṣúfí spiritual guide.
Mutaṣarrif Governor, under the Válí.
Mutavallí Custodian of a religious foundation.
Páshá Honorary title given to provincial governors, ministers and military officers of high rank in Turkey.
Qáḍí See Cadi.
Qá'im 'He Who shall arise', the Promised One of Shí'ih Islám.
Qá'im-Maqám Local governor, under the Mutaṣarrif.
Qalyán Water-pipe.
Quffih Rounded, hooded boat.
Ṣadr-i-A'ẓam Grand Vizier, Prime Minister.
Sardár Sirdar, military commander.
Seraye Government House, administrative headquarters of the government.
Sháṭir-Báshí Chief courier.
Shaykh Elder, teacher, master of a dervish order, etc.
Shaykhí Member of the school founded by Shaykh Aḥmad-i-Aḥsá'í.
Shí'ih(s) Followers of the first Imám, 'Alí, cousin and son-in-law of Muḥammad, and of his eleven hereditary successors; in contrast to the more numerous Sunnís, who uphold the line of elected Caliphs beginning with Abú-Bakr.
Siyyid Descendant of Muḥammad, entitled to wear the green turban.
Ṣúfí Muslim mystic.
Súrih Chapter of the Qur'án.

Táj 'Crown', a felt head-dress.
Takyih Seminary for Ṣúfís.
Túmán Unit of Íránian currency.
'Ulamá 'Those who know', the religiously learned.
Válí Governor-General, governor of a Turkish province.
Vazír (Vizir) Vizier, minister of state.
Vazír-Niẓám Minister of the Army.
Viláyat Turkish province.
Yúz-Bá<u>sh</u>í Centurion, head of a hundred men.

Bibliography

'ABDU'L-BAHÁ. *Memorials of the Faithful.* Translated and annotated by Marzieh Gail. Wilmette, Illinois: Bahá'í Publishing Trust, 1971.

—— *Some Answered Questions.* Collected and translated by Laura Clifford Barney. London: Bahá'í Publishing Trust, 1961.

ABU'L-FAḌL, MÍRZÁ. *The Bahai Proofs.* New York: Bahá'í Publishing Committee, 1929.

ANDERSON, DOROTHY. *The Balkan Volunteers.* London: Hutchinson & Co. Ltd, 1968.

ARBERRY, ARTHUR J. *The Koran Interpreted.* London: George Allen & Unwin Ltd, 1955.

Bahá'í World, The. Vol. VIII. 1938–40. Wilmette, Illinois: Bahá'í Publishing Committee, 1942.

BAHÁ'U'LLÁH. *Epistle to the Son of the Wolf.* Trans. by Shoghi Effendi. Wilmette, Illinois: Bahá'í Publishing Trust, rev. edn 1976.

—— *Gleanings from the Writings of Bahá'u'lláh.* Trans. by Shoghi Effendi. Wilmette, Illinois: Bahá'í Publishing Trust, 2nd rev. edn 1976.

—— *The Hidden Words.* Trans. by Shoghi Effendi. London: Bahá'í Publishing Trust, 1949. Wilmette, Illinois: Bahá'í Publishing Trust, rev. edn 1954.

—— *Kitáb-i-Íqán. The Book of Certitude.* Trans. by Shoghi Effendi. Wilmette, Illinois: Bahá'í Publishing Trust, rev. edn 1974; London: Bahá'í Publishing Trust, 2nd edn 1961.

—— *The Proclamation of Bahá'u'lláh.* Haifa: Bahá'í World Centre, 1967.

—— *The Seven Valleys and The Four Valleys.* Trans. by Ali-Kuli Khan (Nabílu'd-Dawlih), assisted by Marzieh Gail. Wilmette, Illinois: Bahá'í Publishing Trust, rev. edn 1952.

—— *The Tablets of Bahá'u'lláh.* Trans. by Habib Taherzadeh with the assistance of a Committee at the Bahá'í World Centre. Haifa: Bahá'í World Centre, 1978.

BALYUZI, H. M. *'Abdu'l-Bahá. The Centre of the Covenant of Bahá'u'lláh.* Oxford: George Ronald, 1973.

—— *The Báb. The Herald of the Day of Days.* Oxford: George Ronald, 1974.

—— *Edward Granville Browne and the Bahá'í Faith.* Oxford: George Ronald, 1975.

BÁMDÁD, MIHDÍ. *Táríkh-i-Rijál-i-Írán.* 6 vols. Ṭihrán: Kitábfurúshiy-i-Zavvár, 1347/1967–1351/1971.

BLOMFIELD, LADY (Sitárih Khánum). *The Chosen Highway.* Wilmette, Illinois: Bahá'í Publishing Trust, 1967.

BROWNE, E. G. *Materials for the Study of the Bábí Religion.* Cambridge University Press, 1961.

—— *The Persian Revolution of 1905–1909*. Cambridge University Press, 1910.
—— (ed.) *A Traveller's Narrative written to illustrate the Episode of the Báb*. Vol. II, English Translation and Notes. Cambridge University Press, 1891.
BYRON, ROBERT. *The Road to Oxiana*. London: Jonathan Cape Ltd (paper edn), 1937.
CHIROL, SIR VALENTINE. *Fifty Years in a Changing World*. London: Jonathan Cape, 1927.
—— *The Middle Eastern Question and Some Political Problems of Indian Defence*. London: John Murray, 1903.
CHURCHILL, GEORGE P. *Biographical Notices of Persian Statesmen and Notables, August 1905*. Calcutta: India Government, 1905.
DICHTER, B. *The Maps of Acre*. Municipality of Acre, 1973.
Encyclopaedia of Islam. Leiden: E. G. Brill, 1st edn 1913–34; 2nd edn 1960– .
ESSLEMONT, J. E. *Bahá'u'lláh and the New Era*. Wilmette, Illinois: Bahá'í Publishing Trust, 4th rev. edn 1975.
FARLEY, J. LEWIS. *Turkey*. London: Sampson Low, Son, and Marston, 1866.
FERRIER, J. P. *Caravan Journeys and Wanderings*. Trans. by Capt. W. Jesse, ed. H. D. Seymour. London: John Murray, 1856.
GEARY, GRATTAN. *Through Asiatic Turkey*. Vol. II. London: Sampson Low, Marston, Searle, & Rivington, 1878.
ḤALABÍ, 'ALÍ-AṢGHAR. *Zindigí va Ṣafarháy-i-Siyyid Jamálu'd-Dín-i-Asadábádí*. Ṭihrán: 1357/1978.
ḤAYDAR-'ALÍ, ḤÁJÍ MÍRZÁ. *Bihjatu'ṣ-Ṣudúr*. Bombay: 1913.
ISHRÁQ-KHÁVARÍ, 'ABDU'L-ḤAMÍD. *Raḥíq-i-Makhtúm*. Vol. II. Ṭihrán: Bahá'í Publishing Trust, 103 BE (AD 1946).
I'TIMÁDU'S-SALṬANIH. *Rúznámiy-i-Kháṭirát*. Ṭihrán: 1350/1971.
JAHÁNGÍR MÍRZÁ. *Táríkh-i-Naw*. Ṭihrán: 1327/1948.
KAZEMZADEH, FIRUZ. *Russia and Britain in Persia, 1864–1914*. New Haven and London: Yale University Press, 1968.
KEDOURIE, ELIE. *Afghani and 'Abduh*. London: Frank Cass, 1966.
KELLY, J. B. *Britain and the Persian Gulf*. 1795–1880. Oxford: The Clarendon Press, 1968.
KURDÍ, AL-, FÁ'IZ. *'Akká Bayn al-Maḍí wa'l-Ḥáḍir*. 'Akká: Dáru'l-Bashír, 1972.
MULK-ÁRÁ. *Sharḥ-Ḥál-i-'Abbás Mírzá, Mulk-Árá*. Ṭihrán: Anjuman-i-Nashr-i-Áthár-i-Írán, AH 1325/1946–7.
NABÍL-I-A'ẒAM (MUḤAMMAD-I-ZARANDÍ). *The Dawn-Breakers*. Nabíl's Narrative of the Early Days of the Bahá'í Revelation. Wilmette, Illinois: Bahá'í Publishing Trust, 1932. London: Bahá'í Publishing Trust, 1953.
OLIPHANT, LAURENCE. *Haifa or Life in Modern Palestine*. New York: Harper & Bros., 1887.
PARDOE, MISS. *Beauties of the Bosphorus*. Picturesque Europe, 1st series. London: Virtue, Spalding, and Daldy, [1874].
RECLUS, ÉLISÉE. *The Universal Geography*. Vol. IX: South-Western Asia. Trans. by A. H. Keane. London: J. S. Virtue & Co., undated.
ROGERS, MARY E. *Domestic Life in Palestine*. London: Bell and Daldy, 1863.
ROSS, E. DENISON (ed.). *A Persian Anthology*. London: Methuen & Co., 1927.
SHOGHI EFFENDI. *God Passes By*. Wilmette, Illinois: Bahá'í Publishing Trust, 1965.

—— *The Promised Day Is Come*. Wilmette, Illinois: Bahá'í Publishing Trust, rev. edn 1961.

Star of the West. The Bahá'í Magazine. Vol. XIII (1922–3). Chicago: Bahá'í News Service. Reprinted in *Star of the West*. Vol. 8. Oxford: George Ronald, 1978.

SYKES, SIR PERCY. *History of Persia*. Vol. II. London: Macmillan and Co., 3rd edn 1930.

Synopsis and Codification of the Laws and Ordinances of the Kitáb-i-Aqdas. Haifa, Israel: The Universal House of Justice, 1973.

THOMAS, R. HUGHES (ed.). *Memoirs by Commander James Felix Jones, I. N.* Selections from the Records of the Bombay Government, No. XLIII – New Series. Bombay: 1857.

THOMPSON, JULIET. *Abdul Baha's First Days in America*. East Aurora, New York: The Roycrofters, undated.

WILSON, COLONEL, RECB, FRS (ed.). *Picturesque Palestine*. Vol. II. New York: D. Appleton & Co., 1883.

References

INTRODUCTION

[1] Byron, *The Road to Oxiana*, pp. 243–4.
[2] Translation by H. M. Balyuzi.
[3] Translation by H. M. Balyuzi.
[4] From a compilation, made many years ago, by the National Spiritual Assembly of the Bahá'ís of Írán.

THE FAMILY OF BAHÁ'U'LLÁH

[1] Ferrier, *Caravan Journeys*, pp. 503–5.
[2] Bahá'u'lláh, *Epistle to the Son of the Wolf*, p. 170.

THE DAWN

[1] Translation by H. M. Balyuzi.
[2] Translation by H. M. Balyuzi.
[3] Shoghi Effendi, *God Passes By*, pp. 3–7.
[4] ibid. p. 7.
[5] Ross (ed.), *A Persian Anthology*, p. 72. Translation by E. G. Browne.
[6] Nabíl, *The Dawn-Breakers*, pp. 63–5 (Brit.), pp. 92–4 (US).

TO THE CAPITAL CITY OF ÍRÁN

[1] Nabíl, *The Dawn-Breakers*, p. 58 (Brit.), pp. 86–7 (US).
[2] ibid. p. 66 (Brit.), p. 96 (US).
[3] ibid. pp. 71–4 (Brit.), pp. 104–8 (US).

THE FIRST IMPRISONMENT

[1] See Balyuzi, *The Báb*, pp. 166–7.

THE CONFERENCE OF BADASHT

[1] Shoghi Effendi, *God Passes By*, p. 31.

[2] Nabíl, *The Dawn-Breakers*, p. 211 (Brit.), p. 293 (US).
[3] ibid. p. 213 (Brit.), p. 295 (US).
[4] ibid. pp. 213–14 (Brit.), p. 296 (US).
[5] ibid. p. 214 (Brit.), pp. 296–7 (US).
[6] Arberry, *The Koran Interpreted.*
[7] Nabíl, *The Dawn-Breakers*, pp. 215–16 (Brit.), p. 299 (US).

FROM BADA<u>SH</u>T TO <u>SH</u>AY<u>KH</u> ṬABARSÍ

[1] Nabíl, *The Dawn-Breakers*, p. 216 (Brit.), p. 299 (US).
[2] ibid. p. 253 (Brit.), p. 351 (US).

THE SECOND IMPRISONMENT

[1] Verbatim notes of 'Abdu'l-Bahá's talk to pilgrims, August 1919, recorded by Dr Luṭfu'lláh Ḥakím.
[2] Nabíl, *The Dawn-Breakers*, pp. 266–8 (Brit.), pp. 369–72 (US).
[3] ibid. p. 428 (Brit.), p. 584 (US).
[4] Bahá'u'lláh, *Epistle to the Son of the Wolf*, p. 77.

A MOMENTOUS YEAR

[1] Nabíl, *The Dawn-Breakers*, pp. 341–2 (Brit.), p. 464 (US).
[2] ibid. pp. 316–17 (Brit.), pp. 432–3 (US).
[3] ibid. p. 317 (Brit.), p. 433 (US).
[4] Blomfield, *The Chosen Highway*, p. 22.
[5] Nabíl, *The Dawn-Breakers*, pp. 370–71 (Brit.), pp. 504–5 (US).

ONE YEAR AT KARBILÁ

[1] From Nabíl's unpublished history.
[2] Paraphrase of Nabíl, *The Dawn-Breakers*, pp. 23–4 (Brit.), p. 31 (US).

THE FALL OF AMÍR KABÍR

[1] Sykes, *History of Persia*, vol. II, p. 346 (3rd edn).

THE ATTEMPT ON NÁṢIRI'D-DÍN <u>SH</u>ÁH

[1] Bahá'u'lláh, *Epistle to the Son of the Wolf*, pp. 20–21.

THE BIRTH OF THE BAHÁ'Í REVELATION

[1] Bahá'u'lláh, *Epistle to the Son of the Wolf*, p. 77.
[2] Nabíl, *The Dawn-Breakers*, pp. 461–3 (Brit.), pp. 631–3 (US).

[3] Shoghi Effendi, *God Passes By*, pp. 101–2. The words of Bahá'u'lláh are quoted here; the first two paragraphs are taken from His *Epistle to the Son of the Wolf*, pp. 22 and 21.

BÁBÍ MARTYRS OF 1852

[1] Browne, *Materials for the Study of the Bábí Religion*, pp. 268–71.
[2] Nabíl, *The Dawn-Breakers*, pp. 452–3 (Brit.), pp. 619–20 (US).
[3] Browne, *The Traveller's Narrative*, vol. II, p. 334.
[4] Nabíl, *The Dawn-Breakers*, p. 455 (Brit.), pp. 622–3 (US).

THE STORY OF A SHÍRÁZÍ YOUTH

[1] Nabíl, *The Dawn-Breakers*, pp. 59–61 (Brit.), pp. 87–90 (US).
[2] Bahá'u'lláh, *The Hidden Words*, no. 4 (Persian).
[3] Nabíl, *The Dawn-Breakers*, p. 463 (Brit.), pp. 633–4 (US).
[4] Thompson, *Abdul Baha's First Days in America*, p. 34.

RELEASE AND EXILE

[1] Shoghi Effendi, *God Passes By*, p. 105.
[2] ibid. p. 107.
[3] ibid. pp. 108–9.
[4] ibid. p. 108.

BAGHDÁD – THE FIRST YEAR

[1] Bahá'u'lláh, *Epistle to the Son of the Wolf*, p. 166.
[2] Shoghi Effendi, *God Passes By*, p. 115.
[3] ibid. pp. 115–16. The two sentences in brackets are the author's addition, from Nabíl's unpublished history.
[4] From Nabíl's unpublished history.
[5] Shoghi Effendi, *God Passes By*, p. 116.
[6] ibid. pp. 116–7.
[7] From Nabíl's unpublished history.
[8] Shoghi Effendi, *God Passes By*, p. 119.

SULAYMÁNÍYYIH

[1] Bahá'u'lláh, *Kitáb-i-Íqán*, pp. 159–60 (Brit.), pp. 249–51 (US).
[2] Nabíl, *The Dawn-Breakers*, p. 429 (Brit.), p. 585 (US).
[3] Shoghi Effendi, *God Passes By*, pp. 118, 120, with additional passages translated by H. M. Balyuzi.
[4] Thomas (ed.), *Memoirs by Commander James Felix Jones*, pp. 207–8.

[5] Shoghi Effendi, *God Passes By*, pp. 124–5.
[6] ibid. p. 126 (for two references).
[7] ibid. p. 125

BAGHDÁD – FRIEND AND FOE

[1] Shoghi Effendi, *God Passes By*, pp. 125–6.
[2] Bahá'u'lláh, *Kitáb-i-Íqán*, pp. 160–61 (Brit.), pp. 251–2 (US).
[3] Nabíl's account in this chapter is from his unpublished history.
[4] From unpublished diary of Áqá Riḍá.

BAGHDÁD – FINAL YEARS

[1] 'Abdu'l-Bahá, *Some Answered Questions*, chapter IX.
[2] Shoghi Effendi, *God Passes By*, p. 143 (for two references).
[3] Shoghi Effendi, *The Promised Day Is Come*, p. 88.
[4] Nabíl, *The Dawn-Breakers*, pp. 95–6 (Brit.), pp. 137–8 (US).
[5] Shoghi Effendi, *God Passes By*, pp. 131–2.
[6] ibid. p. 131.
[7] ibid. p. 150. The following sentence is from the Qur'án, 8:30.
[8] ibid. pp. 144–5.

FROM THE MOST EXALTED PEN

[1] The verses quoted, in sequence, are: Introduction (Arabic), nos. 3 (A.), 7 (A.), 12 (A.), 14 (A.), 22 (A.), 44 (Persian), 4 (P.), 47 (P.), 48 (P.), 49 (P.), 64 (P.).
[2] Extracts from Bahá'u'lláh, *The Seven Valleys and the Four Valleys*, from 1936 edn. See Bibliography for later edn.
[3] Shoghi Effendi, *God Passes By*, p. 139.
[4] Bahá'u'lláh, *Kitáb-i-Íqán*, pp. 65–7 (Brit.), pp. 100–103 (US).
[5] ibid. pp. 64–5 (Brit.), pp. 99–100 (US).

THE MARCH OF THE KING OF GLORY

[1] Bahá'u'lláh, *Gleanings from the Writings of Bahá'u'lláh*, section XIV.
[2] Shoghi Effendi, *God Passes By*, p. 153.
[3] 'Abdu'l-Bahá, *Memorials of the Faithful*, pp. 145–6.
[4] *Star of the West*, vol. XIII (1922–3), pp. 277–8.
[5] From an unpublished Tablet, translated by H. M. Balyuzi.
[6] *Star of the West*, *idem*, p. 278.
[7] ibid.
[8] The author wishes to acknowledge Reclus, *The Universal Geography*, from which much of the geographical and historical (not Bahá'í) material has been taken.

IN THE CITY OF CONSTANTINE

[1] Shoghi Effendi, *God Passes By*, p. 161.
[2] ibid.
[3] ibid. p. 160.
[4] Bahá'u'lláh, *The Proclamation of Bahá'u'lláh*, pp. 47–54. (See Shoghi Effendi, *The Promised Day Is Come*, p. 37.)
[5] Shoghi Effendi, *God Passes By*, pp. 160–61.
[6] Bahá'u'lláh, *Gleanings from the Writings of Bahá'u'lláh*, section CXIII.
[7] Bahá'u'lláh, *Epistle to the Son of the Wolf*, pp. 68–70.
[8] Shoghi Effendi, *God Passes By*, pp. 157–60, 162.

ADRIANOPLE, THE REMOTE PRISON

[1] The quotation at the head of the chapter is from the Tablet of Aḥmad, included in most Bahá'í prayer books.
[2] Bahá'u'lláh, *Gleanings from the Writings of Bahá'u'lláh*, section CLII.
[3] Shoghi Effendi, *God Passes By*, pp. 163–6.
[4] ibid. p. 166.
[5] ibid. pp. 166–7.
[6] See Balyuzi, *Edward Granville Browne and the Bahá'í Faith*, pp. 83–4.
[7] See ibid. p. 36.
[8] Shoghi Effendi, *God Passes By*, pp. 168–70.
[9] ibid. pp. 170–72.

ADRIANOPLE, THE LAST YEARS

[1] Shoghi Effendi, *God Passes By*, p. 179.
[2] See Balyuzi, *'Abdu'l-Bahá*, pp. 22–3.
[3] See Balyuzi, *The Báb*, pp. 51–2.
[4] See ibid. pp. 185–8.

BANISHMENT TO 'AKKÁ

[1] Shoghi Effendi, *God Passes By*, pp. 179–80.
[2] ibid. p. 180.
[3] Also quoted ibid. p. 181.
[4] Shoghi Effendi, *The Promised Day Is Come*, p. 62.
[5] Shoghi Effendi, *God Passes By*, p. 182.
[6] From Nabíl's unpublished history.

ARRIVAL AT 'AKKÁ

[1] Shoghi Effendi, *God Passes By*, p. 182.

THE LORD OF HOSTS

[1] The quotation at the head of the chapter is from Psalms 24:9–10.

[2] Shoghi Effendi, *God Passes By*, p. 183.

[3] Ezek. 43:1–2, 4.

[4] quoted in Bahá'u'lláh, *Epistle to the Son of the Wolf*, p. 179.

[5] 'Abdu'l-Bahá, *Some Answered Questions*, chapter IX.

[6] Isa. 35:1–2.

[7] Amos 1:2.

[8] Mic. 7:12.

LIFE IN THE BARRACKS

[1] Shoghi Effendi, *God Passes By*, p. 187.

[2] ibid. p. 186.

[3] ibid.

[4] Translation by H. M. Balyuzi.

[5] Shoghi Effendi, *God Passes By*, pp. 187–8.

THE STORY OF BADÍ'

[1] Shoghi Effendi, *God Passes By*, p. 212.

[2] From Nabíl's unpublished history.

[3] Translation by H. M. Balyuzi.

[4] Shoghi Effendi, *God Passes By*, p. 199 (for three references).

[5] Translation by H. M. Balyuzi.

[6] Quoted Browne, *A Traveller's Narrative*, vol. II, pp. 391–2.

[7] From Ḥaydar-'Alí, *Bihjatu'ṣ-Ṣudúr*, translated by H. M. Balyuzi.

[8] Bahá'u'lláh, *The Proclamation of Bahá'u'lláh*, pp. 57, 59–60.

THE GREAT SACRIFICE

[1] Shoghi Effendi, *God Passes By*, p. 188.

[2] ibid. pp. 188–9. See also an account of this event by Amatu'l-Bahá Rúḥíyyih Khánum, *Bahá'í World*, vol. VIII, pp. 253–8.

THE GATES OPEN

[1] Shoghi Effendi, *God Passes By*, p. 189.

[2] ibid. p. 190.

[3] A translation of the *Fire Tablet* revised 1979 by a committee of the Universal House of Justice.

[4] Browne, *Materials for the Study of the Bábí Religion*, pp. 53–4.

[5] Ishráq-Khávarí, *Raḥíq-i-Makhtúm*, vol. II, p. 147, translated by H. M. Balyuzi.

[6] Shoghi Effendi, *God Passes By*, pp. 189–90.
[7] ibid. p. 190.
[8] ibid. pp. 190–91.
[9] ibid. p. 191.

THE TURN OF THE TIDE

[1] Shoghi Effendi, *God Passes By*, p. 191.
[2] ibid. pp. 191–2.
[3] See Balyuzi, *Edward Granville Browne and the Bahá'í Faith*, pp. 21–3.

THE MARRIAGE OF THE MOST GREAT BRANCH

[1] The author has made considerable use of this autobiography in this chapter, as source material and with quotations. The translation is his.
[2] Qur'án 2:81 and 36:29; from Arberry, *The Koran Interpreted.*

LAST YEARS WITHIN THE CITY WALLS

[1] Shoghi Effendi, *God Passes By*, pp. 213–15.
[2] quoted in *A Synopsis and Codification of the Kitáb-i-Aqdas*, p. 3.
[3] Shoghi Effendi, *God Passes By*, p. 192.
[4] ibid. p. 193.
[5] Esslemont, *Bahá'u'lláh and the New Era*, chapter 3.
[6] Shoghi Effendi, *God Passes By*, p. 193.
[7] Esslemont, *idem.*

THE YEARS AT BAHJÍ

[1] Esslemont, *Bahá'u'lláh and the New Era*, chapter 3.
[2] Shoghi Effendi, *God Passes By*, p. 192.
[3] ibid. p. 193.
[4] Browne, *A Traveller's Narrative*, vol. II, xxxix–xl.
[5] Bahá'u'lláh, *Gleanings from the Writings of Bahá'u'lláh*, section XI.
[6] Bahá'u'lláh, *Tablets of Bahá'u'lláh*, pp. 225–6.
[7] Browne, *idem*, xxxvi.
[8] Shoghi Effendi, *God Passes By*, pp. 205–6.
[9] ibid. p. 219.
[10] Mírzá Abu'l-Faḍl, *The Bahá'í Proofs*, pp. 70–72.

THE AZALÍS IN CONSTANTINOPLE

[1] Bahá'u'lláh, *Epistle to the Son of the Wolf*, pp. 106, 108–11.
[2] ibid. pp. 122–6.

PAGES OF AN AUTOBIOGRAPHY

All extracts from this autobiography are translated by H. M. Balyuzi.

[1] Translation by H. M. Balyuzi.

[2] Bahá'u'lláh, *Tablets of Bahá'u'lláh*, p. 85.

[3] Translation by H. M. Balyuzi.

THE ASCENSION OF BAHÁ'U'LLÁH

[1] The words of 'Abdu'l-Bahá are quoted in Shoghi Effendi, *God Passes By*, pp. 238–9.

[2] ibid. p. 239.

[3] Bahá'u'lláh, *Tablets of Bahá'u'lláh*, pp. 219–22.

[4] Shoghi Effendi, *God Passes By*, pp. 239–40.

[5] ibid. pp. 222–3.

ADDENDA

THE REIGN OF NÁṢIRI'D-DÍN SHÁH

[1] Mulk-Árá, *Sharḥ-Ḥal-i-'Abbás Mírzá, Mulk-Árá*, pp. 62–5.

[2] Shoghi Effendi, *God Passes By*, pp. 197–8.

[3] Chirol, *Fifty Years in a Changing World*, pp. 144–58, for the extracts which follow.

[4] Kelly, *Britain and the Persian Gulf*, pp. 557–8.

[5] Translation by H. M. Balyuzi.

[6] I'timádu's-Salṭanih, *Rúznámiy-i-Kháṭirat*, pp. 129, 136, 143, 145.

[7] See Balyuzi, *Edward Granville Browne and the Bahá'í Faith*, pp. 89, 93–4.

[8] See ibid., Index entries for Jamálu'd-Dín al-Afghání, Siyyid.

[9] Kedourie, *Afghani and 'Abduh*, p. 63.

[10] Ḥalabí, *Zindigí va Ṣafarháy-i-Siyyid Jamálu'd-Dín-i-Asadábádí*, p. 8 of Preface.

[11] Browne, *The Persian Revolution*, p. 11.

THE AFTERMATH OF THE SIEGE OF PLEVNA

[1] Anderson, *The Balkan Volunteers*, pp. 148–52, 181–2.

GENERAL GORDON IN HAIFA AND 'AKKÁ

[1] Oliphant, *Haifa or Life in Modern Palestine*, pp. 274–80.

BIOGRAPHICAL NOTES

[1] Shoghi Effendi, *God Passes By*, p. 83.

INDEX

Part I of this index consists of the titles of Tablets and Writings of Bahá'u'lláh described, quoted, or mentioned. Part II contains all other entries. Titles of Tablets, books, and journals are italicized. Footnotes are indicated by the abbreviation n after the page number.

I. TABLETS AND WRITINGS OF BAHÁ'U'LLÁH

II. GENERAL INDEX

Ábájí Qazvíní, a maid-servant exiled to 'Akká, 278

'Abbás, brother of Imám Ḥusayn, 21, 416n

'Abbás the Great, 2, 3

'Abbás Mírzá, father of Muḥammad Sháh, 470, 472

'Abbás Mírzá (Mulk-Árá), illustration (possibly), 34; son of Muḥammad Sháh and half-brother of Náṣiri'd-Dín Sháh, 53, 69, 89; banished to 'Iráq, 89, 432; seeks Bahá'u'lláh's support, 153; autobiography critical of Náṣiri'd-Dín Sháh, 430–1; describes Zanján, 432

'Abbás, Mullá, 39–40

'Abbás, Sháh, 434

'Abbás-i-Núrí, Mírzá, *see* Buzurg-i-Vazír, Mírzá

'Abbás-Qulí Khán, Governor of Ámul, 56, 58–60 *passim*

'Abbás-Qulí Khán, Persian consul-general at Damascus, 286

'Abbás-i-Ṭihrání, Shaykh, martyr of 1852, 89

'Abbásábád, 53, 54

'Abbásids, 106, 122n, 168, 196, 197n

'Abbúd, House of (Bayt-i-'Abbúd), 'Akká, illustrations: exterior, 321, rooms of Bahá'u'lláh, 335, 350, view overlooking the sea, 336; made available to Bahá'u'lláh, 335; room made available for marriage of 'Abdu'l-Bahá, 348; *Kitáb-i-Aqdas* revealed in, 351; residence of 'Abdu'l-Bahá and family, and their removal, 368–9; mentioned, 178, 331, 337; see also 'Údí Khammár, house of

'Abbúd, Ilyás, changes attitude to Bahá'u'lláh, 334–5; intercedes for Governor, 354; presents room for marriage of 'Abdu'l-Bahá, 348; mentioned, 315, 317, 326, 331, 347; see also 'Abbúd, House of

'Abdu'l-Aḥad, of Shíráz, 347

'Abdu'l-'Aẓím, Sháh (Ḥaḍrat-i-), shrine of, 54, 55, 76, 455

'Abdu'l-'Azíz, Sulṭán (reigned 1861–76), illustrations, 209, 263, 284 (his *farmán* banishing Bahá'u'lláh); banishes Bahá'u'lláh to Adrianople, 199; Tablet to, 206–7, 216; addressed in *Súriy-i-Mulúk*, 207–12, 245; ministers decide to banish Bahá'u'lláh to 'Akká, 253–4; his farmán banishing Bahá'u'lláh to 'Akká, 216, 283–5, 337, 359, 379, 425; no reason for banishment, 412; Bahá'u'lláh's warning from Gallipoli, 261–2; loses throne, death, 262; mentioned, 139, 307, 352, 360–1, 426, 476

'Abdu'l-Bahá ('Abbás Effendi): illustrations, 234, 242, 421; names and titles, 378, 416n, 417, 420, 425; birth, 17; recalls Ṭáhirih and Vaḥíd, 63–4; describes Bahá'u'lláh's first imprisonment, 41–2, His stay at Bandar-Jaz, 48, His imprisonment in Ámul, 57–9; tells of deaths in 1852 of Muḥammad-Taqí Khán, 91, and Mullá 'Abdu'l-Fattáḥ 92; extols martyrdom of 'Abdu'l-Vahháb, 97–8, and sings martyr's song, 98; **in Baghdád:** initiates search for Bahá'u'lláh in Sulaymáníyyih, 121; describes plots of Shaykh 'Abdu'l-Ḥusayn and MirzáBuzurg Khán, 142–4, mission of Mullá Ḥasan-i-'Amú, 144–5, change of attitude of adversaries in Baghdád, 155; transcribes original ms. of *Kitáb-i-Íqán*, 165; characterizes Shaykh Murtiḍáy-i-Anṣárí, 147; entertained by Námiq Páshá, 153, 155; migrates to Istanbul, 156; describes journey to Istanbul, 176–7, 179, 183–4 (Mírzá Yaḥyá), 192; **in Adrianople:** advises silence concerning Mírzá Yaḥyá's plots, 229; has friendship of Deputy-Governor, 233; pens undelivered Tablet to Mírzá Yaḥyá, 240; accepts Governor's invitation, 243; tran-

Baṣrah, 144, 148, 224, 480
Bayán, 33, 43, 111, 121, 244, 250, 351
Bayḍún, 'Abdu'l-Ghaní, 316; family, 362n
Bayt-i-'Abbúd, *see* 'Abbúd, House of
Bayt-i-Fanduq, Haifa, where Bahá'u'lláh stayed, 374
Bayt-i-Zahlán, Haifa, Bahá'u'lláh stayed nearby, 374
Beirut, 'Abdu'l-Bahá's visit, 378–9; vilayát of Beirut, 371n; Afnán married to daughter of Bahá'u'lláh in, 388; mentioned, 273, 443
Bellew, Dr, orientalist, 440
'Beloved of the Martyrs', *see* Ḥusayn, Mírzá
Benjamin, S. G. W., first American envoy to Persia, 449
Berdjis, Mas'ud, 119n
Berlin, 352
Bibliothèque Nationale, Paris, 401
Bihjatu's-Ṣudúr, quoted, 298
Bilál Ibn Ribáḥ, first muezzin of Islám, 266n
Birkás, Turkey, 205
Bismarck, Prince, German statesman, 435
Black Sea (Euxine), 193, 195
'Black Standard', 50
Blunt, John E., British consul at Adrianople, 456–9 *passim*
Boghos Agha, Protestant head in Adrianople, 456, 457
Bombay, 11, 165, 388, 405, 473
'Book of Names', 377
Bourée, Nicolas, French minister at Istanbul, 458
Braunschweig, Graf von, first German envoy to Ṭihrán, 435n, 449
Britain: fleet before 'Akká (1840), 273; Treaty of Paris (1856), 290; constructing telegraph system in Írán (1864), 439–40; Persian frontier with Balúchistán, 440; telegraph office in Julfá, 286; visits of Náṣiri'd-Dín Sháh, 445 (1873), 451 (1889); doctors during war of 1877–8, 460–2; ascendancy in Ṭihrán (1884), 435; free passage on Karún river obtained, 449; Mandate for Palestine, 275, 319; mentioned, 476
British diplomatic representatives, Adrianople, 256, 456–9 *passim*; Baghdád, 55, 153; Diyárbakr, 189–90n, 191 Istanbul, 189–90n, 191; Tabríz, 237; Ṭihrán, 53, 435, 436
British Society for the Propagation of the Gospel, 457
Browne, Edward Granville, siege of Plevna inspires oriental studies, 263; translation of Tablet to Badí', 298–9; effect of Mírzá Yaḥyá's defection, 224; visits 'Akká and describes meeting with Bahá'u'lláh, 371–3, 374; describew meeting with 'Abdu'l-Bahá, 379–80; describes Siyyid Jamálu'd-Dín in London, 452–3; mentioned, 392–3, 399
Buddha, 114
Bukhárá, 399
Bulgaria, 460
Bulwer, Sir Henry, British minister at Istanbul, 189–90n, 191
Buq'atu'l-Ḥamrá' (the Crimson Spot), hill near Bahjí, 364
Burj al-Kummandar, 'Akká, 334n
Burju's-Sulṭán, Crusader tower in 'Akká, 327n; illustration, 328
Burning Bush, 377
Burújird, 15
Búshihr (Bushire), 406, 433
Bushrúyih, town in Írán, 32n
Bustán-i-Kabír, garden of (Mazra'ih), 363
Buyúk Khánum, *see* Ásíyih Khánum
Búyúk-Chakmachih, Turkey, 205; illustration of bridge, 205
Buzurg, Ḥájí Mírzá, brother of Ḥájí Mírzá Ḥabíbu'lláh Afnán, 406, 410, 411, 415
Buzurg-i-Vazír, Mírzá ('Abbás-i-Núrí, Mírzá), father of Bahá'u'lláh, illustration, 10; origin of name, 11–12; ancestors, 11n; family, 13–14, 23; father of Bahá'u'lláh, 11, 19, 20; appointed Vazír, 12, and his success, 16–17n; friendship with Mírzá Abu'l-Qásim, 15, 23; antagonism of Ḥájí Mírzá Áqásí, 12, 15–16; governorship, 15, 25; divorced by last wife, 16, 18; financial and other difficulties, 16–17; death (1839) and burial, 17; calligraphy: illustration, 20, *see* 18, 19, 25; houses of, in Ṭihrán, 16, 17, 19, in Tákur, 16, 19, 93; character described, 35; mentioned, 59, 90, 478
Buzurg Khán-i-Qazvíní, Mírzá, Persian consul in Baghdád and his campaign against Bahá'u'lláh, 136–8, 140, 142; 'Abdu'l-Bahá speaks of his plots, 142–4; Shaykh 'Abdu'l-Ḥusayn's promise, 145; recalled to Írán but continues vendetta, 152; reason for dismissal, 157; mentioned, 150, 152, 222, 390,

Nayríz, 61, 71; mentioned, 81
Vaḥíd, Mírzá, son of Mírzá Muḥammad-Qulí, exiled to 'Akká, 278
Vakílu'd-Dawlih (Muḥammad-Taqí, Ḥájí Mírzá), 388
Varna, Bulgaria, 460, 461
Victoria, Queen, 153, 445, 451

William I, of Prussia and Germany, 352, 435n
Will and Testament, of Bahá'u'lláh (*Kitáb-i-'Ahd*), provisions of, 420, 422–3, 425; quoted, 422–3
Windsor Castle, 445
Word of God, 166
World Order, of Bahá'u'lláh, 351, 422
World War, First, 440

Xerxes, 3

Yaḥyá, Ḥájí Shaykh, Imám-Jum'ih of Shíráz, 108n
Yaḥyá Khán (Mushíru'd-Dawlih, Mu'tamidu'l-Mulk), 448, 449
Yaḥyá, Mírzá (Ṣubḥ-i-Azal), illustration, 15; half-brother of Bahá'u'lláh, 14; nominee of the Báb, 224; Báb commits him to Bahá'u'lláh's care, 63; arrested at Ámul, 56, 59–60; goes to Tákur, then flees to Baghdád, 90; Bahá'u'lláh wishes him to return to Persia, 107–8, 224; behaviour in Baghdád, 107, 108, 112, 114, 119–22, 144, 224, 418; his book *Mustayqiẓ*, 123; incites murder of Dayyán, 121, 123; refuses to meet Nabíl, 129; in Baṣrah, 144, 148; names 'Witnesses of the Bayán', 158; flees Baghdád, 158; abandons writings of Báb, 224; reaches Mosul and 'Abdu'l-Bahá describes, 183–4, 224; joins caravan, 184, 190; begs Bahá'u'lláh to accept banishment to Adrianople, 202–3; his intrigues in Adrianople, 220, 222; open rebellion, 223–5; attempts to poison Bahá'u'lláh, 225–6; ignorance revealed, 226–7; plots Bahá'u'lláh's murder, 227–30; his rupture with Bahá'u'lláh 230–3; partisans in 'Iráq, 233, 238; fails to meet Bahá'u'lláh, 239–41, 246; Bahá'u'lláh's description of, 240–1; arch-breaker of Covenant of the Báb, 225; banished to Cyprus, 253; journey from Adrianople, 259, 260 269; wives, 337, 418, see Badrí-Ján; children, 337, 385, 390, 402; Bahá'u'lláh's assurance to, 352; obtains freedom (1878), 426; activities of supporters in Constantinople, 383–4, chap. 40; death in Cyprus (1912), 426; mentioned, 111–13 *passim*, 122, 131, 173, 193, 204, 219, 221, 236, 237, 248, 323, 325, 343, 361, 401–2
Yaḥyá, Mírzá, of Qazvín, 395
Yaḥyá Páshá, 476
Yaḥyá, Siyyid, brother of Munírih Khánum, 344, 347
Yaḥyáy-i-Dárábí, Siyyid, *see* Vaḥíd
Yálrúd, 21, 22, 478
Yazd, 1, 9, 61, 409, 431, 481
Yazdigird III, 9, 11
Yazíd I, Umayyad caliph, 419
Yazídís (Kurds), 185, 186
Yirkih, village, 364
Yúsuf Kamál Páshá, biographical note, 484; mentioned, 213
Yúsuf Khán-i-Vujdání, Mírzá, tutor at Bahjí, 411, 415
Yúsuf, Shaykh, Muftí of Nazareth, 368
Yúsuf-i-Ashtíyání, Mírzá (Mustawfíyu'l-Mamálik), illustration, 447; becomes Grand Vizier, 445; character, 446; biographical note, 483–4; mentioned, 307, 449

Záb, Great and Little, rivers, 182
Za'farán Khánum, exiled to 'Akká, 279
Zagros mts., 1, 3
Ẓáhir, Arab Bábí, 183, 224
Ẓáhiru'l-'Umar, Governor of province of 'Akká, 271, 273, 274
Zahrá Bigum, sister of wife of the Báb, 403, 406
Zahrá Khánum, exiled to 'Akká, 278
Zákhú (Zakho), 'Iráq, stage of march from Baghdád, 185
Zanján, upheaval in, 61, 70, 81, 89, 250, 470; murder of Mírzá Muḥammad-'Alí, physician, 238; condition three decades after upheaval, 432
Zarand, 64
Zargandih, 77
Zaynab (Rustam-'Alí), in Zanján upheaval, 71
Zaynu'l-'Ábidín, Áqá Mírzá, arrives Adrianople, 247
Zaynu'l-'Ábidín, Ḥájí Mírzá, father of Áqá Mírzá Áqá, Núri'd-Dín, 403

BLACK AFRICA

MASKS

SCULPTURE

JEWELRY

This book is to be returned on or before the last date stamped below.

14 DEC 1995
13 MAR 1996
27 JAN 1997
14 FEB 1997
11. APR. 1997
13. JUN. 1997
13 NOV 1997
-1. DEC. 1997
10. FEB. 1998
10. MAR 1998
17. APR. 1998
-9. JUL. 1998
12 OCT 1998
-1. FEB 1999
10. FEB 2000
12. MAY 2000
17. FEB 2001
15. MAY 2001
-2 NOV 2001
7 NOV 2003
28/01/04
8 FEB 2010
24 FEB 2010

LIBREX

709.6
Mey
05168

S.K.C
JEMMETT ROAD
ASHFORD
South K... Library,
Jemmett Road, Ashford, Kent TN23 2RJ

SOUTH KENT COLLEGE
R27770K0589

E-Hub
Resource